W9-AWL-667

Freedom's Daughters

The Unsung Heroines
of the Civil Rights Movement
from 1830 to 1970

LYNNE OLSON

SCRIBNER
New York   London   Toronto   Sydney   Singapore

SCRIBNER
1230 Avenue of the Americas
New York, NY 10020

SCRIBNER and design are trademarks of Macmillan Library Reference USA, Inc.,
used under license by Simon & Schuster, the publisher of this work.

Designed by Kyoko Watanabe
Text set in Bell

Manufactured in the United States of America

1 3 5 7 9 10 8 6 4 2

Library of Congress Cataloging-in-Publication Data
Olson, Lynne.
Freedom's daughters: the unsung heroines of the civil rights movement
from 1830 to 1970/Lynne Olson.
p. cm.
1. Afro-American women civil rights workers—Southern States—History.
2. Afro-American women civil rights workers—Southern States—Biography.
3. Women civil rights workers—Southern States—History.
4. Women civil rights workers—Southern States—Biography.
5. Afro-Americans—Civil rights—Southern States—History.
6. Civil rights movements—United States—History.
I. Title.

E185.043 2001
323'.092'275—dc21
00–041306

ISBN 0-684-85012-5

To Stan and Carly
With love and thanks

contents

Preface		13
1.	*"Far More Terrible for Women"*	19
2.	*"She Has Shaken This Country"*	33
3.	*"Getting Them Comfortable with Rebellion"*	52
4.	*Lighting the Fuse*	75
5.	*"There Had to Be a Stopping Place"*	87
6.	*"Our Leaders Is Just We Ourself"*	110
7.	*"She Kept Daring Us to Go Further"*	132
8.	*"The Most Daring of Our Leaders"*	151
9.	*"Being White Does Not Answer Your Problems"*	163
10.	*"She Never Listened to a Word"*	182
11.	*"We Are Not Going to Take This Anymore"*	200
12.	*"The Cobwebs Are Moving from My Brain"*	213
13.	*"I Had Never Heard That Voice Before"*	225
14.	*"Black and White Together"*	239
15.	*"A Woman's War"*	248
16.	*"We Assumed We Were Equal"*	264
17.	*"We Can't Deal with Her"*	278

18. *Standing in the Minefield*   291

19. *"We Didn't Come All This Way for No Two Seats"*   313

20. *"This Inevitable, Horrible Greek Tragedy"*   331

21. *The "Woman Question"*   350

22. *"We Were Asked to Deny a Part of Ourselves"*   369

23. *"We Got to Keep Moving"*   382

Epilogue   397

Abbreviations for Sources   411

Endnotes   413

Bibliography   435

Acknowledgments   441

Index   443

... The great force of history comes from the fact that we carry it within us, are unconsciously controlled by it in many ways, and history is literally *present* in all we do.

JAMES BALDWIN

Freedom's Daughters

preface

When the March on Washington took place in August 1963, the women of the civil rights movement were all but forgotten.

In later years, the march would be remembered as the most glorious moment of the civil rights struggle, the culmination of years of bloodshed, arduous work, and incredible hardship. Yet on that red-letter day, women, who had played such vital roles in launching the modern movement and propelling it forward, were thrust into the background. No woman marched down Constitution Avenue with Martin Luther King, Jr., A. Philip Randolph, Roy Wilkins, and the rest of the male civil rights leaders. No woman went to the White House afterward to meet with President John F. Kennedy.

Indeed, until a week or so before the march, no woman was to receive any recognition at all. But the committee planning the event, prodded by its only female member, finally agreed that women were far too important to be excluded entirely. So after all the months of pinpoint planning, down to the number of portable toilets and cheese-sandwich bag lunches needed for the hundreds of thousands of people expected to flood Washington, committee members, as an afterthought, put together a brief, backhanded "Tribute to Women." The plan called for the venerable leader of the march, A. Philip Randolph, to introduce some of the movement's heroines for a quick bow at the Lincoln Memorial rally. None of them, however, was to be given a chance to speak.

There would be no voice for Rosa Parks, whose refusal to get up from her seat on a Montgomery bus had set in motion a social revolution that would, in less than a decade, turn the country upside down. Parks was far more than the image that Martin Luther King, among others, had crafted for her—a seamstress too tired to move, who had been less a free agent than a vessel of the forces of history, someone who had been "tracked down by the *Zeitgeist*—the spirit of the times." In fact, she had been a committed civil rights activist since the 1940s, a staunch member of the NAACP with a history of rebellion against the casual cruelties of white bus drivers.

Daisy Bates, too, would make no speech. The major force behind the integration of Little Rock's Central High School, she had braved mobs and death threats in 1957 to shepherd nine black teenagers through the hell of attending a previously all-white school. In doing so, she had helped awaken the country to the violence of its racism.

There would be no say, either, for Diane Nash, a former beauty pageant contestant with the delicate features of a porcelain doll, who had taken over command of the Freedom Rides in the spring of 1961, after the first Riders had been brutalized by mobs in Alabama. Badly battered and stunned by the violence, the Riders had decided to give up their heavily publicized bus trip through the South, designed to test a federal court decision desegregating bus terminals and other interstate public facilities. The twenty-two-year-old Nash, a veteran of countless sit-ins and jail cells herself, dispatched a group of students to Birmingham to take up where the first group had left off, then oversaw successive waves of Riders who poured into the South. The revival of the Rides succeeded in reinvigorating the civil rights crusade.

But the vast crowds that gathered at the Lincoln Memorial on that hot late-summer day in 1963 were given little inkling of the importance of Nash or Parks or Bates to the cause they were celebrating. And there was no mention at all of other women who had been essential to the movement's birth and growth. Women like Ella Baker, who had helped establish the Southern Christian Leadership Conference, headed by Martin Luther King, and then had become the guiding force behind the burgeoning student crusade. Or Septima Clark, the tough but motherly former teacher whose adult literacy and citizenship schools were now the engine for the movement's voter registration work throughout the South. Or Jo Ann Robinson, the demure college professor who was the real architect of the Montgomery bus boycott.

No mention, either, of the hundreds of poor, unlettered women in Mississippi, Georgia, and the rest of the Deep South who daily were braving bombings, beatings, and other forms of terrorism in their blazing determination to win the right to vote. Women like Ida Mae Holland, an eighteen-year-old prostitute in Greenwood, Mississippi, who had been transformed into one of Greenwood's boldest activists. Or the older women of Greenwood who inspired Holland—"mamas" like Mrs. Laura McGhee and Mrs. Belle Johnson, who, in Holland's words, "would walk their walk, and when they'd see the human barricade of police, they'd start talking their talk and singing their songs and saying, 'I ain't scared of your jail because I want my freedom. Ain't going to let nobody turn me around. Going to keep on marching.'"

*   *   *

Lillian Smith, a white Southern writer who had called for an end to racial segregation as early as 1941, noted in 1962 that the images of women throughout history had largely been crafted by men. It was time, Smith believed, for women to engage in the "great and daring creative act" of discovering and declaring their own identities. In my view, the story of the women in the civil rights movement is truly one of discovery. Until recently, the pivotal role that women played in the movement was largely ignored, just as it had been overlooked during the events of the March on Washington. The oversight of women began with contemporary newspaper and broadcast accounts of the civil rights cause, which focused almost entirely on Martin Luther King, Jr., other male civil rights leaders, and the groups they led. Karl Fleming, who covered civil rights for *Newsweek* and is widely thought to have been one of the best reporters on the beat, said in 1998: "There were no women, period. No women covering [the movement] as journalists, and no visible women on the front lines." The only activists he ever dealt with were men, Fleming said. "It was very macho." Yet, according to civil rights activist Stokely Carmichael, "the ones who came out first for the movement were the women. If you follow the mass meetings, not the stuff on TV, you'd find women out there giving all the direction. As a matter of fact, we used to say, 'Once you got the women, the men got to come.'"

For the most part, historians followed the journalists' lead: Virtually all the major early works about the period portray the movement through the filter of the men and their organizations. Only in the past few years has significant attention been paid to movement women and their singular achievements. A number of scholarly studies has been published, as have biographies of such major figures as Ella Baker, Fannie Lou Hamer, Ruby Doris Smith Robinson, and Septima Clark. Women who were active in the Student Nonviolent Coordinating Committee banded together to put down on paper their own accounts of what happened. But the broader story of the movement's women—the leaders and foot soldiers, firebrands and strategists, white Junior Leaguers and black sharecroppers—remained unwritten.

When I began work on *Freedom's Daughters*, it soon became clear that the story I was planning to tell began much earlier than the 1950s and 1960s—the period generally recognized as the time frame of the modern civil rights movement. The struggle for racial freedom, in fact, is a multi-layered saga that spanned several generations, originating before the Civil War and finally reaching its climax at mid–twentieth century. It was a struggle that women helped to mold, lead, and organize from its very beginning. In order to adequately recount the story of the women of the 1950s and 1960s, I realized I would also have to write about their forebears and the remarkable legacy of activism, courage, and rebellion that these early pioneers handed down.

Their story—and that of their twentieth-century counterparts—is a rich and vibrant one, filled with conflict and drama. It's a tale of women making difficult choices, trying, in many instances, to balance lives as wives and mothers with their all-consuming work. It's women boldly defying presidents and sheriffs and the Ku Klux Klan; defying their male leaders' admonitions to be more cautious and more political; defying, too, society's standards of proper female behavior. It's women wrestling with the complexities of their relationships with the men they worked alongside.

And, finally, it's the story of the complicated, often tortured connection between African-American women and white women in the civil rights cause. Black women were always in the vanguard of the movement but, from the beginning, white women were involved as well. At times, black women and white women worked closely together, supporting and nurturing each other. Yet there was also considerable tension and anger between them, the poisonous by-products of the intertwining of sex, gender, and race going back to the days of slavery. The ways in which black and white women were perceived and treated during slavery profoundly affected the ways in which they would be regarded by society in later years—and how they would regard each other. As writer Marita Golden has noted: "We have been defined as symbolic and actual opposites. The white woman weak/the black woman strong, the white woman undersexed/the black woman oversexed, the white woman the symbol of sexual desire/the black woman neutered. And this mumbo jumbo of imprisoning, corrupting imagery still rages in our heads and in our hearts, and makes it all the more difficult to throw a life or love line to one another."

Twice in the history of the United States, the fight for black freedom and equality gave birth to movements for women's rights. Launched in the wake of the abolitionist movement of the early 1800s and the civil rights battles of the 1960s, both women's rights crusades were begun by white women who won their activist spurs in the civil rights struggle. In both cases, black women felt torn between loyalty to their race and loyalty to their sex. Most of them chose race, insisting that their own liberation could not be separated from black men's freedom. They would discover, however, that their needs and interests would be largely ignored by black male activists, just as they would be overlooked by white leaders of the women's movement. The relative invisibility of black women is a problem that persists to this day.

One final note: In writing about women in the civil rights movement, I do not mean to dismiss or minimize the leadership or accomplishments of male activists. Their work was obviously essential to the movement. I have not written much about the men because their achievements have already been well documented. As I see it, both men *and* women played crucial roles in the civil rights movement, and both deserve due recognition as the history of that movement continues to be written.

"Far More Terrible for Women"

Pauli Murray

IT WAS APRIL 22, 1944, A WARM Saturday in Washington, D.C. The skies threatened rain, but the cherry trees near the Jefferson Memorial were in bloom, and hundreds of people, many of them soldiers and sailors in uniform, strolled the banks of the Tidal Basin to admire the lacy pink and white foam of the blossoms. News from the war was mostly good: The Marines had recently captured blood-soaked Iwo Jima, the Fifth Army was about to liberate Rome. In the capital city of the United States, however, a small, thin black woman named Pauli Murray had a different sort of liberation in mind.

Murray, due to graduate in June from Howard University Law School, was standing with some other Howard students outside Thompson's cafeteria, a few blocks northeast of the Tidal Basin. She watched as her fellow students slipped, two and three at a time, inside the cafeteria. Finally, Murray took a deep breath and joined them. Once inside, she picked up a tray and entered the serving line. When the stone-faced employees behind the steam tables refused to serve her, as they refused to serve any black, Murray silently carried her empty tray to a table and sat down among the other black students who had been turned away.

The silent demonstration at Thompson's cafeteria, led by Murray and three other Howard activists on a cloudy afternoon in wartime Washington, was a harbinger. But it did more than prefigure many similar actions almost two decades later. It also symbolized the importance of women to a movement that always *seemed* to be dominated by men. Of the approximately fifty black students who sat in that day at Thompson's, most were women, and *all* of the leaders were. Together, they had stepped from behind a historical curtain and, for the moment, were deferring to no one. Sitting at Thompson's table, waiting to be served, they read textbooks and poetry. Some were glancing at the latest issue of the liberal tabloid newspaper *P.M.* Others watched apprehensively through the windows as a crowd of whites gathered on the sidewalk, where another group of students walked a picket line, carrying placards. One of the placards read: "Are You for HITLER'S Way (Race Supremacy) or the AMERICAN Way (Equality)? Make Up Your Mind!" And another: "We Die Together. Why Can't We Eat Together?" Some soldiers jeered and taunted the pickets. A woman spat at them. Through it all, "[o]ur demonstrators were thoroughly disciplined," Murray wrote to her friend Eleanor Roosevelt several days later. "No response was made to any taunt. . . . We clamped down on our teeth and kept our eyes straight ahead."

The manager of Thompson's pleaded with the students to leave, but they replied, politely, that they would stay till they could eat. By dinnertime, the cafeteria's trade had dropped by half. After several desperate telephone calls from Thompson's manager to his superiors, an order finally came down from the chain's national headquarters: Serve the demonstrators. Even with that, two of Thompson's waitresses refused, so the manager and the chain's district supervisor quickly filled in. For the first time since Reconstruction, a downtown whites-only eating establishment in Washington, D.C., was serving black customers.

"It is difficult to describe the exhilaration of that brief moment of victory," Murray wrote long afterward. The sit-in at Thompson's was the culmination of months of intense planning and training. The participating students had been carefully selected, then rigorously schooled in the nonviolent principles and tactics of Mahatma Gandhi. Each student had signed a pledge not to retaliate against harassment or violence. And it had all worked! Soon, however, the glow of victory vanished. The press wasn't much interested, and the president of Howard University, fearing a backlash from a Congress dominated by Southern racists, ordered the students to suspend further action. Murray was furious that the students' "brief act of imaginative defiance, a commando raid against entrenched racism . . . which, if expanded, could have brought new hope to millions of black Americans," was so abruptly and completely throttled. But throttled it was, and, with the pressure lifted, Thompson's went back to "no Negroes allowed."

Not until sixteen years later would civil rights demonstrators use the same kind of nonviolent resistance employed by Murray and her fellow students. By then most activists didn't even know who Pauli Murray was. When Eleanor Holmes, a brilliant young Yale law student and member of the Student Nonviolent Coordinating Committee, returned to Yale for classes after a summer of civil rights work in 1963, she met Murray, who was then studying for her doctorate in law. Holmes, who as Eleanor Holmes Norton would later become a noted civil rights lawyer and the chair of the Equal Employment Opportunity Commission, had never heard of the 1944 Howard sit-in. She recalled being stunned on learning about the "nerve and bravery of this little woman who had already done what we were only beginning to do [but without] the safety and protection of the full-blown movement and reformist national mood that cushioned our risk."

Important as Murray was to the history of the early civil rights movement in the United States, she and the other Howard women with whom she demonstrated were merely in the middle of a long line of female soldiers of change, black and white, that stretched from the nineteenth-century abolitionist movement forward to twentieth-century civil rights and feminism. Indeed, the interconnections between race and gender, and between racism and misogyny, have helped place women at the very center of social ferment and conflict over the last two centuries of American history. Pauli Murray thus stands as a bridge between present and past. The granddaughter of a slave and great-granddaughter of a slave owner, she sprang from a family whose history, like the histories of countless others, illustrates how far the United States has come since the days of slavery, unbridled racism, and pernicious sexism—and how far it has still to go.

From the beginning, from the days of slavery and the drive for abolition, women of both races were deeply involved. Wrote Frederick Douglass in

1881: "When the true history of the antislavery cause shall be written, woman will occupy a large space in its pages; for the cause of the slave has been peculiarly woman's cause." For women, there was a particular spur, a special urgency in the nineteenth-century struggle to abolish slavery. Harriet Jacobs, an escaped slave who wrote a book about her experiences in captivity, put it this way: "Slavery is terrible for men; but it is far more terrible for women. Superadded to the burden common to all, they have wrongs, and suffering, and mortifications peculiarly their own."

Slave women were expected to work as diligently and as long as men in the fields, but they also had to bear children, raise them, cook, sew, clean, and perform other household chores for their families. Because the field work was so harsh, and medical care and nutrition so poor, miscarriages and stillbirths were all too common. Many women were weak and in constant physical pain, many looked and seemed old by the time they reached their twenties and thirties. Nor did their gender shield women from whippings and the other brutal punishments and treatments of slavery. If their children managed to survive babyhood, they still could be lost forever at the whim of a master who decided to sell them. "Babies was snatched from deir mother's breasts and sold to speculators," one old ex-slave recalled after the Civil War. "Chillens was separated from sisters and brothers and never saw each other again. I could tell you about it all day, but even den you couldn't guess de awfulness of it."

Yet brutality and degradation were not the mortifications that Harriet Jacobs wrote about. Uppermost in her mind, as in the minds of most slave women, was the ever-present danger of rape by white men. The silent menace of interracial rape and concubinage hung over the eighteenth- and nineteenth-century South like a dense miasma. Teenage girls were especially vulnerable, never knowing when they might be preyed upon by their master, the master's son or other relative, the overseer, a neighbor. As hard as black women might fight against such assault, they were, more often than not, forced to submit. According to sociologist Louis Wirth, the sexual assault of slave women by white men was ubiquitous throughout the South. Indeed, it was regarded in some quarters as a rite of sexual passage for young white men. "[N]o likely looking Negro, or more especially mulatto, girl was apt to be left unmolested by the white males," Wirth wrote. "[V]ery few of the young white men grew up 'virtuously' and their loss of virtue was scarcely to be attributed to cohabitation with white women." For generation after generation, young black women in the South were refused what most cultures deem the birthright of women: They were, as Maya Angelou put it, "denied chastity and refused innocence."

Pauli Murray's maternal grandmother, Cornelia Smith Fitzgerald, was born into slavery as a result of just such a rape, a fact that haunted Murray until the end of her life. Her great-grandmother, a beautiful light-skinned slave named Harriet, had been given as a gift to Mary Ruffin Smith, the daughter of a North Carolina plantation owner, on the young white woman's eighteenth birthday. Harriet became Mary Ruffin Smith's personal slave. A few years later, she married a free black farmer and bore a son. But Smith's two bachelor brothers—Sidney, a lawyer and politician, and Frank, a doctor—had had their eyes on Harriet, too. Sidney, in particular, took to following her around, frequently cornering her and trying to kiss her. She resisted and began nailing the door of her cabin shut at night. Then, in 1843, Sidney Smith finally made clear who was master and who was slave. After ordering Harriet's husband off the plantation, Sidney broke down her cabin door and raped her. He returned to her night after night, until his brother, Frank, waylaid him one evening outside Harriet's cabin and beat him bloody. Sidney stayed away from Harriet after that, but she was already pregnant with his child, Cornelia.

Frank Smith's throttling of his brother was hardly a protective act. Frank just wanted Harriet for himself, and she ultimately bore him three daughters. Yet he paid no attention to her outside the bedroom. When around others, she invariably approached him with the same servility that she displayed to the other slave-owning Smiths. Her four girls were raised in a kind of limbo in the Smith home. They were regarded as better than field hands yet were not—quite—house slaves and were not acknowledged as blood kin, either. Their white aunt, not their mother, was the dominant figure of their lives. The two women were linked in a strange kind of motherhood in which, Pauli Murray noted, "[t]he same overpowering forces which had robbed the slave mother of all natural rights had thrust them unwanted upon the childless spinster."

Mary Ruffin Smith, still unmarried, suffered great shame over her brothers' behavior. After Harriet gave birth to her second daughter, the family moved to another part of North Carolina to flee their neighbors' gossip. Probably, though, Mary's shame was relatively mild compared with the humiliation of countless Southern white wives, who discovered that their husbands were forcing themselves on slave women. A wife might pour out her fury, jealousy, and pain in a diary or journal, but she usually didn't dare confront her husband openly. For as cosseted and supposedly hallowed as the white Southern belle famously was, her legal status, in the final analysis, was not much different from that of a slave woman. Declared slavery apologist George Fitzhugh in 1854, "Wives and apprentices are slaves, not in theory only, but often in fact." A wife had no rights to speak of—no rights over her property or her children, no right to vote, no right to participate in public life. She was, in effect, the possession of her husband, barred from education, prevented from entering business or the professions. "In truth, woman, like children, has but one right, and that is the right to protection," Fitzhugh wrote. "The right to protection involves the obligation to obey . . . if she be obedient she stands little danger of maltreatment."

A white woman's reward for her submission was to be idealized beyond measure, to be pictured as the quintessence of ethereal loveliness, an angel who devoted her life to caring for her husband, children, and anyone else who needed her help. It was unthinkable for a woman to put her own needs first, unpardonable for her to show any spark of spirit, ambition, or independence. She was expected to perform her wifely duties without complaint—which, in the case of a slave owner's wife, included not only duties toward her own family but also attending to the feeding, clothing, medical care, and other needs of slaves. In many cases, she had far more daily contact with slaves than did her husband.

Fanny Kemble, a strong-willed young English actress who married a Georgia plantation owner in 1834, was astonished at how much her life was intertwined with those of her husband's slaves. From morning to night, they came to her with their cares: "[N]o time, no place, affords me a respite from my innumerable petitioners; and whether I be asleep or awake, reading, eating, or walking—in the kitchen, my bedroom or the parlor, they flock in with urgent entreaties and pitiful stories . . ." Opposed to slavery, Kemble raged at her helplessness in the face of the misery she saw every day. One morning, she was visited by a slave woman who was the mother of sixteen children, fourteen of them now dead. The woman also had suffered four miscarriages, one of which occurred after she'd been tied by her wrists, hung from a tree, and whipped. "And to all this I listen," Kemble declared, "—I, an English woman, the wife of the man who owns these wretches, and I cannot say, 'That thing shall not be done again; that cruel shame and villainy shall never be known here again.' I gave the woman meat and flannel, and remained choking with indignation and grief long after they had all left me to my most bitter thoughts." (Kemble's thoughts on marriage were just as foreign for that time and place as her opinions about slavery. When her husband, Pierce Butler, divorced her in 1849, he blamed the end of their marriage on his wife's "peculiar views which . . . held that marriage should be a companionship on equal terms. . . . [A]t no time has one partner a right to control the other.")

Although few wives and female relatives of slave owners shared Kemble's views on the immorality of slavery, many, nonetheless, detested the institution. They bridled at the constant psychological and physical impositions it made on their lives—rendering them, as one put it, the "slave of slaves."

Above all, the wives hated their husbands' sexual betrayal that slavery had made so easy. The Southern white woman "was confronted with a rival by compulsion, whose helplessness she could not fight," Pauli Murray said. "Nor could she hide the mulatto children always underfoot who resembled her own children so strongly that no one could doubt their parentage." Wrote one planter's bitter wife: "We are complimented with the names of wives, but we are only the mistresses of harems."

Unable to strike out directly at their husbands, wives often took out their rage on the husbands' victims. Fanny Kemble was horrified to learn that the wife of her husband's overseer had personally supervised the flogging of three slave women, all of whom had recently given birth to children he had fathered. "Jealousy is not an uncommon quality in the feminine temperament," Kemble observed, "and just conceive the fate of these unfortunate women between the passions of their masters and mistresses, each alike armed with the power to oppress and torture them."

In the nineteenth-century South, black and white women alike were caught in a tangle of sexual contradictions, repressions, and lies. Perched firmly on their pedestals, white women—supposedly timid, modest, and pure—were forced to deny any sexual feelings of their own. Black women, on the other hand, were pictured as passionate animals. Thomas Jefferson, who is believed by some to have produced at least one son with his Monticello slave Sally Hemings, once wondered if black women mated with orangutans. Jefferson's thinking was not unusual for his time. Female slaves were seen as lusty temptresses who seduced white men, luring them away from the sanctity of their homes and wives, causing men to violate standards their society held sacred. Of course, the roles that Southern white males assigned to women of both races—purity for the white woman, animal lust for the black—served to assure male domination of both. Neither was allowed to be fully human. Each was "only half of a self," yearning for the missing piece of identity assigned to women of the other race.

Moreover, placing all blame on slave "temptresses" for interracial sex helped ease white men's consciences and explain away the contradictions of a society that trumpeted a chaste and soulless ideal of white womanhood. It also had far-reaching consequences for the relationships between blacks and whites—and blacks and blacks—from then on. The image of sexual wantonness has haunted black women, shaping the way they've been treated by American society since slavery. Writer Willie Morris, for example, grew up in Mississippi in the 1940s believing that white women didn't engage in sex for pleasure, that "only Negro women engaged in the act of love with white men just for fun, because they were the only ones with the animal desire to submit that way."

The pitting of black women against white women produced suspicions and rivalries that affected the nineteenth-century abolitionist movement, the civil rights movement of the 1950s and 1960s, and the women's movement. Likewise, white Southerners' attitudes toward sexuality, sexual predation, the South's devotion to the ideal of "pure white womanhood"— all had profound repercussions on the region and the rest of the country during slavery, Reconstruction, and the century of rigid racial segregation that followed. Yet these suspicions and rivalries, these attitudes and acts, were largely ignored in the popular press of the day and were long consigned to the shadows of history. Even today, they are seldom publicly discussed.

Sex, nonetheless, has always been inextricably entwined with race and racism. "[At] the heart of the American race problem the sex factor is rooted, rooted so deeply that it is not always recognized when it shows at the surface," declared James Weldon Johnson, the noted black poet, writer, and civil rights leader. ". . . [T]he race situation will continue to be acute as long as the sex factor persists."

When Sarah Grimké, the daughter of a wealthy slaveholder, was growing up in the genteel South Carolina city of Charleston, she hated many things about slavery. Above all, she hated the psychological havoc it played on women, black and white. For Grimké, whose father once told her she could have been the greatest legal scholar in the country if she had only been born a boy, the helplessness of Southern white women was akin to that of slaves.

From an early age, she rebelled against the treatment of both. As a girl, she taught her "little waiting-maid" to read and write: "The light was put out, the keyhole screened, and flat on our stomachs before the fire, with the spelling-book before our eyes, we defied the laws of South Carolina." There clearly was no room in the South for this budding young abolitionist, and in 1821 she moved up North. Grimké's younger sister, Angelina, joined her there eight years later. The Grimké sisters, two well-brought-up white women from the South, became noted lecturers and writers in the vanguard of the battle for abolition and women's rights.

According to the law, white women were as subordinate in the North as they were in the South. Lacking legal rights, they were consigned to the home and family. By the 1830s, the "cult of true womanhood," encouraging domesticity, subservience, and piety in middle-class and upper-class white women, was firmly established in the North. In truth, though, Northern women had been tiptoeing away from the hearth since the beginning of the century, organizing charitable and temperance societies, missionary groups, literary clubs. As these activities were largely sponsored by churches, they were considered perfectly respectable: Their main priority was to help others less fortunate—sinners, the heathen, the poor. Few church leaders (or, for that matter, husbands) thought they would encourage women's independence.

Free black women in the North were organizing, too, but with different goals. Unlike white women, most black women had to work outside the home, yet were still hemmed in by legal and social constraints. Theirs was not the "do-gooder" mentality of helping the unfortunate with whom they had little in common. Their societies were more often aimed at mutual relief, designed to help themselves, their families, neighbors, and other blacks for whom poverty and discrimination were realities or ever-present threats. Black women established schools and orphanages, founded settlement houses, aided their down-and-out sisters. They also organized literary and moral improvement societies, determined to prove that they were just as genteel, just as culture-loving, just as free from moral taint as any white woman.

With antislavery sentiment swelling in New England in the early 1830s, women, black and white, rushed to the abolitionist cause. Maria Stewart, a fiery young black abolitionist and former domestic, caused a furor in 1832 when she urged an audience of men and women at Boston's Franklin Hall to join the fight. "It is of no use," Stewart declared, "for us to sit with our hands folded, hanging our heads like bulrushes, lamenting our wretched condition; but let us make a mighty effort, and arise." She aimed her message particularly at black women: "How long shall the fair daughters of Africa be compelled to bury their minds and talents beneath a load of iron pots and kettles?" Stewart's speech, sponsored by the Afric-American Female Intelligence Society, was the first public lecture ever delivered by a woman in America. Church and civic leaders were so appalled at her audacity—the very idea that a woman dare get up in public and make a speech!—that she was forced to leave Boston.

Still, the walls had been breached. Women soon organized antislavery societies in Boston, New York, Philadelphia, and other cities throughout the Northeast. Collecting money through fairs and other fund-raising events, they played a crucial role in financing the abolitionist movement. They inundated Congress and state legislatures with hundreds of thousands of signatures collected on antislavery petitions. With mounting confidence, they published magazines, wrote articles, spoke out at meetings, and organized conventions. Along the way, they encountered increasing opposition from men, even from some of their own male allies in the abolitionist cause. In a passionate retort, abolitionist writer Lydia Maria Child asserted: "Some will tell you that women have nothing to do with this question! . . . When Bonaparte told a French lady that he did not like to hear a woman talk politics, she replied, 'Sir, in a country where women are beheaded, it is very natural they should like to know the reason.' And where women are brutalized, scourged and sold, shall we not inquire the reason? My sisters, you have not only the right, but it is your solemn duty . . ."

In 1837, black and white women abolitionists gathered in New York City for the first Antislavery Convention of American Women. They formally declared that a woman had the right to carve out her own role in fighting slavery, independent of men, the right "to do all that she can by her voice, and her pen, and her purse, and the influence of her example, to overthrow the horrible system . . ." Church leaders viewed such bold assertions with growing alarm. All the same, audiences jammed meeting halls throughout the Northeast to hear the Grimkés and others link the question of women's rights with the antislavery movement. "It is not only the cause of the slave that we plead," Sarah Grimké said at one such meeting, "but the cause of woman as a moral, responsible being. . . . Men and women are *created equal!* . . . whatever is right for man to do is right for woman." As far as most churches were concerned, this was akin to heresy. In 1837, the same year as the women's antislavery convention, an organization of Congregationalist ministers attacked the Grimkés and their upstart female associates, thundering: "The appropriate duties and influence of woman is in her dependence. But when she assumes the place and tone of a man as a public reformer . . . we put ourselves in self defense against her . . ."

Consternation over this new female spirit of independence wasn't the only reason for the widespread anger and hostility toward women abolitionists. Only a small minority of Northerners actively supported the antislavery cause. Many in the North held views that were as racist as those held in the South. The notion that black and white women would meet together—even stay in each other's homes!—was regarded as an abomination. There was fury over the resolution against racism passed by the delegates to the 1837 convention, which stated that whites and blacks should treat each other "as though the color of the skin was of no more consequence than that of the hair or the eyes." Fury turned to violence at the women abolitionists' 1838 convention in Philadelphia. A mob hurled stones through the windows of a hall where black and white delegates were meeting, then blocked the doors and threatened the women as they left. That night, the hall was set ablaze. Unswayed, the women gathered the next morning to insist they would continue to sit together, eat together, and even have tea together in each other's parlors.

In Boston and other Northern cities, unruly crowds heckled women abolitionists, sprayed them with ice water, threatened them with bodily harm, and sometimes roughed them up. One Boston newspaper ridiculed that city's female antislavery society as a "parcel of silly women, whose fondness for notoriety has repeatedly led them into scenes of commotion and riots." On several occasions, female abolitionists rushed Northern courthouses and rescued fugitive slaves about to be sent back South. Reporting on one such raid, an antiabolitionist newspaper described in horror how "a colored woman of great size who scrubbed floors for a living . . . threw her arms around the neck of one officer immobilizing him."

Other women smuggled fugitive slaves out of the South, via the Underground Railroad, and into the North and Canada. Harriet Tubman, herself a runaway slave, became a legend by leading more than three hundred slaves to freedom during nineteen trips to the South, boasting that she "never lost a single passenger" on her underground railway. With a $40,000 bounty on her head, Tubman carried a pistol to defend herself against bounty hunters. But she also sometimes used the pistol to encourage hesitant runaways. "You'll be free or die," she barked.

Black and white women provided stops along the way on the Railroad—refuge in their homes for escaped slaves. Among them was the mother of Laura Spelman, the future wife of John D. Rockefeller. Another was the wife of the chief justice of the Michigan Supreme Court. Shortly after the Fugitive Slave Act was passed in 1850, making it a crime to harbor runaway slaves, the judge confronted his wife. "What am I going to do?" he asked. "You know I must enforce the new law and I know what you are doing." She answered simply, "Just walk right out of the front door and never look back to see what's going on."

*   *   *

For all their daring, for all their ringing speeches and awe-inspiring fund-raising, women in the antislavery crusade found they were still regarded as inferior and subordinate, even by many male abolitionists. "Verily," wrote a sympathetic male supporter, "some of our northern gentlemen abolitionists are as jealous of any interference in rights they have long considered as belonging to them exclusively, as the southern slaveholder is in the right of holding his slaves."

That fact was made abundantly clear in 1840, at the first worldwide abolitionist gathering in London, when women delegates from the United States were refused seats on the floor and confined to a railed-off section on one side. Twenty-four-year-old Elizabeth Cady Stanton, the daughter of a wealthy New York landowner whose abolitionist husband took her to the convention as part of their honeymoon, was so outraged that she promptly enlisted in the fight for women's rights. In 1848, she and her close friend Susan B. Anthony were the key figures behind the first Women's Rights Convention, held in Seneca Falls, New York. The convention marked the beginning of the generations-long struggle for women's equality in this country.

Before and during the Civil War, Stanton and Anthony regarded the antislavery cause to be inseparable from the fight for women's rights. Anthony, in particular, was an ardent abolitionist. She traveled nonstop throughout the North as an organizer for the American Antislavery Society, her uncompromising lectures often drawing hostile, catcalling crowds. With Stanton, she lobbied Congress and the country for passage of the Thirteenth Amendment to free the slaves, and urged other white women to do the same. When the Civil War broke out, Anthony and Stanton put aside the campaign for women's rights and focused exclusively on ending slavery.

When the war was over and the Thirteenth Amendment a reality, however, Stanton and Anthony argued with more vehemence than ever that it was time for women to be allowed into the tent. Republicans, who dominated Congress, and male abolitionist leaders had other ideas. The newly proposed Fourteenth Amendment, providing "equal protection of the laws" to all citizens (thus, in effect, granting full citizenship to former slaves), included the word "male" as a qualification for voting. Anthony and Stanton urged congressional Republicans to omit the word, but were turned down. Arguing that "this hour belongs to the Negro," Republican leaders insisted that their party could not bear the political strain of try-ing to enfranchise women, white or black, along with black men. The "hour of the Negro," in their view, did not extend to Negro women, let alone white women.

After ratification of the vaguely worded Fourteenth Amendment, it quickly became clear that yet another amendment was needed to assure voting rights for blacks. As debate raged over the Fifteenth Amendment, Stanton, Anthony, and their forces once again lobbied for the inclusion of women and once again were turned down. Even their male allies in the abolitionist movement—including one of their staunchest supporters, Frederick Douglass—urged them to step aside. The men argued that while it was important for women to have the vote eventually, it was *essential*— immediately—for the physical and economic survival of black men.

Stanton and Anthony felt profoundly betrayed. For well over a decade, they and hundreds of other women had risked a great deal, sometimes even their lives, for the antislavery movement. Was this ... *indifference* to be their reward? Their pain was understandable. So was their fury. What was incomprehensible was the stunningly racist way in which they vented it. Racism, in some form and degree, had always been present in the abolitionist movement. While there were white abolitionists who treated their black colleagues as equals, many others were unable or unwilling to reconcile their opposition to slavery with the idea of equality for blacks. In this connection, it is instructive to note that women's antislavery societies in New York and several other cities would not permit blacks to join.

As for Stanton and Anthony, instead of simply continuing to demand voting rights for men *and* women, they denounced Congress for favoring "degraded, oppressed" men over the "daughters of Jefferson, Hancock and Adams." While the Republicans had "lifted up two million black men and crowned them with the honor and dignity of citizenship, they have dethroned fifteen million white women—their own mothers and sisters, their own wives and daughters—and cast them under the heel of the lowest orders of manhood." On this basis, Stanton and Anthony went so far as to urge the amendment's defeat. Their racism alienated many of the women who had been their allies in the suffrage and abolitionist causes, resulting in a fateful schism in the crusade for women's rights.

As the abolitionist and women's movements tore themselves apart over the Fifteenth Amendment, the quarreling players—white women, and white and black men—largely ignored the interests of the other major actors in the drama: black women. Seeking a political voice for themselves, white women turned their backs on allies who had fought with them for women's rights and an end to slavery. Black newspapers, meanwhile, urged black women to be "true women" and defer to their men.

Black female activists were caught in a terrible dilemma. If they backed Stanton and Anthony, they would be throwing in their lot with women who were prepared to deny the major right of citizenship to black women's fathers and brothers and husbands, thereby assuring continued white hegemony over blacks. But if black women supported voting for black men only, they would be endorsing a plan that would give *them* no voice at all. The failure to recognize the interests of black women in the battle over the Fifteenth Amendment was not an isolated event. In the century to come, black women would remain largely invisible to the public eye—in the renewed fight for women's suffrage in the early 1900s, in the modern civil rights movement, and in the blossoming of the women's movement in the late 1960s. When one talked about "blacks," one usually meant black *men*. When "women" were discussed, the emphasis was on *white* women.

Anguished by the choice they were forced to make after the Civil War, many African-American women gave up the struggle for their own suffrage and aligned themselves with black men. As Frances Harper, a noted black abolitionist writer and lecturer, wrote about herself: "When it was a question of race, she let the lesser question of sex go." Other women, like the celebrated Sojourner Truth, insisted that neither side was right, that this was not an either/or proposition, that black men deserved their rights along with women, black and white. The tall, gaunt, elderly abolitionist, whose deep, Dutch-accented voice had thundered throughout the country on behalf of antislavery and women's rights, demanded that she and her black sisters not be overlooked. "There is a great stir about colored men getting their rights, but not a word about the colored women," she observed, "and if colored men get their rights, and not colored women theirs, you see the colored men will be masters over the women, and it will be just as bad as it was before."

In the end, Congress passed and the country ratified the Fifteenth Amendment for men only. Despite the racist attitudes of the leading white suffragist leaders, black women continued to work with them in the drive for passage of a women's suffrage amendment. Sojourner Truth set out again to lecture for women's rights, and Harriet Tubman joined a Geneva, New York, suffrage club. "Do you really believe that women should vote?" a white woman asked her once. Tubman, who added to her Underground Railroad exploits by risking her life repeatedly as a Union scout and spy during the Civil War, replied simply, "I suffered enough to believe it."

"She Has Shaken This Country"

Ida B. Wells

SHE WAS A LITTLE SLIP OF A THING, a few inches short of five feet tall. Even with her hair swept up and her linen duster on, twenty-two-year-old Ida Wells still looked like a small girl playing grown-up as she took a seat in the first-class ladies' car on the train heading from Memphis to Woodstock, Tennessee. She opened a book and began to read.

When the conductor came by to collect tickets, he took a look at her and barked, *You're not allowed in this car. Move to the next one—the smoker, the one set aside for niggers.* Wells shook her head. She had bought a first-class ticket, she was a lady, and she was going to stay in the ladies' car. In the post-Reconstruction South, however, no black woman was ever considered a lady. No matter how rich, educated, or refined, she was to be banished to the smoking car, where the windows were filthy, the passengers' drinking heavy, the air foul, and the boisterous conversation equally so.

Ida Wells wasn't moving. When the conductor grabbed her arm to pull her up, she bit him on the back of the hand and braced her feet against the seat in front of her. He ran to get help and came back with two men from the baggage car. After struggling for a few moments, the three finally were able to yank the tiny schoolteacher from her seat. They dragged her down the aisle to the smoking car, as the white passengers stood and applauded. At the next stop, she left the train, her carefully arranged hair now disheveled, her duster wrinkled, dirty, and torn, and the cheers of the whites still ringing in her ears.

Those cheers reflected the triumph many whites surely felt: Finally, almost twenty years after the end of the Civil War, these uppity blacks were getting their comeuppance. For Southern whites, the loss of the war had meant the death of their world, with their towns and plantations reduced to piles of ash, their economy ruined. Perhaps worst of all, a society in which they had been unequivocal masters had been totally destroyed. Blacks no longer bowed their heads and said, "Yes, massa," and "No, massa," obeying without question. Now they thought they were as good as whites, sitting in first-class train cars, shopping in white stores, demanding to be served in restaurants, and talking back. And the hated Yankee government did everything it could to encourage them. In 1875, Congress passed a Civil Rights Act banning discrimination in public places and on public transportation. But the South was determined not to abide by the act, and, to its delight, it discovered that the federal government was not very intent on enforcing it. Indeed, in October 1883, the U.S. Supreme Court declared the law unconstitutional. Within a few years, Southern states would erase the rights, political and civil, that blacks had so recently and dearly won, and enact Jim Crow laws throwing up impenetrable walls of segregation.

When Ida Wells was thrown out of the ladies' car, it was September 1883, one month before the Supreme Court tossed the Civil Rights Act aside. But that ruling, in the view of this determined young woman, would not be the last word. Hot-tempered and independent, considered a "heartless flirt" by the many male admirers she had rejected, Wells had "plenty of nerve," as one admirer put it. In early 1884, she filed suit in a local court against the railroad—an action that the Supreme Court had advised blacks to take if they thought they had been wronged. Amazingly, she won. The judge hearing the case had fought for the Union during the war, and he awarded her two hundred dollars. The railroad appealed. Later that year,

Wells again was denied access to a train's ladies' car, and when she protested, the conductor stopped the train and she got off. Again, she sued the railroad, and the same judge who heard her first case ruled once more in her favor, awarding her five hundred dollars, a ruling later overturned by the state supreme court. Wells's second victory caused a sensation among both blacks and whites. "A Darky Damsel Obtains a Verdict for Damages Against the Chesapeake & Ohio Railroad," proclaimed the headline in a Memphis newspaper.

The story of Wells's ejections from the ladies' car, and her demands for justice, struck a special chord with other black women. At a time when white women were treated, at least in public, with exaggerated politeness and respect, black women, no matter how cultured or educated or well dressed, were thrown out of theaters, tossed off trains and streetcars, pushed off sidewalks, roughed up by conductors and policemen. It had happened to legendary abolitionist Sojourner Truth, as it had happened to so many others, and, Truth, like Wells and others, had fought back. Truth was sixty-eight years old when a streetcar conductor in Washington tried to push her off the car. When she resisted, he grabbed her right arm and wrenched it. She went to the president of the streetcar company and demanded that the conductor be fired, which the president agreed to do. She then had the conductor arrested for assault and battery.

The flagrant humiliation of black women was tied to the widespread belief, stemming from the days of slavery, that they did not deserve respect or consideration, because they were sexual wantons who led men astray. After slavery, white men did not have the same free sexual access to black women as before, but they still considered them fair game. Women were assaulted on the street, in stores and other public places, the assaults ranging from obscene comments and gestures to physical attacks. The risk of rape was ever-present for black women working in white homes and businesses. And always, so the theory went, the women were asking for it.

In the late 1800s, Southern blacks began their great migration to the North—200,000 alone between 1890 and 1910—to seek better economic opportunities and to flee Jim Crow. According to historian Darlene Clark Hine, many of the black women who left the South did so for yet another reason—to escape sexual exploitation and the possibility of rape.

A black church magazine asked Ida Wells to write a story about her experience on the train and the lawsuit that followed. Her defiant message that blacks must stand up for their rights was so well received that other black newspapers and magazines asked her to write stories and columns for them. Soon, her outspoken pieces decrying "the contemptuous defamation of black women" and other injustices to blacks were in wide circulation around the country. In 1889 she became co-owner of the Memphis *Free Speech*, a small black weekly, and began using the paper as the chief forum for her condemnation of white society's treatment of blacks.

Then, on a March day in 1892, her life turned upside down. She was in Mississippi on business when she was handed a Memphis newspaper reporting the lynching of a black grocery store owner named Tom Moss. The circumstances of Moss's death, horrifying as they were, weren't particularly unusual: In 1892, a record 255 people were lynched in America. Most were black, and most of the killings were in the South. But for Wells, this was no routine story. She was godmother to Tom Moss's daughter.

Wells rushed back to Memphis and immediately wrote an editorial demanding that the killers be arrested and brought to trial. Everyone knew who they were, but they remained free. When it became clear to Wells that nothing would be done, she proposed a radical retaliation. Blacks, she declared in an editorial, should move out of Memphis. And, as whites watched in astonishment, they did just that—six thousand of them in only two months. White housewives began complaining about a shortage of cooks and maids, and white businesses that depended on black patronage were close to collapse.

Then Wells did something even more audacious. She turned the spotlight of her editorial page on the general subject of lynching. According to the white shibboleth, most black men who were lynched were "lustful brutes" who had violated white women. But Tom Moss had been killed because he had become too successful. His grocery store had lured customers from a white-owned store across the street, and the white grocer had collected a mob of armed men to drive him out. Moss and his co-owners, fighting it out with the mob, wounded three of its members, sheriff's deputies in civilian dress. The black merchants and several friends who came to their aid were arrested, the store looted and razed. Four days later, Moss and his partners were moved from the county jail during the night, taken on a switch engine to a lonely spot outside town, and shot to death.

What was going on here? Tom Moss was not a rapist, yet he had been lynched. Wells decided to investigate how many others like Moss there had been. She pored over court records, read old newspapers, tracked down witnesses—in short, delved deep into this vigilante form of justice, of which there had been more than a hundred examples each year since the first days of Reconstruction. According to widespread belief, such summary and awful executions were the only way to punish "the most terri-

ble crime on the face of this earth" and to deter other black men from fulfilling their heart's desire: "the opportunity to enjoy, equally with the
white man, the privilege of cohabiting with white women." For close to
two centuries, white men had preyed with impunity on black women in the
South. Now they projected their desires, guilts, and behavior onto blacks.
What if black men, flush with freedom and new political power, decided to
sleep with—maybe even marry—*white women*? And, even more terrifying,
what if white women acquiesced?

That was unthinkable, for in the Southern male psyche, the sacrosanct
white goddess had become the symbol of white male supremacy—indeed,
of the South itself. "Woman! The center and circumference, diameter and
periphery, sine, tangent and secant of our affections!" declared one fulsome
toast at a celebration of Georgia's centennial in the 1830s. In *The Mind of
the South*, W. J. Cash wrote sardonically: "There was hardly a sermon that
did not begin and end with tributes in [woman's] honor, hardly a brave
speech that did not open and close with the clashing of shields and the
flourishing of swords for her glory. At the least, I verily believe, the ranks
of the Confederacy went rolling into battle in the misty conviction that it
was wholly for her that they fought."

After the South's defeat, the confidence of white men in themselves,
their native land, and the submissiveness of their women was unsparingly
stripped away. Many women had stepped in to run businesses, plantations,
and farms during the war, and when the men returned, they often discovered that their wives, sweethearts, sisters, and daughters were not the
demure belles to whom they had bade farewell. For white men, there was
a sense of impotence as a result of the humiliations of the war and what
they saw as an emerging matriarchy. "I think there was a huge amount of
anger on the part of Southern males—unspoken anger, probably unreal-
ized anger—about all that," observed journalist Karl Fleming, a North
Carolina native. "They felt their manliness had been destroyed."

For both white and black men, manhood also was inextricably linked
to the holding of political and economic power. Thomas Rainey, a black
congressman from South Carolina during Reconstruction, complained
that white men retaliated against black men "[j]ust as soon as we begin
to assert our manhood and demand our rights . . ." Black males made up
the majority of the electorate in several Deep South states after the Civil
War. If they actually voted in those numbers, they could control the tax
assessor's office, the local courthouse—they could take over the South as
well as its white women! "The closer a black got to the ballot box," one
black writer observed, "the more he looked a rapist."

Interestingly, in the pre-Reconstruction South, black men were not widely viewed as dangerous brutes with prodigious sexual appetites, and they were rarely accused of the rape of white women—even during the war, when most white men were gone from home. When rape *was* charged, blacks were hardly ever lynched; they were given trials, which, for the most part, were conducted fairly. In more than a few instances, black men and white women became lovers and even spouses, and, while such liaisons were hardly accepted by white society, most did not meet with lethal retribution. The key, of course, was that, as slaves, black men were valuable property. Their lynching would mean significant financial losses for their masters, who, in any case, felt little threat from men over whom they had total control.

This attitude changed with the slaves' emancipation. Only after blacks were free did Senator Ben Tillman of South Carolina declare that the black man was "a fiend in human form." Since blacks weren't property anymore, whites no longer had a financial incentive to keep them alive and healthy, nor did whites have the legal power to keep blacks in line. Once they were granted the rights of all Americans, black men, and any children they might have with white women, were seen as powerful threats. Now, if a black man fathered a white woman's baby, the child still would be considered black, but he would now have the right to inherit his white relatives' property. The specter of such potential competition for the South's wealth was as terrifying for its white male elite as any fears of sexual impotence. All this helped lead to the creation of the equally terrifying apparition of the black male rapist, which served to ensure the political and economic hegemony of white men, as well as to keep black men and white women rigidly separate—and subservient. "The killing may be done in our name, but the real reason is much deeper and has been there forever," observed Virginia Durr, a gregarious, strong-willed granddaughter of an Alabama slaveholder who turned to civil rights activism in the 1940s. "[A]nd that is the desire of one man to keep another man in bondage to him, so he may live at ease and the other man must do the hard work."

After the war, the fear of black rape spread through the white South like a virus, a fear that was accepted as truth even by reputable newspapers and magazines in the North. Writing matter-of-factly about "the new Negro crime," *Harper's Weekly* declared that in aiming for social equality, black men were losing "the awe with which, in slavery times, black men had learned to respect the woman of the superior race."

Despite the fact that the odds of a white woman being raped by a black man were, in the words of W. J. Cash, far less than being struck by lightning, the fear burrowed deep into the Southern psyche. White females were taught to be constantly on guard against black men. Black males were raised never to look a white woman in the eye, to step off the sidewalk when she came near, to avoid any close proximity to her—in short, never to do anything that would give her (or anybody else) the pretext for crying "Rape." Any violation of the taboo could bring terrible retribution. Black men might be free in the eyes of the federal government, but the federal government would do little or nothing when white-hooded riders of the newly organized Ku Klux Klan carried them off into the night. Nothing would be done, either, when their bodies were found hanging from trees, smoldering in the remains of bonfires, mutilated beyond recognition, dismembered. Lynching victims were often castrated or otherwise sexually tortured, a reminder from their assailants that real manhood belonged solely to white men. (Black men weren't the only victims of KKK rampages. Black women were occasionally lynched as well—and routinely raped.)

The lynchings, which continued even after the imposition of Jim Crow laws, served as powerful warnings to the black community as a whole that whites were still in charge, that any attempt at independence or rebellion would meet with a horrible end. Even if they never were the targets of lynching, even if they never saw one themselves, young blacks grew up in a climate of unremitting fear and terror, knowing full well that they once again were under the white man's heel.

After her three-month investigation into more than seven hundred lynchings, the facts uncovered by Ida Wells debunked the view that most blacks who were lynched were guilty of sexual assault. Of the cases she probed, only a third of those lynched had even been accused of rape. Many of the others had been killed for affronts to white superiority—acquiring money or property, attempting to vote, fighting a white man, talking back, refusing to obey an order. In some instances where rape had been alleged, what Wells discovered was even more of a bombshell. The so-called rapes had been liaisons between willing adults. After reading about a black man's rape of an eight-year-old white girl in Indianola, Mississippi, Wells traveled there and found that the girl was eighteen and had visited the man frequently and voluntarily in his cabin. As Wells put it later, black men were being lynched for being "weak enough" to "accept white women's blandishments."

For a black woman to publish such revelations was all but suicidal in the South, and friends tried to warn Wells off. She was dragging into the light the South's dirtiest and most deeply hidden secrets and fears, putting the lie to its sexual myths. The South's rapists were not black men, but white. And it was the hallowed white belle, not the black female wanton, who sometimes found sexual pleasure with men of a different race.

Brushing aside her friends' warnings, Wells got her pistol, which she had bought after Tom Moss was killed, and put it beside her typewriter as she worked on an editorial for May 21, 1892. Eight Negroes had been lynched since the last issue of the *Free Speech*, she began. Three for killing a white man, and five for "the same old racket"—raping white women. Wells went on to report the sensational results of her investigation—that most black men were lynched for economic or political reasons, that others were killed for engaging in love affairs with consenting white women. "Nobody in this section of the country believes the old threadbare lie that Negro men rape white women," she declared. "If Southern white men are not careful, they will over-reach themselves and public sentiment will have a reaction. A conclusion will then be reached which will be very damaging to the moral reputation of their women."

Her editorial hit white Memphis like a lightning strike. One of the city's newspapers printed it on its front page, thundering in its own editorial: "The fact that a black scoundrel is allowed to live and utter such loathsome and repulsive calumnies is a volume of evidence as to the wonderful patience of Southern whites. But we have had enough of it. There are some things the Southern white man will not tolerate . . ."

It was fortunate for Wells that she was in Philadelphia on a long-planned trip when this thinly veiled call for her murder appeared. Spurred by the editorial, a mob of whites looted and burned the *Free Speech* office to the ground. Her co-owner barely escaped with his life, and Wells was warned that she herself would be lynched if she ever returned to Memphis. Thumbing her nose at the threats, Wells wrote a story providing proof of her claims, giving names, dates, places, and circumstances surrounding hundreds of lynchings. The New York *Age*, one of the nation's most influential black newspapers, printed the piece on its front page and distributed thousands of extra copies throughout the country. The story caused a sensation, planting the seed for what would soon become a full-blown international campaign against lynching. Wells was its Joan of Arc, touring the country and Great Britain, lecturing, investigating, organizing, and writing—in general, adding further fuel to the fire. Southern white men, "to justify their own barbarism . . . assume a chivalry which they do not possess," she wrote. "True chivalry respects all womanhood, and no one who reads the record, as it is written in the faces of the million mulattoes in the South, will for a minute conceive that the southern white man had a very chivalrous regard for the honor due the women of his race or respect for the womanhood which circumstances placed in his power . . ."

Shortly before he died, an elderly Frederick Douglass wrote a letter to Wells saying: "Brave woman! You have done your people and mine a service which can neither be weighed or measured." A prominent black clergyman in Boston remarked of Wells: "She has shaken this country like an earthquake."

But no group was more energized than Wells's own generation of young Southern black women, come of age in the late 1800s, many born in slavery but young enough to have escaped some of the institution's emotional shackles. Articulate and assertive, they were much less inclined to submit easily to white domination, much more inclined, like Wells, to protest and fight back.

Like their mothers, these young women knew that for them the Victorian dream of womanhood—staying home, raising the children, being protected and sheltered—was precisely that: a dream. Just as in slavery, most blacks were mired in poverty or teetered dangerously close to the edge, and most black women had to work, along with men, in order to eke out even a bare living. But many in the younger generation had a precious opportunity not available to the women before them—the chance to be educated—and, urged on by their mothers, they grabbed it with alacrity.

In the antebellum South, schooling had been considered a privilege belonging to white males. White girls were rarely educated, and it was a crime to teach slaves of either sex to read and write. With the coming of emancipation, the Freedmen's Bureau and Northern church-sponsored organizations sent thousands of teachers to the South to start schools for blacks. Voracious for the knowledge so long denied them, black children flocked to the schools, spurred on by their parents, mostly their mothers, who saw learning as the gateway to a better life and the first step toward racial equality. When public education for blacks was cut back or abolished after Reconstruction, mothers worked day and night to pay for their children's education. "The men talk about it," wrote Frances Harper, ". . . but the women work most for it."

Mothers pushed both sons and daughters to complete basic schooling. But more often than not, daughters were the ones encouraged to go on to college—a reverse image of white society, where higher education was generally thought wasted on girls. A young black woman grew up knowing she probably would have to be self-sufficient, and a college degree allowed her to teach—the only realistic alternative to a life spent in domestic service or in the fields. Most other jobs, unskilled work and professions alike, were basically closed to her. And there was more incentive for her to finish college than for her brother, who would have even fewer job opportunities demanding a college degree.

So young black women by the thousands, with a self-confidence and independence unknown to most white women of the time, poured their energies into education. They did so with the understanding that they were working for their race as much as or more than they were for themselves. In the process, many became social and political activists: Most of that era's prominent black women leaders started their careers as teachers or remained educators all their adult lives.

Just as in slavery, black women placed enormous importance on helping others within their community. Family and community relationships were always tightly interwoven, with people depending not just on their families for emotional, social, and economic sustenance but on everyone living around them. Eleanor Holmes Norton's memory of her own upbringing—"black children [being] raised, not simply by their parents, but by their neighborhoods"—was true in American black culture from the days of slavery. As black women fought for satisfying lives for themselves, they organized to establish schools, clinics, orphanages, homes for the elderly, lodging for women workers, and other social services. (In many communities, if it hadn't been for black women's organizations, there would have been little or no provision of social services for blacks, since white-controlled government and private agencies routinely ignored their needs.) Women's groups were formed to fight for better health care, housing, and education. And when Ida Wells began making headlines with her antilynching crusade, these young black women jumped into that fray as well.

In their activism, they were following the example of their early-nineteenth-century female forebears, and their example, in turn, would be followed by their daughters, granddaughters, and great-granddaughters in the twentieth century. "I think that women's voluntary organizations have been in the forefront for whatever social change there is," Dorothy Height, longtime president of the National Council of Negro Women, declared in the 1970s. "The fact that this is a male-dominated society . . . indeed a white-male-dominated society, means that males are so involved in the systems and institutions . . . that they don't feel the need to do anything to bring about change. . . . As a black woman, I would have to say that it's been the women . . . who have dared to tackle the racial issues."

In 1896, black women coalesced around the issue of lynching as the result of a vicious attack on their character. Ida Wells had long been used to such attacks: Most whites in the country paid little attention to her campaign or to her, except to cast aspersions on her character and morals. Northerners were often just as bad as Southerners, with even the sober, respectable *New York Times* chiming in to label Wells "a slanderous and nasty-minded mulatress" and to declare that a proclivity to rape was part of the nature of black men. But in 1896 the president of the Missouri Press Association went even further. In an assault on Wells, he wrote a letter calling all black women "prostitutes, thieves and liars." In an enraged response, more than a hundred local and regional organizations of black women joined together in forming the National Association for Colored Women, the first national black women's network. Realizing that the images of the black rapist and the sexually loose black woman were designed to rationalize white society's determination to keep blacks of both sexes under its heel, the NACW listed as two of its main goals the elimination of lynching and an end to the image of black women as morally defective.

As the first national black organization to focus on issues of racial discrimination, the NACW paved the way for the work of the National Association for the Advancement of Colored People, the National Urban League, and, eventually, the civil rights movement of the 1950s and 1960s. As historian Paula Giddings wrote about these black women activists: "They had defended the race when no one else had. They had defended themselves when their men had not."

In the minds of many female activists in the 1890s, black men had fallen short in the fight for racial justice, doing little but talk about it. An editorial in the NACW newspaper, *Woman's Era*, urged "timid men and ignorant men" to stand aside. This was a "woman's age," NACW leaders felt, a time for black women to assume leadership in promoting the advancement of their race. Many black men, however, took emphatic exception. John Hope, the president of Atlanta Baptist College, for one, chided members of Atlanta women's clubs for their "brow-beating spirit" and the "caustic remarks" they had made about men, and charged the women with being "more masculine than feminine." Black men should be encouraged to assert their authority and demonstrate their masculinity, Hope declared, adding that "the surest way for our men to become more manly is for our women to become more womanly." In other words, women should focus less on assuming leadership in the fight against racism and concentrate more on supporting their men.

Hope's remarks reflected a tension between black men and women that had been growing since the Civil War and emancipation. During Reconstruction, the federal government had encouraged newly freed slaves to emulate the gender and family roles of the country's dominant white culture, asserting that husbands should act as heads of their families and wives should be subservient and stay home with their children. Even though staying home was a financial impossibility for most black women, they still were expected to submit to their husbands' control. In 1855, a gathering of free black men had complained about how slavery had stripped away manhood from their brothers in bondage. "As a people," the men declared, "we have been denied the ownership of our bodies, our wives, home, children, and the products of our own labor." Once male slaves were freed, they sought to claim what they saw as those rights of ownership, particularly the control over black women to which white men had previously laid claim.

In the years following the war's end, the Freedmen's Bureau received frequent complaints from black women about physical abuse by both white and black men. When Frances Harper toured the South in the late 1860s, she reported, "Part of the time, I am preaching against men ill-treating their wives." And a black nurse wrote to a Northern magazine that "[w]e poor colored women wage-earners in the South are fighting a terrible battle. . . . On the one hand, we are assailed by white men and on the other hand, we are assailed by black men, who should be our natural protectors . . ."

Black women activists often paid a high personal price for their independence and assertiveness, pressured as they were to conform to Victorian standards of female respectability and subservience. In a diary she kept in her early twenties, the headstrong Ida Wells, for example, revealed a constant internal struggle between her desire for male companionship and attention and her reluctance to get married and give up her freedom. Her ambition and unconventional lifestyle (she didn't marry until she was thirty-two, to Chicago lawyer Ferdinand Barnett) made her the target of a number of scurrilous rumors, among them the stories that she was involved with a white man "for money" and that she'd had an illegitimate child. The rumors, she noted, were started by men.

Wells's outspoken leadership of the antilynching crusade in the 1890s also aroused masculine anger. Once, she said, she almost refrained from going to the scene of a lynching because of complaints from black men that she was stealing their thunder. "I had been accused by some of our men of jumping ahead of them and doing work without giving them a chance," she declared.

It was an accusation that would be revived in the late 1960s, leveled against Wells's female successors in the civil rights battle.

*   *   *

Despite intense social pressure on them to be "proper ladies," many Southern black women had plunged wholeheartedly into the turbulence of political and social action by the turn of the century, and they were increasingly impatient with white women for not doing the same, particularly in the battle against lynching. "[W]hat a mighty foe to mob violence Southern white women might be, if they would arise in the purity and power of their womanhood to implore their fathers, husbands and sons no longer to stain their hands with the black man's blood!" proclaimed Mary Church Terrell, first president of the NACW, in 1904.

But only a few white women in the South would dare even think about violating one of its most rigid taboos and work together with blacks, let alone align themselves with blacks against white men. Indeed, after the Civil War, Southern white women were often more ardent than their men in bemoaning equality for blacks and in promoting the idea of the Lost Cause—the transmutation of the South's defeat into a romantic, heroic crusade. Throughout the South, the United Daughters of the Confederacy, an organization of rebel soldiers' female descendants, erected hundreds of monuments to Confederate fighting men on courthouse and state capitol lawns, emblazoned with the inscription "Lest We Forget."

Notwithstanding their taste of independence during the Civil War, many white women in the South were anxious to return to the world of their past. Instead of challenging the authority of husbands and fathers, they were content, at least outwardly, to return to the submissive life of a Southern lady. "The self-respect of the home-coming, defeated Confederate demanded that manliness be thus buttressed; moreover, in a very primitive sense, Southern women had to compete with each other for the men they outnumbered," according to Mississippi newspaper editor Hodding Carter. "Coquetry, charm, the ability to attract became practical necessities for the woman who sought a mate or would heal a husband's wounds of the body and the spirit."

When the battle for women's suffrage revived in the early 1900s, the movement's leaders, in an attempt to win the support of white Southern women, once again cast off their black allies. Ida Wells-Barnett, who had fought just as hard for women's suffrage as for an end to lynching, was ordered not to march in a massive woman's suffrage parade in Washington in 1913, for fear her presence might offend white Southerners. Defiant as ever, Wells-Barnett slipped into line with the Illinois delegation and marched anyway.

Efforts by white suffragists to gain Southern support, however, turned out to be fruitless. The former Confederate states rejected the Nineteenth Amendment. Particularly frightening to white Southern politicians was the idea of black women being given the vote. "Experience has taught us that Negro women are much more aggressive in asserting the 'rights of the race' than the Negro men are," said Senator Tillman. Another archracist, Senator J. K. Vardaman of Mississippi, warned, "The Negro woman will be more offensive, more difficult to handle at the polls than the Negro man."

Determined to keep a tight rein on women, regardless of race, white male Southerners paid little attention to the evidence that a small minority of white women were, in fact, emerging from their cocoons. Like Northern women more than half a century before, they were doing so through their churches, even though most churches adamantly opposed any change in women's subordinate role. By the early twentieth century, Methodist, Baptist, and Presbyterian women had organized societies throughout the South to support foreign missionary work and help the poor and needy at home. Church leaders, only too happy to have women assume these responsibilities, would have been horrified to know they were giving women the tools to break the fetters of dependence forged in part by their own institutions. Finally allowed a voice, Southern white women, particularly Methodists, quietly set about exercising it, although they were careful to talk of their newfound freedom as the assumption of responsibilities, not of rights.

The Methodist Church was noted in the South for its concern for social issues, but its women members were much bolder in their social activism than the church itself. Methodist women's groups built and supported dozens of settlement houses for mill workers and coal miners, and created other social welfare institutions. They urged equal pay for women workers, the abolition of child labor, and aid for black education. And when the South's first interracial movement took shape in the 1920s, Methodist women were among its most vocal supporters.

The Commission on Interracial Cooperation, formed in 1919 after a spate of riots and lynchings, was, for its time, a radical social experiment—blacks and whites coming together to foster interracial understanding and dialogue and to fight racial violence. Initially, the CIC was a male-only group, with considerable resistance to the idea of including women, but the CIC's head, Methodist minister Will Alexander, quickly realized that if the organization was to have any chance of success, it must include those who actually were doing most of the work of social activism. In October 1920 the CIC Women's Council was formed, pledging itself to work for the end of both lynching and the sexual exploitation of black women.

For the first time, black and white women began meeting together in groups across the South, with whites getting an education from blacks on the sexual double standard and other consequences of racial oppression. Yet, dedicated as they might have been to improving racial understanding, both black and white women fumbled badly in the struggle to communicate with one another. They were divided by a chasm of expectation and experience that most, in the end, could not bridge. Regardless of their race, they also were trapped in a web of dissemblance, accustomed to hiding their true feelings behind a nonthreatening facade, unable, in the final analysis, to get much beyond what poet Adrienne Rich has called "the caricatures of bloodless fragility and broiling sensuality." Carrie Parks Johnson, the first head of the women's council, breathlessly revealed just how little she had known about black women: "I saw these colored women, graduates of great institutions of learning. I saw doctors, lawyers, poets, sculptors and painters. I saw women of education, culture and refinement. I had lived in the South all my life, but didn't know such as these lived in the land."

Black women were hostile toward white women for not taking more of a lead in fighting racial violence and discrimination, not realizing how much nerve it took for a Southern white woman during that period merely to espouse racial justice. And white women in the interracial movement were unable to shed fully their racism or their deeply ingrained feelings of superiority. While they opposed racial injustice, the CIC's whites did not advocate social equality between the races, and they believed that white and black women in the organization should work, for the most part, in parallel committees. When blacks and whites joined forces, black women sometimes were subjected to social indignities, including being told to enter meetings by the back door.

While the Commission on Interracial Cooperation deserves credit for its steps to organize a dialogue between the races in the South, no matter how halting or marred by bias, it achieved little of substance in its fight against racial violence. By 1930, one of the commission's white female leaders had decided to take matters into her own hands. Talk was fine, Jessie Daniel Ames believed, but it was far from enough. By nature, Ames was a woman of action. It was time, she resolved, for white women to accept the challenge flung at them for so many years by black women. Time for white women to confront their men openly about lynching.

The wife of an Army surgeon, Jessie Ames had been widowed young and left with three small children. As wife and widow, however, she had never

been a homebody. Involved in the fight for women's suffrage and racial justice from her early twenties, the red-haired Texas native referred to herself as "a born rabble rouser." Her children often felt "orphaned and
neglected" by her work, she acknowledged, and she never made enough
money to support them properly. She complained of being always in
debt—"furniture mortgaged, car mortgaged . . . bank notes up to the hilt."
But, in her single-minded view, all that paled in importance compared with
the need to prevent lynching.

She had begun this work as a paid CIC field secretary in the Southwest, appearing before audiences who believed "that no Southern woman
of fine sensibilities would speak the word 'lynching' in private, to say nothing of talking from a platform about it by name." Hate mail and gossip
didn't stop her from speaking, nor did they stop her from conducting personal investigations of individual lynchings, much as Ida Wells had done
more than twenty years before.

In 1928, Jessie Ames was put in charge of women's activities for the
CIC, but she soon ran afoul of Will Alexander and the other male leaders,
who had a hard time coping with a woman who did not fit the stereotype
of a Southern lady. They considered Ames too assertive and domineering,
too insistent on her own way. She, on the other hand, saw them as not
aggressive enough in the antilynching battle. "The men were out making
studies," she said years later, "and so the women had to get busy and do
what they could to stop lynching."

Ames agreed with black women that she and other white women had
a moral responsibility to fight lynching. Just as important, she felt, was the
need to combat the *notion* underlying lynching—that killing black men
was a form of chivalry toward white women. The idea that white women,
powerless and weak, had to rely on white men to guard them from rape
kept the women in line as much as it did black men. It was an idea that still
permeated Southern society decades after Reconstruction. At the University of Alabama, for example, members of a prestigious men's honorary
society still hewed to the custom of dimming the lights at their dances and
carrying in a cart filled with ice. One of the members would then raise his
glass and make the following toast: "To woman, lovely woman of the
Southland, as pure and chaste as this sparkling water, as cold as this
gleaming ice, we lift this cup, and we pledge our hearts and our lives to
the protection of her virtue and chastity."

According to this idea, a woman's right to protection depended on
her remaining an ice goddess. If she violated the Southern code of proper
feminine behavior, she could no longer count on men galloping to her

rescue. Chivalry was "pressed like a crown of thorns against our heads," Jessie Ames asserted. Beneath its facade lay the belief of white men that "white women are their property [as] are Negro women."

The number of lynchings had declined considerably since the late 1800s, but every year black men were still meeting horrible, lawless deaths in the South. In 1930, an upsurge of lynchings propelled Ames into action. On November 1, she and twenty-five other white women activists, most of them leaders of church women's groups, gathered in Atlanta to form the Association of Southern Women for the Prevention of Lynching. It was an event of profound social and psychological importance— a confluence of proper white Southern ladies rejecting their role as object and symbol, declaring their independence from the tyranny of the female ideal, mounting a public protest against the heinous crime supposedly committed on their behalf. "Public opinion has accepted too easily the claim of lynchers and mobsters that they were acting solely in the defense of womanhood," the new association's members declared. "Women dare no longer to permit the claim to pass unchallenged nor allow themselves to be the cloak behind which those bent upon personal revenge and savagery commit acts of violence and lawlessness."

Within months of the association's formation, state councils had formed in all fourteen Southern states, with thousands of women, most of them from small towns and rural areas, pledging themselves to take action against lynching. By the early 1940s, more than forty thousand women— the mainstays of Southern churches, who made cookies for bake sales and raised money for missionary societies and arranged flowers on the altars—had become ASWPL members.

This was a ladies' group without precedent. Instead of sipping tea and engaging in genteel conversation, they confronted Southern politicians, reminding them they now had the vote and were prepared to use it as a weapon. They sent telegrams to all Southern governors promising their political support if the governors used their "power and influence" to halt lynchings. Local sheriffs and other law enforcement officers were urged to sign pledges declaring they would do everything they could to prevent mob violence. When Southern members of Congress and other officeholders continued to argue that lynching was needed to stop rape, women showered them with letters and telegrams ordering them to "quit dragging the good name of Southern white women through the mud."

But association members didn't stop with words. Like Ida Wells, some of them turned investigative reporter, driving down rutted back roads in their hats, their white gloves, and their polite demeanor to interview witnesses to lynchings that allegedly stemmed from assaults on white women. Quite frequently, they discovered there had been no such assault. Realizing that investigations alone, while rebutting the main rationale for lynchings, probably would not deter the killings, the women decided on a much bolder course. They would work to halt mob violence themselves, no matter what rationale was used to justify it.

Lynch mobs often let everyone know about their plans hours, and occasionally even days, before they took action—a fact that helped ASWPL women mobilize opposition. The women frequently were tipped off by newspaper and wire service reporters, who called them with news of impending lynchings. In one such case, an AP reporter phoned Jessie Ames on Christmas Day, 1934, to tell her that a mob was gathering in Georgia's Schley County to lynch a black man who had reportedly murdered a policeman. Ames, in turn, called Mary Addie Mullino, who lived in the county. Leaving her family in the middle of Christmas dinner, Mullino rushed to call the sheriff and everyone else she could think of who might be able to stop the violence. Not until she was assured that a lynching had been averted did Mullino finally leave the phone.

Not surprisingly, such unladylike behavior by the women of the ASWPL was often met with taunts of "nigger lover," attacks in the local newspaper, and threatening letters and phone calls. Some women, fearing that their husbands and families would try to stop their work, kept what they were doing a secret. Montie B. Greer, of Potts Camp, Mississippi, for example, didn't tell her husband about her lynching investigations, or the threats that followed, until long after she'd finished her work with the association.

And what were the results of this unparalleled campaign? By 1941, more than 1,300 law enforcement officers had signed antilynching pledges, and many of them had actually saved prisoners from mobs. In counties where association members flexed their muscle, the number of lynchings had declined far more dramatically than in counties where the group had no influence. Even though lynchings had hardly been eradicated, their main rationale—protecting white women from black men—had lost much of its social force.

But while Ames and the members of her group had shown extraordinary courage in their antilynching campaign, they, like the Southern white women before them, found it impossible, in the end, to transcend completely the taboos and shibboleths with which they had been raised. In the late 1930s and 1940s, the women of the ASWPL refused to lobby for a federal antilynching amendment, contending that it violated states' rights.

Defending the exclusion of black women from their organization, they felt that whites, not blacks, were the most effective instruments of social reform. While protesting racial injustice, they supported social barriers between blacks and whites.

Subversive in their early thinking and actions, these women had played an important role in the battle for human freedom, but they couldn't take it to the necessary next step. The stage had to be yielded to women who could.

Women like the two unlikely friends Pauli Murray and Eleanor Roosevelt.

3

"Getting Them Comfortable with Rebellion"

Lillian Smith, Mary McLeod Bethune, Eleanor Roosevelt

"DON'T TOUCH ME. I'M FULL OF splinters," Pauli Murray often told friends. The "splinters" were the anger and pain, self-doubt and confusion, that were such an integral part of her. But the anger was paramount on a December day in 1938 when Murray sat down to write a letter to Franklin D. Roosevelt.

She had just read in *The New York Times* that the President had been awarded an honorary degree by the University of North Carolina, that he had praised the school as a bastion of liberal thinking, the academic vanguard in the struggle for social reform. That, of course, was the conventional wisdom about Chapel Hill—it was an intellectual oasis in an otherwise arid Southern landscape.

But to the twenty-eight-year-old Murray, Roosevelt's speech, as reported in *The Times*, was nothing but windy political platitudes. What about the reality of Chapel Hill—the fact that even this beacon of rationality refused to admit black students? What about the other ugly sores of segregation in the South? What was Roosevelt doing to heal them? Why couldn't he forget politics for once and summon enough courage to defy the Southern leadership in Congress and support a federal anti-lynching law? Why was he so concerned about Hitler's suppression of freedom in Germany and Austria, yet so seemingly unconcerned about the suppression of freedom at home?

In her letter to the President, Murray spilled out her fury. "I am a Negro, the most oppressed, most misunderstood and most neglected section of your population," she wrote. "Do you feel as we do, that the ultimate test of democracy in the United States will be the way in which it solves its Negro problem? . . . Have you raised your voice loud enough against the burning of our people?" Having praised the University of North Carolina, was Roosevelt prepared to pressure the school to accept African-American students? Or did his support of social change merely "mean that everything you said has no meaning for us as Negroes, that again we are to be set aside and passed over for more important problems?"

There was an intensely personal reason for Murray's stinging questions. Only days before, she had applied for admission to Chapel Hill's graduate school, to study race relations with sociologist Howard Odum and his colleagues. She knew what the answer would be but was determined to make the university go on record with it. Her qualifications spoke for themselves—at least until she got to the line on the application asking her race. A native of North Carolina and a graduate of Hunter College in New York City, Murray was the great-granddaughter of a University of North Carolina graduate, and the great-great-granddaughter of a former university trustee. Both, of course, were white.

Ever since Murray was a little girl, the injustice of not being able to attend an institution so intimately connected to her family nagged at her like an aching tooth. Raised by her grandparents, her aunts, and the rest of a large extended family in Durham, she had lived in a world of bewildering contradictions, whipsawed between an ex-slave grandmother, Cornelia Smith Fitzgerald, who prized above all her white Smith ancestry and who even mourned the death of the Confederacy, and a grandfather, Thomas Fitzgerald, who had fought for the Union. Cornelia Fitzgerald, who could pass for white, had implicitly denied the duality of her heritage: She insisted that she was a Smith first and foremost, and rarely mentioned her mother, Harriet, a tragic wraith who was largely ignored by her four daughters whom two white men had sired. By contrast, Thomas Fitzgerald, whose mother was white, was a "race man" with a strong sense of black pride.

Murray thus grew up unsure not only of her place in the world but of her place in her own family. Light brown in complexion, the color of coffee with cream, she was considered too dark at home, too white at her all-black school, and invisible to the white world around her. The only important thing about her was her color, she thought—and felt stripped of any personal identity. At school, some of her darker classmates taunted her about her lightness and yelled, "Black is honest, you half-white bastard!" At home, relatives issued a succession of orders: "Brush your hair, child, don't let it get kinky! Cold cream your face, child, don't let it get sunburned! Don't suck your lips, child, you'll make them too niggerish!" Like much of the black community, many members of Murray's family were obsessed with whiteness. They considered it a mark of distinction. In fact, light skin usually meant that black mothers or grandmothers or great-grandmothers had been forced to have sex with white men. Nevertheless, as Murray later wrote, it provided incredible advantages—"the ability to pass unnoticed in the crowd, the power to avoid humiliation and abuse." It also caused, then as now, tremendous friction and stress within families and communities. At home, those who had the whitest skins "were the family showpieces, the ones to whom most deference was given," Murray observed. "Away from home they had easy access to a white world from which the others were shut out and faithfully reported back the details of their fine treatment . . ."

Murray felt herself a minority within a minority, "shoved down by inexorable pressures from without, thrust up by intolerable frustrations from within." It was all too much for the strong-willed little girl, who met the pressures and frustrations of a segregated society with defiance. From an early age, she rebelled against Jim Crow laws. She avoided segregated streetcars, walked almost everywhere she had to go, and refused to go to movies, because if she went, she would have to sit in the "colored balcony."

Murray hated the South and was determined not to go to a segregated college, so she moved to New York and put herself through Hunter College. There, she lived hand to mouth during the first years of the Depression and suffered from malnutrition. She finally graduated in the winter of 1933. If that year was the worst possible time for a white male college graduate to find a job, it was many times worse for a black woman. Murray's ambition was to be a poet, but she had to settle for work as a sales representative for the National Urban League magazine, then was forced to quit when she came down with pleurisy. Unemployed for more than a year, she finally was hired by the New Deal's Works Progress Administration as a remedial reading teacher in New York and later as a teacher of labor union members.

In 1938, unhappy with what she had accomplished thus far in her life and prompted by the political ferment around her, she decided to enlist in the cause that had consumed her as a little girl—the struggle for racial equality. To that end, she decided to return to the South and face her demons.

It was then that she filled out the application to the University of North Carolina—and waited.

Nine days after President Roosevelt's speech, Murray received her rejection, with the curt explanation: "Members of your race are not admitted to the university." But it was not that simple anymore. The U.S. Supreme Court had ruled two days earlier that the state of Missouri must permit black students to attend the University of Missouri Law School if no substantially equivalent state-run facilities were available for blacks. In his letter to Murray, the graduate school dean at Chapel Hill implicitly acknowledged the ruling and promised vaguely that the North Carolina state legislature would soon make some sort of provision for black graduate education in the state.

This was not good enough for Murray, and she fired off an appeal to UNC president Frank Porter Graham, regarded as an icon of Southern progressivism. "It is the duty of Negroes to press for political, economic and educational equality for themselves and for disinherited whites," Murray wrote. As historian John Egerton pointed out, this was a belief that Graham shared, expressed in "words he might have written himself." But Graham, like Roosevelt, had his finger up to test the political wind and knew that public sentiment in the state was violently opposed to desegregation. As much as he might sympathize with her, this was not the time, he wrote back, for "a popular referendum on the race issue," pointing out that the state constitution specifically required separation of the races. He begged her, in an exchange of several letters, not to stir up trouble, to trust that the legislature, at some unspecified date, would provide blacks with a separate but truly equal graduate education. Murray replied: "We of the younger generation cannot compromise with our ideals of human equality."

Franklin Roosevelt sloughed Murray off, too. He referred her letter to the WPA, since she had once worked for that agency. But she did get a personal letter from an unexpected source—Eleanor Roosevelt. Murray had sent Mrs. Roosevelt a copy of her letter to the President, with a personal covering note. More outspoken against racial abuses than her husband, Mrs. Roosevelt nonetheless had never gone so far as to espouse an end to segregation, and her reply to Murray was cautious. She understood "perfectly" Murray's desire to go to the university, but "great changes come slowly. I think they are coming, however, and sometimes it is better to fight hard with conciliatory methods. The South is changing, but don't push too hard."

Mrs. Roosevelt's message to Murray may have been similar to Frank Porter Graham's, but while Graham defended the status quo, Mrs. Roosevelt was soon to launch an all-out assault on it. Indeed, she had already been widely vilified for her efforts on behalf of racial justice. She had been photographed with black miners and sharecroppers, and had been an ardent advocate within the administration of improving blacks' living and working conditions. She was a member of the NAACP and the National Urban League, and had lobbied in 1937 for congressional passage of a federal antilynching bill while her husband sat back and did nothing. Her activism had led Barry Bingham, the son of the publisher of the Louisville *Courier-Journal,* to write a presidential aide that Mrs. Roosevelt "has made herself offensive to Southerners by a too great affection for Negroes."

As outspoken as Eleanor Roosevelt was in 1938, however, she would become even more of a firebrand in the next few years, affected greatly by her growing circle of black friends, which would soon include Pauli Murray. It was a fascinating pairing, this angry young black militant and aging white aristocrat. For Murray, who had lost her own mother at the age of three, Eleanor Roosevelt would act as a kind of surrogate mother, comforting and soothing her, scolding her, visiting her when she was sick. Murray, in turn, would spur Mrs. Roosevelt on, influencing her to take bolder and bolder stands, until it reached the point where, according to an FBI report, the wife of the President was regarded by many in the South as "the most dangerous individual in the United States today." Eleanor Roosevelt's metamorphosis from sheltered and socially unconcerned socialite to one of the foremost champions of human rights in this century was nothing short of extraordinary.

She had roots in the South and grew up listening to antebellum tales, romantic and horrifying, of her slave-owner forebears. Her maternal grandmother had been raised on a plantation in Georgia, with a "little black shadow"—a young slave girl who slept on a straw mat outside her room and who was always at her beck and call. Eleanor's great-uncle once flew into a rage at his own "shadow" and killed him; his punishment was banishment to Europe for a year. Two other great-uncles were killed fighting for the Confederacy, in a war that Eleanor, like her Southern relatives, preferred to call the War Between the States. Until a few years before she became First Lady, her only knowledge of blacks was as servants, and she often referred to them as "pickaninnies" and "darkies." Indeed, that was one habit she found hard to shed, even as her views on race underwent an astonishing transformation in her White House years and beyond. She used the term "darky" in her autobiography, published in 1937, and a young graduate of Tuskegee Institute wrote her that she couldn't believe that Mrs. Roosevelt, whom she considered "the paragon of American womanhood," had used such a "hated" and "humiliating" word. Mrs. Roosevelt wrote back: "'Darky' was used by my Georgia great-aunt as a term of affection and I have always considered it in that light. I am sorry if it hurt you. What do you prefer?"

As Pauli Murray pointed out, Eleanor Roosevelt was "a nineteenth-century woman . . . born in the nineteenth century and . . . formed in the nineteenth century." For much of her adult life, she struggled to rid herself of deeply ingrained prejudices, of ways of talking and thinking that were so offensive to others. What's remarkable is not how often she failed, but how much, overall, she succeeded.

Once she had made the plunge into the real world, Eleanor Roosevelt never saw poverty and joblessness and racial injustice merely as issues, as her husband and others in his administration tended to do. For her, the issues had unforgettable faces—babies in a Mississippi shack with empty eyes and bloated bellies; a laid-off Detroit mill worker whose children were crying with hunger; the terrified family of a sharecropper who had been lynched by a faceless mob. As she traveled around the country in the early New Deal years, serving as the paralyzed FDR's eyes and ears, she realized that however poor many whites were, blacks, as a whole, were in much more desperate shape.

As First Lady, Mrs. Roosevelt developed close ties with several black leaders, among them Walter White, executive secretary of the NAACP. But the leader to whom she listened most closely, the one with whom she formed the deepest friendship, was a tall, imposing woman who looked like an African monarch and maneuvered in Washington with the wily skill of a consummate politician. Mary McLeod Bethune had joined the Roosevelt administration after serving as president of Bethune-Cookman College in

Daytona Beach, Florida. She had built the school from a shack, five pupils, $1.50 in the treasury, and a few packing cases for desks into a thriving campus of several hundred students and eight modern buildings. Mrs. Bethune was a woman of staunch independence and dignity, due, in part, to her having been born and raised in freedom, unlike the fourteen brothers and sisters who came before her. Like many other black women educators, Mrs. Bethune was a determined activist for civil rights: Her repeated efforts to encourage blacks in Daytona Beach to vote, for example, had prompted several nighttime raids by the Ku Klux Klan on her school.

Eleanor Roosevelt had met her in 1927. When Franklin Roosevelt was elected President in 1932, the First Lady sought a job for her friend. In 1935, Bethune was named to head the office of minority affairs for the National Youth Administration. Her influence far exceeded her job description. As the first black woman appointed to a major federal government position and the most prominent African-American in the Roosevelt administration, Mrs. Bethune launched a crusade to improve the living and working conditions of blacks throughout the country, increase their job opportunities, and halt racial violence. An admiring male government colleague once described her as "a one-woman employment agency trying to get black professional people placed in every bureau of the federal government." Another male admirer said she had "the most marvelous gift of affecting feminine helplessness in order to attain her ends with masculine ruthlessness." She fiercely challenged any personal racial slight. When a White House guard called her "auntie," she stared at him for a moment, then asked, "Which one of my brother's children are you?"

Her trump card was her easy access to Eleanor Roosevelt. Influenced by Mrs. Bethune and others, Mrs. Roosevelt put pressure on her husband and his advisers to give blacks a larger slice of the New Deal pie. In 1935, the President signed an order banning discrimination in the WPA. From then on, according to historian Doris Kearns Goodwin, "the Negro's share in the New Deal expanded." Added Goodwin: "Though the New Deal never succeeded in giving full justice to the economic needs of black Americans, Eleanor was largely responsible for the steady increase over the years in the number of Negroes on public relief and in the funds they earned."

Even though Roosevelt and his administration never saw themselves as civil rights champions of blacks, black voters did. A political sea change occurred in 1936, when blacks shifted their longtime allegiance from the party of Lincoln and voted in massive numbers for Roosevelt and the Democrats, a shift to the Democratic electoral column that would continue into the next century. Still, in the view of Roy Wilkins, then an assistant to

Walter White, Roosevelt was a friend to blacks "only insofar as he refused to exclude the Negro from his general policies that applied to the whole country. . . . The personal touch and the personal fight against discrimination were Mrs. Roosevelt's. That attached to Roosevelt also—he could hardly get away from it—and he reaped the political benefit from it."

As war erupted in Europe and the United States edged closer to the conflict, the President's priorities diverged more and more dramatically from those of his wife. For Roosevelt, the New Deal, having lost considerable political support, was basically over. His energies were now largely devoted to providing aid to the British and preparing his own country for war. Eleanor Roosevelt, on the other hand, had become far more militant. Increasingly, she insisted on social reform and racial justice, particularly on the need to wipe out Jim Crow laws and practices. No longer was she merely advocating the expansion of economic opportunities for blacks and a federal crackdown on lynching. No longer was she counseling patience, as she had done with Pauli Murray in 1938. Now, she was asking the same question Murray had asked: How could America claim to defend democracy when millions of its own people were denied basic civil rights?

In 1939, when the Daughters of the American Revolution refused to allow Marian Anderson to sing in their Constitution Hall, Mrs. Roosevelt resigned from the organization and saw to it that the government invited Anderson to give an Easter Sunday concert at the Lincoln Memorial. Responding to rising discontent and anger among blacks, the First Lady declared: "The nation cannot expect the colored people to feel that the United States is worth defending if they continue to be treated as they are treated now." In a passionate speech to the 1940 convention of the Pullman porters' union, she pledged her best efforts to help make America a place of true equality for everyone. When she finished, the porters gave her a prolonged standing ovation.

Mrs. Roosevelt's increasing boldness in speaking out on what was arguably the country's most explosive social issue infuriated administration officials afraid of antagonizing white voters and the Southern Democrats who controlled Congress and thus had power over the President's legislative agenda. Secretary of War Henry Stimson, for one, blamed her for growing pressure to end discrimination in the military and criticized her "intrusive and impulsive folly." Although President Roosevelt had generally supported his wife's social activism in the past, as the war drew near, he grew increasingly irritated at her insistence that civil rights was not an issue to be swept under the carpet for the duration.

In June 1941, a young theology student at Howard University named

James Farmer witnessed an abrasive encounter between the President and his wife that underscored their disagreements. A pacifist and head of a group called Youth Committee Against War, Farmer received an invitation from Eleanor Roosevelt for dinner at the White House and a chat with the President, along with some thirty other national youth leaders. The only African-American at the dinner, Farmer was put at ease by Mrs. Roosevelt, who sat at his table and "listened to my views with seriousness and responded as an equal." Later that evening, when Franklin Roosevelt asked for questions from the students, Farmer pushed him to justify his characterization of Britain and France as "champions for freedom" in view of what Farmer called their racist colonial policies in Africa. Roosevelt's trademark grin disappeared. He took his cigarette holder from his mouth, blew a few smoke rings, and watched them float away. Then, jabbing his cigarette holder in Farmer's direction, he said: "Let's not put it that way. Let's put it this way. In which country would you rather live today— France or Nazi Germany?"

Before Farmer could reply, Eleanor Roosevelt stood up, pointed her finger at her husband, and snapped: "Just a minute. You did *not* answer the question!"

Obviously nettled, Roosevelt bit down hard on his holder's ivory mouthpiece. "The question was *this*," he retorted. "Why do I consider Britain and France to be more on the side of freedom than Nazi Germany despite their colonization laws? And I answered it thus. You will please let *me* handle the questions!" Mrs. Roosevelt sat down, but Farmer interpreted the expression on her face as saying to her husband, "I'll see *you* later."

As he left the White House that night, Farmer told Mrs. Roosevelt he hoped he and the other students had not been too presumptuous in putting Roosevelt on the spot. "Not at all," she replied. "The questions you asked needed to be asked. I'm glad you asked them, and I'm glad you came."

Farmer, who counted Eleanor Roosevelt among his heroes, had already decided by the time of the White House meeting to devote his life to fighting for black civil rights. Less than a year later, he and twenty-five other activists took seats at a white-only Chicago restaurant. From that incident came the birth of the Congress of Racial Equality, which Farmer eventually headed as one of the leading civil rights figures of the 1960s.

Once the United States entered the war, Eleanor Roosevelt campaigned for an end to racial discrimination in the military and an expansion of employment opportunities for blacks. A meeting she arranged beween the President and civil rights leaders led to the War Department's pledge to form African-American units in each of the armed forces and to train black pilots. Later, when the crack unit of black combat pilots trained at Tuskegee, Alabama, couldn't get Washington to assign them to combat duty, the commanding officer of the unit turned to Mrs. Roosevelt. One month after she took up the matter with Secretary of War Stimson, the Tuskegee Airmen were on their way to North Africa, a staging area for much of the Allied air action before D day.

Responding to a barrage of complaints from black soldiers, Mrs. Roosevelt also bombarded the War Department with letters and calls about the maltreatment of blacks in the military. So insistent was she and so voluminous was her correspondence that General George Marshall, the Army Chief of Staff, assigned one of his underlings to full-time Eleanor Roosevelt duty. The First Lady's relentless demands for the end of discrimination in the armed forces helped spawn two War Department orders that proved to be the first steps toward final desegregation of the military. Under one directive, military recreational facilities could no longer be designated as white-only or colored-only. Under the other, black soldiers could no longer be sent to the backs of buses owned and operated by the government.

Mrs. Roosevelt was just as insistent when it came to job discrimination against blacks in the booming defense industry. Her travels had confirmed for her what civil rights leaders had claimed, that blacks were being shut out of most jobs in munitions plants, airplane factories, and other defense facilities. When A. Philip Randolph called for a march on Washington in 1941 to pressure Roosevelt to sign an order outlawing job discrimination in the defense industry, Mrs. Roosevelt helped broker an agreement between the administration and Randolph. In exchange for Randolph's giving up on the march, Roosevelt signed the executive order and established a Fair Employment Practices Commission to oversee compliance.

For many blacks, Eleanor Roosevelt was a true heroine, whose willingness to stand virtually alone and speak out for racial justice and equality was a source of great encouragement. At moments when he was inclined to give up on white people, the NAACP's Walter White once wrote, he would think of Mrs. Roosevelt and decide there was hope for the race after all.

Many whites, however, considered Mrs. Roosevelt to be a traitor to her race. No other woman in American public life (and few men) has had to endure the calumny and rage that Eleanor Roosevelt endured during her White House years and afterward. It wasn't just her perceived effrontery in comparing American racism with German fascism, or her very public fight against discrimination; it was much more visceral than that. Mrs. Roosevelt insisted she had never advocated social equality between the races, which she knew were code words in the South (and in the North, too) for interracial sex and marriage. But, in her personal life, she practiced social equality all the time. Her relationships with blacks were not just political: Many were deeply personal. She invited blacks to the White House and visited them in their homes. She ate with them, socialized with them, sent them flowers and gifts and cards, became their friend. She acknowledged remnants of personal prejudice and tried to eradicate them. A warm woman who liked to hug and kiss friends hello and good-bye, she considered it a triumph over her own prejudice when she finally was able to greet Mary McLeod Bethune in an openly affectionate way without giving it a second thought.

Despite the mores of the day, she didn't hide these relationships. Nor did she shrink from public appearances at which blacks mingled with whites. In February 1944, she presided over the opening of an integrated servicemen's club in Washington, and, together with a group of young white hostesses, handed out refreshments to a crowd of black soldiers. When photographs of the occasion appeared in newspapers, angry letters poured in to the White House, and papers all over the South inveighed against her. In a fierce diatribe on the House floor, a Louisiana congressman cried: "How can anyone be party to encouraging white girls into the arms of Negro soldiers at a canteen dance . . . ? Do these people have no regard for the traditions of the South and the culture of the white race?"

Many whites, especially those in the South, clearly felt that Mrs. Roosevelt was not due the customary respect and courtesy paid to the President's wife. She had forfeited such consideration, in their view, by stepping outside her role as a "proper" white woman and violating the tradition of First Lady as demure shadow. Mrs. Roosevelt had claimed her independence and challenged the system in so many ways it was hard to count them all. She was everything the compliant, sweet-talking Southern belle was not. And everything the belle might become. No wonder Mrs. Roosevelt's Southern opponents hated her so. She was, said *The New Republic*, the most despised "symbol the middle-class white South has had since Harriet Beecher Stowe."

During the war, the South turned into an anti–Eleanor Roosevelt rumor mill, churning out one scare story after another. According to the most common one, black maids and other servants throughout the region had established "Eleanor Clubs" to pressure their white employers for higher pay, shorter hours, more courtesy—and no more criticism of Eleanor Roosevelt. This story was so widely believed that the FBI launched an investigation to see if it was true. When it was determined to be false, the First Lady reignited the fire by declaring that black domestic workers would be better off if they joined a union. Another rumor had it that black women had pledged to go out every Tuesday ("Eleanor Tuesday") with the goal of knocking to the ground any white woman they saw. In a variation on the theme, black bus passengers in the South were said to have vowed to jostle at least one white passenger a day in honor of Mrs. Roosevelt. Then there were the scurrilous and obscene tales that were widely circulated about the First Lady, most of them depicting her engaging in the ultimate taboo—sex with a black man.

While the First Lady was fending off vitriolic attacks, she was, at the same time, handling criticism from supporters like Pauli Murray, who repeatedly censured the President for not doing enough for blacks and urged Mrs. Roosevelt to do more herself. One of Murray's denunciations of FDR came in the aftermath of bloody race riots in Detroit in 1943 and Roosevelt's remark that "every American regrets" such incidents, which, he said, "endanger our national unity and comfort our enemies." Outraged that the President would blame the rioters while ignoring the racial injustices that led to the disturbance, Murray wrote a scathing poem about the incident and sent it to the Roosevelts.

"I am sorry," Mrs. Roosevelt wrote back gently, "but I understand."

She wasn't always so pacifying. When Murray wrote a particularly withering letter to the President, chastising him for his lack of moral outrage over treatment of blacks in the South, the reply from the President's wife was biting. "[Y]our letter," she began, "seems to me one of the most thoughtless I have ever read." Somewhat chastened, Murray replied that the letter had been "written from a depth of desperation and disgust, such as every thinking Negro often experiences." At that point, Mrs. Roosevelt held out an olive branch and invited Murray to tea.

Still, Murray did not retreat. She was, as Eleanor Holmes Norton has noted, "a central figure in Mrs. Roosevelt's conscience on race," often sending the President's wife letters or newspaper clippings pointing out the latest instances of discrimination, the most recent examples of racial violence. Murray saw her relationship with Mrs. Roosevelt as representing a slow evolution of understanding, "a painful meeting of the minds." As Murray put it: "She grew closer to my point of view, and I matured and grew closer to her point of view . . ." Although Mrs. Roosevelt never told her so, Murray had the impression that the First Lady admired "my spunk and my guts." For her part, Murray had been wary of Mrs. Roosevelt at first, intent only on influencing her so that she in turn could influence her husband. But she soon fell under the First Lady's spell, her pain and rage assuaged, in part, by Mrs. Roosevelt's caring. "We used to say, if you got anywhere . . . within her field of magnetism, that she could get anything she wanted out of you," Murray said. "Whenever I was speaking to her she gave me her complete attention, as if in that moment I was the most important person in her world."

The two remained friends for the rest of Mrs. Roosevelt's life. In 1940, when Murray was arrested and jailed in Petersburg, Virginia, for refusing to get up from a whites-only seat on a Greyhound bus, the First Lady asked the governor of Virginia to investigate. Murray regularly visited Mrs. Roosevelt for tea, which Murray called her "morale-building ses-sions." They exchanged letters and poems. Once, when Murray was ill, Mrs. Roosevelt visited her in the hospital, thereby turning the facility, as Murray remembered it, "completely upside down."

At the 1944 commencement ceremonies for Howard University Law School, a huge bouquet of flowers stood on the platform in full view of the audience. An excited buzz swept through the crowd after someone read the card and passed the word along: The flowers, for cum laude graduate Pauli Murray, were from Eleanor Roosevelt.

Mrs. Roosevelt got most of the attention, but other liberal white women, some from the South, were also pressing for racial justice and other social reforms during the New Deal and war years. At the center of the women's activist network, the President's wife worked with these mavericks to influence legislation and policy. On Capitol Hill, Virginia Durr lobbied for an end to the poll tax, a device Southern states used to keep blacks from voting. Durr, an Alabama native who later would become a close friend of Rosa Parks's and play a supporting role in the Montgomery bus boycott, was one of the guiding forces behind the Southern Conference for Human Welfare, an organization of liberal Southerners.

No Southern white woman was more liberal on racial issues, however, than Lillian Smith, a writer and magazine editor, who, from her roost on a lonely mountaintop in northern Georgia, ventured forth to call for the end of segregation at a time when other white Southern liberals still sup-ported it. Smith also dared to dissect the intimate and taboo issues that Ida Wells had brought to public attention half a century earlier. In Smith's view, the intertwining of race and sex was the central reality of the South, contributing to a regional schizophrenia, a chasm between conscience and behavior. Southerners, she declared, were "lost in a maze of fantasy and falsehood that had little resemblance to the actual world they lived in."

From 1936 until 1945, Smith and her partner, Paula Snelling, published and edited a magazine they first named *Pseudopodia* and then finally changed to *South Today*, a journal of fiction and opinion, both literary and political, whose influence as a liberal voice for Southern reform was far greater than its small circulation suggested. In 1942, Smith wrote an open letter in the magazine "to intelligent white Southerners" in which she urged the abolition of voting restrictions, job discrimination, segregation in transportation, education, housing, and the military—in other words, an end to Jim Crow in the South. Making the same argument as her friend Eleanor Roosevelt—that racial justice must be part of the war effort—Smith contended that blacks had to share in "democracy's privileges as well as its duties," that they should be given their full constitutional rights if they were expected to fight and give their lives for their country.

Confronting the Southern way of life head-on was a breathtaking move at a time when other white liberal writers and editors, such as Ralph McGill and Hodding Carter, were considered radical merely for advocating improved race relations and an end to racial violence. "It was one thing for Northerners—or liberal Southerners gone north—to speak out against the evils and injustices of the South," historian Richard King observed, "but another for a woman like Smith to remain there and risk ostracism and even bodily harm for her beliefs."

Smith also plowed new racial ground in providing a forum for black writers, including Pauli Murray. Another mentor and mother figure for Murray, Smith advised her, praised her, critiqued her poetry and nonfiction writing, and in 1944 published what became Murray's best-known poem, "Dark Testament." Smith also encouraged Murray to write about her tangled ancestry. The result, finally published in 1954, was a book entitled *Proud Shoes*. "You should know that your spirit was looking over my shoulder through every chapter," Murray told Smith.

From the beginning of their magazine, Smith and Snelling published stories and articles by blacks and reviewed black writers' books. "If anyone can be said to have 'discovered' the Negro writers of our country, it was . . . *South Today*," said Harry Golden, a noted Southern white liberal and editor of the *Carolina Israelite*. "Until they put this magazine together, no Southern newspaper had ever reviewed a book by a Negro novelist, no Negro poet had ever lectured to a local writing group, no professor or clergyman had ever discussed the meaning of Negro writing from his desk or pulpit."

Perhaps Lillian Smith's boldest challenge to her native South was her own flouting of the taboo against social mixing between blacks and whites. In September 1943 she wrote Pauli Murray, asking her to a two-day gathering of some twenty black and white women at her home on Old Screamer Mountain, near Clayton, Georgia. "We hope to become friends, simple, natural friends," Smith declared. "I want you as friends to come together and begin personal relationships that may give us all deep pleasure. . . . There are many white women who should know you."

From the days of slavery onward, women civil rights activists generally were much less inclined than men to separate the personal from the political: Women focused on the links between personal behavior and issues, rather than on issues in a vacuum. For Lillian Smith, the personal was paramount. If there was to be true racial equality, she felt, whites and blacks had to get to know each other as individuals. Women, she thought, had to lead the way in breaking down the barriers of ignorance and suspicion that had divided the races for centuries. "We are primarily interested in the psychological interactions of white and Negro women who have for three hundred years lived in such remote intimacy with each other," she wrote. "We think their relationships and the relationships they have had with the men of the white race especially have had a tremendous effect upon the culture and literature of the South."

From 1936 until the 1960s, Smith and Snelling hosted biracial dinners and house parties on Old Screamer, many of them for women only. One of the most memorable occurred in September 1943, when legendary black activist Mary Church Terrell and Eslanda Goode Robeson, wife of Paul Robeson, were among the guests. When the women weren't playing tennis or hiking or learning the samba from Eslanda Robeson, "we talked our heads off," Smith later remarked. "The talk was very candid, and we had sudden arguments, sudden antagonisms [that] rose to the surface and were then laughed away; it was a matter of raw nerves meeting raw nerves." For much of the time, Smith felt "that I was doing a gay little tap dance over a barrel of TNT," not least because this gathering was being held deep in Klan country.

As much controversy as Lillian Smith had stirred up before, however, nothing matched the furor caused by the 1944 publication of her first novel, *Strange Fruit*. The story of a doomed love affair between a white man and black woman in a small Georgia town, *Strange Fruit* examined a society torn by guilt, fantasy, and secrets. In it, the white man, Tracy Deems, abandons the pregnant Nonnie, whom he loves, because she is nothing but a "nigger girl." Tracy plans to marry Dot Pusey, a young white woman who has long pursued him, but hopes to continue seeing Nonnie on the side. "There'd always be Nonnie. . . . When Dot got behind him too much with her paintbrush he'd go to Nonnie and she would peel the new paint off down to the old Tracy. And she'd let him get everything out of his system and would sit there, not talking but there. And whatever he wanted she would give him. That was Non." Tracy would have it all— respectability with a white woman, sex and unquestioning warmth with a black woman. In the end, however, Tracy is killed by Nonnie's brother, and another black man, Tracy's closest boyhood friend, is lynched for the crime. Nonnie and Dot are left with nothing but grief and despair.

With its explosive topic and frank language, *Strange Fruit* jumped to the top of the national bestseller list within days of its publication, selling more than a million copies in hardcover and two million more in paperback. It was banned in Boston and briefly from the U.S. mails, until Eleanor Roosevelt interceded with her husband, who ordered the ban lifted.

After publication of *Strange Fruit*, Smith was a target of threats and hate mail from what she called "the lunatic fringe of the fascist groups and the white supremacy crowd." But what bothered her most was the cold shoulder she received from white Southerners whom she considered intelligent and reasonable. "People were rarely nasty-rude," she recalled, they "just froze me out, stared through me, wouldn't wait on me in stores, etc."

In 1949, Smith set another literary brushfire when she again examined sex and race through the prism of Southern history and culture. This time she was writing nonfiction. "Real history, in my opinion, has never been written and won't be until historians are willing to deal seriously with men's feelings as well as with events," she once wrote. In her book, *Killers of the Dream*, she examined the feelings stemming from her own "haunted childhood" to show the warping effects of race, sex, and religion on the Southern psyche, white and black.

When Lillian Smith was born in 1897, her father was a successful businessman and prominent civic leader in Jasper, Florida; her mother was active in Methodist Church affairs. They were considered moral pillars of the community, yet to Smith, her parents betrayed disturbing contradictions. "The mother who taught me what I know of tenderness and love and compassion taught me also the bleak rituals of keeping Negroes in their 'place.' The father who rebuked me for an air of superiority toward schoolmates from the mill and rounded out his rebuke by gravely reminding me that 'all men are brothers,' trained me in the steel-rigid decorums I must demand of every colored male." From her parents and other adults, Smith learned that it is possible "to be a Christian and a white southerner simultaneously; to be a gentlewoman and an arrogant callous creature in the same moment; to pray at night and ride a Jim Crow car the next morning and to feel comfortable in doing both."

As a little girl, she also learned that both sex and race were taboo topics. Neither was to be openly discussed; both had to do with moral transgression and damnation. "When we as small children crept over the race line and ate and played with Negroes or broke other segregation customs known to us we felt the same dread fear of consequences, the same overwhelming guilt we felt when we crept over the sex line and played with our body," she wrote. "Each was a 'sin,' each 'deserved punishment.' . . . The lesson of segregation was only a logical extension of the lessons on sex and white superiority and God. Not only Negroes but everything dark, dangerous, evil must be pushed to the rim of one's life." Outwardly pushed to the rim, perhaps, but remaining firmly rooted in one's own secret consciousness. White men learned from the example of their slave-owning ancestors to put white women on pedestals, and turn to black women for sex, often coerced. White women denied their sexual and emotional needs and turned to religion, which reinforced the denial.

For Smith, the etiquette of race relations was an intricate, soul-stunting minuet that Southern children, white and black, were forced to master from the time they were toddlers. "[S]ome, if their faces are dark, learn to bend hat in hand; and others, if their faces are white, learn to hold their heads high. Some step off the sidewalk while others pass by in arrogance. Bending, shoving, genuflecting, ignoring, stepping off, demanding, giving in, avoiding. . . . So we learned the dance that cripples the human spirit, step by step by step, we who were white and we who were colored, day by day, hour by hour, year by year, until the movements were reflexes and made for the rest of our life without thinking."

Shortly after *Killers of the Dream* was published, Howard University bestowed an honorary doctorate on Smith with the declaration: "You are a dangerous revolutionist. There is enough dynamite in what you say to blow up the very foundation of segregated civilization." In the South, she was again inundated with criticism, particularly from male writers and newspaper editors who supposedly shared her liberalism. Men like Hodding Carter, editor of the *Delta Democrat-Times* in Greenville, Mississippi, and Ralph McGill, editor of *The Atlanta Constitution*, both of whom would win Pulitzer prizes for editorials challenging racial violence and hatred. Carter and McGill, along with a few other Southern editors like Virginius Dabney of the *Richmond Times-Dispatch*, came to be known throughout the country as courageous exemplars of Southern liberalism, thanks in part to the national press, which regarded—and consulted—them as *the* Southern experts on race relations.

Their reputations and their influence with Northern liberals and government officials drove Lillian Smith wild. For while Carter and McGill opposed the Klan and other white supremacist groups and advocated improved economic and educational conditions for blacks (suffering ridicule, insults, and threats as a result), they did not dare advocate racial equality as early as Smith did. Indeed, as historian Anthony Newberry put it, they were "fair play segregationists," who merely called for a more human segregation, claiming that any attempt to end Jim Crow in the South would lead to violence.

Even before *Killers of the Dream* was published, the quick-tempered, often irascible Smith was locked in a bitter feud with Carter and McGill. The conflict was fueled by a scathing letter from her that was published in *The New York Times* in April 1948 and that was clearly directed at both editors, among others. "As a Southern woman, I am deeply shocked that our liberals are putting up no real fight for human rights in the South . . . ," she wrote. "Not one Southerner has taken a strong stand in a Southern newspaper against segregation. . . . It is hard to understand such timidity at a time like this, unless we remember that Georgia, U.S.A., still has a lot in common with Georgia, U.S.S.R. Totalitarianism is an old thing to us down here. . . . We just don't love human freedom enough to take real risks for it."

Smith thought Carter and McGill, like other Southern liberals, were trying to have it both ways, occupying the moral high ground while taking pains not to become pariahs. The Southern liberal, she once snapped, "cannot bear not to think well of himself, nor can he bear for the world not to think well of him." While Smith had always been an outsider, both McGill and Carter were part of the business and political establishments of their communities, which clearly were reluctant to cede any power to blacks (or women). As members of the white male elite, the editors subscribed to the prevailing Southern progressive view, as noted by historian William Chafe, that "conflict is inherently bad, that disagreement means personal dislike, and that consensus offers the only way to preserve a genteel and civilized life." Of McGill, Smith once wrote dismissively: "Ralph has a great way of hedging on all things that may offend his big-business buddies, then speaking out 'most courageously' when the issue is something that will not offend them."

For their part, Carter and McGill never had much patience with what they saw as Smith's incessant harping on Southern shortcomings, but her baring of the South's soul in *Killers of the Dream* was particularly grating.

They were pragmatists, thinking in terms of politics, not psychology. The idea of probing the hidden recesses of one's own mind to ferret out the reasons for one's behavior was anathema. They also felt, Smith believed, that she was betraying white Southern men in her merciless dissection of the male psyche. (Never mind that she did the same with the female mind.) While the *Saturday Review of Literature* praised *Killers of the Dream* for exposing to the light "the real problem" of the South, Carter called Smith "a sex-obsessed old maid" and McGill and his newspaper denounced her and *Killers*. Another editor at the *Constitution* reviewed her book as "a stinker! . . . Talk about [Smith's] devious demagoguery. Not only is this claptrap, but very badly done claptrap." In his column, McGill wrote: "A woefully unsound book. Miss Smith is a prisoner in the monastery of her own mind. But rarely does she come out of its gates, and then, apparently, seeing only wicked things to send her back to her hair shirt and the pouring of ashes on her head and salt in her own psychiatric wounds."

What particularly infuriated Smith about these attacks was their patronizing nature, summed up by Smith's biographer Anne Loveland as: "We know the situation better than you, we are being realistic whereas you are too idealistic, we are rational whereas you are too emotional . . ." But Smith continued to insist that any hope of solving America's racial problems was dependent on understanding men's minds, that "putting a loaf of bread, a book and a ballot in everyone's hand," while important, was not enough.

Of course, she was right. Racial tensions continued in the United States even after massive desegregation in the 1960s. Smith didn't live long enough to witness the validation of her views, but she did live until 1966, time enough to be hailed for her moral courage by young civil rights workers, many of whom packed *Killers of the Dream* in their suitcases before heading off for the battlefields of the Deep South.

By the end of World War II, the irony of a nation espousing democracy abroad while practicing segregation at home had galvanized thousands of blacks. Anger and rising expectations led to increased militancy, with the NAACP in the vanguard. Membership in the organization had exploded—from fewer than fifty thousand in 1940 to more than half a million in 1946. The NAACP had established itself as the premier group fighting for the rights of blacks. It put down roots in every major city and hundreds of small towns across the South, and it scored an impressive string of legal victories, including filing the suit that ended in a 1944 Supreme Court decision banning all-white primary elections.

In a New York City apartment, a frail, eighty-one-year-old white woman named Mary White Ovington viewed the NAACP's growth and success with quiet satisfaction. "The end is in the clouds with all other great social problems," she wrote Roy Wilkins, "but we've gone a good piece of the way on earth." Though few were aware of it, the National Association for the Advancement of Colored People was largely Ovington's creation. She had come up with the original idea, had been its principal founder in 1909, and had been responsible for bringing the legendary W. E. B. Du Bois to the NAACP as director of publicity and research and as editor of its magazine, *Crisis*. Moreover, Ovington had nurtured the organization through its difficult infancy and childhood, calmly mediating among the massive egos of Du Bois and the NAACP's leading white male leaders. Always in the background, never seeking credit (and rarely given it), Ovington was an early model for women who would follow her as major civil rights activists in the 1950s and 1960s.

Mary White Ovington was a daughter of privilege, born to a prosperous New York businessman and his wife three days before Lincoln's assassination. From an early age, she followed in the footsteps of her abolitionist grandmother. Tall and blonde, Ovington had large pale-blue eyes and was, in the words of a male friend, "austerely beautiful." Like a number of other middle- and upper-class white women who attended college at the turn of the century, she was unwilling to confine herself to domesticity and instead chose a career of social reform. After a stint at Radcliffe, she threw her prodigious energies into settlement work in New York, persuading a wealthy industrialist to build a model tenement house for black workers and then moving into it herself.

In 1908, Ovington sponsored an interracial dinner at a New York restaurant that exploded into a nationwide cause célèbre. The staid affair, attended by doctors, ministers, and social workers, was transformed by newspapers from New York to the Deep South into a drunken orgy of white women and black men. Ovington was the main target of the slurs, which included a flood of "nauseatingly obscene" letters. The Savannah *News* railed that the chief transgressor was "the high priestess, Miss Ovington, whose father is rich and who affiliates five days in every week with Negro men and dines with them at her home in Brooklyn, Sundays. She could have had a hundred thousand Negroes at the Bacchanal feast had she waved the bread tray."

That same year, savage race riots and lynchings in Springfield, Illinois, prompted Ovington to suggest to several white male reformer friends that they establish an organization for racial justice. "We formed our little group almost in desperation," she later said, "feeling someone must voice an opinion against the lynchings and riots and the constant taking away of privilege." The group drafted a Call for an organizational meeting of prominent black and white social activists on February 12, 1909, Lincoln's hundredth birthday. The meeting was interracial, thanks primarily to Ovington, who was the only one of the NAACP's initial founders to have close ties with black intellectuals and reformers. Ovington was also responsible for the fact that more than a third of those who signed the Call and who attended the meeting were women, among them Mary Church Terrell and Ida Wells-Barnett. The signers of the Call demanded voting rights and equal educational opportunities for blacks, as well as an end to lynching and other racial violence. An antilynching campaign became the fledgling organization's first priority, for which it soon became widely known and was severely attacked.

From the day of the NAACP's birth, Ovington was caught in the middle of the constant turmoil created by its split personality. An organization championing the cause of blacks, it was founded by white reformers and funded by white philanthropists, most of whom, except for Ovington, had little direct contact with blacks and who, like many Southern liberals, opposed "social equality" between the races. At the same time, the NAACP's only black executive, W. E. B. Du Bois, was calling for nothing less than total equality. Over the objections of cofounder Oswald Villard, Ovington had recruited Du Bois from his teaching post at Atlanta University. For more than five years before that, the attractive female reformer and the imperious intellectual with the neatly trimmed Vandyke beard had enjoyed a deep friendship spiced with mild flirtation. According to Du Bois biographer David Levering Lewis, Ovington "would come about as close as any white person ever would to being a confidante and advisor" to Du Bois.

Her conciliatory skills would be much needed in the following years as Du Bois clashed again and again with white NAACP leaders, primarily the enormously wealthy Villard, editor of the *New York Post* and *The Nation*. As the men fought over ideology, position, and recognition, Ovington was constantly called upon to smooth the waters. She tried to make Villard see how important Du Bois was and how justified was his rage. "He does do dangerous things. He strikes out at people with a harshness and directness that appalls me, but the blow is often deserved and it is never below the belt." When Du Bois made incendiary antiwhite statements in *Crisis*, Ovington gently suggested he had gone too far. Wasn't it better for blacks and whites to work together, she asked, rather than treat whites as "reactionary heathen" and feeling that they were insulting him "when they have no insult in their heart?"

Ovington, who would have preferred that the NAACP remain an interracial organization, was nonetheless supportive when the transition was made to mostly black leadership and membership in the 1930s. Having served as board chairman in the 1920s, she became treasurer in 1932, mounting ambitious fund-raising campaigns, while at the same time urging black members not to give up on whites. "Don't blame people too much for being indifferent to your ills when you don't ask them to drop their indifference and join with you," she exhorted black audiences. The same year that Ovington became treasurer, the NAACP's board of directors passed a resolution calling her "the Mother of the New Emancipation."

Largely because of Ovington's influence, women played major roles in the NAACP from its earliest days. She pressured the organization to hire women and give them important positions: The NAACP's first executive secretary was a woman, and when Ovington was chairman, six of her fellow board members were women. In 1920, she successfully campaigned for the election of antilynching activist Mary Talbert as vice president, and she pressed for the hiring of Addie Hunton and later Daisy Lampkin as regional field secretaries.

Mary White Ovington was fighting illness and old age and was no longer as intensely involved with the organization by the time Ella Baker became the NAACP's Southern field secretary in the early 1940s. But Ovington and Baker almost assuredly would have hit it off, for in many ways these two daring, strong-minded, independent women were kindred spirits. Both believed that African-Americans must be persuaded to mount the fight for justice and equality for themselves, and that the NAACP, as the largest mass-membership civil rights organization in the country, was ideally suited to encourage that. But the two women also felt that the increasingly bureaucratic organization, with its strong emphasis on legal battles, was ignoring its membership, thus wasting this golden opportunity. "No one pays attention" to the local NAACP branches "except to beg them for money," Ovington once complained.

Baker, then in her late thirties, set out to change the situation, determined, as she sardonically put it, to "place the N.A.A.C.P. and its programs on the lips of all the people . . . the uncouth MASSES included." Leaving New York each February during World War II, she headed South, to spend the next four or five months traveling from one small town to another, encouraging local black residents to join the NAACP. More than that, she was planting seeds. She would ask local people about the most glaring inequity or the most obvious injustice they had faced. It might be the lack of streetlights or paved roads in the black part of town, or it might be an outrageous arrest, even a lynching. Whatever it was, Baker worked hard to make the people see that they were not helpless in the face of vicious white racism, that "in the long run they themselves are the only protection they have against violence or injustice." By themselves, they had no power, but if they joined together and fought, they would have the collective force of an army. As Lawrence Guyot, a young civil rights activist in the 1960s, put it, Baker was "getting them comfortable with rebellion." Such talk was extraordinarily dangerous, both for Baker and for the local blacks listening to her. As the only organized resistance to racial injustice within many Southern communities, the NAACP was considered the devil incarnate by white supremacists. Just being found with an NAACP membership card, let alone engaging in protests or trying to register to vote, invited beatings and lynchings.

Although the heavy repression of the late 1940s and early 1950s succeeded in choking off most mass protest at the time, Baker's ideas took deep root. Rosa Parks never forgot what she learned as a participant in one of the regional leadership training conferences Baker staged for NAACP branch leaders in 1946. And in Greensboro, North Carolina, a high school student named Randolph Blackwell was so inspired by Baker's call to action that he went out in 1943 and organized a local NAACP youth council. Seventeen years later, on December 1, 1960, two current members of the council joined two fellow freshmen from North Carolina A&T at a Woolworth's lunch counter in downtown Greensboro. Refusing to move until they were served, the four young men sparked a chain reaction of student sit-ins across the country, which in turn touched off a crusade the likes of which this country had never seen.

Ella Baker's seeds had borne remarkable fruit.

Lighting the Fuse

4

Mary Church Terrell

LIKE AN ACCELERATING TRAIN, the fight to end institutionalized racism in America picked up more and more speed after World War II. It would gain a monumental victory in 1954, when the Supreme Court ruled on a school-desegregation case entitled *Brown* v. *Board of Education.* The court's decision in *Brown* provided the fuse for the modern civil rights movement. In little more than a decade, American society would be transformed.

It was perhaps predictable that the first major battle of the postwar civil rights struggle would be waged over the public schools of the South, where "separate but equal" and "states' rights" had become segregationist mantras and where the aspirations of blacks—especially their aspirations for their children—were rising as never before. African-American soldiers had returned from fighting freedom's war to find their children—and themselves—still oppressed in freedom's homeland. Black women, attuned as always to the deepest racial ironies of American life, were less willing than ever to see those ironies destroy their hopes for the future. And in the amazing burst of optimism and opportunity that followed the war, black children were learning that gradualism and compromise were not always the right answer, although courage might be.

As the desegregation train gathered momentum, more and more blacks (and more than a few whites as well) climbed aboard. Women, and even young girls, did so with particular enthusiasm and commitment, many inspired not only by their own deep yearnings but also by the memory of all the deeds of all the mothers, grandmothers, great-grandmothers, and great-great-grandmothers who went before them. Some of the pioneers, in fact, were still around, still setting examples. One of them was Mary Church Terrell.

It was fitting that Mrs. Terrell, born the year that Abraham Lincoln issued the Emancipation Proclamation, would live until two months after the *Brown* ruling. A teacher herself and a child of a former slave, she was a person of such indomitable will and clarity of vision that at least two generations of black women would extol and emulate her. Indeed, just a year before she died, "Mollie" Terrell, who had fought for women's suffrage and against lynching at the turn of the century, would celebrate, at ninety, a new civil rights victory of her own, when she completed the struggle that Pauli Murray and the Howard University students had begun almost a decade earlier at Thompson's cafeteria.

Mary Church Terrell's life is a tapestry of black American life, of blacks' perseverance and struggle, from Reconstruction to segregation. In 1881, the dazzling seventeen-year-old danced at President James Garfield's inaugural ball. Just a few years later, after the introduction of Jim Crow practices, Mary "Mollie" Church Terrell, now the college-educated wife of a successful black Washington lawyer, Robert Terrell, was manhandled on streetcars and turned away from restaurants and theaters she had once frequented. "As a colored woman," she wrote bitterly in 1940, "I may walk from the Capitol to the White House, ravenously hungry and abundantly supplied with money with which to purchase a meal, without finding a single restaurant in which I would be permitted to take a morsel of food . . ."

Such treatment was particularly galling for a woman who was raised to believe she was as good as anybody else—and better than some. Her father was a former slave who had defied all the odds to become a millionaire real estate entrepreneur in Memphis. Mollie Church, from the age of six, was sent to white schools in Ohio. Fun-loving and popular, a nonstop talker, she was in perpetual motion and found it "extremely difficult . . . to keep still in school from the day I entered till I received my degree from college." She had many white friends but was quick to stand up for herself at the first sign of racism. When a teacher assigned her the role of a cowering black servant in a school play, young Mollie refused to take it.

At Oberlin College, the first white college in the United States to admit blacks, she opted for the rigorous four-year Classical Course, including the study of Latin and Greek. Friends urged her to enroll instead in the "ladies'" Literary Course, which took only two years to complete. Too much education would harm her chances of getting a husband, they advised. "Where will you find a colored man who has studied Greek?" one friend asked her. Mollie ignored them and received her bachelor's degree in 1884.

Later, she studied French and German for two years in Europe, where several smitten young men, including a German baron, proposed marriage. As an old woman, Terrell would recall those lovestruck white youths as she tartly reflected on the widespread belief of whites that blacks were eager to marry them. "I am persuaded that the average Caucasian in this country believes that there is nothing which colored people desire so much as to marry into their group," she wrote. "It seems to me it is my duty to inform those who entertain this opinion that at least one colored woman voluntarily rejected such a proposition three times."

As one of the new generation of independent, well-educated black women activists who came of age at the turn of the century, Mollie Church plunged into the fights for civil rights and women's rights. Her father had wanted his headstrong daughter to be a "lady," like white women, and enjoy the luxury of staying at home and not working. But she considered that a "purposeless existence." Insisting on a life where "I could promote the welfare of my race," she went, instead, into teaching.

From childhood, she had advocated the right to vote for women, once saying she could not "recall a period in my life . . . that I did not believe in woman's suffrage with all my heart." As a freshman at Oberlin, she wrote an essay called "Resolved, There Should Be a Sixteenth Amendment to the Constitution Granting Suffrage to Women." Though angered at white suffragists' lack of concern about black women, Terrell nonetheless worked closely with white leaders in the suffrage campaign. During World War I, she joined other suffragists in a months-long picket line in front of the White House. She was also active in efforts to improve living conditions for blacks. When the National Association of Colored Women was formed in 1896 to combat racial injustice and to organize social services for the black community, Terrell was elected its first president. In 1909, she signed the Call for creation of the NAACP and attended its organizing conference. Later, she was elected vice president of the organization's Washington branch.

Terrell was in her mid-eighties when World War II ended, and some regarded her as a throwback to a bygone era. Virginia Durr recalled that "Mrs. Terrell looked old and dressed old." But Terrell rejected the very idea that she might actually *be* old. "I can dance as long and as well as I ever did," she wrote at the age of seventy-seven, "although I get very few chances to do so." If there were any doubts about her strength and endurance, she put them to rest when she charged back into the public spotlight, more radical than ever, to lead an antisegregation battle in the nation's capital.

During Reconstruction, ordinances had been enacted to prohibit discrimination against blacks by restaurants, theaters, and other public places in the District of Columbia. Early in the post-Reconstruction era, when American-style apartheid was imposed, the city's white fathers didn't bother repealing the antidiscrimination laws; they simply ignored them. Segregation by fiat soon became as much a part of life in Washington as segregation by law in any city in the Deep South. Then, in 1946, the eighty-three-year-old Terrell was named head of an interracial committee demanding that the laws be enforced. She and the committee became the guiding force behind an extraordinary several-year campaign of picketing, leafleting, and boycotts. During a December snowstorm, the stooped, white-haired old lady, in her fur coat, gloves, and pearls, marched outside a downtown five-and-dime, one hand holding a "Don't Buy at Kresge's" placard, while, with the other hand, she leaned heavily on a cane. In the sweltering humidity of July, she was outside Hecht's department store, directing the action and inspiring her fellow marchers, among them a seven-year-old boy named Carl Bernstein and his mother. (Bernstein would later team with Bob Woodward at *The Washington Post* to help expose the Watergate cover-up.) "When my feet hurt," said another demonstrator, "I wasn't going to let a woman fifty years older than I do what I couldn't do. I kept on picketing." Said Eleanor Holmes Norton, a native Washingtonian who became a prominent figure in her own right in the civil rights struggle: "When I was a youngster, I didn't understand why black people were not protesting, had not found a way to protest. And then came Mary Church Terrell."

On January 7, 1950, Terrell, accompanied by three companions, hobbled into Thompson's cafeteria near the White House, where Pauli Murray and the other Howard students had conducted their 1944 sit-in. Terrell got further than they did. She managed to place a bowl of soup on her tray before she and her friends were ordered to leave. That afternoon, their lawyers filed suit in a local court, alleging that Thompson's had broken the never-repealed Reconstruction laws. Three years later, the Supreme Court heard arguments in the Thompson's case, and on June 8, 1953, it handed down its decision: Racial segregation was against the law in Washington, D.C. "EAT ANYWHERE!" proclaimed a black Washington newspaper in a banner headline.

As immensely satisfying as the Supreme Court ruling was and as much as she delighted in the results of her long years of activism, Mary Church Terrell looked back on her life and thought wistfully about what might have been. At the age of seventy-seven, she had observed: "While I am grateful for the blessings which have been bestowed upon me and for the opportunities which have been offered, I cannot help wondering sometimes what I might have become and might have done if I had lived in a country which had not circumscribed and handicapped me on account of my race, but had allowed me to reach any height I was able to attain." Nothing that happened afterward, not even the victory in the Thompson's cafeteria case, changed her mind.

A teacher born during the Civil War, who lived to see the Supreme Court strike down "separate but equal" public education, might, however, have taken some satisfaction in the knowledge that her example, and that of many others like her, had helped to embolden a new generation of female activists. One such young woman, sixteen-year-old Barbara Johns, lived in the drowsy town of Farmville in rural Virginia. A decade before the mass civil rights demonstrations of the 1960s, she was already pondering how she and her friends could force changes in a school system that was as separate and as decidedly unequal as Farmville's.

Although she had spent much of her early life there, Farmville was a place where Barbara Johns never really felt she belonged. The seat of Prince Edward County, Farmville was a trading center for tobacco and lumber, a town that didn't seem to have changed much since Robert E. Lee and Ulysses S. Grant had separately stopped there in April 1865 on their way to end the Civil War at Appomattox Court House. In 1951, local blacks were barred from the hotel where the generals had rested, just as they were barred from Farmville's restaurants, its drugstore counters, and its only movie theater, bowling alley, and swimming pool. And, of course, its all-white public schools. The school Barbara Johns attended, Moton High School, featured "temporary" buildings that were really just tar-paper shacks, and classrooms that were usually too stuffy and hot in the fall and spring and too cold in the winter. For years, the all-white school district had been promising the black community a new school, but somehow it was never built. The blacks, despite their resentment, did not dare complain too loudly.

Barbara Johns could not understand such docility. Pretty and bright, she had always been an outspoken child; family members said she took after her uncle Vernon, the pastor of the Dexter Avenue Baptist Church in Montgomery, Alabama. The family didn't mean that as much of a compliment, but Barbara, who idolized her uncle, took it as one anyway. Vernon Johns was a hot-tempered crusader for civil rights, who railed at his congregation and other blacks for their complacency in the face of racial and other social injustice. Not much loved by the affluent black members of his church, he was destined to have a powerful influence on his young successor at Dexter Avenue, Martin Luther King, Jr.

When Johns visited Farmville, Barbara loved to hear him talk. "He was beyond the intellectual scope of everyone around the county," she said. "I remember that white men would . . . listen to him speak and shake their heads, not understanding his language." As much as she hero-worshiped her uncle, however, she didn't shy away from disagreeing with him. "We'd always be on opposite sides in an argument. I'm afraid we were both very antagonistic."

At Moton High School, Barbara Johns participated in the drama club, the chorus, and the student council. Those activities made it possible for her to travel to other black high schools around the state. Many, she couldn't help noticing, were in better shape than Moton. What bothered Johns and her fellow students most about their school were the tar-paper shacks, with their leaky roofs and pathetic woodstoves. An occasional motorist, driving by the school, would stop to ask the students what the shacks were. One man, told they were part of the school, responded: "School? Looks like a poultry farm!"

In the fall of 1950, Johns decided to take action on her own. She brought five other student leaders together for a clandestine meeting in the bleachers of the school's athletic field. Farmville's black adults, she said, had made no headway in getting a new school. "Then," recalled one of the other students at the meeting, "she said our parents ask us to follow them but in some instances—and I remember her saying this very vividly—a little child shall lead them. She said we could make a move that would broadcast Prince Edward County all over the world."

For six months, the students planned their strategy. They put it into effect on April 23, 1951. Late that morning, Moton's principal, Boyd Jones, received a phone call from one of the conspirators, advising him that two of his students were about to be arrested by police at the Greyhound bus station. Jones left school in a hurry, never suspecting that the summons was a ploy to get him safely away so that a note with Jones's forged signature could be sent to each classroom, announcing an immediate school assembly. After the teachers and the school's 450 students gathered in the auditorium, the curtains on the stage parted and revealed Barbara Johns, not Boyd Jones, standing at the podium. She declared that the meeting was for students only and asked the teachers to leave. When some teachers protested, Johns removed one of her shoes and smacked it on a bench. "I want you out of here!" she shouted. At that, all the teachers left, some with student escorts. Then Johns got down to business. The time had come, she said, for dramatic action. Joined by the other student organizers, she called for a student strike and produced hand-lettered picket signs proclaiming "We Want a New School or None at All" and "Down with the Tar-Paper Shacks." The students cheered and marched out of the auditorium, with Barbara Johns in the vanguard.

The strike leaders sent a letter to the NAACP in Richmond that same afternoon. "We hate to impose as we are doing," the letter began, "but under the circumstances that we are facing, we have to ask for your help." Three days later, two top civil rights lawyers were on their way to Farmville. By this time, the NAACP had already decided to challenge "separate but equal" in favor of total desegregation. Although there may have been, as Richard Kluger has written, "no less promising place in all Virginia to wage the fight for equal schools," the NAACP lawyers were willing to try. In a shabby basement meeting room of a local church, they told the students and some parents that the NAACP would help them *only* if they were prepared to go for broke—desegregation or nothing—and then only if the students could demonstrate that they had the support of the adults in the black community. The strikers were stunned but enthusiastic. "It seemed like reaching for the moon," said Barbara Johns.

The toughest part would be getting the adults to go along. When Farmville's blacks held a mass meeting the following week, there was increasing pressure on the students to end the strike and return to school. Moton High's principal had written a letter to every parent, warning of repercussions for their children if the strike continued. At the meeting, a for-

mer principal, J. B. Pervall, stood up to denounce the very idea of an
NAACP lawsuit. At that, Barbara Johns, who earlier had delivered a pro-
strike speech, claimed the microphone again. Looking Pervall straight in
the eye but speaking to the crowd, she said: "Don't let Mr. Charlie, Mr.
Tommy, or Mr. Pervall stop you from backing us. We are depending on
you." And that did it. The audience roared its approval—and its opposition
to "separate but equal." A short time later, only a month after Johns had
summoned her schoolmates to battle, the NAACP lawyers filed suit on
their behalf in federal court. Joined with four other complaints, the suit
became part of perhaps the most significant Supreme Court decision of the
twentieth century—*Brown* v. *Board of Education*. And a sixteen-year-old
girl had led them.

Her family, however, had helped make her what she was. There was her
uncle Vernon, of course. But there was also her maternal grandmother,
Mary Croner. As a girl, and later as a young woman, Croner used to
seclude herself in the woods near her home and deliver passionate,
unheard speeches about the degradation to which she and other blacks
were subjected. "I would speak out and pretend the trees was listening,"
she said. When she married and had children, "I gave the speaking up, it
left my mind," partly because her family did not share her passion. But
then came Barbara. When Barbara spoke up at the mass meeting, "I got
real frightened," her grandmother said. "She had a microphone and I
thought, My goodness, she don't know what to say . . . [But] the people
in the audience were nodding and saying 'That's good.' . . . It came to me
that it was my grandchild who was carrying on the speaking . . . I felt that
God had instilled in her what I was trying to do."

To be sure, there were costs for Johns and her family. The Ku Klux
Klan burned a cross in front of Barbara's house. Terrified that worse
might happen, her parents shipped her off to stay with her uncle Vernon
in Montgomery. She never returned to Farmville to live. But the difficulties were outweighed by the satisfaction of knowing that she and the others in the Farmville suit had helped change the face of a nation.

For months before *Brown* v. *Board of Education* was finally handed down,
the South—and much of the rest of America—awaited the Supreme Court
decision with feverish anticipation. From Montgomery, Virginia Durr
wrote a friend: "This schools thing is like dynamite." Indeed, it threatened
to destroy the racial framework—the rigid separation of races—on which
Southern society was based. The explosion occurred at 1:20 P.M. on May
17, 1954, when Chief Justice Earl Warren announced the decision. By a

unanimous vote, he said, the Supreme Court had found racial segregation of public schools to be unconstitutional. "Separate but equal" in education was a legal dead letter.

Amid the jubilation and despair that followed, few paid attention to the decision's silence on the question of enforcement. As one journalist wrote: "It was the first time that the Court had vindicated a constitutional right and then deferred its exercise for a more convenient time." Immediately after the decision, several Southern cities and states announced they would comply. But when it became clear that the Supreme Court was not about to implement the ruling anytime soon, Southern white supremacists swung into action. They exploited long-festering grievances and fears to whip up a paroxysm of rage and racial hatred throughout the region. Even so, the Supreme Court, a full year after *Brown*, continued to dither on compliance. It vaguely decreed that desegregation should be implemented "with all deliberate speed" but failed to set a deadline.

Southern demagogues took full advantage of the time they had been given. They were stirring a potent brew that had been simmering since the Civil War—a mixture of fury at the North and the federal government, racial antagonisms, sexual fears and anxieties, and a nostalgic yearning for the phantom glories of the lost Old South. In the mid-1950s, statues of Confederate soldiers still stood guard in virtually every Southern town square (as statues of Union soldiers still guarded countless Northern cities). The South's pulverizing defeat in the Civil War had been transmuted into a heroic crusade of gray-uniformed chevaliers—a romantic and doomed crusade that captured Southern hearts. As immediate as the war was for most white Southerners, so, too, were the Reconstruction-era humiliations and affronts that had been heaped on a prostrate South. And nothing had been more degrading, in the view of many whites, than being ordered to treat ex-slaves as equals. Now, the despised Yankee government, through its despised court, was again dictating to them, attacking their most hallowed traditions. Unless the South resisted, its whole way of life would be swept away, some politicians thundered. It was time to mount the ramparts again, under the banner of "states' rights."

Sex, as usual, underlay much of the fear. According to segregationists, the mixing of blacks and whites in the classroom would inevitably lead to the bedroom, with the worst possible result: "mongrelization" of the races. In his book, *Black Monday*, a masterpiece of racist demagoguery about the *Brown* decision, Judge Tom Brady, a Yale-educated white supremacist who later would be appointed to the Mississippi Supreme Court, put the issue in overheated terms that every white Southerner could understand. First, you have the "negroid man," whom Brady compared to "the modern lizard." Then you have "the loveliest and the purest of God's creatures, the nearest thing to an angelic being that treads this terrestrial ball . . . a well-bred, cultured Southern white woman or her blue-eyed, golden-haired little girl." In language resembling that of florid antebellum Southern novels, Brady spelled it out: At all costs, the animal must be kept far away from the angel.

In Philadelphia, Mississippi, a young white woman who expressed approval of *Brown* learned to her shock that even the mildest dissent from the point of view espoused by Brady and other segregationists would not be tolerated. "After commenting that Jim Crow laws had made a mockery of the Constitution and being met by surprisingly unfriendly responses, I ceased to express my opinion," Florence Mars later wrote. "Other Mississippians learned the same lesson. It was the issue of 'mongrelization,' the fear of Negro men desecrating white women, that more than anything stirred the emotions of the white population."

Mars, who ten years later would help the FBI track down the killers of three civil rights workers, had discovered how lonely a white Southern liberal could be. For while white supremacists whipped up anti-integration fury in the South, most so-called liberal and moderate leaders lay low. For the most part, they declined to call forthrightly for compliance with the Supreme Court decision or to provide any other alternative to defiance. As historian C. Vann Woodward put it: "In this atmosphere . . . words began to change their meanings so that the moderate became a man who dared to open his mouth, and an extremist someone who favored eventual compliance with the law, and compliance was something which was equated with treason." Carl Rowan, a black *Minneapolis Tribune* reporter who traveled throughout the restive South a year after *Brown*, offered his own bitter definition: "Apparently a 'moderate' is any white southerner who can prove that he hasn't lynched any crippled old Negro grandmothers during prayer-meeting hour."

The South's two most famous liberals—Lillian Smith's old nemeses, Hodding Carter and Ralph McGill—did not think *Brown* should be resisted, but they didn't like it and weren't in favor of immediate compliance by the South. Both counseled the federal government and the North to let the South work out on its own a gradual path to school desegregation. Smith, one of a handful of influential white Southern liberals who openly championed *Brown*, was incensed at what she considered Carter's and McGill's insidious influence in persuading many in the North to adopt their point of view. She wrote in a letter to a friend: "There is an increasing group of appeasers [in the North] who have been won over by our Hodding Carters and Ralph McGills and who now say 'The South must be let alone; they must take their own time about this.'" In the avalanche of news coverage following *Brown,* Carter and McGill, and their views, gained nationwide fame. In January 1955 *Time* wrote that "even liberal Editor Hodding Carter . . . who opposes segregation on 'moral grounds,' feels that the Supreme Court decision has hurt the gradual progress of desegregation in the South by forcing both segregationists and desegregationists to 'extremes.'" The two prominent editors insisted that putting the screws to the South would result only in an upsurge of racial hatred and violence. They did not seem to consider that a vicious campaign of racial hatred was already raging, in the *absence* of pressure on the South.

In contrast, Lillian Smith, after *Brown,* wrote in delight to Pauli Murray that the decision was "a Magna Carta for the world's children." While Smith felt that Southern racism "has always been too involved, too tangled up with sin and sex and God and money to be unravelled by a Supreme Court decision," she strongly believed that desegregation of public schools was an essential first step for overall integration. Her book *Now Is the Time,* written in 1955, was aimed at persuading white Southerners not only to comply with *Brown* but to end other forms of discrimination and segregation as well.

In the poisonous post-*Brown* climate, Smith found herself the target of a heightened intimidation campaign, including hate mail and threats. On July 4, 1954, she invited a group of forty-five children, black and white, to Old Screamer Mountain for hot dogs and ice cream. She found out later, she wrote a friend, that "the colored folks were warned never to do that again" and that the whites "were warned that if they did, certain jobs would never be available to them." A little more than a year later, a fire set by arsonists roared through her house, destroying her bedroom and study, reducing to ash a twenty-year accumulation of letters, manuscripts, books, and notes, "everything on my writing career, everything about *Strange Fruit . . . Killers of the Dream* and so on," she sadly wrote Pauli Murray. "It was about as awful . . . as anything could be."

A week after Lillian Smith held her interracial picnic on Old Screamer, fourteen civic and business leaders from Indianola, Mississippi, met in their small, sleepy town, just a few miles from the sprawling Sunflower County plantation of Senator James O. Eastland. In their outrage at the *Brown* decision, these respectable, middle-class men voted to form an organization aimed at thwarting any attempt to end segregation. The White

Citizens Council, its founders insisted, would not be like the redneck Ku Klux Klan, with its absurd Halloween-like costumes. The council would use more subtle means to terrorize. Anyone promoting integration—or for that matter, improved conditions of any kind for blacks—would find himself facing the severest of economic penalties. Mortgages would be called in, credit refused, jobs lost, insurance policies canceled. Despite its attempts to distance itself from the men in bedsheets and hoods, the White Citizens Council became widely known as the "uptown Ku Klux Klan." Within months after the council's founding, local chapters, claiming as members bankers, judges, lawyers, doctors, congressmen, and governors, had spread, first through Mississippi and then through the rest of the Deep South, wreaking economic, psychological, and even physical violence wherever they sprang up.

It was no accident that the council was founded next door to the plantation of the "Massa of Sunflower County." James Eastland was the organization's godfather. He called for its creation, he encouraged its growth, he urged its members on. More than that, he was, and would continue to be, the field marshal of racist forces in the South, fighting just as hard against young civil rights workers in Mississippi in 1964 as he did against the *Brown* decision in 1954. As chairman of a Senate investigations subcommittee, he accused leading civil rights activists of being Communists; as chairman of the Senate Judiciary Committee, he bottled up one federal civil rights bill after another. Eastland, wrote one historian, was "the most influential individual shaping the direction of the white supremacy movement . . ."

Within days of the *Brown* decision, Eastland, who was up for reelection in 1954, was racing across the South, giving speeches that played skillfully on white Southerners' deepest fears and resentments. Eastland all but ordered his audiences to disobey the federal government's mandate. "Southern people will not be violating the Constitution or the law when they defy this monstrous decision," he thundered. "They will be defying those who would destroy our system of government. You are not required to obey any court which passes out such a ruling. In fact, you are obligated to defy it." Of Eastland's crusade and his outpouring of rhetorical bile, Carl Rowan noted: "You follow the words of Mississippi's senior senator and you see that the South did not revolt, it was manipulated."

Eastland and others like him, however, were on the losing end of a moral argument. Their first, instinctive response was defiance. Soon they would learn that defiance is a two-edged sword.

"There Had to Be a Stopping Place"

*Rosa Parks being fingerprinted after 1956 boycott arrest,
one year after refusing to give up her bus seat*

FOR SOJOURNER TRUTH, IT HAD
been a streetcar. For Ida Wells, a train. For the black women of Montgomery, Alabama, it was the city buses.

Throughout the Jim Crow South, riding on public transportation was regarded by African-American women as a particular torment, whether they were pushed to the back of a bus or streetcar or to the smoking car of a train. Their shame was all the more acute when it occurred, as it often did, in the presence of white passengers, most of whom seemed to look on with approval or, at best, indifference.

The racial rules on Montgomery's buses in the 1950s were appallingly detailed, obviously designed to inflict as much humiliation as possible on black riders, most of them female domestic workers. Blacks had to pay their fare in the front of the bus, then get out and reboard through the rear door. The first ten rows of each bus were reserved for whites. The last ten were supposedly for blacks. The middle seats were considered "no-man's-land." If a black was sitting in one of the middle rows, she could be ordered by the driver to get up and give her seat to a white. If the front and middle sections were filled, any seated blacks would have to yield their places to boarding whites, although there were *no* exceptions to the whites-only rule for the first ten rows. Thus, when a bus reached the black area of the city at the end of a workday, the seats in the front were usually empty while the rest of the bus was filled with blacks, including a line of exhausted maids, cooks, and other workers who clutched the overhead bars, swaying and falling as the bus jolted down the street. "Buses weren't something optional, like restaurants," said Fred Gray, a black Montgomery lawyer. "Every day, the bus situation put the issue of what it meant to be black squarely before you."

The bus drivers, all of them white, were, in the words of a white city commissioner, "mean as rattlesnakes." It was not unusual for them to drive past a stop where blacks were waiting, or to engage in the sport of driving off just as a black passenger, having paid her fare, was about to board through the back door. Some especially perverse drivers would accelerate or slam on their brakes to knock standing black passengers off balance, or open the windows on winter days if a black asked for more heat. Drivers heaped obscenities and curses on blacks, calling them "black bitches," "heifers," "apes," "whores," among other things. Any African-American who complained or answered back risked being thrown off the bus, assaulted, or arrested.

By the 1950s, however, the black women of Montgomery had had enough. Like Sojourner Truth, Ida Wells, and others before them, they decided to fight back. This time, however, they would not act alone. They would join forces—and when they were done, Montgomery, and the rest of the country, would never be the same.

Montgomery's mayor in those days was a man named Tacky Gayle, who blithely ignored the first indication that the racial status quo of his city was about to be altered forever. Less than a week after the *Brown* decision was handed down in May 1954, Gayle received a letter demanding that Montgomery's bus drivers stop humiliating and insulting their black passengers. If the city didn't put an end to the constant abuse, blacks, who made up three-quarters of the ridership, might decide to stay off the buses altogether. Gayle impatiently brushed the warning aside. He figured that the author, Jo Ann Robinson, and the group of black women she headed were just trying to stir up trouble again. Nothing would come of the threat, he was convinced, just as nothing had come of the women's earlier complaints about the mistreatment of blacks on buses.

Mayor Gayle, whose political success was largely attributed to his marriage into an old Montgomery family, was not, to put it charitably, regarded by the rest of the white establishment as an especially bright light in the municipal firmament. On this issue, however, the establishment and the mayor were as one. A black bus boycott in the cradle of the Confederacy? The idea was ludicrous. Montgomery, the capital of the great state of Alabama, was a civilized, genteel place. It was, claimed Joe Azbell, the city editor of the Montgomery *Advertiser*, "one of the most liberal cities in the South," a place where "race relations were better than in any other city I know of." Warming to his theme, Azbell said: "The white people here did everything for the Negro—they gave them their schools, their hospitals—everything." The female agitators who sent that regrettable letter to Mayor Gayle would never rouse Montgomery's blacks from their torpor. If Gayle and the rest of the city fathers were sure of anything, they were sure of that.

In short, the white male leaders of Montgomery were blind to the rage bubbling beneath the seemingly placid surface of the black community. They also underestimated the Women's Political Council; its current president, Jo Ann Robinson; and its founder, Mary Fair Burks. Professors at the all-black Alabama State College, Robinson and Burks did not like taking a back seat to anyone.

By her own account, Robinson had been angry ever since she boarded her first—and last—bus in Montgomery a few days before Christmas in 1949. School had just let out for the holidays. Robinson had reservations on a flight to Cleveland, where she was going to spend two weeks with friends. She decided to leave her car at home and take a bus to the airport.

When she stepped on the bus that December day, Robinson was "as happy as I had ever been in my life." Having joined the Alabama State faculty just three months before, she was proud of how much she had achieved in her thirty-three years. Born on a farm near Macon, Georgia, the youngest of twelve children, she had been valedictorian of her high school class and, later, the only one of her family to go to college. She had earned a master's degree, then taught at a black college in Texas before coming to Montgomery. She fit in well at Alabama State. She liked her colleagues and her students. Life was wonderful. Until she boarded that bus.

When she struggled through the door with her suitcase, there were only two other passengers, a white woman in the third row and a black man in a seat near the back. Robinson took a seat in the fifth row, so lost in thought about her upcoming vacation that she paid no attention to the bus driver yelling at her. Finally, he slammed on the brakes, turned around, and shouted, "If you can sit in the fifth row from the front of other buses in Montgomery, suppose you get off and ride in one of *them!*" Shocked, Robinson didn't respond until the driver jumped out of his seat and raised his hand as if to strike her, screaming, "Get up from there!" The terrified Robinson, tears streaming down her face, stood and stumbled to the closed front door, then realized that she was supposed to get off at the back. But she couldn't make herself move. At last, the driver grudgingly opened the front door, and Robinson lurched off. She walked back to the college, "[t]ears blind[ing] my vision, waves of humiliation inundat[ing] me." The degradation she suffered—"I felt like a dog," she later said—seared her for the rest of her life. When she talked to historian David Garrow about the incident almost forty years later, her voice trembled and her eyes filled with tears. "In all these years," she once wrote, "I have never forgotten the shame, the hurt of that experience. The memory will not go away."

Even though she never rode another bus in Montgomery, Jo Ann Robinson became a woman with a mission—to force the city to treat the black riders on its buses as human beings. She was joined in that crusade by the Women's Political Council, an organization of middle-class black women, most of whom, like Robinson, rarely or never rode the buses. Among them was the equally ladylike, equally militant Mary Fair Burks.

Born and raised in Montgomery, Mary Burks rebelled, even as a child, against being treated like a "nigger." She launched her own "private guerrilla warfare," invading rest rooms with signs FOR WHITE LADIES ONLY and strolling through whites-only parks. When Burks went to the University of Michigan to study for a master's degree, she thought Ann Arbor was "almost Eden" because "for the first time I knew what it meant to feel and live like a whole human being."

In 1946, three years ahead of Robinson, she joined the faculty of Alabama State as a professor of English. Finding herself immersed again in Montgomery's unrelenting racism was a shattering experience for Burks, made that much worse when, driving in the city one day, she found herself involved in a right-of-way dispute with a white woman. The woman pressed vague charges against Burks, who was promptly arrested and jailed. Although the charges were dropped a few hours later, her brief stay in jail convinced Burks to do something more about segregation than just wage a personal war. The following week, Burks contacted fifty women and sounded them out about forming an organization to protest the city's treatment of blacks. Forty signed up immediately. The Women's Political Council was born.

The women who joined were the core of Montgomery's black middle class—public school teachers and principals, Alabama State professors, social workers, nurses. In the beginning, the council's main goals were to increase voter registration, to teach black high school students about the possibilities of political action, and to protest various forms of discrimination. Over the next nine years, as some two hundred fifty more women joined, the council's members all became registered voters themselves (a daunting achievement, even for Ph.D.'s, in light of the arcane literacy test), and then set up registration schools in churches to help others register as well. Mock elections were held and mock government sessions staged by black Montgomery teenagers, some of whom later became lawyers, judges, and state legislators. But little headway was made in the fight against discrimination.

Not until the energetic Jo Ann Robinson became WPC president in 1950 did the council turn its attention almost exclusively to the abuse of blacks on city buses. Robinson's anger at her own mistreatment flared into several confrontations with city and bus company officials over the next five years, as she and Burks helped shape the council into the best-organized, boldest, most aggressive black community organization in Montgomery. As they sharpened their attack, the women worked closely with E. D. Nixon and Rufus Lewis, the city's two leading black male civic activists. Nixon, the president of the Montgomery chapter of the NAACP, was particularly noted for his fearless challenge of the white establishment over repeated instances of racial violence and injustice, including police brutality and white men's rape of black women. Since the early 1940s, Nixon had also worked hard to persuade the city's blacks to register and vote. Rufus Lewis, a funeral home owner, was head of a group of black businessmen who had made voter registration a priority as well.

Sometimes joined by Nixon and Lewis, the women of the WPC met with the City Commission again and again to present their grievances over the buses. Invariably, the commission treated them politely, listened carefully, then ignored them. After one unproductive session, Mayor Gayle reported later, a furious Robinson called him and "said they would just show me: they were going in the front door [of the bus] and sit wherever they pleased." But despite that threat, and Robinson's warning of a possible boycott in May 1954, she and the other WPC members knew that the city's blacks were loath to band together and confront the white power structure.

Part of the problem was the rivalry and friction among various groups in the black community, as well as among their leaders. E. D. Nixon, who vied for influence with Rufus Lewis, told Virginia Durr that "the Negroes were all split up and jealous of each other and divided in cliques and you couldn't get them to stick together on anything." With the prominent exception of the Women's Political Council, most members of Montgomery's upwardly striving black middle class were unwilling to align themselves with domestic workers and laborers, who were the majority of the city's black population. Many in the middle class, particularly the public school teachers and college professors, were afraid of losing their jobs and did everything they could to stay out of controversy. Although Alabama State College was a black institution, it was funded by the state legislature, which could be counted on to take a very dim view of any challenge to the racial status quo.

Those who stood to gain the most—workers who rode the buses—also were fearful of being fired by their white employers. Whenever the possibility of a boycott was raised, people would generally shy away from the subject. Long before her own galvanizing action, Rosa Parks, later the living symbol of the boycott, tried to talk to friends and acquaintances about how a boycott would "really hurt the bus company in its pocketbook." But when she asked them if they would be willing to stay off the buses, they told her they couldn't because "they had too far to go to work." Said Mary Fair Burks: "Everyone would look the other way."

Then came the arrest of Claudette Colvin.

She was fifteen years old, a slender, pretty, loquacious junior at Booker T. Washington High School who wanted to be a lawyer when she grew up. Her mother thought her choice was perfect. Claudette, she said, could "outtalk forty lawyers."

For as long as she could remember, Claudette Colvin had hated the segregation that confronted her at every turn. When she was about nine years old, she wanted more than anything to go to a rodeo that had come to town. In response to her pleading, her father bought her a cowboy hat. "That's as much of the rodeo as we got," she recalled. "The show was at the Coliseum and it was only for white kids." As a freshman in high school, prompted by a history teacher who had "pricked my mind" about the injustice of discrimination, she wrote an essay denouncing the humiliation that black teenagers like herself had to endure.

By her junior year, Colvin saw herself on a mission of change. She had that on her mind when she boarded a crowded bus on her way home from school on March 2, 1955. She sat down in the middle, a place usually secure from a driver's harassment. But several whites got on, and the driver stopped the bus and ordered the teenager and the woman sitting next to her to give two of the whites their seats. Both refused. When the driver jumped off the bus to find a policeman, the older woman found another seat. Colvin stayed put. When two policemen arrived and told her to move or they would arrest her, she still would not budge. "No," she said, "I do not have to get up. I paid my fare, so I do not have to get up. It's my constitutional right to sit here just as much as that [white] lady. It's my constitutional right!" The cops called her a "black bitch" and a "black whore" and dragged her off the bus. In the melee, they hit her at least once with a nightstick, and she kicked and scratched them. She was handcuffed and taken to the city jail, where she was charged with violating the state segregation law, disorderly conduct, and resisting arrest.

By nightfall, news of Claudette Colvin's arrest had electrified Montgomery's black community. The women expressed particular shock and outrage. Other riders had been arrested in previous years, but this was different. This was just a child! *She could be my daughter, or your grandbaby, and here were these white cops, manhandling her and dragging her off to jail!* Mixed with the anger, however, was pride in the fifteen-year-old girl who had stood up for her rights. "Bless her heart, she fought like a little tigress," said Irene West, the affluent widow of a prominent black dentist.

For the blacks of Montgomery, the Colvin arrest was like the opening of a sluice gate. As all the pent-up rage and resentment spilled out, there was intense talk in every black neighborhood of boycotts and court battles. Virginia Durr wrote to her close friend Jessica Mitford that the teenager's case had "created tremendous interest in the Negro community and made them all fighting mad and may help give them the courage to put up a real fight on the bus segregation issue." Jo Ann Robinson and Mary Fair Burks were exultant: Finally, they thought, the time had come. They and the other women of the WPC did everything they could to stir up debate, to fan the flames of outrage. They composed a notice calling for Montgomery blacks to boycott the buses and were ready to turn out thousands of copies. All they needed to add was the date on which the boycott would start.

On the legal front, Fred Gray, one of only two black lawyers in Montgomery, was poised to file the biggest civil suit of his neophyte career—a suit on behalf of Colvin, challenging the city's and state's segregation laws. A Montgomery native and a graduate of Alabama State, the boyish-looking, bespectacled Gray was only twenty-five years old and just one year out of Cleveland's Case Western Reserve Law School. His inexperience, though, was more than matched by his passion for this case. He had told friends in law school that once he had his degree, he planned to return to Montgomery and "destroy everything segregated that I could find." Now he was preparing to take a giant step in that direction, while Jo Ann Robinson, Rosa Parks, and other black women joined with Virginia Durr to start raising money for what was expected to be a long and difficult battle in the courts.

Then everything fell apart. E. D. Nixon announced that Claudette Colvin would not do as the focus of a test case. Colvin was pregnant, he said. The black community could not risk using a girl of less than sterling character in a role as important as this. The whites of Montgomery would destroy her and the entire effort. Some WPC members agreed. Others were furious. It wasn't Colvin's character that was the issue, they argued; it was the injustice done to her on that bus! Still, without Nixon's support, a bus boycott might fail, so plans for the boycott and preparation of the lawsuit were canceled. Claudette Colvin, represented by Fred Gray, was found guilty in state court of the charges against her and placed on indefinite probation. After the verdict, dozens of blacks stayed off the buses for a few days, but nothing ever came of the spontaneous demonstration.

Throughout the summer and early fall of 1955, the distress of many WPC members over the failure to unite behind Colvin was exacerbated by the steadfast refusal of city officials to respond in any substantive way to blacks' complaints about the buses. On October 21, the flames were fanned again when another black teenage girl was arrested for refusing to obey the rules for black bus riders. Ordered by a white woman to relinquish her seat, eighteen-year-old Mary Louise Smith said no. She explained to the driver, "I am not going to move anywhere. I got the privilege to sit here like anybody else." Once again, there was talk of a boycott and lawsuit, and once again, E. D. Nixon scotched the plans. Mary Louise Smith was not suitable either: according to Nixon, she lived in a tar-paper shack on the edge of town. Besides, her father was a drunk.

Many years afterward, both Claudette Colvin and Mary Louise Smith would challenge Nixon's version of why they were rejected. Colvin said that she was *not* pregnant at the time of her arrest, that she became pregnant later that year. Nixon didn't want to use her, she suspected, because she came from King Hill, a poor neighborhood once described as "the forgotten back yard of Montgomery among the railroad, stockyards, junkyards." Her mother was a maid; her father mowed lawns for a living. "We weren't in the inner circle," Colvin said. "The middle-class blacks didn't want us as a role model." Likewise, Smith and others denied Nixon's characterization of her living conditions and her father. She grew up, she said, in a two-story, three-bedroom frame home; a former neighbor of the Smith family claimed that Mary Louise's father was sober and "rock solid."

Whatever the truth, Jo Ann Robinson, Mary Fair Burks, and the other WPC members were tired of searching for the perfect symbol for their cause. No longer would they consult with male leaders about whether to stay off the buses. Their plans for a boycott were ready, and, at the very first opportunity, they would be put into effect, no matter what the men said. The black women of Montgomery, Robinson said later, "were ready to explode."

The woman who would provide the fuse was a light-skinned, forty-two-year-old seamstress who wore rimless glasses and pulled her graying hair back into a neatly braided coil. Quiet, unassuming, polite—the perfect lady, so everyone said who knew her. Soon, she would stun them all, revealing some of the tortured complexity that lay beneath the prim facade. There was so much that was hidden about Rosa Parks. Even her appearance was deceptive. The coil at the nape of her neck, for example, concealed the fact that her hair was long, straight, and silky—a legacy, she said, from her Indian ancestors. When she pulled out the pins at home, her hair spilled down her back in luxuriant waves. "I never cut my hair because my husband liked it this way," she told a friend years later.

Just as few people ever saw Rosa McCauley Parks with her hair down, few knew about her Indian and white heritage, her deep racial pride, her smoldering anger, her lifelong rebellion against being pushed around by whites. Three of her four great-grandfathers were white. Her maternal grandfather, in whose home she was raised, was the son of a white plantation owner and light enough to pass for white himself. Sylvester Edwards loved to use his appearance to embarrass and upset whites, shaking hands and speaking familiarly with those who didn't know him, then laughing when they found out the truth. He delighted in calling whites by their first names and made jokes about them behind their backs. When the Ku Klux Klan rampaged through their small community outside Montgomery, Rosa McCauley's grandfather kept a double-barreled shotgun by his side at all times. "I don't know how long I would last if they came breaking in here," he told her, "but I'm getting the first one who comes through the door."

His standing up to whites made a deep impression on his small, slight granddaughter, who received a further dose of racial pride when, at the age of eleven, she enrolled in Miss White's school in Montgomery. Officially known as the Montgomery Industrial School for Girls, Miss White's was founded by white teachers from New England to teach domestic skills, as well as academic subjects, to black girls. The teachers at Miss White's were shunned by the rest of the city's white population, and the school twice was set afire. The white community's fear that the school's curriculum included racial equality as well as cooking and sewing was not misplaced. It was no accident that several of the women most active in the Montgomery bus boycott had attended Miss White's. "What I learned best" at the school, Parks wrote, "was that I was a person with dignity and self-respect, and I should not set my sights lower than anybody else just because I was black."

More than once as a child, she put those lessons into practice. When she was ten, a white boy threatened to hit her. She responded by threatening to smash his head in with a brick. Another time, a white boy on roller skates, careening behind her on the sidewalk, tried to push her aside. She turned and pushed back. His mother, standing nearby, told the little girl that "she could put me so far in jail that I never would get out again for pushing her child."

In the tenth and eleventh grades, Rosa McCauley attended the laboratory high school on the Alabama State College campus, where one of her classmates was Mary Fair Burks. Her principal memory of Rosa was of a girl with a gentle, quiet demeanor. "Rosa's schoolmates did not impose themselves on her," Burks recalled. "Instead, we respected her and admired her from a distance."

When her grandmother became ill after her junior year, McCauley had to drop out of school. As intelligent as she was, there was no hope of college, and she wasn't even able to finish high school until a few years later. She got a job in a shirt factory, did some domestic work, and took care of the family farm until, at the age of nineteen, she married a barber named Raymond Parks and moved to Montgomery.

When she first met her future husband, she thought he was too light-skinned—"I had an aversion to white men, with the exception of my grandfather," she later explained—but she soon discovered that Parks was as much of a race man as Sylvester Edwards. Indeed, he was the first civil rights activist she had ever met. A longtime member of the NAACP, he and several other men were clandestinely raising money for the defense of the Scottsboro Boys, nine young black men arrested in 1931 for the rape of two white women in northeastern Alabama. Raymond Parks refused to let his young bride accompany him to his group's secret night meetings; it was far too dangerous, he said. One night, the men held their meeting at the Parkses' home, with their numerous guns spread out on the kitchen table. Rosa sat, terrified, on her back porch, her feet on the top step, her head on her knees. She didn't move for several hours. Later, two of the men in the group were killed, and she worried that Raymond would be next. "Every time he was at those meetings with those people," she recalled, "I wondered if he would come back alive . . ."

By the 1940s, the fire in Raymond Parks had damped down. He had tried for years to register to vote but had not succeeded. Finally, he just gave up trying. Now, Rosa took up the banner. Raymond Parks had long discouraged her from joining the NAACP—too dangerous for a woman, he said. But in 1943, Rosa found that the local chapter had at least one female member—her old friend from Miss White's school, Johnnie Carr. Rosa decided to go to the December meeting to see Carr and take a look at the organization for herself. The meeting, which Carr didn't attend, turned out to be the annual election of officers. The men said they needed a woman to take the minutes, and Parks, the only woman present, agreed. "I was too timid to say no," she explained. She paid her membership dues, was elected secretary on the spot, and, from that moment on, threw herself into civil rights work with singular passion.

Despite her modern image as a simple seamstress who just happened to get on a bus one day and ignite a movement, Rosa Parks, together with E. D. Nixon, was the mainstay of the Montgomery NAACP through the 1940s and 1950s. On her lunch hours, in the evenings after work, and on weekends, Parks would be in Nixon's office, answering phones, handling correspondence, sending out press releases to newspapers, keeping track of the complaints that flooded in concerning racial violence and discrimination. As much as he depended on her, Nixon had little use for women as activists. One time he told Parks that "women don't need to be nowhere but in the kitchen." She shot back: "Well, what about me?" Realizing he had painted himself into a corner, Nixon came back with a lame reply: ". . . I need a secretary and you are a good one." She was much more than that. In the early 1940s, she helped organize the local NAACP Youth Council and became its adviser, encouraging its teenage members to try to integrate the local white library. Childless herself, she loved working with youngsters, who, in turn, responded to her warmth and enthusiasm.

As devoted as Rosa Parks was to the NAACP, however, her work with the organization often left her in despair. She had intimate knowledge of

Montgomery's secret injustices—the mysterious killings of black men, the unpublicized rapes of black women by white men, the beatings and burnings that went unnoticed because the victims were black. "Everything possible that was done by way of brutality and oppression was kept well under cover," she later said. "There were several cases of people that I knew personally who met the end of their lives without even a ripple being made publicly by it." Johnnie Carr recalled several instances of young black girls raped by whites. Nixon and the NAACP would push for prosecution, but nothing would ever happen because, Carr said, it always turned out that the assailant's "granddaddy was the judge, or his uncle was the sheriff. But if it was a black man accused of raping a white woman, you just knew that it was the electric chair! All these types of things just made us bitter, bitter!"

At times feeling "overwhelmed by all the violence and hatred," Rosa Parks, nonetheless, refused to kowtow to white authority. Twice, she tried to register to vote, and both times was told she had failed the voter registration test. On her third try, she made a copy of all her answers, determined to use it to bring suit against the voter registration board if she were denied again. This time, she passed. But it was the constant mistreatment on the buses that bothered her the most. For Parks, the greatest indignity about the buses was being forced to pay her money in the front, then get off and go to the back door. Time after time, she'd had run-ins with drivers about the practice; on occasion, they would order her off or drive away before she could reboard. Her worst experience occurred in the winter of 1943, when, having paid her fare, she refused to obey the driver's order to get off and enter through the rear door. He grabbed her coat and yanked her to the front door, raising his arm threateningly. "I know one thing," Parks said quietly. "You better not hit me." Instead of striking her, he threw her off the bus. Parks had noted what the driver looked like— "tall and thickset with an intimidating posture . . . a mole near his mouth"—and from then on, she would carefully examine the face of a driver before getting on his bus. "I didn't want any more run-ins with that mean one," she said.

Because of Parks's own past confrontations with bus drivers and because of her fondness for young people, the arrest of Claudette Colvin, whose mother had been a childhood playmate of hers, hit her hard. She threw herself into raising money for Colvin's defense but refused to accompany Jo Ann Robinson and other local activists when they tried to wring concessions from city and bus officials. "I had decided," Parks said, "that I would not go anywhere with a piece of paper in my hand asking white folks for any favors." After so many years of working for racial justice without seeing tangible results, she had become profoundly bitter and depressed, feelings that were heightened when plans for a boycott and lawsuit in the Colvin case were dropped.

Not long after the Colvin incident, Virginia Durr told Parks about a workshop to be held that summer at the Highlander Folk School, an interracial meeting place and training ground for labor union and civil rights activists in the mountains of northeastern Tennessee. The workshop would focus on ways to implement *Brown* v. *Board of Education,* Durr said; if Parks was interested, Durr would arrange for her to attend. Parks agreed to go, not for her own benefit—"I felt that I had been destroyed too long ago"—but for the young people she worked with.

Highlander would change Rosa Parks's life forever. It is ironic that her attendance was suggested by a white person at a time when Parks had just about given up on white people. But then Virginia Durr was no ordinary white person. A reformed racist who as a freshman at Wellesley College had thrown a fit because she had to sit next to a black in the dining hall, she was now among the strongest antisegregation voices in Montgomery. She and Rosa Parks, each in her own way, one black, the other white, were on long voyages of self-discovery that intersected from time to time in dramatic ways.

Of Virginia Foster Durr, writer Studs Terkel, a close friend, observed: "The woman would not behave. She was simply non-adjustable to the fashion of the day." Durr, who from childhood had made a close study of well-brought-up Southern white women, finally decided that there were only three options available to her: become an actress and play the Southern belle; go crazy like Blanche DuBois; or become a rebel, step outside the magic circle, and challenge the Southern way of life. Durr chose the third option. She went to college, unlike most white Southern girls of the day; married a liberal Alabama lawyer and former Rhodes scholar; and then flouted virtually every tradition her native region held dear.

But for the first years of her life, Virginia Foster, who was born in 1903, was ensnared in those traditions as firmly as any other wellborn white Southern girl. Her paternal grandfather had owned slaves and a plantation in Union Springs, Alabama. Her maternal grandfather, a Confederate soldier and later a congressman from Tennessee, was a member of the Ku Klux Klan. Her beautiful older sister, Josephine, married Hugo Black, a future Supreme Court justice, who at the time was himself a member of the Klan. Growing up, Virginia thought of the KKK as "something noble and grand and patriotic that had saved the white women of the

South" from rapacious black men. Noticing that some blacks had complexions almost as light, or as light, as her own, she had no trouble accepting her father's explanation: "Dear, that was all due to the Union army."

Yet from an early age, she also was keenly aware of the contradictions, deceits, and secrets of the South, aware of the "maze of fantasy and falsehood" that Lillian Smith wrote about. "I am not so Freudian as Lillian but I do think that Sex and Sin and Race are all mingled in this somehow to an astonishing degree," Durr wrote a friend many years later.

Her seventh birthday was burned in her memory as an early indication of those contradictions. Until then, she had always celebrated her birthday at a backyard barbecue at her grandparents' Union Springs plantation, attended by the children of the plantation's black employees, who had been her playmates since infancy. But when she turned seven, her mother announced that from then on the celebration would consist of a traditional birthday party in the front yard, and the guests would be white children only. Never a docile child, Virginia threw a tantrum, and her mother compromised: a barbecue with the black children and some of her white relatives in the morning, and the party with white children in the afternoon.

At the barbecue, all was going well until Virginia's best friend, Sarah, the daughter of her black nurse, offered Virginia's cousin a piece of chicken. "I'm not going to eat any chicken that your black hand has touched, you little nigger," the white girl replied. Virginia told her cousin to go to hell. At dinner that night, when her aunt said that Virginia was the worst child she'd ever seen, Virginia threw a glass of water at her. Dismissed from the table in disgrace, Virginia ran crying to her black nurse, who had cared for and comforted her since she was born. Virginia was sitting on her nurse's lap on the back porch when she heard her aunt say from the dining room that Virginia's main problem was the woman now cuddling her. "She spoils her to death. And besides, I think it's terrible that you let her sit in her lap and sleep with her and kiss her and hug her. You know all those black women are diseased." Virginia's mother said nothing, but later that night, while saying good night to her daughter, she whispered: "I think it would be better if you didn't kiss and hug Nursie."

The next morning, the anchor of Virginia's life was gone. Her nurse, insulted, had quit and gone to Birmingham with Sarah. Virginia was devastated, and some sixty years later was still trying to sort out her pain and confusion, talking in a sort of stream of consciousness as if it had happened yesterday. "If you have . . . slept in the bed with your Negro nurse, if you have kissed and hugged and sat on [Negroes'] laps and have loved them so much and have been so close to them, and all of a sudden you are told by your mother and your father and your aunts and your uncles and the whole white society that they are inferior people and they should not be treated like other people . . . it makes you feel that there is something wrong with *you.* I think it sets up a terrible conflict in people and I think they get to be schizophrenic . . ." Added Durr: "That's why I think so much of the literature of the South is full of conflict and madness, because you can't do that to people."

There were other contradictions that young Virginia noticed—the discrepancy, for example, between the ethereal, romantic ideal of Southern white womanhood and the all too often disillusioning reality. Taught at an early age that spinsterhood was the worst fate that could befall her, she intently studied the come-hither tactics of her wildly popular sister and other Alabama belles such as Zelda Sayre, who would later marry F. Scott Fitzgerald. The main requirements for popularity with men, Virginia concluded, were "beauty, lovely clothes, stupidity, and also enthusiasm, to have lots of pep and to be admiring and make the men feel good." Marriage was discussed endlessly, but never sex—except when white girls were told to be on guard against black men because they liked to rape white women. When Virginia was given that warning, she had no idea what rape was, "so I was rather confused over what to guard against."

As a child and young woman, Virginia was torn by conflicting emotions. She desperately wanted to be popular like her sister, to "be a belle and have a lot of proposals and have everybody adore me and get flowers and candy . . ." But, obstinate and opinionated, she also wanted to avoid the fate of her female relatives, including her mother, who waited hand and foot on her father and who was institutionalized more than once with what everyone called melancholia. And later when her sister married Hugo Black, the onetime Klan member who became one of the South's leading liberals, Virginia said that as much as she loved and admired her brother-in-law, she hated the way he robbed her sister of any life of her own. "He did everything in his power to make her happy, except give her her freedom," Virginia later said. "She was Mrs. Hugo Black. He expected her to subordinate herself to his life and his ambitions. . . . [A]fter she was married, I don't think Sister ever was able to have a free moment."

Following two years at Wellesley, Virginia fell in love with and married a young Birmingham lawyer named Clifford Durr, whose many virtues included giving free rein to his irrepressible wife. When Durr became one of the New Deal brain-trusters in the Roosevelt administration, Virginia finally was able to break free of the bonds of Southern belledom. Aligning herself with the women's division of the Democratic National Committee, she jumped into the fight to end the poll tax—but only on behalf of white Southern women, not blacks. Still believing in white supremacy when she arrived in Washington, Virginia was incensed that white women, most of whom were not encouraged by their husbands to vote and who didn't have money of their own to pay the poll tax, were as effectively disenfranchised as blacks. As she went from one congressman's office to another, lobbying against the poll tax, she realized how deeply ingrained was the idea of women's subordination. "[T]he only time you got any attention was when they would hug and kiss you and say what a really pretty lady you were ... but you were treated with utter contempt, really, when you were trying to get the fundamental right to vote."

Not until she encountered Mary McLeod Bethune, the most prominent African-American in the Roosevelt administration, did it occur to Durr that the interests of white women might indeed coincide with the interests of blacks. "You sweet Southern ladies are never going to get the laws changed," Mrs. Bethune told Durr and other Democratic women one day as they debated the best strategies for ending the poll tax. "Your husbands have power, but *you* don't have any power. And the only way you're going to get the right to vote is to line up with the blacks who are trying to get the right . . ."

In the ferment of the New Deal years, Durr became friends with Mrs. Bethune and with Mary Church Terrell, and later she would credit them with transforming her feelings about blacks and starting her on her own tumultuous journey toward civil rights activism. In Alabama, the only blacks she had ever encountered were servants. In Washington, she was meeting educated, influential black women who had the same warmth, vitality, and independence of spirit displayed by her childhood nurse. Her mother used to tell her that black women should never be called ladies, but when she met Mrs. Bethune and Mrs. Terrell, she decided her mother didn't know what she was talking about. "[T]hese were ladies in every sense of the word," Durr said. "I mean these were great ladies—women who commanded. . . . They took me under their wing and began to try and teach me the facts of life." Mrs. Bethune, in particular, "taught me about all the practical politics I know."

In 1938, Durr became a founding member of the Southern Conference for Human Welfare, an organization of liberal Southerners who hoped to use the New Deal to eliminate poverty and racism in the South. She also spearheaded a major new assault on the poll tax, bringing together an interracial coalition of organizations, from the NAACP to the CIO, advocating federal protection of voting rights in the South. The Durrs' rambling white farmhouse in Alexandria, Virginia, across the Potomac from Washington, served as a magnet for young Southerners drawn to Washington by the New Deal, from a gangling freshman congressman from Texas named Lyndon Johnson to Aubrey Williams, the controversial, left-leaning head of the administration's National Youth Administration, who had hired Mary McLeod Bethune.

In the center of the action, as always, was Virginia, whose fervor for civil rights was matched only by her enthusiasm for entertaining and gossip—she "elevates gossip to an art form," an acquaintance once said of her—and for involving herself in the lives of others. Virginia loved Jane Austen's novels, which didn't surprise her dear friend Jessica Mitford, since Virginia, with "her insatiable appetite for meeting new people" and her penchant for saying exactly what she thought, resembled nothing so much as one of Austen's endearingly talkative, inquisitive heroines. "She was a real spellbinder . . . ," Mitford said, "whose peculiar charm lay in her enormous curiosity about people, her driving passion to find out things, to know about details and motivations, to trace big events to their small human beginnings."

In the late 1940s, as anticommunist hysteria was sweeping through Washington, Cliff Durr, a member of the Federal Communications Commission since 1941, emerged as one of the administration's most outspoken critics of the government witch-hunt. The FBI investigated him and, even more tenaciously, Virginia. In less than two decades, this former vice president of the Birmingham Junior League had become a radical champion of racial and social justice. Besides heading the National Committee Against the Poll Tax, she was chairman of the Washington committee of the Southern Conference for Human Welfare, which called for the end to all Jim Crow segregation in the South. In 1948, she supported leftist Henry Wallace for President, and, much to the dismay of her husband and Hugo Black, ran for the Senate in Virginia on Wallace's Progressive Party ticket. She even managed to win a respectable six thousand votes.

In 1951, the Durrs moved back to Alabama. Virginia Durr had come into her own in Washington, and the thought of returning to the Deep South, with what she considered its "utterly evil" social fabric, sickened and terrified her. But Cliff was determined to replant his Southern roots and to open a law practice in Montgomery. Reluctantly, Virginia went along—but with a strong sense that she was now entering alien, even enemy territory. From her first days back in Alabama, she mourned the "lack of any sympathetic political companionship," feeling she was "out of touch with the living world." It could not get any worse, she thought. Then it did.

Tension and anger were building in the South over the Supreme Court's pending decision in *Brown* v. *Board of Education,* and the Durrs, as relatives of the most liberal justice on the Court, began feeling the effects. Hugo Black was considered a traitor in his native Alabama, and the Durrs' three daughters were bombarded at school with jeers and taunts about their "coon-lover" uncle. "We could hardly have come to Alabama at a worse time . . . ," Virginia wrote a friend in February 1954. "[O]f course whatever Hugo does or doesn't do we are held responsible for it." She was at a loss in deciding how to cope with this "smothering atmosphere": "To adjust to it means giving up everything I ever believed in or fought for, not to adjust means no living, and to stay in conflict means stomach ulcers . . ." A month later, Senator James Eastland helped her make up her mind.

With the 1954 election in mind, Eastland used the pending *Brown* ruling as campaign fodder, roaring that a decision rejecting the "separate but equal" doctrine would prove that the Court was under the sway of Communists. There was nothing Eastland could do to Hugo Black, his bête noire on the Court, but, as chairman of the Senate Internal Security subcommittee, he found other targets to his liking. In March, his subcommittee announced an investigation of the Southern Conference for Human Welfare and issued several subpoenas. One of them was for Virginia Foster Durr.

Durr was a woman of extravagant loves and hates, and there was probably no one she hated more than Jim Eastland. "A vicious little fat toad of a man," she called him, not to mention "the most disgusting character I have known." Once, while lobbying against the poll tax in the 1940s, Durr took a group of her allies, Methodist churchwomen from Mississippi, to meet with Eastland in his Senate office. Eastland was the quintessential Southern gentleman, all sugar talk and compliments, until the women got to the point of their visit and urged him to vote against the poll tax. At that, Eastland's face reddened and his jowls quivered. Jumping to his feet, he screamed at his shocked constituents, "I know what you women want— black men laying on you!" But while he accused white women of wanting black men and vilified black men for preying on pure white women, at home on the plantation he would invite his male weekend houseguests to pick out, as he put it, a "nigger girl and a horse," Durr said. "That was his way of showing hospitality."

Any fear that Virginia Durr felt over receiving the subpoena was overwhelmed by her scalding anger that this vulgar man, who was "just as common as pig's tracks," had dared question her patriotism. The night before her March 18 appearance before the subcommittee in New Orleans, she sat down at a typewriter and, in her fury, pounded out a statement. "This hearing is no valid exercise of the investigatory powers of the United States Congress, but a kangaroo court where people, called as witnesses, are being tried as criminals, as traitors to their country, without any of the safeguards set up around such trials by the Constitution of the United States . . . My life and my work are an open book. I have nothing to conceal and I have no apologies for anything. . . . I refuse to submit to the authority of this committee and I stand in utter and total contempt of it."

Appearing before Eastland the next day in a mahogany-paneled hearing room in New Orleans' main post office, Durr gave only her name and then, having been told that she would not be permitted to read her statement, sat mute. She occasionally took out her compact and powdered her nose in an ostentatious show of defiance, as the frustrated senator hurled one question after another at her. Afterward, she handed reporters her statement and departed.

Durr was followed to the witness stand several days later by Paul Crouch, a former Communist and key FBI informer, who had been a star witness at several celebrated previous loyalty hearings, including that of physicist Robert Oppenheimer. Asserting that Durr "had full knowledge of the Communist conspiracy and its works," Crouch spun a fanciful tale of her accepting government secrets from Eleanor Roosevelt in the White House and passing them on to a ring of Communist spies. The usually mild-mannered, taciturn Clifford Durr was so enraged by this libelous fantasy that he jumped over the jury rail and lunged at Crouch, shouting, "You goddamn son of a bitch, I'll kill you for lying about my wife like that!" After marshals pulled him out to the hall, Durr collapsed to the floor, suffering a mild heart attack.

Eastland's hearing, for which he had such high hopes, had turned into a fiasco. Its circuslike atmosphere had produced the wildest of accusations, which nobody but the most rabid right-wingers believed. Nonetheless, the Durrs felt they had been irrevocably tainted by the accusation of Communism. It was, Virginia said in her inimitable style, like being "peed on by a polecat. You know you are clean; you know you are free of all this and yet you smell bad and people don't want to be associated with you." Clifford Durr's law practice dwindled to practically nothing, and, with a few exceptions, longtime friends now cut the couple dead.

For all the losses, however, there were important gains. In New Orleans, Virginia had received a telegram of support from a group she had never heard of. "As members of the Women's Political Council of Montgomery we are with you one hundred per cent," it read. It was signed by Jo Ann Robinson. When Durr returned to Montgomery, she contacted Robinson and found out what the WPC was. "Why was it you, of all the people in Montgomery, who stood by me?" she asked Robinson, who replied, "We knew that if Jim Eastland was after you, you were our friend."

Just as Washington had changed Durr's life, so, too, had the Eastland hearing and its consequences. Thanks to the senior senator from Mississippi, she now stood outside the magic circle. Her feeling was one of exhilaration. "I didn't get over being scared of my father and scared of the Southern society I lived in . . . until I got ruined," she later explained. "Jim Eastland freed me . . . by hauling me down to New Orleans and exposing me as a nigger-loving communist, as he called me. . . . I am no longer in prison, in jail, and I am not scared to death all the time anymore."

Not long afterward, she joined the only interracial political group in the city, the Council on Human Relations, as well as a prayer group of black and white women, and she became friends with Rosa Parks, E. D. Nixon, and other black Montgomery activists. She was particularly close to Parks, who did occasional sewing for her and who often talked to Durr about the humiliations and abuses she and other blacks had to endure. Durr helped Parks raise money for the Claudette Colvin case. Even more important, she suggested to Parks that she might benefit from attending a training session for activists at the Highlander Folk School in Tennessee.

Parks reclaimed herself at Highlander. She had arrived "tense, nervous and . . . upset most of the time," generally hating whites but loath to confront them because of the sheer hopelessness of the effort. When she left Highlander ten days later, she had shed some of her own racial prejudice. She also had taken to heart the message hammered home by Highlander: Real social change could come only from grassroots pressure, not from "some government edict or some Messiah."

For ten days, Parks had lived on an equal basis with whites, sharing a room, eating, talking, and arguing with them. She found herself laughing, too, something she hadn't done in a very long time. "We forgot about what color anybody was," Parks later said. "I was forty-two, and it was one of the few times in my life up to that point when I did not feel any hostility from white people." One of her greatest delights, she added, was waking up in the morning, smelling bacon frying and coffee brewing, and "knowing that white folks were doing the preparing instead of me."

Bolstered by her sense of equality with the workshop's white participants, Parks was also strengthened and soothed by the leader of the sessions, a fifty-six-year-old former South Carolina teacher named Septima Clark. Clark, who had been fired from her teaching job the year before for refusing to give up her NAACP membership, was destined, like Parks, to become one of the legendary figures of the civil rights movement. "A healing presence," writer Josephine Carson called the profoundly maternal Clark. "Somehow the world seems to land in her arms. She fondles it idly, demands little, waits, receives, inspires, endures. The world gets up, staggers, finds it can walk a little; it leaves her but it will be back."

Reluctant to talk during workshop sessions, Parks finally got up and spoke only with gentle but persistent pressure from Clark. Parks "was afraid for white people to know that she was as militant as she was," Clark recalled. "She didn't want to speak before the whites that she met up there, because she was afraid they would take it back to the whites in Montgomery." Later, responding to the question all the workshop's participants were asked—what she planned to do when she got back home—Parks said she doubted she could accomplish much. Montgomery was the cradle of the Confederacy, she reminded Clark and the others; she was sure that "nothing would happen there because blacks wouldn't stick together."

Despite her doubts, Parks had come into her own at Highlander. Leaving its exhilarating atmosphere was hard. After being treated as an equal by whites, it was hell to return to Montgomery and her job at the Montgomery Fair department store, where "you had to be smiling and polite no matter how rudely you were treated." As the weeks and months passed, the discrimination she experienced became increasingly unbearable— especially on the buses.

On December 1, 1955, less than two months after Mary Louise Smith's arrest, Rosa Parks waited for a bus to take her home from work. She was just steps away from the Winter Building, where the order had been given in 1861 to fire on Fort Sumter and ignite the Civil War. Shortly after five o'clock, a bus pulled up to the stop. Absorbed in thought about an NAACP workshop she was planning for that weekend, Mrs. Parks didn't notice the driver until after she had paid her money and boarded. As she sank into a seat in the black section's front row, she realized with a jolt that he was the same man who'd thrown her off some twelve years before. The bus lumbered down Montgomery Street and stopped in front of the Empire Theater, where several whites got on and sat down in the first ten rows. One man was left standing. The driver turned to Parks and the other blacks sitting in the next row. "Let me have those front seats," he said. When nobody moved, he barked, "Y'all better make it light on yourselves and let me have those seats." The man in the window seat next to Parks stood up and moved back, as did the two women across the aisle. Parks simply moved over to the window seat.

She sat there, remembering how her grandfather kept his shotgun by the fireplace or in his wagon, remembering how he refused to be terrorized by the Klan, even when everyone else was. She remembered, too, how wonderful it had been at Highlander to feel like an equal with whites. At that moment, she decided it was "time that other white people started treating me that way." Years later, she would declare: "People always say that I didn't give up my seat because I was tired, but that isn't true. I was not tired physically, or no more tired than I usually was at the end of a working day. I was not old, although some people have an image of me as being old then. I was forty-two. No, the only tired I was, was tired of giving in. . . . There had to be a stopping place, and this seemed to have been the place for me to stop being pushed around. . . . I had decided that I would have to know once and for all what rights I had as a human being and a citizen, even in Montgomery, Alabama."

The driver asked Parks if she was going to stand up. She looked at him. "No," she replied. "Well," he said, "I'm going to have you arrested." She answered quietly: "You may do that." It was a moment of profound personal significance. For most black Southerners, the idea of agreeing to go to jail, of voluntarily submitting themselves to a dreaded legal system that had oppressed and killed so many blacks before them, was unthinkable. But doing the unthinkable, rising above the fear and shame of the jail experience, would turn out to be an exhilarating act of personal liberation—for Rosa Parks and the blacks, young and old, who followed her. "Here was an individual, virtually alone, challenging the very citadel of racial bigotry," Pauli Murray said ten years later. "Any one of us who has ever been arrested on a Southern bus for refusing to move back knows how terrifying this situation can be, particularly if it happened before the days of organized protest and we had neither anticipated nor prepared beforehand for the challenge. The fear of a lifetime . . . is intensified by the sudden commotion and the charged atmosphere in the cramped space of the bus interior."

As the driver, James Blake, got off the bus to call the police, Parks sat in her seat, trying hard not to think about what might come next, trying not to worry about being manhandled as Claudette Colvin and countless others had been. A few minutes later, two officers boarded the bus. One of them asked Parks why she didn't stand up. She replied with a question of her own: "Why do you all push us around?" "I don't know," he said, "but the law is the law, and you're under arrest." The policemen picked up her purse and shopping bag, escorted her off the bus, and put her in a squad car for the ride to the city jail. At the jailhouse, Parks asked if she could have a drink from the water fountain and was told it was for whites only. She then was fingerprinted, booked, and put in a cell with two other black women, one of whom gave her a drink of water from a dark metal mug.

Meanwhile, word of Parks's arrest had begun to spread throughout black Montgomery. A neighbor of E. D. Nixon's saw her being escorted by the policemen off the bus and immediately notified Nixon, who, in turn, called Clifford and Virginia Durr. Nixon and the Durrs rushed down to the jail to bail out Parks. As Parks emerged from her cell, matrons on either side of her, the first person she saw was Virginia Durr. Tears in her eyes, Durr threw her arms around Parks. They hugged and kissed, Parks later recalled, as if they were sisters.

6

"Our Leaders Is Just We Ourself"

Mass meeting at First Baptist Church during Montgomery boycott. Most of those present are women.

"OH, ROSA, ROSA, DON'T DO IT, don't do it!" Raymond Parks begged his wife. "The white folks will kill you!" Once, he himself had challenged their cruelty and injustice, but it was like challenging a bulldozer: They had crushed him, just as they would crush her. Couldn't she see that?

But Rosa Parks refused to back down. Yes, she told E. D. Nixon and the Durrs after her release from jail Thursday night, she would stand and fight. Nixon was as gleeful as a child on Christmas morning. "My God," he exclaimed, "look what segregation has put in my hands." Central casting couldn't have done better: a perfect lady, who had to work for a living and ride the bus every day, but who had the proper manners and speech of the middle-class women with whom she had gone to school.

When Nixon got home later that night, he made dozens of phone calls, one of them to Johnnie Carr. "Mrs. Carr, they have arrested the wrong woman," he declared, scarcely able to contain his delight. Puzzled, Carr asked, "Who have they arrested?" "Rosa Parks," he replied. Carr couldn't believe it. "You're kidding," she told Nixon. He chuckled. "No, they arrested Rosa Parks. They arrested the wrong woman."

Thus began the transformation of Rosa Parks the person into Rosa Parks the icon. When she commented later on being chosen as the central figure in what was to follow, one could detect a touch of asperity in how she came to be selected over other brave women like Claudette Colvin and Mary Louise Smith: "I had no police record, I'd worked all my life, I wasn't pregnant with an illegitimate child. The white people couldn't point to me and say that there was anything I had done to deserve such treatment except to be born black."

As news of Rosa Parks's arrest reverberated through black Montgomery that night, the lawyer who would represent her in court, Fred Gray, got in touch with Jo Ann Robinson. Gray had a personal interest in the case, as well as a political one. In the year he had been back in town, he had developed a close friendship with Mrs. Parks, who often joined him for brown-bag lunches in his bare little office above an auto shop. They would talk about the mistreatment of blacks in Montgomery and what could be done about it. When Gray worried about his lack of clients and his ability to do anything to end segregation, she "gave me the feeling that I was the Moses that God had sent to Pharaoh and commanded him to 'Let my people go.'"

The young attorney was also close to Robinson—they had worked together on the Claudette Colvin case—and when he contacted her about Parks's arrest, she told him of her plan. The Women's Political Council was going to call for a boycott the following Monday, the day of Parks's trial, and this time no one was going to stand in the way. "Are you ready?" Gray asked. She said she was. After they talked, she scribbled some notes on the back of an envelope outlining her plan of attack: "The Women's Political Council will not wait for Mrs. Parks's consent to call for a boycott of city buses. On Friday, Dec. 2, 1955, the women of Montgomery will call for a boycott to take place on Monday, Dec. 5."

It was close to midnight Thursday, and time was short. After her conversation with Gray, Robinson called Mary Fair Burks and the other officers of the WPC, as well as the principals of the black schools in Montgomery, most of whom were WPC members. Finally, she said, the time had come to implement the detailed plan they had worked out so long ago. She would produce the boycott leaflets, while the rest of the women contacted other council members around the city, who would help distribute them.

Then she sat down to draft the women's call to arms: "Another Negro woman has been arrested and thrown into jail because she refused to get up out of her seat on the bus for a white person to sit down. . . . If we do not do something to stop these arrests, they will continue. The next time it may be you, or your daughter or mother. This woman's case will come up on Monday. We are, therefore, asking every Negro to stay off the buses on Monday in protest of the arrest and trial. Don't ride the buses to work, to town, to school, or anywhere on Monday."

When she was finished, she drove in the midnight darkness to Alabama State College, where, along with a male colleague and two of her students, she slipped like a thief into the mimeograph room in the basement of the administration building. Here she was—a state employee about to use the resources of a state institution to plot a revolt against segregation laws to which the state was fiercely committed. Shrugging off the possible consequences, Robinson and her accomplices worked through the night, duplicating, folding, and bundling some thirty-five thousand fliers. About two in the morning, she had taken time out to call E. D. Nixon and let him know what she and the other women were doing. This time, there was no hesitation from Nixon, who had been up all night himself on the Parks case. He heartily agreed with the boycott plan, telling Robinson he had come up with a similar idea, although he had not done anything about it. He also said he was summoning Montgomery's black ministers and other leaders of the black community to a meeting later that day to organize Mrs. Parks's defense. They would discuss the boycott as well.

By seven Friday morning, the leaflets were stacked in neat piles, the distribution routes mapped out. After loading the fliers in her car, Robinson and her students made it to the eight o'clock class she was scheduled to teach, with just moments to spare. Later, she called her WPC allies. Get the women ready, she said; we're on our way. For hours on that dark, rainy day, Robinson and the two students crisscrossed Montgomery, handing bundles of leaflets through her car windows to women standing on residential street corners, to women waiting in front of schools, beauty parlors, stores, barbershops, and pool halls.

After handing out her stacks of fliers Robinson rushed back to Alabama State in time for her 2 P.M. class, only to find a message from H. Councill Trenholm, the college's president, ordering her to come to his office immediately. When she was ushered in, he stared at her in cold fury, a copy of the flier in his hand. A colleague of hers had found the flier and identified her as the person probably responsible. What was going on here? What was she doing, putting the school in jeopardy like this? She couldn't stay on the faculty after this! He would have to fire her!

As Trenholm shouted, Robinson realized she didn't care if she was dismissed or not. Struggling to remain calm, she told the ASC president about Rosa Parks's arrest and reminded him of the outrageous way that black Montgomery residents had been treated on the buses. A member of the city's black elite, Trenholm had had little personal experience with such humiliations, and Robinson could see that her passionate outburst had affected him. His voice softened, the anger slowly drained from his face. Besides, she assured him, no one but her closest allies would ever know of her role in starting the boycott. Alabama State would never be dragged into the picture. Somewhat reassured, Trenholm dropped his threat to fire her. Whatever her future role in the boycott, he warned, she must not do anything to focus attention on the college nor must she neglect her teaching duties. Oh, and another thing. She must pay for all the paper she'd used.

When Rosa Parks awoke that Friday morning, with the rain streaming down outside her window, her first thought was one of tremendous relief: No matter what happened in the future, she would never ride a segregated bus again. She called a cab and went to work.

At the Dexter Avenue Baptist Church, meanwhile, its twenty-six-year-old pastor was trying to resist the pleas of his best friend to get involved in planning for the boycott. Martin Luther King, Jr., had been at Dexter Avenue a little over a year, and he wasn't ready to take on such a commitment, he told Ralph Abernathy, the pastor of the First Baptist Church. King and his wife, Coretta, had just had their first baby, and he was struggling to finish his doctoral dissertation, as well as meet all the responsibilities of his first pastoral post. He had enough to do to prove himself to his well-educated congregation, which included Jo Ann Robinson and Mary Fair Burks. (When she first saw the small, boyish-looking King, Burks commented to a friend: "You mean that little boy is my pastor? He looks like he ought to be home with his mama.")

He was dedicated to preaching the social gospel—his eloquent sermons on the need for racial justice had already impressed Burks and others in his congregation—and he had accompanied Robinson, Abernathy, and other black leaders to meetings with city officials after the Claudette Colvin incident. But he told Abernathy when he first came to Montgomery that he needed time to get to know the city and its leaders before joining any crusades. How much time? Abernathy asked. "At least several years," King replied. "We must move slowly and carefully, so that when the time does come, we'll be sufficiently prepared."

Now, ready or not, the time had come. Here, Abernathy told King, was an opportunity for leadership that could not be ignored. Until now, with a few exceptions, the black ministers of Montgomery had shied away from any attempt to fight segregation and discrimination. They were far more interested, according to Jo Ann Robinson, in "preaching God and raising their salaries." If they didn't respond this time, who knew what would happen to their credibility, not to mention their authority? The people might just go ahead without them. King finally agreed. As long as he did not have to do any of the work of organizing the boycott, he would publicly support it, as well as turn over his church's basement meeting room for the planning meeting.

When some seventy ministers and other black leaders gathered at the Dexter Avenue Church that evening, they were met with a fait accompli. Realizing, as Jo Ann Robinson wryly put it, that their congregations "were planning to support the one-day boycott with or without their . . . leadership," the ministers "decided that it was time for them, the leaders, to catch up with the masses." Actually, as the women were well aware, the ministers' support was crucial. For one thing, blacks had no access to Montgomery's white-controlled newspapers or radio and television stations, and had no press of their own. Other than word of mouth, churches were the main medium of communication within the black community. The ministers at the meeting promised to lobby for the boycott from their pulpits on Sunday, and all the leaders agreed that a mass meeting should be held Monday night to decide whether the boycott would be limited to one day or continued indefinitely.

Left unspoken was the nagging question on everyone's mind: Would the blacks of Montgomery, so long divided, answer the call?

Monday morning dawned damp and chill. A restless Johnnie Carr couldn't stand the suspense: What was going on out there? She got in her car and drove behind buses all over town to see how many black passengers were riding. She was amazed by what she saw—or, rather, what she did not see: The buses "didn't pick up a single soul. They were just moving on down the street empty." The sidewalks, meanwhile, were crowded with black women—every single one of them walking to work. "The maids, the cooks, they were the ones that really and truly kept the bus running," said

Georgia Gilmore, a cook herself. "And after the maids and the cooks stopped riding the bus, well, the bus didn't have any need to run."

For the first time ever, the blacks of Montgomery had banded together to challenge those who mistreated them. As they marched to their jobs Monday morning, it seemed to Rosa Parks that a tremendous weight had been lifted from her shoulders. "I could feel that whatever my individual desires were to be free, I was not alone," she said later. "There were many others who felt the same way." When she went downtown for her trial that morning, she found hundreds of black supporters milling in front of the courthouse and in the corridor outside the courtroom. Several members of her NAACP Youth Council had played hooky to be there, and one, a girl named Mary Frances, shouted when she saw Mrs. Parks: "They've messed with the wrong one now."

Parks's trial lasted all of five minutes: She was found guilty of violating the state segregation statute and fined ten dollars, a verdict that Fred Gray said he would immediately appeal. When it was over, Parks, wearing a white-collared black dress, white gloves, and a black velvet hat, went to Gray's office to help out, answering a stream of phone calls from people who wanted to know the outcome. She never told the callers who she was.

That afternoon, Montgomery's black leaders formed a new group called the Montgomery Improvement Association to organize any future activity, and elected as president the Reverend Martin Luther King. Abernathy, sure that King would turn the post down, was astonished when the young minister accepted it. For their part, many of the other ministers, who still had their doubts about the wisdom of confronting the white establishment, were happy to let this newcomer to Montgomery take the hot seat. Most were also reluctant to volunteer as speakers at that night's mass meeting, knowing that white reporters and news photographers would be there. Wouldn't it be possible, some asked, to keep their names out of this altogether? At this point, an already seething E. D. Nixon exploded in disgust and anger. "What the hell you people *talkin'* about?" he shouted. "How you gonna have a mass meeting, gonna boycott a city bus line without the white folks knowing it? You guys have . . . lived off these poor washwomen all your lives and ain't never done nothing for 'em. And now you got a chance to *do* something for 'em, you talking about you don't want the white folks to know it." Unless they cooperated, Nixon thundered, he would take the microphone at the church that evening and "tell 'em the reason we don't have a program is 'cause you all are too scared to stand on your feet and be counted." Black men had been cowed long enough, he said. "We've worn aprons all our lives. It's time to take the aprons off. . . . If we're gonna be mens, now's the time to be mens." Jumping in to second what Nixon said, King made clear to the furious older man that he, for one, was "not a coward."

When the ministers arrived, one by one, for the mass meeting that night at the Holt Street Baptist Church, they found no timidity. To make their way into the church, they had to push through a crowd that had massed in front and for several blocks beyond—"more people than I had ever seen in my life," Ralph Abernathy later remarked. These were the thousands who had arrived too late to join the lucky ones inside, those packed in the sanctuary, balcony, basement, aisles, and on the steps. As Abernathy and King approached the church to preside over the meeting, the massive crowd broke into wild applause and cheering, and in the church itself, the thousand or so present leaped to their feet and did the same for at least fifteen minutes, tears streaming down the faces of many in the pews. They were crying, Abernathy said, "out of a sense of new-found freedom, not cheering us so much as cheering themselves for what they had done that day, what we had all done." With dignity and courage, they had done what Mayor Tacky Gayle and the rest of the whites had said was impossible. And they would continue to do it. When Abernathy asked whether they wanted to end the one-day boycott, the crowd in the church joined the loudspeaker-listening army outside in shouting as one: "No!" They vowed to continue the boycott until their demands were met.

As the leaders realized the depth and breadth of support for the boycott, their fear melted away as fast as an April snowfall. "Once we got in there, everybody wanted to preside because this thing was hot," Abernathy recalled. The pulpit and platform were jammed with ministers and others anxious to speak. Rosa Parks, also on the platform, had asked before the meeting if she should talk, too. "Why?" one of the leaders said. "You've said enough." So she sat there, mute, as King introduced and praised her, and the audience gave her a standing ovation.

That Monday, the people had spoken, but the woman who had shown them the way was denied a voice of her own.

For the next 381 days, the fifty thousand blacks of Montgomery stunned their city, the South, and the rest of the country by staying off the buses. Never before in American history had there been such a massive, prolonged defiance of racial discrimination, putting the lie in the most dramatic way possible to white Southerners' arguments that blacks were content to live under Jim Crow. In its attempts to explain these confounding events, the national press focused on the inspiring oratory and leadership of Martin Luther King. But important as King was, most journalists missed the real key to the boycott's success: the black population's new-found sense of community. Riven for so long by class differences and personal rivalries, African-American residents of Montgomery were able to put those divisions aside and, for more than a year, come together in glorious unity. And the way was led by women.

Women like Irene West, the regal, haughty grande dame of black Montgomery, who lived in an imposing home filled with antiques, where she and her guests dined at a mahogany table covered with a damask cloth, replete with crystal, china, and monogrammed silver napkin rings. This woman, who had grown up in affluence, who'd never worked a day in her life, was close to eighty and bent with arthritis. But every morning during the boycott, she would back her green Cadillac out of the garage and drive through town for several hours, picking up people needing a ride. Friends were stunned when they found out what she was doing, not least because she'd hardly ever driven before. She had always had a chauffeur to take her around.

Yet as much as middle- and upper-class black women contributed to the boycott, the true heroines were the ones doing the walking. During the first days of the boycott, whites in Montgomery predicted that blacks would be back on the buses with the first heavy rain. When that downpour came, Johnnie Carr stopped her car alongside a group of women walking down Decatur Street and offered to take as many as could fit in the car. "No, no, Mrs. Carr," one replied, "just let us walk in the rain." As she watched them go, "rain just dripping off of 'em," Carr sat in her car and cried —"because people were willing to do these things, to sacrifice."

No matter the weather—rain, cold, scorching heat—they walked by the thousands, traversing distances that sometimes took hours. Virginia Durr, who often drove for the MIA car pool, once stopped for an elderly woman who had already covered seven miles of a twelve-mile journey to apply for a job. "Well, I appreciate it very much," she told Durr as she got in the car, "but if nobody picked me up, I was going to walk. . . . [I]f my walking is going to help my people get justice, I will walk."

At the weekly mass meetings, attended predominantly by women, the maids were "the soldiers who rallied and prodded the leaders," recalled the Reverend Robert Graetz, one of the few white Montgomery ministers to support the boycott. Maids and cooks and cleaning ladies would stand up and tell about losing their jobs because of their support of the boycott, about defying their employers and other whites, about besting whites in arguments over what was going on. After all the tensions and hardships of the previous week, the meetings, held at various churches, were a needed balm, giving those who attended a renewed sense of community and purpose. They were always jammed, and people would arrive at the church three hours early in order to be sure of a seat. Teachers would go straight from school, maids and cooks from their jobs, and beauty parlor operators wouldn't accept any customers after four o'clock. Once inside, they took any seat available, doctors sitting next to maids, college professors side by side with janitors, lawyers next to yardmen. "Everybody would . . . clap and hold hands in the meeting," Jo Ann Robinson recalled. "Oh, you just loved everybody."

For women who had spent all of their lives being told they were inferior because of their race, sex, and social status, challenging the authority of those who had forced them into submission was a heady, if frightening, experience. In the tradition of slave ancestors who concealed their militance from their owners, some of the boycotters told their white employers what they wanted to hear, that they were not involved in "that mess." When Virginia Durr overheard her mother-in-law's maid say that she and her family had nothing to do with the boycott, Durr was incredulous. Pulling the woman aside, she whispered, "You're the biggest storyteller in the world. You know very well you're supporting the boycott, and all of your family are." The maid laughed. "Well, I tell you," she replied, "I learned one thing in my life and that is, when your hand's in the lion's mouth, it's just better to pat it on the head."

Others were emboldened to stick their hand in the lion's mouth and dare the beast to bite. After the boycott began, the white employer of a maid named Dealy Cooksey had given her rides home. But when the white woman denigrated Martin Luther King, the normally reticent Cooksey exploded in rage. "Don't you say *nothing* about Dr. King!" she exclaimed. "Y'all white folks done kept us blind long enough. We got our eyes open now and we *sure* ain't gonna let you close 'em back. I don't mean to be sassy, but when you talk [about] Dr. King, I get mad. Y'all white folks work us to death and don't pay nothing."

"But, Dealy, I pay you," said her startled employer.

"What do you? Just tell me. I'm ashamed to tell folks what I work for."

"Dealy, I didn't mean to make you mad. I was just talking."

"I walked to work the first day and I can walk now. If you don't want to bring me I ain't begging and I sure ain't getting back on the bus and don't you never say nothing about Reverend King."

Recalling her outburst later, Cooksey said with satisfaction: "We got these white folks where we want 'em and there ain't nothing they can do but try to scare us. But we ain't rabbits no more, we done turned coon. My daddy use to tell me 'bout coon huntin'. If he's in a tree and you shake him down, he'll kill three dogs, and if he's in the water, he'll drown every dog that come in the water. It's just as many of us as the white folks and they better watch out what they do."

It was a complicated dance between the black women and white women of Montgomery, whose ties with each other were much more personal and intimate than those between black and white men. Black women worked as maids and cooks for white women, taking care of their children, fixing their meals, cleaning their homes. While the relationship was clearly unequal, while many whites demeaned and exploited their black employees, others developed a close bond with those who worked for them. Regardless of the relationship, white women considered black women essential to the running of their households, and when the boycott began, many white women, even those who opposed the action, gave rides or taxi fare to their maids, to the great displeasure of city officials and sometimes of their husbands. A number of white women backed the boycott, if only secretly, giving extra money to their employees for the MIA, calling to support the few white women who dared to write letters to the Montgomery *Advertiser* endorsing the boycott.

In one of the letters, Clara Rutledge, a prominent civic activist and friend of Virginia Durr's, told of riding a bus when she was the only person in the first ten rows, while in the back, blacks were jammed together, many standing in the aisles. "'Why,' I asked the driver, 'can't you let these people sit down?' 'I don't mind,' he said, 'but I'm afraid someone will criticize me.' In the years since this incident, in which I have talked about the bus situation, I have yet to find one white person who feels that it is right that a Negro be made to stand that a white person may sit . . .'"

After her letter appeared in the paper, Rutledge was deluged with phone calls. One man asked her if her husband were "the big buck nigger Rutledge" whom he knew, adding that she would "be the next one on the end of a rope." Most of the male callers wanted to know if her husband was a "nigger" and did he satisfy her sexually. "I came to the conclusion years ago, along with Lillian Smith and some of the others, that guilt feelings on the part of white men and fears that Negro men are more virile play a large part," Rutledge said during the boycott. "Sex is the basis of a lot of fears."

For Mayor Gayle and the rest of Montgomery's white male establishment, the fact that white women were collaborating with their black employees, giving them rides and money for taxis, was both an embarrassment and a major affront to white supremacy. In a stinging rebuke, Gayle demanded that whites stop such subversive practices and, rather than helping blacks who supported the boycott, fire them. The blacks, he declared, "are fighting to destroy our social fabric just as much as the Negro radicals who are leading them." The women's response was hardly what Gayle had in mind. As Virginia Durr described it: "[T]he white women got so furious at the mayor that they kept . . . writing letters to the paper saying, 'If the mayor wants to do my wash and wants to cook for me and clean up after my children let him come and do it. But as long as he won't do it, I'm certainly not going to get rid of this wonderful woman I've had for 15 years.'" And they kept on driving.

Still, the white male leadership of Montgomery was not about to stand for such defiance, either from their women or from black boycotters. In January 1956, little more than a month after the boycott began, Gayle, Police Commissioner Clyde Sellers, and other city commissioners announced they had joined the White Citizens Council. A month after that, more than ten thousand people jammed the Coliseum for a WCC rally, complete with the waving of Confederate flags and the playing of "Dixie." The audience cheered and whooped rebel yells as the rally's main speaker, Senator James Eastland, entered the Coliseum in a state highway patrol car, sirens screaming, lights flashing. "There is only one course open for the South to take," Eastland declared, "and that is stern resistance . . ."

As the White Citizens Council gained strength in Montgomery, whites who had demonstrated any support at all for the boycott found themselves the targets of a vicious campaign of fear, hate, and social ostracism. Virginia Durr reported that for a time she was getting more than a dozen obscene, threatening phone calls a day. Women who drove their maids to and from work got similar intimidating calls, many of them in the middle of the night. WCC members and sympathizers received letters like the following: "Dear Friend: Listed below are a few of the white people who are still hauling their Negro maids. This must be stopped. These people would appreciate a call from you, day or night. Let's let them know how we feel about them hauling Negroes."

No one felt the venom of the antiboycotters more keenly than Juliette Morgan, a member of a respected, prominent Montgomery family, who had the pale red-gold hair, delicate features, and ethereal air of a model for a pre-Raphaelite painting. A city librarian, Morgan graduated Phi Beta Kappa from the University of Alabama, marking the fifth generation of women in her family to attend college. Although Morgan never considered herself a social activist, in previous years she had been one of a small group of white women, led by Clara Rutledge, who worked with E. D. Nixon to guard against abuse and discrimination of blacks in the courts. At Nixon's request, Rutledge and the other women would fill the courtroom for trials, putting the judge and lawyers on notice that they were being watched. "Sometimes, I'd walk in the courtroom," Nixon recalled, "and I'd look over there, and Mrs. Rutledge would have [those] women sitting there, and it had its effect on the judge, just to see them."

But the shy, retiring Juliette Morgan was best known as a letter writer. Identifying closely with the views of Lillian Smith, she deplored the way her fellow whites treated blacks, and she made her feelings public and clear over the years in a succession of letters to the editor of the *Advertiser* and other Alabama newspapers. She had once lost a job at a city bookstore after writing a letter to the *Advertiser* criticizing segregation. Retaliation never seemed to faze her, but until the boycott she had not realized how fearsome retaliation could be.

Morgan sent a long letter in praise of the boycott to the *Advertiser* a little more than a week after it began. "One feels that history is being made in Montgomery these days," she wrote. ". . . It is hard to imagine a soul so dead, a heart so hard, a vision so blinded and provincial as not to be moved with admiration at the quiet dignity, discipline, and dedication with which the Negroes have conducted their boycott." The city's blacks, she observed, seemed to have taken a lesson from Gandhi and his famous "Salt March" in India boycotting the British government's salt monopoly.

"It is interesting to read editorials on the legality of this boycott," Morgan added. "They make me think of that famous one that turned America from a tea to a coffee drinking nation. Come to think of it, one might say that this nation was founded upon a boycott. . . . Instead of acting like sullen adolescents whose attitude is 'Make me,' we ought to be working out plans to span the gap between segregation and integration, to extend public services—schools, libraries, parks—and transportation to Negro citizens."

From the day her letter appeared, Morgan received a flood of obscene calls and letters. Her doorbell rang late at night, rocks were hurled through her windows. She endured taunts, insults, and threats from strangers, and old friends and family acquaintances turned their backs on her. Tacky Gayle, once a close family friend, publicly called for her to be fired. The library board declined to do so, but warned her not to write any more letters. For a while, Morgan complied, but in the end she couldn't bear to remain silent. Months after the boycott ended, her final speaking out would exact a terrible price.

*   *   *

As much as whites who supported the boycott were vilified by the WCC's hate campaign, those who bore the major brunt were the boycotters themselves. Occupants of speeding cars showered black pedestrians with water balloons and containers of urine, pelted them with rotten eggs, potatoes, and apples. Martin Luther King's house was bombed. Crosses were burned on boycotters' lawns; many were fired from their jobs. Rosa Parks, who lost her seamstress position two weeks after the boycott began, was besieged by threatening phone calls. "You're the cause of all this," callers would tell Parks. "You should be killed."

One night, as Jo Ann Robinson was chatting with Fred Gray and his wife in her living room, a policeman got out of a squad car in front of her house and hurled a stone through the picture window. As the Grays and Robinson dove to the floor, the officer got back in the car and, with his partner, drove slowly away. Two weeks later, Robinson came outside one morning to find that holes had been eaten through the body of her car by acid. Two men in police uniforms had done it, neighbors told her later.

In late January 1956, Montgomery police launched a campaign of harassment against drivers, both white and black, who gave rides to boycotters. The drivers were stopped, searched, and questioned, then given tickets for infractions that ranged from minor to nonexistent. Robinson, who prided herself on obeying traffic laws to the letter, received seventeen tickets over the next couple of months, "for all kinds of trumped-up charges."

At a January 30 MIA board meeting, several ministers expressed frustration and discouragement that city and bus line officials remained so intransigent over the boycott's three mild demands: that whites be seated in buses from the front toward the back and blacks from the back toward the front, until all the seats were taken; that discourteous drivers be disciplined; and that some black drivers be hired. Wasn't it time, several ministers asked, to consider calling off the boycott, to come to terms somehow with the white establishment? In his response, Martin Luther King made it clear who was in charge: "[I]f we went tonight and asked the people to get back on the bus, we would be ostracized. They wouldn't get back. . . . I believe to the bottom of my heart that the majority of Negroes would ostracize us. They are willing to walk." Trapped by grassroots determination and support, the leaders had no choice but to vote to persevere.

During that same meeting, they came under still greater pressure. Fred Gray had been after them for weeks to authorize the filing of a suit in federal court that would go far beyond the modest demands they were making of city officials. Gray wanted to challenge the whole idea of segregated seating on public transportation, branding it unconstitutional in light of *Brown* v. *Board of Education.* That had been his and Jo Ann Robinson's goal from the beginning, despite King's declaration to journalists that "blacks were not seeking integration." "Certainly [King] was not demanding integration," Robinson recalled more than forty years later. "However, the women of the WPC had started the boycott, and we did it for the specific purpose of finally integrating those buses."

Gray had been encouraged to file a federal lawsuit by Virginia Durr's husband, Clifford, who acted as the young lawyer's behind-the-scenes mentor and who "more than any other person," Gray said, "taught me how to practice law." If Montgomery's blacks were serious about a legal challenge to segregation on city buses, Clifford Durr told Gray, they should not bother with an appeal of Mrs. Parks's conviction in state court, since the state would make sure that the case was not heard for years, if ever. Far better, said Durr, to find four or five new plaintiffs and file suit directly in federal court, knowing that whatever the outcome, the decision would be quickly appealed to the U.S. Supreme Court.

Taking Durr's advice, Gray, who consulted every day with Jo Ann Robinson as well, set out to find black Montgomery residents who had been discriminated against on the buses and who were not afraid to expose themselves to public intimidation. No black men were willing to volunteer as potential plaintiffs, but Gray managed to find four women, among them Claudette Colvin and Mary Louise Smith. At the MIA board meeting on January 30, Gray asked that at least one minister join the women as plaintiffs. King, whom Gray had ruled out as a possible plaintiff, because "he's too much in the limelight," seconded Gray's appeal. Which of the twenty-five clergymen present would volunteer? They had dragged their feet on filing the federal suit in the first place, and now they looked at the floor and each other. Ten minutes went by. No one accepted the challenge.

The next day, Fred Gray filed suit in federal court on behalf of the four women, disputing the constitutionality of Alabama's public transportation segregation ordinance. The dry-as-dust name of the case, *Browder* v. *Gayle*, gave no hint of the unprecedented personal drama it signified: a midwife and mother of twenty-one children named Aurelia Browder, along with three other black women, was taking on the white mayor of Montgomery, Tacky Gayle.

Throughout the course of the boycott, the city's white leaders, who had predicted that blacks would get on the buses with the first hard rain, were bewildered as much by the boycotters' talent for organization as by their determination and resolve. "I'll tell you this, it's the best-organized group anywhere . . . ," said the president of the bus drivers' local union. "They have mass meetings every week, and all of 'em go, by the thousands. I guess they've got a world of confidence or something. . . . What puzzles me is how they got organized so good."

The intricate structure of the boycott—from the mass meetings and car pools to welfare services for boycotters who had lost their jobs —was assembled and kept in place by a network of men and women from a wide array of black organizations and institutions. But while men like E. D. Nixon and Rufus Lewis made significant contributions, it was women who did most of the day-to-day organizing, who provided much of the boycott's direction. At the center of the action, then as before, was Jo Ann Robinson.

Robinson, it seemed, did everything. She conferred with Fred Gray on legal strategy, helped make policy as a member of the MIA's executive board, was part of the MIA delegation that negotiated with city officials, and edited the organization's newsletter. For six hours a day, she drove for the car pool, starting at 6 A.M. and sandwiching time in between her classes. "More than any other person," wrote Martin Luther King, she "was active on every level of the protest."

Why, then, after the boycott, did Robinson fade into almost total obscurity? For that matter, why—*during* the boycott—did she and the other women organizers remain so quietly in the background, ceding center stage to King and the other male leaders, never talking publicly about their crucial roles until many years later? The most obvious reason is that the women in many cases had much more to lose than the men. While most of the male leaders were ministers, professionals, or entrepreneurs, and thus not beholden to local white employers, many of the women were public school employees or Alabama State professors, who would have been fired if their involvement in the boycott had been publicized. Robinson, in particular, was in jeopardy, and her fellow boycott leaders took great pains to shield her from public scrutiny, particularly after Montgomery's White Citizens Council asked the state legislature to investigate state-supported colleges and universities for possible subversive activities.

As much as they tried, city officials never were able to find out who was responsible for the December 2 leafleting of the city. When the protest's leaders were asked who had initiated the boycott, they would respond in the vein of Irene West, who coyly told one interviewer: "Well, really, no one knows. It was an instantaneous combustion." Yet there were some who were not fooled. After several weeks of interviewing participants in the boycott, a researcher from Nashville's Fisk University wrote his superior: "I sense that in addition to Reverend King, there is another leader, tho[ugh] unknown to the public, of perhaps equal significance. The public recognizes Reverend King as THE leader, but I wonder if Mrs. Robinson may be of equal importance. The organizational process is being kept secret, as well as the organizers. Superficially it appears to be a spontaneous move, but listening and talking with different leaders, after a time you receive an altogether different impression." In another letter, the researcher was even more emphatic: "Mrs. Jo Ann Robinson seems to have been the key organizer for the protest. She is the backbone of this collective effort."

But while Robinson and the other women were protecting their jobs, they were also conforming to the then-current norms of American society, black and white, that men should be the leaders, women (no matter how much work they did) the followers. For more than a century, black women's organizations had been in the forefront of the battle against racial injustice. But when women joined forces with men, they tended to slip into the background. "Women listened to men," said one female boycott leader. "They passed the ideas to men to a great extent. Mary Fair Burks and Jo Ann Robinson were very vocal and articulate, especially in committee meetings. But when it came to the big meetings, they let the men have the ideas and carry the ball. They were kind of like the power behind the throne." Another female boycott activist mused many years later: "[S]omehow the male comes up and gets the attention. Others seem to just respect male leadership more. I think the men have always had the edge."

The relationship between male and female leaders of the Montgomery bus boycott would set a pattern that would continue into the civil rights movement of the 1960s: Women would operate behind the scenes, acting as organizers, strategists, fund-raisers, and foot soldiers, while the men would be in the public eye, dealing with the white power structure and the press. Women might occasionally bridle at the sexism of male colleagues, but most, in those prefeminist days, spent little time worrying about being shortchanged personally. Nothing, they believed, was more important than the cause.

When the boycott finally ended in December 1956, Martin Luther King and Ralph Abernathy boarded a bus outside King's home and, in Rosa Parks's words, "made a great show of riding the first integregated bus in Montgomery." The day before, U.S. marshals had formally served city officials with a Supreme Court order striking down Alabama segregation laws as unconstitutional. Celebrating the boycott's success, King and Abernathy sat in what had once been the reserved whites-only section, as a mob of news photographers jostled each other to take pictures. Parks was not with them. The woman who launched the boycott was at home, taking care of her mother.

Whether she was even invited to accompany King and Abernathy is uncertain, but she clearly was not averse to riding an integrated bus herself on that historic morning. When a reporter and photographer from *Look* came to her door and asked her if they could take pictures of her on the buses, she accompanied them downtown, where she got on and off several buses as the photographer snapped away. To Parks's dismay, one of the drivers was James Blake, the very man who had thrown her off the bus in 1943 and had had her arrested in 1955. Blake stared straight ahead as he wheeled the bus into traffic. "He didn't want to take any honors," Parks observed. Later, Irene West mischievously speculated that "if the man who had called the cop had known it would come to this, he would have let [Mrs. Parks] sit in his lap."

Now that the boycott was over, there was some carping, particularly by whites who opposed it, that the protest, in fact, had accomplished nothing, that the Supreme Court, not the boycott, had ended Jim Crow on the city's buses. "What could they possibly gain from the boycott that they can't gain from the federal courts?" Joe Azbell, city editor of the *Advertiser*, had grumbled early in the protest. What could they gain? A sense of dignity, self-respect, and power; a feeling of community; a determination to claim basic rights; a loss of fear—victories that were nothing short of revolutionary for blacks in the Deep South in the 1950s. The Ku Klux Klan of Montgomery discovered for itself what blacks had achieved when, on the night after the Supreme Court ruling, some forty cars loaded with white-hooded thugs cruised slowly through black neighborhoods. There was no panic, no dread; instead, blacks jeered and laughed and shook their fists as the Klan drove by. Disconcerted by their failure to terrorize, the Klansmen drove away.

The courage, passion, and unity of Montgomery's boycotters would ignite a flame in thousands of young blacks throughout the South, inspiring them to follow their elders' example and to launch their own mass campaign for civil rights a little more than four years later. Future movement activists were particularly mesmerized by the sight of black maids and cooks, women who might have been their mothers or grandmothers, willing to sacrifice everything for freedom. "I'll never forget the pictures of old black women walking in the sun," said Charles Jones, one of the Student Nonviolent Coordinating Committee's early strategists. "When you see an old black woman in her seventies walking with her shoes in her hand, you know that there is something very profound about that. . . . The system had no defenses for black folks walking with their bodies into the system, talking about its contradictions, but prepared to put their bodies there rather than guns or bullets or violence."

For many others around the country, however, it was not the boycotters who were the stars of the protest but rather their charismatic young spokesman, Martin Luther King. The MIA president never pretended to be more than he was: He acknowledged he hadn't begun or organized the boycott, and he never wanted to be its leader. "If anybody had asked me a year ago to lead this movement, I tell you very honestly, I would have run a mile to get away from it," he said in 1956. But once involved, however reluctantly, King was brilliant in fostering the black community's sense of purpose, in making the blacks of Montgomery feel they were on a historical mission, that they truly were God's chosen people. Exhorting, persuading, encouraging, the youthful minister was unparalleled in his eloquence. "King has captured the imagination and the devotion of the masses of the Negroes here and has united them—no doubt about it," Virginia Durr wrote a friend.

King was masterful, too, in dealing with the national press, which focused on him as the key figure of the boycott. A *Time* cover story about the protest was written as a profile of King, and a major story in *The New York Times* on the boycott's history focused on him as well. As months, then years passed, King became firmly fixed in the minds of most Americans as the person chiefly responsible for the Montgomery boycott. But many of those who were with him then, as much as they revered him, would gently disagree. They would echo Claudette Colvin, who, when asked at the federal trial who the boycott's leader was, responded: "Our leaders is just we ourself."

As Martin Luther King was being catapulted into prominence by the Montgomery boycott, many of the women involved suffered retribution, and later were all but forgotten.

Shortly after the boycott's end, Juliette Morgan wrote a letter to the publisher of the Tuscaloosa *News*, praising a speech he had given criticizing the White Citizens Council. "You help redeem Alabama's very bad behavior in the eyes of the nation and the world," Morgan said. "I had begun to wonder if there were any men in the state—any white men— with any sane evaluation of our situation, with any good will, and most especially any moral courage to express it." The publisher asked if he could print her letter in his paper, and, disregarding the earlier warning of her employers to stay out of the public eye, Morgan agreed.

Violent as the reaction was to her letter in the *Advertiser* praising the boycott, it did not compare with the uproar over this one. In Virginia Durr's view, most of the rage stemmed from Morgan's depiction of Southern white men as "cowardly," which "really made them determined to get her at all costs, thereby proving her words." Morgan was harassed and hounded wherever she went. "The WCC has given her the full treatment, telephone calls, threats, letters, and the demand that she be fired . . . ," Durr wrote a friend. In July 1957, distraught by the harm she felt she was doing to the library, Morgan resigned from her job. A week later, she was found dead, an empty bottle of sleeping pills by her side, along with a note that said in part, "I can't go on."

An angry, bitter Virginia Durr laid the blame for Morgan's suicide squarely at the feet of white Southern men. "This," she declared, "is Southern chivalry in all its glory." Durr, who did not have Morgan's emotional fragility, reacted to her own continuing persecution by white supremacists with the same finely honed sense of outrage. Yet she was also deeply anguished over the fact that she, her husband, and their daughters had been so thoroughly repudiated by the world in which they lived. The price that the Durr girls paid for their parents' and uncle's beliefs was a source of special pain, with even the baby of the family, Lulah, suffering from the fallout. Once, after getting Lulah ready for a friend's sixth birthday party, Durr called the child's house to get the address. After she identified herself, there was a pause. "Mrs. Durr," said the child's father, "there will be no party this afternoon as far as your daughter is concerned because I wouldn't have a child of yours in the house." In the end, Virginia and Clifford Durr sent their two younger daughters to Northern boarding schools to remove them from the hate.

Clifford Durr's law practice, already shrunken after the Eastland committee hearing in 1954, diminished further, to the point where the family had to rely on loans and handouts from affluent Northern friends to keep going. Virginia repeatedly urged Clifford to leave Alabama but he refused: This was their home, and no matter what, this is where they would stay. Since Clifford Durr was not a particularly social man, the snubbing didn't bother him nearly as much as it did his outgoing wife, for whom talking and socializing were very nearly as important as life itself. "I am not a lonely martyr and want lots of other martyrs around," she once wrote, adding: "[I]t is the isolation that I mind, and I mean the lack of any group to belong to, the lack of any feeling of being a part of the community."

Virginia Durr remained close to Rosa Parks, whose own life had also become much more difficult. During the boycott, Parks had devoted herself to the cause, traveling, making speeches, raising money. She served on the MIA's executive board, worked as a car pool dispatcher, handed out clothes and food to people who had been fired because of their civil rights involvement. After the boycott was over, she tried to get another job in Montgomery, but no one would hire her. She had little income except the money she made from sewing at home and from funds that Virginia Durr had raised for her in appeals to the Highlander Folk School and to some of the Durrs' more affluent Northern friends. "To be a heroine is fine, but it does not pay off," Durr tartly observed.

Parks had much closer ties to E. D. Nixon than to Martin Luther King and his ministerial circle, and when disagreements among MIA leaders, particularly between Nixon and the ministers, boiled up after the boycott's end, Parks allied herself with Nixon. The NAACP leader, bitter about his own invisibility where the boycott was concerned, criticized King for turning the MIA into "a one-man show" and complained that ministers were siphoning off the organization's money for personal use. He also felt that King and his allies had used Parks for their own purposes and then turned their backs on her, refusing to hire her for one of the MIA's paid positions. In a letter to a friend, Virginia Durr described the "blazing row" going on within the MIA. Rosa Parks, she wrote, "has received money for the MIA and been a heroine everywhere else, [but] they have not given her a job here although she has needed one desperately.... She is very, very disgruntled with MLK and really quite bitter which is not like her at all."

Beset by money worries, Parks also had to cope with a mother who was often ill and a husband who had suffered a nervous breakdown as a result of the constant harassment of the Parkses during and after the boycott. An intensely private woman, she often found herself on emotional edge, trying to keep her personal life together while at the same time struggling to meet the heavy demands of being the boycott's most powerful symbol. Sometimes the pressure and strain proved too much, as when a reporter from a San Francisco newspaper announced to her during an interview that he was going "to take me apart and see what made me tick." She sat there, with an empty cup and saucer in her hand, pretending to sip tea for a newspaper photographer taking pictures. Suddenly, the strain of "being as polite and nice as I possibly could" became unbearable. "I just couldn't stand [the reporter] any longer. I went into hysterics. I started screaming. . . . The reporter just walked away and went on about his business. And nobody paid me any attention. I just stood there crying." Years afterward, she was still trying to figure out the reason for her loss of control. "I was not accustomed to so much attention," she said. "There was a time when it bothered me that I was always identified with [not standing up on the bus]. Then I realized that this incident was what brought the masses of people together to stay off the buses in Montgomery."

In August 1957, Parks and her family moved to Detroit, where her brother lived. She would not talk much about why she was leaving the area where she had lived all her life, but a columnist for the Pittsburgh *Courier*, one of the country's leading black newspapers, speculated about a possible reason—the fact that she'd gotten lost "in the shuffle of events" after December 1, 1955. "Mrs. Parks was seldom mentioned as the real and true leader of this struggle," Chester Higgins wrote. "Others more learned— not to take a thing from Dr. King—were ushered to the leadership and hogged the show. They basked in the glory of the battle and the eventual victory thereof. Perhaps as a proud and sensitive personality, she resented standing in the wings while others received the huzzahs." Higgins noted that Parks herself refused to comment.

However she may have felt about not being given credit, there is no question that Parks moved to Detroit primarily because she needed a job. Even there, she had difficulty finding work. She finally took a position as hostess at a guest house at Hampton Institute, a black college in Virginia, but when Hampton reneged on an implied promise to provide an apartment for her, her husband, and her mother, she returned to Detroit, where she first worked for a seamstress friend and then in a clothing factory. Not until 1965, when Representative John Conyers, Jr., hired her as a receptionist in his Detroit office, was she finally able to achieve more than a hand-to-mouth existence.

Her friends, meanwhile, were appalled that she had been allowed to slip into the shadows of civil rights history. Her image, as crafted by King and the other male boycott leaders, was that of a tired seamstress who had been "tracked down by the *Zeitgeist*—the spirit of the times." When Septima Clark saw a documentary about the boycott, she noted that Parks was hardly mentioned. "We talked about it, she and I," Clark said. "She gave Dr. King the right to practice his nonviolence. . . . [I]t was Rosa Parks who started the whole thing." E. D. Nixon made the same point to a woman sitting next to him on a plane one day. When the woman found out Nixon was from Montgomery, she said she did not know what would have happened to black people if King had not been there to lead the boycott. Nixon replied: "If Mrs. Parks had got up and given that white man her seat you'd never aheard of Reverend King."

*   *   *

For a while after the boycott, Jo Ann Robinson and Mary Fair Burks seemed to have escaped unscathed from its repercussions. But in the late 1950s, word spread on the Alabama State campus that a special state legislative committee was investigating professors thought to have been boycott leaders. Suddenly, state "evaluators" began appearing in the professors' classes, listening and taking notes, in a clear attempt at intimidation. Then, in February 1960, an investigation of a student sit-in at the state capitol—in which Robinson and Burks had *not* been involved—cost the two women their jobs. "Everybody who had been involved in either protest paid for it," Robinson later said.

Burks moved to Maryland's Eastern Shore, where she taught at a branch of the University of Maryland. Robinson went to Grambling College in Louisiana, but she never felt at home there. She keenly missed Montgomery and Alabama State, where she had spent the happiest, most exciting years of her life. After a year at Grambling, she moved to Los Angeles, where she taught English in public schools until her retirement in 1976.

In 1984, historian David Garrow, then researching his magisterial biography of Martin Luther King, was sifting through documents in Montgomery when he came across the May 1954 letter from Robinson to Mayor Tacky Gale threatening a boycott. Realizing that Robinson and the women of Montgomery were the true boycott organizers, he nonetheless found Robinson reluctant to claim credit for what she as an individual had done. "The black women did it," she told Garrow.

Looking back on the boycott, Mary Fair Burks compared the contribution made by Martin Luther King, Jr., with that of the women of Montgomery: "[A] trailblazer is a pioneer in a field of endeavor. [A] torchbearer . . . indicates one who follows the trailblazer. Rosa Parks, Jo Ann Robinson and members of the Women's Political Council were trailblazers. Martin Luther King, Junior, was a torchbearer."

7

"She Kept Daring Us to Go Further"

Ella Baker

F ROM HER APARTMENT IN N EW
York, Ella Baker had carried on her own campaign in support of the Montgomery bus boycott. She was fifty-three in 1956, a small, slender woman with a commanding voice and queenly manner, still fiercely devoted to the idea of inspiring other blacks to wage their own battle for equality. During her travels throughout the South in the 1940s, she had risked her life to urge blacks to join the NAACP and band together to fight injustice. But she received little backing from NAACP executives, who were far more interested in increasing the organization's membership and raising money

than in mass protest. Infuriated by what she considered their myopia, Baker resigned as the NAACP's director of local branches in 1946.

Ten years later, she viewed the unfolding events in Montgomery with exhilaration. The blacks of that city had taken the collective action that she had spent much of her life encouraging others to take, and now she put her formidable organizing skills to work on their behalf. Along with several other New York activists, including her friends Bayard Rustin and Stanley Levison, she set up In Friendship, a Northern group that provided publicity and financial assistance to boycotters and other Southern blacks who had suffered reprisals for their civil rights activities. But the urge to help was not Baker's sole motivation. For her, there was enormous significance in this boycott, extending far beyond the immediate goal of ending discrimination on the city's buses. Shuttling back and forth between Montgomery and New York, she saw the Confederacy's former capital as the launching pad for the Southern civil rights movement that she had so long envisioned, a "mass force" emerging as a counterbalance—and rival—to the NAACP.

Much to her frustration, her vision did not seem to be shared by the minister who had led the boycotters to glorious victory. After the Supreme Court ordered the desegregation of the city's buses, Martin Luther King remained head of the Montgomery Improvement Association, yet he and the ministers who were his chief allies showed little interest in seizing the moment and organizing other mass action. Baker was disturbed by what she viewed as almost "a complete letdown. Nothing was happening." Just as upsetting was the failure of the male leadership to encourage the continued activism of the thousands of women whose work and sacrifice had made the boycott a success. "These were women who had demonstrated a kind of dedication, and who had enough intelligence and had enough contacts with other people to have been useful, to have found a role to help move people along," Baker said. But "no role was provided for them . . ."

At a meeting after the boycott, Baker challenged King about the failure to continue the fight. King, who had been spending much of his time giving speeches around the country, was visibly nettled by her question. "[H]is rationale was . . . that after a big demonstrative type of action, there was a natural letdown and a need for people to sort of catch their breath," Baker said. "I don't think that the leadership in Montgomery was prepared to capitalize . . . on [what] had come out of the Montgomery situation."

The loss of momentum in Montgomery was particularly disquieting because blacks across the South had viewed the boycott with such great hope and optimism. Yet the boycott remained an isolated event, with black leaders in other Southern cities initiating no mass protests of their own against segregation on buses—or in the schools. More than two years before, the Supreme Court had struck down school segregation, but white supremacists were making clear to the world, through intimidation and violence, that they still were in firm control of the region, no matter what the Supreme Court said. In 1956, 101 Southern members of Congress signed what came to be known as the Southern Manifesto, defying the court's despised *Brown* decision. After that, school desegregation in the South came to a virtual standstill.

It might have stayed that way had it not been for Arkansas NAACP president Daisy Bates. Like Ella Baker, Bates was a firm believer in mass protest, and she also believed that the NAACP should be doing more to stimulate such activism. Even before the *Brown* decision, Bates had been agitating for desegregation of Little Rock schools. Shortly after *Brown*, the city's school board, under heavy pressure from Bates, announced limited plans to desegregate. In 1957, the school board reported that nine black students would be admitted to Central High. Segregationists, however, were determined to prevent this break in the wall of massive resistance. One of their major targets would be Daisy Bates.

She was no stranger to white terrorism and brutality. When she was eight, she discovered that the couple who had raised her were not her real parents, that her real mother had been raped and murdered by several white men when Daisy was a baby. Her grief-stricken father had handed her over to friends and then vanished. Distraught, Daisy asked her adoptive father who killed her mother. "There was some talk about who they were," he said, "but no one knew for sure, and the sheriff's office did little to find out." From that moment on, the little girl forgot about her dolls and other favorite pastimes and focused her energies on hating whites—and finding her mother's killers.

One day, as she was about to enter the town's general store, she noticed a white man, sitting on a bench on the porch, staring at her. Inside the store, she looked back. His eyes still fixed on her, the man jumped to his feet and walked quickly away. The next day, she returned to the store. The man was on the same porch bench. She advanced slowly toward him, then stopped, never taking her eyes from his. Leaping up, he shouted, "Stop staring at me, you bitch!" and started toward her, then abruptly turned away. Daisy was convinced he was one of her mother's murderers. Day after day, she returned to the store to haunt him, staring at him on his bench, while he, often drunk, would return the stare, or, sometimes, pretend not to see her. "I had come to enjoy tormenting [him]," she recalled. "I felt as if I were making him pay for his sin . . ." One cold, windy afternoon, he was asleep on the bench. She shook his arm lightly. He opened his eyes and looked at her in panic, then lurched to his feet. "In the name of God, leave me alone," he pleaded, then stumbled down the street. A few days later, she was told he had been found dead in a nearby alley.

Her hatred of whites continued. A few years later, as her adoptive father lay dying, he urged her to channel her anger toward more constructive ends. "Don't hate white people just because they're white," he told her. "If you hate, make it count for something. Hate the humiliations we are living under in the South . . . and then try to do something about it, or your hate won't spell a thing." She took his admonition to heart, "a priceless heritage," she declared later, "that was to sustain me throughout the years to come."

While still in her teens, she married L. C. Bates, a former journalist. In 1941, the couple moved to Little Rock and started a weekly black newspaper, the *State Press*, which they transformed into the city's most outspoken voice for racial justice. When a black soldier was shot and killed by Little Rock police in 1942, the *State Press* mounted a crusade against police brutality, one that continued despite cancellation of all advertising by white-owned stores. The paper took on other targets as well: slum housing, job discrimination, injustice in the legal system. In 1946, Daisy and L. C. Bates were jailed briefly after Daisy criticized a local judge in the paper. They were released on bond, and later the Arkansas Supreme Court ordered the judgment quashed.

But that earlier intimidation paled in comparison with the campaign leveled against Daisy Bates during the school desegregation fight. Less than two weeks before the first day of school, she received a hint of what was to come. A rock crashed through her living-room window as she sat reading the newspaper. Attached was a note, with the scrawled warning: STONE THIS TIME. DYNAMITE NEXT.

Under relentless pressure from white supremacists to prevent Central High's desegregation, Arkansas governor Orval Faubus announced on September 2, 1957, the night before school was to start, that he had called out the National Guard to bar black students from entering Central. It was, he insisted, for their own protection. The next day, a federal judge ordered the city to admit the six girls and three boys. Early the following morning, eight of the students, accompanied by Bates and a couple of local ministers, tried to enter Central but were turned away. The ninth student had not gotten the message that all the students were to go together, and as a result, fifteen-year-old Elizabeth Eckford, who was barely five feet tall, attempted on her own to push through the hundreds of screaming whites outside the school. Once the mob realized who she was, they surrounded the terrified teenager, their faces contorted with rage, shaking their fists, baseball bats, and other potential weapons. "Get her! Lynch her!" they shouted.

For the next three weeks, the crisis in Little Rock escalated as Faubus defied the federal court, which, in turn, cited the governor for contempt. On September 20, Faubus unexpectedly ordered the National Guard to withdraw, which left the black students in the middle of a war zone. In a frenzy of hatred, a mob of more than five hundred whites swarmed past police barricades and invaded the school, smashing windows, breaking down doors, beating any blacks in their path, and nearly capturing the nine students. The savage brutality of the mob, whose members, once they realized the students had escaped, took out their fury on any African-American they encountered, stunned and appalled the nation and the world. Realizing he could no longer equivocate, that the integrity of the Constitution was at stake, not to mention the integrity of his administration, President Eisenhower ordered paratroopers from the Army's elite 101st Airborne Division to take control of the high school.

Protected by the paratroopers, the nine black teenagers finally became students at Central, and the crisis seemed to be over. But it had not ended for the students, who were subjected to unrelenting intimidation and harassment by white students and their parents. Having helped get the children into Central, Daisy Bates now devoted her energies to nurturing them and helping them make it through the torments of that school year. Time after time, they were beaten, kicked, knocked to the floor. A stinging liquid was thrown in the eyes of one of the girls; another time, she was scalded in the shower after gym class.

Every morning, the nine students would gather at the spacious, elegantly furnished house that Bates and her husband had built just the year before, and go to school together. Every afternoon, they would meet in Bates's basement to talk to her and each other about the day's experiences. Several of the students later said that these sessions, which Bates compared with group therapy, were essential in giving them support and the will to go on. "There were times when the desegregation effort turned on [Bates's] raw courage," declared Harry Ashmore, the liberal white editor of the *Arkansas Gazette*, who would later win a Pulitzer prize for his editorials denouncing the violence. "I doubt that the black students could have withstood the pressures of that disoriented school year without her undaunted presence."

Ashmore was harassed and threatened by segregationists, but as he noted, it was Bates, with "no assurance of even routine police protection," who was the main target of their terrorism campaign. She was hanged in effigy. A six-foot gasoline-soaked cross was set afire on her lawn, a note at its base proclaiming: GO BACK TO AFRICA! KKK. Not long afterward, her house caught fire from another flaming cross, but the blaze was extinguished before serious damage was done. Night riders fired shots into the house, hurled sticks of dynamite onto the lawn. All the glass in the front of the house was blown out, and steel screens covered the windows. Bates's husband and some of their friends set up a twenty-four-hour guard, shotguns and revolvers at the ready.

One afternoon in the fall of 1957, a white woman came to Bates's house and said she represented a group of "Southern Christian women" who wanted Bates to withdraw her support from the students. If she didn't do so, the woman warned, "you'll be destroyed—you, your newspaper, your reputation, everything." She gave Bates until nine o'clock the next morning to come up with an answer. After a sleepless night, Bates called the woman, said she was "truly sorry for her and all of her ilk—bigots parading behind the standard of 'Christianity'"—and declared she would not back down.

Bates's enemies made good on their threat. Within days, the Bateses' newspaper lost almost all its most important advertisers. Small businessmen who advertised in the *State Press* were warned that if they didn't cancel their ads, they would be bombed or suffer other reprisals themselves. Some of the threats were delivered in person by local thugs. "In a matter of a few weeks, we watched sixteen years of our lives being quickly chopped away," Bates said. She and her husband fought back, just as they had in 1942. This time, they were not successful. The paper was forced to shut down in 1959.

Vital as her role had been in the integration of Central High, Bates herself soon disappeared from view. When the NAACP announced in 1958 that it was bestowing its most prestigious honor, the Spingarn Award, on the nine Little Rock students, there was no mention of Bates. A storm of protest arose, and the students petitioned the NAACP to award the Spingarn medal to their mentor and chief supporter as well. Many NAACP members, including Pauli Murray, were astounded by what they saw as a slight to Bates. Murray wrote to the selection committee: "[J]ust as a baseball fan cannot think of the Dodgers without thinking of Jackie Robinson, or the New York Yankees without thinking of their manager, Casey Stengel, it is impossible to think of the Little Rock Nine without thinking of their manager, Daisy Bates." The NAACP finally capitulated and issued a joint award to Bates and the students.

Bates never publicly sought recognition, but years later, during the height of the civil rights movement, she wrote to Murray: "During these hectic times while we are fighting for human dignity, and many times for survival, one forgets the contribution made by women."

The Little Rock crisis made clear what Ella Baker and other black leaders already knew: The federal government could not be counted on to take an active role in implementing the *Brown* decision or the 1957 Civil Rights Act just passed by Congress. If real progress was to be made in the struggle for freedom and equality, blacks were going to have to start making it themselves.

Even though Martin Luther King had initiated no new confrontation after the Montgomery boycott, he was considered by many to be the most important black leader in the South, and any new mass civil rights movement would have to take him into account. Since the Montgomery Improvement Association seemed unable to continue and expand the fight, a new organization would have to be created, with King at its center. Baker and her colleagues Bayard Rustin and Stanley Levison set out to do just that. In late 1956, the three met night after night to design the framework for a new Southern movement, with black ministers as its leaders and Martin Luther King at its head. Less than two months after the end of the Montgomery boycott, some one hundred of the best-known black ministers in the South—"superstars of the black pulpit," one historian later called them—gathered at Atlanta's Ebenezer Baptist Church to form the Southern Christian Leadership Conference.

That August, with great fanfare, SCLC announced its wildly ambitious first program—a voter registration drive, called Crusade for Citizenship, which hoped to register more than one million new black voters before the 1960 presidential election. The Crusade would be launched with rallies in twenty-two Southern cities on February 12, 1958. A little more than a month before the Crusade's kickoff date, however, it appeared that SCLC was heading for disaster. Nothing at all had been done to prepare for the rallies, let alone the voter registration work that supposedly was to follow. SCLC was an organization in name only.

Greatly disturbed, Rustin and Levison met with King and suggested that Ella Baker become SCLC's executive director and pull together the

Crusade. King, who had little use for professional women, did not like the idea, even though Baker had been one of SCLC's creators, had helped devise its structure and formulate its strategy. He preferred Rustin for the job, but he also knew there was no way he could name this homosexual, pacifist ex-Communist to such a position. When Rustin and Levison argued that Baker had more organizing experience than anyone in SCLC, King grudgingly agreed, but only on the condition that Baker be considered "acting" director. He would use her for the Crusade, but had no intention of keeping her around for long.

Rustin and Levison had not consulted Baker before offering her services to King, and she was furious at them for their effrontery. At the same time, she realized that if she didn't get involved, her dream of a mass civil rights movement might never be realized. On January 9, 1958, she left New York for Atlanta. This strong-willed, independent woman, who often referred to ministers as "glory seekers," was about to join forces with the most famous black minister in America, who believed that a woman's place was in the home. The consequences of that tumultuous pairing would have a profound effect on the civil rights movement for years to come.

When Ella Baker was a little girl in North Carolina, her grandmother would tell her stories about growing up in slavery as the daughter of her master. The tale Ella loved most was the one about her grandmother refusing to marry the light-skinned slave picked out for her by her mistress. When the pretty young house slave held out for the dark-skinned man who became Baker's grandfather, she was banished to the life of a field hand. The banishment did not faze her. She simply plowed all day and danced all night, she told her granddaughter. "Grandma had a fighting spirit," Baker said. "She would not be broken."

While her grandmother passed down a legacy of rebellion, Baker's grandfather, a minister and farmer, instilled in her a deep sense of social responsibility and involvement in the community. After the Civil War, he bought the house and land on which he once had worked as a slave, and parceled out plots to relatives. His household was constantly providing food, shelter, and medical care to those who needed them. "Where we lived," Baker later said, "there was no sense of hierarchy, in terms of those who have, having a right to look down upon, or to evaluate as a lesser breed, those who didn't have. . . . There was a deep sense of community that prevailed in this little neck of the woods."

Baker's grandfather, whom she adored, called her Grand Lady. She often accompanied him on long buggy rides, when they would discuss the state of the world. When he preached, he seated her in the visiting minister's chair near his pulpit, where she could gaze down at the congregation, her little legs not yet touching the floor. Her mother was horrified: In church, whether the congregation was black or white, females belonged in the pews, not on the altar. Although barred from the pulpit because of her sex, Baker still was able to hone her formidable speaking skills through the church; she practiced her oratory at the meetings of the women's missionary societies to which her mother belonged. As an adult, she was known for her deep and resonant voice, her clear, crisp diction, her theatrical flair, her astonishing gift for mimicry.

From her earliest days, she kowtowed to no one. Once, she hit a white boy who called her a nigger. Another time, she threw rocks at a boy for the same offense. A baseball-playing tomboy and a champion debater in high school, Baker was later known as a troublemaker at Shaw University, a black school in Raleigh. She was always protesting something, whether it was the school's strict student dress code, its tradition of students singing black spirituals for white visitors, or its refusal to allow men and women students to walk across campus together. The white president of Shaw grew so tired of Baker's protests that he tried to have her expelled during her senior year. The effort failed when the faculty intervened. For all Baker's agitating, she still managed to graduate first in her class in 1927. That summer, she moved to New York, where the Harlem Renaissance was in full swing; young black writers and activists were focusing on racial identity, injustice, and oppression—and stirring up trouble was the thing to do.

Baker wrote for several black newspapers, helped form black consumer cooperatives, and later got a job with the Roosevelt administration's Works Progress Administration. As the Depression deepened, she was swept up in Harlem's social ferment. "[W]herever there was a discussion, I'd go," she said years later. "It didn't matter if it was all men. I've been in many groups where there were men, and maybe I was the only woman, or the only black. . . . I was open to all kinds of discussions. I'd never heard any discussions about the social revolution . . . New York was the hotbed of radical thinking. You had every spectrum of radical thinking on WPA. We had a lovely time!"

Hired by the NAACP in 1941, Baker began what would become a lifelong dedication to grassroots civil rights organizing. Faultlessly dressed in a suit, gloves, and a hat, a purse stuck firmly under her arm, Baker roamed the South, setting up NAACP adult and youth chapters, meeting and befriending thousands of people, and creating a network of current and future activists. True to form, she rebelled when personally confronted with the South's Jim Crow practices. Once, when ordered out of the dining car of a train, she refused to budge. A military policeman, asked by the steward to eject her, yanked her up from her seat, bruising her leg. "You are overstepping your bounds!" Baker thundered in a voice that traveled throughout the car. When she got back to New York, she wanted to sue, but the NAACP decided against it.

Adamant about standing up for herself, she also ferociously guarded her independence. In 1940, she married T. J. Robinson, a former college classmate. The marriage lasted until 1959. During that time, many of Baker's friends and acquaintances did not even know she had a husband. She retained her maiden name, a highly unusual step in the 1940s. As she later explained: "I never considered myself a feminist in the sense of championing the rights of women, but I may have felt the need to exercise this right by retaining my name . . . the right of the individual to be an individual." During the early 1960s, she told Mary King, a young civil rights activist: "I have always been very happy that I didn't change my name. I didn't think that I belonged to any man."

No man could dominate her. Not her husband. And certainly not Martin Luther King, Jr.

The world that Baker was about to enter, however, was controlled entirely by men. The Southern Christian Leadership Conference was an organization of black ministers, most of whom shared the predominant view of virtually all American churches, black and white, that God meant women to be subordinate. Black clergymen might be coming to the forefront of the fight against the racism of white society, but, as theologian James Cone pointed out, they "shared much of the typical American male's view of women . . ." Lawrence Guyot, a young civil rights activist in the early 1960s, put it more bluntly. "Equality of women in the Baptist Church was like having a rabbi conduct the Baptist service," he said. "It was openly antithetical." Guyot's observation applied to most other black denominations as well.

Yet women had been the heart of American black churches since their founding in the days of slavery. As historians Darlene Clark Hine and Kathleen Thompson have noted: "Men stood in the pulpit and sat on the church board; women did everything else." Women raised the money. They taught Sunday school. They sang in the choir. They operated the women's missionary societies, youth groups, and other church activities. They cleaned, decorated, and maintained the churches. They also made up most of the congregation at midweek and Sunday services. "If Baptist women decided to stay away from the church for one month," Guyot declared, "there would be no church." Ministers often referred to women as the backbone of the church, a term meant as a compliment, emphasizing their vital role. But as theologian Jacquelyn Grant wryly observed: "[T]he telling portion of the word 'backbone' is 'back.' It has become apparent to me that most of the ministers who use this term are referring to location rather than function. What they really mean is that women are in the 'background' and they should be kept there: they are merely support workers."

Although black clergymen mirrored American society's attitude toward women at that time, there was another explanation for their insistence on being treated as dominant authority figures by their congregations and others around them. The ministry was one calling in which black men could demonstrate their manhood, could throw off the submissiveness they had been forced to adopt as the result of slavery and post–Civil War terrorism and intimidation. They had been denied dignity and self-respect, had been required to behave like boys, not men. "The dominant mood in the black community emphasized the need for black male assertiveness," James Cone observed. "Black men, most agreed, needed to assert their masculinity . . ."

And many black men viewed the traditional strength and independence of black women as a threat to that masculinity. Martin Luther King expressed a widely held opinion when he said on the CBS program *Face the Nation*: "The Negro man in this country . . . has never been able to be a man. He has been robbed of his manhood because of the legacy of slavery and segregation and discrimination, and we have had in the Negro community a matriarchal family . . . in the midst of a patriarchal society . . ."

King seemed to feel particularly stifled by the strength and assertiveness of his own mother, whose husband, Martin Luther King, Sr., was the pastor of the Ebenezer Baptist Church before their son came to join him in 1960. Andrew Young, who became one of the younger King's key SCLC lieutenants, said that King, among others, "had a hard time with domineering women in SCLC because Martin's mother, quiet as she was, was really a strong, domineering force in that family. She was never publicly saying anything, but she ran Daddy King, and she ran the church and she ran Martin . . ." King certainly was not alone in his feelings about mothers. Other black men, including Andy Young, complained that their mothers dominated not only them but their fathers, too. "My father was the head of our household and my mother ran his life," Young declared. He acknowledged that his attitude toward his mother influenced his later perceptions of Ella Baker and the younger women, both black and white, who would soon flood the movement. "[T]hey all set off one defense reaction: They were too much like my mother. Strong women were the backbone of the movement, but to young black men seeking their own freedom, dignity and leadership perspective, they were quite a challenge."

When Martin Luther King married Coretta Scott, he made clear to her that her role was to stay in the background, caring for him and their future children. "I want my wife to respect me as the head of the family," he told her. "I *am* the head of the family." She and he both laughed at "that slightly pompous speech," and he retreated, saying, "Of course, I don't really mean that. I think marriage should be a shared relationship." But, in fact, Coretta King wrote later, "he really did mean it." Bernard Lee, another close SCLC associate of King's, declared: "Martin . . . was absolutely a male chauvinist. He believed that the wife should stay home and take care of the babies while he'd be out there in the streets."

When Ella Baker arrived in Atlanta to take over running SCLC, she had to start from scratch. Her "office," she quipped, was her purse and the nearest phone booth. She was allowed to use the mimeograph machine at Ebenezer, but only after 5 P.M., when the church office officially closed. Baker was SCLC's sole staff member, and she had almost no contact with King or the organization's other leaders as she worked virtually around the clock, racing to get ready for the kickoff of the Crusade. When February 12 arrived, she had managed to organize church rallies in twenty-two Southern cities, collect and distribute information about state voter registration laws and the ways blacks could overcome the barriers to registration, and recruit local workers. She looked mainly to women for help: "All of the churches depended, in terms of things taking place, on women, not men. Men didn't do the things that had to be done."

Considering that Baker had few resources and little support from her new ministerial associates, the fact that thirteen thousand people turned out for the rallies was remarkable. But all the enthusiasm and oratory of that day produced few tangible results. After their rousing speeches at the rallies, SCLC's ministers did almost nothing to follow up with the organizational work that was needed. Most of them made no attempt to recruit potential voters, teach them what they needed to know to register, and take them down to the courthouse. The plan for local registration committees never got off the ground.

Baker had planned to stay in Atlanta only six weeks. But she agreed to extend her stay when SCLC's selection committee still had not come up with a nominee for permanent executive director. Despite Baker's impressive work on the Crusade's kickoff rallies, there was never any thought about giving her the job. On April 30, 1958, the SCLC board named John Tilley, a Baltimore minister, as executive director and Baker as his associate director.

But Tilley, like the other ministers in the organization, had no intention of giving up the pastorship of his church to devote all his time to SCLC. So, once again, Baker was virtually on her own. She traveled widely throughout the South, drawing on her network of personal contacts from her NAACP days to put together voter registration and citizenship training drives, trying desperately to keep the flame of Montgomery burning. As hard as she worked, however, she knew she could not organize or inspire a mass civil rights movement by herself. In the summer of 1958, she warned King that "we are losing the initiative in the Civil Rights struggle in the South mainly because of the absence of a dynamic philosophy or spiritual force." King agreed. Then he took Coretta to Mexico for a two-week vacation.

As the months passed, Baker grew increasingly frustrated, angry, and annoyed. Frustrated that SCLC's ministers refused to get involved in registering voters in their own hometowns. Angry that King spent more time and energy giving speeches and pastoring Ebenezer Baptist and writing his memoirs on the Montgomery bus boycott than he devoted to SCLC. Annoyed that the organization seemed more interested in establishing King as a national icon, a Moses-like savior who would free his people from modern-day slavery, than in working on grassroots organizing.

King ran SCLC in the same authoritarian manner that he and most of the other ministers ran their churches. To them, power meant control over others. Baker had a completely different view of power. She believed that King's job, and SCLC's, should be to nurture people, to help them find the power within themselves to change their own lives and the society in which they lived. No one person could do that for others, no matter how eloquent he was, she was convinced. She was certainly talking about King when she said years later that "because a person is called upon to give public statements and is acclaimed by the establishment, such a person gets to the point of believing that he *is* the movement. Such people get so involved with playing the game of being important that they exhaust themselves and their time and they don't do the work of actually organizing people."

Baker was not the only associate of King's who was critical of him.

After reading the manuscript of *Stride for Freedom*, King's Montgomery memoir, Stanley Levison warned King not to imply that "everything depended on you." Fred Shuttlesworth, a firebrand Birmingham minister, reminded King in a letter that "when the flowery speeches have been made, we still have the hard job of getting down and helping people." SCLC, Shuttlesworth wrote, "must move now, or else [be] hard put in the not too distant future to justify our existence."

King was not fond of any criticism—he "loved to be surrounded by people who said 'yes,'" Bayard Rustin remembered—but Baker's complaints were particularly galling. Old enough to be King's mother, Baker felt no awe for the twenty-nine-year-old SCLC leader and was never as deferential to him as those in his inner circle were. "I was not a person to be enamored of anyone," she later remarked. The two clashed repeatedly, and Baker got a reputation within the organization as "difficult." "I wasn't an easy pushover because I could talk back a lot. Not only could, but did," she said. On at least one occasion, according to Rustin, Baker managed to reduce King to tears. "Ella Baker was very tough on Martin," Rustin said.

For his part, King treated Baker more as a secretary than as SCLC's top organizer. He was often unavailable to take her calls. He would wave aside her advice, ideas, and suggestions. "She always felt persecuted as a woman and I cannot say that she was not justified," recalled Coretta Scott King, who harbored her own share of grievances about being kept in the background. Baker encouraged King's wife to step out of her husband's shadow. "Coretta, you need to be among the councils of the men," Baker declared. "You have a lot to say."

In the spring of 1959, King fired the ineffectual John Tilley as SCLC's executive director and, despite his difficulties with Baker, asked her to become "acting director" again while the SCLC board searched for a permanent replacement. For all their discord, Baker and King remained dependent on each other, at least for the moment. King had no one else on whom to call, and although Baker intensely resented King's treatment of her as well as his autocratic leadership style, his organization was the only one that was working, however falteringly, on voter registration. She agreed, and once again threw herself into work to which only she, among the SCLC hierarchy in Atlanta, seemed truly devoted.

She came up with an idea for a new SCLC campaign that included recruiting black women from across the South to teach basic reading, writing, and political skills to illiterate blacks so they could register to vote. Getting blacks past the fear of reprisals if they tried to register was only the first hurdle in putting them on the voting rolls: They still had to pass arcane literacy tests in several Southern states. And nobody had bothered to explain to unschooled blacks why they *should* vote or how getting involved in political action could change their lives. Baker had long been intrigued by the work of Septima Clark at Highlander, whose citizenship school program had made impressive strides in giving a basic education to blacks who needed it.

But there was little interest, at least at that point, in Baker's plan. The ministers did not share her enthusiasm for the enlistment of women, nor were these products of the black middle class, who promoted the idea of a well-mannered, cultured "new Negro," all that eager to focus attention on lower-class, unlettered blacks. Baker, Clark, and other women were dealing with reality; many of the men, as Baker perceived, were dealing with image.

Having vetoed Baker's plan, however, the ministers had nothing to put in its place. King acknowledged that the Crusade for Citizenship had been a disappointment. When SCLC leaders gathered in Birmingham in December 1959 to discuss plans for 1960, he put forth a sweeping if unfocused alternative to voter registration. "This is the creative moment for a full-scale assault on the system of segregation," he said. "We must practice open civil disobedience. We must be willing to go to jail en masse . . ."

Less than two months later, the assault that King had envisioned was indeed launched—but not by him or SCLC. Four North Carolina college students were its shock troops, followed by hundreds, then thousands of young people. As spellbinding as King was in his speeches and sermons, neither he nor his organization had managed to rekindle the spirit of the Montgomery boycott. It was college students who had relit the torch, with a seemingly new form of nonviolent confrontation—the sit-in. This was what Ella Baker had been waiting for, what she had worked for, for so many years. And now she would work to make it succeed.

On February 1, 1960, four male freshmen from the North Carolina Agricultural and Technical College walked into the downtown Woolworth's in Greensboro and sat down on stools at the dime store's lunch counter. When the waitresses wouldn't serve them, the students refused to move. Two of them were members of the Greensboro NAACP youth group, which, impatient with the glacial pace of school desegregation and the lack of momentum after the Montgomery boycott, had been agitating to get things moving again. The Youth Council had been founded seventeen years before, after a visit to Greensboro by NAACP official Ella Baker.

After being refused service at Woolworth's, the four returned the next day, and this time they brought with them more than twenty fellow students. The day after that, sixty-six students from A&T and other colleges and universities throughout the area showed up. By the end of the week, more than a thousand young people were involved in the sit-in, shocking not only the residents of Greensboro but the rest of the South and the nation.

Few realized that this dramatic technique of protesting discrimination, far from being new, had been used by Pauli Murray and her fellow Howard University students, among others, as far back as the early 1940s. None of the early sit-ins, however, had triggered the kind of national press coverage and student interest drawn by the Greensboro sit-ins and those that followed. Soon, students in nearby Winston-Salem and Durham launched their own demonstrations. Hundreds of students staged sit-ins in downtown Nashville. Protests erupted in South Carolina, Florida, and Virginia, igniting each other like a string of firecrackers. By April, more than fifty thousand people throughout the South had taken part in sit-ins in seventy-eight cities and towns, and more than two thousand demonstrators had been arrested.

Although the four students in the first Greensboro sit-in were men, young women joined the ranks of the demonstrators after the first day. Among them were whites—three students from the University of North Carolina Women's College campus in Greensboro, one of the elite schools for white women in the South. North Carolina papers had a field day with this news, and the college's chancellor put pressure on the three not to participate again. By contrast, dozens of female students from Greensboro's all-black Bennett College joined the sit-in movement with the enthusiastic support of Willa Player, their school's president. No stranger to fearlessness when it came to civil rights, Player had offered the use of her school's chapel in 1958 to Martin Luther King when no other black school or church in Greensboro would allow him to speak.

The sit-in movement, in both the North and the South, caught the country completely by surprise. American college students, for the most part, were seen as politically apathetic, interested more in the material trappings of success than in changing the world. That was as true for black students as for white, with most black schools encouraging their students to conform to the values of white society, to aspire to middle-class respectability. Many African-American students in the late 1950s and early 1960s represented the first generation of their families to go to college, and their attendance often came as a result of great sacrifice by their parents. Theirs was a generation with the potential to become doctors and lawyers and professors, so when they sat in at local lunch counters, when they risked arrest and expulsion from school, they were also putting their futures at risk—the futures in which their parents had invested so much.

By their willingness to take such a gamble, by seizing the initiative and finally igniting a mass civil rights movement, they also had wrested the spotlight away from the older black leadership, who, in their view, had delivered too little, too late. The stage was being set for a power struggle between the old and the new, a struggle in which Ella Baker would prominently figure.

In Atlanta, Baker watched the unfolding of the sit-ins with worry as well as excitement. She had seen the momentum of the Montgomery bus boycott fade away, and despite her best efforts, the promise of SCLC's voter registration campaign had been squandered. Now, she feared, the same thing might happen again with this new student movement. One month after the sit-ins began, there seemed to be no communication among the scattered groups of demonstrators, no idea of joining together and forming one potent source of mass protest. If the potential of this infant movement was to be realized, she felt, it was up to her to provide the stimulus. Baker persuaded Martin Luther King to bring student sit-in leaders together for a conference at Shaw University, her alma mater, and cadged eight hundred dollars from SCLC funds to pay for it.

On a bright, warm weekend in early April, more than three hundred students from all over the South—two hundred more than had been expected—flooded Shaw's small campus, arriving by train and bus, in Volkswagen Beetles and on motorcycles. Some still wore bandages as evidence of their encounters with local police. They had read about each other's exploits, but this was the first time they had had a chance to exchange war stories, to take each other's measure. The Greensboro contingent was given its due for being first in the fray, but the group inspiring the most awe was from Nashville. They were the real battle-scarred veterans—the best trained, the best led, the best known. Their exploits had made front-page headlines around the country, and they would soon become the subject of an NBC television documentary. Receiving much of the attention was the young woman acknowledged as their main leader, a twenty-two-year-old Fisk University student named Diane Nash. Her courage and cool daring were legendary, but it was her delicate beauty that bedazzled many of the male participants at the conference.

As the students got to know one another, they also began realizing the value of what Baker was trying to do. Julian Bond, a handsome, elegant

Morehouse College student and one of the leaders of the Atlanta movement, recalled how the light dawned for him: "As you began to meet these
people from all these various different sit-in places and you said, 'Oh yeah,
I remember reading about what you all did there,' the idea began to seep in
that we might be real hell on wheels in Atlanta, but if we can coordinate
what we're doing in Atlanta with what they're doing here, we would really
be tough stuff."

As the students worked out plans for an organization to coordinate
their activities, Ella Baker worked equally hard to ensure their independence. SCLC, in particular, was casting longing eyes at their youthful daring and vision, with Martin Luther King generously applauding them for
doing what he and his organization had only thought about. It was clear to
Baker that King and his key lieutenants wanted the students' new group
to become SCLC's youth arm. At a meeting of SCLC leaders at the Shaw
conference, King and the other ministers discussed how they would influence the students to go along with their plan. "They were most confident
that this would be their baby, because I was their functionary and I had
called the [student] meeting," Baker said. "Well, I disagreed . . . I was outraged. I walked out." For the rest of the conference, Baker lobbied the students individually and collectively, urging them to decide their own future,
independent of already established civil rights organizations. "She didn't
say, 'Don't let Martin Luther King tell you what to do,' but you got the real
feeling that that's what she meant," Julian Bond said. "You know, 'He's a
good man and so on, but don't let him tell you what to do.'"

By the time of the student conference, Ella Baker had begun to sever
herself from King and SCLC. The month before, King had offered the job
of permanent SCLC executive director to Wyatt Tee Walker, an aggressive, arrogant young pastor from Petersburg, Virginia, who later said,
"One big piece of evidence about the greatness of Martin Luther King is
that a man as vain as I am is willing to play second fiddle to him." Walker
told Baker she could stay on in Atlanta if she wished, so long as she understood she would be working for him. Baker was having none of that. She
was tired of all the macho posturing, tired of not having a voice. In years
to come, she would tell interviewers that the way she was treated by King
and the other SCLC ministers never really bothered her, but in private, she
complained angrily to friends about such treatment. "[S]he was concerned about not being recognized in a man-made world," recalled Septima Clark. "She felt that the men wanted all the glory . . . [S]he wanted
her just deserts, which would have been right, you know. But they weren't
about to give [them] to her, and so she decided that she couldn't take it."

With the students, Baker had finally found a group that valued her wisdom and experience. As the young people agreed to band together in what would become the Student Nonviolent Coordinating Committee, Baker urged them not to limit their sights. She told them they must look beyond lunch counter sit-ins, focus on "more than a Coke and a hamburger," and work to change the entire social structure of the country. At the Raleigh conference and in coming years, "she kept daring us to go further," said John Lewis, who would later become SNCC chairman. Lewis said he considered Baker "our personal Gandhi. The spiritual mother, I guess I would call her, of SNCC."

Baker's ideas on participatory democracy, her unshakable belief that people must fight for their own freedom and not rely on leaders to do it for them, were adopted by SNCC as its own. As the idealistic and inventive organization, which welcomed women, both black and white, to its ranks, began to develop an office, staff, and program, Baker served as its guiding force. Without Ella Baker, said James Forman, who became executive secretary of SNCC, "there would be no story of the Student Nonviolent Coordinating Committee."

Antagonists during most of their relationship, Baker and Martin Luther King never appreciated each other's strengths. Baker discounted King's generosity, his eloquence, his astonishing ability to inspire Mississippi sharecroppers and Manhattan business leaders alike. Blinded by sexism and holding a different view of leadership, King rejected Baker's bold vision, her experience, and her skills at forming a mass movement. When Baker left SCLC, she became one of the most important figures in the civil rights movement, emerging, in a very real way, as the movement's chief rival to King. Indeed, in the eyes of some youthful civil rights leaders like Stokely Carmichael, her influence overshadowed King's. "The most powerful person in the struggle of the sixties," Carmichael said firmly, "was Miss Ella Baker, not Martin Luther King."

Although Baker was never a formal leader of SNCC, her enormous influence on the students would have profound repercussions for the United States—and cause major headaches in the years to come for the young minister from Atlanta, whom most Americans thought of as the man in charge of the movement.

8

"The Most Daring of [Our] Leaders"

Nashville students sitting in at lunch counter

WHEN DIANE NASH ARRIVED AT

Fisk University in the fall of 1959, it seemed a perfect match: a lovely, intelligent, cultured young woman and a prestigious black school that would give her not only an excellent education but an introduction to some of the most eligible young African-American men in the South. A college degree was desirable, of course, but for middle-class young women who came of age in the 1950s, black or white, real fulfillment lay in finding the right man to marry and having children. Or so almost everyone said.

Adlai Stevenson, for example, informed members of Smith College's graduating class of 1955 that they should focus their energy on "the humble role of housewife," regardless of any other ambitions or talents they might have. "The assignment to you, as wives and mothers, you can do in the living room with a baby in your lap or in the kitchen with a can opener in your hand," lectured the paragon of modern American liberalism. "If you are clever, maybe you can even practice your saving arts on that unsuspecting man while he's watching television." A few years later, Dr. Benjamin Mays, president of Morehouse College, delivered the same message, somewhat less patronizingly, to new Spelman College graduates: "[O]ver and above business, politics and the professions, you Spelman women will be called upon to be wives, mothers and homemakers. . . . The husband and father will make exacting demands of you, and he will expect certain things of you in spite of your education and degrees."

If all that were true, what better place for a young black woman to look for the right man than Fisk, Nashville's academic citadel of black privilege? Renowned as one of the best black universities in the South, Fisk was founded in 1866 by Northern Congregationalist missionaries to educate newly freed slaves. The famed Jubilee Singers, who popularized black spirituals in the late nineteenth century, had been Fisk students. So was W. E. B. Du Bois. James Weldon Johnson had capped his brilliant, amazingly varied career as civil rights activist, poet, novelist, and diplomat by teaching at Fisk.

With its sterling pedigree, Fisk, along with Morehouse, Spelman, Howard, and a few others, attracted the cream of the South's black middle and upper class. But the schools' lineage was white as well as black—white missionaries had founded them, white philanthropists helped fund many of them—and they had taken on much of the coloration of white society, including white standards of proper behavior and white ideals of beauty and femininity. On such campuses, light skin, Caucasian features, and straight hair were the sine qua non of attractiveness, and students of both sexes who did not meet those criteria often suffered the pain of rejection. For young college women, who were expected to get a husband as well as an education in college, such rejection was particularly hurtful.

Diane Nash had no such problem. Light enough to pass for white, she also was astonishingly pretty. When asked about Nash, men who knew her in the late 1950s and early 1960s invariably praised her beauty. "The first thing you have to say about Diane—the first thing anyone who encountered her noticed, and there was no way *not* to notice—is that she was one of God's beautiful creatures, just about the most gorgeous woman any of us had ever seen," raved John Lewis, one of her Nashville civil rights comrades. Lewis went on to describe Nash as "[s]mall and shapely, with honey brown skin and bright green eyes." In the late 1990s, Kwame Ture, formerly known as Stokely Carmichael, who worked with Nash in SNCC, dropped his customary revolutionary fervor when reminiscing about her. "Ah, Diane, Diane," he said with a fond laugh. "Everybody wanted to marry Diane. She was warm, she was gentle, she was so brave, she was so intelligent, she was so pretty. . . . Everybody wanted Diane Nash. Everybody."

For the first twenty-one years of her life, Nash, the product of a middle-class Catholic upbringing in Chicago, had not done much to challenge the white society whose values her family had largely adopted. In high school, she had even dreamed of becoming Miss America and in 1956 was a runner-up in a local pageant leading to the Miss Illinois contest. (In the pageant's talent competition, she sang "Take Back Your Mink" from *Guys and Dolls*, wowing the judges when she unfastened her evening gown to reveal a leotard underneath.) She had been raised in a home that tried to overlook race, influenced greatly by a grandmother who believed that emulating whites was the best way for blacks to get ahead. Educated by nuns, at one time thinking about becoming a nun herself, Nash had an intellectual understanding of racial discrimination, from whose harshest effects she had been sheltered. Even when she first went away to college, attending Howard University in Washington, she experienced little overt prejudice. After a couple of years at Howard, she decided to transfer to Fisk.

Like many other young women, regardless of race, Nash wanted more than she was getting out of life. As products of the postwar teenage culture, women of her generation had been encouraged to believe they were special, to do well in school, to develop their talents and abilities. Then they were expected to exchange that early independence and assertiveness for a lifetime of self-denial and dependence on men. Young women of the 1950s faced a classic double bind—the bind that Margaret Mead described when she said a woman could define herself as "a woman, and therefore less an achieving individual, or an achieving individual and therefore less a woman." If she chose the former, she was on her way to becoming "a loved object, the kind of girl whom men will woo and boast of, toast and marry." But if she followed her own interests, she risked forfeiting "as a woman her chance for the kind of love she wants." While women had faced this dilemma for many years, young women growing up after World War II were questioning its validity even as they outwardly conformed to the era's political and social conservatism.

African-American women, especially, were enmeshed in contradictions. Forced since slavery to be more self-sufficient and assertive than white women, many were nonetheless faced with the same middle-class expectations, subjected to the same pressure to get married, to subordinate their own interests and desires to those of others, particularly their husbands and families. In a 1960 article entitled "The Negro Woman," *Ebony* editor Lerone Bennett declared, "One result of the traditional independence of the Negro woman is that she is more in conflict with her innate biological role than the white woman." Young black women might have been influenced by that point of view, but they were not necessarily buying it. Like white women, many were seething with questions and doubts about the future. Their questioning, however, extended beyond their role as women to the abuse and discrimination to which they and other blacks were subjected because of their skin color. They were about to join black men of their generation in challenging the very underpinnings of white Southern society: racial segregation. And in the vanguard would be the soft-voiced, seemingly demure Diane Nash.

Nash's moment of epiphany came at the Tennessee State Fair in 1959. She had gone to the fair on a date, and wanted to use the ladies' room. She found two—one marked WHITE WOMEN, the other COLORED WOMEN—and for the first time in her life suffered the degradation of Jim Crow. This was no longer an intellectual exercise: She was being told in the most searing way imaginable that *she* was beyond the pale, unfit to use the same facilities as white women. Outraged by the experience, she was even more upset that her date, a Southerner, did not share her fury. Neither did most of her fellow Fisk students. They did not seem to care that they could shop at downtown stores but not eat at the stores' lunch counters, or that they had to sit in the balcony to see a movie. The more Nash found out about segregation in Nashville, the more she felt "stifled and boxed in." In the rest of the country, Nashville had the reputation of being more racially progressive than most Southern cities. Blacks could vote in Nashville. The city's schools and buses were integrated. Blacks served on the police force, fire department, City Council, and Board of Education. But segregation still firmly ruled in theaters, restaurants, hotels, and libraries, and Diane Nash, a deep-dyed moralist, decided then and there that Nashville was in a "stage of sin." She couldn't believe that "the children of my classmates would have to be born into a society where they had to believe that they were inferior." Above all, she could not believe that her classmates were willing to let that happen.

Since they did not seem to share her anger, she looked elsewhere for support. Paul LaPrad, a white exchange student at Fisk, told her about a black minister named James Lawson, who was training college students in

the use of nonviolence as the framework for an all-out attack on segregation. For Lawson, who had spent three years in India studying the principles of Gandhi, nonviolence was more than just a protest technique: It was
the means by which he ordered his life. The young minister talked about
the power of nonviolent confrontation with evil, about overcoming the
forces of hate and transforming society through love and forgiveness. At
first, Nash was skeptical. How could such high-flown idealism be har-
nessed as a weapon against gun-toting sheriffs and club-swinging racists?
Even after attending several of Lawson's workshops, she still was sure
"this stuff is never going to work." But since, as she said, it was "the only
game in town," she kept going back, and after weeks of studying theology
and philosophy, of reading Thoreau and other advocates of passive resistance, of discussion and arguments with the workshop's other participants, the intense young woman from Chicago was finally captured by
Lawson's vision. She was particularly drawn to his belief that to be effective, these young would-be activists would have to transcend self-hatred
and a sense of inferiority, that they would have to learn to love themselves.
Having been raised in a milieu that downplayed her blackness, she now
found herself part of a group "suddenly proud to be called 'black.' Within
the movement . . . we came to a realization of our own worth . . ."

Many students at the workshops did not know what to make of Nash.
She was one of only a handful who attended from Fisk, where the notion
of protest was antithetical. So what was this beautiful, light-skinned, quintessential Fisk type doing at the workshops? Whatever the reason for her
being there, her presence entranced virtually every man in the group.
"Plenty of fellows attending those sessions gave a go at hitting on Diane,"
said John Lewis, an American Baptist College student who was one of the
participants. "You saw resentment among some guys because they
thought another guy was making an inroad with her." Several women in
the group were jealous of the attention she was getting. Even so, sexual
and romantic undercurrents remained generally in the background of the
Nashville movement. In time, Lewis said, Nash "came to be seen more as
our sister than as an object of lust. . . . We all became brothers and sisters,
a family."

In the late fall of 1959, the students at Lawson's workshops formed a
central committee to act as the decision-making body for the group. Nash,
who had impressed everyone with her clear-eyed thinking and the intensity of her developing commitment to nonviolence, was named to the committee. More and more, the students were turning to her as one of their
main leaders.

The committee had chosen the lunch counters and restaurants of Nashville's downtown stores as the target of the students' first protest, scheduled for February 1960. For the next several months, the students underwent rigorous training to prepare for the upcoming sit-ins, and on February 13, 124 students left a Nashville church and made their way to the lunch counters of several downtown stores. There, they took their seats and asked for service. The men wore suits and ties, the women, dresses, stockings, and high heels. They were poised and polite and gave little outward sign of the fear many of them felt. Diane Nash, for one, was terrified—a terror that would never leave her, no matter how many sit-ins and protests she would participate in afterward.

As frightened as the students were during that first sit-in, however, they had to struggle to keep from laughing at the stunned, panicky reactions of white store workers and patrons, who acted, Nash recalled, as if these well-dressed young people were "some dreadful monster . . . about to devour them all." Waitresses dropped dishes, cashiers broke down in tears, an elderly white woman almost had a seizure when she opened the door of a store's "white" ladies' room and found two young black women inside. Throwing up her hands, she screamed, "Oh! Nigras everywhere!"

There were no arrests and no violence. After a couple of hours, the students left the stores, jubilant that their first foray had gone without a hitch. A second sit-in was planned for the following week. In the meantime, several members of the students' Central Committee came to Nash and asked her to head the group. She was hardworking and outwardly fearless, and she did not seem to have the ego problems that a lot of the men had. "Because she was a woman and not a man, I think Diane never had to go around and do any posturing," said Bernard Lafayette, an American Baptist College student and one of the Nashville movement's leaders. But Nash had no desire to become the recognized head of this movement. Like most young women of that time, she had been raised to stay in the background. The men pressured her into accepting, however, and when she returned to her dorm room, she was so frightened by what she had done that she could hardly keep her legs from collapsing under her. "This is Tennessee, and white people down here are *mean*," she told herself. Not only that, but "we are going to be coming up against . . . white Southern men who are forty and fifty and sixty years old, who are politicians and judges and owners of businesses, and I am twenty-two years old. What am I *doing*? And how is this little group of students my age going to stand up to these powerful people?"

Once again, she managed to damp down her fear. She joined the other students in the second sit-in, which was as quietly successful as the first. Nevertheless, the city was losing its patience. Nashville officials, deluged by complaints from store owners that the sit-ins were causing whites to stay away from downtown, warned the students not to continue. If the warning wasn't heeded, they made clear, the kids could forget about being treated with kid gloves any longer. Worried about the possibility of violence and arrests, the ministers connected with the movement urged the students to reconsider their plans for another demonstration on February 27.

With their numbers swelling, the young people refused. In the middle of another snowstorm, more than three hundred of them poured into downtown Nashville. No sooner had some of them sat down at the Woolworth's lunch counter than the ministers' fears proved justified. The demonstrators were met by an opposing force of cursing young white toughs, who yanked them from their stools and threw them to the floor, beat them with fists and clubs, kicked them, spat on them, extinguished lighted cigarettes on their backs and in their hair. The police were nowhere in sight, and when they finally arrived, they approached not the white attackers, but the bruised and shaken demonstrators, who were spattered with mustard and ketchup, spit and blood. "Okay, all you nigras, get up from the lunch counter or we're going to arrest you," one of the cops barked. When no one obeyed, the students were ordered to their feet, arrested for disorderly conduct, and marched out, through a gauntlet of hostile whites, to police paddy wagons. When they looked over their shoulders at the lunch counter, they saw a new wave of students quietly moving in to take their place.

As the police wagons pulled away, the demonstrators inside steeled themselves for an experience for which there was no adequate preparation. They had rehearsed the sit-ins, had tried to get a sense of what they would be like, how it would feel when someone beat them or called them nigger. But it was impossible to simulate how it felt to go to jail for the first time, to give themselves up voluntarily to this dreaded system, to risk incurring a stigma that could mark them forever. Like others in the wagons, Diane Nash was wrestling with an almost paralyzing fear. Only bad people went to jail, she had been taught, and bad things happened to them once they were there.

The eighty-one arrested students were released on bail that evening. Monday morning, they reported to the city courthouse for their trials. Nashville's black community had been shocked by the arrests, and more than 2,500 blacks surged around the courthouse in an impressive show of solidarity. Inside the courtroom, the trials proceeded with bureaucratic efficiency—one after another, the students stood, were found guilty of disorderly conduct, and given fifty-dollar fines. Then, suddenly, Diane Nash threw a monkey wrench into the works. Nash told the judge that she, John Lewis, and fourteen others had decided to go to jail instead of paying the fines. Drawing on the principles of Gandhi, Nash declared, "We feel that if we pay these fines we would be contributing to and supporting injustice and immoral practices that have been performed in the arrest and conviction of the defendants." Stunned by Nash's announcement, the students who already had agreed to pay their fines declared that they, too, would go to jail.

Until then, most students arrested in sit-ins nationwide had spent little, if any, time behind bars. The idea that young people who had done nothing more than politely demand their rights would be sentenced to jail for thirty-three days electrified Nashville's blacks and touched off protests throughout the country. The city put the demonstrators to work, and the sight of the men shoveling snow and cleaning city streets and the women polishing the marble staircases of the courthouse threw the black community into even more of an uproar.

The jailing of the students had clearly backfired. Nashville's mayor, Ben West, a political moderate who had courted black votes in his last election, proposed a compromise: He would let the jailed students go and appoint a biracial commission to consider steps to desegregate the downtown stores if the demonstrations stopped. Nash and the others agreed and were released. Nash, however, was not content to sit around and wait for the committee's report. Two days after her release, she and three other students sat in at the city's Greyhound bus terminal, which was not covered by the demonstration cease-fire that the mayor had arranged. To the astonishment of everyone, including the demonstrators themselves, they were served at the bus station without any problem. It was one of the first sit-in victories in the South.

But there was little time for celebration. When the mayor's biracial committee failed to make any serious recommendations for desegregating downtown lunch counters and restaurants, the students resumed their sit-ins. At the same time they launched a boycott of downtown stores and picketed the city's central square and courthouse. Racial tension escalated, and this time the mayor seemed powerless to do anything about it.

On April 19, just two weeks after Nash and the other leaders of the Nashville movement attended SNCC's organizing conference in Raleigh, a tremendous explosion ripped through the home of Alexander Looby, the students' lawyer. The early-morning bombing was so powerful that it shattered more than a hundred windows in nearby Meharry Medical College, yet, miraculously, Looby and his wife were not injured. Outraged, the students called for a mass march to City Hall and sent a telegram to Mayor West, asking him to meet them. When the marchers, now numbering more than three thousand, reached City Hall, the mayor was waiting for them at the top of the steps. An activist minister named C. T. Vivian made a short speech, and the mayor began to reply, pointing out all that he had done for Nashville's blacks and reminding them that he was mayor of all the community. Listening to him, Nash grew increasingly frustrated: "He was making a political speech, and I remember feeling like, 'This is not getting us anywhere. What can I do? What can I say?'"

What she did was ask a simple question, one that would have far-reaching consequences for the city of Nashville. "Mayor West," she said, "do you feel it is wrong to discriminate against a person solely on the basis of their race or color?" The question went to the heart of nonviolence, bypassing all the political boilerplate and appealing directly to West's conscience. The mayor did not disappoint. He nodded—and then said yes. "They asked me some pretty soul-searching questions—and one that was addressed to me as a man," West said years later. "And I found that I had to answer it frankly and honestly—that I did not agree that it was morally right for someone to sell them merchandise and refuse them service. And I had to answer it just exactly like that."

Stunned by West's honesty, the marchers burst into thunderous applause, and the next day, the Nashville *Tennessean* ran a huge headline: INTEGRATE COUNTERS—MAYOR. Three weeks later, six downtown stores targeted by demonstrators opened their lunch counters to blacks.

It was an enormous victory for the fledgling movement. The day after the march, Martin Luther King came to Nashville to honor the students. Calling their campaign the "best organized and the most disciplined" in the South, he said he had come "not to bring inspiration but to gain inspiration from the great movement that has taken place in this community."

The Nashville students would become models for thousands of young people in the burgeoning Southern civil rights movement, and the Nashville leaders, including John Lewis, James Bevel, Bernard Lafayette, and Marion Barry, would be among the movement's foremost activists. But in the early days, at least, no one was better known or more awe-inspiring than the intrepid Diane Nash. Lewis called her "the most daring of [our] leaders." Demonstrators on trial in Nashville were often asked, "Do you know

Diane Nash?" Suddenly, she was everywhere—on the cover of *Jet*, on television, on the front pages of the Nashville newspapers. Her fame was not much to her liking—she was not fond of personal publicity, and she was often singled out by racists who recognized her from her picture in the paper. Once, at a sit-in, she was terrified when one of the toughs surrounding the students spotted her and yelled, "That's Diane Nash! She's the one to get!"

But if that was the price that had to be paid, so be it. She had been transformed by her experiences, and now she was a true believer, surrendering her heart and soul, in a way few people ever would, to nonviolence and the fight for freedom. In early 1961, her reputation as one of the most daring young firebrands in the movement would be burnished even further by a monthlong stint in jail. At the request of local students, Nash and three other SNCC activists, including a Spelman College sophomore named Ruby Doris Smith, had joined a sit-in at a drugstore in Rock Hill, South Carolina. They were promptly arrested, but rather than post bond, they opted to go to jail for thirty days.

Not long after the four were released, Nash dropped out of Fisk. "The Chaucer classes," she said, "became unbearable after Rock Hill." She was hired by both SNCC and the local SCLC affiliate. Her combined salary was about twenty-five dollars a week, and she rented a room at Nashville's YWCA. When *Jet* magazine asked her about her plans for the future, she said, "I'll be doing this for the rest of my life."

Logically, Diane Nash should have been elected first chairman of the Student Nonviolent Coordinating Committee at the end of its founding meeting in Raleigh. At that point, she was the Nashville movement's acknowledged leader, and in a struggle for influence between the two most powerful student groups—Nashville and Atlanta—it had been decided that the first SNCC chairman would come from Nashville, while the organization would be headquartered in Atlanta. After the balloting, however, the new chairman turned out to be Marion Barry, Jr., a suave, politically astute Fisk graduate student in chemistry who, while an activist in Nashville, had not been as involved in the movement as Nash and some of the others. The vote was taken while Nash was absent from the meeting; the timing, John Lewis was convinced, was deliberate. "Diane was a devoted, beautiful leader, but she was the wrong sex," Lewis said. "There was a desire to emphasize and showcase black manhood." The students were products of a time in which men, not women, customarily held formal positions of authority. With Nash as its leader, the Nashville movement was clearly an aberration. "Before the women's movement, men and women tended to see the males as naturally in leadership positions," Nash said years later. "The thing that we didn't do is take the out-front positions, and when the TV cameras were around I know I, for one, and I think many other women, were content to let the men who were interested in dealing with the press be with the press."

But for black women, it was more than following the norms of society. Prathia Hall, who would become a leading SNCC organizer, said black women had no problem with men being out front because women felt it "important to our community that black males be seen as competent, standing up and giving strong leadership. I don't think . . . that women felt that taking that posture was depriving them or taking anything away from them."

Because men occupied the formal leadership positions in SNCC, as they did in SCLC, because men were the ones sought out by the press, it was not surprising that most Americans had little idea of the key roles women played in the movement from the beginning. SNCC, in particular, would be unprecedented in the way it welcomed women—young and old, black and white, college students and illiterate sharecroppers—to its ranks and gave them the latitude to become major strategists, organizers, and activists. In other words, they were leaders in all but title and outside recognition. From the beginning, this daring, idealistic, adventurous organization insisted that everyone have an equal voice. Many of the women in SNCC came to see the group as having a distinctly "feminine" ethos, especially as compared with the authoritarian, masculine cultures of civil rights organizations like SCLC and the NAACP. SNCC was "very nurturing, very loving—it really *was* the beloved community," said Sandra "Casey" Hayden, a prominent white SNCC activist. In short, SNCC reflected the philosophy of its spiritual mother and guiding force, Ella Baker.

Baker was still working for SCLC when the student organization was founded, but from the moment of SNCC's birth, it became the recipient of most of her formidable energy and devotion. She carved out working space for SNCC's first office at SCLC headquarters, and gave the students access to SCLC's mimeograph machine and mailing facilities. She recruited Jane Stembridge, a young white theology student from Virginia, to run the office. Along with Stembridge and Connie Curry, another young white woman, Baker kept SNCC running that summer of 1960, all the while trying to figure out how to use SNCC as the engine for transforming the student crusade into a mass movement, embracing blacks of all ages and classes throughout the South. Both Stembridge and Curry had been at the Raleigh conference, welcomed from the beginning, as were other white observers. The "beloved community" envisioned by SNCC embraced whites as well as blacks, and the organization's logo showed a white hand and black hand clasped in friendship. "There was a time," recalled Casey Hayden, "when if one was willing to punch a hole in the consensus of the times, one was welcomed into a community with others who were doing the same. . . . [A]ll you had to do to be in it was punch that hole and join up."

9

"Being White Does Not Answer Your Problems"

Casey Hayden

LOOKING BACK AT THE DAWNING
of the 1960s, it is not surprising that young white women would be
attracted to a fight for equality waged by blacks of their age. They knew
very well how it felt to be discriminated against, even if their skin color
shielded them from Jim Crow segregation and the terror of racial violence.
"The truth is that women are . . . second-class citizens," declared an article in *The New York Times Magazine* on September 2, 1962. "[I]n the middle of the twentieth century, women are subject to prejudices that smack
of the nineteenth century." Women, white as well as black, were denied

certain jobs, were barred from many of the nation's most prestigious colleges and graduate schools, were paid lower wages than men, even when they were allowed to do the same work. Most churches refused to ordain women, the New York Stock Exchange banned them from its floor, many states would not allow a married woman to start a business of her own without a spouse's consent or get a credit card or loan in her own name. Three states wouldn't accept women as jurors. In Texas, a man who caught his wife flagrante delicto could kill her lover, claim justifiable homicide, and escape punishment. The president of a New York advertising agency was quoted by the *Times Magazine* as saying, "No woman can successfully deal on equal terms with men—and remain a woman. If she tries it, she becomes ridiculous or repulsive."

In an October 1962 editorial entitled "In the Same Boat," *Ebony* magazine warned America's white male leaders to pay attention to the needs and demands of "the country's most hated and her most loved minorities: Negroes and women." Indeed, said *Ebony*, "emancipation of women is more tardy than the emancipating of Negroes. . . . The fear that prompts Senators to bar women [members] from their Capitol Hill swimming pool is the same fear that prompts white residents to bar Negroes from their neighborhoods. . . . The real fear is not so much in how the newcomer fits into his new environment as how much competition he will offer the old-timer."

Such fear was present after World War II, when white women, as well as African-Americans, were pressured to leave their wartime jobs to make way for returning white servicemen. Women were subjected to an intensive propaganda campaign by political and social leaders and the national press to return home and devote themselves to their husbands and children, no matter how much they needed the money or the psychic satisfaction of salaried jobs. In the view of sociologist Wini Breines, U.S. culture in the immediate postwar years was aimed at repressing both blacks and white women, in defense of white male prerogatives. "American politics and culture were structured by a defense of masculinity and whiteness . . . ," Breines argued. "[T]he fifties were white men's last time of undisputed dominance," a time in which both "women and black people were to be kept separate and contained . . ." The fear of white women's independence spawned the same accusations of domination and emasculation of their men that had plagued black women for generations. "There has been a tendency in recent years to picture the American woman . . . as a domineering Mom who exploits the male, destroys his masculinity and reduces him to a quivering Milquetoast," *The New York Times* observed in 1962.

Unlike African-Americans, however, middle-class white women in the 1950s expressed little discontent. They were privileged, weren't they? Many now lived in new, postwar comfort, with a house, a car, gleaming appliances, and other heavily advertised consumer goods. Any concerns about their own psychological well-being were usually dismissed as ridiculous and trivial. Unlike blacks, white women tended to live in isolation, their lives focused on their immediate families, often in all-white suburbs (referred to in the mass media as centers of "suburban matriarchy"). If they were unhappy, they had no one to turn to, no community of like-minded women to offer support or guidance or to serve as a catalyst for change. Taught that any discontent they felt was selfish and unnatural, believing, in any event, that it was their own individual cross to bear, white women adopted a policy of dissemblance and concealment, hiding their dissatisfactions behind a facade of suburban bliss. And their daughters were encouraged to do the same. But for a good many young white women in the postwar generation, the indoctrination didn't work. They, like black women their age, had grown up with higher expectations, with a greater awareness of options, and they struggled against the suffocating conformity of the era and the stereotyped "feminine" roles they were supposed to play. Struggled against what Wini Breines called *the* fact of cultural life in the 1950s: that anything different was wrong, be it the color or texture of one's hair, the color of one's skin, the clothes or the makeup one wore, one's attitude. "The parameters of feminine beauty, personality, intelligence and ambition were so narrow that minor deviation meant exclusion and discomfort, and often unintentionally, became a wedge that grew into insurgence," Breines noted.

As narrow as the boundaries for female behavior were in the rest of the country, they were positively expansive when compared with those in the South, where white women were still expected to act like belles. Indeed, wrote sociologists Maxine Atkinson and Jacqueline Boles, "the southern lady today is a slightly modernized version of the plantation mistress, without the plantation." In a 1962 *New York Times Magazine* article, Hodding Carter, in his heyday as the cynosure of Southern liberalism, ridiculed playwright Tennessee Williams' depiction of Southern women as stifled, unhappy, and sexually repressed. That image tarnishes the good name of the South, declared Carter, who hastened to defend the modern Southern belle. "What's wrong with femininity?" he wrote. "What's wrong with a girl soft-pedaling her mental capacity when she wants a man who wouldn't like to find out that she's smarter than he is? . . . One of life's great objectives for a gal should be to make men like her, and another is to

make a home for the man she decides will do. . . . What's wrong with pretending helplessness and being wide-eyed and bearing down on an accent
which a great many men prefer to the clipped or the twanged or the
detachedly English tones of lovely women elsewhere?"

In fact, a growing number of young Southern white women thought
a great deal was wrong with Carter's portrayal of this fluttery-eyed,
honey-voiced, duplicitously subordinate creature. Most of the white
women who worked with SNCC in the early days—Jane Stembridge, Connie Curry, and Casey Hayden, among them—were from the South. Spiritual heirs to Lillian Smith and Virginia Durr, they understood the close
links between the repression of blacks and the subordination of women. By
rejecting the symbol of sacred white womanhood, they, like Smith and
Durr, were cutting themselves loose from the moorings of the society in
which they had been raised. In the words of historian Barbara Ransby,
these young women had become "race traitors," embracing "African-
Americans, men and women, as leaders, mentors, friends and family." In
Dixie, there could be no greater transgression.

The early white women in SNCC made clear they had not come to the
movement to play Lady Bountiful in the cause of racial justice, as some of
their nineteenth-century sisters had done. They were not there to dominate or dictate or lead. They were there to serve. And in serving, perhaps
they would find their own freedom. "I came here because I, too, needed to
be free, respected, a person, understood," Stembridge wrote a friend.
"Being white does not answer your problems, being able to go in anywhere
does not end your needs."

Intellectual and intense, Jane Stembridge was a poet and writer. An English literature major in college, she was not the kind of person you would
expect to find juggling all the administrative details inherent in starting
up and running an organization. But, then again, SNCC was not anyone's
typical organization. In her early twenties, Stembridge was small and
blonde, with hypnotic blue eyes. She had been part of the student civil
rights movement since its beginning, taking a couple of days off from her
graduate studies at Union Theological Seminary in New York to attend
SNCC's founding conference in Raleigh. Soon after, she was recruited by
Ella Baker to come down to Atlanta and take charge of the SNCC operation, much as Baker had done for SCLC.

The daughter of a Baptist minister who had been forced to leave several pastorates in the South because of his liberal beliefs on race, Stembridge grew up as a good Southern white girl was supposed to—making

good grades in school, joining the right clubs. But she always felt stifled, as if she'd been poured into a mold that was squeezing the life out of her. "I fit exactly. I was made to fit," she wrote about her upbringing. "Sometimes I wiggle and stretch. I get smashed. . . . [F]reedom is a kind of historical concept about people and governments, unrelated to me."

Unlike Jane Stembridge, Connie Curry, on the surface at least, never seemed to have any trouble fitting in. Tall and dark-haired, with lively brown eyes and a strong chin, Curry was outgoing and warm, and possessed of a quick, dry wit. She had been student body president at Agnes Scott College, a woman's school in Atlanta hardly known for its political liberalism. "We were a finishing school," Curry said. "At Agnes Scott, people were mostly trying to get pinned or engaged by the time they were seniors—or death was imminent." In truth, Curry was much more a tangle of contradictions than most of her Agnes Scott classmates: an attractive young woman who adored men but refused to pretend she did not have a mind or a strong will.

Curry's parents were émigrés from Northern Ireland, and the family was considered "different"—even worse, Yankees—by the folks in Greensboro, North Carolina, where Curry spent much of her childhood. Her mother, unlike many white women in the South, was "totally straightforward," Curry said. "She was very independent, very outspoken." Hazel Curry tried her best to instill those qualities in Connie and her sister, Eileen. "My mother never taught me to play the game," Curry said. "I never knew how to be quiet or be the power behind the throne. I don't think I ever learned to flirt." She also never learned to be a racist. One day, when she was in fourth grade, the boy ahead of her in the cafeteria line referred to one of the cafeteria workers as a nigger. Connie told him off, saying the woman was just as good as his mother. At recess, he got his revenge, knocking her into a mud puddle.

But she really didn't get involved in civil rights until college, when she joined the National Student Association, a confederation of student governments founded in 1947. She initially signed up because of the men, she confessed later: They were so much more interesting than the Southern good old boys she met during mixers at Emory and Georgia Tech. Since its founding, NSA had been a strong supporter of integration, and its meetings had always been interracial. In 1953, Curry was elected chair of NSA's Great Southern region, which consisted of only one white college—Agnes Scott—and several black schools, including Morehouse and Spelman.

After graduation from Agnes Scott in 1955, Curry went to France on a Fulbright scholarship and then worked for the Collegiate Council of the United Nations in New York. In late 1959, NSA asked her to return to the South to organize a series of intensive race relations seminars for Southern students of both races backed by the Field Foundation. Curry had just opened her new office in Atlanta when the sit-in movement was launched in her hometown of Greensboro. She realized that the thrust of her project would have to change: "It just wasn't important anymore to hold integrated tea parties or conferences or anything; it was a whole new thing." She attended SNCC's organizing conference in Raleigh and was elected an adult adviser, along with Ella Baker. Later Curry was named to the organization's executive committee, the only white woman to serve on it. Then in her mid-twenties, Curry was not much older than the students she was supposed to be advising, but she had already graduated from college, had a job, and, perhaps most important, had access to Field Foundation money.

From that point, she threw herself into the student movement, paying SNCC's telephone and other bills, and conferring and debating for hours at its executive committee meetings. She traveled the South recruiting white students for the movement, observing their sit-ins and marches, and reporting on them to the NSA, which was helping to coordinate sit-ins in the North against national store chains that refused to serve blacks in the South. "Connie was a bridge between the overwhelming number of black sit-in students and white students who were predisposed to join with us," said Julian Bond, who became a good friend. "She got us into the NSA network. It was an invaluable resource for recruiting money and political support."

Although Curry was never arrested or jailed (the NSA made clear that was not in her job description), she did not escape harassment. She was evicted from her apartment because one of her roommates had invited a black man there, she received threatening phone calls, and her sporty red-and-white Karmann Ghia was spray-painted with KKK symbols. (Mary King, who later joined SNCC, was astonished at Curry's boldness in zipping around Atlanta and the rest of the South in a car that King considered "outrageously racy for someone under surveillance.")

During a trip to Austin in March 1960, Curry recruited a University of Texas graduate student named Sandra Cason, called Casey by her friends. Though beautiful and blonde, Cason was, nonetheless, an anomaly at this university noted for its football team, beauty queens, and hard partying. She had emerged as one of the leaders of Austin's sit-in movement, and lived with an interracial group called the Christian Faith and Life Community, an oasis of liberalism on the UT campus. Cason, who called herself a Christian existentialist, termed the Community "a lay seminary," a place of intense study and worship, whose members read the works of theologians like Tillich and Niebuhr and existentialists like Sartre and Camus, then debated how to use their tenets in the fight for social justice. Dorothy Dawson, a fellow member and close friend of Cason's, remembered the Community as "the most intellectually alive" place at the university. It was also one of the few places where blacks and whites could live under the same roof.

Like most of the black students and many of the white women who joined the civil rights movement in the early days, Cason came from a strongly religious background. She grew up in Victoria, a small town in southeastern Texas, near the Louisiana border. Her father, a labor organizer, was an alcoholic, and her parents divorced when she was six months old. She was raised by her mother, whom Cason described as self-supporting, intellectual, and liberal and who encouraged her daughter to think for herself.

Cason also was heavily influenced by the YWCA, whose longtime fight against segregation, crucial in its day, has been pushed into the remote shadows of history. Black women first became YWCA members in 1893, but for half a century they were confined to all-black chapters, despite decades of opposition to the policy by prominent black women. Finally, in the 1940s, well before any other white-led women's organization, the YWCA committed itself to fighting for the full integration of black women into "the mainstream of association life" and launched a campaign against segregation and discrimination in general. Many women, both black and white, who would become active in the civil rights movement, had close ties to the Y. While Ella Baker worked with SNCC for no pay in the early 1960s, she was on the YWCA payroll as director of a Y campus race relations project in the South. Cason and Mary King worked on the project at different times before joining the SNCC staff. Anna Arnold Hedgeman, a prominent black government official and civil rights activist, got her start as a YWCA official, as did Dorothy Height, who later became president of the National Council of Negro Women.

The student YWCAs were particularly active in the fight for racial equality and justice. They sponsored integrated conferences and discussion groups and invited black speakers to white campuses as early as the 1920s. Centers of social activism on many campuses in the years leading up to the 1960s, student Y's also helped develop leadership skills in young women like Cason and Dawson. Even before the sit-in movement began in February 1960, the university Y in Austin, a joint YMCA-YWCA operation, had started a campaign of its own. Cason and Dawson led Y picket lines at local segregated restaurants and, along with other students, went to the restaurants in integrated groups, sitting down and asking to be served. When told to leave, they did so, but the whites among them left behind cards reading *I'll patronize this restaurant if you integrate.* When Connie Curry came calling that March, Cason had already been "introduced to the stuff that the student movement was putting forward—but through the Y . . . I already had my orientation to it. I already had been there."

That summer, at Curry's invitation, Cason attended the annual NSA congress in Minneapolis. A group of SNCC members appeared before the hundreds of mostly white student delegates to describe the sit-ins and their nonviolent philosophy and to ask for NSA's support. Such backing was crucial for SNCC. It would help the students raise badly needed funds and also would bring to the movement a network of white supporters. But a number of NSA members opposed any expression of support and demanded to appear on a panel to explain their reasons. Concerned that the antimovement delegates might persuade the rest of the convention, Curry asked Cason to take part in the discussion. A story about Cason's performance appeared in the next day's *Minneapolis Tribune,* headlined WHITE COED BACKS SIT INS, GETS OVATION. The article began: "A beautiful University of Texas coed with honey blond hair and a southern voice so soft it would not startle a boll weevil made a statement of ethical principles on the Negro sit-in movement Thursday."

"I cannot say to a person who suffers injustice, 'Wait,'" Cason declared. "Perhaps you can. I can't. And having decided that I cannot urge caution, I must stand with him. If I had known that not a single lunch counter would open as the result of my action, I could not have done differently than I did. If I had known violence would result, I could not have done differently than I did." She described a visit by Ralph Waldo Emerson to his close friend Henry David Thoreau, who was in jail for refusing to pay taxes to a government that supported slavery. "Henry David," Emerson said, "what are you doing in there?" "Ralph Waldo," replied Thoreau, "what are you doing out there?"

Cason paused, gazing out at the hundreds of students before her. "What," she asked, "are you doing out there?"

For a moment, those in the audience seemed transfixed. Then they leaped to their feet on a wave of applause. Afterward, the congress voted by an overwhelming margin to endorse the sit-ins and support them nationally and on a local level. "There is no question," said Curry, "that [Cason's speech] was a personal turning point for many of the white delegates and probably a decisive moment in the history of NSA's civil rights activism."

Among those mesmerized by Cason's message and by Cason herself was a University of Michigan student leader named Tom Hayden. The editor of the university's student newspaper, Hayden had been much impressed with the cool courage of all the SNCC students who had spoken, but like a number of other male delegates, he was especially dazzled by Cason, and he followed her wherever she went. "I idolized her," he later said. She had clarified for him the dilemma he was facing—whether to pursue his ambition to become a foreign correspondent, and thus remain an observer, or to follow the lead of the SNCC people and throw himself into full-time social activism. He admired how the black students, impatient with their elders, had assumed moral leadership. They were living, Hayden thought, "on a fuller level of feeling than any people I'd ever seen, partly because they were making modern history in a very personal way, and partly because by risking death they came to know the value of living each moment to the fullest." Once he saw them in action at the NSA congress, once he had heard Cason, he made up his mind about his future. "Here were the models of charismatic commitment I was seeking—I wanted to live like them."

Back in Michigan, he wrote about Cason's speech for the *Michigan Daily* and exchanged letters with her. She sent him a copy of *Let Us Now Praise Famous Men*, by James Agee and Walker Evans, which he read "urgently." More and more, he found himself pulled toward the South, the civil rights movement, and "the most interesting woman I'd ever met." In October, he flew down to Atlanta for the big SNCC conference organized by Ella Baker and Jane Stembridge. Hayden was ready to become involved in the student campaign, but he was even more eager to become better acquainted with Cason.

In Atlanta for the same conference was a sixty-four-year-old woman whose entire adult life seemed to have been directed toward that moment. Lillian Smith was seriously ill, had been battling breast cancer for seven years, but she was not about to let illness keep her from savoring this, her ultimate triumph. For two decades, she had carried on her lonely campaign for racial equality, enduring vilification, ridicule, threats, and terrorist campaigns. In the late 1950s, as her strength ebbed, she called on young people of the South, both black and white, to take up the fight. "We need a fresh approach," she wrote to a friend. "Something younger, more vital, more risky, full of fun and ardor. We need to get the youngsters involved. . . . The rest of us have broken down walls, filled up ditches, defined problems, put a sharp edge on dilemmas, we've shaken everybody's souls with the moral issue—now something more has to be done. And what we who are more experienced, more aware, can do is encourage the young ones to try, to take over, TO DO SOMETHING . . ."

Three years later, when the sit-in movement was ignited, she summoned all the energy she still possessed to support it. She gave speeches, wrote letters, hosted gatherings of students at her home on Old Screamer Mountain. She paid for a full-page newspaper advertisement taken out by the Atlanta student movement to explain its purpose and activities, and raised money for SNCC and CORE, as well as donating some money of her own. She demanded that Atlanta's department stores integrate their lunchrooms, threatening to cancel her accounts with them unless they did, and urged the city's newspapers and television stations to support the student demonstrators. She became a mentor and friend to Jane Stembridge, as she had to Pauli Murray almost two decades earlier.

But there was a measure of sadness mixed with Smith's enthusiasm. The students were finally doing what she had been calling for since the early 1940s, but she was too old and too sick to become an active member of their community. In her visits to Old Screamer, Stembridge said, "what I mostly did was listen. Because she needed to talk about what she'd done and what she'd been through and the [lonely] stands she had taken. She was eaten up with the whole thing, with never having really been understood and appreciated. . . .There wasn't a SNCC around her; there wasn't a group support system." Connie Curry, who went with Stembridge on one of her visits, was struck by Smith's "yearning to have been part of a movement where people believed and marched and sang for freedom."

As the final speaker at SNCC's conference, Smith looked out at Stembridge, Curry, Diane Nash, Sandra Cason, Bob Moses, John Lewis, Julian Bond, and dozens of other young activists, many of whom had never heard of her before the sit-in movement began. She talked of their journey toward freedom and justice, talked of how she and others had made the first steps down that road years before. "We of the older generation cannot go on that great journey with you," she said. "But there is something we can do: We can make of our lives, our knowledge, our experiences, our wisdom . . . a bridge, a strong, sure bridge over which you can cross into the new, unmade world."

*   *   *

Like Ella Baker and Septima Clark and many others before them, Smith had passed on to the students a precious legacy. Listening to her poignant valedictory address in Atlanta was another Southern white woman who had contributed to that legacy—but, at the age of thirty-six, Anne Braden was still very much on the front lines. For Diane Nash and Jane Stembridge, as for other young women activists who would come later, Braden served as both a role model and a source of comfort and support. Defying the upper-class culture in which she had been raised, she had opposed racism and had withstood the intimidation of mobs, death threats against her two toddlers, and a stint in jail on a sedition charge. After her jailing in Louisville in 1954, a steady stream of friends and relatives, bearing flowers and covered dishes for supper, had come to console Braden's heartbroken parents in Anniston, Alabama. It was, Braden said, as if they were mourning her passing, ignoring the fact that the "corpse . . . was alive and healthy."

When she was four or five, Anne Gambrell McCarty used the phrase "colored lady" in front of her mother. "You never call colored people ladies, Anne Gambrell," her mother reproved her. "You say colored woman and white lady—never a colored lady." In Anne's household and in the circles she was part of, everyone used the word "nigger," except when one was talking directly to a black person, and then the term was "colored." It was not until Anne was a teenager that she discovered the word "Negro."

Growing up in Anniston, the adored daughter of a genteel Old South family, she was raised to believe she was better than most people because of her superior bloodlines. But even when she was small, she sensed that something was wrong with this life she was expected to lead. "I was so horribly well-brought-up and polite and reared in the 'best' Southern tradition of smoothing over all the rough edges of things," she recalled. "Actually, I think that is one of the worst aspects of Southern life—the phoniness of it, the smearing of sweet sugar over ugliness . . ."

She would see occasional flashes of that ugliness. As a teenager, she had a discussion with an old family friend, a man known for his kindness, about the antilynching legislation then being debated by Congress. When Anne argued in favor of the law, the friend replied, "We have to have a good lynching every once in a while to keep the nigger in his place." Anne was speechless. "To the day I die I think I will hear those words ringing in my ears. Words of murder from one of the gentlest people I ever knew."

But she was far more conscious then of her society's attitude toward its women than its racism. As she got older, she realized that "[t]he whole idea of settling down in a small Southern town and being a Southern white woman was just the most appalling, boring life that I could possibly think of. I did not intend to spend my life just waiting on a man who treated me like a toy or a plaything . . ." In 1941, Anne went away to college, first attending Stratford, then finishing up at Randolph-Macon. Both were elite women's schools in Virginia, known for putting the finishing educational and cultural touches on well-bred Southern ladies. For Anne, these institutions nonetheless managed to provide an intellectual excitement she had never experienced before and gave her "an inkling of what it is to seek the truth." She discovered Lillian Smith, and saw *Strange Fruit* when it was produced as a Broadway play. Reading Smith's work, Anne finally was able to articulate what had been bothering her most of her life—the discovery that Southern white women were prisoners and, at the same time, oppressors.

For the first time in her life, segregation was no longer a forbidden topic, and she explored it thoroughly in discussions with professors and fellow students. Her awakening, however, carried a heavy price. She had always been close to her mother and father, but her changing views on race were anathema to them, and when she let them know how she felt, "my parents and I could not communicate anymore." Still, it wasn't until after college, when she became a newspaper reporter on the courthouse beat in Anniston, then in Birmingham, that she realized how ugly the reality of race in the South really could be.

She learned that justice for blacks was, more often than not, a contradiction in terms. She covered the trial of a young black man whose crime was passing a white woman on the opposite side of a country road and looking at her in an "insulting" way. He was declared guilty of assault with intent to rape and sent to prison. And for years afterward, Anne would be haunted by the memory of a chat with a Birmingham deputy sheriff, who, making small talk with this attractive young reporter, told her there had been only one unsolved murder in the county in the last two years. She asked what it was, and he said, "Come on, I'll show you." He took her into a room, pulled open a drawer in a filing cabinet, and took out a skull. He laid it on the table. "There it is," he said with obvious relish. "And it never *will* be solved—that man was a nigger and he was killed by a white man." The deputy smiled, obviously thinking she would appreciate the joke. Horror-stricken, she turned and left without a word. This, she thought, was "the end of the road where segregation led—death and decay, death in the skull on the table." She had to get out of the courthouse, out of Birmingham. She decided to move to Louisville, a city with a reputation for racial progressivism, much like Nashville's.

When she arrived in 1947, however, she found that Louisville, like Nashville, was schizophrenic when it came to race. The city buses were integrated, as were its golf courses and libraries. Blacks could vote. But schools, parks, restaurants, and most other public accommodations were strictly segregated. After being hired as a reporter for the Louisville *Times*, Anne started attending NAACP meetings, and soon found herself on a committee working to end segregation in public parks. She also met Carl Braden.

Their subsequent romance seemed straight out of a Katharine Hepburn-Spencer Tracy movie. She, the well-brought-up, bright, quick-witted career woman; he, the rough-hewn, blunt blue-collar journalist, who, as his future wife would say, "was off somewhere else when they passed out the tact." The labor editor for the Louisville *Times*, Braden came from a working-class, union background. When Carl and Anne started seeing each other, he introduced her to his world of union organizing, and she got him involved in her growing passion, the fight against racial injustice.

Carl and Anne were married in 1948. Soon after, both quit the *Times* to handle public relations for a group of CIO unions. Two years later, with Anne expecting their first baby, Carl got a job as copy editor on the Louisville *Courier-Journal*. But the Bradens continued their battle against racism, working on campaigns to end job discrimination in Louisville, as well as segregation in hospitals, schools, and bus stations.

In 1954, a casual acquaintance of the Bradens', a young black electrician named Andrew Wade, asked them a favor. Wade, a World War II veteran, wanted a bigger house for his growing family—he and his wife had a two-year-old daughter and another baby on the way—but he could not find anything suitable in the black sections of town. While there had been an explosion of home construction in the white areas of Louisville since the end of World War II—eighteen thousand houses in all—only three hundred new houses had been built in black neighborhoods. Wade told the Bradens that he had tried to buy a house in a new all-white subdivision on the outskirts of town but was rejected. Would the Bradens consider buying a house there and reselling it to the Wades?

The Bradens immediately agreed. "[W]e never considered saying 'no' . . . ," Anne later said. "He needed a house, and we were the people who, because of the accident of having been born with white skin, could help him." Louisville had never had much racial trouble to speak of, and the Bradens' action was not illegal. In 1948, the Supreme Court had struck down restrictive housing covenants banning blacks from all-white residential areas, even though Louisville, like most American cities, continued to practice housing segregation.

But the Bradens had not reckoned on the fear and hate being stirred up in the South over the pending *Brown* v. *Board of Education* decision. *Brown* was handed down four days after the Bradens had transferred the house's title to the Wades and the black family moved in. In retrospect, it occurred to Anne Braden that Louisville's white supremacists saw the house sale as a gauntlet flung down by this young white couple. "The people who were determined to preserve segregation at any cost," she said, "evidently decided that now was the time to teach a lesson to the Negro people and the white people who join with them to oppose segregation."

There now began a campaign of terror against both the Bradens and the Wades, a fright-filled period of telephoned death threats and cars driving slowly back and forth in front of both families' houses. It was a time when Anne Braden, who was pregnant with her third child, moved her children's beds into the hall every night to shelter them from possible gunfire, a time when she sat up until three or four o'clock each morning, waiting for Carl to come home from his job on the *Courier-Journal* desk, a gun by her side. (She had hated the very idea of weapons in her house but had finally borrowed one from Andrew Wade after a car forced Carl's car to stop one day and its occupants threatened the life of her son, Jimmy, who was sitting next to Carl.) Physically exhausted, drained emotionally by the tension and fear, Anne lost the baby she had been carrying.

Through it all, she and Carl had few allies. No one in Louisville's white community appealed for tolerance and compassion, no one pricked the city's conscience. The *Courier-Journal*, touted as one of the South's leading liberal voices, decried the violence but blamed the Bradens for indirectly causing it. The paper sympathized with the Wades' neighbors and their concerns about plummeting property values. With no one standing up for the Bradens and the Wades, their enemies were free to go after them with impunity. On the night of June 26, the Wades' house was dynamited. Three months later, with no arrests made, Louisville's district attorney turned the matter over to a grand jury. The Bradens were summoned to testify. In the grand jury room, Anne, to her astonishment, found herself being questioned by the DA not about the bombing or other violence to which the two families had been subjected, but about her membership in alleged subversive organizations. She had never heard of most of the groups, had known of others but never joined them, had belonged to a few. Nonetheless, she indignantly refused to answer any of the questions, telling the grand jury that the queries had no relevance to the bombing, that the DA had no business interrogating her about "matters I had always been so sure were my private business, freedoms I had always been so sure were mine." Carl took the same position.

For the Bradens, Louisville had turned into the kind of world Alice discovered after tumbling down the rabbit hole. It was apparent that *they* were being investigated, not the segregationists who had spent the summer terrorizing both families. The buying of the house, as well as its bombing, were a Communist plot to stir up race trouble in untroubled Louisville, according to the district attorney. The Bradens, he said, were the ringleaders.

Such accusations were not uncommon in the South following the *Brown* decision. The influence of Senator Joseph McCarthy himself might have been on the wane in 1954, but McCarthyism was still virulent and was being used by the anti-*Brown* forces as their chief weapon in fighting integration. Led by James Eastland and his Senate internal security subcommittee, segregationists branded as subversive or Communist anybody with the effrontery to challenge Jim Crow or advocate any other drastic social change. For Eastland, Anne Braden said, the issue was simple: "All who did not support segregation were Communists." White Southerners were the main targets of the smear campaign, whose strategy of harassment and intimidation was brilliantly effective: Victims of the witch-hunt were isolated and often rendered impotent, and other whites, afraid of being called subversive, remained silent, no matter how sympathetic they might be to the cause. Following in Eastland's footsteps, a number of Southern states set up their own committees to ferret out "subversives"— that is, integrationists, and ambitious politicians like Scott Hamilton, Louisville's district attorney, hopped on the bandwagon.

While the *Courier-Journal* disapproved of the Bradens' buying a house for a black family, it could not stomach what Hamilton was now doing to the couple. In an editorial, it supported the Bradens' refusal to answer questions before the grand jury, saying, "Mr. Hamilton has produced not the slightest evidence to uphold his theory of a communist plot. He has paid very little attention to the alternative and much more likely theory that the bombing was the work of hoodlums who resented a Negro's purchase of a house in a white area." Nevertheless, the next day, the grand jury indicted the Bradens, along with four other whites who had supported the Wades, on charges of sedition.

Sitting in a jail cell that night, Anne could not believe what had happened. "What had I done?" she remembered thinking. "Sold a house? How much can they do to you for selling a house? Threaten your life for five months, kill your unborn child, and then put you in jail for twenty-one years? All for one little house?" The next morning, after some sleep and more thinking, she realized she had done more than sell a house. "I had challenged a whole settled world, a way of life, and this world had struck back. What had I expected?"

She was released on bond a week later, but while she and Carl were in jail, Louisville police raided their house twice, confiscating dozens of books from their voluminous library, books that Scott Hamilton later labeled as seditious. The charges against Anne and four other defendants were eventually dropped, but Carl was tried and convicted on charges of sedition and "conspiracy to destroy property to bring about a political end, to wit communism." Sentenced to fifteen years, he spent eight months in prison, including two months in solitary confinement, until the Kentucky Court of Appeals struck down the statute under which he was convicted and ordered his release. The Kentucky court's decision was upheld by the U.S. Supreme Court.

Friends urged the Bradens to leave Louisville and the South, to move to a place where they could free themselves and their children from the hate and enmity that surrounded them. Both Anne and Carl adamantly refused to consider such a thing. They would not be terrorized into silence. "The only way that I was going to leave Louisville was in a coffin," Anne said later. And Carl declared he was "not going to live under a system where a man could be put in prison for selling his house to a Negro. I decided I would spend my life trying to change that system."

Three years after the bombing of the Wades' house and little more than a year after the Montgomery bus boycott, the Bradens were recruited by the Southern Conference Educational Fund to set up, among other things, a communications and support network for those scattered white Southerners courageous enough to confront segregation. SCEF wasn't fearful of hiring people tagged with the "red" label; it, too, had been branded as Communist by none other than Jim Eastland himself.

SCEF had been founded in 1942 as an arm of the Southern Conference for Human Welfare. The newer group was created with only one purpose: to eliminate all segregation in the South through the joint action of black and white Southerners. SCEF officials were among Eastland's chief targets (along with Virginia Durr) when the senator from Mississippi went hunting for Communists in 1954. In his committee report, Eastland accused SCEF of being Communism's principal voice in the South.

News of the affiliation between the Bradens and SCEF only increased the anticommunists' ire. In July 1958, the House Un-American Activities Committee scheduled hearings in Atlanta to investigate Communist subversion in the South. The Bradens were among those subpoenaed. In the end, Anne was not called to testify, but Carl, who *was* summoned, refused to answer any questions, just as he and Anne had done before the Louisville grand jury. Citing the First Amendment, he told the committee that his beliefs and associations were none of its business. The committee cited him for contempt of Congress, and he served ten months of a one-year sentence.

Alarmed by the campaign against SCEF and the Bradens, fearful of too close an association with them, a number of civil rights and other liberal organizations began distancing themselves from their former allies. Anne appealed to them to recognize that they were playing right into Jim Eastland's hands. "*Any* white person in the South who acts for integration (not just talks, but *acts*) is going to be labeled a Communist," she said in an impassioned letter to CORE officials. " ... [I]f you adopt a policy of refusing to work with people who have been called Communists, *who* in the South are you going to work with? . . . You are urging white people to speak out, to take action, to stand up and be counted. Is it right for you to ask people to do this if you run from people who have been labeled because they did the very thing you are asking others to do?"

Not everyone pulled away. Eleanor Roosevelt remained a supporter of SCEF and wrote a blurb for *The Wall Between,* Anne Braden's book about her family's ordeal in Louisville. Infuriated by the red-baiting of integrationists, the former First Lady was even angrier that the smears were accepted at face value by some of the victims' natural allies. "Like the scream of 'red,' the scream of race has become a political symbol and each man thinks he has to outscream the other to prove his purity," she wrote. Another stalwart champion of SCEF was Ella Baker, who became a close friend of Anne's. Thanks largely to Baker's influence, SNCC sloughed off the warnings of other civil rights leaders and developed strong ties to the Bradens and SCEF, an alliance that would prove invaluable for the student organization in years to come.

For all the red-baiting they endured, the Bradens managed to turn SCEF into a civil rights organization of major importance in the South in the late 1950s and early 1960s. They saw their role as providing financial, psychological, and other kinds of support for movement activists, both black and white, and linking them together in a communications network. Working for SCEF "means defending the people who, alone and on their own, have shown initiative and are getting their heads chopped off . . . ,"Anne wrote to Ella Baker. "It means providing a framework to which people can turn, friends who will rally around when they are needed."

Drawing on their experience as newspaper reporters, the Bradens turned the organization's monthly paper, the *Southern Patriot*, into an essential source of information about the budding fight for freedom. They gave publicity to local campaigns and activists at a time when the civil rights movement was not yet in the national headlines and when the local media, hostile to the movement more often than not, either ignored or distorted what was going on. "[I]f it had not been for Carl and Anne Braden, I'm sure I would have been dead already," declared Fred Shuttlesworth, the leader of the Birmingham movement. Whenever Shuttlesworth was threatened or under attack from Public Safety Commissioner Bull Connor and the other racists in his city, he got the word out to the Bradens, who, in turn, would call the Associated Press, or United Press International, or a newspaper outside the South, and suggest they investigate what was going on in Birmingham. "We did that in other places, too," Anne said. "People would be in jail or in trouble, nobody was paying any attention, and we'd sound the alert. It was a whole information program."

SNCC benefited from the network, too. The *Southern Patriot* gave extensive play to the students' activities, and in turn SNCC modeled its own communication and public relations machinery, including its newspaper, the *Student Voice*, on the program developed by the Bradens. For many of the student activists, Anne also served as a surrogate mother. She housed and fed them when they were in Louisville, gave them advice and comfort, tried to find money for them to finish college. They looked up to her and Carl as role models, whose courage and determination seemed unquenchable despite the seemingly endless harassment they had to endure. "There are no adjectives to describe Anne's contribution [to SNCC and the movement]," said Jane Stembridge. "I wouldn't know what to say. I'm absolutely astounded at a person, male or female, who makes that kind of commitment."

Young women, in particular, saw Anne as a mentor. She had made it a point to encourage women, no matter what their age, to participate in the movement, explaining, "I always considered I had a mission in life to get women out of the kitchen and involved in things . . . to get past the husband to the kitchen and get the woman out." (Once, at a meeting at Martin Luther King's home, she literally did that, persuading King to retrieve his wife, Coretta, from the kitchen so that she could join the discussion.)

Anne knew what the young activists, particularly the white women, were going through. She had been there. She knew the difficulty of rejecting the ideal of Southern white womanhood, the pain of severing oneself from one's past and one's family, of wanting to be a good girl and please everybody. She knew, probably better than anybody else, how hard it was to juggle the conventional woman's roles—wife, mother, cook, house-keeper—with other work. At the time of the October 1960 SNCC conference, she had three small children, nine, seven, and eight months old. The baby, Beth, had been born the week after the sit-in movement started in Greensboro. Describing the frantic rat race of her typical day, Anne said: "I squeeze office work in when I can—after the house is cleaned up in the morning and before it's time to feed the baby again, after the older children get home from school and I've talked to them a little and feel they are settled for a while—and mostly late at night after everybody is in bed. I've sometimes counted up and I usually manage well over eight or ten hours of actual office work in a twenty-four-hour period, but I still don't catch up."

Just as younger women leaned on her as a source of support, she reached out to older women in the movement, friends like Ella Baker and Virginia Durr, for the same kind of solace. In a letter, Anne apologized to Baker for burdening her with talk of her problems, "[c]onflicts I've been living with too long and unable to resolve . . . the principal one the conflict between the demands of being a mother and the demands of being 'a worker in the cause.' . . . I keep feeling that a woman *should* be able to do both these things, but in practice it never quite works out—and I constantly feel I've done a half-way job at both, and at the moment I feel that I have utterly failed to organize my life correctly . . ."

Braden's intense commitment to the movement took a heavy toll not only on her but on her children, who hungered for more of her attention and time, according to Jane Stembridge, who spent considerable time with the Bradens in Louisville. Stembridge recalled how Anne would ignore preparations for Christmas until about 3 P.M. Christmas Eve, when she would reluctantly stop work and embark on an hours-long frenzy of shopping and cooking. "She would take that much of Christmas Eve and all of Christmas Day, and then the day after Christmas she was back to work," Stembridge said.

The traditional expectations of what a woman should be and do, instilled in Anne Braden from birth, haunted her. They would similarly haunt the newer generation of female activists, no matter how hard they struggled to break free.

10

"She Never Listened to a Word"

Diane Nash (second from right)

IN THE SPRING OF 1961, HUN-
dreds of civil rights activists boarded Greyhound and Trailways buses and
headed deep into Dixie, raising the movement's temperature as well as its
stakes. The bloody mob scenes that followed their forays focused national
and international attention on the South's brutal racial injustice and threw
the new Kennedy administration into confusion. When the Freedom Rides
were finally over, they had joined the Montgomery bus boycott and the
sit-ins as epochal events of the movement, inspiring thousands more people, from black sharecroppers in Mississippi to white students at Smith
and Yale, to become part of this historic crusade.

And Diane Nash, as usual, was in the thick of it all.

While she would end up directing the Freedom Rides, Nash had no role in their initial planning. They were the brainchild of James Farmer, the director of the Congress of Racial Equality. Known for its adherence to nonviolence, CORE had pioneered the use of sit-ins and other direct action protests in the early 1940s, and now Farmer was anxious to test *Boynton* v. *Virginia*, a recent Supreme Court decision that struck down segregation in interstate train and bus stations. According to the Court, it was no longer legal for stations to confine blacks to separate waiting rooms, rest rooms, and lunch counters. The South was well known for ignoring Supreme Court rulings on integration, but, with the Freedom Rides, Farmer was determined to make this one a decision that Southerners— and the new Kennedy administration—could not overlook.

On May 4, the Freedom Riders recruited by CORE—seven black men, three white men, and three white women—left Washington in two buses, at the start of what was supposed to be a two-week trip to test their right to mix, black and white, in bus stations throughout the South. They encountered few major problems until they reached Alabama. In Anne Braden's hometown of Anniston, a mob of whites surrounded one of the buses when it pulled into the terminal. They beat at the windows with pipes and clubs and slashed the tires as the bus pulled away. A few miles outside town, the tires went completely flat. The pursuing mob caught up with the bus and set it ablaze. The choking Riders stumbled off, just before the fuel tank exploded, and were greeted with blows from baseball bats, bricks, and fists.

Meanwhile, the second bus managed to get away and head for Birmingham, a tough iron and steel center notorious for its bigotry and racial violence. CBS correspondent Howard K. Smith was at the Trailways terminal when the bus arrived. Some thirty or forty men were milling around outside the station. They were Klansmen, a local reporter told Smith. The men dragged the Freedom Riders off the bus, pushed them into a nearby alley, and clubbed them with lead pipes, brass knuckles, key rings, fists, and feet. One of the passengers was paralyzed (for life, as it turned out) by the beating. Another fell at Smith's feet, his face a bloody, unrecognizable mess. "They . . . just about slaughtered these kids," Smith said later. After a while, one of the toughs glanced at his watch, and the mob dispersed. Only then did Bull Connor's officers, whose station house was just three blocks away, arrive at the terminal. Later Smith saw some members of the gang standing in front of Connor's office, laughing and talking. Badly shaken, Smith, who had covered Nazi Germany before World War II, felt he had witnessed another Kristallnacht. He told CBS Radio listeners that the mob reminded him of the worst Gestapo thugs.

Diane Nash and other members of the Nashville student movement were spending that lovely Sunday afternoon at a picnic celebrating the students' most recent victory—desegregation of the city's movie theaters. The fun was interrupted by several news flashes over a portable radio someone had brought—first, reports about the burning of the bus in Anniston, then the mob violence in Birmingham. James Bevel, who had become chairman of the Nashville movement, wanted to continue the picnic, but Nash, who felt "as though *we* had been attacked," demanded that they take immediate action to support the Ride. So insistent was she that Bevel, the master debater, finally capitulated, muttering to his friends, "She's going to keep talking nasty about us." He called an emergency meeting of the movement's central committee in a nearby church. For more than twelve hours, the group and its adult advisers argued about what they should do.

On Monday morning, the debate still raging, they heard that the badly battered Freedom Riders, nudged by the Kennedy administration, had decided to give up on their plan to ride all the way to New Orleans. Nash and the other Nashville activists were appalled by the news. How could the Riders allow violence to vanquish nonviolence? The Ride *had* to continue. The movement's future depended on it.

Nash phoned James Farmer, who had dropped off the Ride in Atlanta after receiving word that his father had died. Would Farmer object if some of the Nashville students went down to Birmingham to continue the Freedom Ride? The head of CORE could not believe what he was hearing. It would be suicide. Farmer warned that a massacre was possible. "Well, we realize that," Nash said with an edge of annoyance. "We're not stupid. But we can't let them stop us with violence. If we do that, the movement is dead. Every time we start something, they'll just answer with violence . . ." Farmer finally agreed and offered to try to recruit some new troops himself.

From that moment, Nash was all but running the show. She lined up and prepared students for the trip, at the same time fending off frightened parents, worried ministers, and angry Kennedy administration officials, who were trying to smooth things over after arranging for the first Riders to escape Birmingham by plane. When the ministers who advised the students were reluctant to advance money for the journey, Nash and the other student leaders held firm until they got the funds. From the ministers, from Farmer, from others, Nash got the same dire warning: She was risking a bloodbath. When she called Fred Shuttlesworth in Birmingham to let him know that replacements were coming, the activist minister, who had gambled with his own life just a couple of days before to retrieve the injured Riders in Anniston, said, "Young lady, do you know that the Freedom Riders were almost killed here?" "Yes," she snapped, "that's exactly why the ride must not be stopped . . . We're coming. We just want to know if you can meet us."

In New Orleans, Justice Department official John Seigenthaler, who had flown there with the first Freedom Riders, was jolted awake by a phone call from Assistant Attorney General Burke Marshall. "You know Diane Nash in Nashville?" barked Marshall. Seigenthaler, a Nashville native, knew who she was. Make her stop these new Riders, Marshall ordered. Seigenthaler tried but failed, as did just about everyone who tangled with Diane Nash. All hell is going to break loose, he warned. She replied, "I couldn't turn them back if I wanted to." She advised him to stay where he was, adding that he could talk to the new Riders himself when they ended their trip in New Orleans. Frustrated, Seigenthaler flew back to Birmingham instead. "It was as if I were talking to a wall," he remarked to a reporter. "She never listened to a word."

However unbending she may have seemed to all these male authority figures, Nash agonized over the very real possibility that the ten students heading for Birmingham, most of them close friends and comrades of hers, might be killed. The Riders, who included John Lewis, were no less fearful. Several of them made out wills before they left. Others gave Nash letters to be mailed in the event of their death.

When the bus arrived in Birmingham, it was surrounded by police and a screaming mob. Three hours later, the students were allowed off the bus and were arrested by Bull Connor himself—for their own protection, he said with a little smile. The following night, Connor loaded the Riders into two cars and said he was taking them back to Nashville. Instead, they were dropped off at the edge of a tiny, isolated settlement near the Tennessee state line. Leaving the terrified students and their luggage in the middle of the road, the police cars zoomed away, but not before one of the Riders, Katherine Burke, shouted to Connor, "We'll be back in Birmingham by the end of the day." Connor just laughed. But, in fact, they were.

To Bull Connor and, for different reasons, to Kennedy administration officials, it must have seemed like a bad dream: The Freedom Riders had returned to the Birmingham bus station, now reinforced by twelve other students, including Ruby Doris Smith, Diane Nash's cellmate in the Rock Hill jail. The Justice Department had not been averse to Connor's highly unorthodox way of handling the Riders—quietly spiriting them out of town. Anything to get them out of the news and out of the President's hair. When Kennedy heard that the Ride was continuing, he angrily ordered his aide Harris Wofford to stop the students. "I don't think anybody's going to stop them right now," Wofford said.

The President and Attorney General Robert Kennedy were nearly beside themselves, and much of their fury was aimed at the Ride's young field marshal. The administration had only just recovered from the Bay of Pigs debacle, and Kennedy was now preparing for a crucial summit meeting in Vienna with Soviet leader Nikita Khrushchev. Now, suddenly, the administration had to cope with this mere girl and her friends. From the White House, it seemed that the Riders were intent on giving the South a national and international black eye, not to mention plunging the administration, which had been totally unprepared for this crisis, into chaos. For a group of men who proudly cultivated a reputation of macho toughness and who believed, according to one Washington newsman, that "women were put on this earth to please men," it must have been particularly infuriating to have to deal with the outspoken, assertive Nash. They regarded her as arrogant and uncompromising, and treated her, she thought, with the most maddening condescension. She was as hostile to them as they were to her, and in the coming months they would do their best to seek her comeuppance.

When the Greyhound bus finally rumbled out of the Birmingham station to continue the Freedom Ride, Ruby Doris Smith was the only Rider on board not from Nashville. When she had heard that Nash was recruiting students to join the Ride, she raced around Atlanta trying to raise enough money to go, too. Her appalled family and friends tried to dissuade her, but the headstrong teenager, money in hand, managed to get to Birmingham anyway. Now she and the others were bound for Montgomery.

As the bus pulled into the city's downtown terminal, the students peered from the bus's windows and saw a ghost town. Only when the Riders disembarked did people slip out of alleys and side streets and from around the corners of office buildings. There were hundreds of them, men, women, and children, carrying bats, chains, tire irons, bricks, and pipes. "Git them niggers!" several women screamed. The crowd fell on the fleeing Riders and the reporters who were there to cover them.

The male students tried to push the seven women into a cab, but the black driver refused to admit Susan Wilbur and Susan Hermann, who were white. It was against the law for him to have whites in his taxi, he shouted. When Wilbur and Hermann attempted to get into a second cab, members of the mob pulled the driver from his seat. As the cab containing the black women left the parking lot, the women looked back at the carnage. John Lewis was on the ground, beaten senseless. Another male Rider was being held by several men while women and children clubbed and clawed his face. Like a swarm of bees, others surrounded a stunned and dazed Susan Wilbur. One man was punching her while a woman hit her over the head with a shoulder bag.

At that moment, John Seigenthaler arrived on the scene from Birmingham. The woman with the shoulder bag knocked Wilbur down in front of Seigenthaler's car, and he jumped out to rescue her, elbowing his way through the mob. Grabbing Wilbur by the shoulders, he pulled her to her feet, yanked open the front passenger door of his car, and pushed her toward it. "Come on," he shouted, "get in the car!" Wilbur, who had no idea who Seigenthaler was, pleaded with him not to get involved. "Mister, this is not your fight," she said. "Please don't get hurt on account of me. I don't want anyone to get hurt. I'm nonviolent." Losing all patience with this display of Gandhian principles, Seigenthaler screamed, "Young lady, get in the damn car!" But it was too late. "Who the hell are you?" someone demanded of Seigenthaler, and just as he was explaining that he was a federal official, someone else fractured Seigenthaler's skull with a lead pipe. As the mob focused its rage on the man from the Justice Department, both Wilbur and Hermann managed to slip away. Pursued by several toughs, they made it to a nearby church, where the exhausted, panicked young women took asylum.

Virginia Durr had been watching all this from her husband's office overlooking the parking lot. She felt "absolute, stark terror" as she saw the melee unfold like a scene from a horror movie. "[T]he people who were shouting and holding up their babies to 'see the niggers run' were just ordinary Montgomery people who had come downtown on Saturday as they usually do," she said years later. "These were the people I was living among, and they were really crazy. . . . I still have nightmares about it sometimes."

In Nashville, Diane Nash and those helping her tried frantically to account for the whereabouts of all the Riders. Several, including John Lewis, were injured. Amazingly, no one was killed. As the battered students called in from wherever they had taken refuge, Nash directed them to a local minister's house. By early evening, all but those who were hospitalized had gathered there and were jubilantly celebrating their survival. News of the bloody confrontation had already swept across the country: The television networks were scrambling to get footage of the beatings on the air as quickly as possible, while newspaper editors were getting ready to run photos of the event on their next day's front pages. The Freedom Ride was big news again.

When he heard about the rampage, Martin Luther King flew in from Atlanta, as did James Farmer. As soon as she had accounted for all the students, Diane Nash came down from Nashville. They and the Riders assembled the following night for a mass meeting at Ralph Abernathy's First Baptist Church, along with more than a thousand Montgomery residents. The gathering, with its fervent singing and speeches, brought back memories of all the bus boycott mass meetings in Montgomery five years earlier. But there were differences: The earlier meetings did not have policemen, armed with arrest warrants, in front of the church; nor did they have a mob of whites outside, waving Confederate flags and screaming epithets at those within.

Downstairs at the church, King was on the phone to Robert Kennedy in Washington. The two men urgently discussed the mob and the future of the Freedom Ride, while Farmer, Abernathy, and other leaders clustered around King. But field marshal Diane Nash was nowhere in sight. She was undoubtedly the last person the Attorney General wanted to talk to, and King and the others never considered including her in their inner circle. Instead, she thought, they patronized her and pushed her aside. (She said decades later that she never would have put up with such treatment if it had occurred after her exposure to the women's movement.)

Kennedy urged that the Ride be stopped so that tempers could cool and so that the administration could gain time to try to work things out. Shaken by the violence and concerned that continuation of the trip into Mississippi might be considered needlessly provocative and thus antagonize possible white supporters, King was inclined to agree. "Don't you think that maybe the Freedom Ride has already made its point and now should be called off . . . ?" King asked Farmer. The CORE head would not commit himself until he had consulted with Nash, who flatly rejected King's suggestion. "No," she told Farmer, "we can't stop it now, right after we've been clobbered." Farmer returned to King. "Please tell the Attorney General that we have been cooling off for three hundred and fifty years," he said. "If we cool off any more, we will be in a deep freeze. The Freedom Ride will go on."

After more than eight hours of terror, in which the mob came close to invading the church, the National Guard finally arrived in the darkness of early morning. The exhausted congregation was escorted outside under armed guard, loaded into jeeps and trucks, and taken home.

As planning began for resumption of the Ride, Diane Nash nursed her anger over the way King and his cohorts had tried to exclude her from the decision making. She and the other students had been responsible for forcing the Kennedys into action, yet they had been ignored by everybody but Farmer. King and his men now acted as if the Ride were their show and were being treated by the media and administration as if that were true. The fact was, however, that before the new crop of Riders had left Birmingham for Montgomery, Nash had failed to persuade King to join them on the journey. When he first demurred, she and a couple of others kept pressing until he erupted: "Do not tell me when my time has come! Only God can tell me that! How dare you try and tell me!" He declined again in Montgomery when a group of students led by Nash urged him to board the bus when it left for Jackson, Mississippi.

Initially, James Farmer had decided not to go to Jackson either. There was too much to do back at the office, he told the CORE members who had joined the original Riders. But his real reason for choosing not to rejoin, as he confessed later, was his conviction that he would be killed if he did. "I was scared spitless," he said. Farmer was far from alone in believing that some Riders would die. As bad as Alabama had been, everyone was sure that Mississippi, unmatched for its brutality and hatred for blacks, would be far worse. John Lewis remembered how, growing up, he had heard all kinds of "unbelievably horrible things about Mississippi, stories of murders and lynchings, bodies dumped in rivers . . ." Staying alive in that deadly state would require every bit of ingenuity and courage Lewis and the others could muster.

On the morning of May 23, Farmer and King were at the station to say good-bye to the Riders. Farmer reached his hand through the window of one of the buses to shake hands with seventeen-year-old Doris Castle, a CORE member from New Orleans. After he wished her a safe journey, the petite teenager looked at him, her eyes wide. "But, Jim, you're going with us, aren't you?" she whispered. He said no and gave several excuses. She ignored them all. "Jim, please!" she implored. The appeal of this young girl, about to risk her life, shamed Farmer into action. Turning to an aide, he said, "Get my luggage and put it on the bus. I'm going."

When the bus finally headed for Jackson, the two-hundred-eighty-mile trip seemed more like the first stage of a military assault than a bus ride. Rifle-bearing National Guardsmen stood watch inside the bus; hundreds of National Guardsmen lined the highway all the way to Mississippi's capital. Helicopters clattered overhead. The Riders sat quietly, scribbling down the names of next of kin on stray pieces of paper, trying to ignore the clumps of bystanders they raced past, who were shaking their fists and screaming obscenities.

When the bus arrived in Jackson, Farmer looked out the window and saw a large crowd milling around the station. "I guess this is it," he said. "Let's go. We can't sit here and die." He got up and stepped down off the bus, all the while fighting a desperate urge to flee. Then Lucretia Collins, one of the original Riders from Nashville, linked her arm in his. "I couldn't duck and run," Farmer said later. "This pretty young lady had my arm. How could I run?" The two of them, their arms entwined, headed toward the crowd, which parted and allowed them to enter the station's white waiting room. There, they saw a cluster of reporters and policemen, one of whom ordered them to leave. When Farmer and Collins refused, they were arrested on charges of disturbing the peace, disobeying an officer, and inciting to riot. They were thrown into a paddy wagon, followed by the rest of the Riders.

When they arrived at the Jackson jail, they were met by cops who brandished their guns and shouted obscenities. As each Rider was taken into a room for questioning, those waiting outside could hear the sound of blows, followed by groans and crying. One after another, the Riders were found guilty in assembly-line trials and sentenced to a year in prison. Most refused bail and chose to stay in jail forty days, the longest they could serve time in Mississippi and still file an appeal. After their trials, they were herded from the courthouse to the Hinds County jail. On the way, they passed through a gauntlet of police clutching rifles, shotguns, and submachine guns. More police stood guard on nearby rooftops. By now Diane Nash was in Jackson, too, watching her friends and associates disappear into the jailhouse.

Nash had wanted to be on the bus with the first group—with John Lewis and Bernard Lafayette, with James Bevel, who had joined the crew in Montgomery—but they argued that she must continue directing the Rides, something she could not do from a cell. So she drove to Jackson with a lawyer for the Riders to observe what was happening and to report back to Nashville. She was alone, trying to keep track of all the Riders pouring in, making sure each was accounted for, in a place where blacks had been terrorized into silence. At first, Medgar Evers, Mississippi's NAACP head, was the only black leader in Jackson willing to help her, but she had to be very careful, since Evers' office was under heavy surveillance by state authorities. Nash felt like a spy operating behind enemy lines, passing occasionally for white, one of the few times in her life she did so on purpose.

*   *   *

As the first Freedom Riders disappeared into the maw of the Mississippi legal system, an emergency call went out from Nash, Anne Braden, and others for volunteers willing to head immediately for Jackson. Hundreds responded. Soon, groups of new Riders, black and white, began pouring into Jackson's bus stations from all over the country. About half of them were students. More than a hundred were women. As soon as they arrived, they headed for the whites-only waiting rooms and were immediately arrested and taken off to jail. There, they learned what the first Riders already knew: Mob terror, covered by the world's press, had been replaced by hidden violence. The streets of Jackson seemed calm enough, but in the jailhouse Mississippi was living up to its reputation.

With the mounting arrests, the cells of the county jail became massively overcrowded. In the beginning, Ruby Doris Smith occupied a four-bunk cell with thirteen other female Riders. Four more were packed in, six more after that. In the end, there were twenty-three women in a space the size of a small bedroom. Sweltering in the early summer heat, forced to use stopped-up toilets and eat bug-infested food, the women tried to keep up their spirits by sharing with each other their particular talents: One woman taught rudimentary Spanish, another taught beginning ballet steps. Above all, they sang. "The jailhouse rocked with the songs of Freedom Riders," said James Farmer. ". . . Jackson had never heard the likes of it before."

Two weeks later, a few hours before sunrise, the Riders were roused from their restless sleep, ordered out of their cells, and loaded onto trucks and paddy wagons. Not knowing where they were going, they sang then, too, to distract themselves from their fear. When the vehicles finally stopped at dawn, the passengers found themselves staring out at cotton fields worked by black convicts in black-and-white-striped prison clothes, watched over by mounted white guards carrying shotguns and bullwhips. In the dim, rosy light, four guard towers loomed, and razor-wire fences stretched to the horizon. For the crime of walking into a bus station waiting room, the Riders had been sent to one of the most fearsome penitentiaries in the South, a place whose brutality was made legend in the novels of William Faulkner and Eudora Welty and in the blues songs of Leadbelly and others who had done time there. Used as a bogeyman to scare the black children of Mississippi into being good, Parchman penitentiary was a twenty-thousand-acre prison farm in the middle of the Mississippi Delta, just a few miles from James Eastland's plantation. The only modern thing about the prison was its maximum security unit, a brick and concrete building built in 1954 to house its gas chamber and the cells for its most dangerous criminals. Maximum security was a place, said one former inmate, "where they just beat the living crap out of you. It was death row in one wing, crazy people in another wing and folks sent to be kicked and stomped in the rest." Maximum security was where the Riders were to be housed.

But first came the sexual humiliation of the Parchman admission procedure. Ushered into different rooms, under the scrutiny of guards with cattle prods, both men and women were ordered to strip naked for thorough body searches. The women endured rough, painful vaginal searches by female guards, who used the same gloves dipped in Lysol over and over in their "examinations." Issued striped prison dresses, the barefoot female Riders were sent to death row and assigned to cinder-block cells whose floors were carpeted with a layer of dead bugs at least half an inch thick.

Aware that Parchman was in the world spotlight, Mississippi governor Ross Barnett ordered prison authorities to refrain from flagrant physical violence to the Freedom Riders. But there were other ways to torment them. Once, as Elizabeth Wyckoff, a white classics professor from Vassar, was telling some Greek myths to her cellmates, a guard ordered her to be quiet. When she continued, the women's mattresses were taken away. In defiance, they sang "The Star-Spangled Banner." Then their sheets were removed. They kept on singing as their toothbrushes and towels were whisked away. When that didn't shut them up, the fans were turned off and the cell became a sweatbox. That night, cold air was forced into the cell, as the shivering women tried to sleep on the bare steel platforms of their bunks.

Most of the Riders, women and men, resisted the orders of their jailers at one time or another. Their nonstop singing drove the guards crazy, which only caused them to sing all the louder, their repertoire running the gamut from spirituals to rhythm and blues to rock and roll. As they sang, women prisoners taught each other the latest dance crazes—the Twist, the Watusi, the Hully Gully—gyrating madly in their cells.

Occasionally, a rabbi would come up from Jackson to visit, and many of the young women enjoyed the visits so much that they became, as one put it, "instant converts to Judaism." But the conversions had a decidedly secular motive. The women would cluster around the rabbi as he began chanting Hebrew prayers. When the bored guards tuned out, he would slip in news, in the same singsong drone, about what was going on in the country and the world, along with communications from their families. "Did you get your glasses?" he chanted to one young woman. To another, "Are you taking your medicine?" The women would chant back their replies. "He was our main contact with the outside world," said Rider Joan Trumpauer. "I don't know if the guards ever caught on to what we were saying . . ."

The good times, however, were more than balanced by the bad. As the weeks dragged on, the wet-blanket heat, execrable food, lack of exercise, harassment, and, above all, the intense boredom tested the prisoners' physical and emotional endurance. Most vulnerable were the later Riders, who had little or no training in the techniques and philosophy of nonviolent direct action. Riders like Judy Frieze of Newton, Massachusetts, who went directly from her Smith College graduation to Jackson, not fully realizing what she was getting into until she saw some of her fellow Riders writing wills and farewell letters on their way to the Mississippi capital. In Parchman, there was anger and fear, homesickness and depression, occasional fights, backbiting, and arguments. But for the most part, a spirit of camaraderie and community prevailed.

Following the philosophy of nonviolence to the letter, some of the Riders tried to draw their guards into that community. From their first day at Parchman, Marilyn Eisenberg, a Rider from California, and other women in her cell made it a point to speak to the matron in charge of their cubicle. Initially hostile and rough, the matron finally began to return their greetings. Then she responded to their jokes and allowed herself to be drawn into longer and longer conversations. "Before I left Parchman, she was singing for us on our make-believe radio programs and was often heard humming our freedom songs," Eisenberg recalled.

When their forty days were up, Eisenberg and the rest of the Riders departed the penitentiary, tired, dirty, some of them sick, all of them profoundly relieved. At the same time, there was a sense of exhilaration. They had come face-to-face with the beast, had stood their ground, and had survived. None of them would ever be the same, certainly not the more than one hundred women Riders, who had abandoned feminine respectability to wear convict's stripes in the most terrifying prison in the most terrifying state in the country.

On the day of James Farmer's release from Parchman, he stood outside its gates in a rumpled, dirty suit now a few sizes too large. As he waited for his ride, a van filled with a new crop of young white women Riders pulled up. The gate opened and the van disappeared inside, but not before the women recognized Farmer and waved, singing "We Shall Overcome" at the top of their lungs. "Jails were not a new experience for the Riders," Farmer later mused, "but the Freedom Riders were definitely a new experience for Mississippi jails."

The Riders' commitment to racial justice, their willingness to go to prison, drew others to their cause. Among them was Eleanor Roosevelt. Captivated by the student movement like her friend Lillian Smith, the former First Lady confided to her secretary one morning that she had had "the most wonderful dream last night, Maureen. . . . I dreamt I was marching and singing and sitting in with the students in the South." She supported the movement in her newspaper columns and her speeches, gave money to SNCC and CORE, and lambasted the Kennedys and the Democrats in Congress, both publicly and privately, for dragging their feet on civil rights.

When the Freedom Rides began, Eleanor Roosevelt was seventy-six years old and suffering from tuberculosis and aplastic anemia. She was bone tired, but, outraged by the mob violence in Birmingham and Montgomery and by the administration's failure to protect the Riders, she summoned up enough energy for one more fight. In May 1962, five months before her death, she chaired a CORE-sponsored conference in Washington to investigate the lack of government protection for the Riders, declaring at the meeting's beginning: "Never has a tinier minority done more for the liberation of a whole people than these few youngsters of CORE and SNCC."

With the Freedom Rides, civil rights activists had succeeded in alerting the world to the extent of racial injustice in the South. In doing so, they also had shifted their focus from scattered local movements to a common cause. Said one Freedom Rider: "There were a lot of little movements going into Parchman, but one big one coming out."

And, more than ever, it was the students who were setting the movement's pace. James Farmer had hoped the Rides would propel CORE and himself into the front lines of the civil rights fight, but, by jump-starting the Rides in Birmingham and continuing them for three months, Diane Nash and SNCC proved to be the shock troops of the movement. With the Rides, SNCC began transforming itself from a clearinghouse for local movements to an organization of sixteen full-time field workers and a distinctly confrontational identity. Large numbers of black and white students from all over the country, attracted by SNCC's daring, idealism, and courage, rallied to its banner.

The Freedom Rides marked the first influx of non-Southerners, both black and white, into the movement, and many stayed on after their term in Parchman. To young whites rebelling against what they saw as the materialism and moral ambiguity of American society, the civil rights cause seemed wonderfully unambiguous. There was no difficulty at all distinguishing the good guys from the bad.

Yet many other people in the country, including some of the nation's top newspaper and magazine editors, objected to the idea of an all-out civil rights revolution and the prospect of more confrontations, more violence. Sympathetic though they might have been to the goals of the movement, they, like the Kennedy administration, had seen the continuation of the Rides as needlessly provocative. The students "are challenging not only long-held customs but passionately held feelings," said a *New York Times* editorial. "Nonviolence that deliberately provokes violence is a logical contradiction." According to a Gallup Poll taken in June 1961, 63 percent of Americans disapproved of the Freedom Rides.

Diane Nash, of course, was having none of that. "I'm interested now in the people who call for gradualism," she said. "The answer, it seems to me, is to stop sinning and stop now! How long must we wait? It's been a century. How gradual can you get?" Freedom, she declared, "is worth the price you have to pay. And all of us are willing to pay that price."

That's what John and Robert Kennedy, deeply concerned about alienating their party's base in Dixie, were afraid of. It was time, the Kennedys believed, to press the students to tone down their protests. While the Freedom Rides were still going on, Robert Kennedy and Burke Marshall met with Nash and other members of the Rides' coordinating committee in the Attorney General's office. Nash repeated to Kennedy what she had already said publicly: "Here are people acting within their constitutional and moral rights; they have done nothing more than ride a bus or use a facility that anyone else would normally expect to use any day of the year, but they have been confined and imprisoned for it. And somehow the Attorney General and the President of the United States . . . can do nothing about such a gross injustice."

Bobby Kennedy swept her concerns and criticisms aside. He told the young activists that the Rides were accomplishing nothing. If the students really wanted to see the end of segregation in the South, he said, they should switch their emphasis from direct action confrontations to registration of black voters. And if they did that, they could rely on the administration's support and protection. Burke Marshall offered another carrot. If the students agreed to such a voter registration plan, said the head of the Justice Department's Civil Rights Division, they could count on getting thousands of dollars from charitable foundations interested in promoting civil rights. The administration already had a commitment from several foundations to support the proposal. And there was yet one more inducement: Government officials would make sure that male students working on voter registration would be exempt from the draft.

Nash was suspicious. To her, such a tempting cornucopia of promises meant nothing but trouble. Why were the Kennedys, who had done so little in the area of civil rights, getting involved now? They were trying to co-opt the student movement, she thought, trying to move it away from the confrontational tactics with which it had shaped its identity. Nash didn't oppose voter registration as such, but she did challenge the idea of its replacing nonviolent direct action as SNCC's chief tactic. "I became terrified that the Kennedys would take over and control the movement . . . ," she said. "If we started depending on the money from foundations and from Kennedy," the question would then become "Whose song do you sing?"

Adamant that SNCC should resist such blandishments, she was perturbed that some of her male colleagues at the meeting, Charles Jones and Chuck McDew among them, seemed receptive to the administration's promises. The way the male students welcomed the idea of draft exemptions "really scared me," Nash said more than thirty years later at a conference of former civil rights activists, "because, again, it represented control, and I had extreme objections to that." To that, Jones, who was also at the conference, retorted: "Diane wasn't facing the draft, bless her heart. We were." Nash shot back: "Yeah, but I was part of SNCC, and my life was on the line, and everybody's was . . . If there was an arrangement with the government, we all needed to know about it."

In fact, at the time of the meeting with the Attorney General, Jones and McDew were among several SNCC leaders already in the voter registration camp. The chief agent of their recruitment was Tim Jenkins, vice president of the National Student Association, who had close ties to SNCC as well as to Burke Marshall and the Kennedy administration. Jenkins, a recent Howard University graduate who was to attend Yale Law School that fall, had aligned himself totally with the Kennedy voter registration plan. Like the Kennedys, he believed that registering blacks to vote would not touch off the kind of resistance and violence engendered by the sit-ins and Freedom Rides. It seemed the perfect solution—putting African-Americans on the road to equality without stirring up racial tension and more political problems for the administration.

Jenkins persuaded a number of prominent SNCC activists, including McDew and Jones, that voter registration was the key to the organization's future. They were not from Nashville, and most didn't need much convincing. Like Nash, McDew, who would soon succeed Marion Barry as chairman of SNCC, was one of the few non-Southerners who had played a major role in SNCC from its founding. He considered himself a practical man, and he knew how much his organization, teetering close to insolvency, needed the infusion of funds promised by the Kennedy administration. In addition, the idea of moral suasion as a major weapon in the fight for racial justice seemed to him highly impractical.

For the rest of the summer of 1961, Jenkins, Jones, McDew, and their allies tried to convince Nash and her camp, which included Marion Barry, John Lewis, and James Bevel, of the wisdom of the voter registration position. The key was Nash, who adamantly refused to consider giving up the strategy that, until now at least, had served as the cornerstone of the student movement. The pressure on her was so intense that Nash suffered dizzy spells after these discussions. She did not realize until years later how condescendingly the voter registration proponents had behaved toward her. They were not as bad, from her point of view, as the Kennedy people or Martin Luther King and his men. Nash, after all, was a major figure in SNCC, which welcomed the participation and informal leadership of women, whose guiding force from the beginning had been a woman. Yet, if it had not been for the fact that "I was taken seriously by a lot of people . . . ," Nash recalled, some of the male leaders in SNCC "would have wiped me out." For all SNCC's respect for women, the men in the organization still were products of a time in which men were used to taking center stage and to dominating the opposite sex. "I was the only female in this group of good old boys, [and] sexism was a serious issue . . . ," Nash said some thirty years later. "They regarded me as this troublesome female who [was] a pain in the neck . . . and causing really unnecessary problems . . ."

Her refusal to consider jettisoning direct action as the main tactic of the student movement prompted the calling of a SNCC leadership meeting at the Highlander Folk School in August. For three days, the two sides thrashed out the issue in a debate that grew angrier and more hostile as the hours dragged on. Several of those attending had just been released from Parchman and were hardly in the mood to be told that the kind of confrontational tactics that had sent them to jail were no longer valuable.

For most of those three days, Ella Baker sat and listened, as she usually did, while the students shouted at each other. Finally, though, she couldn't take it anymore. Here were the leaders of her beloved SNCC about to tear the organization apart in this raging argument over its future. "Wait a minute," she said. "Doesn't nonviolence mean that we listen to our brothers and sisters?" She went even further, startling many of the students by violating her policy of staying out of their way and letting them come up with their own solutions. Why not a two-pronged attack? she asked. Why not have programs devoted to direct action *and* to voter registration?

Once they got down to the "nitty gritty," she predicted, they would discover no substantive difference in the two. Recalling that meeting years later, Baker dryly said she knew that if the students "went into these deeply prejudiced areas and started voter registration, they would have an opportunity to exercise nonviolent resistance. They began to see that they wouldn't have to abandon their nonviolence. In fact, they would be hard put to keep it up."

The SNCC leaders adopted Baker's suggestion, which, in the view of Anne Braden, saved the organization. "Diane and the rest were ready to leave," said Braden, who was present at the marathon meeting. "It would have been the end of SNCC, if Ella hadn't intervened." As Charles Jones saw it, "Ella reached out and pulled us lovingly back together."

At the end of the Highlander meeting, Nash was named to head SNCC's direct action wing, and Jones was put in charge of voter registration, with both projects deciding to focus their initial efforts on Mississippi. The voter registration faction had come up with an extraordinarily ambitious plan aimed at nothing less than upsetting the balance of political power in the United States by defeating the Southern barons who ruled Congress, many of whom represented predominantly black areas. If enough black voters could be registered in these congressional leaders' states, the political power of Southern racists could be ended forever. And what better place to begin waging that campaign than in the home state of the archfoe of civil rights, Senator James O. Eastland? No less audacious was the plan of the direct action team. Called "Move on Mississippi," it envisioned a massive campaign of sit-ins, boycotts, and other confrontational tactics aimed at the desegregation of every facility and institution in the state, from restaurants to schools to churches.

But while SNCC vowed commitment to both programs, it did not take long for voter registration to emerge as the organization's main thrust. It would continue to dominate until the mid-1960s. The Kennedys had gotten their way, but the outcome was not quite what they had envisioned. Having dismissed Nash and her allies for their naiveté and lack of knowledge about the real world, neither the Kennedy administration nor the SNCC advocates of voter registration had any idea of what they were getting into. Administration officials did not realize that while SNCC might agree to pursue voter registration, it would do so in its own uniquely confrontational way, heading immediately for the most implacably racist state in the Union. John Doar, the Justice Department official who worked most closely with SNCC organizers in the South, compared them with "young people who, when asked to go out and gather some firewood, immediately sink their ax into the biggest tree in the forest." And neither the government nor the students were prepared for the ferocity of Mississippi's resistance to SNCC's voter registration efforts.

Imbued with the gentleman's code of their Ivy League alma maters, the Kennedys and other top administration officials believed that it would be, as John Lewis put it, "morally difficult for even the most dedicated white supremacist to make a frank argument that Negroes should not be allowed to vote." But Southern segregationists had no interest in debate. They understood that the student activists wanted to topple them from power, and they fought back with every weapon they had, from beatings and jailings to burnings and murder. As it turned out, the sit-ins and Freedom Rides would be mild stuff compared with the drama and danger of trying to help rural blacks seize voting rights in the South. For the students under assault, the promises of government protection would come to be seen as a chimera. Disregarding Diane Nash's warnings that SNCC should not count on the administration as its ally, the voter registration leaders had put their trust in its pledge to support them, only to feel betrayed when government officials maintained they were powerless to intervene.

But all that was in the future. Now, SNCC workers were on their way to Mississippi. And they would find there, as they would find elsewhere in the South, that their direct action tactics, soon to be eclipsed, had become the stuff of legend. Stunned by the fact that young outsiders had stood up to the South's feared white establishment, rural blacks called all civil rights workers, whether they had seen the inside of a bus or not, by one common name—Freedom Riders.

"We Are Not Going to Take This Anymore"

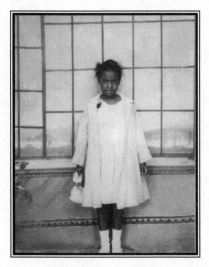

Jessie Divens, one of McComb's young activists

IN 1961, WHEN CIVIL RIGHTS workers set up shop in Mississippi, it was the poorest, most backward state in the Union. Its blacks lived and worked in conditions mimicking slavery and were made to understand that, for them, equality and freedom were unattainable dreams. As bad as the records of other Southern states were in regard to racial outrages, Mississippi's was worse. It had the largest number of lynchings, the most lynchings of women, the worst mob atrocities. Nearly six hundred blacks were known to have been lynched in Mississippi between 1880 and 1940. The actual number may have been far higher.

By the time of the *Brown* v. *Board of Education* decision in 1954, lynchings had become quite rare in other Southern states. Mississippi, however, had seven racial murders in 1955 alone, among them that of a fourteen-year-old-boy named Emmett Till. In 1959, a man named Mack Charles Parker, arrested for the rape of a white woman, was taken by a mob from his cell in Poplarville, beaten, shot, and thrown in chains into the Pearl River.

And just in case murder and intimidation didn't do the trick in keeping blacks servile, the Mississippi legislature in 1954 passed laws making it virtually impossible for would-be black voters to register. In addition to the longtime poll-tax requirement, applicants had to fill out a four-page form, including a section in which they had to copy and interpret an excerpt from Mississippi's constitution. The excerpt was chosen by the county registrar of voters, who was empowered to decide if the interpretation was acceptable. Blacks, no matter how highly educated, rarely seemed able to interpret the constitution to the liking of the registrars, whose own education in many cases did not reach even an eighth-grade level. Whites, on the other hand, were almost always able to satisfy the registrars' standards of constitutional scholarship.

For most Mississippi blacks, the idea of attempting to register to vote was as far-fetched as the hope of earning a profit on a cotton crop. Many could not read or write, and thus could not fill out the application. Isolated on plantations and farms, with no protection by the law, the impoverished blacks of Mississippi did everything they could to avoid conflict with whites, just to stay alive. Jane Stembridge called Mississippi "the ultimate in hatred, not that the hatred is of greater intensity, but that the hatred is everywhere and there *is* no escape."

All this, then, was what the young SNCC activists faced when they arrived in Mississippi. They had come to join forces with Bob Moses, a former math teacher from New York, who, at the urging of Jane Stembridge and Ella Baker, had traveled to Mississippi the year before to stir up interest in SNCC and the movement. Moses had set up a voter registration project in the tough little hill town of McComb, in the southwestern part of the state—dangerous country for anyone encouraging blacks to vote.

Still there'd been a small nucleus of black adults in McComb ready to help Moses, and he located another group of eager recruits almost as soon as he and a couple of other SNCC workers set up a voter registration school in the town's black Masonic Temple. They were students from McComb's Burgland High School, and most of them were girls. It was a pattern that would occur again and again, as the movement spread throughout the Deep South in the early 1960s. Almost invariably, the first group of local people to throw themselves wholeheartedly into civil rights work were teenagers, who, full of the fire of youth, were impatient with the caution shown by their elders. And at least in the beginning of the local movements, the majority often were girls, who had grown up relatively free of the fear of stepping out of line instilled from childhood in their brothers and male friends. "[T]he brunt of the violence in the South was directed toward the black male," noted James Bevel. "The females had not experienced that kind of negative violence, so they didn't have the kind of immediate fear of, say, white policemen as the young men did." Bevel's observation echoed what black sociologist E. Franklin Frazier wrote in the 1940s—that a black man in the South "is not only prevented from playing a masculine role, but generally he must let the Negro woman assume the lead in any show of militancy."

The local girls in the movement had been raised, for the most part, to be feisty and independent. "My mom brought me up to believe that I could do anything, that I could be anything I wanted to be," said Jacqueline Byrd, who was fourteen when Bob Moses came to McComb. One of ten children, Byrd was not inclined to let anyone, regardless of color, push her around. Not long before Moses' arrival in town, she had been in McCrory's five-and-dime store in downtown McComb. She stood in line to make a purchase, but whites kept pushing her aside "as if I had no value at all." Finally, a white girl not much older than Byrd told her, "Well, if you want to get waited on in this store, you'll have to say, 'Yes, ma'am,' and 'No, ma'am' to everyone here." Byrd looked at her. "No," she said. She put down the item she wanted to buy and stalked angrily out of the store. "I could have punched her lights out," she later told one of her brothers.

Byrd, Johnnie Wilcher, and Brenda Travis were among the students recruited to go door-to-door asking people to come to Bob Moses' voter registration school. Moses had already taught the students about the poll tax and instructed them on how to fill out the complicated registration form at the courthouse. Eager to share with others what they had learned, they were shocked and hurt when people they had known all their lives slammed the door on them or pretended not to be at home or, in at least one case, slapped a young canvasser. "We felt our own people were not really listening to something that was worthwhile," Byrd recalled. "It wasn't until I was an adult that I understood how afraid they were of losing everything."

One of those who felt most thwarted by the adults' reaction was fifteen-year-old Brenda Travis, whose lifelong rebellious spirit had finally found an outlet. Like Jackie Byrd, Travis did not tolerate insults from whites. Once at a bus stop, a white woman tried to elbow her out of the way. If

Travis didn't move, the woman said, she would slap her face. "Well, you can imagine what I told her," Travis recalled. "My best friend said, 'Girl, you're crazy!'" When the teenager got involved with the voter registration effort, her mother ordered her to stay home. She was told that "what I was doing was dangerous, and I should get all that mess out of my head." Travis ignored the warning. "I decided that I was going to do it anyway, and I did."

Not all the girls, however, let their parents know what they were doing. Ruby Divens, the mother of twelve-year-old Jessie Divens, was a cook for Phoebe Jones, a white woman in McComb. One day, Jones asked Ruby Divens if she knew Bob Moses. *No*, Divens replied. *Well*, said Jones, *your daughter sure knows Moses. She was over at the Masonic Temple the other day.* When Divens got home, she asked Jessie if she knew this outsider from the North. Jessie admitted she did. Her mother had told her never to talk to strangers, but Moses had brought hope and excitement to town, and Jessie wanted to be part of it. "I always knew I was equal to everybody else, and he had come to prove that to us," Jessie Divens said later. "To me, it was a revolution that had started . . . something I had to be a part of or just burst wide open."

For Jessie and the others, Moses' charisma had nothing to do with eloquence or oratory. More than anyone else in SNCC, Moses was the spiritual offspring of Ella Baker. Profoundly influenced by Baker's philosophy of leadership, he did not preach, did not tell people what to do. He listened to them, worked alongside them, became involved in their lives, convinced them they had the power to tear down the walls of segregation and to overcome racial injustice. "We would have followed him to the ends of the earth," said Jackie Byrd.

Jessie Divens certainly felt that way. Obeying the letter of her mother's instruction, if not the spirit, Jessie at first followed Moses wherever he went without engaging him in conversation. Finally, however, Moses' diminutive shadow could not restrain herself. Standing outside a cafe, watching him eat his lunch one day, she jerked the door open, walked in, and announced to Moses, "I'm Jessie, and I'm going to help you." When Ruby Divens found out about Jessie's involvement, she was frightened, but unlike Brenda Travis' mother, Divens did not forbid her daughter from canvassing. "I just didn't get on Jessie, like a lot of mothers . . . ," she said. "I figured that Jessie had a mind of her own. And a good mind, at that."

From then on, whenever Divens' employer asked her if she knew Moses yet, she always said no.

What is he teaching the children?

I don't know, was the invariable reply.

Jones took to sitting for hours on her front porch, waiting to see if Moses would pass by, "thinking, I guess, I'd holler, 'Hi, Bob!'" Ruby Divens said. "Everywhere you went them days, white folks was asking, 'Who is Bob Moses?'"

Besides the early participation of teenage girls, another pattern would soon become apparent to Moses and the organizers who followed him. Wherever they went, older local women would join the girls, many of whom were their daughters and granddaughters, in the vanguard of the movement. Warm, generous, and fearless, the older women served as role models for the younger ones. "Those women stood up to the system," said Jackie Byrd. "They talked back, and in the process, taught me how to be a strong woman." Local women also welcomed the young civil rights workers into their homes, feeding them, housing them, mothering them, and marching with them to the courthouse.

And they were almost always out front. "Violence is a fearful thing," said SNCC activist Avon Rollins. "People don't realize how frightened you get. I remember . . . where the words wouldn't come out of my mouth, where my teeth were just crushing together, chattering because the fear was so strong in me, not knowing what was going to happen. Then I'd see these black females out there, and I knew I couldn't let them take the beating, and the words would come out, and I would make my stand."

But, more often than not, women took the beatings, too. They risked all they had—their families, their homes, their jobs, their lives—in this chancy fight for equality. Many said they were on the front lines because it was too dangerous for men to be there, that men would be killed for doing what they were doing. It was generally thought that Southern whites did not see black women, who worked in their houses and took care of their children, as much of a threat. But racists in Mississippi, as in the rest of the South, did not seem to share that point of view, never thinking to spare women in their terrorist campaigns. Women lost their jobs; their houses were bombed and torched; they were shot, beaten up, and thrown into jail. Family members were assaulted. If no black women activists lost their lives in the movement, many came perilously close to doing so. "I think the women *were* stronger," said Ivanhoe Donaldson, another SNCC organizer. "Many of the men were beaten down."

Hardships were nothing new for these women. Toughened by poverty, brutal racism, and myriad other forms of adversity, they believed that the civil rights struggle held out the glimmering hope of a better life—for them, but, more important, for their children and grandchildren. "You could see it in their eyes and hear it in their voices," said Fred Powledge, who covered the movement for *The Atlanta Journal* and later *The New York Times*. "They were standing up, saying, 'I'm not going to take any more of this shit. Send me to jail, shoot me, but no more.' It was the fiercest, most courageous, heaviest battering ram against segregation in the whole movement."

Few of the women activists in Mississippi had to be pushed very hard to get involved. Like Rosa Parks in Montgomery and countless other black women throughout the South, many had already been involved in their own battles for freedom; the movement was the same war on a larger battlefield. Among them was Aylene Quinn, who owned a popular diner in McComb called South of the Border. One day, an NAACP activist came by to tell her Moses was in town. If Moses should drop in, the man said, Quinn should feed him, even if he happened to find himself without any money. Quinn did not need any convincing. An NAACP member, she had long wanted to register to vote; in fact, she had paid her poll tax eight years before and tried to register two years after that, as the law required, but was told she had not passed the test.

When Moses did drop in at South of the Border, Quinn not only welcomed him, she soon transformed her little neighborhood cafe into a hub of movement activity. She knew the risks and understood how vulnerable she was to official retribution. Mississippi was a dry state by law, but the law was universally flouted. Like many restaurant owners, white and black, Quinn sold liquor under the table. Everybody knew it, including the local police, whom she regularly paid off. She wasn't comfortable breaking the law, but she had children to support and educate. "I seen where I could make a living, and that's what I did," she said. "And if I could outsmart the law, I did that." But she knew, as she got even more deeply involved in Moses' voter registration work, that it was only a matter of time before the law struck back.

While most blacks in McComb seemed to want little to do with Moses and his voter registration school, sixteen residents gathered enough courage to attend the school and then go down to the county courthouse in Magnolia in early August to take the test. To everyone's surprise, six passed and were registered. Impressed, local activists in Amite and Walthall counties, where no blacks had been permitted to register in anyone's memory, persuaded Moses to come and work his magic in those areas. On August 15, he took three blacks to the Amite County courthouse in Liberty, where all three were turned away and Moses himself was arrested and sent to jail for a night. Fourteen days later, he returned to Liberty with another small group and was badly beaten outside the courthouse by a cousin of the sheriff.

When he returned to McComb, his head swathed in bandages, he found the Masonic Temple in an uproar. Fresh from the Highlander free-for-all, a dozen SNCC activists had descended on the town, and the direct action advocates, led by Marion Barry, had recruited several local young people for nonviolent protests. Indeed, the first demonstration—a sit-in at the lunch counter of the downtown Woolworth's—had already taken place, ending with the arrests of two of the protesters, Curtis Hayes and Hollis Watkins.

Many students in McComb, including the impetuous Brenda Travis, were fired up by the drama and excitement of direct action. Moses was less than enthusiastic. He had asked SNCC to send people to help with the voter registration project, not to conduct sit-ins. Such protests would inflame the area's hard-core racists—who, as far as Moses was concerned, were inflamed enough as it was—and might also antagonize the middle-class, middle-aged NAACP activists who had invited him to McComb in the first place. Moses, however, did not feel he could order Barry and the others to desist. So planning for the next sit-in went ahead, with Brenda Travis determined to play a part.

Because the SNCC organizers had decreed that demonstrators must be eighteen or older, the fifteen-year-old lied about her age to Barry, who approved her participation. On August 30, with a toothbrush and a fresh set of underwear in her purse, she and two young men set out for the train station and its whites-only waiting room. The police knew of their plan and kept the demonstrators under surveillance. When the young people got to the station, they found the door locked. They proceeded to Woolworth's, where the lunch counter waitresses were conducting a sit-in of their own, occupying all the stools to prevent the demonstrators from sitting down. Undeterred, the three walked over to the Greyhound bus station, where they had less than a minute to enjoy the air-conditioning in the white waiting room before they were arrested. That first night in jail, Travis felt more exhilaration than fear. "To be honest," she said later, "I was really excited because there wasn't much going on in McComb . . . so this was sort of like the highlight of our being, the highlight of our existence . . ." The only thing she worried about was what her mother would say when she found out.

Stunned by Travis' arrest, black McComb received an even greater shock when she was sentenced to four months in jail. The idea of a young girl behind bars with violent criminals was horrifying, and Mrs. Quinn and

other women in town did what they could to support her, including bringing in food to her and the young male activists who were jailed with her.

After a month, Travis was released, and her classmates at Burgland
High School rallied around her. She had not been a student leader at Burgland, but now she was the one they all looked up to. She had missed the
first month of the new school year, and there was a rumor afloat that Burgland's principal, hoping to appease the town's whites, did not intend to
readmit her. The night before she tried to return to school, SNCC staged
a mass meeting, during which James Bevel, in town from Jackson, ignited
the crowd with his spellbinding exhortation for more direct action. Many
of Travis' fellow students were at the meeting and, fired up by Bevel's oratory, held a rump session afterward to decide what to do if Travis was
turned away from Burgland. If that happened, declared Johnnie Wilcher,
they must all walk out behind her. Everyone agreed. After making some
protest signs and hiding them in the Masonic Temple, they went home to
await the morning.

When Travis reported to school the next day, she was indeed told by
the principal that she could not return. At a school assembly later that
morning, a senior named Joe Lewis stood up and asked the principal what
he was going to do about Brenda. If she was not readmitted, Lewis said,
the rest of the students would walk out. As the principal began to remon-
strate, the students stamped their feet, clapped their hands, and yelled.
Suddenly, more than two dozen got to their feet and marched out of the
auditorium. Outside, they decided they needed more students if their
demonstration was going to have real impact. So they returned to the
school and its adjacent junior high, bursting into the classrooms and urging the students to come with them. "The teachers said, 'Get away from
here ... You can't pull anybody else out,'" recalled Annie Pickett, one of the
ringleaders. "We said, 'Come on.' . . . The kids ran out after us." As teachers braced themselves in the classroom doorways, attempting to block
their charges from leaving, the students, some as young as eleven and
twelve, wriggled through their legs and under their outstretched arms.
Watching her fellow students pour out of the building, Jackie Byrd had the
unsettling feeling that she and they were about to change their lives, leaving behind everything that was comfortable and familiar, and heading off
into "something totally unknown." When one student said nervously, "My
parents are going to kill me for doing this," another responded, "If we do
this, then they will have to follow us."

More than one hundred students formed themselves into a ragged line
outside the building. Their leaders decided they would march all the way

to the county seat in Magnolia, but first they had to stop off at the Masonic Temple to pick up their signs. As they started out, the older students walked up and down the line, giving a quick primer in the discipline of nonviolence, urging the younger students to keep their cool.

At the temple, meanwhile, SNCC leaders had gathered from throughout the South to hold their fall executive committee meeting. It had been Ella Baker's idea: to close ranks, after the wounding Highlander sessions, in a place where the two SNCC wings had already joined forces.

Engrossed in debate in a second-story room at the Masonic Temple, the SNCC leaders first heard the faint strains of "We Shall Overcome," then were confronted by a swarm of teenagers who had come to claim their placards. Although some of the SNCC people had covertly encouraged the walkout, others, including Bob Moses, were opposed, fearing the kids would be chewed up by McComb's racists. Still, in the face of so much youthful determination, the SNCC grown-ups felt they had little choice but to join the march. "We have to direct these kids," said Chuck McDew, "or they're going to get their heads busted . . ."

Outside, the SNCC people organized the Burgland students into a double line, girls on the left, boys on the right. Instead of going all the way to Magnolia, they were persuaded to march to McComb City Hall. Remain on the sidewalk, they were told. Don't talk back to the police or anybody else. Stay off the grass. And so they set off, singing lustily, waving their banners, a bunch of black kids marching defiantly toward the downtown of one of the meanest, most violent places in the South. When they got to the red-brick, white-pillared City Hall, they found a large crowd of whites, cursing and yelling and shaking their fists. As she looked up, Annie Pickett saw a noose dangling in a front window. Undeterred, the students, one by one, climbed the steps to pray. "Throw those niggers in jail," roared someone in the crowd. The police promptly complied.

After spending several hours in jammed cells, the marchers under eighteen were released to the custody of their parents. While some parents were furious, most were supportive. When Annie Pickett's mother came to pick her up, one of the policemen told her, "Grace, we want you to have that girl back here for court." A bootlegger, Grace Pickett knew the cop well, since she paid him off regularly. She said, "I'd rather for a snake to spit in my face than you say anything to me. Come on, Annie May." With her daughter in tow, Mrs. Pickett marched out of the station.

Ruby Divens retrieved her daughter, Jessie, from jail. She was nervous about the repercussions but by now she endorsed what Jessie was doing even though her husband, Jessie's stepfather, had already lost his garbage-collecting job because of it. (A few nights later, dynamite was thrown at a house across the street from the Divenses', and cars filled with white men were parked in front of their house early in the morning. Night after night, Ruby Divens stayed up until dawn, a shotgun in her lap.)

When Aylene Quinn's daughter, Caroline, returned home after her brief time in jail, she was treated like "a big star." She asked for a glass of milk, even though she usually did not drink milk, because "I thought that since I had been in prison—that was what I should drink." Her family's reaction, she said, "was wonderful. My mother was very proud of me."

There was no such hero's reception for the SNCC activists, who stayed in jail for several days before their release on bail. When they got out, they discovered that most of the students who took part in the march had been expelled from Burgland after refusing to sign a pledge that they would never get involved in such action again. The SNCC organizers set up a makeshift high school at the Masonic Temple, and later arranged for them to attend at Campbell College, a black school in Jackson.

The students' lives had been turned upside down. For many, the idea of spending more than six months in Jackson, separated from everything that was familiar, was even more frightening than the walkout and march. Thirteen-year-old Willie Martin, for one, had never spent a night away from home in her life, and now she would be apart from her close-knit family, in a strange city, for what seemed an eternity. "I was terrified," she recalled, "but it was something I believed in, something I had to do."

Jessie Divens was too young to attend the classes at Campbell, so she and a few others attended a Catholic school in Jackson, riding city buses to and from classes. Jessie had never ridden a municipal bus before, and on one of her first days in Jackson she sat in the front seat on the way to school. When a white woman got on a few stops later, the bus driver yelled, "All the niggers go to the back." Jessie had been poised to get up and give the woman her seat, not because she was white but because she was older, but when she heard the driver's demand, she sat back down again. He repeated his order, and she replied, "I paid my money just the same as she did. I am not budging out of this seat." At the next stop the driver got off the bus and summoned the police, who arrested Jessie and carted her off to jail.

The defiance of this tiny girl, who looked considerably younger than twelve, threw the Jackson legal system, and SNCC, into an uproar. A city judge threatened her with reform school if she didn't apologize and promise never to disobey the city's segregation laws again. Jessie refused. No one could get her to change her mind—not the judge, not the lawyer SNCC had retained for her, not James Forman, SNCC's new executive sec-

retary, who had come from Atlanta to mediate the crisis. "They kept asking me, 'Are you going to do what we're telling you to do?'" she recalled.
"I told them, 'No, just lock me back up, and let's forget the whole thing.'"
Stymied, the Jackson authorities and the SNCC leader finally reached a
compromise: Jessie would stay in Jackson and out of reform school, but she
would be sent to a new school. A school that she could attend without having to ride the bus.

Brenda Travis was not so fortunate. Clearly wanting to make an example of her, a judge in McComb sentenced the fifteen-year-old to an inde-
terminate term in reform school on the grounds that, by marching with the
other students, she had violated the probation she had been granted after
her sit-in conviction. She ended up spending more than six months there.

The sentence infuriated McComb's blacks, and many blamed SNCC.
Adding to the anger and fear was the September murder of Herbert Lee,
a farmer in Amite County, who had been helping Moses with voter registration. Moses and the others realized that, for the time being at least, their
voter registration campaign was dead in McComb and the outlying counties. They retreated to Jackson, and made plans to head north, to the Delta.

McComb, meanwhile, seemed to return to its somnolent, pre–children's
crusade racism. Appearances, however, were deceptive. As Jessie Divens
pointed out, things started changing the day that "children reared in
this community publicly stood up and went against the grain and said,
'We are not going to take this anymore. And here we are. Deal with it.'"
Imbued with a passion for freedom, Jessie, Jackie Byrd, Annie Pickett, Caroline Quinn, and all the other young McComb activists bided their time,
waiting for the outsiders' return to stoke the fires of rebellion once more.
"It was a job incomplete," Divens said. "It was a job that had to be done.
And because we were kind and loving to them, I knew they would come
back."

When they did reappear in 1964, McComb would erupt in an even
greater wave of terror and violence.

SNCC's assault on McComb was just one campaign in "Move on Mississippi," the war against segregation that the direct action wing was planning to wage in the state. In Jackson, Diane Nash, along with James Bevel
and Bernard Lafayette, attempted to recruit high school and college students as the vanguard for the mass protests they had in mind. Terrified,
however, by the almost certain repercussions of getting involved in
protests, most blacks in Jackson wanted nothing to do with the young
integrationist outsiders. When SNCC sent a group of kids out to demon-

strate and sit in, the Jackson authorities cracked down on the outsiders from Nashville, not the young protesters. Bevel, Lafayette, and Nash were arrested, and convicted of "contributing to the delinquency of minors" for encouraging youths under eighteen to violate the segregation laws in Mississippi. They each received two-year prison sentences, which they promptly appealed.

In the midst of all this, Diane Nash, the incandescent beauty of the student movement, married its most controversial hell-raiser, James Bevel. Many of their colleagues were confounded by the news. "Diane and *Bevel?*" Julian Bond asked incredulously when he found out. Every man in the movement, it seemed, had had a crush on Nash at one time or another. Every man, Stokely Carmichael said, wanted to marry her. But the one who actually captured this proper, middle-class Midwest native was a quarrelsome, woman-chasing cyclone of energy from Itta Bena, Mississippi, a thoroughgoing eccentric who wore a yarmulke and claimed to hear the voice of God. In many ways, however, their union made perfect sense. They had the same intensity, the same ardent commitment to nonviolent direct action, a commitment that bordered on obsession. Both had no patience with the pragmatism of their SNCC coworkers. They opposed making political deals with the Kennedy administration. This was a holy crusade, and in their view, one couldn't be a politician and a crusader, too. As would be true of other movement love affairs and marriages, Bevel's and Nash's passion for each other was inextricably tied to their passion for the movement. For the moment, at least, both passions would serve to mask their obvious differences (not to mention Bevel's incessant philandering).

Nash's marriage effectively ended her position of leadership in the movement. From that point on, the dynamic young woman who had led the Nashville sit-ins and saved the Freedom Rides was eclipsed by her charismatic husband, who soon would join the staff of SCLC. "Bevel's a genius," observed SNCC organizer Ivanhoe Donaldson. "He's crazy but he's a genius. He's overwhelming, and I think he just overwhelmed Diane. And so she faded into his background while his star was out there shining."

She had been one of the most daring, creative, committed leaders of the student civil rights movement, as well as a brilliant strategist and tactician. But she was also a young woman who had grown up in the conservative 1950s. Independent and strong-minded as she was, she had been raised with the notion that a wife should defer to her husband, even if that wife once had stood up to the President and Attorney General of the United States. She became pregnant almost immediately after their marriage, and while she remained a key behind-the-scenes strategist, she soon had to juggle her movement work with the responsibilities of caring for her infant daughter and her husband. Yet before the baby was born, Nash showed once again the dramatic inventiveness for which she was famed.

In the spring of 1962, when she was five months pregnant, she announced she was abandoning the appeal of her conviction in Mississippi and would go to prison for two years. She was upset that most movement activists had abandoned the "jail, no bail" policy that she and other SNCC activists had implemented by spending thirty days in the Rock Hill jail the previous year. Especially disappointing to her was the fact that Martin Luther King had been quickly bailed out of jail in Albany, Georgia, a couple of months before. Nash asked Anne Braden to help get the word out about what she was doing. As much a purist as Nash, Braden felt a deep kinship to the younger woman, knowing full well the conflicts implicit in being a wife and mother as well as a civil rights activist. "As I think you know, I have a special sense of identification with Diane and will be willing to do anything you want me to in order to make her sacrifice more meaningful," Braden wrote to James Bevel.

She helped Nash write an open letter to explain her determination to go to jail and to urge others to follow her example. "I can no longer cooperate with the evil and corrupt court system of this state," Nash declared. "Since my child will be a black child, born in Mississippi, whether I am in jail or not, he will be born in prison. I believe that if I go to jail now, it may help hasten that day when my child and all children will be free—not only on the day of their birth but for all their lives." Nash's statement, circulated by Braden and widely publicized in the black press, hit the civil rights movement—and Mississippi authorities—like a jolt of electricity. Nash was well on her way to becoming a martyr in the eyes of the American public, and state officials wanted none of it. Judge Russell Moore, who had imposed the initial prison sentence, begged her to continue with her appeal, but she refused. The judge asked Bevel to intercede with her.

"Judge Moore, you don't understand Christianity," Bevel said. "All the early Christians went to jail."

Answered the judge: "Maybe so. But they weren't all pregnant and twenty-one."

In the end, Nash served only ten days—for refusing to move from the white side of the courtroom. Moore simply refused to implement the earlier sentence.

12

"The Cobwebs Are Moving from My Brain"

Septima Clark and Rosa Parks

IT WAS A BEAUTIFUL, BUCOLIC setting for the boot camp of a revolution. Majestic live-oak trees, draped with Spanish moss, sheltered the handsome brick buildings of Dorchester Center from the blinding rays of the sun. Inside, in the cool dimness, ordinary folks—sharecroppers, beauticians, storekeepers, and the like—were taught how to teach others to read, write, and, not incidentally, protest.

Located near the Georgia coast, some thirty miles south of Savannah, Dorchester was the nerve center of the citizenship schools, which by 1962 had become the foundation of the movement's voter registration drive in the Deep South and the engine for transforming the fight for civil rights into a mass crusade. Under the motherly tutelage of Septima Clark, would-be citizenship teachers from all over the South, many of them barely literate themselves, learned the rudiments of teaching basic literacy and political skills to their friends and neighbors back home.

On the surface, what went on at this former Congregationalist retreat did not seem so earthshaking. Clark and those who worked with her simply adopted the methods that she had employed for years to teach literacy to adults, using practical materials like Sears order forms, voter registration material, money orders, driver's license exams, and checks. But even a little knowledge could pose a threat to white supremacy, as the antebellum South understood full well. Most Southern states had made it a crime to teach slaves how to read and write, realizing that knowledge fostered independence and thinking for oneself. Learning about civil rights, politics, and government was even more subversive. Fannie Lou Hamer, one of the many rural women who went to Dorchester and later became civil rights leaders in their communities, had no idea that she had any rights of her own until she encountered the movement, an ignorance typical of other rural Southern blacks. "I never learned anything about voting or democracy in school," she said. "I never even heard what was in the Constitution." At Dorchester, Clark would draw a diagram on the blackboard, with "the government at the head and all the people who would come under. Then on down to the masses, [to] show how you too can become a part of this great governing body, if you will register and vote."

It was like a chain letter, blacks from all over the South being taught that they had the power to change their lives and then going back home and passing the word along. At Dorchester, "people would speak. They would unburden themselves, talk about what they had lost, about what they wanted, about how they had come to be there," reported Dorothy Cotton, who worked with Clark. "One woman said, 'The cobwebs are moving from my brain.' That's how it felt to all of us." Cotton added: "People stayed in these workshops five days and returned home doing things they had never dreamt they would do."

Some of them, however, had doubts in the beginning. When Victoria Gray returned home to Hattiesburg, Mississippi, after her week at Dorchester, she wondered, on the night of her first citizenship class, how she and her six students, most of them elderly, could change anything in that bulwark of racism. They sang "We Shall Overcome" at the end of class, and as they were singing, Gray glanced around at her students, "two or three who were learning their ABCs, for all practical purposes; another two or three who were just a little bit further on than that." *We shall overcome?* she thought. *This is the most ridiculous thing I've ever seen. What are we going to overcome?* But when Hattiesburg became a hotbed of civil rights activity several months later, Gray's citizenship school students were in the thick of the action. The class "freed those people," Gray said. "They became convinced they had rights. And once they realized it was their birthright to be participants in policymaking, they asked, 'If that's the case, why don't I have that right? Why aren't I doing what I have the right to be doing?' And they set out to change things."

Like her friend Ella Baker, Septima Clark had a genius for convincing people that they themselves could be leaders, that they did not have to depend on others to show them the way. So it was more than slightly ironic that the citizenship school program at Dorchester, while directed by Clark, was under the aegis of the Southern Christian Leadership Conference and Martin Luther King, whose philosophy of leadership could not have been more radically different.

In the late 1950s, Ella Baker, while still at SCLC, had tried to persuade King to adopt a citizenship school program like the one Clark had started at the Highlander Folk School. King had little enthusiasm for the idea then. In 1961, Highlander, which had been harassed and investigated by the Tennessee legislature for years because of its civil rights work, was on the brink of being shut down by the state. Myles Horton, Highlander's cofounder, urged King to take over administration of Clark's citizenship school. This time, the prospect was appealing to the SCLC leader because, among other things, it would attract foundation money to his organization. That spring, at the age of sixty-four, Clark joined the SCLC staff as director of education and teaching, responsible primarily for the citizenship school program. Her alliance with King and SCLC would be an uneasy one. Never as outspoken as Ella Baker, Septima Clark nonetheless was a strong-willed, independent woman who did not hesitate to point out in her gentle way what she considered to be the folly of King's and the other SCLC leaders' authoritarian rule.

Septima Clark grew up in Charleston, South Carolina, the daughter of a woman who, unlike her husband, had never been a slave and who never let her family forget it. Clark's mother, who had been born in Charleston but reared in Haiti by her two brothers, was afraid of no one and taught her children to follow her example. "[S]he wanted you to be able to stand your ground, regardless of where you were or whatever happened," Clark remembered. Her mother, who took in washing, was proud that she never had worked directly for whites, and she and her husband refused to allow their daughters to work in white households. "Being in a white home might lead to temptation with the white man of the house or even delivery boys," Clark said. "'They might mark your legs,' my mother would say." It was her way of warning against sexual assault.

After she finished high school, Clark became a teacher on Johns Island, a tiny spot in the Atlantic just off the South Carolina coast. She stayed there three years, teaching children during the day and, on her own time, instructing adults at night after they came in from the fields. It was on Johns Island that she developed her methods for teaching illiterate adults, basing their learning on their life experiences and their own needs, rather than on primers that featured pictures of white children and their pets ("See Spot run").

In 1918, at the age of twenty, Clark joined the NAACP, and the following year came back to Charleston to teach in the school that she had attended as a child. In 1922, she married a sailor named Nerie Clark. She loved children (in the area where she grew up, she was known as Little Ma because she mothered all the neighborhood kids), and she was distraught when her first child, a girl, lived only twenty-three days. Shortly thereafter, she got pregnant again and moved to Dayton, Ohio, with her husband. She was in the hospital, after giving birth to a son, when she discovered that her husband was living part-time with a mistress in Dayton. He asked Septima to leave the city as soon as she was able, and she complied. Ten months later, Nerie Clark died. To add to all these emotional hammer blows, Clark, like so many other black women, had to leave her ten-month-old son with his grandmother while she went back to work in Columbia, South Carolina. She was devastated by the fact that economic necessity prevented her from raising the boy she loved so much, and at the end of her visits to him, she would burst into uncontrollable tears. Unable to mother her own child, she would, in later years, become a mother figure for anyone who needed her care.

She eventually returned to teaching in Charleston, and earned a bachelor's degree, then a master's. She became even more involved in the NAACP, working to equalize the salaries of black teachers with those of whites. In the course of her burgeoning civil rights activism, she entered into an unlikely friendship with a white federal judge, the scion of one of Charleston's most patrician families, and his attractive second wife. Once a key figure in the city's social and civic life, Judge J. Waties Waring was the second most hated person in Charleston in the late 1940s, when Clark came to know him. His Northern wife, Elizabeth, was the first.

Something happened to sixty-one-year-old Waties Waring when he became a federal judge in 1942. Until then, he had lived his life as custom demanded, practicing law in a prestigious Charleston firm, living in a historic old house on Meeting Street, belonging to all the right clubs, married for thirty-two years to a woman with the same impeccable social credentials as he. He was a true son of the Old South, devoted to its credo of white supremacy, and nobody—certainly not South Carolina's two racist senators, who blessed his appointment to a federal judgeship—ever thought he would be anything but.

However, becoming a federal judge, with all the job's responsibilities and freedom, seemed to touch off a restlessness in Waring. In 1945, he shocked Charleston society by divorcing his wife and marrying Elizabeth Avery, a woman fifteen years his junior from Connecticut, who had taken to spending her winters in Charleston. For the ruling elite of the city, the divorce and remarriage were bad enough; the refusal of the judge's assertive, independent new wife to adopt a Southern lady's demure demeanor made matters even worse. But the final straw was Waring's stunning change of heart on race, and the crucial role played by Elizabeth Waring in that transformation. After their marriage, the transplanted Yankee read everything she could find on race relations, including *The Mind of the South* by W. J. Cash and *An American Dilemma* by Gunnar Myrdal. In the evening, she gave the books to her husband to read. Until then, he had not given much thought to the South's treatment of blacks, but these books' description of the inequality and injustice they faced greatly disturbed him. "I'd put the books down, so troubled I couldn't look at them," he later remarked. He and his wife would then "get in our car and drive through the night, miles and miles, just thinking and talking."

Over the next few years, his views on race underwent a seismic shift, and his behavior in court, not to mention his rulings, reflected that change, causing consternation and fury throughout the South. Waring outlawed segregated seating in his courtroom, hired a black bailiff, ordered that racial designations be stricken from lists of prospective jurors. He ruled in favor of equal pay for black and white teachers, the cause for which Septima Clark had been fighting, and struck down as unconstitutional the state's attempts to bar blacks from voting in Democratic primaries. "It is time for South Carolina to rejoin the Union," he declared in his ruling on white primaries. "It is time to . . . adopt the American way of conducting elections." Assigned one of the cases that would eventually be grouped together and presented to the Supreme Court as *Brown v. Board of Education*, Waring persuaded Thurgood Marshall and the other NAACP lawyers to jettison their early argument for "separate but equal" schools and directly challenge the constitutionality of school segregation.

Waring was even more outspoken off the bench, attacking segregation as "unreasonable, unscientific, and based upon unadulterated prejudice" and decrying what he called "the sickness" of Southern society. His wife voiced similar views. Elizabeth Waring was such a pariah in Charleston that when Septima Clark invited her to speak at the city's black YWCA, Clark came under intense pressure to withdraw the invitation for fear that local white civic leaders who gave money to the Y would cut off its funding. Despite a flood of obscene phone calls and phone threats, Clark refused to disinvite Mrs. Waring, just as she later resisted pressure from the principal and other teachers at the school where she worked to stop associating with the Warings.

Mrs. Waring's speech at the Y proved even more incendiary than expected. A condemnation of the "decadence" of white Southerners, it was printed verbatim in local newspapers, and from then on, the Warings were subjected to a nonstop barrage of harassment and abuse. A cross was burned on their lawn, a block of cement hurled through their living-room window. The judge received so many threats that he couldn't go anywhere without a bodyguard, and Elizabeth Waring was shoved and jostled on the street. All Waring's old friends had long since shunned him, and the only people in Charleston who would associate with him and his wife were blacks financially or emotionally secure enough to ignore warnings to stay away from the Warings.

Most of the couple's new friends were members of Charleston's black elite—lawyers, doctors, ministers, businessmen, who were independent of white financial support. All but Septima Clark. She had no economic security—as a public school teacher, she was paid by the state—but she did have an abundant supply of loyalty and courage. If she had any uneasiness about her friendship with the Warings, it stemmed from her association with the couple's other black friends, not with the judge and his wife.

In this socially stratified city, the caste system for blacks was as rigid as it was for whites. Whites' identity and social status depended on their family lineage; that of blacks was dependent on the bloodlines of the white families who owned them during slavery, or of the white men who had fathered their ancestors. The black upper crust of Charleston tended to be light-skinned and straight-haired, and not inclined to befriend someone like Septima Clark, who was dark, had kinky hair, and was the daughter of a washerwoman.

Clark had a tangle of emotions about her encounters with these people. On the one hand, she tried to measure up to their standards of proper dress and behavior—when she went to the Warings', she always felt she needed to get her hair straightened beforehand and wear a new dress, even though Elizabeth Waring told her none of that was necessary. On the other hand, this intensely proud woman deeply resented being considered socially unacceptable, especially by members of her own race. After being entertained several times at the Warings', she insisted that the judge and his wife, along with a couple of their black friends, come for tea at her modest home before she would agree to go to the Warings' again.

Clark remained a staunch champion of Waties and Elizabeth Waring for the rest of their lives. In 1952, the judge retired and, with his wife, moved to New York City, where they died within a few months of each other in 1968. Both were buried in Charleston. There were two hundred blacks and twelve whites at his funeral; nine blacks and no whites at hers. "She said she didn't want none of the hypocrites at her funeral—and she didn't have any," said Clark, who attended both services.

By the mid-1950s, Septima Clark had acquired a reputation as somewhat of an agitator, a person to be wary of if one wanted to stay out of trouble. Not only was she an NAACP activist and a friend of the hated Warings; she had started spending her summers at Highlander, that supposed hotbed of Communist activity in the Tennessee hills. The good citizens of Charleston would have been even more unsettled if they had known that in the summer of 1955, Clark, during a Highlander workshop on leadership, had helped inspire Rosa Parks to challenge segregation on Montgomery buses.

That same year, in response to the NAACP's role in *Brown* v. *Board of Education*, the South Carolina legislature passed a law making it illegal for any city or state employee to belong to the civil rights organization. Clark refused to resign her membership and was promptly fired. After teaching for forty years, this fifty-seven-year-old woman had lost not only her job but all her retirement benefits as well. Making matters worse, no one in Charleston would hire her, and few would have anything to do with her. A black teachers' sorority held a testimonial dinner for Clark, but none of the members would have their pictures taken with her, fearing that if any photos were made public, they would lose their jobs.

In the end, it was Myles Horton who came to Clark's rescue, hiring her in early 1956 as director of workshops at Highlander. Founded in 1932 as a school for poor adults in Appalachia, Highlander became a training ground for labor union organizers, then shifted its emphasis in the 1950s to developing community leaders for the emerging civil rights movement. It was Clark's idea to set up a program to teach unschooled Southern blacks to read and write, to prepare them to register to vote. Horton, she said, thought it would be enough to go into a community and simply recruit potential black voters. "But I knew . . . that if they were illiterate, with the laws that we had, they would not be able to read enough to register in most Southern states . . . ," Clark said. "We had to get them trained to read those laws and answer those questions." Winning the argument, she set up Highlander's citizenship school program, training dozens of future teachers by 1961.

But even as citizenship schools began spreading throughout the South, the institution that birthed them was threatened with extinction. Since its founding, Highlander had been a target of state officials, who were infuriated not only by its fomenting of civil rights activism but also by its housing blacks and whites under the same roof. Like SCEF and similar groups headed by white Southern liberals, Highlander was tarred with the Communist brush brandished by Senator James Eastland and other red-hunters. In the summer of 1959, while Myles Horton was away, a squad of police raided Highlander, claiming to find moonshine in a jug and arresting Clark, a teetotaler, for possession of homemade liquor. It was a ridiculous charge, but it served the purpose of shutting the school down, at least temporarily. The state then pursued Highlander through the courts, seeking to close the school for good and confiscate its property. In 1961, that effort succeeded. A judge ordered Highlander's land, buildings, and other possessions sold at auction, but by that time Clark's citizenship school program was being run by SCLC. Her immediate boss was Andrew Young, a Congregationalist minister and New Orleans native, who had been hired from the staff of the National Council of Churches to coordinate the program and administer the foundation grants that funded it. Dorothy Cotton, a former college administrator from Petersburg, Virginia, who had come to SCLC with Wyatt Tee Walker, was responsible for recruitment of students. At that point, the only other member of the citizenship school staff was Clark's cousin, Bernice Robinson, a beautician by profession who had a gift for teaching and who helped Clark with the training sessions themselves.

For one week every month, future citizenship school teachers came to Dorchester for training. The rest of the time, Clark, Cotton, Robinson, and, sometimes, Young traveled throughout the South, enlisting new recruits for Dorchester and checking on the progress of the schools already in operation. Such trips were made at great personal risk, but the potential for violence never seemed to faze Clark. Often traveling alone by bus, she always took the fifth seat from the front, where whites normally sat, to test government desegregation regulations. "They asked me to move," she recalled, "but I didn't. I reminded them that we had a law now that said we could sit anywhere in the bus." When she presided over her gatherings, members of the Ku Klux Klan or the local White Citizens Council sometimes ringed the building; in Grenada, Mississippi, a church in which she was working was set ablaze five minutes after she and citizenship school participants left.

One night, when she was staying with Virginia Durr in Montgomery, a parade of cars and motorcycles traveled back and forth in front of the Durrs' house. Virginia told Clark that the vehicles' occupants undoubtedly were members of the Klan. At three o'clock the next morning, the phone rang, and a man identifying himself as the chief of police informed Virginia that her husband's office had been broken into and, since Clifford was out of town, would she mind coming down and reporting on what was missing. Sure that the call was a ruse to get her out of the house and leave Clark alone, Virginia refused. Greatly upset, she rushed to Clark's room to reassure her that everything would be all right, only to find that Clark was considerably calmer than she. Clark was more frightened, she confessed later, of riding with Virginia in Virginia's car than she was of any nightriders. Her hostess had an unsettling habit of stopping at a green light and powdering her face, then when the light turned red, shooting through the intersection. "I said, 'I'm really more afraid of riding with you than I am of those Klansmen' because I was so afraid that a policeman was going to stop her . . . ," Clark said. "[Then] they would have gotten me."

Like many of the women who came to Dorchester for training, Septima Clark was known for her great warmth and generosity. People, both black and white, were drawn to her by the dozens for encouragement and comfort. They stayed at her house, called, wrote letters seeking her help with troubled marriages and love affairs, problems in finding a job or enough money to stay in school, difficulties with parents or children.

But Clark balanced her nurturing with counsel and sometimes reproof when she felt that friends and associates were going astray. Much of her criticism was aimed at her male SCLC colleagues, whose style of working and living was so different from her own. When she spent time at SCLC headquarters in Atlanta, Clark lived in a run-down church-operated rooming house on the edge of a slum, her room illuminated by a single seventy-five-watt lightbulb hanging from the ceiling. The material niceties of life meant little to her, and she disapproved when SCLC leaders spent movement money on such things, such as Andrew Young's chartering of a plane once to bring him from New York to Dorchester to greet a new group of citizenship school students from Mississippi. Clark was upset that Young indulged himself in such a way at a time when no money for food had been given to the students for their long trip to Georgia. "Here you are," she recalled telling Young. "You can charter a plane and sit in an airport in Savannah and eat a good dinner and then ride out here in a rented car. And you wouldn't send this man six dollars and he didn't have anything coming to this workshop, and you want him to go back there and work."

It bothered Clark, too, that King and the other SCLC leaders seemed so determined to be in the civil rights spotlight and so reluctant to do the unglamorous work of actually organizing people. She once sent a letter to King urging him not to feel he had to lead all the marches by himself. Instead, he should "develop leaders who could lead their own marches." King read Clark's letter aloud to the rest of the SCLC staff. "It . . . tickled them," she said. "They just laughed." Such a suggestion would inevitably be discounted by the SCLC inner circle, but the fact that it came from a woman undoubtedly made it seem more absurd. Like Ella Baker before them, Septima Clark, Dorothy Cotton, and the other women of SCLC were never taken seriously by the men, no matter how great their contributions. "Those men didn't have any faith in women, none whatsoever," Clark said. "They just thought that women were sex symbols and had no contributions to make." Clark herself had been responsible for creating the base on which the civil rights movement had been built, but at SCLC meetings, she said, "I was just a figurehead. . . . Whenever I had anything to say, I would put up my hand and say it. But I did know that they weren't paying attention."

King employed his considerable talents of charm and flattery on Clark in much the same way he used them on members of the Altar Guild at the Ebenezer Baptist Church, Andrew Young recalled. "He was not aware of his tendency to ignore her substantive comments or undervalue her work," Young said. When Clark wrote her autobiography in the early 1960s, King was asked to write the preface. In a letter to her publisher, the young SCLC head emphasized Clark's difficulties in combining motherhood with work, rather than her legendary accomplishments in the movement, which he regarded as imposed upon her and, in any event, distinctly secondary to her maternal duties. "*Echo in My Soul,*" King declared, "epitomizes the continuous struggle of the Southern Negro woman to realize her role as a mother while fulfilling her forced position as community teacher, intuitive fighter for human rights and leader of her unlettered and disillusioned people." It's hard to imagine fainter praise.

In the late 1960s, an author named Josephine Carson wrote a book on forgotten Southern black women, using pseudonyms for everyone she mentioned. Her main character, Septima Clark, was called Charity Simmons. Asked by Carson how the civil rights movement treated women, Clark talked about the way King (whom Carson referred to as Mr. L) introduced her to important visitors to the SCLC office. "[W]hen he gets to me, he says, 'This is Charity Simmons, Mother of the Movement.' Here I'm carryin' on this big project and he doesn't even mention it . . . He'll do the same thing with Beulah. There she is, manager of the whole office work force, and he'll say, 'This is Beulah Handley. She's got a beautiful singing voice.' And those men go off thinking all we can do is sing and play Mama! . . . Seems like a man like him with all that fame and power could give the credit, but he can't."

Despite her outward serenity, Clark was at times profoundly discouraged and disillusioned by SCLC's sexism, its autocratic style of leadership, its dismissive attitude toward her citizenship school program, which was, in fact, its greatest contribution to the voter registration effort in the South. In a memo to King, she complained that SCLC staff members working with her seemed to feel that "the work is not dramatic enough to warrant their time." Indeed, she declared, "[i]t seems as if Citizenship Education is all mine, except when it comes time to pick up the checks."

Clark expressed her unhappiness to confidantes like Anne Braden, telling Braden that she was thinking of quitting, of joining the Peace Corps and going to Africa. In another example of the support network that women activists had set up for themselves, Braden served as a source of encouragement and solace for Clark. "I believe it would be a tragedy if you should leave—not so much for you but for the South," Braden wrote back. "Our part of the country needs you, Septima, more than any one person that I can think of right now. I know the whole struggle gets discouraging at times, and there are times when I feel like retiring to my garden and forgetting it all too. I guess we all go through these moments but in my saner moments I know that all of the things that we are doing are worthwhile and that someday we will see how it all adds up to progress. And some way we must keep in touch and bolster each other when the going seems rough . . . Don't let things get you down. You can't always see the good that you're doing until you look back at it from a distance. But I don't know of anyone who has made the contribution that you have . . ."

Despite the problems she faced, Clark stayed on at SCLC until 1970, when she retired at the age of seventy-two. By that time, some ten thousand citizenship school teachers trained by her and her colleagues had taught more than one hundred thousand blacks to read and write and demand their rights of citizenship. In 1964 alone, close to two hundred schools were operating throughout the South—in living rooms, beauty parlors, churches, general stores, even outside, under the trees. It was an astonishing achievement that would help transform the political face of the region. "From one end of the South to the other, if you look at the black elected officials and the political leaders," Clark observed in 1985, "you find people who had their first involvement in the training program of the citizenship school."

13

"I Had Never Heard That Voice Before"

Freedom Singers, including Bernice Johnson Reagon (far left)
and Bertha Gober (third from left)

IN ALBANY, GEORGIA, BERNICE
Johnson was growing impatient. She had read all about the sit-ins, the
Freedom Rides, the McComb school walkout. It seemed to her and to
other students at Albany State College that the civil rights movement was
bearing fruit all over the South—with the major exception of southwestern Georgia. "[W]e would say, 'When is it going to happen here?'" Johnson recalled.

People talked about how bad Mississippi was, but in fact, much of
Georgia was not much different when it came to repression of blacks.
Southwestern Georgia was a particular throwback. This was the heart of
the state's cotton plantation country, a region that W. E. B. Du Bois
described as "perhaps the richest slave kingdom the modern world ever

knew." The countryside around Albany, the area's largest town, was still dotted with vast plantations, only now they were owned by people like Robert Woodruff, the chairman of Coca-Cola, and the fabulously rich Mellon family of Pittsburgh. The owners' overseers roamed the cotton, corn, and peanut fields on horseback, keeping a close watch on the black sharecroppers working the land.

The "plantation mentality" of the sharecroppers—their submissiveness to, and dependence on, white authority—was shared by most of the black population of Albany, including the administration of all-black Albany State College. Dependent on the state for the school's funding, the administration did nothing when white men routinely harassed and humiliated female students. Men raced their cars through campus, throwing eggs and bags of urine at Albany State coeds, acting as if they were going to run them down. Sometimes, white men would slip into the women's dorms and proposition the students. More than once, the women had to call on members of Albany State's football team to help repel the intruders. And still the college's administration did nothing.

In early 1961, Bernice Johnson helped organize a rally of Albany State students to protest, among other things, the failure of the college and the city to crack down on the women's white persecutors. Albany State's conservative president, who had already prohibited any mention in the student newspaper and other publications of harassment by white men, was so alarmed by the rally and so fearful of retaliation by the state's Board of Regents that he suspended student government activities for the rest of the year. He also fired the dean of women, the only college official to support the students. Outraged, Johnson and the other protesters yearned all the more for the civil rights movement to set up shop in Albany. And then, at last, Charles Sherrod and Cordell Reagon arrived in town.

Sherrod and Reagon had been in McComb but left after the student walkout at Burgland High School and went in search of a likely site for a new voter registration campaign. Sherrod, an early SNCC leader and one of those jailed in Rock Hill with Diane Nash, was the architect of SNCC's bold plan to overturn the South's control of Congress by registering enough black voters in Southern states to defeat key members on Capitol Hill. While the campaign continued in Mississippi, he decided to target southwestern Georgia.

As usual, students were the first to join the SNCC drive. Reagon spent much of his time on the playgrounds of black Albany, recruiting junior high and high school students, most of them girls. And there was, of course, the fertile ground of Albany State, where students were as eager to listen to the organizers as authorities were to keep them off the premises. One day, Bernice Johnson was in the student center with Sherrod and Reagon when one of the college deans saw them and shouted, "Get off this campus or I'll call the police!" Said Johnson: "It was like I was sitting with the bogeyman."

While voter registration was their ultimate goal, Sherrod and Reagon turned to direct action to get things going, using as their fuse a September 22 order by the Interstate Commerce Commission barring segregated facilities in interstate travel. The order implemented the Supreme Court ruling in *Boynton* v. *Virginia*, which the Freedom Riders had tested in their attempts earlier that year to integrate interstate bus stations. With the new ICC regulation, there now could be no doubt of the federal government's position on the illegality of discrimination in interstate travel.

On November 22, 1961, Bertha Gober, an Albany State student from Atlanta, and a classmate, Blanton Hall, broke away from the crowd of black students waiting in the Trailways station's "colored" waiting room to board buses for their Thanksgiving vacations, and darted into the white side of the building. They were arrested for "tending to create a disturbance" and were carted away. Three high school students were also arrested for trying to integrate the whites-only waiting room. The high school students were bailed out within an hour, but Gober and Hall decided to remain in jail over the holiday.

The trials of Gober and the other students arrested at the bus station were held the following Monday. Bernice Johnson joined other Albany State student leaders in calling for a march to City Hall. In a scene reminiscent of McComb, they went from classroom to classroom urging people to walk out. While a number of professors tried to prevent their departure (one student leader actually picked a professor up and moved him away from the doorway of his classroom), at least one teacher urged them on. "Get out," history professor Trois Latimer told the kids sitting in front of her. "Go do something for your freedom. You ain't doing nothing here."

From her position at the front of the parade to City Hall, Johnson looked back and saw only a few people. "My God," she said, "I guess we failed." When she glanced back a little later, she couldn't see the end of the line. More than five hundred people, adults as well as students, had joined the march and gathered outside City Hall that Monday. The police made no arrests, and the demonstrators later marched to the Union Baptist Church. "Nothing like this," Johnson exulted, "had ever happened before in Albany."

SNCC was determined to keep the pressure on. To that end, James Forman, SNCC's executive secretary, organized a Freedom Ride, this time by train, from Atlanta to Albany to test the ICC ruling. He put together an eclectic, integrated group that included himself; SNCC's office manager; Bob Zellner, SNCC's first white organizer; and newlyweds Tom and Casey Hayden. Tom and Casey's relationship had blossomed after the October 1960 SNCC conference in Atlanta. They began living together in the summer of 1961, following Hayden's graduation from the University of Michigan, and were married in the fall.

Also in the group was a shy, soft-spoken white teenager who had stumbled into the movement by accident. Nineteen-year-old Joan Browning bore about as much resemblance to a firebrand as Georgia governor Ernest Vandiver did to a liberal. Although a Georgian, Browning had known little about the racial chasm dividing the South until abruptly confronted with it the previous autumn. Now, here she was on the morning of December 10, putting on her new plaid vest, green corduroy skirt and jacket, and penny loafers, getting ready to confront the white authorities of Albany. With clean underwear and a toothbrush in her purse, she was also set for jail.

The second oldest of eight children, Joan Browning grew up on a farm in rural Georgia, some seventy-five miles from Albany. Her parents were poor truck farmers, but when she recalled her upbringing, what she remembered was not the poverty, but the love, warmth, and sense of community she received from her family and neighbors. "I could walk anywhere, and somebody would always look out for me," she said.

After finishing high school at sixteen, Browning attended Georgia State College for Women as a premed major. Two years younger than most of her fellow freshmen, she was lonely and homesick on the Milledgeville campus. She missed the warmth and closeness of the people back home and chafed under the school's many restrictions and regulations, meant to foster proper conduct in young Southern ladies. She did not mind the required attendance at church on Sunday—religion was important to her—but she disliked having to wear the girdle, garter belt, and stockings mandated for church attendance. Above all, she hated the atmosphere at the Methodist church she attended near the campus. Compared with the tiny Methodist chapel she and her family attended, she found it stiff and formal, unwelcoming and unfriendly. At home, everybody sang the hymns; at the church in Milledgeville, the choir performed for a passive congregation.

Looking around for an alternative, she discovered a black AME church across the street from the college. Now *this* was more like home! The minister and congregation welcomed her enthusiastically. The singing was "lusty and joyful," exactly what she was used to. "I found myself in a place where I felt safe and accepted," she recalled. The fact that she and a college friend were the only white faces in the pews did not bother her. She had had almost no contact with blacks while growing up, and her family and neighbors did not talk much about racial matters. The taboos of race had not gained much of a hold on her psyche. "I went to a black church, not because it was black but because it was warm," she later wrote. "I went there not to break some racial barrier, but to worship."

Soon enough, though, she learned about the taboos. The president of her college called her in one day and ordered her to stop attending the black services. Not only did she refuse, she soon deepened her rebellion by slipping off campus to attend interracial student conferences. Finally, early in her junior year, the college had had enough of her independence. Her financial aid was canceled, and she was told to leave. If she did not go voluntarily, she would be expelled. At the age of eighteen, Joan Browning found herself in Atlanta, working in the library at Emory University, going to night classes at Georgia State, and searching again for a community that reminded her of home. She discovered it in SNCC, and spent most of her limited free time doing volunteer office work in the organization's dingy Auburn Avenue headquarters. Then Jim Forman asked her to consider another assignment—the Freedom Ride to Albany.

Boarding the train in Atlanta, the racially mixed SNCC group claimed one small victory before reaching Albany: Despite the initial protests of the conductor, they sat together all the way to their destination in a whites-only car. Maybe their luck would hold, some thought, as the train rumbled into what seemed to be a deserted Albany station. As they entered the empty white waiting room, they could see through the window a crowd of blacks gathered across the street. Walking out of the station, to the welcoming shouts of the crowd, the Freedom Riders were arrested by Albany police chief Laurie Pritchett and his men, on charges of "blocking the sidewalk" and "obstructing traffic." Casey Hayden was not arrested; as the designated observer, she had the job of slipping away and reporting back to SNCC. But three bystanders, including Bertha Gober, were caught up in the police net. They had been at the station to welcome the Riders, and were also taken into custody. For the second time in less than three weeks, Gober was on her way to jail.

The next morning, several of Albany's leading black women organized a prayer vigil outside City Hall. Within a few minutes, they were under arrest, too, charged with the same misdemeanors as the Freedom Riders. With their arrest, the town's black community, already angry over the arrests of the Albany State students and the Freedom Riders, finally erupted. The following day, some four hundred African-American residents of Albany marched in the rain from the Shiloh Baptist Church to City Hall; it took more than two hours for Laurie Pritchett's men to put them all under arrest. The day after that, another two hundred or more marchers turned out and were also put behind bars.

For the first time in the history of the civil rights movement, a direct action protest was supported by an entire black community, a large segment of which was now in jail. The South had not witnessed such grassroots involvement since the Montgomery bus boycott. And never before had such a large number of people—more than seven hundred in all—been arrested in a single city. This was a big story, and national news reporters converged on Albany to find out what was going on.

Alone in her cell, Joan Browning, up to then the only white woman to be arrested in Albany, had little knowledge of what was happening around her. The worst part, she thought, was the loneliness, the lack of someone to talk to. She had gravitated to SNCC because of its emphasis on "the beloved community"; now, because of the color of her skin, she was cut off from that community, separated from Bertha Gober and the two black women on the Ride. "Being alone was torment, just plain torment," she recalled. At one point, she tried to work loose the bricks in the wall separating her cell from that of the three black women, thinking if she could get rid of just one brick, she could see them. She stopped only when jail officials threatened to put her in a straitjacket.

Browning was released on the evening of her fifth day in jail. Cold and dirty, still woozy from a short-lived hunger strike, she was taken, along with several other freed Riders, to that night's mass meeting at the Mount Zion Baptist Church. Having grown used to the dim light of her unheated cell, she was bedazzled when she walked into the warm, brightly lit church. "It was," she later said, "just like walking into the face of the morning sun." She looked around her in awe. There were people everywhere, standing against the wall, up in the balcony, even spilling out onto the front lawn. And they were all on their feet, smiling, weeping, applauding, shouting out encouragement, hugging her as she and the other Riders slowly made their way to the choir stand in front of the church. Asked to say a few words about her experience, Browning tried to pull her scattered thoughts together. "It's a funny, mixed-up feeling to hate being in a dirty place—but to be glad you're there for a good reason," she said. "We hope you'll keep going."

That experience of going from dark to light, from silence to an explosion of joyous sound, from cold to warmth, would always stay with Browning. "Instead of people shunning me, now they were accepting me. I could have wallowed in that the rest of my life," she said. For a few moments, at least, "I was home."

By the middle of December, Albany's jail was filled to overflowing, and Chief Pritchett had to farm out more than half of those he and his men had arrested to jails in adjoining counties. Everybody agreed that conditions in the city jail were bad. ("I do feel that for the size of the town we have a most terrible jail," Bernice Johnson said in a report sent to SNCC headquarters. "It seems that the taxpayers of Albany should demand more and better facilities for their prisoners.") But the county jails were far worse. Demonstrators were horrified when, after being loaded into buses, they were told they were on their way to Terrell, Baker, Lee, and other counties. Albany was an oasis of civility compared to these places, where many of the white residents, including the sheriffs and their deputies, were known to take pride in their own meanness, especially where blacks were concerned. Only six months before, the sheriff of Baker County, who was said to have killed at least four blacks in his custody, had arrested a black plantation worker on trumped-up charges, then shot him twice in the neck as the man sat handcuffed in the sheriff's car. Still suffering from his wounds, the man was later thrown in jail on charges of assaulting the sheriff.

In the Mitchell County jail in Camilla, fifty-eight women, most of them teenagers, were stuffed into one cell, some for two weeks or more. They received no food the first day, and that night the heat was adjusted constantly, from stifling hot to freezing cold. On the way to the jail, sixteen-year-old Brenda Boone reported, "the police officer known as Big Red used vulgar language and tried to frighten us, but it didn't work, for most of us were not easy to be made afraid." Annie Sue Herrin, another sixteen-year-old held at the jail, answered "No," instead of "No, sir," when a deputy asked her if he had spelled her name correctly on a report. He told several other deputies to hold her, then closed the door of the room in which he was questioning her, and hit her as hard as he could. "That is just a sample of what you're going to get," he warned.

But for all the hardships and extreme discomfort, there were compensations, particularly the joy and exhilaration of breaking down class and age barriers in those cells and coming together as a community. Maids were thrown together with the wives of doctors and lawyers, fourteen-year-olds with women old enough to be their grandmothers and great-grandmothers. Norma Anderson, the wife of the local movement's head, was in a cell with eleven other women, most of them cooks and maids. A leading member of Albany's black middle class, Anderson had had little opportunity to get to know women like these. Later, when she thought back about her days in that cell, she remembered one event in particular: When the women were very thirsty, they were given an old mayonnaise jar filled with lukewarm water. The women made a small, cramped circle and passed the jar around, one to another, taking tiny sips, making sure there was enough for everyone. Said Anderson: "I have never been to a church service of Communion that moved me more deeply than the experience in that jail cell."

In the history of the civil rights movement, the Albany campaign would be remembered for the depth and breadth of its community involvement, a model for future community-wide campaigns in Birmingham and elsewhere. But it would also be remembered for something else—its singing. Even hard-bitten white journalists fell under its spell. "Such music cannot be described—or recaptured . . . ," Pat Watters, an *Atlanta Journal* reporter, wrote ten years later. "Even now, hearing it more thinly on tapes, I return to the mystical, inspired and excited, ecstatic—and reverent mood of those meetings."

Music had always been an integral part of the civil rights movement, beginning with the singing at mass meetings during the Montgomery bus boycott. Singing bolstered spirits and created community whenever activists marched or sat in, whenever they went on Freedom Rides, whenever they went to jail. To pass the long days at Parchman penitentiary, Freedom Riders made up new songs and learned others from their cellmates. The Nashville Riders, including gifted songwriters James Bevel and Bernard Lafayette, were especially important in the cross-fertilization of freedom music that took place in prison.

Cordell Reagon, a good singer himself, taught his repertoire to the high school and college students whom he recruited early in the Albany movement. Moreover, he made it a point to recruit gifted singers like Bernice Johnson and Bertha Gober to lead songs at the mass meetings. Then he got out of the way. For when the freedom songs were combined with black Albany's rich tradition of congregational singing, Reagon recalled, "we made something unbelievable, a total spiritual experience." Said Johnson: "Ordinarily you go to church and you sing, but sometimes the congregation takes the roof off the building. *Every* mass meeting [in Albany] was like that."

Until they got involved in the movement, many of Albany's young blacks had not paid much attention to the lyrics of the spirituals and hymns they had known since babyhood. Now, however, those words were overwhelming in their aptness and force. "They were saying what I was feeling," Bernice Johnson said. "Somehow, it felt like all those words that black people had been praying and saying was a language for us, a language we could not understand unless we were involved in a practical, everyday struggle."

It was a language that Johnson and others could change to suit their own purposes, one that would empower and strengthen them in ways they could scarcely imagine. Johnson got a hint of this when she was asked to sing a song at one of Albany's first mass meetings. She knew she was not supposed to solo. She was meant to "plant a seed," to start a song that would be picked up by everyone. Johnson had just come from her first march to City Hall, and when she stood in front of hundreds of people at Mount Zion, this tiny, sturdily built teenager discovered a force and energy in her rich contralto that had not been there before. Head thrown back, eyes closed, she started to sing the spiritual "Over My Head I See Trouble in the Air." But when she got to the word "trouble," she realized she did not feel troubled, and so she substituted the word "freedom." "Over My Head I See Freedom in the Air"—the change of one word transformed a lament to a triumphant call to arms. Repeating the line, the crowd at Mount Zion joyously endorsed the change.

"I was given permission to mess with a sacred song," Johnson said later. "The permission came because I had walked around City Hall. And if you're bad enough to walk around City Hall in Albany, you can change the words to this old song." Those few minutes forever altered Johnson's life. "I had never heard that voice before. I had never been that me before. And once I became that me, I have never let that me go . . ."

The words to other songs were changed, and other people's lives were transformed. Bertha Gober and another young woman activist, Janie Culbreth, passed time in jail reworking the lyrics of the spiritual "Oh, Mary, Oh, Martha," to "Oh, Pritchett, Oh, Kelley," referring to police chief Laurie Pritchett and Mayor Asa Kelley. "Open them cells," the song went. "Can't you hear God's children crying for freedom?" Singing that song when they marched, the blacks in Albany jettisoned all caution. To stay out of trouble and alive, they had been taught, they must cloak themselves in an aura of invisibility around white folks, must never call attention to what they were doing or thinking, must stay in their place. Now here they were, not only as visible as they could possibly get but verbally challenging the town's leading white authorities as well. On their own, most of Albany's African-Americans would never have dreamed of asserting themselves in such a way. But together, in song, they could do it.

"With a song," said Bernice Johnson, "there was nothing [the authorities] could do to block what we were saying . . . Singing is different than talking because no matter what they do, they would have to kill me to stop me from singing . . . Sometimes they would plead and say, 'Please stop singing.' And you would just know that your word is being heard."

With hundreds of people in jail, local leaders of the movement had no clear idea what to do next. They were newcomers to this business of civil rights agitation and were not prepared to cope with the magnitude of their newborn campaign. So they decided to turn to the man that so many others had sought when they needed help—Martin Luther King.

It was not a task King was eager to assume. Although most people in the country regarded him as *the* leader of the civil rights movement, he had done almost nothing to help organize and mobilize local protests. Speechmaking and fund-raising were still his main occupations. Unlike SNCC and CORE, SCLC still had not come up with any new major civil rights initiatives of its own.

Several members of the SNCC contingent in Albany, including Ella Baker, vehemently objected to the local leaders' decision to invite King in. They felt that the Albany drive was doing just fine without him, that his involvement would lead to a Messiah complex among the people, making them believe that only he could win victory for them. But the SNCC activists had another reason for their strong opposition to King's participation in Albany. They did not want the spotlight of the national press, now shining on SNCC and the local organization, to switch to King, as it almost certainly would if the charismatic leader became involved. More and more, the leaders of the various national civil rights organizations were vying with one another for the public's attention. Personal and organizational prestige were at stake, and so was the ability to raise money. The more publicity, the easier it was to raise funds, particularly among Northern white liberals. In its early days, SNCC did not have an effective fund-raising apparatus and constantly teetered on the brink of financial insolvency. Its leaders were infuriated that King and SCLC raised so much money and gave so little of it to SNCC—particularly since much of the money came in response to the sit-ins and Freedom Rides, for which the students had been largely responsible.

If SNCC disliked SCLC's tactics, its own way of operating was deeply resented by the NAACP. The country's oldest civil rights organization, which emphasized negotiation and legal action rather than demonstrations, was furious at these young upstarts for coming in and stirring up a commotion in Albany. Ruby Hurley, director of NAACP operations in the South, and other leaders of the organization tried—and failed—to get members of the NAACP youth chapter in Albany to end their involvement in the protests.

With the exceptions of Hurley and Baker, however, few women took part in these internecine squabbles. Men were the acknowledged leaders of the movement, and they were the ones most intimately involved in the competition and rivalry. "The civil rights revolt, like many social upheavals, has released powerful pentup emotions, cross currents, rivalries and hostilities . . . ," Pauli Murray wrote in 1963. "There is much jockeying for position as ambitious men push and elbow their way to leadership roles. Part of this upsurge reflects the Negro male's normal desire to achieve a sense of personal worth and recognition of his manhood by a society which has so long denied it."

News coverage, which the leaders sought, was, as Murray pointed out, a matter of men reporting on men. Stories on the movement often read like accounts of sports contests or wars, keeping score of who was up and who was down, who won and who lost. Conflict was always emphasized, whether between civil rights organizations or between local white authorities and activists. The behind-the-scenes activity that women specialized in—organizing, building consensus, sustaining a sense of community— did not make good television, nor did it lend itself to dramatic newspaper or magazine headlines. There were no reporters around, for example, when Ella Baker sat in a corner of Albany's Shiloh Baptist Church in December, writing down the names, addresses, and money needs of hundreds of protesters who had just gotten out of jail, many of whom had been fired from their jobs. Nor was any attention paid to Septima Clark, who stood at the door of the Albany courthouse from morning until late afternoon, urging blacks to register to vote. Howard Zinn, a Spelman College professor and veteran white activist, once described Ella Baker as "mov[ing] silently through the protest movements in the South doing the things the famous men didn't have time to do." He could have been talking about other women activists as well.

*   *   *

On December 16, more than 1,500 blacks packed Albany's Mount Zion and Shiloh churches to hear Martin Luther King speak, first to one congregation, then the other. He had responded to the appeal from the town's black leaders, and just as SNCC organizers feared, no sooner had he taken the pulpit than he became the focal point of the Albany movement. The next afternoon, he headed a march of more than two hundred blacks to City Hall. Chief Pritchett's men herded them into an alley behind the jail and arrested them. Thus began a monthlong chess game between Pritchett and King, who soon realized he was facing a wily opponent indeed.

On the surface, Laurie Pritchett, who was in his mid-thirties and had the beefy frame of an ex–football player, seemed much like Bull Connor and other notoriously racist Southern lawmen. "There are three things I like," he once told *Newsweek* correspondent Karl Fleming. "Drinking buttermilk, putting niggers in jail, and kicking reporters' asses." In fact, though, Pritchett was a shrewd, fascinatingly complex man who was determined to avoid the horrendous publicity received by Birmingham and Montgomery law enforcement officers for sanctioning the bloody mob violence in their cities. For that, he would ultimately have a major impact on the media's perception of Martin Luther King's role in the movement in Albany. In Pritchett's town, whites were kept under control, his officers were not allowed to use nightsticks or guns when rounding up demonstrators, he himself was polite and affable in packing them off to jail. He soon got the reputation of meeting nonviolence with nonviolence, of conducting arrests, according to Ralph Abernathy, "the way crossing guards helped schoolchildren."

Pritchett made a special point of trying to be nice to Martin Luther King and his men. When King was arrested on December 17, he and Abernathy were transported to the Sumter County jail in the chief's own new Buick Roadmaster. King pledged to stay in jail, without posting bail, "as long as necessary" to change Albany's system of segregation. Two days later, he walked free after city officials agreed to desegregate the train and bus terminals and turn loose all jailed demonstrators on their own recognizance. King explained that he didn't need to stay in jail after all, because the city had made significant concessions. But SNCC workers and the media scoffed at that argument, noting that the agreement to desegregate interstate transportation facilities was merely a recognition of the ICC ruling that had become law two months before. "A devastating loss of face" for King, the New York *Herald Tribune* called the situation, as well as "one of the most stunning defeats" of his career. In Mississippi, Diane Nash's attempt to spend two years in prison was prompted in part by her deep disappointment with King's decision to accept bail after promising to stay in jail.

For the rest of his involvement with the Albany campaign, King would be stuck with that image of an overeager compromiser, outmaneuvered by Pritchett and other city officials. He would go to jail in Albany two more times but would obtain no major concessions from the city fathers. When he finally left town, most journalists left with him, convinced that the effort in southwestern Georgia was over, with nothing much gained, no lunch counters or parks or libraries integrated. Pat Watters of *The Atlanta Journal*, who became one of the severest critics of the way reporters, including himself, covered civil rights, said journalists "resisted the movement and ignored its meaning . . . writing of it in conventional terms, doing our part in pushing toward the conventional, reshaping it, destroying its meaning." By focusing on conflict and controversy and on the most visible leaders, the media failed to see what lay under the surface of events, failed to see the dramatic changes that *were* occurring—in the hearts and minds of local blacks.

For Bernice Johnson and others in Albany, the true meaning of the movement there was their realization that centuries of black submissiveness had finally ended. "When I read about the Albany Movement, as people have written about it, I don't recognize it," Johnson observed. "They add up stuff that was not central to what happened. Discussion about Pritchett, discussion about specific achievements, discussion about whether it was a failure or success for King. For me, that was not central." What *was* important, Johnson said, was acquiring a sense of power "in a place where you didn't feel you had any power. There was a sense of confronting things that terrified you, like jail, the police, walking in the street—you know, a whole lot of black folks couldn't even walk in the street in those places in the South. So you were saying in some basic way, 'I will never again stay inside these boundaries.' . . . The civil rights movement gave me the power to challenge *any* line that limits me."

When Johnson talked about boundaries, she was not only referring to the limits placed on her as a black. She meant as a woman, too. One of the most liberating aspects of the Albany campaign, she came to believe, was the emergence of women, including herself, as informal leaders. Before the movement came to Albany, the only time women were allowed in church pulpits was on the annual Women's Day. Now, she and other women were in the pulpit all the time, leading songs and speaking at mass meetings.

Johnson's passion had always been music; since childhood, she had dreamed of becoming an opera singer. But it was made clear to her early on that such an aspiration was foolish for a black girl from Albany, that she should pick a more suitable career. So whenever anyone asked her what she wanted to be, she would say, "A doctor." At Albany State, she majored in biology. Then, in December 1961, she was expelled from school, along with Bertha Gober and the other student demonstrators. Traumatic as her expulsion was, it freed her: Now she was going to do what *she* wanted to do, regardless of what her parents or anybody else thought. Enrolling at Spelman a few months later, she switched her major to music, and from then on, her life would be devoted to her original passion. By the end of 1962, she had married Cordell Reagon and become one of SNCC's famed Freedom Singers, a group that traveled throughout the country giving concerts, raising funds, and inspiring thousands to join the struggle.

14

"Black and White Together"

Penny Patch

WHILE THE NATIONAL MEDIA focused on Albany in the summer of 1962, Charles Sherrod turned his attention to the launching of a voter registration campaign in the neighboring counties. Sherrod's plans for staffing the new project came as a shock to some of his SNCC colleagues. In addition to black men, he proposed to recruit whites and nonlocal black women as organizers—something that SNCC had never done before in the Deep South. Bob Zellner, a white Southerner, had been involved briefly in McComb, and white women were working in the organization's Atlanta office, but no whites or outside black women, except Diane Nash, had been brought in to do full-time field work. In Mississippi, Bob Moses believed that such a staffing plan was far too dangerous, although he would later change his mind.

What Sherrod wanted to do, essentially, was to affirm SNCC's ideal of "black and white together." "We want to strike at the very root of segregation," he said. "The root is the idea that white is superior. That idea has eaten into the minds of the people, black and white. We have to break this image. We can only do this if we see white and black working together, side by side, the white man no more and no less than his black brother, but human beings together." Overcoming blacks' fear of and submissiveness to whites may well have been Sherrod's principal reason for recruiting an integrated group of workers, but there were other, less idealistic reasons that he didn't voice publicly. The use of white students, he hoped, would bring greater publicity and more money to the southwestern Georgia project. He told the skeptics in SNCC that "white people don't care anything about us, but they care about their children. . . . If their children came South—the children of these white people, the good guys, the good thinkers—then money [and attention] would come with them." Those same arguments would be used two years later to bring hundreds of white volunteers to Mississippi for Freedom Summer.

In the end, Sherrod won the argument, and, as a result of his victory, a white Swarthmore College freshman received a phone call at her dorm in May. Would she be interested in spending her summer doing voter registration work in southwestern Georgia? Without a second thought, Penny Patch said yes.

Years later, Patch would trace the roots of her civil rights activism to ravaged postwar Germany, where she spent much of her childhood. Her father was an American diplomat, and when she was two, her family went abroad for most of the next eleven years, living in Manchuria and Czechoslovakia but mostly in Germany. Patch, who attended German schools, loved the country and its people, but was haunted by the Holocaust. Her parents, who were socially and politically liberal, took her to the Dachau concentration camp, an encounter with evil that seared itself in her memory. Later, she met many Jewish refugees and camp survivors. The little girl could not understand how the Germans she liked so much could have stood by and allowed the murder of millions of innocent people. "How could you not do anything?" she once asked the parents of a friend. They did not answer, and she soon realized "there were some questions I should not ask if I wanted to be welcomed into the homes of my friends."

When she was thirteen, Patch and her family returned to the United States, and she entered Dalton, one of New York City's most prestigious private schools, and promptly lapsed into profound culture shock. It was the late 1950s. The pressure to conform was overpowering. But Penny Patch was not like everyone else. "I was not an American child," she said. "I got back here, and I really didn't fit in. That primed me, I think, to do things that were not the usual."

In 1961, she went to Swarthmore and "dove right in" to political activism. She and other Swarthmore students took part in sit-ins at a segregated roller-skating rink near the Swarthmore campus in Pennsylvania. Later, they picketed and sat in at whites-only restaurants on Maryland's Eastern Shore. The baby-faced eighteen-year-old was arrested several times in the spring of 1962, spending weekends in jail and returning to Swarthmore in time for Monday classes. For the first time since coming back to the United States, she felt as if she belonged. Having been uprooted so many times in her life, she was captivated by the warmth and sense of community she found in the movement. But her involvement also stemmed from a deep sense of personal responsibility, the result of her childhood preoccupation with Germans' guilt for the Holocaust. "Here was evil, and I could go and do something about it," she remembered thinking. "If I didn't, I would be just like all those people in Germany."

In June, Patch's parents, frightened for their daughter's safety but nonetheless supportive, took her to La Guardia Airport and put her on a plane to Georgia. Also aboard and headed for the same project was Peggy Dammond, who had been a year ahead of Patch at Dalton. The two young women didn't know each other well, but from their superficial acquaintance, Patch believed that Dammond, even though she was black, had fit in much better at Dalton than Patch had. Dammond didn't see it that way. Although she was light-skinned and could pass for white, she had no desire to be part of the white world. "All my life," she later said, "I can remember resenting the fact that people would not know that I was Negro . . . something that I was very proud of."

For several years, Dammond, whose great-uncle had been editor of a black liberation newspaper, led a dual life. During the day, she attended her tony white prep school on the East Side of Manhattan; at night, she returned to the thriving black street life of Harlem. She organized some of the teenagers in her Harlem neighborhood into a group called the Harlem Brotherhood Group, whose members swept streets, cleaned up litter, and in general tried to improve conditions in some of Harlem's poorer sections. Ever since she was small, Dammond said, she had "felt a sense of mission toward changing the Negro's position in this world and in the country"—an ambition stemming from an intense desire to affirm her blackness.

After Dalton, she had attended Hunter College for a year, then decided to stay out of school the next year, having accepted a part in an off-Broadway play. As it turned out, the play was never produced, but by the time it fell through, Dammond had gotten involved in the movement. Like Patch, she had joined the sit-ins on the Eastern Shore of Maryland and had been arrested and jailed.

On the surface, the two young women had much in common, but the legacy of their "blackness" and "whiteness"—the way they thought about themselves and the way others thought about them—would result in starkly different experiences during the long and frightening summer that lay ahead.

Patch was the only white woman in the first integrated band of student workers in southwestern Georgia. She and her coworkers, including several white men, drove and walked down miles of dusty back roads, knocking on the doors of sharecroppers' cabins, urging people to attend mass meetings and to go to the courthouse to register to vote. It was hot, tedious, dangerous work: Blacks in those notoriously violent counties were terrified of white reprisals, and sometimes the workers would have to make ten or fifteen visits to a cabin before its inhabitants would agree to go to a mass meeting. Sometimes, they refused to go at all.

In time, Patch lost her consciousness about being white. She identified so completely with the blacks around her that when she was with them, "I would see people just like me." It was a dangerous illusion, since no one else in the South, black or white, could see it that way. More than thirty years later, she remembered how naive she had been when she first arrived in Georgia, how oblivious she was to the ramifications of being a white woman in the South. No one had explained to her how the ideal of "sacred white womanhood" served as a justification for white supremacy, how a young white woman's association with blacks could become a flash point for white rage and a potential peril for the blacks, particularly black men, seen in her company. It was painfully ironic: She was more at home in Georgia than she had been in any place since Germany, and yet her mere presence was a threat to the lives of the people to whom she felt so close.

Wherever she went that summer, Patch was the unwilling center of attention. After a Terrell County mass meeting at which she made a brief speech, the local paper carried a story with the headline: "White Girl, Handful of Negroes Hold Undisturbed Meet at Sasser." Sometime later, while she was canvassing in Lee County with several black women organizers, the women's car was stopped by the sheriff. "What are you doing, driving around with these nigger gals?" he demanded of Patch. She had riled up the county's white residents, he told her, and if she ever returned, he would not be able to stop them from throwing her in a nearby swamp.

For a time, Patch lived with Dammond and several other female organizers at the Lee County home of the indomitable "Mama Dollie" Raines, a farmer and former midwife who was fast becoming a legend among SNCC workers for her protective mothering of them, her intrepid commitment to the cause, and her enormous courage. Charles Sherrod once described Mama Dollie, who had delivered more than a thousand babies, black and white, as "a gray-haired old lady of about seventy who can pick more cotton, slop more pigs, plow more ground, chop more wood, and do a hundred more things better than the best farmer in the area." She was used to being threatened for housing civil rights workers—she often stayed up all night with a shotgun in her lap—but when she took in Penny Patch, the threats against her and other blacks in Lee County reached such feverish intensity that she finally had to ask Patch to leave. From then on, the white teenager lived with black families in Albany, working there and in the nearby counties.

During her time in southwestern Georgia, which eventually stretched to more than a year, Patch grappled constantly with the complexities of being a white woman in the South. "I learned a lot, very fast, and never knew enough," she later wrote. Her life and behavior were considerably more circumscribed than those of the black women she worked with. She was not allowed to ride in a car or to canvass with black male coworkers, nor was she permitted to socialize with them in public. When she greeted a black male leader of the Albany Movement with a kiss on the cheek at a mass meeting one night, she was told afterward that "I was never to make that sort of contact with a black man in public ever again, that I could cost someone his life."

It pained her that being white separated her from the blacks she was trying to recruit, that while they were all invariably polite, many were also intensely wary. Why should they trust her? Was she just going to create more trouble for them? She sensed wariness, too, on the part of Dammond, Kathleen Conwell, and some of the other black women organizers. In a report to SNCC headquarters, Conwell noted "a degree of hostility" between Patch and the black women. "I think they always felt I brought more trouble than benefit" to the project, Patch said.

There was no question in Peggy Dammond's mind that the presence of whites inhibited blacks with whom the organizers worked. Some of them, thinking *she* was white, often clammed up when they first met—a source of great frustration for her. "[W]henever we were in an integrated group many people just wouldn't talk," she recalled. "They'd stand up when a white person came over to talk to them. They'd call them 'madam' or 'sir.' . . . But the minute that it was an all-Negro group there, people relaxed . . . their whole attitudes changed, and we felt comfortable with our own."

Yet for all the problems, Penny Patch on occasion managed to surmount the formidable barrier of race. Her quiet friendliness and obvious commitment to the cause won the trust of a number of local blacks. With several, she developed close, lifelong friendships. One Lee County resident who became active in the movement wrote that before he met Patch and Ralph Allen, another white civil rights worker, "I referred to my white brothers as crackers and I hated all of them." But as he got to know Patch and Allen, the man observed that "my whole opinion of white people changed" and the two young outsiders became "just like a brother and sister to me."

One day, while Patch and several other women were canvassing in Lee County, they went to the home of a black woman doctor. On the walls of her farmhouse were pictures of a number of her forebears—some black, some Indian, some white. "We must come to flow freely among ourselves," the doctor told Patch and the others. It was a bit of wisdom that Patch wholeheartedly accepted. "We are confronting the community with what should be and what will be," she wrote to Wiley Branton, head of the Voter Education Project, the conduit of foundation money for the Southern voter registration campaign. "We are showing here and now, rather than talking about black and white together, that a dream can be reality, and that words can mean something. There are few things that in my mind are designated as totally, absolutely and completely right. Integration is one of those things."

Terror and violence swept through southwestern Georgia that summer, as racists did their best to prove Patch wrong. To a small degree, she felt the effects of that intimidation: Arrested five times, she spent several weeks in jail, and was roughed up a bit. But while her gender and race made her the object of vilification, they also seemed to protect her from the worst of the violence visited on white male workers and, of course, on blacks, male and female.

Carolyn Daniels, a thirty-two-year-old black woman who ran a beauty shop in her Terrell County home, was one of the terrorist campaign's chief targets. Like Dollie Raines, Daniels housed several of the young organizers, in addition to teaching citizenship school classes and canvassing and marching herself. One night in September 1962, nightriders fired several shotgun blasts into her cinder-block house, hitting Jack Chatfield, a white worker, in the arm and slightly wounding Prathia Hall, a black divinity student, and a couple of others. There was blood everywhere, recalled Charles Sherrod, who was also there.

Several months later, terrorists returned to Daniels' house, which had become SNCC's voter registration headquarters in Terrell County. They riddled the house with bullets, and this time Daniels was shot in the foot. She was rushed to the hospital, and while she was away, a carful of men hurled a firebomb into her house, blowing half of it away. But the violence "did not unnerve [Daniels]," Prathia Hall said. "She was a single mother struggling to make it, but she was steel, she was strength for all of us . . ."

In 1963, the violence spread to Albany. The press was off to Birmingham and other civil rights hot spots by now, and Pritchett and his men felt free to retaliate against the demonstrators, including the many student volunteers, white and black, who had flooded the town. Almost all the volunteers ended up in jail for weeks at a time. Most were harassed and intimidated. Some of the harassment was petty: Pritchett made a point of eating a piece of lemon meringue pie outside the cell where Penny Patch and a couple of other white women were staging a hunger strike. Some of the intimidation involved sexual humiliation: When Faith Holsaert, a white woman from Brooklyn, was arrested, the cops interrogating her fondled her breasts and threatened to strip her. Two other white women, Joyce Barrett and Joni Rabinowitz, were forced to strip to their bras and panties.

Once again, however, the real brutality was reserved for blacks, including the girls and young women who increasingly dominated the Albany campaign. While the local male leaders seemed burned out by this time, unwilling to get involved in any more demonstrations, a group of girls, ranging in age from eleven to sixteen, kept pushing. "They were a wonderful bunch," said Patch, who, like many of her SNCC coworkers, regarded the girls with awe. One of the most intrepid was fourteen-year-old Joanne Christian, who was arrested thirteen times and jailed for sixty days and who, during her various stints in jail, was beaten, thrown down stairs, kicked, and dragged by her hair. Nothing ever seemed to daunt Joanne or her eleven-year-old sister, LaVette, known as Dear, who was jailed seven times, for a total of forty-seven days. Joanne spent her Saturdays patrolling downtown Albany, buttonholing black passersby and pressuring them to register to vote. "I almost feel sorry for the people she approaches—they hardly stand a chance," SNCC organizer Joyce Barrett wrote in a report. In another report, Faith Holsaert described how Joanne "found one of her teachers downtown shopping and the poor woman practically bowled me over in her attempt to avoid the militant Miss Christian." SNCC organizers recalled seeing Joanne at the head of one of the marches, standing next to Dear. Hands on her hips, Joanne glared at Laurie Pritchett, who was looming in front of her. "Sing, Dear, sing!" she ordered her little sister. At the top of their lungs, the two girls serenaded Pritchett with "We Shall Overcome."

For the Christian family and several others in Albany, going to jail had become a badge of honor. Indeed, according to Penny Patch, members of these families would argue over whose turn it was to get arrested, since "someone would have to stay out to go to work or tend to the baby." After one mass meeting, Jack Chatfield asked eleven-year-old Marion Gaines when she was next going to jail, noting that her fourteen-year-old sister, Pat, had been arrested that afternoon. "Tomorrow," Marion said. "I couldn't go today on account of I had to go to music." Said Patch: "Every member of the Gaines family was arrested at different times, including two-year-old Peaches, who was jailed while on a picket line with her mom."

When protests and demonstrations broke out in Sumter County, some forty miles north of Albany (where a future President of the United States, Jimmy Carter, was born), young women once again were in the vanguard. The police in the county seat, Americus, were even more brutal than their Albany counterparts, subduing the more than two hundred participants in an August 8 march with guns, clubs, fists, and cattle prods. Most of the demonstrators were carted off to jail, among them more than two dozen girls, most of them under fourteen, who were taken to the Lee County stockade. Taken there—and forgotten.

It was a horror story to end all horror stories. Children, having been burned with cattle prods and bruised from beatings, locked up in a cell with a toilet clogged with feces, forced to sleep on a concrete floor slick with urine and other waste, and given cold, rancid hamburgers to eat. The stench was unbearable. Attracted by the waste, flies, gnats, and mosquitoes swarmed through the bars of the screenless, broken windows and feasted on the little girls. Eliza Thomas found a cockroach in her hair one night, and Robertina Freeman spotted a rattlesnake crawling into the cell. The girls had to shout for half an hour before a guard came and killed it.

Such inhumane treatment horrified one of Sumter County's top officials, County Attorney Warren Fortson. "I could not comprehend we could do anything like that to children," he said thirty years later. The girls' degradation caused Fortson to start questioning his own previously unshakable belief in white supremacy, a process that eventually led to his conversion to the civil rights cause. His efforts to establish communication between whites and blacks in Americus led to a petition campaign demanding he be removed as county attorney. He eventually resigned, and left Americus in 1965.

Despite Fortson's revulsion over the treatment of the young demonstrators, the girls remained in jail for weeks, apparently having fallen through the legal system's cracks. No one outside Americus seemed to know—or care—what had happened to them. Then one day, Danny Lyon, a University of Chicago student who worked during the summers as a SNCC photographer, came to Americus, and a local teenager volunteered to drive him out to the stockade. When they arrived, the teenager went to the front of the jail to distract the guard, while Lyon crept around to the back, camera in hand. Peering through the bars, he was stunned by what he saw—the garbage, the flies, the stinking, overflowing toilets, but above all those "beautiful teenage girls" standing and sitting in the middle of that hellhole. They, in turn, were mesmerized at the sight of the curly-haired white man and the camera he was aiming at them. They ran over to the window and reached for his hand through the bars, smiling and laughing and whispering, "Freedom." Emotionally overwhelmed, Lyon took shot after shot of the girls in their squalor. When he had finished his roll of film, he whispered good-bye and sneaked back to the car, lying on its floor as his accomplice spirited him out of the county.

Lyon's pictures were developed as soon as he arrived back in Atlanta and were sent to a sympathetic Northern congressman in Washington. Brandishing the photos, the congressman took the floor of the House and told the story of the girls' incarceration. After almost a month in jail, they were finally released.

For all their torment, the young women activists of southwestern Georgia, along with Mama Dollie Raines and the older women, remained undaunted. Like their sisters in Mississippi, they never stopped defying white authorities, never gave up the struggle. "A new day's a-come!" Mama Dollie would declare to those she encountered in her canvassing forays. "Time to wake up and take a stand!"

15

"A Woman's War"

Woman demonstrator carried to paddy wagon by jail trusties
during Jackson, Mississippi, civil rights protest

AS ALBANY DISAPPEARED FROM
the headlines and evening news broadcasts, civil rights workers were fanning out across Mississippi, including the notoriously violent Delta. Once again, it was mostly local women who welcomed the organizers and persuaded others to listen to them, who marched and canvassed with them, who housed and fed them, who suffered retribution with them, and who gave them the courage to continue. Most of the organizers were young men; at that point in the Mississippi movement, Bob Moses did not want women from outside the state doing any field work. Nevertheless, the campaign was, in the words of one organizer, "a woman's war."

The obstacles were staggering. It was difficult to win the confidence of people who had little reason to believe in this bold notion of self-empowerment, who felt themselves at the mercy of white racists. The only certainty was the reprisals they would suffer if they became involved.

No wonder so many blacks in the Delta—and in the rest of Mississippi, for that matter—referred to the movement as "that mess."

One of the organizers, a cocky nineteen-year-old from Jackson named Charles McLaurin, was beginning to understand how the locals felt. McLaurin was riding in a car through the Delta one day with three elderly black women who had agreed to try to register to vote. Even before they left Ruleville, bound for the county seat of Indianola, McLaurin had started to shake. Now, as the car rolled along the highway, he could feel the fear surge through his body. Here he was, taking these women to register to vote after telling them there was nothing to fear, and he was scared witless himself!

But then this was very scary country they were traveling through on that breathless August day in 1962. It was Sunflower County, home of James Eastland and Parchman penitentiary, and spawning ground of the White Citizens Councils. In targeting the Mississippi Delta, civil rights activists were going up against some of the most die-hard segregationists in all of die-hard, segregationist Mississippi. Blacks elsewhere in the South considered Mississippi the heart of darkness, which is how Mississippi blacks felt about the "seething, lush hell" of the Delta. And these days the local authorities were doing all they could to make sure that the Delta lived up to that reputation. When civil rights workers moved into the town of Greenwood, its mayor drawled: "We gonna see how tight we can make it, gonna make it just as tight as we can. It's gonna be rougher, rougher than you think it is."

In the car, McLaurin listened with half an ear as the women chatted quietly. Would a mob be waiting for them in Indianola? he wondered. Much too soon to suit him, the car arrived at the old brick courthouse. As McLaurin sat there, hesitating, the three women calmly got out and walked up the courthouse steps "as if this was the long walk that led to the Golden Gate of Heaven, their heads held high." McLaurin watched in amazement. "I sat there," he said, "trying to figure out why it was that all these years people had been saying that the folks in the Delta were afraid to register, afraid to vote. And here I was—younger, stronger—and I was hanging back while those three old ladies were walking right up to the Man and telling him what they wanted."

Scrambling after them, McLaurin realized that he "was no longer in command. The three old ladies were leading me, I was following them." Later, in a report to SNCC about what had happened that day, he said: "The people are the true leaders. We need only to move them, to show them. Then watch and learn." Although the women were turned away by the county registrar, the example of their strength, courage, and quiet dignity transformed McLaurin's life. "I'll never forget those old ladies. Never. They were my beginning. That's when I started to become a man."

Besides marching to the courthouse, local women also played crucial roles in enlisting support for the movement among leaders in their communities, particularly among ministers, who were often strongly opposed. Indeed, the reputation of black churches in the South as a guiding force of the civil rights movement is somewhat misleading. While Martin Luther King and the rest of the SCLC leadership were ministers, many rural preachers (and a good number in the cities as well), fearing financial and physical retaliation, wanted to have as little to do with the movement as possible. Ministers like King and Ralph Abernathy, with their large, urban congregations and national reputations, might be able and willing to take the risks they did, but unknown country preachers and their largely impoverished flocks often felt otherwise. In the first six months after civil rights organizers arrived in the Delta town of Greenwood, they could find only two churches that would allow them to hold mass meetings. The local women who first became involved in the Mississippi movement did so knowing they were defying their ministers—and ended up putting so much pressure on those clergymen that many finally enlisted, too. In Ruleville, Rebecca McDonald told her board of deacons that she had given more money to the church than anyone else and therefore the movement was going to use the church "whether the white people liked it or not." The deacons yielded.

In Hattiesburg, located in southeastern Mississippi, organizers Curtis Hayes and Hollis Watkins initially found all the churches there shut to them. They were discussing their predicament in a Hattiesburg shop when its owner overheard them. He told them to get in touch with his sister, Victoria Gray, who had been speaking out against racism since she was a child. When Hayes and Watkins contacted her, Gray, a cosmetics distributor, realized that, at last, she was not alone. "All my life," she said, "I had felt kind of odd, the way I thought, the way I felt, the things I was willing to do, and then here were some people who talked my language, apparently thought the way I did, willing to take risks. I just felt like, 'Hah, finally!'" Gray convinced her pastor to open the doors of his church to the two young men. "The Hattiesburg movement," she said, "was born in St. John's," an AME church in the nearby settlement of Palmer's Crossing.

If women were the key to bringing the black churches along, and they were, it was simply confirmation of their traditional role. As Unita Blackwell, a former sharecropper who became one of the Mississippi movement's most effective organizers, put it: "Who's the people that really keeps things going on? It's women. The women is the ones that supports the deacon board. They holler the amen. The women is the ones that supports the preacher. . . . So in the black community the movement quite naturally emerged out of all the women that carried out these roles.We didn't know we was leaders. You knew you did things, but you never saw it as a high political leadership role."

At first, the ebullient Blackwell was afraid that civil rights organizers would overlook her obscure little Delta community of Mayersville. "I sure do hope that them folks show up here," Blackwell told a neighbor. The neighbor replied: "Well, ain't nothing going to ever happen here, child, because nothing don't never happen in Mayersville." But then Blackwell and her neighbor were sitting and gossiping on Blackwell's porch one day when two young men came down the street "with a new kind of stroll that we weren't used to." They smiled at the women and said hello. "That's them, Corinne," Blackwell urgently whispered. "You reckon that's them sure enough?" Corinne asked, staring intently at the strangers. Blackwell nodded emphatically. "I know that's them."

Soon Mayersville's first mass meeting was held, and Blackwell was there. When those same two young men—Charles Cobb and Ivanhoe Donaldson—asked for volunteers to go down to the courthouse and register, Blackwell's hand shot up. She made an immediate impression. Donaldson later recalled telling Cobb: "Hey, if she took over here, this would be great." But then he realized "she had *already* taken over." Laughing, he said, "It was like Christopher Columbus: You're discovering what's already there. Well, that was discovering Unita Blackwell. She was already in charge, and she was just waiting for us to recognize it."

Whenever civil rights organizers arrived in a new place, many would make it a point of seeking out women as contacts. Recalled Stokely Carmichael: "You'd come into a town, not knowing anything about it, and [women] were always there to guide you, protect you." Since slavery, black women in the South had been the glue of their community, the ones who sustained and nurtured its close-knit ties. They came to each other's aid, took care of each other's children, made the community an extension of their own families. For these women, the young civil rights workers became cherished members of that larger family.

"I'm reminded . . . of an expression from the Bible, which is: 'He loved me before he knew me,'" said Jean Wheeler, a SNCC organizer who worked in southwest Georgia and Mississippi. "In Georgia and in Mississippi the local people were like that. They loved us before they ever saw us. When you showed up, they didn't even ask you if you were hungry. They would just do for you like you were their own children." For an organization as perennially short of funds as SNCC was, such support was invaluable. It enabled the organizers to move from one community to another with virtually no money, secure in the knowledge that they would be welcomed at their next stop with shelter and food. Perhaps even more important was the nurturing warmth they received. SNCC's metaphorical idea of itself as "the beloved community" was strengthened by the love it found in the larger communities it entered, enabling its workers to keep going, despite the grinding pressure of knowing that violence and death could be awaiting them down the next lonely road.

As loving and warm as they were, however, local women emphasized to the activists that the workers had responsibilities to the community as well—that they had to get along with others, had to heed others' point of view. For young black men convinced that *they* knew the right and wrong way to do things, that wasn't always easy to accept. Organizers from SNCC and CORE could be brash and arrogant at times, telling people what to do, rather than consulting with them first. CORE organizer Matt Suarez, a native of New Orleans, recalled how he and his coworkers first charged into Canton, in the central part of the state, "trying to bust down brick walls by running our heads through them. We understood very little about Mississippi . . ." The outsiders let the blacks of Canton know that they were there to save them and that the local people should follow their orders. It didn't take long for Annie Devine, an insurance agent in her fifties and the divorced mother of three children, to set them straight. "She agreed with our goals," said Suarez, "but she believed in approaching people with more subtlety and sensitivity, and she was more successful."

Devine, whom Suarez called a "country diplomat," played a vital role in CORE's work in Canton, serving as mediator and go-between for the community's black leaders and the kids from outside. She knew everybody in town and advised CORE activists on the best ways to approach each of them. According to one organizer: "There wouldn't have been no movement in Canton without Mrs. Devine."

Devine, like other black women in Mississippi, believed that the alliance between civil rights workers and local people had to be a genuine, long-lasting partnership. A close friend of Devine's, a woman who would emerge as the guiding force of the Mississippi movement, made that point clear to John Lewis. "[I]f you're going to come to Mississippi, you can't just come here and stay for one day or one night," Fannie Lou Hamer advised the young activist. "You've got to stay here for the *long* haul. I know Mississippi and you'd better be ready to move *in.*"

Hamer had worked for years as a sharecropper on a plantation near Ruleville. On occasion, she had confronted her white boss about the way she and the other black workers were treated. She also talked to her fellow field hands about their dreadful pay and working conditions. "I just steady hoped for a chance that I could really lash out, and say what I had to say about what was going on in Mississippi," she later said.

The youngest of twenty children in a sharecropping family, Hamer remembered her early life as "worse than hard. It was horrible!" She and her siblings often went hungry, and since there was no money for shoes, their mother would tie their feet in sacks when they worked in the fields. On cold days, Fannie Lou, who walked with a pronounced limp after a bout with polio, would stand in the spot where the cows had been resting to warm her cracked, chilblained feet.

School came as a revelation, opening hitherto unimaginable new worlds. Hamer loved to read and was a whiz at spelling, winning one spelling bee after another. But her family needed her to pick cotton, and she had to drop out of school after the sixth grade. When she was twenty-seven, she married Perry (Pap) Hamer, a sharecropper, and they settled down on the Marlow plantation outside Ruleville. Fannie Lou loved children, but her several pregnancies ended in miscarriages, so she and Pap adopted two little girls. In 1961, Fannie Lou underwent surgery for the removal of a small benign uterine tumor. She later learned that the white doctor had sterilized her during the operation. Beside herself with grief and fury, she went to the doctor's office and confronted him. "He didn't have to say nothing—and he didn't," she later said. She didn't know then that sterilization of poor black women without their consent was common in the South; all Fannie Lou Hamer knew was that a white man had felt free to violate her body.

She had been under the heel of whites all her life and was no better off now than she had been as a child. She earned less than four dollars a day in the cotton fields, lived in a small, unpainted frame shack on the plantation, with no running water and a privy out back. When civil rights workers arrived in Ruleville the year after her sterilization, she was more than ready to answer their call.

She attended a mass meeting at her church one hot summer night and heard James Forman and James Bevel talk about how blacks, by registering and voting, could get rid of all the white officials who had persecuted them for so many years. A lightbulb clicked on in Fannie Lou Hamer's mind. "Just listenin' at 'em," she said, "I could see myself votin' people out of office I know was wrong and didn't do nothin' to help the poor. I said, you know, that's somethin' I really want to be involved in." When Bevel and Forman asked for volunteers to register, Hamer immediately raised her hand, unconcerned about the virtual certainty of white reprisal. "The only thing they could do to me was kill me," she said, "and it seemed like they'd been trying to do that a little bit at a time ever since I could remember."

When she went to the Indianola courthouse to try to register, the county clerk instructed her to write out and interpret Section Sixteen of the Mississippi constitution. She copied it without trouble, but there was no way she could interpret it, since it was a section dealing with "facto laws, and I knowed as much about a facto law as a horse knows about Christmas Day." Later that day, she was confronted by the "blazing mad" owner of the plantation on which she had worked for eighteen years. He told her she had a choice: withdraw her application to register or get kicked off the plantation. "Mr. Dee," she replied. "I didn't go down there to register for you. I went down there to register for myself." She had until morning to decide, he said. The next day, Fannie Lou and Pap Hamer were without jobs or a place to live. A friend took them into her house, but the refuge did not last long. A carload of white nightriders pumped sixteen bullets into the bedroom where the Hamers had slept. No one was hit, but, later that same night, thugs shot into another home, seriously wounding two young women from Jackson State University who had come to Sunflower County to help with the registration drive.

Hamer, concerned that her presence was putting everyone around her in danger, for a time moved in with a niece in nearby Tallahatchie County. But she soon returned home and began working with civil rights activists in Sunflower County, all the while intently studying the Mississippi constitution. On December 4, she took the voter registration test again. This time, she passed. Now Hamer and her husband, by this time living in a dilapidated rental house, were under virtual siege. After dark, cars and trucks, shotguns poking from their windows, would crawl past the house. The Hamers made sure to turn off all lights at night, to stay away from windows, and not to open their doors to strangers. Harassment by local officials reached petty extremes. One month, the Hamers received a $9,000 water bill—in a house with no running water.

In the fall of 1962, Bob Moses invited Hamer to come to a SNCC rally in Nashville and tell the story of her attempt to register and her eviction from the plantation. The students were mesmerized by her account, faulty grammar and all, and soon she was traveling throughout the country as one of SNCC's most potent speakers, raising money and spellbinding audiences with her call for struggle, sacrifice, and action. Always, she made clear where her allegiance lay. "If SNCC hadn't of come into Mississippi, there never would have been a Fannie Lou Hamer," she said. "I was respected with the kids and they never told nobody what to say, nobody. . . . This is what's been there all the time, and we had a chance to get it off our chests, and nobody else had ever given us that chance."

Young activists were awed as much by the courage and fortitude of this indomitable woman as they were by her eloquence, her powerful singing, and her facility for coming up with colorful, ironic one-liners. She referred to Mississippi as "the land of the grave and the home of the tree," and said the real name of the NAACP should be "the National Association for the Advancement of *Certain* People." She once told an FBI agent who had done nothing to protect black demonstrators: "If I get to heaven and I see you there, I will tell St. Peter to send me on back to Mississippi."

Indeed, there were those who believed that but for Fannie Lou Hamer's gender and lack of education, she could well have become the most important figure of the civil rights movement. "Fannie Lou had the ability to get the people worked up, much more so than Martin Luther King," declared Henry Kirksey, one of the first blacks elected to the Mississippi Senate in the late 1960s. Eleanor Holmes Norton said she believed that Hamer was as eloquent and charismatic as King, if not more so. "She was an unbelievably brilliant orator and conceptualizer," said Norton. "[Y]ou've never heard a room flying [like one] that Fannie Lou set afire." When Hamer would finish speaking, Norton said, her listeners realized she had "put her finger on something truly important that all of us had felt but she had said. . . . You never needed to hear anybody else speak again."

During 1964's Freedom Summer, Tracy Sugarman, a white writer and artist, accompanied Hamer one Sunday to a little country church near Ruleville. The pastor of the church had not involved himself in the movement, and Hamer was on his case. When she and Sugarman arrived at the church, the minister was in the middle of a reading from Exodus about God's deliverance of the Israelites from bondage in Egypt. For blacks, the story of the Israelites' slavery and persecution by the Egyptians was particularly meaningful because it reminded them of their own experience in America. After the reading, the minister smiled at Hamer. "I'm right pleased that Mrs. Fannie Lou Hamer has joined our service this mornin'," he said. "We are all happy to see you, Mrs. Hamer, and your friend. Would you like to say a few words to the congregation?"

This was what she had been waiting for. By now forty-six years old, she rose slowly, painfully to her feet—a short, heavy, large-boned woman with huge sad eyes and a voice that rolled, Sugarman remembered, like thunder. She transfixed the congregation as she equated their plight with that of the children of Israel, unfurling one biblical allusion after another. "Pharaoh [is] in Sunflower County!" she declared. "Israel's children [are] building bricks without straw—at three dollars a day!" Her voice trembled, and her eyes filled with tears. "They're tired! And they're tired of being tired!" She paused, then turned to the minister and pointed her finger at him. There was silence as her audience strained to hear what she would say. "And you, Reverend Tyler, must be Moses!" she cried. "Leadin' your flock out of the chains and fetters of Egypt—takin' them *yourself* to register—*tomorra*—in Indianola!"

In Greenwood, some twenty miles to the southeast, a number of black women were in the forefront of demonstrations and marches that erupted there in the early spring of 1963. A widow named Laura McGhee particularly impressed civil rights workers with her utter fearlessness. Said McGhee's son Silas: "She is the type of person that would do anything she could for you, anything, irregardless of what it is. [B]ut on the other hand, if you try to mess over her, you got trouble . . ."

Mrs. McGhee's determination to resist any challenge to what she considered her God-given rights was already legendary by the time the organizers came to town. In the 1950s, a white neighbor coveted her farm, but she refused to sell. One day, she saw the neighbor on a bulldozer cutting a ditch through her property. She ran down, climbed up on the bulldozer, and pulled the man off. When the sheriff came, she told him he had ten minutes to get the bulldozer off her property or she would burn it. Sometime later, the neighbor succeeded in having McGhee committed to the state mental hospital and started foreclosure proceedings on her farm. With the help of a lawyer, she managed to get herself released from the asylum and to keep her land.

When SNCC organizers arrived in Greenwood, McGhee was among the first locals to welcome them and was among the first to try to register and to urge others to do the same. When the citizenship school program was introduced in Greenwood, she became one of its first teachers. She allowed workers to stage mass meetings and rallies on her farm, and when the students were arrested after marches and demonstrations, she used the land as security for their bail. When the sheriff came out to warn her about such activities, she told him that he was trespassing and that since he seemed powerless to stop white thugs who used her home for nightly target practice, she certainly didn't want his advice on other matters.

The McGhee boys—Silas, Clarence, and Jake—took after their mother. Silas and Jake, in particular, rarely missed an opportunity to try to clip Jim Crow's wings. Laura McGhee urged them on, even as she worried about their safety. One time, when Jake was arrested, she asked Bob Zellner to go with her to the Greenwood jail to find out what was happening. They were accompanied by a white volunteer lawyer, who was told by Zellner to make sure Mrs. McGhee was included in any conversation the lawyer had with police. Once they got to the station, however, the chief ushered the lawyer into his office, leaving McGhee and Zellner standing outside. Jake's mother, steaming, tried to follow, but a policeman stepped in front of the door and pushed her away. "But that's my son," she said. "They're talking about my son." And before the cop could say anything, she "reared back," as Zellner recalled, "and socked him right in the eye as hard as you could ever want to see anybody hit." The policeman's head hit the back of the door and he started sliding to the floor, woozily trying to draw his gun. Zellner attempted to move McGhee out of the way, so he could grab the gun, but she was intent on "following up on her advantage." She kept jabbing the policeman like a prizefighter, and every time she hit him, his head banged into the door.

Finally, Zellner got hold of the cop's gun and held him down. "Mrs. McGhee," he said, "I think you've hit him enough there. You've got him pretty well subdued." Meanwhile, the chief, on the other side of the door, was shouting, "What's going on out there?" He repeatedly pushed against the door, each time delivering yet another blow to his officer's battered head. Funny as the incident seemed later, Zellner feared at the time that it would have serious consequences. "Here's this policeman," Zellner said, "and he's got this huge black eye, and Mrs. McGhee is totally unrepentant." Although McGhee was arrested, she was promptly freed on bond, and the case never went to trial. The reason for such leniency, Zellner believed, was that the police were embarrassed to have "to explain that Mrs. McGhee had completely beaten the guy up."

The story only added to the legend of Laura McGhee, and in the months and years to come, many local residents would refuse to try to register to vote unless she went with them. What's more, McGhee helped set an example that inspired and further emboldened several of Greenwood's outspoken and rebellious young black women, among them an eighteen-year-old former prostitute named Ida Mae "Cat" Holland.

During one march in Greenwood, while Laura McGhee was trying to yank a nightstick away from a policeman who had been shoving her with it, Ida Mae Holland was confronting the Greenwood police chief himself, Curtis Lary. Someone had pushed Holland to the head of the march, and she announced to Lary: "We're going to the courthouse to register to vote. . . . Our rights are guaranteed by the U.S. Constitution." Lary looked stunned. How could this be—a local whore, who had served time in jail for theft and assault, leading a civil rights march? "For the first time in my life, I saw indecision in Chief Lary's face, and that made me feel so proud," Holland said later. "People started looking up into my face, into my eyes, saying, 'That Cat is sure enough tough, isn't she?' I wasn't so tough. . . . But I knew I couldn't turn back." In more ways than one, the movement helped Holland find her freedom.

She had grown up poor in Greenwood, the daughter of "Aint Baby" Holland, an unmarried laundress who rented the woodshed behind her house to whores and their customers. Raped at eleven by a white man who gave her five dollars afterward, Cat, who, like many of her girlfriends, had discovered that white men could "take us just like that, like lightning striking," was turning tricks at twelve, charging black men five dollars and white men ten. At sixteen, she was pregnant, and shortly before giving birth to a son, she was sent to the county prison farm for shoplifting. A year later, she spent another two months in prison for assaulting the new girlfriend of the man who fathered her child. Then in the summer of 1962, Holland heard that some young outsiders had come to town "to stir up trouble," which to her meant new customers. Spotting one of them on a Greenwood sidewalk, she sashayed suggestively behind him. "I got it. Come an' git it," she chirped. The stranger turned, smiled, and kept on walking. He stopped at a small brick building with a sign on the front door showing interlocking black and white hands. The stranger was Bob Moses. He opened the door and invited her inside.

She walked into an entirely new world. People were scurrying around, answering phones, making plans for canvassing, interviewing impoverished Greenwood residents about their food and clothing needs. A large map of the Delta, covered with pushpins, hung on one wall. Holland stood behind the chair of a young woman who was typing a report. She was sure the typist was tapping out nothing but p's and q's—a black woman couldn't possibly type that fast—but, looking over the woman's shoulder, Holland saw complete, perfectly spelled words and sentences. The young woman was Emma Bell, one of the kids who had walked out of Burgland High School in McComb the year before and who now was working full-time for SNCC. Moses pointed to a nearby desk. "This is your desk," he said, pulling out a chair for Holland "like a gentleman on a date." She sat down, rolled a sheet of paper into a typewriter, and joined the movement. It was, she said, "the beginning of me finding myself."

Before long, she was canvassing, demonstrating, and teaching the first citizenship education class in Greenwood. She also was arrested—thirteen times in all. In fact, going to jail turned out to be one of her greatest con-tributions. A savvy jailhouse veteran before she joined the civil rights bat-tle, she became a mentor and leader for movement women who had never been behind bars before. In the process of all this, she became a different person: "Neighbors who used to look down at me for my whoring and fighting and stealing now looked into my eyes and said, 'How do.'"

Even her mother, who had opposed her involvement with the move-ment, changed her mind. "I glory in yo' spunk, gal!" Aint Baby Holland exclaimed.

Another of Greenwood's young female rebels was June Johnson. Four years younger than Cat Holland, Johnson had also grown up feeling like a misfit. Although she had never been in any serious trouble, she was con-sidered a problem child at school and at home, constantly involved in con-frontations with her classmates, teachers, mother, other members of her family—and whites. As a child, she objected when her grandmother ordered her and her sisters to pick cotton, because the white foremen often fondled young female workers in the fields. She was told to pick cotton anyway. When a foreman smacked her on the bottom with a hoe and ordered her to work harder, she spun around and hit him back. She was ten at the time.

At one of the first mass meetings in Greenwood, fourteen-year-old June was captivated. The organizers took her seriously, and even more important, offered her work that provided an outlet for her anger, rest-lessness, and rebellion. Bob Moses walked her to school in the mornings, talking about the movement and how it could change her life. "My fun," she recalled, "was walking down the street learnin' from Bob Moses."

She agreed to canvass for him and hid her canvassing notebook under her mattress, so her mother would not find it. But one of her sis-ters told on her, and her mother, who cooked for Greenwood's top white restaurant and was fearful of white retaliation, ordered June to take the notebook back. She obeyed, but soon was sneaking out of the house again to go to the movement headquarters. Belle Johnson was furious, but neither scoldings nor whippings could keep her daughter away from the movement.

Early in the summer of 1963, soon after school let out, June begged her mother to let her go for a week to Septima Clark's citizenship school training class. A few months before, SCLC had sent a new colleague of Clark's, Annell Ponder, to Greenwood to organize teacher training sessions in the Delta. Laura McGhee, Cat Holland, and Fannie Lou Hamer were among the first to sign up. Within a couple of weeks, they and twelve other women were teaching the basics of literacy and citizenship to more than two hundred students. Ponder had recruited a few of the new teachers, including Hamer, to go to Charleston for additional training, and June Johnson, who had become one of the local movement's most committed workers, had been invited to go, too. Her mother was against the idea at first, but, after appeals by Bob Moses and Ponder, she reluctantly said yes. Belle Johnson was particularly fond of the reserved, austerely beautiful Ponder, who had won the hearts of many black Greenwood residents since her arrival in April.

The women from the Delta were exhilarated by their experience in Charleston. During their all-night bus ride back home, they decided to put into practice the tactics of nonviolent confrontation they had discussed during the previous week. At an early-morning stop in Columbus, Mississippi, they unsuccessfully tried to integrate the bus station, which enraged their driver. As they started to reboard the bus, he pushed them toward the back. Fannie Lou Hamer told him he was breaking the law and demanded his name and badge number. That made him even angrier, as did the women's singing of freedom songs as the bus pulled out. At each stop after Columbus, the driver got off the bus and made a phone call.

Late that morning, the bus rumbled into Winona, a tiny place on Highway 82 and the last stop before Greenwood. It was Sunday, June 9, 1963. Hamer and a couple of others stayed on the bus, while Ponder, Johnson, and two other women went into the station's white waiting room and sat down at the lunch counter. The waitress took one look at them and hurled her dishcloth at the wall behind them. "I can't take no more!" she cried. Just then, two police officers, presumably alerted by one of the bus driver's calls, emerged from the back of the waiting room and ordered the women to leave. When Ponder declared that such a demand was against the law, one of them snapped, "Ain't no damn law! Get up and get out of here!" The women left, but when they got outside, Ponder wrote down the license plate numbers of the officers' cars. With that, the officers arrested all four women and shoved them into cars. Watching what was going on, Hamer rushed off the bus and was arrested, too.

At the Winona jail, one officer told the women: "I been hearing about you black sons of bitches over in Greenwood, raising all that hell. You come over here to Winona, you'll get the hell whipped out of you." He ordered them into cells, all except June Johnson. "Not you, you black-assed nigger!" he shouted. The fifteen-year-old was wearing a "beautiful pink dress," but the next thing she knew, "I didn't have anything on. They had torn my clothes off. And they just started beating me. With billy sticks, fists, kicking me, stomping me . . ." Writhing in pain on the floor, she was told, "Get up, nigger." She raised her head, and one of the men hit her in the back of the head with a club wrapped in black leather. Her assailants finally yanked the dazed, naked teenager to her feet and dragged her to a cell.

Annell Ponder was next. They shouted questions at her, and when she answered, one of them yelled, "Can't you say, 'Yes, sir,' bitch?" She stared at the men. "Yes, I can say, 'Yes, sir.'" "Well, say it," the cop demanded. She responded, "I don't know you well enough." With that, Ponder's beating began. They worked her over for about ten minutes with blackjacks and a belt, fists and open palms. She crept back to her cell, her clothes torn from the waist down, head swollen and bloody, eyes blackened, teeth chipped. As she passed Fannie Lou Hamer's cell, she whispered, "Pray for me."

But Hamer would soon need prayers herself. The cops apparently had found out who she was, and when she was dragged into an empty cell, one of them snarled, "You bitch, we going to make you wish you was dead." She was thrown facedown on a cot, and a black prisoner was ordered to beat her with a blackjack. They brought a second prisoner in to sit on her legs, and when the first man gave in to exhaustion from beating her, the second took his place. At one point, her dress started to move up her thighs and as she tried to pull it down, one of the cops yanked it over her head. From their nearby cells, the other women could hear Hamer's agonized screams.

When the beating was finally over, the cop's prediction proved to be right. "[B]efore they stopped beating me, I wish they could have hit me one more lick that could have ended the misery that they had me in," Hamer later said. Later, neither she nor the other women were given medical treatment. Indeed, she was convinced that the cops planned to kill them. She overheard one of them say that the women could be thrown into a nearby river and nobody would ever find them.

Alarms, meanwhile, were being set off in Greenwood. The citizenship school teachers who had stayed on the bus reported the arrests of their coworkers as soon as they arrived home. Lawrence Guyot drove to

Winona to investigate, whereupon he, too, was arrested, viciously beaten, and thrown into a cell. Now it was Eleanor Holmes's turn. Holmes, who was working in Greenwood for the summer, went to see police chief Curtis Lary before heading off to Winona. She urged him to call the Winona cops and tell them that she was coming, that she was a student at Yale Law School, and that "there would be all kinds of hell to pay" if they tried to put her in jail, too. He apparently did as she suggested, because she was not arrested and was allowed to see Guyot and the women, although she did not have enough money to bail them out.

In Birmingham, Martin Luther King ordered two of his top lieutenants, Andrew Young and James Bevel, to go to Winona and secure the release of Annell Ponder, an SCLC employee, as well as the others. Neither man had a car, and they asked Dorothy Cotton, who was also in Birmingham, for the use of hers. Only if she could go herself, said Cotton, a coworker and close friend of Ponder's. Young and Bevel replied that going to Mississippi was too dangerous for a woman—an argument that Cotton dismissed as ridiculous. "Those are women in jail in Winona," she pointed out. "If Mrs. Hamer's brave enough to challenge Mississippi, I'm brave enough to help get her out."

At the Winona jail, Young insisted that Cotton stay outside. As it turned out, he and Bevel could have used some of her forcefulness. By Young's own admission, the two men froze when they were ushered into the sheriff's office, afraid to tell him why they were there. He, in turn, "acted as if it was the most normal thing in the world for us to be hanging around that morning." Finally, after a phone call came in from Atlanta about the women and Guyot, Young and Bevel got up the nerve to acknowledge they had come to bail out the sheriff's prisoners.

When the six were finally freed, the two SCLC officials tried to hide their dismay at the shocking appearance of Hamer, Ponder, Johnson, and Guyot. Their eyes were blackened, swollen, and bloodshot; their faces and bodies were covered with huge dark bruises; they could hardly speak. Hamer was taken to a hospital in Atlanta and would not let her family see her for a month. One of her kidneys was permanently damaged. "To the day that she died, she suffered" from the whipping, Johnson said.

The beatings of the women and Guyot were among the most savage assaults in the history of the civil rights movement, made worse by the sexual humiliation involved in the partial or complete disrobing of Johnson, Hamer, and Ponder. The Justice Department, which usually refused to get involved in such attacks (to the great dismay and anger of civil rights workers), filed civil and criminal charges against the white officers who inflicted the beatings, one of the first cases in which such charges were leveled. But when the case came to trial in Oxford, Mississippi, the cops were acquitted of all charges by an all-white jury. "We wondered why we'd come there," recalled June Johnson. "There was no justice." While the beating and its aftermath scarred Johnson emotionally as well as physically, her resolve seemed undamaged. "I'll tell you, all these experiences made me a fighter," she observed. "I was fifteen years old, and I was a fighter."

Little more than a week after her beating, she helped instill that fighting spirit in others. At a voter registration rally in Itta Bena, a few miles from Greenwood, she gave an impassioned speech describing what had happened to her in Winona and declaring that if her listeners registered, they could get rid of people "who beat you up for nothing." After a smoke bomb was thrown into the church, Johnson's audience marched out of the church and to the sheriff's house to demand protection. Scores were arrested, and the next day, forty-five of them, including a seventy-five-year-old woman, were sentenced to six-month terms at Parchman.

As it turned out, however, Johnson's most important convert was her mother. The day that Belle Johnson found out what had happened to her daughter, she quit her job at the white restaurant and decided to join the civil rights fight herself. She started cooking for the workers at the movement headquarters in Greenwood, then began canvassing and speaking at mass meetings. In time, she became a key local leader.

When mass demonstrations erupted in Jackson, Belle Johnson took off for Mississippi's capital. She stayed away so long that her children became alarmed and June set out to look for her. "I took a chance, picketed the state capitol, and when I went to jail," June said, "I found my mother there."

"We Assumed We Were Equal"

*SNCC organizers in Albany, Georgia, in summer of 1963.
On wall: extreme left, Dorie Ladner; third from left,
Martha Prescod; second from right, Penny Patch*

DESPITE EVERYTHING—DESPITE
the grudging attitude of the Kennedy administration and Congress,
despite the hostility of the solid white South, despite beatings and jailings,
despite the Klan and the White Citizens Councils—despite all this and
more, the civil rights movement continued to gain momentum in the early
1960s. Now dozens of young Northern blacks were heading South toward
Mississippi, Georgia, and other battleground states to devote a few
months—or, in some cases, years—of their lives to the cause. In its early
days, SNCC had only a sprinkling of non-Southerners, Diane Nash among
the most notable. But as the organization expanded its voter registration
efforts, it desperately needed more people. Charles Sherrod's project in

southwestern Georgia marked the first time that Northerners, both black and white, were actively recruited. And by 1963, the rapidly growing campaign in Mississippi was taking in Northern blacks, too.

For young black women who joined the cause from outside the South, it was a particularly mind- and life-altering experience. Most of them were fresh from college—and from the restrictions that most campuses placed on female students. Now, suddenly, they were given free rein to challenge Southern sheriffs, provided they had the nerve to do so. According to Lawrence Guyot, "SNCC was truly an open society . . . gender didn't mean a thing. If you were able to risk your life, if you were able to mobilize people and operate through the fear that we all knew was there, that's how you were judged."

Even though men dominated SNCC's official positions of leadership, being a formal leader was not considered to be very important. The organization retained its old freewheeling, egalitarian ways, much to the chagrin of executive secretary James Forman, who kept trying to impose some discipline and order on its engaging anarchy. Jean Wheeler, a Howard University student who first worked in Georgia, then in Mississippi, recalled: "People had titles, but the titles didn't matter. And especially they didn't matter when you were in Mississippi by yourself and there was some sheriff coming toward you with his gun drawn." Wheeler canvassed, organized mass meetings, accompanied local blacks to the courthouse—in short, "did anything I was big enough to do. . . . I just had so much freedom to decide how I was going to work and so much support for my decisions that I never ever felt [a] sense of limitation . . ."

As role models, Wheeler and others from the North, most of whom were raised according to conventional middle-class standards, looked to local women like Fannie Lou Hamer, Dollie Raines, and Belle Johnson, who inspired the younger women with their courage and commitment and their refusal to abide by traditional standards of female behavior. But there were younger local women who were also inspirational, in their own right and in their own way. They included Emma Bell from McComb and the Ladner sisters from Hattiesburg, women who had grown up under the most brutal racism yet had inherited a legacy of defiance from their mothers, grandmothers, and countless others before them.

"We came," Joyce Ladner said, "from a long line of . . . strong black women who had historically never allowed anyone to place any limitations on them." Joyce and Dorie Ladner's mother, whose education had ended with the third grade, had never heard of Sojourner Truth or Harriet Tubman, but she "inherited the tradition that a Sojourner Truth or a Harriet

Tubman set before her." The Ladner sisters were taught by their mother not to allow whites to abuse or misuse them and to always look white men straight in the eye. Joyce and Dorie first got involved in the movement in high school, when they set up the first NAACP Youth Council in Hatties-burg, then as students at Jackson State College. Their mother was terrified that something would happen to them, but her example had been too strong: Her daughters would allow no one to dissuade them from what became an all-out rebellion against discrimination and abuse. Feeling like caged animals all their lives, stifled and humiliated by "ignorant whites whom we regarded as the scum of the earth," the Ladner sisters leaped at the opportunity to claim their freedom. They began meeting other Mis-sissippi women who felt as they did, women who, in Joyce's words, "had ideas they wanted to express and . . . couldn't, [who had] things they wanted to do with their lives and [felt] totally constrained." Like the Lad-ners, none of these women "knew they were oppressed because of their gender; no one had ever told them that."

Joyce and Dorie were eventually asked to leave Jackson State because of their civil rights activity. After enrolling at nearby Tougaloo College, a black church-run school sympathetic to the burgeoning local move-ment in Jackson, they emerged as two of the movement's most militant student leaders. They became organizers for SNCC, where they just nat-urally assumed they would have the same responsibilities and opportu-nities as the men. "When we got into SNCC I would have been ready to fight some guy if he said, 'You can't do this because you're a woman,'" Joyce Ladner declared. "I would have said, 'What the hell are you talking about?' A lot of the women in SNCC were very, very tough and indepen-dent-minded. . . . We assumed we were equal. We were treated that way."

The power relationships between men and women in SNCC were com-plex and did not lend themselves to easy explanations. As *The New York Times*'s Fred Powledge put it: "All these folks were way ahead of everyone else. They were in the vanguard. But you also have to remember that they were functioning at the limits of their sensibility then. One thing that they had not publicly confronted was what we now take for granted as the issue of women's rights, women's equality." While a few men in SNCC did believe in the equality of women, many others did not. Yet because of the nature of the group, and the strength of the women who joined it, many women felt as Joyce Ladner did—that they and their male coworkers were equals. "If you wanted to go into the field and somebody didn't want you to go into the field because you were a woman, that was their opinion," said Bernice Johnson Reagon. "But it never stopped you from doing it. . . . I am not describing an organization where men were progressive when it came to women, and they were for women being equal. I'm not saying that. I *am* saying that . . . the structure of that organization was such that you were the only person who could limit what you did. And you had to find the courage to challenge anything that didn't feel right to you . . ."

The comparatively few white women in SNCC prior to 1964 did not have the same authority or freedom enjoyed by their black counterparts. But they, too, were exhilarated by their sense of power and achievement in an era when white women their age were supposed to be focusing their energies on finding the right man to marry. Penny Patch's early experiences in southwestern Georgia had shown how dangerous it could be for white women to work in the field—although less dangerous for them than for their black coworkers and the local people whom they were organizing. "That was the red flag," said Chuck McDew. "It's one thing to have white women work in the office. It's another [for a black man] to be driving around in rural areas with a white woman sitting by your side. Whites can't handle that. Imaginations just ran wild." The sight of such interracial couples, echoed *Newsweek* correspondent Karl Fleming, only added to the rage and sense of impotence of white segregationists. "That is what it was *all* about, *all* the time, everywhere. It was the great underpinning of the whole damn thing—just pure sexual fear."

Because of the fury of Georgia whites over her presence, Patch was not allowed to operate as freely in the countryside as her coworkers, but she said she didn't resent such restrictions. "I was a white woman, and even given that, I was able to do so much more than [I could have] anywhere else in society." Yes, she was occasionally given traditional woman's work to do—cooking, typing, working in the office. "But," she pointed out, "I also learned to drive a car, listen and persuade, organize people to register to vote or go on demonstrations, develop strategy, act independently if necessary, speak in public, and keep working despite fear and exhaustion."

The white women who followed Patch to Georgia in subsequent summers also spent considerable time out in the field. And by the end of 1963, Bob Moses had invited a handful of white women, all seasoned SNCC veterans, to work in Mississippi. One of them was Casey Hayden, who, as a result of her marriage to Tom Hayden, had a unique vantage point from which to compare SNCC's treatment of women with that of white-dominated student activist groups.

For a brief time after they married, Tom Hayden stayed in Atlanta with Casey, running the Southern office of the newly formed Students for a

Democratic Society, and working closely with SNCC. But he soon decided he would rather lead a student movement of his own than serve as a cog in the SNCC machine. In the fall of 1962, he was elected SDS president, and he and Casey moved to Ann Arbor, where he enrolled in graduate school at the University of Michigan and set out to build SDS into a national organization. Casey, meanwhile, had exchanged the civil rights work to which she was passionately committed for a humdrum secretarial job at a Presbyterian church in Ann Arbor. She missed the movement's warm, collegial atmosphere and its involvement in life-and-death issues, hated the chilly intellectualism of her husband's and his SDS cohorts' endless debates about esoteric issues. One night, she interrupted a "particularly rambling" argument at the Haydens' apartment to say, "I seriously believe y'all are discussing bullshit," then got up and went to bed. On other occasions, she organized walkouts of the women present; they'd adjourn to another room to drink tea and talk about their lives.

Although Casey Hayden was a veteran activist in her own right and contributed to the writing of the Port Huron Statement, SDS's famed articulation of its principles, most SDS leaders, including Tom, viewed her mainly as his appendage. His infatuation with her waned, and he began an affair with another female activist. Such casual relationships were the norm in the student movement, which, as Tom Hayden later wrote, was "a chauvinist's paradise [in which] the positions of power were dominated primarily by men and the opportunities for unequal sexual liaisons were legion."

Tom's paradise was Casey's nightmare. Less than two years after they were married, she left him and returned to Atlanta and SNCC, becoming the organization's Northern coordinator, in charge of fund-raising and working with outside support groups in key Northern states. In the scruffy Atlanta headquarters, she joined another white woman—Dorothy Miller, a quick-witted, fast-talking, petite New Yorker who, as Julian Bond's assistant in SNCC's sophisticated news and public relations operation, turned out volumes of press releases and newsletters. Miller, who had graduated from Queens College and had served as managing editor of one of the college's two newspapers, had come South looking for a way to translate her liberal ideals into real life. She had grown up in leftist circles; but she had been dissatisfied in that hothouse atmosphere. "Everybody always talked about these great ideals, but nobody ever did anything about them," she said.

When Miller left the Atlanta office in the spring of 1963 to marry Bob Zellner, Mary King took her place. King, a tall, serious brunette, was also from New York, the daughter of a liberal Methodist minister who had imbued his daughter with a belief in racial equality. At the age of fifteen, King had stood in front of her high school social studies class, her voice breaking, and talked about the senseless murder of Emmett Till. A story about the murder in *Life*, along with a photograph of Till's mutilated body in his casket, had had "a powerful and traumatic effect" on the white teenager. It was, she later said, "my first graphic confrontation with [the] social evil" of racism. After graduation from Ohio Wesleyan University, King worked on a YWCA campus race relations project directed by Ella Baker, then took the job with SNCC. She and Casey Hayden shared an apartment in a black housing project in Atlanta.

Unlike the black women in SNCC, King, Hayden, Miller, Penny Patch, and most of the other early white women never felt they played anything but a supportive role in the organization. And that's the way they thought it should be. "We were on [blacks'] turf," said Hayden. "We had entered their world. . . . If we had all been in a women's organization and we'd been all white, it would have been different. We were yielding everything, right and left, all the time, because in this setting it was appropriate to do that."

Yet while white women may have been satisfied to remain behind the scenes, the responsibilities they were given helped develop in them a new sense of strength and independence. The work performed by Hayden, King, and other white women was vital for the continued survival of the organization and its workers. Fund-raising kept SNCC financially afloat, if only barely, and generating news stories and maintaining contacts with the Justice Department helped protect the safety of organizers in the field. Twenty-three-year-old Mary King marveled that a phone call from her to a *New York Times* reporter could result in a *Times* story the next day. Her efforts to focus the media's attention on what SNCC was doing "gave me a sense of . . . personal power . . . that few people my age had the opportunity to experience," she later wrote.

More and more, King and Hayden found themselves analyzing the traditional roles of women in society, questioning society's expectations of female subordination and submission. During the year they lived together, the young women were heavily influenced by two authors who would later become feminist icons—Simone de Beauvoir and Doris Lessing. King and Hayden's underlined, marked-up copy of Beauvoir's book *The Second Sex* finally fell apart from so much use. They spent hours studying its complex, scholarly attack on man's domination of women throughout history, just as they spent hours discussing Lessing's *The Golden Notebook* and its female characters' attempts to develop egalitarian relationships with the men in their lives.

The struggles of the women in Lessing's book were particularly relevant for Casey, still trying to come to terms with her marriage to Tom Hayden and its breakup. *The Golden Notebook* was an "enormously supportive book" that "mirrored my own life," she said. Within the civil rights movement, no one was focusing on the relationships between men and women, even though such personal ties were "just so central." Lessing's "psychological insights were invaluable because there was no place for psychology in the movement."

Intent on forging a world of racial equality, the men and women of SNCC spent little time examining the complexities and contradictions inherent in their own relationships and in their work. There was, for example, the apparent contradiction between SNCC's male leadership and "macho" persona and what many considered to be its "feminine" style of operation, focusing on the creation of community and the empowerment of others. Then there was the intricate relationship between the sexes, in which strong, independent black women deliberately pushed men to the forefront, content to remain in the background themselves and to have their men protect them. For centuries, black men in America had been cowed into submission by the brutality of racism, unable to defend themselves, let alone their wives and daughters, against abuse by whites. But now the young African-American men of SNCC had come forward, defying white authority and courting danger and death on a daily basis. "How can you not support these guys for doing that?" said Casey Hayden. "Of course you want them to be head [of the group]."

The black men in SNCC tended to be very protective of their female coworkers. Traveling through the Georgia or Mississippi countryside, the men usually would insist on driving and often would push female passengers to the floor when potential danger approached. In local projects, men sometimes tried to keep women out of the field. Ivanhoe Donaldson thought such protectiveness "wasn't something actually born out of chivalry. It was kind of a reinvestment in one's sense of manhood, and the idea 'You can't mess with our women.' So there was this concern about exposing women to brutality . . . and situations where they could be subjected to abuse."

A number of women, black and white, didn't mind being shielded in this manner. Joyce Ladner, for one, remarked: "I didn't want to sit in the front. . . . For black people, black Southern people especially, we understood that as a kind of protectiveness, like a brother would protect." But there were other women who objected. The issue, according to Donaldson, "created a lot of stress in the organization because the women felt like . . . they wanted to stand side by side and engage in all the struggles that everybody else did."

There was stress even in the southwestern Georgia project, where, thanks to Charles Sherrod, women performed the same work as men. But Sherrod also could be "quite patriarchal," in the view of Penny Patch, imposing a strict code of behavior on women that did not apply to men. "Men just had a lot more freedom," Patch said. "Women had to be extremely well behaved." Women, for example, were barred from becoming romantically involved with local men, while male SNCC workers were free to go out with local women.

In the summer of 1963, Martha Prescod, an African-American student from the University of Michigan, was exposed to Sherrod's protectiveness when she stopped off in Albany on her way to work in Mississippi. She had been told that Bob Moses was finally welcoming outside women, but when she got to Georgia, Sherrod informed her that she could not continue on to Mississippi, that it was too dangerous. So Prescod and Jean Wheeler, also en route to Mississippi, stayed on in Albany to work. Then, one day, they called Moses to find out how things were going. "Where are you?" he asked. "I've been waiting for you." Sherrod "wanted to keep us and protect us," recalled Wheeler, "[but] we thought that Greenwood was a much more sexy place to be, much more exciting and dramatic and powerful . . ." Unwilling to confront Sherrod directly, Prescod and Wheeler waited until the next time he was arrested and then slipped out at midnight, on their way to Greenwood.

In SNCC's early years, the roles of women and whites were not the emotional, divisive issues they later became. In the early 1960s, race was the sole focus of SNCC and the rest of the movement. Just about everyone considered questions raised by gender to be utterly beside the point. Anne Braden was one of the few to disagree. "Women, like Negroes, still aren't totally free," she wrote a friend in 1962. "In fact, I think that my next crusade—after we integrate—will be to see if we can't win real freedom for my sex. In a way, I'm working on the two battles simultaneously, I guess." Braden once confronted Chuck McDew, then chairman of SNCC, about his views on women during a discussion over who would take Bob Zellner's place when Zellner returned to school. "It doesn't have to be a man, does it?" she asked McDew. He looked at her with horror, "as if to say, 'What other kind of creature is there in the world?'" But she persisted, saying, "I mean, it could be a girl, couldn't it?" Looking even more horrified, he responded with an emphatic "No!"

McDew, like other SNCC activists, was wary of the danger created by white women in the field, but Braden was convinced that the major reason for his opposition to a woman was a sense of "male supremacy." Recalling the incident a few months later in a letter to Joan Browning, Braden wrote: "My feminist blood was boiling—but at that moment we were in the courthouse in *Magnolia*, Miss., of all places, for the McComb trials, and surrounded by the enemy, so I did not feel that it was the time or place to have a full-dress argument with him. So I just said, 'OK. But when you all get ready to fight for the *whole* human race, let me know.'"

Braden had raised an issue that SNCC workers did not want to think about. As they saw it, they were bound together in an exuberant closeness unfathomable to those outside the movement—and even to some of those in it. Sharing suffering and danger, working against all odds to transform the social structure of their country, they saw themselves as the true "beloved community"—"a band of brothers and sisters in a circle of trust." Chuck McDew remarked: "I don't think I've ever loved, or felt, as intensely about people as I did back then. How many people would you tell now, 'Yes, I will die for you'?"

Completely consumed by the movement, most SNCC workers lacked any personal life outside it. They depended on each other for emotional sustenance and virtually every other kind of support, and whenever they met would wrap their arms around each other in long embraces and enthusiastic bear hugs. "What sustained us from day to day was an intense feeling of interdependency—the sense that we had only one another to rely on . . . ," said Mary King. "We could not trust anybody else." For Casey Hayden, as for others, ". . . [the movement] was everything: home and family, food and work, love and a reason to live . . ." Adding to the young activists' exhilaration was the knowledge that they were engaging in a remarkable experiment: Not only were they preaching racial integration, but they were experiencing it as well. "We simply dropped race," Hayden declared. ". . . We were living in a community so true to itself that all we wanted was to organize everyone into it . . ."

That passionate closeness, not surprisingly, translated into a consid-erable amount of sex. Bob Zellner recalled "a lot of loving going on," and Jean Wheeler said, "We were twenty years old. What do you expect?" The romantic relationships within SNCC had a feverish intensity, which was only enhanced by the aphrodisiacs of excitement and danger. Many fell under its spell, including young women who had been brought up with the idea that sex should be saved for marriage. "We were young, we were living in wartime conditions . . . ," Penny Patch said. "[W]e never knew whether we would see one another again. We were ready, black and white, to break all the taboos."

At Swarthmore, Patch had been "totally entranced" by the male SNCC activists who had come to her campus on a recruiting trip, finding them "heroic and brave and incredibly smart and very attractive." She was hardly alone in her reaction to the dashing, danger-defying young men. "Twentieth-century cowboys driving broken-down automobiles" was how one older civil rights activist described them.

By 1963, the civil rights movement had become chic among liberal circles in the North and in Hollywood. Dorothy Miller recalled watching movie stars hanging on every word uttered by Bob Moses and Bob Zellner. "We were," she said, "*their* movie stars." But it was the men, more than the women, who were the center of attention, who were feted at cocktail parties and interviewed on national television. For a time, said SNCC organizer Dion Diamond, male civil rights activists had the cachet of rock stars, complete with their own groupies. Which meant, he said, "instant access to . . . sex. Unabated sex. And I think if there were one hundred . . . black civil rights workers, I would dare say that ninety-nine . . . took advantage of it."

That was as true in Greenwood and Ruleville as it was in Los Angeles and New York. "[I]n a town with no heroes, a SNCC organizer who publicly voiced opposition to the status quo and who physically carried that out before the police was sought after as a sexual partner" by local women, Lawrence Guyot said. Such offers were not often refused. "SNCC organizers were no saints," Guyot acknowledged. "We asked [for] discretion. We were never able to enforce it."

Bob Zellner, for one, was astonished by such sexual freedom. He had come from rural Alabama, his father was a Methodist minister, and he definitely was not prepared for the extracurricular goings-on he discovered in SNCC. But he, too, was soon drawn into the romantic roundelay—first with Susan Wilbur, the Freedom Rider whom John Seigenthaler tried to rescue from the mob in Montgomery. Zellner was engaged to Wilbur when he met Dorothy Miller in Atlanta in 1962. Despite his engagement to Wilbur, Zellner began a relationship with Miller. A year after they met, they were married. More than thirty years later, Zellner recalled his whirlwind romance with Miller, musing how "strange" it was because "I was very much in love with Susan." For Zellner, as for the others in SNCC, it was a heady, confusing time.

Sensitive to the history of white men preying on black women in the South, Zellner said he had confined his relationships to white women. Likewise, a number of black SNCC workers got involved only with other blacks. But many other activists freely crossed the racial line in their romances—white men with black women, and more often, black men with white women. Black men and white women—it was the greatest social taboo in the South, and one that civil rights workers defied with as much gusto as they challenged every other racial restriction. "We prided ourselves on being color-blind," said Casey Hayden, "and the black men, of course, were the most desirable because they were the heroes." In having interracial affairs, white women were rejecting their culture's historical fear and suspicion of black men. For black men, the significance of such affairs was even more profound. White women were the sacred totem of Southern white supremacy, the rationale for denying black men their rights and their manhood, the ultimate forbidden fruit. Whether in the North or South, black boys grew up knowing certain things "without ever knowing how you knew them," observed Roger Wilkins, Roy Wilkins' nephew and an official in the Kennedy and Johnson administrations. "You knew that Mississippi was evil and dangerous, that New York was east and the Pacific Ocean was west. And, in the same way, you knew that white women were the most desirable and dangerous objects in the world. . . . Blacks of a very young age knew that white women of any quality went with the power and style that went with the governance of America."

If black men in SNCC were laying claim to their manhood and to future power through their involvement with white women, they also crossed the racial line simply to love and be loved. "We used to talk a lot about our relationships with white people," said Chuck McDew. "You had to have them as friends, you had to have them as lovers, because otherwise you'd go crazy. You'd be burned up by what we called the 'Charlie fever.' You had to know that everybody wasn't like the people who wanted to kill you. You had to reach out."

McDew himself had relationships with several white women, including Dinky Romilly, the daughter of Virginia Durr's old friend Jessica Mitford. McDew and Romilly met when he made a SNCC recruiting trip to Sarah Lawrence College in New York, where she was a student; not long afterward, she joined the SNCC staff in Atlanta. Durr, who took a deep interest in the love lives of her friends and their children, was greatly concerned about McDew's reputation as a ladies' man. "I hear from numerous sources that Chuck is a wonderful guy but has girls all over the place and picks his rosebuds where he may . . . ," she wrote a friend. "I think the

Dink deserves better than that." While the relationship was no casual fling, McDew eventually did get involved with someone else, and Romilly later took up with SNCC executive secretary James Forman.

Many movement romances were like McDew and Romilly's—caring, intense, and short-lived. "Sex, enjoying each other's affection . . . was a way of reassuring each other that we were going to be okay," said Charles Jones. "It wasn't a question of a long-term commitment. It was a question of a mutual need that members of the movement themselves shared with each other." Like Jones, many others in the movement saw sex as a gesture of reaching out and giving to one another—"it wasn't just sex, it was also sharing ideas and fears, and emotional support," one young female worker said. "If you were lucky enough to have a bed," declared Casey Hayden, "you might feel bad if you didn't share it."

But sex could also be used as a form of domination and control. A number of SNCC men engaged in what Charles Jones called "sexual power games." Some were sexually aggressive, trying to "get in bed with every woman—black or white—that they could find," said one white woman active in SNCC. Annie Pearl Avery, a black activist from Alabama, got so tired of unwanted advances from her male coworkers that she put out the word at a SNCC conference in Atlanta: "Anybody that comes to my door and tries to come in there without permission, I'm going to hurt you." Since Avery was known to tote a gun on occasion, the warning had a strong effect.

Although almost everyone involved in SNCC in its early years considered themselves part of a loving, tightly knit community, it clearly was not a utopia. The undeniable closeness of its members had helped paper over—but not altogether erase—the vast differences among them in race, gender, class, and background. From the beginning, there were signs of potential trouble, although many preferred not to see them. When she started working in the Atlanta office, Dorothy Miller recalled "some antagonism" toward her, which she believed stemmed from her assertive, demanding, high-adrenaline style: "When I said I was going to meet somebody at eleven o'clock, I meant eleven o'clock." Her attitude often was at odds with the laid-back Southern way of operating preferred by others, and Miller became known "as a bossy white lady" by some on the staff. While she thought at the time that the criticism was "an individual thing directed at me," she later realized that it was part of a general resentment on the part of certain black staffers that "white people were getting involved who [were] much more skilled and who ended up with skilled jobs." But, according to Miller, little attention was paid then to such tensions. "The attitude was that the problems we were having came from the outside, but inside we shouldn't have these problems because we were one big family . . . and we were. . . . The consensus was that we were not going to let threats divide us. . . . We didn't really come to grips with the fact that there were inherent problems in having a multiracial organization."

In trying to wipe out racial inequality and injustice, the movement was challenging history. Yet history would insist on having its say. The experiences and attitudes of SNCC members, black and white, had been profoundly affected by events that had taken place generations before they were born—by a slave owner's wife beating a female slave for bearing her husband's child, for one, or by a black man lynched after being falsely accused of rape. The emotional legacy of such occurrences often were buried deep in people's psyches, manifesting themselves in unexpected and dramatic ways.

One such drama occurred on a fall night in 1963 when Mary King and Casey Hayden invited several black male coworkers to their Atlanta apartment after a day of SNCC staff meetings. They all were sitting in the living room, continuing a discussion about plans for Mississippi, when there was a sudden commotion outside the front door and three unknown black men burst into the apartment. One was carrying a sawed-off shotgun. Another had a butcher knife. The SNCC men in the living room jumped up and fled out the back door. The women, meanwhile, told the armed strangers, in the calmest tones they could muster, that they had to leave, and, finally, they did.

King and Hayden had no idea what to make of the incident. They didn't know the men, and they were sure their coworkers didn't know them, either. They didn't know what the men had in mind when they broke into the apartment or why they left so readily. Had they invaded the wrong apartment? Above all, King wrote later, she had no idea why her friends had run away, leaving her and Hayden to face the intruders on their own. Certainly, she thought, it was not because of cowardice. The men who fled had proven their courage many times over, standing up to murderous white racists in one Southern town after another. Did they leave, she wondered, because they felt they were in greater danger than she and Hayden? That, in fact, is what Casey Hayden believed. "The SNCC guys split quite simply because we were white women and black men alone in an apartment in the Deep South," Hayden said years later. "They ran from lynching. We, as white women, were not threatened. The guys were at risk of lynching, and we weren't. Of course they would run." It made no difference whether the men at the door were black or white, she said: "Black men were often hired by whites to do their dirty work."

Whatever the reason for their friends' flight, King and Hayden never found out for sure. When the SNCC staff meeting resumed the next day, neither they nor the men brought up what had happened. Although confused and upset, King refrained from saying anything, in part, she wrote, because she disliked confrontation.

The fissures of expectations and experience dividing white women and black men thus remained unexplored, just as other psychological divides would go unexamined by those in the movement. In less than a year, the influx of white volunteers into Mississippi would widen the fissures into unbridgeable chasms.

17

"We Can't Deal with Her"

Gloria Richardson and Attorney General Robert F. Kennedy
at 1963 press conference

THE TEMPERATURE OF THE CIVIL
rights movement rocketed upward in the spring and summer of 1963, as dozens of protests erupted throughout the country and a number of them exploded into violence. In later years, some historians would cite the marches in Birmingham as the inspiration for all this activity. Martin Luther King was in Birmingham, and that, as usual, made it the center of the civil rights universe as far as the media were concerned. In fact, much of the protest in 1963 either predated Birmingham or was nearly simultaneous with it. Cambridge, on the Eastern Shore of Maryland, was one of the early battlegrounds that year. The movement forces there were led by a woman—a divorced, middle-aged mother of two named Gloria Richardson.

In Cambridge, Richardson broke all the rules. In a movement where women tended to exert authority behind the scenes, she was unmistakably out front—the head of the only major grassroots campaign beyond the borders of the South. At a time when most local movements were focusing on the right to vote and access to public accommodations, Richardson wanted to end racial discrimination in housing, education, and hiring. A woman who would not compromise and could not be managed, she stood up to men in authority, whether they were the white power brokers of Cambridge, or Kennedy administration officials, or some of her fellow civil rights leaders—and earned their considerable wrath as a result.

The demonstrations in Cambridge began in March 1963. The spark that ignited them came when the management of a local movie theater that had traditionally confined blacks to the balcony decided to restrict them still further—to the balcony's *rear* seats. By summer, the protests would lead to violent clashes between whites and blacks, and the Attorney General of the United States would intervene.

In the center of it all—to the bewilderment of many in Cambridge— was Gloria Richardson. Richardson came from one of the most prominent, well-connected black families in Cambridge: Her grandfather had been a member of the Cambridge City Council for more than thirty years. A graduate of Howard University, Richardson now lived in her grandfather's stately house on Race Street. In truth, though, Richardson's privilege was as problematic, as complex as the history of blacks in Cambridge. Before the Civil War, many free blacks lived on Maryland's Eastern Shore. Yet Cambridge was a major slave-trading center, whose auction block had been situated downtown, directly in front of the courthouse. Unlike blacks in the South, those in Cambridge never lost the right to vote once it was granted to them in 1869, and beginning in the early 1900s, blacks served on the Cambridge City Council. Nevertheless, the political power and rights of Cambridge's African-American community were severely limited by a rigorous system of segregation. Despite the connections of Richardson's family, her father could not get treatment at Cambridge's whites-only hospital when he was ill. Despite her education, Richardson was unable to find a decent job in Cambridge after her divorce and was forced to settle for work at a local garment factory.

The forty-year-old Richardson had always closely identified with Harriet Tubman, who had been born a slave on a plantation on the Eastern Shore, not far from Cambridge. Richardson grew up steeped in the lore of the legendary liberator of slaves turned Civil War spy. Richardson's children went to school with Tubman's descendants. And when the civil rights movement came to Cambridge in 1962, Richardson, like Tubman, didn't hesitate to take charge. She helped organize and then became head of the Cambridge Nonviolent Action Committee, a group affiliated with SNCC but under local control. The committee's original demands were for an end to segregation in restaurants, theaters, and other public accommodations, but Richardson broadened the campaign to an all-out attack on racial inequality, from inadequate health care to discrimination in jobs, housing, and education. The restriction of blacks to the back of the theater balcony was the tinder that set off the explosion.

With help from Swarthmore, Brown, Morgan State, and Maryland State students, Richardson organized a series of sit-ins and protests. On March 25, she and a number of other Cambridge activists appeared before the City Council to demand immediate integration of all public facilities downtown. Their appearance at the meeting turned into an angry confrontation, and over the next seven weeks Richardson and her cohorts renewed their demands daily by picketing and sitting in at City Hall, the county courthouse, and the jail. More than eighty demonstrators, including Richardson, were arrested. Finally, a local judge ordered the creation of a committee to negotiate the protesters' demands, and the prisoners were released.

For a few days, there was relative peace until twelve black teenagers were arrested on May 25 for picketing the Board of Education. Negotiations broke down, and violence flared, with two white men shot and wounded and several white-owned businesses set afire on June 10. The state police were summoned, and more than twenty blacks were arrested. Undaunted, Gloria Richardson stood on the front porch of her house and called for more demonstrations. She urged nonviolence and appealed to Attorney General Robert F. Kennedy for federal intervention.

On June 13, a melee erupted when a mob of whites chased a large group of black demonstrators back into the black section of town. State troopers sealed off roads, the National Guard was called in, and the next day martial law was declared and a curfew imposed. For three weeks, the Guard kept the lid on, but when the troops were pulled out on July 8 and a group of black students tried to integrate a popular restaurant, whites harassed and beat up the black demonstrators. Three nights later, several carloads of whites sped through black communities, spraying the air with bullets. A number of blacks, crouched behind cars and taking cover in buildings, returned fire. Ordered to return to Cambridge, the National Guard used tear gas and warning gunshots to restore order.

Appalled local government officials had earlier approached Richardson with what they considered an extraordinarily generous offer. In return for her promise to call off demonstrations for a year, they would begin admitting a few black students to four grades in the public schools, hire one black in the city employment office, enact an ordinance desegregating public accommodations, and create an interracial committee to work on other racial problems. It wasn't good enough. Richardson and her followers demanded complete school integration and equal opportunity in all job hiring.

Once again, she urged the Kennedy administration to intervene, warning that continuing white violence against black demonstrators might well touch off an explosion of black violence against whites. Finally, the Kennedys listened—and entered the conflict. The federal government's intervention in Cambridge came as a surprise to most civil rights activists since the administration had adamantly refused to get involved in previous local racial confrontations, such as the one in Albany. But unlike the racial flash points in the Deep South, Cambridge was only seventy-five miles from Washington, and the incidents there, among the worst in the country that spring and summer, made the federal government very apprehensive. Less than a month earlier, prompted by the violence against blacks in Birmingham and other Southern cities, President Kennedy had issued the strongest denunciation of racial discrimination ever made by a U.S. President. Afterward, he sent to Congress a bill that, among other things, proposed to ban segregation in public accommodations throughout the nation. Although some black leaders complained that the legislation wasn't strong enough, it was a significant milestone—and a significant risk—for Kennedy, one that he thought might turn out to be his "political swan song." All the more reason, then, to keep racial tension in Cambridge damped down and not give Southern congressmen another weapon to use against his bill.

On July 22, Gloria Richardson was summoned to Robert Kennedy's office in the Justice Department, along with several state government representatives, and SNCC chairman John Lewis, among others. The meetings were loudly confrontational, with Richardson responsible for many of the sparks. Kennedy and Burke Marshall were as flummoxed by her as the city fathers of Cambridge had been. Wrote Murray Kempton in *The New Republic*: "She is a stranger and cannot be engaged, because she is both a Negro and a woman and thus represents the two largest figures in Southern myth and the two smallest in Southern reality. What deepens her mystery is her entire failure at the conventional commercial and civic response." Kempton quoted a Cambridge official's plaintive observation: "People ask what we did wrong, but when you got a woman like Gloria Richardson in your town, it doesn't make much difference what you did wrong. . . . We can't deal with her and we can't deal without her."

Martin Luther King, Roy Wilkins, and other male civil rights leaders believed in compromise. Richardson, in contrast, looked back on three centuries of slavery and abuse and concluded that the time for compromise had passed. Like Diane Nash, whose own confrontation with Robert Kennedy had occurred two years earlier, she was an outsider and did not care whether or not she was accepted by white power brokers. She believed that Kennedy and Marshall were more focused on ending the violence than on assuring equality for Cambridge blacks, that any promises made would eventually be broken.

Yet, despite Richardson's misgivings, she did finally agree to an accord hammered out in the meetings in Kennedy's office. The terms called for a complete overhaul of Cambridge's race relations—from desegregation of the schools and hospitals to new public housing for blacks. Richardson said later that she signed what became known as the Treaty of Cambridge because she was certain it would not hold. She hoped to prove that Cambridge had no intention of living up to the agreement, that Washington's intervention would prove to be no more effective than local demonstrations.

Her cynicism was justified. Despite the "treaty," Cambridge remained a segregated town. In less than a year, it was convulsed once again by violence. Richardson's many detractors charged that she contributed to the continuing racial disharmony by urging blacks not to vote in a special election on a referendum on whether to desegregate public accommodations. Richardson responded that these rights were guaranteed to blacks by the Constitution and that they should not be subjected to a vote.

In the view of the national media, the government, and many civil rights leaders, it was Gloria Richardson's fault that little or no progress in race relations had been made in Cambridge. The recalcitrance of city officials came up for almost no discussion. Martin Luther King, the Urban League's Whitney Young, and Roy Wilkins accused Richardson of grandstanding. Noting that most of the civil rights leaders who criticized her had never been to Cambridge to see for themselves what was going on, Richardson was convinced that their attacks were made at the behest of the administration, that the Kennedys "wanted things quieted down, and so they told these people then to try to cut the ground from under the movement."

She was shunned as a renegade who did not hew to the traditional civil rights agenda, who claimed more for blacks than the right to vote and to use public accommodations. Her critics in the movement had no inkling that she was a harbinger of what the movement was to become.

*   *   *

In the spring and summer of 1963, however, most mainstream movement leaders, Martin Luther King prominent among them, were more interested in gradualism and compromise. The demonstrations in Birmingham had commandeered the attention of the nation and the world, with searing photos and television footage of young marchers chased and bitten by Bull Connor's lunging police dogs and blasted by fire hoses. But pressured by the Kennedy administration, King and the SCLC had agreed to a settlement with Birmingham's white power structure—vague pledges to desegregate store facilities and to hire blacks sometime in the future—that fell considerably short of what had been demanded at the beginning of the campaign.

As it turned out, the Birmingham crusade had a far greater impact nationwide than on the city where it was waged. Only the smallest dent was made in Birmingham's rigid segregation. Local racists still were allowed to abuse and attack blacks more or less at will. But because of Birmingham, Americans were now focused on civil rights as never before. President Kennedy joined the national and international outcry, telling one audience that the photographs of police dogs attacking demonstrators made him sick. In the two weeks after the first Birmingham march, *The New York Times* printed more stories about race than it had published in the preceding year. A little more than a month after the demonstrations, the President introduced the 1963 Civil Rights Act with the declaration: "The events in Birmingham and elsewhere have so increased the cries for equality that no city or state can prudently choose to ignore them." By the summer of 1963, a tidal wave of protest had swept over the South, with some fourteen thousand persons arrested in demonstrations in almost two hundred towns and cities.

When plans for the March on Washington were announced in midsummer, it was billed as a climax to that season of protests, as well as a way to prod Congress into passing Kennedy's civil rights bill. Martin Luther King and other civil rights leaders hoped that the event would rivet the attention of America and the world, and it did have that effect—even before it occurred. The idea of tens of thousands of blacks streaming into Washington to demand their rights, after a summer of widespread racial turmoil and violence, was disturbing to many whites, who feared and predicted that the marchers would turn violent (even though most of the summer's violence had been committed by whites). "The March Should Be Stopped," declared the headline of a New York *Herald Tribune* editorial. The *Washington Star* proclaimed that if the "misguided pressure" of civil rights protests "is to be capped by some climactic idiocy, like the proposed March on Washington . . . then it will have no happy ending." The Kennedy administration opposed the march, too—at least at first. The Kennedys felt it would hurt the President's popularity, already sagging from his proposed civil rights bill, and would hamper administration efforts to get it passed.

Even within the movement, there was considerable dissension. SNCC activists wanted to use the march as an instrument of mass civil disobedience, including sit-ins and picketing of the Capitol, the Justice Department, and the White House. But King and the other leaders insisted that the march must be peaceful and law-abiding, that it must not provide any ammunition to opponents of the administration's bill, and that Kennedy and his people must not be treated as the enemy.

In the midst of all this, only one person seemed to care that, in the planning for what the leaders hoped would be the most glorious moment of the civil rights struggle, women had been completely ignored. The lone exception was the only woman on the nineteen-person planning committee, Anna Arnold Hedgeman. She was outraged that no woman was to march with the male leaders, or speak at the Lincoln Memorial, or meet with President Kennedy afterward. Finally, bowing to Hedgeman's pressure, the committee penciled in a brief "Tribute to Women," to take place at the beginning of the Lincoln Memorial rally. A. Philip Randolph would introduce Rosa Parks, Daisy Bates, Diane Nash, Gloria Richardson, and a few other heroines of the movement. None, however, would be given the chance to speak. Hedgeman couldn't believe it. Not one of her fellow committee members had voiced any qualms about the plan. No one else seemed to find it extraordinary that the women who had helped launch the movement and kept it going were denied a voice on this singular day.

She was determined that women be given their say. This sixty-four-year-old black woman had spent most of her life as an administrator in predominantly white institutions—the YWCA, the federal government, and the administration of New York mayor Robert Wagner—and in each job, she had been an outspoken champion of racial and social justice. Working for the National Council of the Churches of Christ at the time of the march, she was responsible for recruiting thousands of white Protestants throughout the country to participate in the demonstration. From the start, she had objected to the way the march's leaders regarded women. She didn't like the fact that she was the only woman on the planning committee, but her fellow members ignored her complaints about that, just as they later ignored her objections to the invisibility of women in the march. In her view, the last-minute "Tribute for Women" didn't come close to adequate recognition. At the same time, she didn't want to make a big fuss, didn't want to embarrass Wilkins, Randolph, and the rest. So, as the march date neared, she wrote a letter to Randolph, proposing that one of the women to be honored also be allowed to make a brief speech on behalf of the others. She sent copies of the letter to the other committee members, then sat back and waited, confident that the men would see the justice, the fairness of what she was suggesting.

But she heard nothing, not even at the committee's final meeting just a couple of days before the march. The time for politeness was over. As the meeting neared adjournment, she asked for the floor, picked up her letter, and read it aloud. "In light of the role of Negro women in the struggle for freedom and especially in light of the extra burden they have carried because of the castration of our Negro man in this culture, it is incredible that no woman should appear as a speaker at the historic March on Washington meeting at the Lincoln Memorial," the letter began. Since male leaders of the movement "have not given women the quality of participation which they have earned through the years," it fell to the sole woman on the committee to insist that at least one woman be given a voice at the rally.

After Hedgeman finished, the only response came from Roy Wilkins. "No one can quarrel with that statement," he said. "I think the case is made." Hedgeman was delighted. She sat back and waited—but again, nothing happened. In the end, there were no changes in the program. It would have been difficult to choose one woman to speak "without causing serious problems vis-à-vis other women and women's groups," the march's leaders argued. They seemed to have projected their own attitudes and behavior onto women: In fact, they were the ones who had jockeyed for attention and position, who had fought among themselves over who would speak, and for how long.

In New Haven, where she was studying for a doctorate in law at Yale University, Pauli Murray was as appalled as Hedgeman at the march's snubbing of women. Once again, the fifty-three-year-old Murray was ahead of her time. The petite, chain-smoking activist had been a pioneer in the civil rights struggle: When Martin Luther King was still a schoolboy in Atlanta, she had been arrested and jailed for refusing to move to the back of a bus. Four years later, she had led a sit-in at a Washington restaurant. Now, once again, she was out in front, crusading for the rights of women at a time when most black women in the movement considered that an extraneous issue.

Murray begged to differ. In the course of her peripatetic career, she argued, she had suffered as much from Jane Crow, her term for sexual discrimination, as from Jim Crow. "What does it profit me personally to fight fifty years of my life for the civil rights of Negroes only to have to turn around and fight another fifty years so that I and my sex may benefit from the earlier struggle?" she wrote less than a month before the March on Washington. "I do not have that many years to live, and am frank to confess I am selfish enough to want to enjoy equality in *my* time."

Her three years at Howard Law School had given Murray her first taste of sexism. Howard was the country's major training ground for civil rights lawyers in the 1940s, yet its male professors and students treated female students as "objects of ridicule disguised as a joke." Race was not a factor at Howard since the law school was all black. "Therefore," said Murray, "the problem of sex was isolated and made more visible." Although she was first in her class, she felt like an "invisible woman," ignored by her professors and barred from joining the law students' professional fraternity.

After getting her law degree, she won a fellowship for graduate legal study, but when she applied to Harvard Law School, the alma mater of at least half the Howard faculty, she was rejected. Black men could attend Harvard Law, but women, black or white, were not allowed. For Murray, Harvard's refusal to admit her because of her sex was as painful as the University of North Carolina's turning her down for its graduate school because of her race. But her Howard Law School classmates viewed her exclusion differently. "The fact that Harvard's rejection was the source of mild amusement rather than outrage to many of my male colleagues who were ardent civil rights advocates made it all the more bitter to swallow," she wrote. "The harsh reality was that I was a minority within a minority, with all the built-in disadvantages such status entailed."

Instead of Harvard, Murray did graduate work at Boalt Hall, the law school of the University of California at Berkeley. When she later tried to get a job with a New York law firm, she was unsuccessful, despite her experience and stellar academic credentials. Her problems, she believed, stemmed more from the legal profession's deep bias against women than from her color. After establishing her own practice, she was finally hired in 1956 as an associate—and only the second black lawyer ever hired—at the white-shoe New York law firm of Paul, Weiss, Rifkin, Wharton & Garrison. As a forty-eight-year-old black woman, she was sure she had no chance of making partner, and in any event, she did not particularly care for the firm's corporate work. During the Little Rock crisis, she helped raise money to try to keep Daisy and L. C. Bates's newspaper afloat. "In the process," she recalled, "I kept saying to myself, 'What am I doing sitting up here in a Madison Avenue law firm, with a very good salary and a month's vacation and all the benefits? I'm really in the wrong place.'"

The 1959 lynching of Mack Parker in Poplarville, Mississippi, plunged Murray into a deep depression, and she fled to Africa, to teach at the newly established University of Ghana law school. She believed she would never return to America, but two years later, she changed her mind. "I could not evade the impelling conviction that my own task was *not* to expound democratic values to Africans, but to realize those values in American life." She returned to the United States in 1962 to study for her doctorate at Yale.

While she had been away, the civil rights movement had gathered great momentum. But Murray was disturbed that black women, who clearly were playing an integral part in the movement, were not seen by the public or by black male leaders as leaders or policymakers. It also bothered her that when newspapers and magazines ran stories about America's racial crisis, they almost always sought out men to explain the black community's concerns and goals. The problems, dreams, and roles of black women were almost never discussed. "Negro women need to face some hard questions," Murray wrote. "Are they losing or gaining ground in the transition from a segregated to an integrated society? . . . One thing is crystal clear. The Negro woman can no longer postpone or subordinate the fight against discrimination because of sex to the civil rights struggle but must carry on both fights simultaneously. She must insist upon a partnership role in the integration movement . . ."

The exclusion of women from key roles in the March on Washington only confirmed Murray's belief that many male civil rights leaders "harbored medieval attitudes toward women." She was infuriated, too, by the decision of A. Philip Randolph to deliver a major speech a couple of days before the march at Washington's male-only National Press Club. The club had finally changed its membership policies to allow black men as members, but it still would not admit women. Even women who *covered* events at the club were restricted. While male reporters sat in the audience and were served lunch and could question the speakers, female reporters were confined to a narrow balcony, with no food, no chairs, no access to phones, and no chance to ask questions. "It was one of the ugliest symbols of discrimination against women to be found in the world of journalism— a metaphor for what working women everywhere faced," wrote *New York Times* reporter Nan Robertson.

Susanna McBee of *The Washington Post*, who had been assigned to cover the march, had interviewed its leaders in New York. But for Randolph's appearance at the press club, she would have had to sit in the balcony and keep quiet; so the *Post* pulled her off the assignment and handed it to a male colleague. Ten days before Randolph's speech, Elsie Carper, a *Post* reporter and president of the National Women's Press Club, declared: "It is ludicrous and at the same time distressing that a group fighting for civil rights has chosen a private and segregated male-only club for its first press appearance in Washington. . . . The balcony, as well as the back of the bus, should have special meaning to civil rights leaders." The *Post* itself treated the women reporters' objections with condescension. "The ladies of the Fourth Estate are fuming . . ." was how the paper began its brief story on the protest.

When she read about the controversy, Pauli Murray fired off a blistering letter to the grand old man of the civil rights movement. His decision to speak at the press club, she wrote, "can only be construed to mean that you are concerned with the rights of Negro men only and care little for the rights of all people. Frankly, if I were a newspaper woman and you persisted in carrying out this invitation, I would picket you and question your sincerity about human rights."

Murray made clear to Randolph that her anger went far beyond insensitive treatment of female reporters: ". . . I have been increasingly perturbed over the blatant disparity between the major role which Negro women have played and are playing at the crucial grass-roots levels of our struggle and the minor role of leadership to which they have been assigned in the national policy-making decisions . . . ," she wrote. "The time has come to say to you quite candidly, Mr. Randolph, that 'tokenism' is as offensive when applied to women as when applied to Negroes . . ."

Despite the pressure from Murray and women reporters, Randolph refused to change his mind about speaking at the press club. A cancellation would be "uncivil," he said. On August 28, Rosa Parks, Daisy Bates, and the other female honorees marched unnoticed down Independence Avenue with the wives of the male leaders. Wilkins, King, Randolph, John Lewis, and the rest of the men, meanwhile, strode along Constitution Avenue, while television cameramen and newspaper photographers cruised ahead of them on flatbed trucks to record the scene. At the Lincoln Memorial, the only women heard were Mahalia Jackson and Marian Anderson, who raised their magnificent voices in song. "Those of us who did not sing didn't get to say anything . . . ," Parks mused almost thirty years later. "Nowadays women wouldn't stand for being kept so much in the background . . ."

Still, it *was* a glorious day. Even Pauli Murray was caught up in the huge crowd's joyful mood. She told friends later that she had marched twice that morning. She had stepped out first with her niece and Patricia Roberts Harris, her friend and classmate from Howard University (who in the 1970s would join Jimmy Carter's cabinet as Secretary of Health Education and Welfare). After a while, Murray and her niece reversed course and threaded their way back through the thousands of marchers to find the contingent from Murray's parish church. "It was the nearest thing I've seen to Judgment Day," Murray later marveled. "You know our romantic notions about Judgment Day? Well, these were the great throngs, you know. It was like the 'great gettin' up morning.'"

All the apprehension and worries of whites, all the predictions of violence proved no more substantial than the early-morning mist. Washington had closed its liquor stores and bars that day, the city's major league baseball team had canceled its game, many congressmen had ordered their female staffers to stay home. "The general feeling," said the Washington *Daily News*, "is that the Vandals are coming to sack Rome."

The "Vandals" turned out to be middle-aged and elderly matrons in white gloves and flowered hats; young women in bright summer dresses and young men in jeans and sports shirts; businessmen and government bureaucrats; union members and sharecroppers; priests, rabbis, and ministers in clerical garb; movie stars in sunglasses. They joined forces in what *The Washington Post* called "part picnic, part prayer meeting, part political rally, combining the best and most moving features of each. It was a happy crowd, much more gay than grim, full of warmth and good feeling and friendliness . . . united in a sense of brotherhood and common humanity."

By early afternoon, more than a quarter million people had gathered in front of the Lincoln Memorial, surging against the Memorial steps, lining both sides of the Reflecting Pool, and spilling out over the grassy areas beyond. Alice Walker, then a Spelman College student, was sitting on the limb of a tree far from the Memorial, taking shelter from the hot, bright sun. She couldn't see the speakers very well, but that was all right: She preferred concentrating on the visions conjured up in her mind by their oratory, particularly those evoked by the passion and poetry of Martin Luther King. When King spoke about "letting freedom ring" across the "green hills of Alabama and the red hills of Georgia," Walker realized that she had a claim to the rust-red earth of her native Georgia and that she must fight those who would try to disinherit her. "Those red hills of Georgia were mine," she later wrote, "and nobody was going to force me away from them until I myself was good and ready to go."

The soaring force and eloquence of King's "I Have a Dream" speech transfixed not only the hundreds of thousands at the Memorial but the millions who saw and heard it that day on television and radio. More than any other public declaration, the SCLC leader's speech "made the black revolt acceptable to white America," declared historian Harvard Sitkoff. Even some of the SNCC activists who were wary of King and who resisted the march were greatly moved. "A thing of beauty," Cleveland Sellers called King's address. The young militant found he had tears in his eyes at its end, as did so many others in the crowd around him at the Memorial. It occurred to Sellers that while he and his SNCC colleagues might be unhappy with how the march and rally were conducted, the event had been a "tremendous inspiration" for the local Southern blacks, the real foot soldiers of the struggle, whom SNCC had brought to Washington. King's message, to stand and fight for their native land, had particular resonance for them, but they also luxuriated in the sheer joy of the day itself, in the exhilarating knowledge that "they were not alone, that there really were people in the nation who cared what happened to them."

When a white man asked Hazel Rivers' pardon after accidentally stepping on her foot during the march, the black housewife from Birmingham couldn't believe her ears. "Certainly," she replied to the man, after she recovered her wits. "I believe," Rivers later told *New York Times* reporter Fred Powledge, "that was the first time a white person has ever really been nice to me." Having already been arrested twice in Birmingham for picketing and marching, she was heading back South that night with renewed determination. "If I ever had any doubts before, they're gone now," she told Powledge. "When I get back home I'm going to follow this on out. I've followed it this far."

For one day, black and white America had been taken to the mountaintop and given a glimpse of racial harmony. In that brief, wondrous moment, as James Baldwin wrote, one had the feeling that "perhaps the beloved community would not forever remain that dream one dreamed in agony." But while the exultation of the moment would never be forgotten by those who experienced it, it turned out to be just that—a moment.

Brutal reality set in as soon as the pilgrims to Washington returned to Mississippi, Georgia, Alabama, and any other place where people lived who were resolved to crush the dream.

18

Standing in the Minefield

Freedom Summer volunteer Heather Tobis
with Fannie Lou Hamer

IN THE LATE FALL OF 1963, THE
prevailing mood among civil rights workers in Mississippi was one of deep
gloom. In some cases, there was outright despair. At first glance, such
depression seemed misplaced: Organizers had just staged a mock campaign and election for governor and lieutenant governor, in which more
than eighty thousand Mississippi blacks had cast their votes. Braving
intense white harassment, blacks had gathered at makeshift polling places
in churches, schools, and stores throughout the state, proclaiming to the
country and the world that they laid claim to this basic right of citizenship.

But impressive as the Freedom Vote turnout was, there was no getting
around the fact that it still was just a pretend election. No denying the
even more painful truth that after more than two years of struggle in Mississippi, after all the deaths and beatings and suffering, fewer than four
thousand blacks had been allowed to register to vote. Bob Moses had put

it in the starkest possible terms in a report to SNCC's executive committee: "[I]t is not possible for us to register Negroes in Mississippi." With the federal government making clear it would not intervene to protect civil rights workers in the state, white supremacists felt free to intimidate and attack at will those they considered troublemakers.

Adding to the misery, the Voter Education Project had decided to cut off most of its funding to the Mississippi campaign, citing the disappointing number of blacks registered. Even with VEP money, most organizers were living hand to mouth, subsisting on tiny stipends and the generosity of local people. Without the funds, there were reports of workers going without food and warm clothes, of their "enduring a Valley Forge in Mississippi."

The idealism and optimism of many organizers had been transformed into demoralization, cynicism, and bitterness. The movement had changed radically since the 1960 sit-ins and the founding of SNCC; few knew that better than Jane Stembridge, SNCC's first staff member, who had encouraged Bob Moses to set up shop in Mississippi. Stembridge left SNCC in November 1960 to devote herself full-time to her poetry and other writing, but she came back in early 1963 to join Moses in Mississippi—the first white SNCC staffer to work in the state full-time.

At first, Moses was opposed to the idea of Stembridge—or any white woman—in Mississippi, but he finally allowed her to come down to Greenwood, provided she agreed to certain conditions. She was to stay with a black family who lived across the street from the movement's office. To avoid being seen in public, she had to arrive in the office before daylight, stay in the office all day, and wait until after dark to walk back across the street. Moses escorted her both ways. Eventually, however, he relaxed the rules and Stembridge came out of hiding. Within a year, a few other white women, Casey Hayden and Penny Patch among them, were working in the state.

In November 1963, Stembridge wrote Anne Braden from Greenwood about "severe, albeit temporary personality problems in this office and enough friction to cause some people to refuse to work at all." To Mary King, Stembridge wrote sadly: "With all the forces of human fear and hatred arrayed against us, we must somehow draw together around the fire, around the table. But, instead, we are destroying each other."

The mood of the exhausted organizers, some of whom had been risking their lives in Mississippi for well over two years, was in stark contrast to the high spirits of local people, who were exhilarated by the Freedom Vote's success. "Whether or not we capitalize on [that enthusiasm] remains to be seen . . . ," Stembridge told Braden. "The main problem lies with us."

It was clear that the movement was stalled in Mississippi, that things couldn't go on the way they had. But there was never any question of pulling out, recalled Ed King, the white chaplain of Tougaloo College in Jackson, who participated in the discussions of what to do next. "We decided that if we retreated, a wave of terror would punish the people. . . . We couldn't walk away because the people would still suffer. We had to find a nonviolent way to go forward." Bold changes were needed, changes that would force Americans to pay attention to the state as they never had before. "We wanted to break Mississippi open," said Casey Hayden.

Thus began plans for Freedom Summer. The idea for the summer project has been attributed to Bob Moses and Allard Lowenstein, a liberal white New York activist and former president of the National Student Association, who helped organize the 1963 mock gubernatorial election. But according to Ed King, the project's roots also can be traced to Diane Nash and James Bevel. After four young black girls were killed in the bombing of a Birmingham church in September 1963, Nash and Bevel came up with a proposal to create a nonviolent army in Alabama, which would engage in massive sit-ins and strikes in Montgomery. Nash and Bevel's plan was to immobilize the state capital, with the idea of winning the right to vote for Alabama blacks. Nothing came of the proposal then, but it stayed in the minds of the organizers of Freedom Summer. What if a similar army were created in Mississippi, with hundreds of volunteers imported for an all-out push for voter registration? And what if whites were invited to be part of that immense force?

Recruiting whites was a stunning idea, but there was a precedent. Lowenstein had persuaded a reluctant Moses to allow seventy white Yale and Stanford students, all of them male, to help canvass the state for November's Freedom Vote. The white students' presence infuriated Mississippi racists, and a number of the student workers were arrested and otherwise harassed. Nonetheless, the addition of seventy more people helped create a successful statewide political organizing campaign. And because whites were involved, Bob Moses believed, national journalists covered the Freedom Vote with considerably more enthusiasm than if it had been an all-black effort.

The media's preoccupation with white civil rights workers was obvious even before the Mississippi Freedom Vote. Penny Patch, for one, hated the fact that her work in southwestern Georgia had generated considerable press interest, including a front-page story in the *New York World-Telegram & Sun*, headlined WHITE GIRL IN A MIRE OF HATE. The publicity was "happening because I was white, middle-class, and a woman to boot," she noted. "And it reflected how much more value was placed on my life, and the lives of other white civil rights workers, than on the lives of black people."

Bringing a flood of white students to Mississippi, Moses acknowledged, would greatly heighten the danger for everyone, but he argued that it would also shine a searchlight on the state, making it possible "to get out a whole set of facts about what was really happening." While white America seemed to have no trouble ignoring the terrorism visited on blacks in the state, it could hardly turn its back when its own children were beaten or even killed. But Moses' arguments ran into stiff resistance from his black coworkers, most of whom vehemently opposed the whole idea of Freedom Summer. If they hadn't already lost their faith in the concept of "black and white together," many were fast doing so. White Mississippians had shown them nothing but implacable hatred; white FBI agents and Justice Department officials had stood by while they were beaten and otherwise brutalized. Whites, in short, were responsible for stymieing the movement in the state, and now black organizers were expected to welcome a bunch of cocky white kids, with advantages that African-Americans could scarcely dream of, and watch them be hailed as the movement's saviors. For more than a few, it was an unbearable thought. "We were always making our people depend on white people in one way or another," said Stokely Carmichael, who opposed bringing whites in. "Here again [that's] what was being done." For veteran organizer Willie Peacock, the idea of recruiting white women was particularly grating. At one SNCC meeting, Peacock declared: "We don't want any white people . . . and NO white girls ever. [T]hey are so much trouble."

Local people, however, felt very differently about Freedom Summer, reflecting a growing dichotomy between their outlook on the movement and that of the young organizers. Local blacks, who were rooted in the religious ethos of universal brotherhood, were also "very pragmatic. They wanted things to change, and if it took bringing in a bunch of white kids, [that was] OK," recalled SNCC organizer Charlie Cobb, another strong opponent of white participation. At a meeting to discuss the summer, Fannie Lou Hamer pointed out the contradiction inherent in the organizer's opposition to whites: "You can't tell me you're for desegregation—and at the same time tell me you're opposed to this project because white people are going to be involved. . . . If we're trying to break down the barrier of segregation, we can't segregate ourselves." Victoria Gray, who also strongly supported Freedom Summer, said: "I was not part of the . . . inside political thing. My only concern was: What will this do for the community? Will it be a plus or minus in terms of our goals and objectives? I didn't have any other kind of battles to contend with."

After a number of angry meetings and heated arguments, the summer project was finally approved in early 1964. SNCC workers reluctantly closed ranks and began to prepare for the summer, but many of them were still simmering. For the first time since she joined SNCC almost two years before, Penny Patch, who had come to Mississippi in January 1964 to help get ready for the project, sensed the presence of "serious anti-white sentiment" in the organization she loved. It wasn't really aimed at her, she thought; it was more intellectual, more directed at the white students about to descend on the state. Still, she detected a coolness on the part of Emma Bell, Dorie Ladner, and some of her other black female coworkers. At the time, Patch could not understand why the women were so stand-offish. Later, she concluded that her affair with a black SNCC organizer might be the cause of the unfriendliness. But if so, such resentment seemed puzzling, since the involvement of white women with black men had never been a divisive issue in SNCC before. Such attachments were common, out in the open, and seemed, in the view of Patch and other white women, to be completely accepted.

More than thirty years later, however, Patch wrote that in hindsight she thought the strains between black and white SNCC women had always been there—the legacy of "centuries of degradation, animosity and confusion that preceded our time together in the Movement." As long as there were only a few white women in SNCC, those strains remained mostly subterranean, but when an influx of white women threatened to upset the precarious balance, the tensions became palpable. "It is slavery and oppression which created the distance between black women and white women," Patch declared, "not the fact that white women slept with black men during the Civil Rights Movement." Nonetheless, she acknowledged being "abysmally ignorant" of the feelings of black women and said she probably would have been more sensitive, more discreet in her romantic ties if she had been more aware. But that didn't mean she would not have gotten involved with a black man. "SNCC men were handsome, they were brilliant, they were brave, and I was very much in love."

That winter and spring, Casey Hayden and other SNCC recruiters traveled to college campuses to seek Freedom Summer volunteers. "Mississippi is where it's at," Hayden announced to University of Chicago students. Although she made clear how dangerous the venture would be, she infected the students with such excitement, such moral fervor, such a strong conviction that they were about to become part of history, that many of them rushed right out to apply. "She swept us up in her enthusiasm," said Heather Tobis, then a University of Chicago freshman. "I thought she was just clear as a bell and exactly right: This is what we had to do." The Chicago students' enthusiasm was shared by thousands of other idealistic, socially conscious young people across the country. "[T]hey all wanted to come to where the action was . . . ," Hayden said. "Kids on college campuses were reading the existentialists. The black students were like heroes. They were like existentialist heroes, and people wanted to get close to this."

Applicants were told they had to bring enough money to support themselves during the summer, and as a result, the majority were white and came from middle-class or more affluent families. (Most black students couldn't afford such a venture.) And in an era when women were still expected to confine themselves to conventional feminine roles, almost as many women as men volunteered for a project that defied just about every possible convention for well-brought-up white women. It was unchaperoned, interracial, and fraught with danger, and, as such, offered an unparalleled challenge, a taste of personal freedom and responsibility, to young women chafing at society's demands and restrictions. "It seemed back then that life was so short for me, I had to act then, before everything was over and closed in on me," one female volunteer said later. In other words, before she surrendered to marriage and motherhood.

In general, women faced a more difficult application process than did the men. All applicants under twenty-one had to get permission from their parents, and for many women, such permission was withheld or given only with the greatest reluctance. Most of the female applicants had no idea how explosive their mere presence in the South would be, no knowledge of the tortured connection between white women and racism. They were puzzled when asked questions by SNCC interviewers that were not posed to their male counterparts—questions about sex, about how they would respond if black men wanted to sleep with them. Some were upset when they requested to be assigned to voter registration—the centerpiece of Freedom Summer, the most dangerous, dramatic, coveted work of the project—and were summarily turned down. "In general," declared a summer project memo, "girls will not be involved in the more active elements of the voter registration program." For the most part, white women were given jobs in two new programs—teaching at Freedom Schools and operating community centers—as well as working in local movement offices. Teaching and typing might be traditional "women's work," but they also kept white women out of sight, kept them out of cars with black male organizers on lonely back roads, subject to ambushes by nightriders.

As the women struggled through the application process, most of them had no idea of the minefield they were about to enter. They would not know, in fact, until they were standing right in the middle of it.

In late June, hundreds of Freedom Summer volunteers gathered on the lawn of Western College for Women in Oxford, Ohio. They had just arrived for a weeklong training session before heading off to Mississippi. In their chinos and Brooks Brothers shirts and Villager shirtwaist dresses, they self-consciously formed ragged circles and started to sing, stumbling over the words to a freedom song that few, if any, of them really knew. Then a strong, deep voice boomed out over the others, and the rest of the voices followed its confident lead. Before long, the circle containing the owner of that robust voice—a short, heavy black woman whose nametag read "Fannie Lou Hamer"—had expanded to include dozens of others. Soon there was just one circle, and everyone was singing with gusto, trying to match Hamer's volume and passion.

The new group was the second batch of volunteers to go through training at Oxford. The first had just left for Mississippi, resembling, as one volunteer remarked, both "children headed for summer camps and soldiers going off to war." Almost eight hundred volunteers in all, mostly white, almost half of them women, trekked to that rural Ohio campus for training in the early summer of 1964, brimming with idealism, enthusiasm, and fear. Again and again, the SNCC organizers told them how dangerous it would be, how likely it was that people would be killed that summer. But Hamer, who was also there to train the kids, focused less on the perils and more on the need to understand and to reach out.

She talked about the blacks with whom they would be living and working, talked, too, about the whites. "The white man is the scaredest person on earth," she said. "Out in daylight he don't do nothin'. But at night he'll toss a bomb or pay someone to kill." Yet, she declared, she did not hate white Mississippians, and they must not, either. "We need you," she said. "Help us communicate with white people. Regardless of what they act like, there's some good there. How can we say we love God, and hate our brothers and sisters? We got to reach them. If only the people comin' down can help us reach them."

Hamer's attitude toward the students was straightforward—she welcomed them, expressed gratitude to them for coming to Mississippi. The reaction of younger SNCC workers was far more complicated: Many resented the volunteers, yet some showed compassion and caring. Bob Moses and a few others were calm, polite, and accepting, but a number of the male SNCC veterans "took great pleasure in intimidating these kids," said John Lewis, who was then SNCC chairman. "They strutted and swaggered and challenged these students on everything from race to politics to sexual attitudes."

In the view of Sally Belfrage, a volunteer who wrote one of the most perceptive accounts of Freedom Summer, the blacks' anger and cynicism stemmed from the knowledge that the civil rights struggle "was their life sentence, implanted in their pigment, and ours for only so long as we cared to identify with them." During the training at Oxford and over the course of the summer, Belfrage recalled, black workers engaged in "subtle condescensions which acted to diminish any self-important, bloated white prides."

She and other volunteers were mesmerized by the charismatic SNCC veterans, wanted to be like them, and were deeply hurt when they realized that they would never be fully accepted by their heroes. "And this raised the question: Why, then, am I here? If they're not grateful for my help, if we are supposed to be struggling for brotherhood and can't even find it among ourselves, why am I here? This was each one's private battle, rarely discussed. To do so would have meant admissions, giving words to certain uncomfortable doubts."

They had joined forces in the fight for racial equality, and yet once again, blacks and whites found themselves unable to truly open up to each other, to bridge their age-old gap in experience and understanding. Observing the uneasiness between the newcomers and organizers, a white psychologist taking part in the Oxford training sessions told another outside participant: "They're only alike in that they both think they understand the other, and certainly themselves. They're both wrong."

As Belfrage noted, many of the blacks felt that the volunteers could easily retreat back to their white refuges, not realizing that some of them had severed themselves from their families and communities, had defied the conventions of white society, and could not—or would not—ever really go back. And, according to the white psychologist at Oxford, the white volunteers were naive, believing they understood the SNCC workers because they "feel for the Mississippi Negro." But, he added, "they can't feel *like* the Mississippi Negro. They know it and it makes them unhappy. . . . They don't like to find out they're insensitive about anything."

Yet while they may have been bewildered, even disillusioned, by the prickliness and confrontational attitude of some of the SNCC organizers, most of the volunteers were swept up in the veterans' fervor and passion for the cause. Bob Moses proved to be the main source of inspiration, as he had been for countless black recruits from McComb to Greenwood. "I would have gone anywhere [for him]," recalled Pam Parker, a white volunteer from Philadelphia. "I would have done anything he asked me to do. I trusted him so much."

Moses and others described the myriad dangers awaiting the volunteers in Mississippi. They told the volunteers about the frenzy of anger over Freedom Summer whipped up by politicians and newspaper editors in the state. In some places, men had formed themselves into home guards and practiced close-order drill after work; in Jackson, the mayor hired two hundred new policemen, and bought an astonishing amount of additional weaponry, including a huge tank. Even more ominously, more than two hundred white supremacists, in response to the summer project, had recently organized a new offshoot of the Ku Klux Klan. The group already had attracted nearly ten thousand members. As a result, a new spasm of violence was convulsing Mississippi. Almost two hundred crosses were burned in sixty-four counties on a single night; roaming bands of nightriders shot into black homes and bombed black businesses and churches.

For the summer volunteers, the training session amounted to nothing less than a total immersion in the idea of danger, an exercise in living with fear as a simple fact of life. The young whites learned how to curl up on the ground in a fetal position, how to shield their head with their hands, if they came under physical attack. They learned the mechanics of coping with what Ivanhoe Donaldson called "the stark terror of day-to-day living. . . . Always checking your car before you got in it, because you were worrying about whether someone stuck a piece of dynamite under it. Always making sure your tires were in good condition, because you never know, you may have to race up the road at night."

Andrew Goodman, a volunteer from New York attending the first Oxford training session, had learned all that before leaving for Mississippi. Yet less than a week after the twenty-year-old Goodman's departure from Oxford, the second crew of volunteers was informed by Bob Moses that their colleague had disappeared, along with two CORE organizers, Michael Schwerner and James Chaney. Andy Goodman had been in Mississippi less than twenty-four hours when he and the other two were last seen in a 1963 blue Ford station wagon, heading down a dusty road after investigating the burning of a black church.

That night, eighteen-year-old Heather Tobis talked to her parents from Oxford. They had encouraged her in her social activism since she was small, had supported her in her decision to go to Mississippi. But now they wanted her to come home. Her mother cried. Her father, who had never raised his voice to her before, shouted, "Don't you know what you're doing to your mother? You're killing your mother!" Tobis, who was close to both her parents, was devastated but, nonetheless, refused to do what they asked. "I believed I was carrying out the vision and values my parents also believed in," she said. Fear for their daughter's safety was what drove them now, however, and for the rest of the summer, they were estranged from Heather. "It was terrible for them," she recalled. "And it was terrible for me."

Penny Patch had been in Oxford, working hard during the day, partying hard at night with her SNCC coworkers, all the while feeling "very tense and afraid." She returned to Jackson the same day that Goodman left for Meridian, and was in the Jackson office when word came that he, Schwerner, and Chaney had disappeared. For two weeks, she lived at the office, manning the phones day and night, taking occasional catnaps on a desk in a side office. She and other SNCC staffers called jails in the area, including the one in Philadelphia, where the young men, in fact, had been taken by the Neshoba County sheriff and his deputy. Nobody at any of the jails admitted to having them in custody. She helped relay calls to and from the FBI and Justice Department. All the while, she was haunted by Goodman, for it was she who had handled his application, she who had accepted him into the project. During that period, Patch dreamed that she was standing in a forest and that Goodman's dark eyes were staring at her from the branches of a tree. She was desperate to join her black coworkers when they slipped into Neshoba County at night to search its swamps for the three men's bodies. But since she was a white woman, that was out of the question. So she stayed in the Jackson office, answering the endlessly ringing phones.

Violence and hate were everywhere that summer, and so was the terror that violence engendered. There was a war going on in Mississippi, *The New York Times Magazine* reported, describing the discovery of a cache of high-powered rifles, shotguns, and pistols, fifteen dynamite bombs, and several thousand rounds of ammunition in the home of a

McComb white supremacist. By the end of the summer (the most violent in Mississippi's history since Reconstruction, it was later reported), the bodies of the three missing civil rights activists would be found buried in an earthen dam. Dozens of other workers would be beaten or otherwise manhandled; hundreds more would be arrested; more than sixty buildings would be burned or bombed, including thirty-five churches.

During the months they spent in the state, white volunteers discovered what blacks in Mississippi had always known: how helpless and vulnerable they were in the face of white brutality. Their world had been turned upside down. They had grown up relying on the police for protection, but now they regarded the cops as the enemy, and the police felt the same way about them. ". . . [I]t was several years afterward before I could see a police car and not have an immediate reaction of fear," remarked Jan Handke, a volunteer from Stanford University. The white community was a strange and frightening place, populated as it was with men armed with shotguns and rifles, and driving cars and pickup trucks with their license plates removed or covered up. The volunteers' dread was intense and ever-present, turning "every shadow, every noise—the bark of a dog, the sound of a car—... into a terrorist's approach," one of them wrote. Said Heather Tobis: "I was frightened every single minute I was there. . . . I often didn't sleep at all during the night, just listening for every creak, and thinking: Was this a Klan member at the door?"

In learning to cope with their fear, the young white activists were bolstered and inspired by the remarkable courage shown by the local people, particularly the women, with whom they lived and worked. Hundreds of blacks offered food and shelter to white volunteers, knowing full well that such hospitality could mean the loss of their jobs, homes, and lives. In the town of Marks, Mary Dora Jones took eleven volunteers into her home when no one else would touch them. "My house is your house," she told them. In Indianola, Irene Magruder housed nine volunteers, then turned her home into the local movement office when the original office was destroyed by arson. Later, her house was torched, too, with white firemen waiting until it was gutted before they turned on their hoses. Magruder lost everything she owned in the fire, but her greatest regret, said one volunteer who had been living in the house, "was that she couldn't cook for us anymore."

In nearby Sunflower, Annie Mae King, who had earlier been fired from her job as a cook for trying to register to vote, ignored local whites' warnings about sheltering volunteers, declaring that she considered herself a citizen, was paying her own taxes, and "thought I had the right to have my own decisions about who came in my house . . ." When her home was bombed in retaliation, she was serene in her response: "I didn't worry about that—I said the Lord gave me that one, he'll give me another . . ."

Like Jones, Magruder, and King, other local women defied the dangers of having volunteers in their midst and enveloped the young whites with warmth, generosity, and love. "We had been warned to expect fear and hostility," one volunteer wrote, "but we were immediately invited to live in and eat in Negro homes and to speak in Negro churches. For many local citizens, our coming was a religious event . . ."

In many cases, white volunteers were treated like full-fledged members of the family. One local woman introduced a friend to the volunteer staying with her, saying, "This is Nancy, my adopted daughter." A young woman in Canton wrote home that whenever she and another volunteer took a walk with their hostesses, "one of them invariably greets each passerby with 'Have you seen my girls yet?'"

In Hattiesburg, there was a deluge of volunteers, and some, like Irene Paull, had to find their own housing. Paull trudged from house to house in black neighborhoods, "dusty, hot, exhausted, and close to tears," until the operator of a beauty shop finally took her in. "I can't turn you away from my door," the woman told Paull. "I just can't. I'm scared they'll bomb me out but you folks is here to help us . . ." One evening, a neighbor dropped by for a chat. When she saw Paull in the kitchen, sweeping the floor and washing the dishes, the neighbor looked at Paull's hostess with alarm. The beautician winked at Paull and laughed. "Don't you be so jumpy, Martha," she told her neighbor. "Can't you see. . . . I've gone and got myself a white girl."

Unsure how these privileged white young people would respond to living in impoverished black communities, local blacks expressed surprise at how quickly many of the volunteers adapted. Ida Mae Holland, for one, was convinced that the white students, accustomed to urban amenities like indoor plumbing, would balk at using an outhouse. She was amazed when one young white woman she knew used the outhouse "like she was born to it." Holland also recalled that many black families were initially reluctant to sit down and eat at the same table with the whites they were hosting, because such social interaction with whites had always been a taboo. But that reluctance usually faded away, and many volunteers participated fully in family meals and other gatherings. "What was so funny," Holland remembered, "was that the white students who had never eaten chitlins and all were sitting there, eating like they were very, very happy to do so."

For Unita Blackwell, the opportunity for blacks to get to know whites as people, and vice versa, was one of the most treasured offshoots of that summer. "I remember cooking some pinto beans—that's all we had—and everybody just got around the pot. . . . [T]hat was an experience just to see white people coming around the pot and getting a bowl and putting some stuff in and then sitting around talking, sitting on the floor, sitting anywhere, 'cause you know, there wasn't any great dining-room tables and stuff [like] in the white people's houses. . . . We was sitting on the floor, and they was talking, and we was sitting there laughing, and I guess they became very real and very human, we each to one another. It was an experience that will last a lifetime."

For white volunteers, it was a schizophrenic summer in terms of their relationships with blacks. While they luxuriated in the joyous welcome of their host families and other local blacks, at the same time some were coping with the indignation of black coworkers. One bone of contention, in fact, was the local blacks' warmth toward the volunteers. There was a feeling among some black organizers that local people showed more caring and appreciation to these white movement neophytes than to black workers who had put their lives in danger for years. That friction grew worse after the summer, when a number of the white volunteers stayed on in Mississippi. Gwen Robinson, a black SNCC activist, described "almost knock-down-drag-outs between the black staff and the white staff" in the project in which she was working. "The black staff would say, 'Why did you sit there and let them fawn over you, treat you like you was some kind of royalty? You enjoyed it.' And they would be saying, 'No, I didn't. I was just trying to be polite.'"

Nerves already frayed by fear, tension, and exhaustion were strained even further by resentment and a mutual lack of understanding. As Bob Moses and others predicted, the national media, during the summer and afterward, paid close and lavish attention to the activities of the white volunteers, irritating black staffers, whose work remained unsung. The headline of one *Saturday Evening Post* article declared: AT THE RISK OF THEIR LIVES, HUNDREDS OF NORTHERN STUDENTS ARE CHALLENGING THE HEART OF THE DEEP SOUTH. And the *San Jose Mercury* emblazoned a front-page story about the summer project with the headline: THEY WALK IN FEAR BUT WON'T GIVE UP. The "they" in the headline referred to the white volunteers.

"We've been getting beaten up for years trying to integrate lunch counters, movies and so on, and nobody has ever paid us no attention . . . ," one black female activist complained to Dr. Alvin Poussaint, a black psychiatrist who counseled civil rights workers in Jackson. "But these white girls come down here for a few months and get all the publicity. Everybody talks about how brave and courageous *they* are. What about us?" When the three civil rights workers disappeared, there was a widespread feeling among black activists (and many whites) that the intense federal government investigation which followed was ordered only because two of the three workers, Goodman and Schwerner, were white.

In some Freedom Summer projects, blacks complained that white volunteers were trying to muscle them aside. Black men headed most of the projects, but several had to cope with articulate, aggressive volunteers, with far better educations than they had, coming in and telling them and other blacks how to do things. "I always felt inferior to Northern students," said Curtis Hayes, one of SNCC's legendary organizers. "Personally I felt they were smarter than we were. *They* thought they were smarter than we were. I knew we knew more about Mississippi than they did, but they had the ability to carry out these long analyses, intellectual discussions, about our environment that seemed like a foreign language to us."

A number of volunteers, oblivious to the wounded feelings of their black coworkers, seemed to have a missionary attitude about their work, a belief that they really *were* there to save the blacks of Mississippi. One young woman wrote home about how "completely unorganized" her project director was and how she had "taken on an informal position of leadership. Several times I've had to completely redo press statements or letters written by one of them. It's one thing to tell people who have come willingly to Freedom School that they needn't feel ashamed of weakness in these areas, but it's quite another to even acknowledge such weaknesses in one's fellow workers."

White volunteers had their grievances, too. Some women didn't like the fact that they were automatically assigned to Freedom Schools or clerical work, and few project directors took the time to explain the danger posed to blacks by white women working in highly visible voter registration jobs. A number of female volunteers felt that the traditional "women's work" in which they were engaged, whether they had requested it or not, was less highly valued than what the men were doing. "There was very much a sense [that] . . . voter registration activity was where it was at," recalled Linda Davis, who taught in a Freedom School. "And since we had chosen teaching, we were sort of shoved to the side. . . . You know, here [were the] . . . guys running out, being macho men."

That sense of vague resentment over being second-class citizens was not shared (at least publicly) by white women who had come earlier to SNCC and who had always been careful to stay in the background. As

Casey Hayden and others pointed out, the women who came South during Freedom Summer, although only a few years younger than the early white women in the movement, were very different in their backgrounds and attitudes. While most of the original white women in SNCC were from the South, the majority of female volunteers had been raised in urban settings in the North, with little understanding of Southern cultural mores. They tended to be more assertive than Southern women, and many were already in the throes of developing what Hayden called a "feminist consciousness."

Yet few female volunteers were vocal in their complaints. It was still the first half of the 1960s, and sexism was hardly considered a major grievance, especially when racism was still so murderous. Indeed, some women, like Elinor Tideman Aurthur, were not fully aware of the resentment they felt until years afterward. In Mississippi, said Aurthur, "we were the . . . rear support system, and I remember being content to be part of the rear support system, but there was also a sense in which I didn't like it."

In fact, it was sex, rather than sexism, that emerged as the most incendiary black-white issue during Freedom Summer. When they came to Mississippi, most female volunteers had no idea how the sexual and racial history of the South would rise up to haunt them. They had no idea that their race and gender made them symbols of white supremacy and that, as such, they were lightning rods for racial fear and hatred. The thought of hundreds of young white women invading Mississippi to work for black equality was the ultimate white supremacist nightmare: blacks *and* white women rebelling against being kept in their place. White Mississippians obsessed over the idea that these young women had come South with the primary intention of violating its greatest social taboo—sleeping with black men. One male volunteer reported that whenever he told local whites he was a medical student, they accused him of being in Mississippi solely to perform abortions on "all the white girls who are pregnant by Negroes."

While white volunteers of both genders were considered pariahs by whites in the communities in which they worked, women were treated with particular scorn and derision, subjected to an outpouring of "the vilest type of verbal (and sometimes physical) abuse from the local whites," noted Alvin Poussaint. Because the mere sight of white women associating with blacks was so inflammatory, female volunteers in most projects were under strict orders not to be seen with black men in public. Many abided by the rule, while some, naive and insensitive, flouted it.

"They act like they're visitin' their boyfriends on college weekend!" Fannie Lou Hamer stormed one day, pouring out her worries to Charles

McLaurin, the summer project's director in Ruleville, about several female volunteers. At Oxford, she had told all the young white women that their presence in Mississippi would be a red flag to whites, that they had to stay out of sight in the black community, that they could not wander all over town. "I told 'em and told 'em, 'It ain't gonna be like home,'" she said. But now here they were, chatting with blacks in front of the Freedom House, playing cards with black men in the backyard, walking downtown to buy curlers and Cokes, sometimes cutting through property owned by whites. "If some whites laid hands on one of those young girls, every Negro man in Ruleville would be in trouble," Hamer exclaimed. "That kind of trouble kills people in Mississippi. . . . Mac, I'll tell you the truth! I'm worried sick. You got to spell out the rules for them. All of this just ain't real for them yet. Then, if they can't obey the rules, call their mothers and tell them to send down their sons instead!" Hamer's message was passed on, and, according to one observer, "everybody cooled it."

But whether they obeyed the rules set down for them or not, female volunteers still found themselves in a cross fire, as Poussaint described it, catching hell from their black coworkers on other issues. According to the psychiatrist, white women, more than white men, were regarded as high-handed, trying to tell blacks how to run the projects. "The white girls were periodically made the scapegoats for most of the difficulties any particular project was having," Poussaint wrote. "It was they who were blamed when the program was not running properly or the staff got bogged down in black-white relations." Penny Patch said she believed that white women bore the brunt of growing black skepticism and resentment toward whites in the movement. "To this day, white guys get welcomed [by former black coworkers] in a way that's really different," Patch remarked in 1998. "It's a fascinating dynamic."

Like Patch in southwestern Georgia in 1962, most female volunteers in 1964 knew little about all this history and were unprepared for its effects on them, just as they had little knowledge of, or preparation for, the complications of getting emotionally and sexually entangled with black men. In the ensuing years, the subject of interracial sex has tended to dominate discussion of the summer of 1964. The question of how much sex actually occurred still is vigorously debated. Feminist scholar Sara Evans has written that sex between black men and white women was a "widespread phenomenon" during Freedom Summer, and quoted one black male worker as saying that female volunteers "spent that summer, most of them, on their backs, servicing not only the SNCC workers but anybody else who came . . ." Sally Belfrage, on the other hand, said she saw little evidence of interracial affairs, that the lack of privacy endemic to all projects would by itself thwart any sexual intimacy. "I can't even work out where they did it . . . ," Belfrage said. "My greatest problem in Greenwood was the absolute impossibility of being alone." Other female volunteers said that, while they were aware of a certain amount of sexual activity among coworkers, it never became a major issue.

However common interracial relationships were during Freedom Summer, the issue ignited a firestorm of controversy that has not yet abated. More than thirty years later, feelings about the matter were still raw, arguments still raged among former movement activists, black and white. At the time, black men were blamed for exploiting white women, while white women were accused of enticing black men. The issue was often seen in stark, either/or terms, with little attention paid to the complexity of the psychological dynamics involved in such relationships.

Working in Mississippi had the electric, feverish quality of operating during wartime, with one volunteer remembering the experience as "kind of [a] manic adrenaline high. . . . You just never came down." Swept up in the romance and drama of their cause, the volunteers, like the SNCC staffers who came before them, often found the mix of fear, tension, and excitement to be a strong aphrodisiac. By going to Mississippi, women volunteers had already defied society's boundaries on female behavior. Once they had arrived, some made clear they were challenging strictures on sex as well. "The theme of sexual liberation runs like a subterranean current through the volunteers' letters, journals, and interviews," according to sociologist Doug McAdam, who wrote a book about Freedom Summer volunteers. "It was not yet the full-blown ideology of 'free love' that was to take hold a few years later. . . . Instead it was a discrete, often tentative experimentation that anticipated the explicit connection between personal and political liberation made later in the decade."

As before, black men were the dashing heroes of the movement, and female volunteers were drawn to them just as their older white sisters in the cause had been. Like earlier female activists, too, the volunteers insisted that being part of the "beloved community" meant being free to love whomever they chose, regardless of what society had to say about the choice. "[S]leeping with black men was a way to 'prove' their 'commitment' to black and white equality; some women tried to demonstrate their liberalism in that way," wrote historian Mary Aickin Rothschild.

But the younger women, many of whom were in Mississippi for only two months, did not have the time to really get to know the men with whom they formed sexual attachments, unlike women like Patch and Hayden, who had been in the movement for at least a couple of years. The volunteers had little understanding of the volatile welter of emotions they, as white women, aroused in black men, who, in many cases, came from an environment so completely different from their own. An environment where, as Curtis Hayes put it, "white women sitting down, talking to you like an equal, was unheard of, let alone having sex with one."

As "the supreme tabooed object," white women were both adored and hated by black men, in the view of Alvin Poussaint. One young black man told the psychiatrist: "Whenever I'm around one of these white girls, I don't know whether I feel like kissing her or punching her in the mouth!" Sleeping with a white woman meant an assertion of one's manhood, a laying claim to the most prized symbol of white male America. But in that symbol's name, black men had been oppressed, tortured, and killed for nearly a century. As a result, wrote Poussaint, black male activists, whether consciously or unconsciously, might also "come to view sexual intimacy with white girls as a weapon of revenge against white society."

In the early days of SNCC, when there was little visible resentment of whites, when "black and white together" still seemed an exciting possibility, such sexual tensions were not apparent, at least not in public. But by the time of Freedom Summer, according to Casey Hayden, "black males were feeling more black and white females were feeling more female," laying the groundwork for an explosion of misunderstandings and recrimination. In Mississippi, the line between sexual liberation and exploitation became increasingly blurred. While a number of female volunteers entered willingly into sexual attachments with black coworkers and local black men, some initiating the relationships themselves, other women complained that black men pressured them to have sex. If they resisted, the women said, they were accused of being racist, the worst possible charge that could be leveled against them. One female volunteer recalled: "If you didn't [have sex], you could count on being harassed. If you did, you ran the risk of being written off as a 'bad girl' and tossed off the project. This didn't happen to the guys." All the summer projects forbade interracial sex, but only white women were sent home for violating that rule. Neither the black men with whom they were involved or the white men who had affairs with black women were similarly punished.

At the same time, it's important to remember that there were also close, caring relationships between black men and white women during Freedom Summer. "There've been things written about interracial sex, but little about love," Pam Parker noted. "I fell in love." Parker, who was assigned to teach in the Holly Springs Freedom School, became involved with fellow volunteer Ralph Featherstone, an African-American teacher from New Jersey. When Featherstone encouraged Parker to focus more on her teaching than on him, Parker was nonplussed: "I'd been raised to serve a man.... No man I'd known would have thought a woman's teaching was more important than he was."

Midway through the summer, Featherstone was assigned to go to McComb and open a Freedom School there. The night before he left, he and Parker lay on his cot, and he held her close. She was terrified that he would be killed, that she would never see him again. Featherstone survived the summer. He and Parker eventually married other people, and in 1970 he died in a car bombing. The bombers were never caught.

Thirty years after Freedom Summer, Pam Parker, now known as Chude Pamela Allen, wrote: "The racist whites were wrong. It was not black men's sexual prowess they needed to fear. It was rather the idea that men and women working together could change things."

"Sex is one thing; the Movement is another. And the two shouldn't mix," declared a black female SNCC staffer a few months after Freedom Summer. "The Negro girls feel neglected because the white girls get the attention. The white girls are misused. There are some hot discussions at staff meetings."

Until the summer project, there had been little friction between black and white women in SNCC. While a number of black women had grown noticeably cooler to their white counterparts in the months leading up to the summer, some, like Martha Prescod Norman, retained close friendships with Casey Hayden and other white women. "We were all there facing those bombs and bullets together," said Norman, "and for that reason had a kind of fundamental respect and admiration for each other." But in the fallout over the summer's black-white sexual liaisons, those friendships were put to the test. A number of black female staffers were angry about the involvement of their male coworkers with white volunteers, and while some confronted black men about their behavior, much of the hostility was directed at white women, both volunteers and staffers.

The clash between black and white women in Mississippi seemed to stem, in some cases, from the fact that each appeared to have what the other wanted. Unlike many white women, black women were not restricted to office work or the Freedom Schools. They were out on the front lines with men, canvassing, organizing, going to the courthouse, and in general asserting themselves in no uncertain terms. They had more responsibility and power in the field than ever before. Indeed, several were named directors of local projects at the beginning of Freedom Summer.

Cynthia Washington, a former engineering student at George Washington University, was one of the new project directors. She had joined SNCC less than a year before, but her coolness in the face of danger prompted Stokely Carmichael, who headed the summer project in the state's 2nd Congressional District, to put her in charge of the project in Bolivar County, "one of the roughest spots we had in terms of violence." Carmichael himself was a witness to Washington's sangfroid late one night when Washington drove him in her pickup truck from Greenwood to the Bolivar County seat of Cleveland. Before they set out, she told him, "Well, you know, there's this long way around Cleveland which is kind of safe. And there's a shortcut, but the Klan is always waiting." Then she looked at him and said, "I'm tired." What could Carmichael do but respond "Me too"? So they took the shortcut, and they were indeed chased by the Klan. Washington, said Carmichael, "just went straight ahead."

After several months as a project head, Washington couldn't understand how white women could be upset about not being in the field. It was terrifying, grindingly hard, often thankless work, and being a project director "wasn't much fun," either. But what also bothered her was that her black male coworkers treated her like "one of the boys" during the day *and* at night. When the day was over and there was time to relax, the men took out other women, not her. Other black female staffers, she discovered, had the same grievance. "Our skills and abilities were recognized and respected," Washington declared, "but that seemed to place us in some category other than female."

While white women in the movement were generally regarded as feminine in their behavior, black women, "out in the streets battling with the cops," were perceived as "amazons, less than and more than women at the same time," observed SNCC activist Gwen Patton. For black women, there was pressure, both internal and external, to show how tough they were, how much of a superwoman they could be. But, said Patton, such strength came with a high price: "a very difficult personal life in terms of relations with men."

Struggling with these questions of femininity and self-esteem, some black female civil rights workers watched in dismay as black men, freed from the proscription against associating with white women, turned to female volunteers for companionship and sex. With a shortage of black men in America, it was hard enough for a young black woman to find someone to date and to marry. According to the 1960 census, black women outnumbered black men by more than six hundred thousand. Nearly one in four black women had never been married by the age of forty, compared with one in ten white women. And in a more egalitarian society, black women realized, there would be even more difficulty in finding a mate, as black men were given free rein to pursue women with the skin, hair, and features decreed by American society to be beautiful. "For sisters," black novelist Bebe Moore Campbell wrote almost thirty years later, "the message that we don't measure up is the nightmare side of integration."

While young white women agonized over their looks, too, few had the slightest idea of the hurt that many black women felt when they stood before a mirror and realized that nothing about their appearance met the ideal standards of American beauty. No idea, either, of how black women daubed their faces with bleaching creams like Nadinola, which linked romance and lighter skin in its ads: "Look how men flock around the girl with the clear, bright, Nadinola-light complexion. Don't let dull, dark skin rob you of romance." White women knew little, if anything, about all the time that black girls and women spent, and the pain they suffered, in getting their hair straightened with hot combs—and then worrying constantly about it "going bad" if they went swimming or got caught in the rain or worked up a sweat while dancing. "Many white women may have 'bad hair' days, but they do not have 'bad hair' lives," remarked Midge Wilson and Kathy Russell, authors of a book about the relationships between black and white women.

According to literary critic Gloria Wade-Gayles, black women "know that they are devalued because they are black women." But since they are "socialized to believe their agony is second to the agony of the race and second to the agony of their men," they keep their anger and pain to themselves—or let it flare against the white women whom they believe to be the cause of their grief. "I spent three years hating white women so much it nearly made me crazy," Ruby Doris Smith told a white interviewer in the mid-1960s. "It came from discovering how the whole world had this white idea of beauty. See, the Western world concept of beauty is *your* kind of beauty, not mine. You can't find my African kind of beauty—I mean thick lips and kinky hair—in a picture anywhere. . . . And I mean, I just hated that so much that for three years I wouldn't speak to a white woman."

Since the days of slavery, feelings of jealousy and resentment had poisoned the way that black and white women felt about each other. In the 1960s, women, operating under the same code of silence as their foremothers, fared little better at eliminating that poison than their ancestors had forty, eighty, one hundred years before. Lacking true understanding, white women viewed black women through the prism of stereotypes, and black women did the same. White women, who never experienced the pain of racism themselves, were often oblivious to how black women lived and what they thought.

On the other hand, black women, like black men, had always paid close attention to whites, since doing so had often been a necessary requirement for survival. Many black women viewed white women as helpless, cosseted, and spoiled, unable and unwilling to take charge of their own lives or responsibility for others. "Black women have no abiding admiration of white women as competent, complete people," Toni Morrison wrote in 1971. "Whether vying with them for the few professional slots available to women in general, or moving their dirt from one place to another, they regarded them as willful children, pretty children, but never as real adults capable of handling the real problems of the world."

Unquestionably, a number of black female activists in Mississippi felt that way about their white counterparts. According to Cynthia Washington, Casey Hayden had complained to her in 1964 that the only work given to women in SNCC was office work. Such complaints made little sense to Washington, she remarked, since at the time *she* was in charge of the Bolivar County project. She assumed that if Hayden and the other white women could do something besides type, "they'd probably be doing that."

Hayden, however, did not recall such a conversation. Indeed, she denied ever saying such a thing to Washington. Yes, she was in the Jackson office during Freedom Summer, but she was there helping to organize the movement's challenge to the regular Mississippi delegation at the Democratic National Convention. Washington "just didn't get it," Hayden said. "She'd just arrived. She'd come into the office from working in the field, and there were a lot of white women there. To her, maybe we all looked like secretaries. I am sure I never talked to her about being a secretary. How could I? I wasn't one. And I was hyper-sensitive to the issues surrounding the role of whites. I would never have complained about white women's work assignments."

By the end of the summer, the formerly close-knit "beloved community" was coming apart, a development made inevitable, in the view of some, by the influx of so many white outsiders. "Times had changed," Penny Patch later wrote about Freedom Summer and its aftermath. "It seems to me that ultimately it did not matter how anybody, white or black, behaved. The sheer number of white volunteers simply constituted a perceived threat to the integrity of the black movement, or at least to SNCC, a predominantly black organization in which the leadership had always been (and continued to be) black. Our history as black and white Americans overwhelmed us."

19

"We Didn't Come All This Way for No Two Seats"

Fannie Lou Hamer testifying before
Credentials Committee at 1964
Democratic National Convention

IN THE YEARS SINCE FREEDOM
Summer, the furor over the relationships between black and white civil rights workers has tended to overshadow the revolutionary changes that took place in Mississippi as the result of those tumultuous couple of months. All across the state, the spark of rebellion was finally catching hold.

In early August, students from Freedom Schools throughout the state drew up a lengthy list of demands, many of which focused on the glaring inadequacies of the schools that most would start attending again in the fall. The students were asking "why it was that the people did not have a voice," said Freedom School teacher Liz Fusco, "and to assert that their voices would be heard."

At the same time, the students' elders were demanding that *their* voices be heard in the political arena. Having been denied the right to participate in the political and electoral processes of their state, Mississippi blacks came up with the audacious idea of creating their own political party as a challenge to the militantly segregationist state Democratic Party. During Freedom Summer, that challenge would infuriate not only Mississippi officials but also the President of the United States. More important, it would dramatically illustrate to the world the racial inequities of the South's political system—and forever change the way politics is conducted in this country.

The Mississippi Freedom Democratic Party was born in Jackson's black Masonic Temple on April 26, 1964, with the fewer than two hundred people on hand swallowed up in the hall's vastness. Such a pitiful turnout revealed the utter absurdity of such a venture, declared the party's many critics. Even more ridiculous were the party's plans to run black candidates for Congress in June's Democratic primary, then to send a delegation to the Democratic National Convention in August to call into question the regular Mississippi delegates' right to be seated. The whole thing was nothing but a pipe dream. What could it possibly accomplish? How could Mississippi blacks, most of whom weren't even allowed to vote, pose any sort of threat to the state's white political establishment?

But that was not the way the party's founders viewed their creation. The success of the November 1963 mock gubernatorial election had revealed the intense yearning of Mississippi blacks to be part of the electoral process. The MFDP saw its role as launching blacks on the road to political organization, as well as giving notice to the state's white politicians that the gubernatorial vote was not a onetime shot.

It saw itself as a bulwark of true democracy, a real party of the people of Mississippi, open to both blacks and whites. Although movement organizers had midwifed the party's birth, its key leaders were local blacks who long had been part of the civil rights struggle. And women, who had been in the forefront of that crusade, now played integral roles in the MFDP, at a time when in most state party organizations, Democratic or Republican, women had little voice or influence, even though they did much, if not most, of the day-to-day work. Fannie Lou Hamer was at the center of the

MFDP, along with Victoria Gray, Annie Devine, and numerous other women. There were so many women, in fact, that Lawrence Guyot, who became MFDP chair, once told Hamer, Gray, and Devine that it was time for the women to step back and allow the men to come forward. It didn't take him long to disavow that statement. "I came to the movement a chauvinist and a fool, and I got thoroughly educated very, very quickly," he said.

In the primary races for Congress, Hamer was nominated to run against Representative Jamie Whitten, who had been in the House of Representatives for more than twenty years, and Victoria Gray became a candidate for the U.S. Senate. Despite constant harassment and death threats (according to one SNCC organizer, a primary consideration in Hamer's race was "whether the candidate will get killed"), the women embarked on their Don Quixote–like quests, giving speeches and shaking hands from early morning to late at night. Neither showed concern about the danger of running. "Sometimes it seems like to tell the truth today is to run the risk of being killed," Hamer said. "But if I fall, I'll fall five feet four inches forward in the fight for freedom."

Not surprisingly, the women lost their races, as did the two male MFDP members running for other congressional seats. But their defeats did nothing to slow the party's momentum, which, with the coming of Freedom Summer, kicked into high gear to prepare for its challenge at the Democratic National Convention in Atlantic City. In Washington, Ella Baker took charge of the battle to win Northern Democratic support for the MFDP. Opening an office with borrowed money and several SNCC staffers, Baker buttonholed senators and congressmen and appeared before state Democratic conventions, drawing on the vast array of contacts she had made in the previous twenty-odd years, utilizing all her formidable persuasive and organizing talents. As legal counsel for the new party, Baker enlisted Joseph Rauh, a prominent liberal Washington lawyer who was one of the founders of Americans for Democratic Action. In 1948, Rauh had helped Senator Hubert Humphrey, who equaled Rauh in his support for civil rights, win adoption of a surprisingly strong civil rights plank in the 1948 Democratic Party platform.

In Rauh's view, the MFDP had a strong case to present to the convention. The regular Mississippi Democratic Party had not only excluded blacks—almost half the state's residents—from becoming party members, but it had already made clear it would support Barry Goldwater, the probable Republican candidate, in the 1964 presidential election. According to party bylaws, the Democratic convention had the right to seat any delegation it chose, and Rauh believed he could get enough support in the Credentials Committee to bring the conflict to the full convention for a vote. To help him prepare the legal brief outlining the MFDP's case, he recruited Eleanor Holmes, who had just graduated from Yale Law School.

Back in Jackson, Casey Hayden was spearheading the planning for the precinct meetings and county conventions. To prove beyond doubt that the regular Democrats were purposefully shutting them out, MFDP members throughout the state went through the motions of trying to win access to the regular party's precinct meetings in June. Wherever they went, they found locked doors or changes in meeting times and places. So they promptly called their own meetings, swore allegiance to the national Democratic Party and to President Lyndon B. Johnson, and elected delegates to the county conventions, which in turn elected delegates to the state convention in August.

Less than four months after the birth of the MFDP, the party convened again in Jackson's Masonic Temple, but this time the place was jammed with people who had come to witness the political miracle about to take place. With the outside temperature hovering over one hundred degrees, the un-air-conditioned hall was murderously hot, but no one seemed to care much, certainly not the delegates, who were milling around on the floor in their Sunday church clothes, waiting for the convention to be called to order.

There were balloons and banners, red, white, and blue bunting, and all the rest of the accoutrements of a political gathering. But the handmade placards denoting the counties represented on the floor resonated with meaning that went far beyond the trappings of grassroots politics. AMITE read the placard for one group of delegate seats. NESHOBA was nearby, as were SUNFLOWER and LEFLORE and TALLAHATCHIE. Places where blacks had been murdered, tortured, beaten, and otherwise terrorized for trying to gain their rights, including the right of political assembly that they were exercising here. The majority of delegates were women, and most—Fannie Lou Hamer, Laura McGhee, Belle Johnson, and Unita Blackwell among them—had suffered from such retribution. What they felt that day, however, was satisfaction and hope. Against all odds, they were about to take their quest to Atlantic City, to precipitate a showdown over black inequality in their state before national Democratic leaders, not to mention a countrywide audience. Several key state delegations from outside the South had already rallied behind them, with state conventions in California, Minnesota, Michigan, and New York endorsing the challenge.

A small, regal woman in a plaid suit stepped up to the podium to give the convention's keynote speech. For Ella Baker, the MFDP convention was the culmination of everything she had worked for. For more than twenty years, she had urged Southern blacks to shed their fear and band together to fight the tyranny under which they lived. In Bob Moses' view, Baker's "spirit, consciousness, and teaching infused the Mississippi movement." And now here she was in the Mississippi capital, watching as black residents of that "most depraved" state demanded their rights *now*. Her speech had none of the florid oratory that marked conventional political addresses. Simple and direct, it urged the people sitting before her to remain steadfast in their crusade. "It is important that you go to the convention whether you are seated or not," she said. "It is even more important that you develop a political machinery in this state. The Mississippi Freedom Democratic Party will not end at the convention. This is only the beginning."

They arrived in Atlantic City on August 21, eyes bleary, clothes rumpled after a two-day trip on chartered buses. For the sixty-eight MFDP delegates, many of whom had never been out of Mississippi in their lives, it must have seemed surreal—leaving their homes, where the threat of bombings and burnings was ever-present, and coming to a place where sunburned vacationers lolled on the beach, the air smelled of popcorn and seaweed, and pretty girls wearing "LBJ" straw boaters pranced down the boardwalk. "We . . . were flung with no transition into a world of deals and decisions, ulcers and Dexedrine," wrote Sally Belfrage, one of a number of volunteers accompanying the MFDP delegation.

Unlike other participants at the convention, the Mississippi challengers had no time or inclination to party in the circuslike atmosphere. After checking in at the run-down Gem Motel about a mile from the convention hall, they went to work, lobbying individual delegates and appearing before state caucuses. They had been cautioned by Bob Moses and Ella Baker, among others, not to get their hopes up about ousting the regular Mississippi delegation. The chances of that happening were slight at best, they were told. But many, convinced that the convention would recognize the justice of their cause, were unpersuaded. Their optimism was bolstered by the enthusisam with which they were greeted by other state delegations.

As they talked to delegates in the lobbies and meeting rooms of Atlantic City's fanciest beachfront hotels, however, the MFDP delegates had no inkling that President Lyndon B. Johnson was getting set to wage all-out war against them. The toweringly insecure Texan was determined that nothing would mar his party's coronation of him as its 1964 standard-bearer—or his chances for victory in November. Ever since he became President after John F. Kennedy's assassination in November 1963, Johnson had been terrified that Kennedy's brother Robert would somehow wrest the 1964 Democratic nomination from him. That fear had been laid to rest, and now Johnson, despite his approval rating of nearly 70 percent in the polls, was convinced that a floor fight over seating the MFDP would cost him the South and the election. "If we mess with [this] group of Negroes . . . we will lose fifteen states without even campaigning," the President told Hubert Humphrey. Why were the Mississippi blacks so ungrateful? Why weren't they satisfied with all that he had already done for them—his success in winning passage of the 1964 Civil Rights Act, for example, not to mention the rest of the Great Society programs his administration had introduced? Most of the major civil rights leaders—Martin Luther King, Roy Wilkins, Whitney Young, Bayard Rustin—had agreed with the administration's plea for a moratorium on civil rights demonstrations until after Election Day. It was time to bring SNCC and the MFDP into line, too.

Months before the convention, Casey Hayden had sent a memo to other challenge organizers stressing the need to arouse public sympathy for the Mississippians' cause. The convention delegates, and the rest of America, must be made to feel what it was like to be a poor black in Mississippi in 1964, to have little to look forward to but fear, humiliation, and abuse. At the convention, the MFDP delegation chose its most eloquent speaker to put those feelings into words. On August 22, Fannie Lou Hamer limped to a witness table and sat down in front of the one hundred ten members of the Credentials Committee. Hamer, who was deputy chair of the delegation, knew how much was riding on her testimony and that of the other pro-MFDP witnesses. The challengers needed to win support of 10 percent of the committee—eleven votes—to bring the discussion about seating the delegation to the convention floor. If it got to the floor, the backing of eight states would be enough to force a roll-call vote on whether to oust the regular Mississippi delegation and seat the insurgents.

Hamer told committee members in simple, unvarnished language how she had been fired from her job and thrown off the plantation that had been her home for eighteen years for trying to register to vote. She told them how nightriders had tried to kill her. And she told them in horrifying detail about the savage beating she, June Johnson, and Annell Ponder had endured in Winona on that hot Sunday afternoon fifteen months earlier.

Then she paused, perspiring heavily under the television lights, tears shining in her eyes. "All of this is on account we want to register, to become first-class citizens . . . ," she said, her voice choked with emotion. "[I]f the Freedom Democratic Party is not seated now, I question America. Is this America? The land of the free and the home of the brave? Where we have to sleep with our telephone off the hook because our lives be threatened daily because we want to live as decent human beings, in America?" When her testimony was finished, she picked up her purse and slowly, awkwardly, left the table. For a moment, there was silence, and a number of committee members dabbed at their eyes.

At the White House, however, the response to Hamer's testimony was sputtering rage. Watching the televised committee hearing, President Johnson "saw her and blew his stack," according to Joe Rauh. How dare this *outsider*, this *sharecropper*, this *woman* steal the show at *his* convention? In the middle of Hamer's testimony, the President hastily staged an impromptu press conference and succeeded in wresting network coverage away from her. As Unita Blackwell later put it: "Mrs. Hamer had captured the United States and he knowed it, and that's when he came on to cut it off." But Johnson was unable to prevent the broadcast of her testimony on the networks' news programs that night. The stories led to a deluge of calls and telegrams to the Credentials Committee from all over the country in support of the MFDP challenge.

Johnson moved quickly to put an end to this rapidly growing threat to the peace of the convention. Machiavellian to the core, the President chose as his chief lieutenant one of the country's most liberal politicians, the man whom many saw as the foremost champion of civil rights in Congress. But Senator Hubert Humphrey was also desperate to be Johnson's vice presidential running mate, and Johnson made clear that Humphrey's handling of the MFDP matter would determine whether he would, in fact, be the President's choice. Through Humphrey, the President offered the MFDP what he termed a compromise. Under the plan, members of the regular Mississippi delegation would be seated only if they signed a loyalty oath pledging support to the Democratic ticket, and the MFDP challengers would be given seats as honored guests on the convention floor. In future conventions, state delegations would not be allowed to choose their members on the basis of race.

With tears in his eyes, Humphrey appealed to the MFDP leaders to accept the proposal. He himself supported their cause, he told them, but Johnson had made clear to Humphrey that he would never be Vice President if there was a floor fight over the challenge. Fannie Lou Hamer shook her head in sad disappointment. "Senator Humphrey, I been praying about you, and I been thinking about you, and you're a good man, and you know what's right," she said. "The trouble is, you're afraid to *do* what you know is right. You just want this job. I lost my job, and I know a lot of people have lost their jobs, and God will take care of you, even if you lose this job. But, Mr. Humphrey, if you take this job, you won't be worth anything." From that point on, Hamer, clearly lacking any sense of political expediency, was excluded from the discussions.

After the Mississippians rejected the plan, Johnson sweetened the offer, or so he thought, by proposing that two MFDP members—Aaron Henry, the chairman of the delegation, and Ed King—be seated on the floor as nonvoting delegates at large. Both of them men, both middle-class, one of them white—hardly representative of the predominantly black, working-class delegation, half of whose members were women. When that fact was pointed out to Humphrey, the Minnesota senator said that it didn't matter, that Johnson had made up his mind who would represent the MFDP on the floor. And it certainly wouldn't be the person that the President regarded as his convention nemesis, "that illiterate woman" Fannie Lou Hamer.

"I'm not going to stoop to no two votes at large," Hamer said, and the majority of the delegation agreed. Once again, whites were telling blacks what to do. In this case, it was white liberals, who had supported an end to discrimination and segregation, but on their own terms and timetable. *Accept what we give you now,* the Mississippi blacks were being told in Atlantic City, *and we promise that in the future things will be better.* For Hamer and many of the others, that was untenable. The "white man . . . is saying, 'It takes time,'" she later noted. "For three hundred and more years they have had 'time,' and now it is time for them to listen. We have been listening year after year to them and what have we got? We are not even allowed to *think* for ourselves. 'I know what is best for you,' but they *don't* know what is best for us! It is time now to let them know what they owe us, and they owe us a great deal." She added, "If we are free, I don't think you're supposed to tell me how much of my freedom I'm supposed to have. . . . Well, wait, man, let me have something to do with this. If it's any compromising let me say what I want."

In Victoria Gray's view, accepting Johnson's compromise would have been a betrayal of the blacks back home who had repeatedly gambled their lives (and in some cases, lost them) in the fight to claim their rights. The politicians "said to us, 'Just take this . . . and next time, you know, there'll be more.' I thought about the many people for whom there was not going to be a next time. . . . It made no sense at all, with all the risk that had been taken, to accept what we knew for certain to be nothing."

Lyndon Johnson was a consummate politician, the master of the deal. When Hamer and the rest of the MFDP delegation refused to play by his political rules, he became more than slightly unhinged. He told his wife and others he was close to a mental breakdown, that he might decline the nomination. He told his aide Walter Jenkins that he believed Robert Kennedy to be the mastermind behind the MFDP. Then, with every force he could muster, the President set out to destroy the challenge. At his command, the FBI tapped phones at the Mississippi party headquarters, and agents posing as NBC correspondents sought information from unwitting MFDP delegates. Members of the Credentials Committee were threatened with the loss of government jobs. Johnson sent Walter Reuther, head of the United Auto Workers, to Atlantic City to twist the arms of those beholden to the UAW. Reuther told Joseph Rauh that he would no longer be the UAW's Washington counsel if he did not support the administration's compromise. Martin Luther King, who had backed the challenge before the convention, was faced with the possible loss of substantial UAW funding for SCLC. "The heat was on to a terrific degree," Rauh declared. "There were so many hatchet men that you had to stand with your back to the wall."

Without the MFDP's knowledge, Hubert Humphrey and his lieutenant, Minnesota attorney general Walter Mondale, brought the Johnson compromise to the Credentials Committee, which approved it. The night before Johnson was to be nominated, the compromise was presented to the full convention with the inference that the Mississippi challengers had accepted it. The report was quickly approved, with no debate, no floor fight. All the support for the challenge, built painstakingly over the previous five months, "disappeared in the space of two days," said Julian Bond. "It just completely vanished."

Infuriated by what they viewed as an act of treachery, the MFDP delegates marched that night to the convention hall singing "We Shall Overcome." With credentials given them by sympathetic delegates, Hamer, Victoria Gray, and twenty other Mississippi insurgents slipped into the hall and sat in the seats vacated by the regular Mississippi delegation, most of whom had declined to take the loyalty oath mandated by the compromise and had left for home. The challengers refused to leave when ordered to do so by the convention's sergeants at arms. Surrounded by swarms of television correspondents and cameramen, they denounced the hypocrisy of a President and party that professed their commitment to civil rights but refused to acknowledge an integrated group of delegates fully supportive of Democratic Party principles and policies.

The sight of civil rights activists staging a sit-in as a protest against their professed allies proved alarming—and embarrassing—for party and movement leaders. The next morning, they pulled out all the stops in a last-ditch effort to persuade the MFDP delegates to accept the compromise. One after another, the big names of the civil rights movement appeared before the Mississippians, telling them they didn't know a victory when they saw one, urging them not to damage the electoral chances of Johnson and other Democratic leaders. Some, like Martin Luther King, were diplomatic. Others, like Roy Wilkins, were patronizing and hostile. According to Hamer, the NAACP head told her, "You people have put your point across. You don't know anything. You're ignorant . . . about politics." (In response to such criticism, Unita Blackwell later said, "Ignorant? They [were] exactly right. . . . But we were not stupid, and that's the difference.")

The movement leaders' intense pressure, however, made a number of delegates think twice about opposing the compromise. A few male delegates, mostly from the small minority of middle-class businessmen and professionals in the delegation, already had aligned themselves with the outside leaders. Aaron Henry was one of those who came out in support of the plan, telling his fellow delegates they should be guided by Wilkins, King, and the rest. The women, as SNCC organizer Martha Prescod Norman put it, tended to be "secure in their movement experiences" and to trust their own judgment, refusing to capitulate to outside leaders. "The big niggers talk to the big niggers," said Blackwell, "and the little folks . . . couldn't talk to nobody except themselves, you know. They just going to push the thing on through and have us there for a showcase."

The party's three leading women were the ones who prevented that from happening. Hamer, Victoria Gray, and Annie Devine sensed that sentiment within the delegation, especially among the men, was shifting in favor of the compromise. Hamer, Gray, and Devine were sitting in different parts of the room, but, said Gray, "it was like we had ESP, mental telepathy, going." After the speakers left the room and the delegates were getting ready to vote, each of the three stood up and made an emotional appeal to her cohorts to remember whom they were representing and why they were there. "I said, we didn't come all the way up here to compromise for no more than we'd gotten here," Hamer recalled. "We didn't come all this way for no two seats." When Henry Sias, one of the most intrepid activists in the MFDP, took the floor to recommend acceptance of the

Johnson plan, Hamer and Devine let him know in no uncertain terms how mistaken he was. "When they got through talkin' and whoopin' and hollerin' and tellin' me what a shame it was for me to do that, I hushed right then . . . ," said Sias. "I changed my mind right there. . . .Those two women opened my eyes."

After the women spoke, the vote was taken. The compromise was resoundingly defeated.

For their part, Democratic liberals couldn't fathom the reasoning behind the MFDP's rejection of what they considered significant concessions. What was wrong with this upstart delegation? It had captured the spotlight at the convention, had drawn national attention to the political and electoral inequities in Mississippi. Because of its pressure, the Democrats had promised to begin breaking the hold of white supremacy on their party in the South—a staggering shift for a group so heavily populated by conservative Southerners. And even though the MFDP delegation as a whole had not been seated, the offer of the two at-large seats represented a major triumph for blacks throughout the South—or so white liberals claimed.

The media joined in the scolding of the Mississippians. Anthony Lewis, a liberal columnist for *The New York Times*, declared that the MFDP "could have accepted a rule that they did not altogether like, instead of slipping into unauthorized seats. . . . They could have made a point not of their demand for total victory but of their loyalty to the national Democratic party and to President Johnson." Conservative columnists Rowland Evans and Robert Novak were even more patronizing in their criticism. The compromise, sniffed Evans and Novak, "was far better than [the MFDP] had any right to expect." In the columnists' view, there could be only one explanation for the rejection by these politically immature blacks of their party elders' help and guidance: The MFDP was "dangerously oblivious to the Communist menace to the civil rights movement."

In the months to come, journalists and politicians would increasingly raise the specter of subversive influences on the MFDP and on SNCC. "You could watch it building up in late 1964," said Carl Braden. In the eyes of the White House and the rest of the Democratic establishment, SNCC and MFDP had "committed the unforgivable sin . . . [B]y refusing to compromise they were refusing to play politics. They were really serving notice that if [they] are going to be involved in politics, it's going to be an entirely different kind of politics and different people are going to run things.... I mean this is a threat.... If you're sitting somewhere in power you don't want that happening."

For blacks in Mississippi and the rest of the South, however, the MFDP's refusal to compromise showed that blacks like them, poor and unlettered though they might be, could stand up to powerful white politicians and hold their ground. In that sense, what happened in Atlantic City was a triumph for Southern blacks, although not in the way white liberals claimed. It represented, said civil rights scholar Leslie McLemore, "the coming of political age of Black people in Mississippi in a way that had not been seen since Reconstruction." Listening to local blacks talk about the convention at a mass meeting one night, a Freedom Summer volunteer said she realized that the presence of the MFDP delegates on the floor of the convention "meant something that would have been completely lost if a compromise had been accepted that simply hushed everything up." One woman at the meeting exulted: "I looked at that convention from the time it started. All the time 'til now I never seen no niggers in a convention, but they was there! Lots of them! Big ones and little ones, they was there!"

The repercussions of the MFDP challenge, however, extended far beyond its effect on Southern blacks. It led to a revolutionary overhaul of the Democratic Party, opening the party up to blacks, women, and other groups that had had little or no representation in its councils before. In 1968, the Democrats kept their promise and seated an interracial delegation from Mississippi (which included a number of MFDP members). But the most radical changes came at the 1972 convention and later, when all delegations had to include minorities in roughly the same proportion as their population in the states. In addition, women were to make up at least half of the delegates. "The fact that 50 percent of every delegation must be female can be traced directly to what we did in Atlantic City in 1964," said Lawrence Guyot. "The fact that there will never again be all-white delegations—ever—in the Democratic Party is attributable to what we did in 1964."

But what was to happen years in the future meant little or nothing to most of the young SNCC activists who had worked so hard to make the MFDP a reality. In the days and weeks immediately following the challenge's defeat at Atlantic City, the dominant feeling among the organizers was one of disillusionment and despair. "For many," said Joyce Ladner, "it was the end of innocence." They had done everything according to the rules, they felt they were morally right, and they still had come up short. They were now questioning many of their old assumptions: the wisdom of working with white liberals, their faith in the federal government, and, in a broader sense, the meaningfulness of pursuing civil rights laws when blacks were in such desperate economic straits. "The kids tried the established methods, and they tried at the expense of their lives . . . ," said Ella Baker. "But they were [not] willing to wait and they had paid a high price. So they began to look for other answers." Some even talked of seizing power from the white establishment. "After Atlantic City," Cleveland Sellers declared, "our struggle was not for civil rights, but for liberation."

There was bitterness, too, about the Freedom Summer volunteers, most of whom had left Mississippi by the time SNCC organizers and the MFDP delegation returned from Atlantic City. "[F]or three months they took over—people started depending on them," said Hollis Watkins. "They were educated and spoke well, so people listened to them and respected them, and then . . . they were gone, and the community was scattered. . . . [W]e had to pick up the pieces."

But if the organizers still believed, as some of them had earlier said, that the volunteers would ease back into their privileged lives without a backward glance, they were very much mistaken. For many volunteers, the summer in Mississippi completely transformed the way they felt about themselves and their world. If only for a brief time, they had lived in poverty, had known paralyzing fear, had seen firsthand the terrible effects of racism and discrimination. But they also had known the satisfaction of risking their lives for a morally unimpeachable cause, not to mention the joy of being treated with such caring and generosity by the blacks with whom they lived. "I guess the thing that pulls me back the most are the people who made us a part of their community," wrote one volunteer who went home, then decided to return to the town where she had been working. "In Mississippi, I have felt more love, more sympathy and warmth, more community than I have known in my life."

The summer project proved to be a radicalizing experience for many volunteers, serving as a seedbed for later movements of the 1960s, including the women's movement. When the volunteers returned to their home turf, "intent on bringing the messagᵉ of Mississippi to the rest of the nation," they often found a stiff resistance to that message. At the University of California at Berkeley, for example, Mario Savio and other Berkeley students who had been in Mississippi came back in the fall of 1964 to be greeted by an order from the dean of students barring campus political groups from disseminating literature and engaging in other activity at the entrance to the university. An outraged Savio was in the forefront of student protests of the university's new regulations, and he and other protesters formed the Free Speech movement, which, according to historian Max Heirich, "set the tone for an entire college generation's confrontation with authorities."

In Mississippi, meanwhile, the "closed society" imposed by white supremacists since Reconstruction was being pried open, thanks to the glare of national attention that Freedom Summer focused on the state, and the efforts of local blacks to capitalize on that attention. In McComb, Aylene Quinn helped bring an end to a months-long rampage of Klan bombings and burnings, including the bombing of the house where summer volunteers were staying, and the torching of several black churches and homes. Even after many of the volunteers had left, the Klan continued its bombing spree in McComb, and every night blacks went to bed, nerves taut, waiting for the "sickening, anguishing sound" of the next explosion.

It was only a matter of time, Quinn knew, before her turn came as a bombing target. She was the most visible local activist in McComb, as dedicated and fearless in 1964 as she'd been in 1961, when she first welcomed Bob Moses and the early SNCC workers to town. "Mama Quin [*sic*]is kind and good to everyone, but more than that, she is a towering figure of strength," SNCC organizer Mendy Samstein wrote in a report. "She can't be intimidated. . . . And the pressures increase." When the white owner of the building housing her cafe ordered her to stop feeding civil rights workers, she refused. "When in Rome, do as the Romans," he said. To which she replied, "But I'm not in Rome. I'm in McComb." The police raided her place twice, once planting a bottle of illegal whiskey and then arresting her. The cafe was finally closed.

Then, late in the evening on September 20, a black Ford pulled up in front of Quinn's home. Within seconds, a deafening blast, caused by fourteen sticks of dynamite, ripped through the still night air. When the smoke cleared, Quinn's house lay in partial ruin, with the front wall and much of the roof collapsed. "They weren't out to frighten tonight," Samstein wrote. "Mama Quin was to be killed." But Quinn was not home at the time of the bombing. Her two youngest children, a nine-year-old girl and four-year-old boy, were being cared for by Johnnie Wilcher, who had been one of the 1961 walkout leaders. Miraculously, neither Wilcher nor Quinn's son was injured, although the little boy had been trapped in his bed by the fallen ceiling. His sister suffered a punctured eardrum.

In a scenario worthy of a Kafka short story, police arrested Wilcher and Caroline Quinn Breckinridge, Quinn's oldest daughter, who taught at the McComb Freedom School that summer. After questioning and releasing the young women, the authorities turned to Quinn, accusing her of bombing her own house and children. This was too much for the outspoken activist. She and two other women whose houses had been bombed traveled to Washington to demand justice from the President, the Justice Department, and the American public. At a Washington press conference, Quinn ridiculed the idea that she would destroy her own house: "Do you think I would work eleven years to keep a house and then plant a bomb under it while two of my children were in it?" The women's meetings with Justice Department officials and President Johnson garnered considerable publicity, as did a statement from McComb's chief of police that *if* the women came back to McComb, "I would advise them to ease into town without letting anyone know about it."

Spurred on by the women's stories, the media began to focus on the Klan's campaign of terror in McComb. The nightly television news shows presented a number of reports on the unchecked bombings; *The New York Times* strongly denounced them in an editorial, as did Drew Pearson in his national syndicated column. The deluge of bad publicity became a major embarrassment for McComb's white civic leaders, and shortly thereafter, eleven KKK members were arrested for taking part in the bombings of black homes, churches, and businesses. When the Klansmen were later released on probation, the editor of the McComb newspaper criticized the move, and other members of the white establishment circulated a petition calling for a halt to racial violence and to law enforcement's harassment of civil rights workers. More than six hundred fifty white McComb residents signed.

It would never become a racial nirvana, but the little hill town, regarded by many as the meanest place in the state, had just taken the first step toward civility.

Although local blacks were in the forefront of challenging white supremacy, a scattering of whites also played a role in ending supremacists' iron control of the state. Among them was Hazel Brannon Smith, the crusading owner and editor of several weekly newspapers, including her flagship paper in Holmes County, the Lexington *Advertiser*. In a state where most media outlets were violently segregationist, only a handful of white journalists ever dared to speak out against what was going on. None was more outspoken than Smith. The vivacious former debutante from Gadsden, Alabama, waged all-out war against the White Citizens Council and the Mississippi Sovereignty Commission (which she called the council's "stooge and private gestapo") in her regular front-page editorial column. "Mississippi today is being ruled by a dictatorship of professional leaders of the Citizens Council in Jackson working through Governor Barnett—and anyone who gets in their way they try to destroy," she wrote in the early 1960s.

Smith knew that to be true from personal experience. In retaliation for her barrage of attacks, the Citizens Council pressured local businesses to stop advertising in Smith's paper, then established a rival newspaper in Holmes County. The *Advertiser*'s revenues plummeted, Smith received death threats, the newspaper office was set afire, her husband was dismissed from his job, but she never wavered. In the early 1960s, civil rights activists started their own newspaper, the *Mississippi Free Press*; Hazel Brannon Smith printed it on her presses. In 1964, she endorsed the Civil Rights Act and welcomed Freedom Summer volunteers and Martin Luther King to Hazelwood, her white-columned home. In that year, too, she won a Pulitzer Prize for her hard-hitting editorials. Shortly afterward, she declared: "I long to see the day when all the white people in Mississippi learn what I know—that the white man has nothing to fear from the Negro."

Florence Mars and her aunt, Ellen Spendrup, also spoke out. The two white women helped the FBI track down the murderers of Michael Schwerner, James Chaney, and Andrew Goodman, who were killed near the women's hometown of Philadelphia. "It was not my intention to become involved," Mars later wrote. "But I wanted the community to see that it should oppose murder no matter who committed it."

Florence Mars came from one of Philadelphia's most prominent families. Her father was a lawyer, and her grandfather was the largest landowner in the county, with properties that included Philadelphia's leading department store. She had been brought up as a proper young Southern white woman, but from an early age Mars questioned the treatment of blacks by white society. In 1954, she voiced approval of the *Brown* decision, a view that was greeted by a torrent of criticism from other whites in Philadelphia. After that, "I ceased to express my opinion," she said, and spent much of the next few years away from home, living in New Orleans for a while and then in Europe. But in 1962, she came back to Neshoba County, to raise cattle on a farm her grandfather had left her and to run the county stockyards, which she had bought a few years earlier.

When the three civil rights activists disappeared in June 1964, after being held in the Philadelphia jail, Mars was sure that they were dead and that the county sheriff, Lawrence Rainey, and his deputy, Cecil Price, were somehow involved. Her views were shared by a handful of white women in town, including Spendrup, who didn't shy away from voicing her beliefs. "Well, certainly, I think they're dead," Mars's aunt would tell people. "I think you'll find their bodies over in the Mississippi River somewhere!"

That was a daring thing to say in a place where virtually everyone else was declaring that the workers' disappearance was a hoax. The KKK "owned" Philadelphia, said Joseph Sullivan, who headed the FBI investigation into the men's disappearance. "In spirit, everyone belonged to the Klan." When the FBI descended on Philadelphia, Mars and her aunt were among the few whites willing to defy the Klan and to talk to investigators. Indeed, when the Klan held a meeting at the courthouse to discuss ways to force other civil rights workers to leave town, the two women attended the meeting and took notes on what was said. They then turned their notes over to the FBI, as well as information they'd picked up that contradicted the alibis of several KKK members who were suspects in the activists' disappearance.

In the fall, after the bodies of the three workers were found, Mars and her aunt were called before a federal grand jury in Biloxi inquiring into the murders. Contradicting earlier testimony from white witnesses that Lawrence Rainey had been a respected, impartial sheriff, the women told the grand jury that Rainey was well known for his hatred of and brutality toward blacks. Within two days of Mars's testimony, Klansmen launched a boycott against her stockyards, warning cattle buyers and sellers throughout Neshoba and neighboring counties to stay away. "We intend to ruin you," a late-night caller told Mars. She tried desperately to persuade her customers to defy the Klan and appealed to local officials for help, but with no success. Business fell off dramatically, and a few months later, she was forced to sell the stockyards. Later, she did the same with her farm, when the Klan threatened to poison her herd of Hereford cattle.

But there was no sympathy, no outcry on her behalf from whites in Neshoba County. None, that is, until Lawrence Rainey, in an obvious act of spite, arrested Mars for drunk driving, yanking her from her car late at night, clapping handcuffs on her, and then tossing her and a female friend, who was also in the car, in jail. Their arrests shocked the white community. It was one thing, in whites' view, to brutalize, even murder blacks and white civil rights workers; it was quite another to treat well-bred white women as if they were common criminals. "A longtime family friend said if it was any consolation, it had opened his eyes to the fact that Rainey considered no one immune to his power . . . ," Mars later wrote. "The arrest caused a decline in Rainey's influence. People were indignant . . . because Rainey had violated the southern code by throwing two ladies in jail."

In February 1967, Rainey, Cecil Price, and seventeen other men, most of them members of the Klan, were arrested on charges of violating the three murdered workers' civil rights. That October, seven of the men, including Price, were found guilty in federal court—the first jury conviction in a major Mississippi civil rights case since Reconstruction. The jury couldn't reach a verdict on the guilt or innocence of three of the defendants, and the rest, including Rainey, were acquitted. All the convicted men received prison terms. Despite his acquittal, Rainey, who had stepped down as sheriff in 1967, could not find another job in law enforcement. He moved away from Philadelphia, losing several subsequent jobs after employers learned of his past.

By the summer of 1968, the Klan's hold on Neshoba County—and other parts of Mississippi—had been broken. The organization's membership had dropped from a high of ten thousand in 1964 to fewer than five hundred, with only about fifty considered hard-core members. Likewise, the White Citizens Council, discredited and in disarray, had lost most of its once-considerable influence in the state.

Thanks in part to events set in motion by Freedom Summer and those with the courage to participate in it, racial terror no longer held sway in Mississippi by the late 1960s. Blacks—and whites—were now largely free to say and do as they pleased, without having to look over their shoulder to see who was listening, who was going to retaliate. "Freedom Summer was the beginning of a whole new era," said Unita Blackwell. "People began to feel that they wasn't just helpless anymore, that they had come together. . . . [W]e wasn't a closed society anymore."

20

"This Inevitable, Horrible Greek Tragedy"

Woman marcher lies unconscious after mounted police attack on marchers in 1965 Selma demonstration

AT A SNCC MEETING SHORTLY
after the Democratic convention, Penny Patch approached a friend and close colleague whom she hadn't seen for many months. The young black woman, who was standing with a group of other female black staffers, simply ignored Patch. "She looked through me, around me, anywhere but at me," Patch recalled. "She did not acknowledge my presence." Emotionally shaken, Patch turned and walked away. The two women would not speak again for another thirty years.

The coolness that Patch had felt from black women in SNCC in early 1964 had turned to ice after Freedom Summer. Now and then, she would hear about SNCC parties to which she and other white staffers were not invited—an ostracism that was "tremendously painful but hard to pin down." Nobody ever said anything to her, but there was no way to escape the sense of distance—from both black women and black men.

The estrangement between blacks and whites was just one thread of the complex web of strains and tensions entangling SNCC and the movement that fall. Along with the bitterness over the perceived betrayal of the white liberal establishment at Atlantic City, there was a sense of drifting, of having no idea where this crusade was now headed. "A massive identity crisis," Mary King called it. According to Julian Bond, SNCC had made no plans for what would follow Freedom Summer and the convention challenge.

Adding to the problems were the mushrooming growth and changing character of the SNCC operation. In little more than three years, SNCC had expanded from a nucleus of sixteen organizers to a staff of one hundred eighty. In the early days of the organization, its activists had similar backgrounds and experiences: They were mostly black, from the South, strongly religious, with a commitment to nonviolence and the "beloved community." As black Northerners joined the group, there was more of a questioning of the value of nonviolence and of having whites in the organization. Black nationalism was on the rise. Then, after Freedom Summer, some eighty new people were added, almost doubling the existing staff of one hundred. Many of the newcomers were summer volunteers who had stayed in the South. By the fall of 1964, the mix of people in SNCC was highly combustible. And it was just waiting to explode.

In November, all SNCC staff members were summoned to a retreat at Waveland, a church center on the Gulf coast of Mississippi, to discuss the future of the organization.

Before the retreat, James Forman invited SNCC staffers to write position papers on their own concerns about the organization, as well as to offer ideas for its future. For Mary King and some of the other white women in SNCC, Forman's invitation represented an opportunity to call their colleagues' attention to an issue that they had been debating with great intensity over the last few months.

In the summer of 1964, King had come to Jackson to coordinate the summer project's press operations. She moved in with Casey Hayden, who was living in a house across the street from Tougaloo College. In Jackson, the two young women continued their discussions about the subordinate role of women in American society that they had begun in Atlanta. Soon, other SNCC women were participating in the conversations. Most of them, like Elaine De Lott and Emmie Schrader, were white, from the North, and had just come South that year. But a few black women also occasionally joined in, notably Dona Richards, a University of Chicago graduate in philosophy who was also Bob Moses' wife. Richards had been in Mississippi less than a year. The independent, assertive New Yorker was a controversial figure within SNCC circles, in part because, as a relative newcomer to the movement, she had managed to attract and marry the quietly charismatic head of the Mississippi campaign, to whom many other women had been attracted. Compounding the difficulties for Richards was her later decision not to take Moses' name, still a highly unusual step in the mid-1960s. Penny Patch's "very first feminist glimmering" came in listening to a group of black women in SNCC discuss Richards' keeping her maiden name. "I think that's really disrespectful," one of them said. But for Patch, who had never heard of a woman doing such a thing before, "it was one of those little lightbulb moments." Patch thought to herself, "Why is she doing that? That's kind of neat." In Mary King's view, Dona Richards was "ahead of her time—a woman of the '90s living in the '60s."

Increasingly during that hot, steamy summer, the discussions at the Freedom House turned to the status of women in SNCC. The women's growing sense of self, their belief in their own strengths and skills, all of which had been nurtured by SNCC, had led to a desire for more—more of a voice in the organization, more responsibility, more awareness of their contributions. According to King, they were simply following in the footsteps of Ella Baker and her "vision of the leadership potential in each person, the ability of each of us to take responsibility for him- or herself rather than submit to authority . . ." Such desires, however, conflicted with the complex reality of SNCC. Sexism did not dominate the organization, as it did other civil rights groups. Nonetheless, it did exist there, just as it did in most organizations of that period that included both men and women. Some women in SNCC had taken on great responsibility, but in the Atlanta office and the major local movements, including that in Mississippi, the major decision-making roles were held by men. "Even though the women were in the meetings . . . the men seemed to . . . have the final opinion," noted black SNCC activist Fay Bellamy.

Earlier in 1964, women staffers in the Atlanta office had staged a sit-in in James Forman's office, which, although lighthearted, was a bid for attention to their grievances. Forman acknowledged that "both within and without SNCC subtle and blatant forms of discrimination against women exist." He himself was regarded as being relatively sensitive to women's concerns, yet his later comments about the women's sit-in had a paternalistic quality about them. In his memoirs, Forman said that he was the one who had suggested the demonstration to the women, urging them to dramatize their demands by imitating the student sit-ins of the early 1960s. "I proposed that they role-play, using me as a target," he wrote. It's inconceivable that the women, most of them veterans of sit-ins and jails themselves, were in need of such patronizing advice. In any event, Mary King, who participated in the sit-in, denied that Forman had made any such proposal. "It was certainly not his idea," she declared. "Perhaps what he meant was that he did not feel antagonized by it. That was true; he was very good-spirited about it and entered into the humor of the situation."

By the fall of 1964, however, King and some of the other women believed it was time to get serious. From memos, meetings, and conversations, they began collecting examples of occasions where they thought women had been treated with a lack of respect or relegated to the background. The appointment of an all-male committee to revise SNCC's constitution, for one. A SNCC leader's apologizing for appointing a woman as interim head of a Mississippi project, for another. The women were "looking for some substantiation in the full meaning of the word," King later said. "That is, to give substance, body, solidity to something that [was] very largely perceptional.... We were dealing with awareness here, our own growing awareness and a desire that the movement be broad enough and big enough and democratic enough to accept our awareness."

At Waveland, she, Hayden, Schrader, De Lott, and other white women involved in the Freedom House discussions incorporated those examples into a document that would create a storm of controversy lasting more than three decades. Before the retreat convened, the women gathered in a small room at the church center and poured out their feelings onto paper. Drawing analogies between whites' treatment of blacks and the movement's treatment of women, their manifesto complained of "the assumption of male superiority" within SNCC, one as "widespread and deep-rooted and every bit as much crippling to the woman as assumptions of white supremacy are to the Negro."

"It needs to be made known that much talent and experience are being wasted by this movement when women are not given jobs commensurate with their abilities," the paper went on. "It needs to be known that just as Negroes were the crucial factor in the economy of the cotton South, women are the crucial factor that keeps the movement running on a day-to-day basis. Yet they are not given equal say-so when it comes to day-today decision making." Since SNCC had been founded on the belief of participatory democracy for its members, shouldn't women be allowed to participate as fully as men?

The women laid out their concerns with great trepidation, knowing that "within the framework of the civil rights movement and indeed in the field of civil liberties," as King noted, "women's rights had no meaning and did not exist." In the paper, they acknowledged that their list of complaints "will seem strange to some, petty to others, laughable to most"—a line that Hayden later said was hers. Hayden, who was regarded as a role model and mentor for several of the younger women, said she felt she had to participate in the writing of the paper, but was reluctant to do it and hoped against hope that the document would never be circulated. "I was really nervous about its reception. . . . I remember thinking it was not the right issue for that time. The issue at that time was what we [in SNCC] were going to do next."

Because of their anxiety about how the paper would be received, King, Hayden, and the rest decided not to sign their names to it. Their fears were well placed. The atmosphere at the Waveland retreat turned out to be one of hostility and tension: No one was treated very kindly during its sessions. According to Forman, Waveland "reached a new low in bad vibrations and secretive maneuvers. People were cutting each other up . . ." When the women's paper was read by SNCC staffers, many responded with jeering and mockery, according to Mary King. It was regarded as a bad joke, bringing up an issue that was felt to be trivial and beside the point at a time when the movement itself was floundering. It didn't take long for SNCC staffers to figure out who had written the paper, and although a few people, including Bob Moses and Dona Richards, expressed support, the majority responded to King, Hayden, and the other women with derision.

For King, the widespread antagonism of black women in SNCC was particularly wounding. Through the paper, she had hoped to reach out to her black female coworkers and begin a dialogue about the role of women in the movement. After the summer, however, most black women in the organization wanted little to do with their white counterparts. Likewise, the majority had scant sympathy for the concerns set out in the paper. As Cynthia Washington later remarked, white women and black women "started from different ends of the spectrum," with black women having greater authority and responsibility within SNCC, as well as very different life experiences. Washington, like many other black women in the organization, insisted then that she had always been treated as an equal. It wasn't until years later that she recognized, she said, "that our single-minded focus on the issues of racial discrimination and the black struggle for equality blinded us to other issues. . . . The problems of womanhood have had an increasing impact on us . . ."

The handful of black women who agreed with the paper's main premise believed it was neither the time nor the place to vent such internal grievances, with the movement's mission still unfulfilled and with SNCC coming under increasing attack from outside. Fay Bellamy, who joined SNCC a few months after Waveland, said there was a feeling among black female staffers that "certain things couldn't be shared, not because they should be secret, but if it's not going to be positive, then don't deal with them, don't inflict them on the community. . . . [W]e were always putting the women's struggle aside, for later use, because once again it was like prioritizing your environment . . . and we didn't feel that the movement could stand it right at this point in time."

One evening during the retreat, a large number of SNCC staffers, including King and Hayden, wandered down to a pier overlooking the Gulf for an evening of drinking wine and letting go of the tensions and hurts of the traumatic sessions. They stretched out on the pier, under a golden moon, and listened to Stokely Carmichael launch into one of his famous comic riffs. Carmichael, a Trinidad native who grew up in New York and who loved the spotlight, was known as one of the smartest and funniest men in SNCC. His stand-up routines—comparable, it was said, to those of any professional comedian—invariably reduced his listeners to helpless laughter. That night, as he had done on so many other occasions, he poked fun at everybody and everything he could think of, including himself. He joked about blacks in Mississippi, about the Waveland meeting, about the various position papers. Then he looked at Mary King. With a big grin, he asked, "What is the position of women in SNCC?" As he answered his own question, he shook with laughter: "The position of women in SNCC is prone!"

Those in his audience knew that Carmichael's remark referred to the relaxed sexual mores of SNCC, not to mention the furor over staffers' and volunteers' sexual activity during Freedom Summer. Most, including Hayden and King, responded with uproarious laughter. "It was very funny," Hayden said more than thirty years later. "Stokely was always very funny, and I laughed, and I still think it's funny. . . . Because there's a lot of truth in it. You know, we were young people and very attractive . . . and that's what young people do in their twenties. . . . It wouldn't have been funny if it hadn't been true."

But not everyone would feel that way. In years to come, Carmichael's comment would be interpreted by both white and black feminists as evidence that he and other male SNCC leaders had no use for women except as sexual partners. In *Sisterhood Is Powerful*, a 1970 anthology of essays on women's liberation edited by Robin Morgan, the comment appeared in a section entitled "Know Your Enemy: A Sampling of Sexist Quotes," and was altered to read: "The *only* position for women in SNCC is prone [italics added]." The change in the quote, and its interpretation as a sexist commentary, became accepted wisdom.

Carmichael himself was both furious and pained that a spur-of-the-moment quip would be used to portray him as a thoroughgoing misogynist. "Of course it was a joke!" he said in the spring of 1998, a few months before he died. "How could anyone seriously describe the position of women in one word?" Such criticism was particularly galling, he said, because he had worked to give women in SNCC more responsibility and authority. As one of the leaders of the Mississippi summer project, for example, he had appointed three women, including Cynthia Washington, as local project directors.

Agreeing that Carmichael's remark was taken out of context, Mary King said that the way it had been interpreted had done her former colleague "a terrible disservice." Like many of the other women who worked with Carmichael in the early years of SNCC, King insisted that he had been one of the most sensitive, responsive men in the organization in his interactions with women. "He was really so lacking in bias," said King. "He didn't need to have it explained to him that women were human beings: He was just completely right there." Kathie Amatniek, a white Freedom Summer volunteer who later became a prominent women's liberation activist in New York, recalled how Carmichael came for dinner one night at the Freedom House where she and other volunteers were living. For more than a month, the female volunteers had been unsuccessfully trying to get the men to help with chores around the house. At the end of dinner that night, Carmichael got up and said, "Well, let's do the dishes." Then, according to Amatniek, he "proceed[ed] to do them," to the astonishment of everyone.

Just as Carmichael's remark was widely misunderstood, so, too, according to King and Hayden, was the position paper to which he referred. Feminist scholars and other writers would later point to the paper as proof of rampant sexism within SNCC and portray its white female authors as rebels who, disgusted with the group's chauvinism, went on to help launch the women's movement. Such an interpretation overlooks the complexity of SNCC history and of the relationships between men and women in the organization. It is true that as SNCC and other civil rights groups were disintegrating in the late 1960s and black nationalism was on the rise, women were expected to play increasingly subordinate roles. But in SNCC's early years, at the height of its influence, its female activists, including Hayden, King, and others who were white, felt an unparalleled sense of empowerment.

To those unfamiliar with the dynamics of SNCC, Hayden conceded, it was logical to assume from the paper's seemingly angry wording that it was meant as a denunciation of male activists. But, she added, "we really didn't have that anger. It was like we were having an argument with our brothers. It was a family squabble." Rather than demanding power, what the women were really seeking was the men's attention. "[We were] just trying to educate people. . . . The idea was 'Move over, guys. We've got some stuff to bring in here,' rather than 'Move over, guys, I want to be up there.'"

The Waveland retreat did nothing to resolve SNCC's future or the disputes dividing its staff members; if anything, it made the problems worse. The issues raised in the women's position paper were ignored by the organization, and relationships in the erstwhile "beloved community" continued to unravel. In Mississippi, bitterness and dissension were tearing field projects apart. The still-considerable violence in many communities— bombings, burnings, beatings—only exacerbated the tensions. White and black staffers seemed constantly at odds. By the fall of 1964, interracial romantic involvements had "gone underground," as one longtime organizer put it: "Black men began to creep into white women's beds." A few months later, such relationships would be deemed totally unacceptable. One white female volunteer, who stayed on after Freedom Summer, said she felt "lonely almost immediately. . . . I just never was able to connect . . . with the two black women on our project. They just seemed to hate me. It was probably the sex thing, but I never got close enough to find out."

After the summer, Penny Patch joined a project in Batesville, in the northern part of the Delta. She wanted to get back to the real work of organizing, to join forces again with local people who were far removed from the internecine SNCC feuds. But she couldn't escape the turmoil. A young black man from the North, a recent SNCC recruit, was named project director in Batesville. He came, said Patch, with a "not so incipient black nationalism and I felt it from him. There were times when he lost it and verbally attacked me." Once, he locked her out of the Batesville office while screaming "white bitch." "I stood in the hallway, banging on the door, trying to persuade him to let me in, trying not to make a scene that local black people in the building would notice. I walked off finally in despair."

Lawrence Guyot, chairman of the MFDP, was in despair himself as he watched what was happening in Mississippi. He was a longtime SNCC organizer but also a native Mississippian, and his heart was with the blacks of his state as they struggled to break free of oppression. They had made great breakthroughs as the result of Freedom Summer and the convention challenge, and the fall of 1964 should have been the time to capitalize on those breakthroughs. "That was a crucial time," said Guyot. "We had jolted the country. The state of Mississippi was on the defensive." But instead of keeping the pressure on Mississippi and supporting the MFDP, many of the young outside organizers were giving up, despite Ella Baker's pointed reminder to them that "the people are waiting." Staff members "were wandering in and out of the organization," said Marion Barry. "Some worked. Some didn't work." A number of staffers left the state, and projects were abandoned, Freedom Schools and community centers closed. It was, Guyot declared, "utter chaos."

With the campaign in Mississippi struggling to survive, the last major battle of the civil rights movement—in Selma, Alabama—claimed the national spotlight. As it turned out, the Selma campaign would surpass even Birmingham in its drama and far-reaching consequences. Diane Nash would emerge once more to play a critical, behind-the-scenes role in the events that unfolded there. Events that another woman, Amelia Boynton, had helped set in motion.

In the fall of 1964, Nash and James Bevel, who were now working for SCLC, had headed for Selma, hoping to implement the first stage of their plan, drawn up after the Birmingham church bombing, to organize the blacks of Alabama into a nonviolent army to claim their right to vote. The couple envisioned a statewide campaign of protests, voter education, voter registration drives, and mock elections. Selma, they told Martin Luther King, would be the perfect place to start. King was given the same message by Amelia Boynton, a local businesswoman who had been fighting for voting rights in Selma for more than thirty years and who, according to historian David Garrow, "had as substantial an impact on civil rights development in Alabama as anyone . . ."

Boynton inherited her civil rights activism from her mother, who, when women were given the right to vote in 1920, would drive black women in her horse and buggy to the registrar's office in Savannah and help them fill out the forms. Following graduation from Tuskegee Institute, Amelia moved to Selma in 1929 as a county home economics extension agent, responsible for teaching homemaking skills to local black women. Working with her was a county agricultural agent named Sam Boynton, with whom she fell in love. They were married in 1932, and Amelia quit her job soon thereafter.

In the late 1930s, Sam and Amelia Boynton became the leaders of a campaign to get blacks on the voter registration rolls in Selma and the rest of Dallas County. Such an effort was as risky for the Boyntons, then and later, as it was for anyone fighting the same fight in Mississippi. Located in cotton country some forty miles west of Montgomery, Selma was a hard-core outpost of white supremacy—a former major slave-trading center razed by Union troops in 1865 and onetime home of Ku Klux Klan founder Nathan Bedford Forrest.

In the 1940s, Sam Boynton lost his job because of his voter registration activities, but he and his wife never wavered in their commitment. Their dedication to civil rights was passed along to their son, Bruce, who, on his way to Howard Law School in 1958, refused to leave a Richmond bus station's whites-only lunch counter. His case, *Boynton* v. *Virginia*, prompted the Supreme Court decision outlawing segregation in interstate transportation facilities, which, in turn, led to the 1961 Freedom Rides.

After Sam Boynton was fired, the Boyntons opened an insurance agency, and on the wall of their office, Amelia hung a plaque with the names of local blacks who had tried to register to vote. Attempting to register in Selma took tremendous courage, since applicants courted retaliation not only by an extremely active White Citizens Council but by a sheriff who equaled Bull Connor in his racism and meanness. Jim Clark, a hulking man who dressed himself and the dozens of men he designated as his "posse" in military-style uniforms and helmets, was notorious for beating and otherwise intimidating blacks who he believed had stepped out of line. Faced with the menace of Clark and his equally brutal henchmen, most blacks in Dallas County stayed far away from the county registrar's office, despite the Boyntons' best efforts.

In early 1963, when SNCC organizers Bernard and Colia Lafayette first came to town, fear still had an iron hold on blacks in Selma. The Lafayettes, newlyweds fresh from Mississippi, were looking for a new project to direct. On their first night in Selma, two Justice Department officials warned them of the dangers and advised them to get out of town. They ignored the advice and looked around for local allies. Bernard Lafayette recalled that "it was Mrs. Amelia Boynton who befriended us. We used her office and began to work."

The Lafayettes were subjected to intense harassment, and one night Bernard Lafayette was ambushed and badly beaten. Yet slowly, very slowly, people started to try to register. When Sam Boynton died in May 1963, Clark and his posse, waving wooden bats, surrounded the church where Boynton's memorial service was held, took photographs of the people who entered, and then barged into the church and stood there throughout the service. The crude attempt at intimidation angered Selma blacks and served as an impetus for the new voter registration drive. The Lafayettes went back to school that fall, and other SNCC organizers continued the campaign.

When Nash and Bevel came to Selma and began pressuring Martin Luther King to make his next stand against injustice in Selma, Amelia Boynton added her influential voice to theirs. Boynton was a "determined and persistent" woman, said Andrew Young, and King finally agreed. Starting in January 1965, he led groups of black Selma residents to the county voter registration office, where they were turned away by Clark and his men. On January 19, Boynton, at the front of the line, refused the sheriff's order to disperse. Infuriated by the cool defiance of his longtime nemesis, he suddenly grabbed Boynton by the back of her coat collar, shoved her down the street, and threw her into a patrol car. "I was stunned," Boynton recalled. "I saw cameramen and newspaper reporters and . . . I said, 'I hope the newspapers see you acting this role.' He said, 'Damn it, I hope they do.'" They did. The photographs and film footage of Boynton's manhandling by Clark provoked widespread outrage among the blacks of Selma, as well as throughout the country. Said Ralph Abernathy about Clark: "He had gone for the person who most antagonized him, without thinking that this person was a woman and that in pushing and jerking her around he conformed to almost everyone's stereotype of the southern sheriff and fulfilled our highest hopes for him." In response to the rough treatment of Boynton, hundreds of demonstrators turned out for the next marches.

As Bevel orchestrated the escalating protests, Nash oversaw the day-to-day work of canvassing. Both were remarkably creative strategists and organizers, but Nash now stayed mostly behind the scenes, juggling her movement work with caring for their two small children, while Bevel took center stage with his spellbinding oratory. "[N]o small measure of what we saw as Jim's brilliance was due to Diane's rational thinking and influence," Andrew Young later wrote. Only Bevel was on SCLC's payroll, however. As Young acknowledged, it was common in church circles for the wives of ministers to devote most of their time and energy to their husband's calling—directing the choir, running the Sunday school, organizing women's groups—with no compensation. "It is not to our credit that we followed that model with Diane," he said.

In late February, when a young black man died after being shot in a nighttime demonstration near Selma, an enraged Bevel called for activists to stage a funeral march from Selma to Montgomery, to lay the dead man's coffin on the state capitol steps. That didn't happen, but Bevel's spur-of-the-moment idea sparked plans for a Selma-to-Montgomery march on March 7, to be led by King. On the day of the march, King had a preaching commitment in Atlanta, so the procession was led by John Lewis and Hosea Williams, one of King's key lieutenants.

It was a Sunday afternoon, and many of the marchers were in their best churchgoing clothes—men in suits and women in brightly colored dresses, hats, and high heels—as they headed toward the edge of town. The marchers reached the humpbacked old Edmund Pettus Bridge and began climbing its steep arc. At the top, Lewis and Williams, and the throng behind them, looked down on a heart-stopping sight. At the end of the bridge were arrayed dozens of helmeted state highway patrolmen, with dozens more of Jim Clark's men, some of them on horseback. As the marchers started down the incline, the officer in charge of the state troopers gave them two minutes to disperse. Even if the march leaders wanted to retreat, there was no way they could do so, with hundreds of people behind them on that narrow bridge. But the officers didn't pause to wait. A minute after the order was given, the troopers and deputies rushed the terrified marchers, swinging clubs and bullwhips. "Get those goddamned niggers!" Clark yelled. A cloud of tear gas enshrouded the procession. Screaming and choking, the more than six hundred marchers turned around and tried to run, trampling over each other in their panic. John Lewis was clubbed by a trooper and collapsed to the ground with a fractured skull. Amelia Boynton, who was marching behind Lewis, was hit hard on the arm by a trooper's club. As she gasped for breath, another trooper struck her in the back of the neck, and she also fell unconscious. Later, she would say, "The horses . . . were more humane than the troopers; they stepped over fallen victims." Some of the horsemen pursued the fleeing marchers all the way back to Brown Chapel, the center of the Selma movement.

Americans watching the network television news programs that night were stunned and sickened by the barbarity they witnessed, and thousands of them made plans to head for Selma and join forces with the activists there. The national response to what happened at the bridge "was greater than the Freedom Rides, greater than the March on Washington, greater than Mississippi Summer," Lewis later wrote. "The country seemed truly aroused." Protests were staged in more than eighty cities, condemning the violence and calling for passage of a voting rights act. More than sixty members of Congress fired off a telegram to Lyndon Johnson urging him to introduce such legislation immediately.

Martin Luther King announced he would lead a new march from Selma to Montgomery and filed a request for a federal injunction banning Alabama from interfering with such a protest. A week later, still waiting for the injunction, three white ministers, in Selma for the march, were walking through a white section of town after dinner when they were surrounded by a crowd from a local bar. One of the ministers, the Reverend James Reeb, was smashed in the head with a club. He was rushed to a Birmingham hospital, where he died two days later. Reeb's death sparked more demonstrations throughout the country, including one outside the White House. On Monday, March 15, President Johnson went before Congress to propose the Voting Rights Act, which would finally make the Fifteenth Amendment, enacted almost a century before, a reality for millions of blacks in America. "At times history and fate meet at a single time in a single place to shape a turning point in man's unending search for freedom," Johnson declared. "So it was at Lexington and Concord. So it was a century ago at Appomattox. So it was last week in Selma, Alabama."

The rush of events continued. Federal judge Frank Johnson ruled that the Selma-to-Montgomery march should be allowed to proceed without being hindered by local or state officials. King announced that the march would take place the following Sunday, and throughout the country, people began heading for Selma. Ministers, nuns, blue-collar workers, college students, housewives, members of Congress, movie stars poured into town. On March 21, they took their places in line, alongside the local blacks who had inspired their pilgrimage, and headed across the Pettus Bridge, on the first leg of their five-day journey to Montgomery. At the procession's head were King and the leaders of the other major civil rights organizations.

By the time the march entered Montgomery on Thursday, March 25, its participants had swelled to a crowd of some twenty-five thousand. One of them was the woman who had launched the modern civil rights movement from that city almost ten years before. Few people, however, recognized Rosa Parks. She was supposed to be in the front ranks of the marchers, along with King and the other civil rights leaders, but the young activists who were acting as marshals didn't know who she was and kept telling her she didn't belong there. "I got put out of that march three or four times," she recalled. "Whenever they would put me out, I would just stand on the sidelines until somebody would pass by and say, 'Mrs. Parks, come on and get in the march.' I would say, 'I *was* in it, but they put me out.'" Swept up in the mass of people, she made her way down Court Street, past the Court Square stop where she had caught James Blake's bus on that chilly December night, then onto Dexter Avenue, past the Dexter Avenue Baptist Church, to the grounds of the state capitol. There, she was finally ushered to the front of the line and her picture taken with the march's leaders. But her most vivid memory, she wrote later, was "being put out of that march."

Viola Liuzzo, a white housewife from Detroit, was also among the marchers on that final triumphant leg into Montgomery. When the march had been announced the previous week, the thirty-nine-year-old Liuzzo arranged for a friend to take care of her five children, then got in her car and drove to Selma. A part-time college student, Liuzzo badly wanted to get involved in the fight for social justice. At the same time, she was restlessly searching for an identity apart from her domestic roles. One of her daughters would later describe Liuzzo as being "very conflicted about not fitting in . . . with other women her age. She wasn't traditional, and she wasn't domestic. . . . Mom wanted so much out of life, but sometimes she felt like she was all alone." Liuzzo's closest friend, a black woman named Sarah Evans, remarked: "She knew what was right and couldn't hold back. She wanted to be part of what was happening in this country in the 1960s. That girl had some of that same stuff in her that Dr. King had in him."

In Selma, Liuzzo pitched in to help the organizers prepare for the march. She registered out-of-town marchers, ferried people back and forth from the airport to Selma, helped set up first-aid facilities in Montgomery. She joined the first leg of the march, out of Selma, then worked for the next few days on logistical support. But she insisted on participating in the final day's march to the state capitol. Standing at the foot of the capitol that afternoon, she heard Martin Luther King ask, "How long will it take us to realize the promise of justice in society?" After the march was over, she drove several marchers back to Selma. At SCLC headquarters there, Leroy Moton, a nineteen-year-old black man who had worked as coordinator of the march's drivers, was looking for a ride to Montgomery. Liuzzo volunteered to take him.

As Liuzzo's green Oldsmobile was stopped at a light, waiting to cross the Pettus Bridge, its occupants were spotted by four white men in an Impala. They were members of the Ku Klux Klan, and they had spent the early part of that evening drinking in a local bar with the men who had ambushed and beaten James Reeb. "You boys go do your job," one of Reeb's attackers told the four. "I already done mine." They intended to do just that. After about forty-five minutes at the bar, they were cruising Selma's streets, looking for Northern agitators. At the bridge, they hit what they considered the jackpot—a car with Michigan tags, with a white woman and a black man inside. "Let's take them," said one of the men, Collie Leroy Wilkins, Jr.

The Impala tailed Liuzzo's car on Highway 80 for about twenty miles. Apparently realizing she was being followed, Liuzzo accelerated to close to ninety miles an hour, but the Impala kept pace. Finally, it pulled alongside the Oldsmobile. "The lady just turned her head all the way around and looked at us," recalled Gary Thomas Rowe, another occupant of the car. "I will never forget it in my lifetime, and her mouth flew open. . . . At that point Wilkins fired a shot. . . . He fired three or four more shots." When Rowe said he didn't think Wilkins had hit the car, Wilkins replied, "That bitch and that bastard are dead and in hell. I don't miss."

He was half right. The Oldsmobile skidded off the road and into a ditch. Viola Liuzzo had been killed instantly. Moton was drenched with her blood, but he had not been hit. He pretended to be dead when the murderers came back to check on their handiwork; satisfied, the four drove away. That night, Rowe, who was the FBI's chief informant inside the KKK, called his control agent and told him what had happened. The other three men were soon arrested and charged with Liuzzo's murder.*

But within days, it appeared that Liuzzo, the only woman activist to be killed during the modern civil rights movement, was the one on trial. Her morals were questioned, as was her commitment to her family and to civil rights. FBI director J. Edgar Hoover, who was avowedly hostile to Martin Luther King and the movement, was also highly sensitive to the fact that one of his informants had, at the very least, not stopped a murder that he knew was going to take place. "Evidently aware of the embarrassment the FBI would suffer from the presence of its undercover informer in the murderer's car, Hoover marshaled the Bureau's resources to blacken the dead woman's reputation," columnist Jack Anderson later wrote. Hoover told President Johnson that Liuzzo had been sitting "very, very close to the Negro" in the car—a situation that had "all the appearances of a necking party." FBI agents were ordered to collect—and disseminate—derogatory information about the murdered woman.

---

*Later, Wilkins would accuse Rowe of being the triggerman. In 1978, Rowe was indicted for Liuzzo's murder by the state of Alabama, but a federal court prevented his prosecution, citing his immunity as a government informant.

Many in the media joined in the criticism, dismissing Liuzzo as a civil rights dilettante who abandoned her children to pursue her own selfish ends. "A plumpish perky blonde, belatedly a sophomore at Wayne State University, who liked a cause," was *Newsweek's* condescending description of her. Even members of Liuzzo's own church took part in the attack. "The reaction to her death from the parishioners was 'How dare she leave her children and go down South with *them* people,'" said Pat Fry, a congregant at the same Catholic church. "I was horrified."

When Collie Wilkins was brought to trial, his lawyer made clear he believed that Liuzzo, whom he called "a white nigger," had gotten what she deserved. He all but accused Liuzzo and Moton of having a sexual relationship: "Why [else] would a white woman from Detroit desert her husband and children to ride around in a car with a black man?" Wilkins' lawyer "accused the poor, dead woman of the nastiest sort of sex mania and the Negro boy of even worse," said an appalled Virginia Durr, who attended the trial. "He piled vileness upon vileness until the whole courtroom stank. And all in the name of 'Southern White Tradition and Pure White Southern Womanhood.'"

Wilkins' first trial ended in a mistrial. The jurors in his second trial were all white males (women and blacks were not allowed to serve on Alabama juries), and eight of them were current or former members of the White Citizens Council. Wilkins was acquitted. Two months later, Wilkins and his accomplices, with the exception of Rowe, were tried in federal court and found guilty of violating Liuzzo's civil rights. They were given the maximum sentence of ten years in prison.

Viola Liuzzo, meanwhile, entered history as "the most controversial of the civil rights martyrs," in the words of her biographer. A woman who had defied society's standards for proper female behavior, she would always be tainted by the accusations against her. And she never would be regarded in the same heroic light as the men murdered in the cause.

Liuzzo's wasn't the only death at Selma. For all intents and purposes, the Southern civil rights movement, begun in Montgomery a decade earlier, died in Selma, too. As John Lewis noted: "The road of nonviolence had essentially run out. Selma was the last act."

With the passage of the Civil Rights Act in the summer of 1964 and the Voting Rights Act four months after Selma, the federal government had assumed the initiative in the civil rights struggle in the South. In just a few years, the movement had seen the attainment of its major demands—the outlawing of Jim Crow segregation and a ban on barriers to black voting. The end of legal racism was a remarkable achievement, but it did not mean the end of black inequality, and activists did not see the laws as unalloyed victories. Pointing to the government's less than strict enforcement of previous civil rights laws, they questioned whether the Johnson administration would be any more vigorous in enforcing the new legislation.

In addition, enactment of the laws meant that civil rights workers no longer had clearly defined enemies to organize against. It was no longer "the good guys" versus "the bad guys," brave movement activists facing off against murderous sheriffs and KKK members. The intractable problems that remained for blacks—poverty, institutional racism, unemployment, among them—were not the stuff of drama, "not amenable to romantic crusades and the evangelical approach," as historian C. Vann Woodward pointed out. "They were tough and harsh and brutally raw." Morever, they were national problems, not ones exclusive to the South, and in taking them on, activists would be challenging the attitudes of the entire country. When the movement's emphasis started shifting from the South to the North, from voting and other rights of equal treatment to economic issues, white support dropped precipitously. Adding to the white backlash was the eruption of racial violence in Watts and other urban areas, and a rise in black nationalism among movement radicals, many of whom were members of SNCC.

When Stokely Carmichael first used the term "black power" in 1966, he was talking, he said, about the need for blacks to build political and social institutions within their communities, rather than to rely, futilely, on the white establishment to share its power. But his remark was interpreted by many whites—and some black militants—as a literal call to arms against whites. That same year, the fast-talking, impetuous New Yorker ousted John Lewis as chairman of SNCC. Carmichael's election marked the demise of the old SNCC, created with such hope and optimism in the spring of 1960. Most of its founding members, the advocates of nonviolence and the "beloved community," were already gone. Shortly after his defeat, Lewis also left. "I didn't want to be part of it," he later declared. "It was not the movement that I knew."

The change in SNCC was also a source of pain for Ella Baker. What bothered her was not the new SNCC leaders' militancy but their retreat from the hard work of community organizing. Carmichael seemed more interested in traveling around the country, delivering his inflammatory, confrontational speeches, than in helping the people whom SNCC had pledged to serve. Founded on the ideal of egalitarianism, the organization now seemed to be turning its back on that belief. There was a loss of trust and community, an abandoning of the rituals of courtesy and generosity so highly valued by SNCC's local black supporters in the South. In late 1966, Fannie Lou Hamer sadly complained that many of her SNCC comrades had grown "cold and unloving." One young female activist put it more bluntly: "We were starting to eat each other alive."

In 1965, SNCC began urging its white staff members to abandon their work with Southern blacks and to organize in white communities. Casey Hayden was one of the first to follow the directive. She moved to Cleveland for a while to work with SDS, then moved on to Chicago to help organize a union of white women on welfare. But she felt adrift and lost, severed as she was from the organization that, for her, was "home and family, food and work, love and a reason to live . . ."

Mary King did not leave to work with whites. She stayed on in Mississippi—and felt increasingly estranged from her black coworkers. "I look around in the mass meeting," she wrote at the time, "and see more and more clearly there is no place for me, no real place for others like me . . . I am almost numb. There is so much emotional entanglement, so little sense and so little stamina . . ." In 1965, she left SNCC and married fellow organizer Dennis Sweeney, seeing in him an "escape from this miasma that seemed bleakly without options." The couple moved to Palo Alto, California, where Sweeney and his friend David Harris began organizing resistance to the draft. But marriage provided no escape for King, and a year later, she divorced Sweeney and returned to the East. (Fifteen years after that, Sweeney shot and killed another close antiwar associate, former congressman Allard Lowenstein.) "For a long time after leaving SNCC, I dreamed at night as if I were still there . . . ," King recalled. "I grieved for three years. It was even longer before I could talk without choking about what my experiences meant."

In April 1965, Penny Patch sent a letter of resignation to the SNCC office in Atlanta. She had worked in the field longer than any other white woman in SNCC—longer, indeed, than the majority of organizers, regardless of race or gender—but now, she wrote, "it was no longer an organization I felt able to be part of." She remembered that her letter was short, that she could not write a longer one "because it hurt so much to write it at all. I wrote it and mailed it and felt like I had lopped off an arm, a leg, my head; it felt like I was spilling blood everywhere."

For Patch, as for Hayden, King, and many others, leaving SNCC was an emotionally devastating experience from which she never fully recovered. After a childhood of wandering, the diplomat's daughter had finally found a community, an extended family, and now it was gone. "I was desolate and full of rage—rage at the system, the country, all the white people who opposed change or did nothing. And rage at my beloved SNCC community for what felt like a betrayal."

By December 1966, only seven whites, among them Bob and Dorothy Zellner, still worked for SNCC. At a staff meeting held in upstate New York, the antiwhite hard-liners in the group forced through a vote demanding the remaining whites' expulsion. In the debate preceding the vote, Fannie Lou Hamer, along with a few others, strenuously opposed getting rid of whites, but she was shouted down by black separatists, who derided her as being "no longer relevant" and not at their "level of development." The following May, Bob Zellner, who had been SNCC's first white field secretary and who had repeatedly proven his courage and organizing skill, appeared before the organization's leaders. He and Dorothy had agreed with SNCC's directive to organize within the white community—they had already launched a project to work with poor whites in New Orleans—but they asked to be allowed to operate the project as members of SNCC. Their appeal was rejected. "This was the worst thing that had ever happened to me," Dorothy Zellner said. "I understand it and I accept it. But I'm still mourning. Looking back, to me it's a tragedy. It was this inevitable, horrible Greek tragedy . . . and there was no way to stop it."

Although most white activists quietly accepted their exile from the black movement, a few made quite clear how wrong they thought this division was. Virginia Durr, outspoken as ever, was one of them. In the late 1960s, Durr, who had been invited to speak to a class at the all-black Tuskegee Institute in Alabama about her civil rights work, listened in shocked disbelief as a young woman in the class told her: "You old lady, we don't want to hear you anyway. You just coming down here to take us down. We don't want to hear no white folks." The other students in the class shouted their agreement. Durr tried to argue with them, but to no avail. Afterward she sadly reflected: "They didn't give a damn about politics or about the right to vote or the right to sit down in a bus. . . . That class was, in a way, the most painful moment of my life, because I felt that they didn't give a damn about all I'd worked so hard for."

Later, in a letter to a friend, Durr declared: "I want so much to do something to stop this awful color division, and I blame the young militants at the same time I blame the KKK. I simply do not see why calling a man a 'honky' and saying 'Kill him' is so different or should be forgiven than a white man saying 'Kill the nigger.' I have fought too long against one to accept the other."

21

The "Woman Question"

Eleanor Holmes Norton, EEOC chair

SHELL-SHOCKED BY HER BREAK
with SNCC, Casey Hayden was also very lonely. After working in Cleveland and Chicago, she wandered around the country for a few months and then took refuge with Mary King, at a cottage that King's family owned in southern Virginia. En route to see King, Hayden wrote down her thoughts on the possibility of creating a community of support among like-minded women, "so that we could keep working for radical change." At the cottage in Virginia, Hayden and King fine-tuned what Hayden had written. This new paper would be directed *solely* at women. And this time, the authors would sign their names.

They called it "SEX AND CASTE: A kind of memo from Casey Hayden and Mary King to a number of other women in the peace and freedom movements." The wording of the title—"A kind of"—reflected a lingering insecurity about the wisdom of raising such issues—an unsurprising reaction, considering the hostile reception to the authors' first paper at Waveland. This memo was broader in scope, focusing on women's subordination in society, rather than just in the civil rights movement. It focused, too, on the fact that such subordination was taken for granted by women as well as men. Unlike racial discrimination, Hayden and King observed, sexual discrimination was not considered a significant social problem. Women who questioned the way they were treated were belittled and ridiculed by men, their complaints regarded as trivial. "That inability to see the whole issue as serious, as the straitjacketing of both sexes, and as societally determined often shapes [women's] own response so that we learn to think in [men's] terms about ourselves and to feel silly rather than trust our own feelings."

The civil rights movement had inspired its participants "to think radically about the personal worth and abilities of people whose role in society has gone unchallenged before." Now, Hayden and King said, women in the movement were "trying to apply those lessons to their own relations with men." It was crucial for women to break out of their chrysalis of self-doubt, Hayden and King believed, but there was no public support for doing so. They lamented the fact that "[n]obody is writing, or organizing or talking publicly about women, in any way that reflects the problems . . ." Perhaps, they said, women in the civil rights, antiwar, free speech, and other youth movements percolating in the country could begin a dialogue with one another about these issues, could join together in "a community of support for each other . . ." Perhaps women could work together to try to build a society where personal needs and problems would be treated as social and political issues, and where institutions would be shaped to "meet human needs rather than shaping people to meet the needs of those with power."

The personal is political—that was a link that Lillian Smith, among other women, had made years before, to little effect. This time, however, the idea that personal behavior and relationships belonged on the country's political agenda would land with explosive force—an impact that Hayden and King never anticipated. Their memo, which would come to be viewed as the new feminism's first manifesto, was tentative in its vision: Although it came close, it stopped short of calling for the creation of a women's movement similar to the civil rights movement. Given the dismissive climate in the country to the concerns of women, such an undertaking, the two women thought, would be impossible. "Objectively, the chances seem nil that we could start a movement based on anything as distant to general American thought as a sex-caste system. Therefore, most of us will probably want to work full-time on problems such as war, poverty, race."

They reckoned, however, without women like Heather Tobis. Tobis, who had worked in Mississippi during Freedom Summer, got hold of Hayden and King's memo during the winter of 1965 and read it avidly. Throughout the country, hundreds of other young women were doing the same. Hayden and King had sent the memo that November to women in SDS, NSA, and other student groups, as well as to some of their female former coworkers in SNCC. The women in SNCC showed little interest, but those in other organizations, most of them white, immediately passed the memo on to more women after reading it themselves.

It served as a kind of yeast, prompting the bubbling up of thoughts and feelings that a number of the women harbored but rarely, if ever, expressed publicly. Tobis, for one, had been thinking hard about the status of women since her return to the University of Chicago after spending the previous summer in Mississippi. Like other female Freedom Summer volunteers, she had come back to her old life with a newfound sense of strength and power as a result of her experiences in the South. Ever since grammar school, she had been active in social justice causes, but she had grown up, as had so many other young women, with "enormous insecurities" about her own abilities. Was she smart enough? Did she know enough? Was she brave enough? Watching the work of local black activists in Mississippi, however, she realized that "you didn't have to be the smartest or the best or even have the answers. . . . Whatever *you* knew was enough. You didn't have to know enough according to some white person's standard or some man's standard."

Tobis also saw that the black women in the Mississippi movement did not take a backseat to anybody. They were out front, leading with a boldness that she had rarely seen before in women. She realized, too, that the views of women activists—both local women and those from the outside, including summer volunteers—were heeded. "Maybe not as much as they should have been, but they *were* listened to. It was more of an equal society." After returning to Chicago, she followed the lead of the Mississippi women, putting into practice some of the protest techniques she had learned from the civil rights movement. On one occasion, a friend of hers, who had been raped at knifepoint, was denied a gynecological exam at the university's health service and was instead lectured about her "promiscuity." Outraged, Tobis and other female friends of the young woman staged a sit-in at the health service office.

When Casey Hayden and Mary King's memo came along, with its emphasis on transforming personal (i.e., women's) problems into political issues, Tobis was primed for action. *Oh, boy, this really is true,* she thought when she read the memo. *We're going to have to find some way to work this out.* When SDS scheduled its winter conference at the University of Illinois at Champaign-Urbana, Tobis decided to attend. It was time, she thought, to explore the "woman question."

More than a hundred years earlier, women had used the abolitionist movement as a springboard for the launching of this country's first women's rights crusade. Like their twentieth-century counterparts, the female abolitionists, through their work for racial justice, had developed organizing skills and a commitment to human rights that would lead to their own demands for equality. Those ideas, though, had little relevance or appeal for most American women of that period, subscribing as they did to their Victorian society's ideal of "true womanhood," with its emphasis on female domesticity, subservience, and piety. In 1965, the situation was quite different. Many young white women like Tobis, born during or after World War II, had grown up with high expectations and ambitions. They had been given good educations, had been raised to believe in the idea of personal fulfillment. Such beliefs, however, were at odds with the stereo-typed "feminine" roles that society still expected them to play. At the same time, full-time domesticity was no longer the unquestioned norm: Almost half of all married women were now employed, albeit mostly in low-paying, low-status "women's jobs." Women had broadened their sphere beyond the home, but society, in the midst of wrenching changes in racial relations, had not substantially altered its attitudes toward women or their "place." Small wonder, then, that Hayden and King's memo resonated so strongly with young white female activists.

Although Heather Tobis belonged to a campus organization affiliated with SDS, she was not a member of the national group. She did not fully realize how much of "a chauvinist's paradise" (to quote Tom Hayden) it was. Like most of the Northern student left groups in the 1960s, SDS was thoroughly dominated by white men, who were as concerned about assert-ing their manhood as any black militant. "[T]he new left envisioned a whole society alive with participatory democracy. Yet the young radicals still equated this invigorated citizenship with masculinity, viewing it as a triumph over effeminacy," historian Doug Rossinow observed. It was a movement, said SDS leader Todd Gitlin, that was marked by "arrogance, elitism, competitiveness, machismo [and] ruthlessness . . ."

Yet the Hayden-King memo had caused enough of a stir by the time of the SDS conference that the question of women's status in the student movement could no longer be ignored. A workshop on the subject was penciled in, with both men and women participating. Tobis was stunned by what she heard there: "The men were telling the women what reality was. They were denying our reality in a way that was so shocking." On subjects like Vietnam or civil rights, perhaps, she might never challenge such male certitude. "Maybe on everything else, I might think I'm stupid or don't know enough. But you can't know more about what I actually think than I do. . . . This was a discussion about what our life is like, are women listened to? No, we don't particularly think we're listened to. Then [a man] says, 'Oh, yes, they're listened to' . . . and proceeds to ignore what we just said."

Tobis and the other women walked out of the session. They split up into several groups to compare notes on the way that men treated them as subordinates, as handmaidens. For many of the women, it was the dawning of a realization that other women shared their grievances and, perhaps even more important, that if they banded together, they might be able to do something about their complaints.

Soon after the Champaign-Urbana conference, Tobis launched a women's discussion group at the University of Chicago. Later, she would be a key organizer of the women's liberation movement in Chicago. Indeed, as women's groups began mushrooming throughout the country in the late 1960s, their founders often turned out to be, like Tobis, Freedom Summer alumnae. Pam Parker Allen was central to the early women's liberation movement in New York, as was Kathie Amatniek (who changed her name to Kathie Sarachild). Ann Popkin was one of the first members of Bread and Roses, an influential women's liberation group in Boston. As it happened, more than 70 percent of the women who worked in Mississippi during Freedom Summer became involved in women's liberation, many of them trying to replicate the same spirit of community they had experienced in the South. "The civil rights movement had a . . . personalized politics, a community, a vision of human connection and humanity," Popkin said. "All those things for me [were] there again in the women's movement." Mused Allen: "What I remember about Mississippi was the love I felt . . . from everyone. There was this openness and acceptance of you as a person that I've never really felt since, not even in the women's movement, even though that's what we were trying to re-create."

The core of the early movement was "consciousness-raising"—a gathering together of women to discuss their personal lives and problems in an atmosphere of support and understanding. For the women who participated, such discussions were often life-changing experiences. Most of the women were white, and had grown up in isolation, believing that any dissatisfaction or discontent they felt was theirs alone, unshared by other girls or women. In the consciousness-raising sessions, however, they learned that the opposite was true.

In these sessions, they also talked about transcending their sense of inferiority, about the importance of standing up for themselves, about the need to take action and risks. Such discussions were not dissimilar to those engaged in by young black activists in Jim Lawson's nonviolent workshops in Nashville a few years earlier. The women were realizing, as Diane Nash and her colleagues had before them, that they had to learn to love themselves, to come to "a realization of our own worth." Just as the black students struggled to cast off their psychological subordination to white society, so, too, did white women activists grapple with their psychological and economic dependence on men.

With a supportive community now behind them, the women could also follow in the footsteps of the civil rights movement by mobilizing to force social change. At first, the change that many of them sought was in their own immediate surroundings. Dorothy Zellner, who was active in the fledgling women's movement in New Orleans, pressed her husband, Bob, to take more responsibility for the housework and for the care of their two small children. Both were working on an SCEF project to organize poor whites, but Dorothy was doing all the domestic chores, too. "We went through some very severe struggles around that," Bob Zellner recalled, acknowledging that he often "fell short" in doing his share of the work.

Before long, local women's groups, emphasizing the need for women to take control of their own lives and bodies, began to organize on behalf of themselves and other women in their communities. They founded rape crisis networks, women's shelters, abortion counseling services, day-care centers, women's health-care organizations. Members of Bread and Roses, for example, went on to form the Boston Women's Health Collective, which produced *Our Bodies, Ourselves*, the groundbreaking, bestselling primer on women's health. Women activists protested sexual harassment in the office and on the street. They demonstrated against the media's depiction of women. They called into question even the most routine encounters of daily life, such as women fetching coffee for men and men opening doors for women.

Focusing their energies on the personal aspects of women's lives, the younger, more radical women were a crucial element in the revived feminist campaign. But there were other key players—older professional women who took on the courts and the federal government in their demands for economic and legal equality for women. Chief among them were the two longtime friends Eleanor Roosevelt and Pauli Murray.

Eleanor Roosevelt's role in the women's movement was short-lived but critical. In Pauli Murray's view, "the catalytic event which signaled the rebirth of feminism in the United States" was a visit that the former First Lady paid to President John F. Kennedy shortly after he took office in 1961. Roosevelt, who had supported women's rights as fervently as she had endorsed the black civil rights struggle, was angered by what she considered Kennedy's abysmal record on appointing women to positions in his administration. He was the first President since Herbert Hoover not to select a woman for his cabinet and had named only ten women to policy-making jobs, none of them especially high-ranking or visible. That was unacceptable, Roosevelt told the young President, and presented him with a three-page list of the names of women who she said should be considered for executive appointments. Kennedy countered her proposal with one of his own: He was about to announce the formation of a presidential commission on the status of women. Would Mrs. Roosevelt be its chair?

The seventy-six-year-old Roosevelt was seriously ill, but she agreed to Kennedy's request. He may have thought he was getting rid of two troublesome birds with one stone: silencing the outspoken former First Lady by bringing her into the administration tent and ridding himself of the "woman question" by creating a commission that would meet for years and accomplish nothing. What happened instead was an unprecedented national focus on the role of women in America, and the creation of a nationwide women's network, under Eleanor Roosevelt's aegis, to seek changes in the way women were treated. Members of the network were members and staffers of the presidential commission, as well as organizers of state women's commissions formed by the presidential body. And Pauli Murray was at the center of the action.

Eleanor Holmes Norton, who considered Pauli Murray a mentor, called Murray "a pre-consciousness woman" when it came to both civil rights and feminism. As Norton saw it, Murray "lived on the edge of history, seeming to pull it along with her." Active in the civil rights struggle long before the modern movement, she was campaigning for women's rights well before the feminist groundswell of the late 1960s. Shortly after she graduated from Howard Law School, Murray wrote: "I will resist every attempt to categorize me, to place me in some caste, or to assign me to some segregated pigeonhole. No law which imprisons my body or custom which wounds my spirit can stop me."

When Floyd McKissick, James Farmer's successor as head of CORE, introduced Murray to another activist by saying, "This chick really has something on the ball," the fiftyish Murray was stunned and infuriated. She had to assume one of two things, she later wrote. Either she was being treated as a sex object or she was "on the receiving end of male condescension." In her view, "McKissick might as well have used the term 'Auntie,' long used by patronizing whites in the South when speaking to Negro females of mature age."

"Pauli resonated with feminism at a time when any young black woman who was in the movement would have been far deeper into civil rights," Norton reflected. "I mean, we hadn't even gotten the civil rights laws. . . . Black women were fully included in the civil rights movement, so that talk of feminism, in the way Pauli was absorbed in it, seemed remote to where one's energy and attention had to be."

Murray argued otherwise. It was essential that black women take up both fights, she said, noting that most black women "must prepare to be self-supporting and to support others, perhaps, for a considerable period or for life. . . . Negro women have no alternative but to insist upon equal opportunities without regard to sex in training, education, and employment at every level." She had no patience with black men who argued that black women's main role was to support them as they asserted the manhood previously denied them. "I say I can match you . . . ," Murray said. "Negro women are as much a victim of psychological rape as Negro men are of psychological castration. Until Negro men understand this, we will be at loggerheads; the only way we're going to get out of this particular bag is as partners."

She never hesitated to let others know her feelings about discriminatory treatment resulting from her gender. When she and a woman friend tried to enter a private club in New Haven to have lunch, the black doorman told them to use the "ladies' entrance" in the back. Murray refused. "You and I have been told to use back doors all our lives," she said to the doorman. "I think you'll understand why I have no intention of doing so any longer."

Some years later, at a Postal Service ceremony marking the issuance of a Harriet Tubman commemorative stamp, Murray, the only woman on the dais, was asked to give the benediction. She began her remarks with the comment: "The person who says the benediction has the last word. I'm presumptuous enough to believe I walk in the tradition of Harriet Tubman, and she would come back and haunt me if she knew I was the token woman on this program. So before I give the benediction, will the women and girls in the auditorium stand in silent tribute to Harriet Tubman?" Hundreds of women stood, then followed the moment of silence with a thunderous burst of applause.

When the presidential commission on women was created, Murray, then studying for her doctorate at Yale, was asked to help undertake an extensive review of the differences in the legal treatment of men and women in regard to political and civil rights, property rights, and family relations. Her work on the study gave her an expertise on the legal status of women that would prove an invaluable tool in future campaigns for women's rights legislation. For the moment, however, she saw her work as a tribute to the dying Eleanor Roosevelt. As she wrote her report in the fall of 1962, she thought constantly about Mrs. Roosevelt, who "had filled the landscape of my entire adult life." When the former First Lady died on November 7, the grieving Murray committed herself to continuing what her old friend had started. Murray knew, she said, that "we could never fill this great hole, but that all the women that came under her influence must now try to carry forward what one person had carried alone."

In the winter of 1964, Murray and other women's rights advocates were handed their most important legislative victory since Congress approved the Nineteenth Amendment. The landmark amendment came about because of the civil rights movement. But, in one of the strangest scenarios in Capitol Hill history, the amendment's author turned out to be a crafty Southern baron, one of the movement's most ardent congressional foes.

For years, Representative Howard Smith of Virginia had been as effective in bottling up civil rights legislation in the House as James Eastland had been in the Senate. The tall, rumpled, eighty-year-old Smith was chairman of the House Rules Committee, which gave him enormous power over which bills would be considered by the full House. To get to the House floor, a bill needed a rule—in effect, a permit—from the Rules Committee. Smith was a master at burying bills he opposed. To Virginia Durr, the pipe-smoking Virginia congressman was like "a rock of ages standing there, refusing to let any liberal legislation through at all."

In 1964, Smith was casting about for ways to stymie the Civil Rights Act proposed in 1963 by John Kennedy and pushed hard by Kennedy's successor, Lyndon Johnson. What he found was a proposal by the National Woman's Party, a women's rights organization whose roots lay in the suffragist fight for the Nineteenth Amendment. NWP members were, for the most part, elderly, white, middle- and upper-class women who had little interest in, or sympathy for, the civil rights struggle. Indeed, the party's founder, Alice Paul, had been one of the women's suffrage leaders who, in the early 1900s, opposed black women's participation in the voting rights campaign.

Raising the same argument that Elizabeth Cady Stanton and Susan B. Anthony made about the Fourteenth and Fifteenth amendments, the followers of Alice Paul contended that women should be included within the scope of the Civil Rights Act of 1964. And some of them, in arguing that white women should not be denied rights given to blacks, framed their appeal in language as racist as that used by Stanton and Anthony a century earlier. "Thank God for the members of Congress who are from the South and for those members from the East, North and West, who will use their brains and energies to prevent a mongrel race in the United States and who will fight for the rights of white citizens in order that discrimination against them may be stopped," wrote one NWP leader.

Howard Smith claimed the NWP's idea. During Rules Committee hearings on the civil rights bill, he had warned Emmanuel Celler, the act's sponsor in the House, that the bill was "as full of booby traps as a dog is full of fleas." Now, he had come up with a booby trap of his own. There was too much public and White House pressure on him to be able to prevent the bill from coming to the floor. But once it was there, he could—and would—do his best to sabotage it.

On February 8, Smith stood in front of a microphone on the House floor. "Mr. Chairman," he said, "I offer an amendment . . ." It was a simple amendment, one that required almost no new language in the bill. All it did was add the word "sex" to Title VII of the act, which prohibited discrimination by employers, employment agencies, and unions on the basis of race, color, religion, and national origin. But that one word threw the House of Representatives into pandemonium. If approved, it would give women a formidable legal weapon to fight gender inequities in hiring and promotion that were deeply ingrained in American society. Smith, whose joking remarks about the amendment provoked uproarious laughter from the overwhelmingly male House, hoped that the idea of sex equality in employment would be so controversial, would be considered so outlandish, that it would kill the entire legislation.

When Emmanuel Celler rose to oppose Smith's proposal, he responded with his own attempt at witticism. Based on his personal experience, Celler said, he did not see a pressing need for such an amendment:

In his own house, although he was allowed to have the last two words in any argument or discussion with his wife, those words were always "Yes, dear." In a more serious vein, the seventy-five-year-old Brooklyn congressman warned that passage of Smith's amendment would result in the striking down of state labor laws designed to protect women against onerous and dangerous working conditions. Like supporters of the Fourteenth and Fifteenth amendments, Celler and most other advocates of the 1964 Civil Rights Act believed that this was the "Negro's hour" and that inclusion of women in the bill would spell political disaster.

In the post–Civil War Congress that considered the amendments, there were no women in the body to argue otherwise. In 1964, however, twelve women were House members. Eleven of them, Republican and Democrat, rose to speak for the amendment and to challenge their male colleagues' jocular treatment of it. "I presume that if there had been any necessity to . . . point out that women were a second-class sex, the laughter would have proved it," Martha Griffiths, a Michigan Democrat, snapped. Katherine St. George, a Republican from New York, added: "We are entitled to this little crumb of equality. The addition of that little terrifying word, 's-e-x,' will not hurt this legislation in any way."

Griffiths, the first woman to be named to the powerful Ways and Means Committee, was the congresswoman to whom other House members listened most closely. A shrewd, adroit legislator, she was unabashedly in favor of women's rights and would later become a key congressional sponsor of the Equal Rights Amendment. In the debate over Smith's amendment, this staunch liberal revealed a racist streak again reminiscent of Elizabeth Cady Stanton and Susan B. Anthony. "[I]f you do not add sex to this bill . . . you are going to try to take colored men and colored women and give them equal employment rights, and down at the bottom of the list is going to be a white woman with no rights at all." Celler responded that black women would be protected only on the basis of race, not sex. That argument was not good enough for Griffiths. "It would be incredible to me that white men would be willing to place white women at such a disadvantage except that white men have done this before . . . ," she declared. "[Y]our great-grandfathers were willing as prisoners of their own prejudice to permit ex-slaves to vote, but not their own white wives. . . . Mr. Chairman, a vote against this amendment today by a white man is a vote against his wife, or his widow, or his daughter, or his sister."

Griffiths' views pitting white women against blacks were echoed by Southern male conservatives. Attacking the act as a whole, Mendel Rivers, a Democrat from South Carolina, thundered: "It is incredible to me that the authors of this monstrosity . . . would deprive the white woman of mostly Anglo-Saxon or Christian heritage equal opportunity before the employer."

The amendment passed, 168–133. Those who voted for it were, for the most part, Southerners, Republicans, and women of both parties. Most male Democrats from outside the South opposed it. As it turned out, however, Smith's attempt at sabotage backfired. When the full bill came up for a vote on February 10, it was approved, 290–130, sex amendment and all. Interestingly enough, all but one of the men who had spoken out for the amendment in debate voted against the act.

Women who had been involved with the presidential women's commission were overjoyed. They'd had nothing to do with the amendment's passage; they did not even know Smith was going to introduce it. But now that it was a reality, they planned to do everything they could to get it enacted. The Johnson administration, however, was adamantly opposed to the amendment, believing that its inclusion would make it more difficult for Senate passage. Senator Everett Dirksen, the Republican minority leader, announced he opposed the amendment, too.

Mounting a last-minute lobbying effort, the women enlisted Pauli Murray to write a memo making clear why the provision was necessary. Murray was delighted with the amendment's introduction because she believed it would make it much easier for black women to prove discrimination. "[A]s a Negro woman, I knew that in many instances it was difficult to determine whether I was being discriminated against because of race or sex, and felt that the sex provision would close the gap . . ." Her strongly worded, well-reasoned memo contended that inclusion of the amendment would only serve to bolster the main intent of the bill: "A strong argument can be made for the proposition that Title VII without the 'sex' amendment would benefit Negro males primarily and thus offer genuine equality of opportunity to only *half* of the potential Negro work force." Murray's memo was used by the forces lobbying for the amendment and was sent to senators and administration officials. The memo apparently helped influence a number of senators, and the Senate decided to retain the amendment in the act, which became law on July 2. In a letter to Murray, Marguerite Rawalt, a presidential commission member who had served as leader of the lobbying effort, declared: "To you comes a real measure of credit for the ultimate successful passage of Title VII . . ."

Just as she played an important part in Title VII's enactment, so, too, would Pauli Murray have a key role in ensuring its enforcement. It was not an easy task: For many men (and some women), the idea of enforcing equality of the sexes in the workplace was very much a laughing matter, just as it had been for the men on Capitol Hill. In the media, the "sex" amendment was subjected to merciless ridicule and derision. The EEOC "would be much better advised to worry about the grave and almost intractable problems that have been put in its charge," *The New Republic* snorted. "Why should a mischievous joke perpetrated on the floor of the House of Representatives be treated by a responsible administrative body with this kind of seriousness?" With mock horror, *The Wall Street Journal* presented scenarios of what might happen if there were true employment equality: "a shapeless, knobby-kneed male 'bunny' serving drinks to a group of stunned businessmen in a Playboy Club," for example, or a "matronly vice president" pursuing a male secretary around her desk.

More worrisome for advocates of the sex discrimination provision was the EEOC's backhanded dismissal of it. The agency's chairman, Franklin D. Roosevelt, Jr., talked about how difficult it would be to enforce it, and the EEOC's executive director termed the provision a "fluke" and "conceived out of wedlock." *The Wall Street Journal* quoted an unnamed EEOC official as saying that the agency did not plan to come down hard against violators, as long as "the women's groups will let us get away with it." The EEOC staff was entirely male, and the only female commission member was Aileen Hernandez, a black former union official. According to Hernandez, most men at the EEOC reacted to the issue of sex discrimination with either "boredom" or "virulent hostility."

Three weeks after the EEOC began operation, Pauli Murray wrote other women's rights allies that unless they joined together and pushed for implementation of the sex discrimination ban, "we would lose the little we thought we had gained." A longtime member of the NAACP, Murray began to think about the possibility of forming an "NAACP for women," a national organization that would press for women's rights using the same courtroom and lobbying tactics as the venerable civil rights group. "Do you suppose the time has come for the organization of a strong national ad hoc committee of women who are ready to take the plunge?" Murray wrote to Marguerite Rawalt. ". . . [T]he sex provision will be emasculated beyond recognition unless there is prompt action on the part of women committed to the full equality of all individuals in our society." Noting the EEOC chairman's cavalier attitude toward the amendment, Murray added tartly, "I wonder what Mrs. Roosevelt would have thought of her son's actions."

The idea of a women's rights organization had been percolating in the minds of other women, too. Among them was Betty Friedan, who wrote *The Feminine Mystique*, the bestselling account of the malaise and discontent of white women like herself, struggling with society's dictum that fulfillment could be found only in home and family. The huge success of the book catapulted Friedan into the spotlight as a leading spokeswoman for women's rights. In October 1965, she contacted Murray after reading a *New York Times* story about a speech Murray had made suggesting the possibility of a women's march on Washington, similar to the 1963 civil rights march, to demand enforcement of the sex discrimination ban. Murray spelled out for Friedan her idea of "a network of about five hundred key women around the country who could spring into action whenever issues directly affecting women arise in Washington." She put Friedan in touch with Rawalt and other members of the "feminist underground" in Washington, who pressed Friedan to take action.

At a conference of state women's commissions in June 1966, Friedan, Murray, and twenty-six other women activists formed a temporary group that they called the National Organization for Women. Each contributed five dollars to cover initial expenses. On a napkin, Friedan jotted down the new body's purpose: "to take the actions needed to bring women into the mainstream of American society *now* . . . in fully equal partnership with men." The creation of the first avowedly feminist organization since the suffrage crusade, Murray noted, "had happened so quickly and smoothly that most of the delegates left the conference unaware that a historic development in the women's movement had begun." Three months later, "thirty-two of us set up the permanent organization of NOW, never dreaming that within less than two decades it would have more than 200,000 members and become a potent force in American politics." At a press conference announcing the new group, Friedan made clear that NOW was not a women's club but a "civil rights organization." She declared: "Discrimination against women in this modern world is as evil and wasteful as any other form of discrimination."

NOW's organizers gave notice to the government that they would no longer tolerate the placing of women's issues on the bureaucratic back burner. In October 1966, Aileen Hernandez resigned from the EEOC and was elected vice president of NOW, replacing Friedan as president in 1970. Hernandez, Friedan, and the organization's other leaders continued to make the EEOC their main target, but they also pushed for the appointment of more women to government positions and for affirmative action for women. In time, the organization would launch campaigns for legalized abortions, more and better child-care programs, and other women's rights goals. Other national feminist organizations would soon spring up, but NOW would remain the largest and most dominant body in the women's movement.

As the 1970s dawned, the EEOC finally began enforcing the ban against sex discrimination in employment, in large part because of the pressure put on it by NOW and other women's groups. In addition, the scope of Title VII was expanded, making it a far more potent weapon in the battle against discrimination because of gender. It was used as the legal basis for outlawing the firing of pregnant women. It also served as the basis for affirmative action and for banning sexual harassment. Until the courts began to rule that harassment was a form of employment discrimination banned by Title VII, women were legally powerless in challenging sexual badgering by employers and coworkers. For generations, black women, in particular, had been targets of sexual harassment, and now, at last, they had been given a tool with which to combat such assaults.

The EEOC's most aggressive enforcer turned out to be a Pauli Murray protégée, who carried on her mentor's crusade just as Murray had continued Eleanor Roosevelt's fight. Eleanor Holmes Norton was named to head the EEOC in 1977 by President Jimmy Carter. The Yale Law School graduate and former SNCC activist had already shown her aptitude for vigorous handling of sex discrimination cases. As chair of New York City's Human Rights Commission in the early 1970s, she had been instrumental in winning maternity benefits for women employees of several major New York–based companies; had ordered one of the city's most famous restaurants, "21," not to discriminate against women diners; and had pressured the Biltmore Hotel to change the name of its Men's Bar and to allow women in.

Norton, who had been given her pick of several civil rights posts in the Carter administration, wasted no time in her attempt to whip the inefficient, overburdened EEOC into shape. She appointed a special team to pare down the agency's backlog of 130,000 cases and installed a streamlined process to weed out weak discrimination complaints and move important, high-impact cases into court more quickly. Under her direction, the EEOC also took the lead in filing complaints against large companies that discriminated, rather than waiting for individual complaints about such companies.

Faced with the reality or threat of class-action discrimination lawsuits, American employers began to respond. As a result, young American women entering the job market in the 1970s and later had job opportunities and protections that were scarcely imaginable just a few years before. That was true for black women as well as white. Until the 1960s, most black women had worked in domestic service jobs, but by the 1970 census, only 18 percent of black women with jobs described themselves as domestic workers. In 1990, the majority of employed black women—58.9 percent—were in white-collar positions. Jacqueline Byrd Martin and Johnnie Wilcher, both involved in the McComb school walkout, were among several black women in McComb who, through the EEOC, successfully sued the local telephone company for employment discrimination. In 1973, AT&T, which had more women employees than any other company in the world, settled a massive class-action discrimination suit filed by the EEOC by paying thirty-eight million dollars to women and minority men who had either been denied promotions or been underpaid because of discrimination.

The EEOC was not alone in challenging barriers to women's freedom and equality. In the space of a few years, the Supreme Court struck down sex segregation in newspaper help-wanted ads, ruled that sexual harassment was a form of job discrimination, and made first-trimester abortions legal. Congress passed Title IX, outlawing sex discrimination in educational programs receiving federal assistance. State laws barring women from jury duty were abolished, and divorce laws in most states were made more equitable. Women could now get credit cards and bank loans in their own name, could start their own businesses without a male cosigner.

Barely a decade after the women's movement began, most formerly all-male colleges and universities, including the nation's three major military academies, were admitting women. So were once all-male private clubs. The number of women entering law, medical, business, and other professional schools skyrocketed. Women became astronauts, Episcopal priests, editors of major newspapers, college presidents, heads of companies.

Looking back at the last thirty years, one can say with considerable assurance that the women's movement has had an impact on the life of virtually every woman (and man) in the United States. Indeed, the lives of millions of women were dramatically changed because of it. Only a relatively small number of women were actively involved in the movement, but many who did not participate, even those who rejected any association with feminism, supported—and benefited from—much of its agenda, including day-care centers, equal pay and job opportunities, and fairer divorce laws.

Yet, like the civil rights movement, the new feminism, in the end, fell short of its goals. It profoundly altered the nation's consciousness about women and prompted sweeping changes in women's status, but it failed to achieve the fundamental transformation of public and private life sought by many in the women's movement. With all the progress that had been made, major inequities still existed. Although women's salaries had increased, they still fell far short of men's wages. And despite the significant employment gains of both black and white women, white men still dominated most businesses, as well as professions like the law, medicine, and higher education. As civil rights activists had earlier discovered, the passage of laws outlawing segregation and discrimination did not, by itself, mean the end of inequality. Sexism, like racism, was still deeply woven into the nation's fabric.

Like the civil rights movement, too, the women's movement was badly damaged by growing dissension within its ranks. Female solidarity proved to be a chimera, as conflicts between the movement's two major wings grew sharper and more hostile. Many movement radicals were calling for a complete economic, political, and cultural overhaul of American society. Some demanded an end to the nuclear family and female separatism. Such extremism was anathema to the more conservative wing of the movement, made up of older, professional women. Instead of overthrowing the power structure of this country, they wanted to join it.

As the movement discovered, the call for sisterhood (a metaphor taken from the civil rights movement) could not erase the divisions caused by differences among women in terms of race, class, and cultural and sexual orientation. There were tensions between lesbians and heterosexual women, between married and single women. And black women, for the most part, wanted nothing to do with this crusade, even though many had benefited economically from it. The women's movement was one that white women active in the civil rights and student movements could finally call their own. It was "a battle in which [we] can organize and fight without the constant struggle of being an outsider, playing a dual role," as one white female activist put it. That was not true for black women, whose identities were bound up in both their race *and* their gender. When Betty Friedan attempted to recruit black female SNCC members for NOW, the young women told her that they were not interested, that their goal was to help black men get the "rights they had been denied so long."

For more than a century, black women had been pulled between allegiances of race on the one hand and gender on the other. Almost always, they chose race, insisting that their own freedom could not be won independently of their men's freedom. As it turned out, however, neither black men nor white women paid much attention to black women's needs. Just as their interests were ignored in the post–Civil War battle between abolitionists and women's rights activists, so, too, were those interests largely forgotten in the 1960s and 1970s, when black men and white women once again pursued their own agendas. When the CBS newsmagazine program *60 Minutes* ran a story in 1972 about sex discrimination, the only women shown in the story were white. At the end of the piece, the white female correspondent declared that American women were finally rebelling against being put on a pedestal. It was a statement, however, that applied only to *some* women. Black women in this country had never known what it was like to have such a lofty, exalted perch.

For many black women, the women's movement and its battles, its emphasis on consciousness-raising, had little or no relevance to their lives. Young black women, who more often than not were raised in tightly knit communities, had trouble understanding this new hunger for sisterhood. When writer bell hooks enrolled in a Stanford women's studies class in the early 1970s, she noted how "white women were reveling in the joy of being together—to them it was an important, momentous occasion." Such joy seemed strange to her because "I had not known a life where women had not been together."

Betty Friedan's *The Feminine Mystique*, which served as a bible for much of the movement, focused on the experiences of white middle-class housewives, with no mention of black women at all, let alone the majority of black women who worked for a living. Friedan's observation that "I never knew a woman, when I was growing up, who used her mind, played her own part in the world, and also loved, and had children" revealed a chasm in the experiences of black and white women that seemed as wide as it had been at the turn of the century.

In the view of many black women, Friedan and other white women's rights activists were zeroing in on issues that would benefit white women only, particularly issues dealing with personal fulfillment. The conditions that middle-class white women found oppressive—being a housewife, stuck at home with the kids, for example—seemed like nirvana to many working-class black women, who would have loved to have such options. Meanwhile, the issues that *they* cared about—improved housing and transportation, better health care and nutrition, welfare, and the like—were not priorities for many white women, who'd never had to worry about the basics of life.

Once again, the tangled history of black and white women in America, with its subterranean currents of anger, competition, and jealousy, was intruding on the present. For years, black women had toiled in white women's homes, had suffered their abuse—and now were being asked to call them "sisters." "It is difficult for a black person looking at a white upper-class woman who may derive her position from her husband's prestige to think of her as 'oppressed,'" observed theologian Rosemary Reuther. "To blacks she represents the oppressor." Black women had long considered white women to be, in Toni Morrison's words, "willful children, pretty children, but never . . . real adults capable of handling the real problems of the world." There seemed to be little understanding that, through the women's movement, many white women were now attempting to break out of that childish world and become "real adults."

Still there were some black women who, like Pauli Murray and Aileen Hernandez, believed it was important for black and white women to find common cause in their gender and band together to fight sexual inequality. Among them was Septima Clark. In 1968, Clark joined NOW, at the urging of her good friend Virginia Durr. Both then in their late sixties, the black daughter of a former slave and the white granddaughter of a former slave owner said they had become members of the organization for the same reason: the subordination of women by men. "I am all for women's liberation," Clark later declared. "This country was built up from women keeping their mouths shut. It took fifty years for women, black and white, to learn to speak up."

Fannie Lou Hamer, Anna Arnold Hedgeman, and Shirley Chisholm, the first black woman elected to Congress, were early members of NOW as well. Hamer and Chisholm also were founding members of the National Women's Political Caucus, an organization formed in 1971 to support the election and appointment of women to government office. Hamer, however, made it clear to her white NWPC counterparts at the caucus's first meeting that most black women would never enlist in the women's movement unless it understood and addressed their concerns. "Fannie told them off . . . ," said Chisholm, who was at the meeting. "A lot of the women could not understand what [she] was railing about. They were stuck on the word 'sisters,' and they thought we were all sisters. What we were saying is that sisters had different agendas."

22

"[W]e Were Asked to Deny a Part of Ourselves"

Stokely Carmichael speaks at 1966 Black Power rally

IN OCTOBER 1966, *EBONY* PAID homage to women civil rights activists in a special issue devoted to women. One of the women featured in the civil rights story was twenty-five-year-old Ruby Doris Smith Robinson, who earlier that year had been elected executive secretary of SNCC, replacing James Forman. Robinson was the first and only woman ever to hold a top formal leadership job in SNCC—or, for that matter, in *any* major civil rights organization—in the 1960s. Yet in the *Ebony* article, she raised the possibility that women might someday withdraw from the civil rights arena: "In the past, Negro women had to assert themselves so the family could survive. Fortunately, more men are becoming involved with the movement, and the day might come when women aren't needed for this type of work."

At first glance, it seemed a strange thing for this famously independent, strong woman to say. But given the mood of the times, Robinson's comment was not really odd. While white women were starting to assert themselves, black women had begun to pull back, to downplay their assertiveness. Within the black community, there was a growing sentiment, promoted by advocates of black power and popularized in black publications like *Ebony*, that black men needed to step forward and that black women were obligated to support this male ascendancy. With black male leaders like Martin Luther King and Stokely Carmichael the targets of criticism and investigation by the federal government and some of the leaders' erstwhile white allies, black women were sensitive to the need for racial unity. Many were prepared to fall in step behind their men.

As a result, Ruby Doris Smith Robinson was in a delicate position. She was undeniably a leader, but she did not want to assert herself at the expense of her male counterparts. She solved the dilemma in the *Ebony* article by making clear that, while men's dominance might be a goal, women, in her view, would not be able to abandon the civil rights fight for many years to come: ". . . I don't believe the Negro man will be able to assume his full role until the struggle has progressed to a point that can't even be foreseen—maybe in the next century or so."

For the time being, then, women were needed in the fray, Ruby Doris Smith Robinson prominent among them. In the mid-1960s, Robinson was the unquestioned linchpin of the SNCC operation, fighting hard for the organization's survival while at the same time juggling the demands of a husband and a baby. Robinson had been with SNCC from the beginning; she'd gone to jail in Rock Hill and had been one of the first Freedom Riders sent to Parchman penitentiary. Despite SNCC's later divisions and seemingly insurmountable problems, she remained committed to the organization and its mission with a passion that few, if any, could match.

After her stint in Parchman, Robinson had returned to school at Spelman but continued her association with SNCC. She first started working as James Forman's unofficial assistant, but it soon became clear that she was, in fact, the one running the show day to day. By early 1962, "you got your money from Ruby; you got your orders from Ruby," said SNCC activist Reggie Robinson. According to Ivanhoe Donaldson: "Forman was sort of above it all. . . . He would come in and cruise through. . . . But Ruby had to deal with the nuts and bolts of what made things work. Jim might take credit, but Ruby was in there, actually doing it."

Known for her ferocious energy, Robinson was also noted for a drill-sergeant demeanor that could cow the most intrepid organizer. "Inside SNCC there were these men who would take on ten sheriffs, and if they had to take on Ruby, they were terrified," Dorothy Zellner remarked. Stanley Wise, who worked closely with Robinson in Atlanta, said, "She absolutely did not tolerate any nonsense."

Still, for all Robinson's work and fierce dedication to keep SNCC together, the task facing her was incredibly daunting. "As Ruby Doris received more power to govern . . . SNCC became progressively less governable," noted Cynthia Griggs Fleming, Robinson's biographer. The young woman was in charge of a national civil rights organization, with responsibility for dozens of local organizing projects, a substantial payroll, a sizable car and truck fleet, not to mention fund-raising, lecturing, and printing operations. But it was also an organization on the brink of financial collapse. An organization torn by anger and conflicts, filled with people who wanted to "do their own thing," who insisted they were not responsible to anybody, least of all to the office in Atlanta. "Ruby was always juggling someone's 'creativity' against someone else's urgency, and involved were class issues, racial issues, gender issues, education issues," said Ivanhoe Donaldson. "So she was easy to pick on and she had to deal with all that stress."

She was seen by many in SNCC as hating whites, particularly white women. Mary King, for example, remembered Robinson as "bristl[ing] with antagonism" toward her and other white female SNCC staffers. But, according to others, Robinson, by the mid-1960s, had lost much of the hostility she once had borne toward white women. She told writer Josephine Carson that she had decided to try to rid herself of that hatred when "I realized what I was doing to myself. I was losing my self-respect and even losing my looks. I finally had to work myself out of it. I had to find a new sense of my own dignity, and what I really had to do was start *seeing* all over again, in a new way."

Robinson was, however, unquestionably hostile to the issues raised by King and other white women regarding the role of women in SNCC. That didn't mean she was oblivious to women's complaints: In fact, she was one of the participants in the 1964 sit-in in Jim Forman's office. But her single-minded focus was on the survival of SNCC and its task of organizing black people to fight for freedom and equality. Any other issue, including the question of women's rights, she considered irrelevant and divisive.

She felt the same way about Stokely Carmichael, the man viewed as the architect of black power, and his incessant calls for what she termed "the destruction of Western civilization." Carmichael and his cohorts were so busy goading the white establishment, she believed, that they had given up the job of organizing. At one meeting, Robinson insisted that Carmichael be prevented from holding a press conference at which he, as SNCC chairman, planned to oppose the draft. "Ruby called for the organization to silence Stokely on the grounds that what he was saying was contrary . . . to what the organization had been putting forward," recalled James Forman. "And . . . she felt that if we didn't silence him the organization ran the risk of not being in existence."

Robinson was noted for her toughness and aggressiveness, but she was a far more complex woman than her public persona indicated. When SNCC organizers were arrested and thrown in jail, it was Robinson who showed the greatest concern about their welfare, Ivanhoe Donaldson recalled. "You knew that if anybody in Atlanta knew you were alive, it was Ruby Doris. . . . Ruby was concerned about your psyche, how you were handling the situation. Were you eating? Were you getting beat up? Were you on a hunger strike? Were you going to survive it internally? She'd write you these long letters, telling you how to be strong, how to deal with things. She was very much into people."

She also revealed a wistful vulnerability at times, as she tried to cope with the inhuman pressures of her SNCC job while struggling to be a good wife and mother. At the end of 1963, she had married Clifford Robinson, the brother of her sister's husband. Although Robinson became a mechanic on the SNCC staff, servicing the organization's cars, he had not been involved in the movement. A couple of years later, Ruby Doris told Josephine Carson that she sometimes thought the main reason she married Robinson was because he was the only man she'd met "who is stronger than I am." She loved him, she hastened to add, but "we aren't very much alike. . . . [A] man has to be powerful to handle a woman. We're smarter. There's no question about that. . . . And Negro women can be pretty hard on a man. I mean, white women don't do so much of this as far as I know, but we *fight*!"

In 1965, Robinson became pregnant and worked until the day she gave birth. Two weeks after her son was born, she went back to her job. The already frenzied pace of her life became even more frantic. During the day, Robinson's mother took care of the baby, and Robinson was concerned that her son would become more attached to his grandmother than to her. "He's getting more of her nature than he is of mine . . . ," she fretted to Carson. "But I hope I can stay very close to him. . . . Sometimes I worry about it, though. My mother is a . . . strong woman and she could influence my son if I'm not with him enough. She's good, but he *is* my son." At night and on the weekends, she did most of the child care and housework. Robinson may have been a radical in the fight for racial justice, but she never challenged society's view—a view embraced by her husband—that a woman's main responsibility was to her family and to her home. She was always rushing, always trying to juggle a multitude of concerns at once. Sometimes, a ball was dropped: One day, on the way to her mother's house to drop off her son before going to work, she realized she had left the baby back home.

At SNCC, the stresses were intensifying. She fought a demand from the Internal Revenue Service to provide the agency with its complete financial records, including a list of SNCC contributors—a demand that she and other SNCC leaders considered to be a harassment campaign. According to James Forman, who remained close to her, she also endured "vicious attacks" from certain male SNCC staffers who fought her attempts to impose discipline on the organization. They justified their verbal assault on Robinson, Forman said, "by the fact that their critic was a woman."

Robinson, who had suffered from various ailments since her jailing in Rock Hill, was mentally and physically exhausted. "I have a feeling of . . . death, but it strengthens my feeling of life somehow," she told Carson in 1966. A few months later, she fell ill after attending a fund-raiser in New York and was rushed to a hospital. After extensive tests, she was diagnosed with lymphosarcoma, a rare and deadly type of cancer.

On October 7, 1967, Ruby Doris Smith Robinson died. She was twenty-five years old.

Later, Bernice Johnson Reagon would say about Robinson: "With her life she kept SNCC together. And I think it took her life. That's all. I don't think it's complicated." Kathleen Cleaver, an activist in the Black Panthers, agreed. "What killed Ruby Doris was the constant outpouring of work, work, work, work, with being married, having a child, the constant conflicts, the constant struggles that she was subjected to because she was a woman. . . . [S]he was destroyed by the movement."

As early as 1964, Pauli Murray was warning of a "backlash of a new male aggressiveness against Negro women." She viewed the later black power movement as a "bid of black males to share power with white males" in a world "in which both black and white females are relegated to secondary status."

While black militants might question other values of white culture, they were not averse to the idea of patriarchy. And while they might oppose most actions of the federal government, they, and other black men, would use a report by a white government official to bolster their call for the subordination of women.

One morning in late 1964, Daniel Patrick Moynihan found himself awake at four o'clock. He knew what had roused him at that ungodly hour—his growing worry over the Johnson administration's attitude toward civil rights. Moynihan was an Assistant Secretary of Labor in the administration, a thirty-seven-year-old liberal intellectual with a Ph.D. in political science. What concerned him was the complacent belief of many government officials that the Civil Rights Act, passed just a few months earlier, was the main answer to the civil rights problem. Moynihan, however, was firmly convinced that the act—and other legislation ending legal racism—would not, by themselves, allow blacks in America to reach full equality. The government, he believed, had to mount a major national effort to deal with the more complex, more intractable problems of black inequality, particularly those dealing with unemployment. Moynihan was remarkably prescient in his views: His sleepless morning occurred before the events in Selma, and, at that point, few people, including civil rights activists, were looking much beyond the immediate goal of a bill to guarantee voting rights.

Moynihan decided to write a paper about the issue, which he hoped would serve as an alarm bell for the administration. He wanted, he said later, "to explain to the fellows how there was a problem more difficult than they knew and also to explain some of the issues of unemployment and housing in terms that would be new enough and shocking enough that they would say, 'Well, we can't let this sort of thing go on. We've got to do something about it.'" Those terms focused on the disintegration of the black family, and they would indeed shock—but in ways that Moynihan never anticipated.

In "The Negro Family: The Case for National Action," Moynihan argued that generations of white racism had resulted in the black family's unraveling, which he saw as the underlying reason for many of the economic and social problems that blacks faced. "[H]ere is where the true injury has occurred: unless this damage is repaired, all the effort to end discrimination and poverty and injustice will come to little," Moynihan wrote. In his view, it was a vicious cycle: Because of racism, black men were not able to find decent jobs and support their families properly. As a result, families often broke up, and women became household heads—their families' sole means of support as well as the sole parent of their children. Such situations led to widespread poverty, to an increased reliance on welfare, and to children of these fatherless homes dropping out of school and getting into trouble. In his views on single-mother families, Moynihan did not mince words: "Negro children without fathers flounder—and fail."

His primary purpose in writing the report was to encourage the government to come up with policies that would strengthen black families. But his intentions got lost in the *Sturm und Drang* that arose after the report's release in March 1965. Many blacks accused Moynihan of making the black family a scapegoat for problems directly attributable to racial discrimination. He was also seen as blaming black women for the fix that their men and their children found themselves in. Moynihan protested that he had no such intention, that he was merely describing a situation that existed, not affixing blame to any blacks, women or men. The blame, he said, belonged to the racism of white America.

But the wording of his report contributed, rightly or wrongly, to such an interpretation. Moynihan viewed the problems of black families in this country through the filter of his experiences and attitudes as a white Irish-American male who came of age in the late 1940s and early 1950s. His report, for the most part, was male-centered, focusing on the need to help black men achieve equality in a society dominated by white males. (The need for black women's equality was never mentioned.) Because the "matriarchal structure" of the black community is so at odds with the rest of American society, Moynihan argued, it "seriously retards the progress of the group as a whole, and imposes a crushing burden on the Negro male and, in consequence, on a great many Negro women as well." He added: "Ours is a society which presumes male leadership in private and public affairs. The arrangements of society facilitate such leadership and reward it. A subculture, such as that of the Negro American, in which this is not the pattern, is placed at a distinct disadvantage."

Throughout the report, Moynihan viewed black men as victims, not as autonomous individuals who should take any responsibility for themselves. He repeatedly emphasized the need to help black men claim the manhood that had been denied them since slavery. Moynihan speculated that the introduction of Jim Crow segregation after Reconstruction was more psychologically damaging to black men than to black women because, he erroneously concluded, men used segregated transportation and other public facilities more often, and because "segregation, and the submissiveness it exacts, is surely more destructive to the male than to the female personality." And why was that? Because, explained Moynihan, "[t]he very essence of the male animal, from the bantam rooster to the four-star general, is to strut. Indeed, in 19th century America, a particular type of exaggerated male boastfulness became almost a national style. Not for the Negro male. The 'sassy nigger' was lynched." In his paper, Moynihan urged that more black men be encouraged to enter the armed services, in part, he said, because it was "an utterly masculine world . . . a world away from women."

The Moynihan report sent a shock of seismic proportions throughout black America. Even as Moynihan was attacked for the paper, "black matriarchy" became a catchphrase in a deluge of attacks on black women for allegedly dominating and emasculating black men. "Although [the report] can't be held responsible for the intense Black male chauvinism of the period, it certainly didn't discourage it, and [it] helped shape Black attitudes," wrote historian Paula Giddings. At the very least, it transformed a simmering, generations-long tension between black men and women into what writer Michele Wallace termed a "brainshattering explosion." Forced by history to be assertive and self-reliant, black women throughout the years had found themselves chastised by black men for being "more masculine than feminine," as Atlanta Baptist College president John Hope put it in the early 1900s. Strong black women kept their families and communities together, but they were often seen by black men, including their sons and other male relatives, as domineering, even suffocating presences. According to Septima Clark, black mothers, alert to the dangers facing their sons if they challenged white society, tended to force their male offspring into docility, which resulted in their sons' considerable resentment and a "feeling that women should not have a say in anything."

Burdened with the image of sexual wanton, black women now had to cope, too, with the tag of castrating matriarch. But the term "matriarch" suggests someone with great power, which was not the reality for black women. They might have jobs, but the jobs tended to be low-paying, without any authority over others. At home, they might be heads of the household (often forced into that position by default), yet were still considered second-class citizens by most of society, including many of their own men. "Men may be cruelly exploited and subjected to all sorts of dehumanizing tactics on the part of the ruling class," declared a woman who joined SNCC in the mid-1960s, "but they have someone who is below them—at least they're not women."

Nonetheless, the black media, along with other institutions in black America, picked up the "matriarchy" drumbeat. In the same issue of *Ebony* that carried the paean to women in the civil rights movement, an editorial declared that, while black women had made great contributions to their people in the past, "the past is behind us." Now, the editorial asserted, "the immediate goal of the Negro woman . . . should be the establishment of a strong family unit in which the father is the dominant person." Indeed, black women might consider following the example of the Jewish mother "who pushed her husband to success, educated her male children first and engineered good marriages for her daughters." In another article in that issue, called "A Look Beyond the 'Matriarchy,'" the author fired an additional shot at black women. "The truth is that despite the fact that the Negro woman has done so much to bring the race so far, it has been done at the expense of the psychological health of the Negro male who has frequently been forced by circumstances into the position of a drone."

Even black women's magazines joined the attack. In 1970, *Essence* ran a piece that read as if it came from the pre-feminist-consciousness *Ladies' Home Journal*. Entitled "Make Your Marriage an Affair to Remember," it gave the following bit of advice to newly married black women: "Now that it is just the two of you, you have discarded your independence and you must rely on him. Even if you don't feel that way in the beginning, show him that you do. Make him feel ten feet tall!" (Ten years later, the magazine took it all back. Commenting on the earlier story, a 1980 *Essence* editorial noted wryly: "Many women who followed this philosophy ended up worn out, broke and confused when their husbands got bored and left them for white women, which was another burning issue of the seventies decade.")

The advocates of black power were in the vanguard of the "matriarchy" campaign, using the Moynihan theory as ammunition to ensure women's subservience. Black women had been the mainstays of the civil rights movement, but now they were told they should not exert any kind of leadership role. "The black woman is being encouraged—in the name of the revolution no less—to cultivate 'virtues' that if listed would sound like the personality traits of slaves," declared black feminist writer Toni Cade Bambara. After Ruby Doris Smith Robinson's death, SNCC, approaching its own end, was completely dominated by men, most of whom had not been around in the days when the organization called itself "a circle of trust." Almost all the women from that heady early time were gone, too, many profoundly disillusioned by what had happened to their beloved organization. But a number of the early SNCC women, who had repeatedly demonstrated their leadership skills, spoke out, during this time of turmoil, in favor of black women giving way to black men. Racial loyalty, in their view, was far more important than the question of gender.

Joyce Ladner, who had returned to school and eventually received a doctorate in sociology at Washington University, wrote in 1971, for example, that the strength of black women served as a brake on black men's ability to deal with a male-controlled white society. "What is clear . . . is that an alteration of roles between Black males and females must occur," she declared. "The traditional 'strong' Black woman has probably outlived her usefulness because this role has been challenged by the Black man, who has demanded that the white society acknowledge his manhood and deal directly with him instead of using his woman—considered the weaker sex—as a buffer."

Marian Wright Edelman, who had been a founding member of SNCC, one of the leaders of the Atlanta student movement, and later a power-house civil rights lawyer in Mississippi, also was intent on pushing black men to the forefront. In the early 1970s, she met with Roger Wilkins, a former Assistant Attorney General in the Johnson administration and an old friend of hers. She told Wilkins she was starting a new national advocacy group for children called the Children's Defense Fund. He thought it was a good idea and told her so. Since that was the case, she said, "I want to step down and let you run it."

"Marian," a surprised Wilkins said, "I don't understand." Edelman replied: "Among other things our children need, they need the image of a strong black man running things, changing the course of events." Wilkins couldn't believe what he was hearing. "She had invented this organization, and now she was ready to let somebody else take all the credit," he said later. "Well, I declined, but it was one of the most remarkable conversations I've ever had." (Edelman went on to take charge of the Children's Defense Fund herself.)

Younger black women, who joined SNCC, CORE, and other organizations that had turned to black militancy in the middle and late 1960s, found themselves constantly on the defensive. Angela Davis, who started her radical activist career with SNCC in Los Angeles, tried to organize a rally in 1967 and was told by her male counterparts that her job was to inspire men, not lead them. "Some of the brothers came around only for staff meetings (sometimes)," Davis wrote, "and whenever we women were involved in something important, they began to talk about 'women taking over the organization,' calling it a matriarchal coup d'état." Even women who had already proven themselves as leaders were not exempt from such treatment. When Gloria Richardson, leader of the Cambridge, Maryland, movement, tried to address a Cambridge rally in the mid-1960s, she was shouted down by male CORE members, who called her a "castrator."

In some black militant circles, violence against women was accepted—and even encouraged. Black writers and activists, including Amiri Baraka (the former LeRoi Jones) and Eldridge Cleaver, supported the rape of white women as "a justifiable political act." Cleaver said he himself had raped white women, after "practicing" on black women. SNCC activist Cleveland Sellers wrote about beating up his girlfriend, Sandy, at a New Year's Eve party in the late 1960s, after he found her sitting next to H. Rap Brown, who had replaced Stokely Carmichael as SNCC chairman. Sandy had had an affair with Brown, and Sellers, incensed that she was talking to Brown at the party, called her outside and pummeled her on the face, chest, and back of the head, nearly knocking her down. A few years later, Sellers wrote: "I realize now that I was terribly unfair to Sandy at the time. But then I thought she was being unfair to me. I thought she was being unfair to SNCC. I rationalize that I struck her because I was angry, because I was hurt, because I was frustrated, because I was tired." He noted, almost as an afterthought, that Sandy left him two months after the party.

Hit by a barrage of male charges and demands, most black women did not fight back. Unlike turn-of-the-century black women leaders, who asserted themselves unequivocally as women, the majority of black women in the late 1960s and in the 1970s "did not see 'womanhood' as an important part of our identity," observed bell hooks. ". . . [W]e were asked to deny a part of ourselves—and we did." Many women, accepting the "matriarchy" premise, felt a sense of guilt that they had profited from America's racist white society at the expense of their men. Some began seeking out psychiatrists like Alvin Poussaint to help them "suppress their aggression and dominant personalities." Said Poussaint: "These women, who were victims of black matriarchy propaganda, were erroneously blaming themselves for problems in the black community which were in fact due to and the result of institutional racist practices."

Even if they did not fully agree with the propaganda campaign being waged against them, black women were wary about expressing disagreement for fear of betraying their men and their community, for fear, too, of providing further fuel for white attacks against black male leaders. "The tendency to close ranks, to keep silence in order to protect the community, was strong, too strong for most black women to oppose," wrote historians Darlene Clark Hine and Kathleen Thompson. "Dissemblance had proved a very positive survival skill in the past, and it was difficult for most women to recognize that it might have outlived its usefulness." So once again, black women were left by the wayside, with the black movement and the women's movement generally ignoring their interests.

The relatively few black women who did publicly voice their opposition to male chauvinism within the black community and who did speak out for women's rights were often subjected to a furious onslaught of criticism for being "traitors to their race." In 1973, a group of black women, including Eleanor Holmes Norton, created the National Black Feminist Organization, whose goal was the political, social, and economic equality of black women. The black community must stop thinking of black women "only in terms of domestic or servile needs," the NBFO declared. "[T]here can't be liberation for half the race." That view, however, was attacked by black militants and resisted by most black women. Accused of dividing the black movement, the NBFO survived only until 1975.

Young black women writers like Ntozake Shange, Alice Walker, and Michele Wallace were also targeted for criticism. "I will not be part of this conspiracy of silence. I will not do it," declared Shange, whose award-winning play, *For Colored Girls Who Have Considered Suicide/When the Rainbow Is Enuf*, touched on black men's violence toward women. Male violence and abuse also played major roles in Alice Walker's short stories, poetry, and novels, including her Pulitzer Prize–winning book, *The Color Purple.*

In her short story "Advancing Luna and Ida B. Wells," Walker wrote about the rape of a white female civil rights volunteer by a black male coworker, then imagined a conversation between herself and Ida Wells about what she had just written. "Write nothing," she visualized the antilynching crusader as saying. "Nothing at all. It will be used against black men and therefore against all of us. . . . You are dealing with people who brought their children to witness the murder of black human beings, falsely accused of rape. People who handed out, as trophies, black fingers and toes. . . . No matter what you think you know, no matter what you feel about it, say nothing. And to your dying breath!"

"Which, to my mind," Walker declared, "is virtually useless advice to give to a writer." It was advice, nonetheless, that most black women heeded.

The perils of violating that code of silence were underscored once again in 1991 when Anita Hill accused Supreme Court nominee Clarence Thomas of sexually harassing her several years earlier, when Hill worked for Thomas at the EEOC. Sexual harassment had become a major workplace issue: More and more women were speaking out against harassment and were taking cases to court. Yet the idea of a black woman calling into question the sexual conduct of a black man was, in the eyes of many blacks, as unforgivable in the 1990s as it would have been a century earlier, when Ida Wells was waging her antilynching campaign. Although black men had not refrained in the past from leveling sharp public criticism against black women, it was unacceptable for black women to castigate black men, particularly where sexual issues were concerned.

In his testimony before the Senate Judiciary Committee, Thomas played on the unease felt by many blacks—and whites—in regard to the attacks against him. He described Hill as a vengeful former employee who resented his preference for light-skinned women, and portrayed himself as a black man whose masculinity was being used by racists as a weapon against his nomination. Thomas's skillful use of racial imagery and symbols, particularly his depiction of himself as the victim of "a high-tech lynching," deflected and defused Hill's sexual harassment charges. Once again, emphasis was placed on the physical and psychological harm suffered by black men as the result of slavery and racism, while the damage done to black women was largely ignored.

In the end, Thomas—a conservative Republican whose tenure as EEOC chairman had been marked by a reduced enforcement of laws against workplace discrimination—was confirmed by the Senate and supported by much of the black community. Anita Hill was considered a traitor by many, if not most, blacks. Such an outcome profoundly disturbed a number of prominent black women, who decided they could remain silent no longer. On November 17, 1991, *The New York Times* carried a full-page ad signed by 1,603 black women, most of them writers and scholars. The "malicious defamation" of Anita Hill, the ad declared, was just the latest example of how black women had been maligned throughout American history, "stereotyped as immoral, insatiable, perverse; the initiators in all sexual contacts—abusive or otherwise . . ." Such an "attack upon our collective character" must be met with "protest, outrage, and resistance."

But in making this fight, the ad made clear, black women can expect no outside help. "No one will speak for us but ourselves."

23

"We Got to Keep Moving"

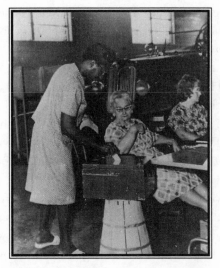

*Black woman voting in 1966 primary in
Jackson, Mississippi*

WHILE MANY YOUNG CIVIL RIGHTS
workers had moved on to the black power, women's, and peace movements
by the late 1960s, the civil rights struggle had only just begun for local
activists who remained in the South. Women like Fannie Lou Hamer and
Unita Blackwell and Johnnie Carr used their freshly acquired political skills
and their newfound sense of power to fight for implementation of civil
rights and voting rights bills and to work to improve the lives and education of their children. Legislating equality for blacks, the women knew,
meant nothing if the white establishment prevented the laws' enforcement.
They knew, too, that court-ordered school desegregation would end in failure unless they and their children forced the white school boards to enforce
the orders.

In Mississippi, Hamer, Victoria Gray, and Annie Devine—the "three great women" of that state's movement, as Unita Blackwell called them—helped lead the way. When the MFDP lost its challenge in Atlantic City, the women did not give up. They announced they were running for Congress and tried to get their names on the ballot as MFDP candidates in the November 1964 election. To the surprise of no one, the state rejected their attempt, but they ran anyway, urging blacks to vote in another mock election. Despite intensified white efforts at intimidation, including bombings and other nightrider activity, more than sixty thousand blacks in Mississippi cast ballots in November.

The following month, attorneys for the MFDP, dusting off a federal statute enacted during Reconstruction, contested the legality of the election of the Mississippi House delegation. The MFDP lawyers pointed to the exclusion of Hamer, Gray, and Devine from the ballot and claimed that the five white men elected should not be seated by the House because blacks had been "systematically and deliberately excluded from the electoral process." To most political experts, this new MFDP challenge seemed like another pie-in-the-sky effort. With less than a month to go before the new Congress was to be sworn in, how could the Mississippians possibly hope to convince the House to unseat five of its own members, most of whom had sat in that body for many years?

Once again, however, the MFDP ignored the seeming impossibility of the task before it and flung itself into the fight. While Hamer, Gray, and Devine spent much of their time organizing support in Washington and throughout the rest of the country, hundreds of blacks back home staged fish fries, cake sales, and other fund-raising events to send a new battalion of lobbyists to the nation's capital. In the first days of the new year, more than six hundred blacks from Mississippi boarded Trailways buses for the trip to Washington and the opening of the 1965 congressional session on January 4.

The first act of the new Congress was to be the ritualistic swearing-in of members. William Fitts Ryan, a liberal Democrat from New York and an MFDP ally, had already announced that he would object to the swearing-in of the five Mississippi congressmen. Most Washington insiders considered Ryan's plan to be quixotic, since the Johnson administration and the House congressional leadership had already made clear they opposed any effort to oust Mississippi's House delegation. When Ryan stood to object, the capital's cognoscenti were sure, he would be standing virtually alone.

But the lobbyists from Mississippi had other ideas. Shortly before noon on January 4, as members of Congress walked through the underground tunnels leading from their offices to the House chamber, they witnessed a civil rights demonstration the likes of which they had never seen before. Lining both sides of the tunnels, as far as the eye could see, were hundreds of blacks, old and young, many of them clad in overalls and other working clothes. They waved no signs, carried no banners, sang no songs. They stood silently as members of Congress walked by, their presence alone serving as a powerful statement of their mission. One congressman later told Anne Braden that he had left his office prepared to vote to seat the Mississippi delegation. But as he made his way through the lines of blacks, he began to have serious doubts. "Finally, I had to say to myself, 'What kind of person are you?'" When he reached the floor of the House, he walked up to Majority Leader Carl Albert. "I'm sorry," he told Albert. "I'm not going with you on Mississippi. I can't vote against those people out there."

But how many more like him would rally to Ryan's side? Hamer, Gray, and Devine, along with other Mississippi blacks, sat in nervous anticipation in the House visitors' gallery as the gaunt old Speaker, John McCormack of Massachusetts, gaveled the 89th Congress to order and began calling the roll of members. It did not take him long to get to the first member of the Mississippi delegation. As McCormack intoned the name of Thomas Abernathy, of the state's 1st District, William Ryan jumped to his feet and shouted, "I object, Mr. Speaker, to the swearing-in of Mr. Abernathy." Throughout the chamber, dozens of other members leapt up, too, and shouted out their objections. McCormack started counting the number of members on their feet, but there were so many of them (more than sixty, as it turned out) that he gave up and acknowledged that enough members had objected to force a roll call vote on the Mississippi delegation's seating. "According to the rules of this House," McCormack said, "the gentleman from Mississippi will step aside until all other members are sworn in." He made the same pronouncement to the state's other congressmen. In the gallery, the MFDP activists and their supporters "could hardly believe" what was happening, recalled Arthur Kinoy, one of their attorneys. Victoria Gray leaned over to Kinoy and in an exultant whisper declared: "We did it! Even if just for this moment, we did it!"

After the swearing-in of all House members except the five Mississippians, Carl Albert took the floor and offered a compromise, which, in effect, recognized the legitimacy of the challenge. If the House would agree to seat the Mississippi delegation for now, he said, the leadership would authorize a later vote on the challenge itself, following an investigation of the allegations against the state's electoral process. By a vote of 276–149, Albert's resolution was approved, and the Mississippi congressmen were finally sworn in. Their satisfaction, however, must have been dampened somewhat by the galling knowledge that a remarkable number of their colleagues—a little more than one-third—had gone on record in unequivocal opposition to their seating.

On September 17, the MFDP challenge came to the floor of the House for consideration, and once again, Mississippians traveled to Washington to lobby for the cause. This time, Gray, Hamer, and Devine were invited by congressional supporters of the challenge to sit on the House floor during the debate. Several black congressmen, including Adam Clayton Powell, Jr., urged the women to turn down the invitation, for fear that their presence on the floor might prompt some members to vote against the challenge. The women rejected the congressmen's request, and shortly before the debate began, William Ryan and two other white congressmen escorted Hamer, Devine, and Gray to seats on the Democratic side of the chamber. It was an event of great moment: The three were the first black women ever to sit on the floor of the House and the first blacks from Mississippi to be there since 1884.

As she sank into her chair, Gray looked up at the galleries, crowded with the people from Mississippi, and felt overwhelmed "with the meaning of it all." Only three years earlier, she had raised her hand at Hattiesburg's first mass meeting when SNCC organizers asked for volunteers to register to vote. She had had an unsettling feeling then that her whole life was about to change. But never in her wildest dreams could she have imagined she would be in Washington, on the House floor, on that September morning. In her view, it was not important that she, Victoria Gray, was sitting in that seat. What *was* important was the message that her presence—and that of the other women—was giving to the country, and especially to blacks in the South. "Regardless of how the vote came out, it was that visible act, that symbol, affirming every reason why we should be there. We had every right. . . . There was not one single doubt in my mind that we had a right to be there."

In the final vote, the challenge was defeated, 228–143. Its chances, slim to begin with, virtually disappeared after enactment of the Voting Rights Act one month earlier. The administration and congressional leadership pointed to the act as the proper tool for correcting voting rights inequities in the future. They refused to consider the possibility of correcting injustices of the past.

Despite failing in Congress, the challenge, nonetheless, was seen as a major influence on the South's eventual capitulation to black voting. The significant number of House members who voted in favor of the challenge in January and September put Mississippi and other Southern states on notice that future congressional delegations might run into similar or greater problems if blacks were not allowed into the electoral process. Mississippi, for one, implicitly acknowledged it was getting the message when state officials began urging local registrars and law enforcement authorities to curb violence against blacks trying to register to vote.

"We showed them we were for real," Fannie Lou Hamer said after the September vote. "And now we have to build solidly in the state. Let's take the challenge right to them in the Sunflower County elections this November." Like the other Democratic dons in the Deep South, James Eastland, the Massa of Sunflower County, was about to confront some new political realities.

The fight to end legal racism in the United States and to guarantee blacks full citizenship rights had lasted more than a century. Its culmination was the Voting Rights Act of 1965. The struggle itself reminded one of a relay race, with early activists like Sojourner Truth handing the baton to Ida Wells and Mary Church Terrell, who, in turn, passed it off to Pauli Murray, Lillian Smith, and others. Fannie Lou Hamer, Victoria Gray, and Annie Devine were among those who crossed the finish line, but their achievement was built on the work and sacrifice of all those women—and men—who had gone before.

As soon as the act went into effect on August 6, long lines of blacks began forming outside registrars' offices throughout the South. The new law wiped out most of the legal devices used by Southern whites to prevent blacks from voting. It banned the infamous literacy tests and other discriminatory registration practices, and it directed the Justice Department to file lawsuits against the collection of poll taxes. It also mandated the use of federal examiners to help register voters and to monitor how well Southern counties were complying with the law.

In fourteen counties in Mississippi, Alabama, and Louisiana, the examiners opened up shop immediately. Almost without exception, they were stunned by the huge number of blacks who turned out, standing patiently for hours in lines that often snaked around the block. "Plain, decent people," as journalist Pat Watters described them, "come at last to what the rest of America took for granted, to the duty that the rest of America was exhorted to perform." In the first three months of the law, nearly two hundred thousand new black voters were registered in the five hard-core states of the Deep South.

That was good news, indeed, but it was only part of the story. About a third of those new registrations occurred in the relatively few counties to which federal examiners had been assigned. In hundreds of other Southern counties, local officials were doing their best to resist enforcement of the new law. President Johnson, reluctant to press the Southern states too hard, preferred to push voluntary compliance with the law and resisted sending in the massive number of examiners necessary for large-scale enforcement. As a result, in counties without federal monitoring, registrars' offices were often closed when blacks came to register, and applicants were still being rejected arbitrarily. They still ran the risk of retaliation in the form of economic pressure and, not infrequently, violence.

In order to force local authorities to register blacks, Fannie Lou Hamer and other MFDP activists turned to lawsuits. In 1963, the Justice Department, thanks to documentation of voting rights discrimination provided by Hamer, Charles McLaurin, and others, had filed a lawsuit against Sunflower County. In the spring of 1965, a federal judge ruled that the county registrar had indeed shown racial bias in deciding who could register and that such practices must stop. Hamer and the MFDP immediately launched an all-out drive to get blacks registered; in just three weeks, more than three hundred had their names added to the registration rolls. In response, county officials declared that the new voters would not be allowed to cast ballots in that year's local elections because they had to be registered for at least four months before the election and to have paid poll taxes for the previous two years. Hamer and four other county residents promptly sued the county, urging the court to delay the local elections and to suspend the poll tax. A federal judge denied the requests in April, and the elections were held as scheduled. Still enmeshed in the congressional challenge, Hamer pressed on with an appeal of the judge's ruling. The following year, the U.S. Fifth Circuit Court of Appeals, in a ruling on *Hamer v. Campbell*, nullified the 1965 Sunflower County elections, marking the first time since Reconstruction that a federal court had struck down an election because it excluded black voters.

By 1967, when those county elections were finally held, it had become much easier for Mississippi blacks to exercise their voting rights, thanks in no small part to the pressure of local activists like Hamer over the previous two years. In the fall of 1967, 181,000 blacks—more than half of those eligible—were on state voting rolls. Violence against potential black voters was far less common than it had been, and white candidates, fully aware that their political futures might well be determined by black votes, abandoned their old race-baiting tactics and began to court blacks.

The Voting Rights Act was not a panacea for blacks in the South, as some had hoped. It did not result in an appreciable change in the quality of most blacks' lives. It did, however, bring them into the political and electoral process for the first time since Reconstruction. Thousands of Southern blacks would be elected to public office in the years to come; in 1992, there were more than 825 elected black officials in Mississippi alone, more than in any other state. Ten black women served in the Mississippi legislature, six were mayors, and seventy-five were members of city councils.

Sarah Johnson was one of the first black women to win public office in Mississippi. The director of a Head Start program in Washington County, Johnson was elected in 1973 to the Greenville City Council, the first African-American ever to become a member of that body. Shortly after her election, she was invited to attend the annual meeting of the local homebuilders' association. Senator James Eastland was to be the guest speaker. Johnson went, and once there, couldn't resist joining the receiving line to meet Eastland and "purposely offer my hand to see if he would shake it." When it was her turn to greet the senator, she told him her name and her new title—and then stuck out her hand. He reluctantly shook it. "It was," said Johnson, "about the shallowest handshake I've ever had."

Just as the civil rights campaign was forcing upheavals in Southern politics in the mid-1960s, so, too, was it finally causing ferment in the South's schools. A decade after *Brown* v. *Board of Education,* many of the public schools in Alabama, Mississippi, and the other die-hard Southern states were still defiantly segregated. But federal courts had finally begun to issue orders to school districts to enforce the ruling. The desegregation drive was strengthened by passage of the 1964 Civil Rights Act, which mandated desegregation for all public schools receiving aid from Washington. In the forefront of that campaign was a loose, ad hoc alliance of women. Black women filed suit against lagging school districts, knowing they were courting violent retaliation not only against themselves but against their children, who would be the first blacks in newly integrated schools. When court orders were handed down, black and white women worked together to make sure the orders were carried out peaceably. And when they were not, white and black women came to the aid of blacks who had defied angry white supremacists to put their children in previously all-white schools. A number of the women in this informal confederation were newcomers to the battle for civil rights. Many, however, were seasoned veterans.

Johnnie Carr, for example, had ties with the movement that went back to the Montgomery bus boycott. One of the boycott's leaders, Carr was president of the Montgomery Improvement Association, the group, originally headed by Martin Luther King, that had coordinated the boycott. When a desegregation suit was brought against Montgomery schools in 1964, Carr and her husband, Arlam, were the only black parents willing to put their names on the suit as plaintiffs.

On the day the suit was filed, the Carrs had scarcely returned home from the courthouse when the obscene phone calls and the threats began. Johnnie Carr took the persecution in stride. She refused offers from neighbors to guard the Carrs' house, but as a precautionary measure, she and her husband did move their bed from a bedroom overlooking the street to one in the back.

A few months later, federal judge Frank Johnson approved the integration of the Montgomery schools' tenth, eleventh, and twelfth grades, and Arlam Carr, Jr., became a tenth grader at Lanier High School. After graduating from Lanier, he went on to the University of Texas at El Paso, then returned to Montgomery and joined the news department of a local television station—the first black to be hired at the station in other than a menial capacity. In 1998, he was a senior news producer and director there. A couple of years before, he'd been inducted into the Lanier alumni hall of fame. He faithfully attends all his high school class reunions.

In Mississippi, many school districts sought to evade school desegregation orders by requiring parents to fill out "freedom of choice" papers, in which they would designate which school they wanted their children to attend. White officials figured most blacks would be too frightened to select white schools, knowing that they and their children would probably be targets of intimidation and harassment. In Sunflower County, a middle-aged sharecropper named Mae Bertha Carter proved them wrong. Mrs. Carter, who had been picking cotton since the age of seven and had been forced to drop out of school after fifth grade, was determined that her children be given a good education. When Sunflower County announced its new "freedom of choice" plan in 1965, Mrs. Carter and her husband, Matthew, were the only blacks in the county to sign the papers sending their children to previously all-white schools.

A few days after the Carters turned in the papers, a fusillade of rifle shots was fired into their cabin, several bullets slamming into the wall above the bed where two of the children were sleeping. When the children started school in the little town of Drew, they were shunned by teachers, jeered at by fellow students, kicked, targeted by spitballs, called "nigger," and told they smelled bad. Their parents, meanwhile, were coping with their own persecution. Their credit was cut off at the plantation store, and the cotton grown on the fields they cropped was plowed under. Their barn was torn down, and they were threatened with eviction from their cabin.

Several organizations, including the American Friends Service Committee and the NAACP Legal Defense and Education Fund, came to the family's aid. A new Friends Service Committee task force, headed by Connie Curry, provided money, clothing, and emotional support for the Carters, helped them find a house in Drew, and pressured the federal government to intervene and stop the reprisals. And in June 1967, Marian Wright, who headed the Jackson office of the NAACP Legal Defense and Education Fund, filed suit in federal court on behalf of Mrs. Carter and her children. In the class-action suit, the former SNCC activist, who graduated from Yale Law School in 1964, argued that "fear of white retaliation, firmly grounded in fact, has deterred other Negroes from choosing the formerly white schools." In 1969, a federal district court ruled in the Carters' favor, striking down all "freedom of choice" plans and ordering full desegregation. "That could not have happened without the Carters," Wright later wrote.

Seven of the eight Carter children who attended formerly all-white schools went on to graduate from the University of Mississippi. In 1998, the Carters' second-youngest daughter, Beverly, became a teacher at the elementary school in Drew that had made her life so miserable more than thirty years before.

Desegregating the schools was just one of the battles waged by the women in the Mississippi movement, in their determination to give their own children and grandchildren, as well as other black children in the state, the leg up on life that they had not had. When the Head Start program came to the state in the summer of 1965, Mae Bertha Carter, like Fannie Lou Hamer, Annie Devine, and many other local women, helped launch centers to supply health care, hot meals, and an education to impoverished preschoolers.

An offshoot of Lyndon Johnson's War on Poverty, Head Start seemed to encourage the kind of community organization and activism that had been nurtured in Mississippi and other parts of the South by the civil rights movement. Indeed, the law authorizing the poverty initiative specifically called for "maximum feasible participation of the poor." In Mississippi, the activists involved in Head Start, many of them MFDP members, threw themselves into the program's development and operation with a commitment and enthusiasm that would make the Mississippi operation a model for other Head Starts in the country. The Child Development Group of Mississippi, as the operation was called, "was one of the most exciting educational programs for poor folk in the nation," said Marian Wright, who sat on the CDGM board.

Mississippi activists were anxious to impart to the youngsters in Head Start the same sense of dignity and self-worth that the civil rights movement had nourished in them. "We wanted to train them to be free . . . and don't have white people over them every time they turn around," recalled Head Start teacher Annie Mae King, whose house had been bombed a few months earlier in retaliation for her housing of white Freedom Summer volunteers. "More than any other Head Start project in the nation," declared *The New Yorker*, "CDGM changed the expectations of the poor people it served—helped them to feel like active participants in the social contract. In that way, it became a major and somewhat revolutionary agency for social change."

That's exactly what the white political establishment of Mississippi was afraid of. With Head Start, blacks had begun to liberate themselves from white economic control, had initiated a black grassroots network for long-term change. The Head Start program had provided employment for local activists when no one else would hire them. For the first time in history, as Marian Wright noted, "black folks in Mississippi had jobs independent of the plantation system," a situation that she termed "revolutionary."

The two senators from Mississippi, John Stennis and James Eastland, charged that CDGM was nothing but a federally subsidized front for civil rights activity. They successfully pressured the Office of Economic Opportunity, the federal agency administering the War on Poverty, to stop funding the Mississippi Head Start program after its first three months. Yet the Head Start centers in Mississippi, despite the loss of federal money, continued to operate. Teachers and parents volunteered their time and gave what little money they had to buy food and school supplies for the children. "You see, we were working for principle and we weren't out for just money alone," Annie Mae King explained. "We were working for freedom and to be able to govern our own affairs and our own businesses and to teach our own children."

In early 1966, OEO, feeling increasing heat from Northern white liberal supporters of CDGM, did another about-face and awarded the Mississippi program a new one-year grant. But time was running out for the Mississippi activists. A few months later, under renewed pressure from Stennis and Eastland, OEO announced that a new statewide organization, made up of a few white moderates and a number of black middle-class professionals and businessmen, had been designated as CDGM's successor in running Head Start in Mississippi. Most of the people in the new organization had not been involved in the early civil rights struggle; indeed, many had actively opposed the movement. In the view of the movement's mainstays, the newcomers were trying to reap the benefits of the political successes that they and other poor blacks had won at such cost, including the plum of federal money. Fannie Lou Hamer, for one, lambasted "these middle-class Negroes, the ones that never had it as hard as the grassroots people in Mississippi. They'll sell their parents for a few dollars. Sometimes I get so disgusted I feel like getting my gun after some of these schoolteachers and chicken-eatin' preachers."

That same alliance of whites and middle-class blacks was also busy establishing its own political base in the state. By the time of the 1968 Democratic convention, the group had formed a political party called the Loyal Democrats, aimed at supplanting the state party organization, which the MFDP had challenged at Atlantic City in 1964. The MFDP found itself in a dilemma: Most members did not want to cooperate with the Loyalists, but neither did they want the upstart group to reap the fruits of what the MFDP had wrought. So they reluctantly joined with the Loyalists in a coalition. When the Democrats met in Chicago, they voted to replace the regular Mississippi party delegation with that representing the Loyalists and the MFDP.

For Fannie Lou Hamer and other MFDP representatives in the delegation, the victory was bittersweet. Their goal of ousting Mississippi's old Democratic Party had been achieved, but they no longer were in control of the effort. Hamer, in fact, had not wanted to go to the convention at first, because of her feeling that poor blacks, particularly black women, were being muscled aside. Hamer felt that the 1968 challenge had "lost the truth," said Unita Blackwell. "It lost the real and basic feelings of the grass roots, because all the guys was in again—the big wheels . . ."

This was not an easy time for Fannie Lou Hamer, and the following years would become even more difficult. Her health, never good after the Winona beating in 1963, was getting worse, and she had to cope with the MFDP's disintegration and other internal problems afflicting the movement to which she was so passionately devoted. But she never wavered in her commitment, and, in fact, became more deeply involved in an even greater array of social issues. Hamer had started out fighting for voting rights, but her activism now ranged from schooling to health care to ending hunger. She filed a lawsuit demanding the protection of black teachers' jobs in Sunflower County, and helped bring Head Start to the county. She launched a cooperative farm, funded by Northern organizations and individuals, on which sharecroppers displaced by farming mechanization could plant crops to feed their families.

The farm lacked professional management, however, and failed within a few years. For Hamer, there were other blows. When new local elections were held in Sunflower County in 1967, thanks to Hamer's lawsuit, more blacks were registered to vote than whites. Yet many black voters cast their ballots for white candidates, and all local MFDP candidates were defeated. In addition, competition for scarce Head Start jobs, as well as other disagreements over the running of the program, led to some serious rivalries and feuds among former movement colleagues. Hamer herself came under severe attack from fellow activists for supporting a merger between a grassroots Head Start program and one run by the county.

In the 1970s, the woman who had been the heart of the grassroots civil rights movement in Mississippi felt abandoned and alone. SNCC was gone, and the MFDP had all but vanished. The up-and-coming young black leaders in the state, college-educated and middle-class, wanted nothing much to do with her. Already suffering from diabetes and high blood pressure, she had a nervous breakdown in 1972, then was diagnosed with breast cancer two years later. In the final years of her life, Hamer, who "thrived on helping people, on having people around her," had few people return the favor.

On April 14, 1977, Fannie Lou Hamer died at the age of fifty-nine. She and her husband, Pap, were penniless, and friends had to raise money to pay for her funeral. At the end of her life, she sometimes felt that no one remembered her or cared about what she had done. She was wrong. She may not have been fully appreciated while she was alive, but she had helped change the South and the rest of the country, and the outpouring of tributes after her death made that clear.

The Mississippi House of Representatives, which had passed laws making all civil rights activity a crime little more than a decade earlier, unanimously approved a resolution a few days after Hamer's death praising her for her contributions to the state. Hamer's funeral in the small white Williams Chapel in Ruleville drew such a huge throng that state highway patrol officers were called in to direct traffic. National political figures packed the chapel, as did her former colleagues (and opponents) in the movement. Ella Baker, Stokely Carmichael, Julian Bond, and John Lewis offered eulogies, as did Aaron Henry and Hodding Carter III. The main speaker was Andrew Young, the newly appointed U.S. ambassador to the United Nations.

Looking out at the crowd in front of him, Young declared of Hamer: "She literally, along with many of you, shook the foundations of this nation, and everything I learned about preaching, politics, life and death, I learned in your midst. The many people who are now elected officials would not be where they are had we not stood up then. And there was not a one of those that was not influenced and inspired by the spirit of this one woman, Mrs. Hamer."

In paying tribute to Hamer, Young saluted, too, all the other women who had influenced and inspired. The other women, mostly unknown, who had infused the civil rights movement with their own indomitable spirit. "It was women going door to door, speaking with their neighbors, meeting in voter registration classes together, organizing through their churches, that gave the vital momentum and energy to the movement, that made it a mass movement," Young pointed out. "Mrs. Hamer was special, but she was also representative. Hundreds of women spoke up and took leadership in the movement, and from the civil rights movement learned the lessons that inspired the women's movement. It was from our movement that a catalyst came, and it is now a global upsurge from village level to parliaments, asserting the rights of women."

Many of the mourners in the chapel that day were the women of whom Young spoke, women for whom Fannie Lou Hamer had served as a mentor and role model. One of them was Unita Blackwell, sitting next to Victoria Gray and Annie Devine in a front row. As she listened to the speakers, Blackwell thought about how much her friend would have enjoyed this gathering: ". . . [S]he loved a great big crowd . . . and she brought all these people back together again, and it was a beautiful thing." Blackwell knew how unhappy Hamer had been the last few years of her life, but Hamer had also taught the younger woman that the movement was bigger than any one individual, that "we got to keep moving."

Blackwell intended to do just that. Urged on in the mid-1960s by Hamer and others, the former sharecropper had become one of the movement's best organizers in the Delta. "SNCC told me I had natural instincts in organizing techniques," she said. "I organized whole counties. . . . I didn't see the bigness of the thing at the time. But I learned that black people weren't so ignorant as people wanted us to believe. We black people were just unexposed."

Along with other local women activists, Blackwell also became adept as a Washington lobbyist for CDGM and other government programs for the poor. With her quick tongue and mind, and her utter fearlessness, Blackwell was particularly skillful at taking on recalcitrant bureaucrats. "People such as . . . Unita Blackwell didn't need anybody to talk for them," said Marian Wright, who organized some of these lobbying trips. Blackwell, said Wright, was "one of the smartest people I know."

During one Washington trip, Blackwell was determined to find out just exactly what the government meant by "maximum feasible participation of the poor" in poverty programs. In Issaquena County, the only poor black involved in running such programs was, in her words, "a straight-out Tom." She sat in the front row at a meeting of poor people that OEO head Sargent Shriver attended, determined to find out "what is this 'maximum feasible'? Does it mean one-third, one-half, or what does it mean?" During the meeting, it was announced that Shriver would not speak. Blackwell, however, was determined to get an answer. She went up to Shriver during a break and said, "Just one question, please." Later news reports said Blackwell pointed a finger in Shriver's face, which she acknowledged was probably true: "Well, that's the way I talk, with my finger out, you know. . . . I reckon that finger was headed toward his face." When she confronted Shriver with her question, "the other folks jumped up behind me and went to screaming, 'You damn right! Tell us what is the maximum feasible participation of the poor!'"

In the ensuing furor, Shriver was hustled out of the meeting by anxious aides, and Blackwell, with her unvarnished style of "speaking truth to power," was branded as a troublemaker. When she later went to the White House to attend a reception hosted by Lady Bird Johnson, the Secret Service stopped her before she could enter the mansion and took her to an office, where they interrogated her about her background. "I told them to quit kidding themselves, they already knew that . . . ," she said later. "They stalled me until the people got through the reception line, shaking Madam Lady Bird's hand. . . . I think they were just scared that I probably would say something to the lady. But I didn't have a word to say to her, not nothing whatever. . . . I wasn't going to bother her." Once the reception was safely over, the Secret Service took Blackwell back to her hotel. "But they haven't ever apologized to me."

Like Fannie Lou Hamer's work, Unita Blackwell's activism extended far beyond voting rights by the late 1960s. She helped launch the first Head Start program in Issaquena County, and worked with the National Conference of Negro Women to build low-income housing for poor blacks.

She and her husband also filed a lawsuit to desegregate the local schools. Later, she studied public policy at Harvard and made several trips to China. She was awarded a MacArthur "genius" grant in 1992.

But her greatest triumph occurred in 1977, when she was elected mayor of Mayersville, a place where, thirteen years before, she had been barred from registering to vote. Mayersville had been newly incorporated, and, shortly after she was elected, Blackwell, the first black woman ever to become a mayor in Mississippi, had to appoint a board of aldermen to help her run the town. One of the people she chose was the white county clerk who had turned her away when she tried to register in 1964. Blackwell's reasoning for picking this onetime foe was simple and pragmatic: "She'd been working for the county twenty-five years. If there was anything I needed to know, she knew it. If I asked, 'Did you know that?' she would look like a fool if she didn't."

In 1984, Mayor Unita Blackwell was invited to address the Democratic National Convention in San Francisco. She followed Jesse Jackson at the podium, and as she made her way to the microphone, she thought of Fannie Lou Hamer, and tears welled in her eyes. Fannie Lou, who had fought so hard and argued so eloquently for the seating of black Mississippians at the 1964 convention, was the one who should be here now, Blackwell thought. It was Fannie Lou who "was standing there in us— in me, in Jesse, in all of us . . ." Blackwell also remembered James Chaney, Mickey Schwerner, and Andy Goodman, who had died "for the right for me to stand there at that podium." As she looked out at the thousands of people jammed into San Francisco's convention center that night, she realized that she, too, was passing the legacy on. "I was standing there," she said, "for all who had died, all who will live, for all the generations to come."

epilogue

Bernice Johnson Reagon once described the civil rights movement as the "borning struggle," the catalyst for the women's movement, the antiwar and environmental movements, and virtually every other campaign for social change that would follow. As a result of the civil rights battles, "protest and opposition became a way of life and a way of thinking in this country," observed Theresa del Pozzo, a white activist who joined SNCC in 1964. "And everybody who opposes polluted water, nuclear power plants, a highway coming through your land, farm closings, plant closings, unemployment, housing—every one of those people is continuing the struggle."

Yet, of all the social movements of the 1960s and afterward, none touched more lives, none had more far-reaching consequences for American society, than did the campaigns for black and women's equality. Challenging the United States to live up to the ideals of freedom on which it was founded, both movements worked to change some of the country's most entrenched cultural values and attitudes, as well as the way its citizens lived their lives. No one would claim that the two campaigns succeeded entirely. Some, indeed, would say that they had failed. Decades later, racism and sexism were still an ingrained part of American life. Many blacks were still mired in poverty, trapped in neighborhoods where crime, violence, and drug use were rampant. Women were still battling for economic parity, for equality in personal, social, and business relationships. Affirmative action programs were being dismantled. Abortion rights were under constant threat.

Yet, in contemplating all the problems, all the goals left incomplete, one also had to remember, as Bernice Reagon once remarked, "how things were before." Denying "the vast accomplishments of the civil rights movement," historian Grace Elizabeth Hale has pointed out, "is to succumb to a numbing fatalism in which its real achievements are forgotten or taken for granted and no better future can even be conceived." The same observation could be made about the women's movement.

If the civil rights crusade did not achieve full equality for African-Americans, it did open up the closed society of the South, eradicate legal segregation, bring Southern blacks into the political process, and create sweeping new educational and economic opportunities for blacks through-out the country. The hundreds of thousands of blacks added to Southern states' voting rolls helped end the political careers of a number of arch-segregationists, including James Eastland, the foremost congressional scourge of the civil rights movement. Eastland decided not to run for reelection in 1978 because "he would not win again," according to Ed Brown, director of the Voter Education Project. He *would* not win, said Brown, because Fannie Lou Hamer and other Mississippi activists "had registered people and gotten things to the point that he *could* not win."

There was yet another major achievement of the civil rights move-ment—one that could not be measured in anything tangible, like jobs or college degrees or elections. Simply put, it was the disappearance of terror. Most Southern blacks could now live without fear of losing their lives or their jobs for stepping out of line, for provoking the ire of whites. A decade after Hamer was beaten in Winona, a white newspaper reporter named Kay Mills visited her at her home in Ruleville. Mills, who would later write a biography of Hamer, wanted to know if things had really changed all that much for Delta blacks in the past ten years. Hamer looked at the young woman, then said slowly, "If you had turned up the road to my house in '63, you might have been stopped before you got here, probably arrested. That's how tense it was. Everybody in town would have known a white lady was here, and would have been driving by to check it out." Hamer did not need to add, Mills later wrote, that more might have hap-pened than just "driving by."

As for the women's movement, one of its greatest victories also proved to be intangible: No longer was the assumption of women's inferiority and subordinate position a basic cultural tenet of American life. As feminist scholars Rachel Blau DuPlessis and Ann Snitow noted, such a premise had profoundly influenced the way women lived and thought, had been "the starting point from which one planned one's moves and shaped one's life. The very difficulty of describing this prefeminist atmosphere is a measure of how dramatically things have changed."

Issues once considered private—sexuality, children and family, male-female relationships, one's personal appearance—were now an integral part of the nation's political discourse. Young women were presented with educational and job opportunities that their mothers could only have dreamed of. Women who never considered themselves feminists in the 1960s and 1970s came to acknowledge in later decades that the women's movement had indeed benefited their lives. Among them was Barbara

Williams Emerson, the daughter of SCLC leader Hosea Williams and a veteran civil rights activist herself. Emerson, who credited the women's movement with helping give her the strength to leave an unhappy marriage, observed that feminism "laid a groundwork for saying: I can, I have a right, I have an entitlement to be a whole, complete person in and of myself."

To gauge the impact of both the civil rights and women's movements, one need look no further than at the later lives of two young black women involved in the civil rights struggle in Mississippi. One of them is Jacqueline Byrd, who, along with more than one hundred other students, staged the 1961 school walkout in McComb. When she was about fourteen, Byrd and four of her girlfriends talked about what they wanted to be when they grew up. One girl said she wanted to be the head of a company, another said she would like to be a doctor, and Byrd had vague dreams of being in charge of some business or organization. The two other girls snorted. "Y'all can't do that," one of them declared. "Think about the times we live in. Y'all are probably going to be fat and old and housewives."

More than three decades later, Jacqueline Byrd Martin reflected back on that conversation. "The two girls who said that we'd be fat and old and housewives are exactly that," she said. The girl who wanted to head a company became a top corporate executive at Honeywell and then a successful consultant. The girl with medical ambitions was a pediatrician in California. And Martin herself? In 1988, she was named head of administration of the McComb city government, ensconced in a large office with French windows that looked out on the City Hall steps where she and her fellow students had stood in 1961, demanding their freedom.

In Greenwood, Ida Mae Holland, who had gone from prostitute to activist, watched her mother die an agonizing death in a local hospital of burns suffered when her house was firebombed. Holland was sure the arson had occurred in retaliation for her work with SNCC, and it strengthened her determination to leave Mississippi. She went to Minneapolis, where she attended the University of Minnesota, first earning a bachelor's degree and then a doctorate in American studies, with a focus in theater arts. Along the way, she added to her name the Swahili word "Endesha," which means "she who drives herself and others forward." "I'm *Dr.* Endesha Ida Mae Holland, and don't nobody ever forget that," she once told an interviewer with a laugh. "That's the funniest thing and the grandest and glorious thing I've ever heard of. Just think, little Cat could achieve that."

Holland became a professor of American studies at the State University of New York in Buffalo, and later joined the faculty of the University of Southern California. She also won considerable success as a playwright: Her prize-winning autobiographical play, *From the Mississippi Delta*, had a six-month run in New York in the early 1990s and was produced in a number of regional theaters throughout the country.

Whatever they did later in their lives, most female civil rights activists of the 1950s and 1960s retained a strong commitment to the fight for racial equality and social justice. "I still think of myself as a movement person, first and foremost," said Eleanor Holmes Norton, who was elected Washington, D.C.'s nonvoting delegate to Congress in 1990. "I don't think of myself as a congresswoman first or a lawyer first. The movement was absolutely central to who I became, who I am still, and how I am regarded." Her major act after being elected to Congress, she noted, was to become a prime mover for the 1991 Civil Rights Act.

Like Norton, many movement veterans entered politics and government. In the Carter administration, Mary King became deputy director of the agency in charge of the Peace Corps and ACTION, the government's domestic volunteer organization. For fifteen years, Connie Curry headed Atlanta's Bureau of Human Services, spanning the administrations of Maynard Jackson and Andrew Young, the city's first two black mayors. Casey Hayden worked with Curry for part of that period. In Washington, Joyce Ladner, a professor of sociology at Howard who also served as Howard's president for a time, was a member of the Control Board, an agency created by Congress in the late 1990s to oversee the troubled administration of Mayor Marion Barry, Ladner's former SNCC colleague.

Marian Wright Edelman was in Washington, too, as the president of what *The New Republic* called "one of the capital's best-known, best-connected lobbies." From her days as a lawyer in Mississippi, the young woman from Bennettsville, South Carolina, had proven extraordinarily skillful at attracting public attention to the plight of the poor. In 1973, she set up the Children's Defense Fund, which, for more than twenty-five years, has been in the forefront of the fight to create and protect federal social programs for children, particularly those who are impoverished.

A number of movement women, meanwhile, continued the struggle for social reform on their home turf. When Bob Moses returned to Mississippi in the early 1990s, bringing with him his newly organized nationwide campaign to encourage math literacy among poor children, Annie Devine was there to greet him. For most of the previous thirty years, Devine had been in Canton, remaining active in the fight for Head Start, better housing, and aid for the hungry, among other pressing local social concerns. She didn't hesitate to scold Moses and David Dennis, who had worked with Moses in the Mississippi movement and who now was his colleague on the Algebra Project, for leaving the state in the mid-1960s. "Mrs. Devine compared Bob and me to runaway fathers," Dennis remarked. "She said, 'You gave birth and you left, and you haven't done anything to support your children.'"

In Montgomery, Johnnie Carr, as head of the Montgomery Improvement Association, continued to lobby city officials for better treatment of minorities and the poor, just as she had for more than forty years. In 1998, at the age of eighty-seven, she was still presiding over MIA meetings, still pressuring the white mayor of the city to be more attuned to the needs of blacks. In a conversation with a visitor, she fondly recalled her close friendships with two other civil rights stalwarts, Virginia Durr and Rosa Parks. In the 1970s and 1980s, Carr and Durr often appeared together to lecture about their civil rights experiences, with Carr not infrequently trying to get her friend to tone down her impulsive outspokenness. When Durr, in her early nineties, went to live in a nursing home in the North, near one of her daughters, Carr felt bereft. "I've missed her so much," she said.

Rosa Parks, meanwhile, remained Representative John Conyers' administrative assistant in Detroit until her late seventies. After her retirement, she devoted most of her time to the cause that had propelled her into the history books. She made dozens of public appearances every year, and in 1987 she founded the Rosa and Raymond Parks Institute in Detroit, to offer career and leadership training for black teenagers. "I am happy to go wherever I am invited and to accept whatever honors are given me," Parks said in the early 1990s. Yet she was still somewhat bemused that nobody was much interested in her life and achievements—except for that one act of defiance so many years ago. "Interviewers," she said, "still only want to talk about that one evening in 1955 when I refused to give up my seat on the bus."

Septima Clark, whose gentle encouragement of Parks nurtured Parks's rebellion, stayed a social activist until her death in 1987. Clark conducted workshops for the American Field Service, helped raise scholarship money for black students, and organized day-care facilities. In 1975, she was elected a member of the Charleston school board, the same body that had dismissed her as a teacher nineteen years before. And in 1976 the governor of South Carolina restored the retirement benefits she had lost when she was fired in 1956 for her civil rights activities.

In Louisville, Anne Braden and her husband, Carl, continued to run the Southern Conference Educational Fund until its demise in 1973. The end of SCEF was yet another blow for the Bradens, who had lost their eleven-year-old daughter, Anita, to a fatal lung disease a few years before. In 1975, Carl died, too. Anne retained her passion for activism, helping to found several new groups, including the Kentucky Alliance Against Racial and Social Oppression, which seeks to combat specific instances of racism in Louisville and the rest of the state. "I still call it the movement, by the way," she said in 1998. "As far as I'm concerned, it didn't end." What *has* changed is the way she is now regarded by individuals and organizations that once shied away from her, Carl, and SCEF. In recent years, she has received awards and commendations from a number of such groups. "I've been transformed from a pariah into a heroine," Braden said with a laugh. "It's really strange. I know how to handle attacks, but I don't know how to handle awards."

In Julian Bond's view, Anne Braden was like Ella Baker—"sort of a legendary figure, a person who has sacrificed a great deal of time and money, almost all of her personal life . . . but who has continued over the years to support the sorts of things that she thinks are right." Braden remained close to Baker, who served as a consultant to SCEF, in addition to maintaining her involvement in a wide array of other human rights causes. A few years before Baker's death in 1986, she challenged the claim that the civil rights movement had been a failure and focused, instead, on the need to keep the torch burning: "The major pressures, the things we considered the most oppressive, are lifted. And people can elect the people they want to elect whether they turn out to be good or not. . . . I don't see the productive value of being bitter. I don't claim to have any corner on an answer but I believe that the struggle is eternal. Somebody else carries on." At Baker's Harlem funeral, Bob Moses asked all those who considered themselves to be Ella's children to come forward. Hundreds of people stood and marched to the front of the Abyssinian Baptist Church.

The victories, those that were personal and those for the social good, often came with a heavy psychological price. Like their male counterparts, a number of movement women, particularly those who were younger, were emotionally scarred by what had happened to them in the 1960s. Some never quite regained their bearings. Bertha Gober, whose arrest helped trigger the Albany movement and whose songs helped keep it going, became mentally ill and slipped from sight. Annell Ponder, who never fully recovered from her vicious beating in Winona, suffered other blows: an unhappy liaison with one of the movement's key male figures and the death of a child. She, too, disappeared from view, a "victim of the movement," Septima Clark called her.

In a number of cases, idealism and passion had been replaced by disillusionment and pain. Friendships had been destroyed, and most of the love affairs and marriages begun in the intensity of the movement's wartime conditions ended shortly thereafter. Cordell and Bernice Johnson Reagon were among those who split up, as did Bob and Dorothy Zellner, Dinky Romilly and James Forman, Bernard and Colia Lafayette, Frank and Jean Wheeler Smith, Silas and Martha Prescod Norman, Bob Moses and Dona Richards, and Diane Nash and James Bevel.

Bernice Reagon was pregnant with her second child when she and her husband separated in 1965. Left alone, with an infant and a toddler to support, she struggled to fulfill her own ambitions and continue her work with the movement while coping with the loss of her marriage. Like a number of black women in SNCC, she aligned herself with black nationalism, and during the late 1960s, joined the Harambee Singers, a female group whose audiences were almost exclusively black.

Eventually, Reagon received a Ph.D. from Howard University, writing her dissertation on the music of the civil rights movement. She became director of the Smithsonian Institution's Black American Culture program and later curator of the Smithsonian's National Museum of American History. She won a MacArthur "genius" grant. But her most celebrated achievement was the founding of Sweet Honey in the Rock, a world-renowned a capella group of black women whose concerts drew large, devoted audiences of every color. In Reagon's view, her work with Sweet Honey was simply a continuation of what she started back in Albany: "I'm still an activist, still a singer, a song leader, as I was then." She moved beyond black nationalism, but her singing, and that of Sweet Honey, remained focused on the lives and legacies of black women—"singing about our lives and our commitment to our community and our commitment to struggle for change."

When Diane Nash's marriage crumbled, she, too, was left with two small children to raise. She and Bevel had long been at odds over his incessant philandering; on occasion, he'd been physically abusive to her. After their divorce in 1968, Bevel, who later acknowledged fathering at least seventeen children in a succession of relationships and marriages, refused to provide any financial support to Nash. (In the early 1990s, Bevel would give Louis Farrakhan the idea for the 1995 Million Man march, which, among other things, urged black men to take more responsibility as fathers and husbands.) Having dropped out of Fisk to work for SNCC and SCLC, Nash had no college degree and no plans to get one. She supported herself and her children with a series of ill-paying jobs, several of them in social service organizations, and devoted much of the rest of her time to the antiwar movement and a variety of civil rights and human rights groups. But her main focus was her children. With considerable scrimping, she brought them up, then helped send them to college.

For all her disappointments, Nash had no regrets about her all-consuming early commitment to the movement, a commitment whose trade-off had been a future with little material comfort or security. She was intensely proud of what she had done in the early and middle 1960s— proud not so much of her own remarkable achievements as of what had resulted from her and others' work. She thought of Selma, for example, and how that campaign had led to the Voting Rights Act, which, in turn, led to the election of hundreds of black officials. "I [am] very satisfied," she said. A satisfaction that "has to do with the fact that . . . my living has made a difference on the planet. And I love that. I really do."

For the young white women who had been involved in the civil rights movement, there was, in many cases, a deep sense of isolation, a feeling of being cut loose from all familiar moorings. No longer welcomed by most black activists, some of them had been rejected by the white world as well. "For me, and for many Southern white women, participation [in the civil rights movement] made us outcasts, women without homes," Joan Browning wrote in the late 1990s. Browning herself was disowned by most members of her family after her 1961 arrest and jailing in Albany. The nineteen-year-old Georgia native, who had been extremely close to her mother and seven brothers and sisters, was heartbroken over the estrangement. Her hope of becoming a doctor had been dashed by being forced to leave Georgia State College for Women because of her civil rights activities, and she had no money to finance going back to school and finishing her education. For most of the next fourteen years, she lived in Atlanta and worked for a series of liberal organizations, including the Southern Regional Council, the Urban League, and the ACLU. In 1976 she moved to rural West Virginia, and in 1994 finally received her bachelor's degree, from West Virginia State College. She earned a living through bookkeeping, fund-raising, and writing, and became deeply involved in local community affairs.

But while Browning found a measure of contentment and satisfaction in her life, she was the first to acknowledge that it had not turned out the way she once had hoped. When she was growing up, she assumed she would marry and have a large family. "Of course, I didn't do either," she said. "The men available to me because I was a civil rights activist shrank and shrank and shrank. The men of my youth were no longer available to me. And the men of my youth would no longer be desirable because I was a different woman. I was a different woman entirely."

For Casey Hayden, there were a number of years of restless wandering, of searching for the kind of meaning and fulfillment in her life that she had found in the civil rights movement. She lived in Vermont, New York, California, and Colorado, among other places, before returning to Atlanta in 1983, to work for the Southern Regional Council and then with Connie Curry in the Atlanta city government. After her divorce from Tom Hayden, her involvements with men were unhappy, for the most part, although one longtime relationship produced a son and a daughter. By the late 1990s, however, Hayden had come to "feel grounded." She was finally in a strong, stable marriage, was coming to terms with her civil rights experiences, was now writing and lecturing about them. Only in the past few years, she said, had she begun to recover from the pain of her separation from the movement. "The loss was huge. . . . I was in shock forever. It's hard to sense that you've peaked in your twenties and that nothing is going to touch this afterwards."

Penny Patch had become a wanderer, too. Only twenty-one when she left SNCC, she moved to northern California with a white male organizer she had known in Mississippi, the two of them struggling to create a life outside the movement "in a world we did not feel was ours." Patch lost virtually all contact with old movement friends, black and white, and felt an overwhelming sense of isolation. "[T]here was hardly anybody to talk to," she said. "We did not talk to each other. It seems to have been pretty universal. . . . Almost everybody felt as if they had lost their home." In time, however, "I numbed myself to the pain and couldn't even feel it, much less articulate it."

In 1967, Patch and her companion moved to Vermont, bought land and built a house, married and had a son, and separated shortly thereafter. It was after the separation in 1970 that Patch finally began to put her life back together. She eventually remarried, had a daughter, and, with her husband and children, moved to the town of Lyndonville, in northeastern Vermont. After earning a degree in nursing, she was a public health nurse, working mostly with pregnant women and children, and then became a midwife. She stashed all her papers and letters relating to the movement under her bed and tried to bury her memories as well. In time, she began to wonder if what she remembered had, in fact, actually occurred the way she recalled it. "Had black-white ever been a serious issue? Did it affect other people profoundly or was it simply that I, with my personal history of serious childhood losses, had been deeply wrenched by something which was only a very minor part of the ... [m]ovement? Had there ever been a beloved community?"

Then, in 1988, she received an invitation to a SNCC reunion at Trinity College in Hartford, Connecticut. One of its organizers was Trinity professor Jack Chatfield, who'd worked as a SNCC organizer in southwestern Georgia and who, like Patch, was haunted by "accounts unsettled, mysteries unresolved, friendships severed, and feelings of serenity, even momentary ecstasy, now lost beyond recovery." The reunion drew dozens of former SNCC activists, black and white, who, like Patch and Chatfield, had felt bereft for years from the loss of their community. For four days, the participants, many of whom had not seen each other in more than twenty years, recalled SNCC during panel discussions, sang, partied, and caught up on each other's life. When the reunion ended late Saturday night, Patch went back to her hotel room, sat on the bed, and sobbed uncontrollably, her husband and children holding her close.

For Patch, as for other former activists, the healing continued. At another movement reunion in 1994, this one marking the thirtieth anniversary of Freedom Summer, she went out to eat in Jackson with MacArthur Cotton, a black Mississippian with whom she had worked closely in SNCC. They talked about what they were doing now, talked, too, about their families. She said she had heard he had become a Muslim for a while and wouldn't talk to whites. That was true, he said. That was just the way things had been back then. He asked her if she had been hurt when she heard that. Very much, she replied. Throughout the meal, they couldn't stop smiling at each other.

But there were some divisions that would not close. Black women and white women, for one, remained wary of one another. The centuries-old gap in understanding, all the long-standing resentments and jealousies, were still there. A number of black women passionately defended SNCC against the charges of sexism that had cropped up in the intervening thirty years, insisting that the organization had done nothing but empower women and criticizing those with a different opinion. At the Trinity reunion, when Kathie Sarachild talked about both positive and negative experiences as a white female Freedom Summer volunteer, Jean Wheeler Smith chastised her for what Smith thought was an overemphasis on the negative. Put on the defensive, white women, at the reunion and afterward, tended to downplay any gender-related problems they had encountered in the movement. According to Cheryl Lynn Greenburg, a Trinity professor who helped organize the reunion, a "certain romanticization of the past" dominated the gathering, overlooking the actual complexities of life in SNCC and the rest of the movement.

"The intersection of gender and race is still such a hot spot," said one white woman who was active in SNCC. "It's a minefield. Every place you step—there's no way to do the right thing. It doesn't matter what you do. If you don't do anything, you're wrong. If you do something, you're wrong."

That's a reality that Penny Patch accepted, just as she accepted other realities about SNCC, herself, and her former comrades. While "so much is healed," the conclusion was inescapable, she felt, that SNCC's early vision of "black and white together" had been lost. "After the initial ecstasy of reunion," she wrote in the late 1990s, "it becomes clear there is a great deal of distance between us. . . . There are a few white and black SNCC people who have succeeded in maintaining and developing close interracial friendships since the movement time, but these are small in number. And I am not one of those people. I understand well that what was between us will never be again."

Yet, Patch insisted, it was important to remember that such a community did exist, if only for a moment. "The fact that some of us had deep friendships that crossed all racial lines is simply a miracle. For short periods of time, in those early years, we leaped over the history and the minefields between us. . . . No matter what came after, there was a brief time when we were black and white together."

If Pauli Murray had been around in the 1990s to counsel her younger black and white sisters (and brothers) in the movement, she undoubtedly would have urged them not to give up on the vision of interracial community, no matter how unrealistic it might now seem. Murray, who died in 1985, had always been a woman ahead of her time, first in her struggle for black freedom and equality, then for women's rights. In the last years of her life, the message she pushed was one of reconciliation.

In 1967, she had been hired by Brandeis University as a professor of American civilization and politics, with the task of helping to create an African-American studies program. From the moment she arrived on the Brandeis campus, she was confronted by militant black students who espoused an "ideology as alien to my nature and as difficult for me to accept as white ethnocentrism. This emerging racial rhetoric made absolutely no sense to me; in turn, some of my most deeply held values about universal human dignity were considered obsolete by young black radicals."

She began to see feminists behaving in the "same hostile extreme way." It greatly troubled Murray that the struggles for freedom from racism and sexism had led to so much alienation. "My feeling is that if this country is to survive, we must live together in harmony . . . ," she later said. "There-fore, there is a need for people to be involved with and concerned about reconciliation even as we are working on liberation." While at Brandeis, she asked herself, "What do you want to do with the time that you have left?" The question haunted her for months, until she resolved it by resign-ing from her tenured Brandeis professorship. At the age of sixty-three, she entered the Episcopal seminary in Cambridge, Massachusetts.

The Episcopal Church in the United States was still strongly opposed to the idea of women priests at that point, and Murray, who long had been active in the fight for the ordination of women, had no idea what she would do if the church had not changed its mind by the time she graduated. But she was convinced that the ministry was where she belonged, where she could pursue what she saw as her mission of healing. In 1976, shortly before Murray's graduation from the seminary and after three years of emotionally wrenching turmoil over the issue, the Episcopal Church in the United States, in one of the most significant victories for the women's movement, voted to allow women's ordination.

On an icy January morning in 1977, Pauli Murray, her small, erect frame clad in white and gold vestments, was ordained in Washington's majestic National Cathedral, with the jubilant congregation erupting in "happy chaos," as one news account of the ordination described it. Murray was the American church's first black female priest.

One month later, Murray traveled to Chapel Hill, North Carolina, to celebrate her first Holy Eucharist service. It was a day to remember the past. She had grown up near Chapel Hill, had been rejected by the Uni-versity of North Carolina, which was located there. Now she was stand-ing in the Chapel of the Cross—the same tiny brick chapel where her grandmother, Cornelia Fitzgerald, had worshiped as a girl, from the bal-cony reserved for slaves.

For so many years, Murray, the granddaughter of a slave and great-granddaughter of a slave owner, had struggled with the question of who she was, where she fit in. "Don't touch me," she used to tell friends. "I'm full of splinters." In Chapel Hill, however, the pain was gone. It was time, she had decided, to embrace all of her complicated heritage, to gain strength from all of her roots. And it was time for the rest of the country to do the same. "Black, white, and red are related by blood and by culture and by history and by common suffering," she would later tell an interviewer. "And so what I am saying is look, let's level with one another. Let's admit we are related and let's get on with the business of healing . . ."

Remembering the past on that mild Sunday afternoon, however, involved more than reconciliation. It was also a triumphant celebration of the legacy handed down by Murray and the countless other women who had fought so long and so hard for freedom. From Sojourner Truth and the Grimké sisters, to Ida Wells and Mary Church Terrell, to Ella Baker and Pauli Murray, to Diane Nash and Fannie Lou Hamer, the traditions of defiance, commitment, and community had been passed along, from one generation of women to another, in a great, tightly linked chain.

That afternoon, Pauli Murray's thoughts focused on two women in particular: her grandmother and Eleanor Roosevelt. Cornelia Smith Fitzgerald's tattered, yellowing Bible was Murray's most treasured possession, and she now carried the Bible to the pulpit and opened it to a passage she would read later in the service. Marking the page was a faded purple ribbon, which, more than thirty years before, had adorned the bouquet of flowers sent by Mrs. Roosevelt to celebrate Murray's law school graduation.

Clutching her grandmother's Bible, this lawyer, activist, scholar, poet, and priest looked out at the mostly white congregation and reflected on how far she—and this little church—had come. "There is no black Christ, white Christ, or red Christ," she declared. "There is only one Christ, the spirit of love and reconciliation, the healer of deep psychological wounds." As she spoke, she felt the nearness of her grandmother's spirit. Not in the balcony, though. Cornelia Smith Fitzgerald was in the pulpit, directly behind her.

abbreviations for sources

BP	Carl and Anne Braden Papers, State Historical Society of Wisconsin
BWOHP	Black Women's Oral History Project, Schlesinger Library, Radcliffe College
CRDP	Oral History Collection, Civil Rights Documentation Project, Moorland-Spingarn Research Center, Howard University
OH/CU	Oral History Collection, Columbia University
OH/FDRL	Oral History Collection, Franklin D. Roosevelt Library
OH/LBJ	Oral History Collection, Lyndon B. Johnson Library
OH/USM	Oral History Collection, University of Southern Mississippi
PM	Pauli Murray Papers, Schlesinger Library, Radcliffe College
PV	Preston Valien Collection, Amistad Research Center, Tulane University
RP	Anne Romaine Papers, State Historical Society of Wisconsin
SCLC	SCLC Papers, microfilm, Library of Congress
SHSW	State Historical Society of Wisconsin
SNCC	SNCC Papers, microfilm, Library of Congress
SOHP	Southern Oral History Program, University of North Carolina
VD	Virginia Durr Papers, Schlesinger Library, Radcliffe College

endnotes

Chapter 1

20 "[o]ur demonstrators were": Pauli Murray letter to Eleanor Roosevelt, 5/4/44, PM.

20 "It is difficult": Pauli Murray, *Song in a Weary Throat: An American Pilgrimage* (New York: Harper & Row, 1987), p. 224.

21 "brief act of": Ibid., p. 228.

21 "nerve and bravery": Ibid., pp. x–xi.

22 "When the true": Quoted in Alma Lutz, *Crusade for Freedom* (Boston: Beacon Press, 1968), epigraph.

22 "Slavery is terrible": Quoted in bell hooks, *Ain't I a Woman?: Black Women and Feminism* (Boston: South End Press, 1981), p. 24.

22 "Babies was snatched": Quoted in Dorothy Sterling, ed., *We Are Your Sisters: Black Women in the Nineteenth Century* (New York: Norton, 1984), p. 10.

22 "[N]o likely looking": Quoted in Gunnar Myrdal, *An American Dilemma: The Negro Problem and Modern Democracy* (New York: Harper, 1941), p. 126.

22 "denied chastity": Brian Lanker, *I Dream a World: Portraits of Black Women Who Changed America* (New York: Stewart, Tabori & Chang, 1989), p. 9.

23 Pauli Murray's maternal: Pauli Murray, *Proud Shoes: The Story of an American Family* (New York: Harper & Row, 1978), p. 47.

23 "[t]he same overpowering": Ibid., p. 48.

23 "Wives and apprentices": Quoted in Myrdal, p. 1073.

24 "In truth": Quoted in William H. Chafe, *Women and Equality: Changing Patterns in American Culture* (New York: Oxford University Press, 1978), p. 16.

24 "[N]o time": Fanny Kemble, *Journal of a Residence on a Georgia Plantation in 1838–1839* (New York: Harper & Brothers, 1863), p. 73.

24 "And to all this": Ibid., p. 200.

24 "peculiar views": Quoted in Margaret Ripley Wolfe, *Daughters of Canaan: A Saga of American Women* (Lexington: University Press of Kentucky, 1995), p. 92.

25 "slave of slaves": Quoted in Jacqueline Jones, *Labor of Love, Labor of Sorrow: Black Women, Work and the Family, from Slavery to the Present* (New York: Basic Books, 1985), p. 25.

25 "was confronted with": Murray, *Proud Shoes*, p. 37.

25 "We are complimented": Quoted in Dorothy Sterling, *Black Foremothers: Three Lives* (Old Westbury, N.Y.: Feminist Press, 1988), p. 6.

25 "Jealousy is not": Kemble, p. 228.

25 "only half of a self": Minrose C. Gwin, *Black and White Women of the Old South: The Peculiar Sisterhood in American Literature* (Knoxville: University of Tennessee Press, 1985), p. 11.

26 Writer Willie Morris: Willie Morris, *North Toward Home* (Boston: Houghton Mifflin, 1967), p. 79.

26 "The light was": Anne Goodwyn Jones, *Tomorrow Is Another Day: The Woman Writer in the South, 1859–1936* (Baton Rouge: Louisiana State University Press, 1981), p. 29.

27 "It is of no use": Quoted in Sterling, *We Are Your Sisters*, p. 154.

28 "Some will tell": Quoted in Lutz, p. 65.

28 "to do all that she can": Ann D. Gordon, ed., *African American Women and the Vote 1837–1965* (Amherst: University of Massachusetts Press, 1997), pp. 3–4.

28 "The appropriate duties": Quoted in Lutz, p. 115.

29 "as though the color": Gordon, p. 4.

29 "parcel of silly women": Lutz, p. 75.

29 "a colored woman": Gordon, p. 36.

29 "What am I going to do?": Murray, *Song*, pp. 215–16.

30 "Verily": Henry Mayer, *All on Fire: William Lloyd Garrison and the Abolition of Slavery* (New York: St. Martin's Press, 1998), pp. 247-48.

30 Twenty-four-year-old: Elisabeth Griffith, *In Her Own Right: The Life of Elizabeth Cady Stanton* (New York: Oxford University Press, 1984), p. 37.

31 "degraded, oppressed": Quoted in Paula Giddings, *Where and When I Enter: The Impact of Black Women on Race and Sex in America* (New York: Morrow, 1984), p. 66.

32 "When it was": Quoted in Sterling, *We Are Your Sisters*, p. 415.

32 "There is a great stir": Ibid., p. 411.

32 "Do you really believe": Ibid.

Chapter 2

33 She was a little slip: Linda McMurry, *To Keep the Waters Troubled: The Life of Ida B. Wells* (New York: Oxford University Press), p. 26.

34 "heartless flirt": Sterling, *Black Foremothers*, p. 74.

35 Truth was sixty-eight years old: Sterling, *We Are Your Sisters*, p. 254.

35 According to historian: Darlene Clark Hine, "Rape and the Inner Lives of Southern Black Women," in Virginia Bernhard et al., eds., *Southern Women: Histories and Identities* (Columbia: University of Missouri Press, 1992), p. 181.

35 A black church magazine: Sterling, *Black Foremothers*, p. 73.

37 "the opportunity to enjoy": Quoted in Walter Lord, *The Past That Would Not Die* (New York: Harper & Row, 1965), p. 30.

37 "Woman!": W. J. Cash, *The Mind of the South* (New York: Knopf, 1941), p. 86.

37 "I think there was": Interview with Karl Fleming.

38 Interestingly, in the pre-Reconstruction South: Martha Hodes, *White Women, Black Men: Illicit Sex in the 19th-Century South* (New Haven: Yale University Press, 1997), pp. 209-10.

38 "The killing may be done in our name": Virginia Durr (pseudonym, Eliza Heard), "Economics and a Murder Trial," *New South*, October 1965, p. 5.

40 "Nobody in this section": Sterling, *Black Foremothers*, p. 82.

40 "to justify their own barbarism": Quoted in Gerda Lerner, *Black Women in White America* (New York: Vintage, 1972), p. 203.

41 Shortly before he died: McMurry, p. 174.

41 "The men talk about it": Giddings, p. 72.

42 "black children [being] raised": Lanker, p. 147.

42 "I think that women's": Interview with Dorothy Height, BWOHP.

43 "a slanderous and nasty-minded mulatress": Giddings, p. 92.

43 "prostitutes, thieves, and liars": Sterling, *Black Foremothers*, p. xxxvi.

43 "They had defended the race": Giddings, p. 135.

43 An editorial in the NACW: Deborah Gray White, *Too Heavy a Load: Black Women in Defense of Themselves, 1894–1994* (New York: Norton, 1999), p. 36.

43 John Hope: Ibid., p. 57.

44 "As a people": Quoted in Giddings, p. 60.

44 "Part of the time": Ibid.

44 "[we] poor colored": Ibid., p. 114.

44 Her ambition: Miriam DeCosta-Willis, ed., *The Memphis Diary of Ida B. Wells* (Boston: Beacon Press, 1995), p. 114.

44 "I had been accused": Giddings, pp. 116–17.

45 "[W]hat a mighty foe": Lerner, p. 210.

45 "The self-respect": Hodding Carter, "Yes, Tennessee, There Are Southern Belles," *New York Times Magazine*, Oct. 7, 1962, p. 93.

46 "Experience has taught us": Giddings, p. 123.

47 "the caricatures": Adrienne Rich, *On Lies, Secrets and Silence* (New York: Norton, 1979), p. 298.

47 "I saw these colored women": Quoted in Gordon, p. 127.

48 "orphaned and neglected": Jacquelyn Dowd Hall, *Revolt Against Chivalry: Jessie Daniel Ames and the Women's Campaign Against Lynching* (New York: Columbia University Press, 1979), pp. 119–20.

48 At the University of Alabama: Wolfe, p. 148.

50 Mary Addie Mullino: Hall, pp. 230–31.

Chapter 3

52 "Don't touch me": Pauli Murray to Barbara Ann Lucas, 1/19/77, PM.

53 "I am a Negro": Murray, *Song*, p. 111.

54 "the ability to pass": Murray, *Proud Shoes*, p. 89.

55 As historian: John Egerton, *Speak Now Against the Day: The Generation Before the Civil Rights Movement in the South* (Chapel Hill: University of North Carolina Press, 1995), p. 233.

56 "great changes": Murray, *Song*, p. 113.

56 "has made herself": Allida M. Black, *Casting Her Own Shadow: Eleanor Roosevelt and the Shaping of Postwar Liberalism* (New York: Columbia University Press, 1996), p. 37.

57 Eleanor's great-uncle: Blanche Wiesen Cook, *Eleanor Roosevelt, Vol. 1* (New York: Viking, 1992), p. 28.

57 She used the term: Joseph Lash, *Eleanor and Franklin* (New York: Norton, 1971), p. 522.

57 "a nineteenth-century woman": Pauli Murray interview, OH/FDRL.

58 "the most marvelous": Lash, p. 523.

58 "Which one": Giddings, p. 227.

58 "the Negro's share": Doris Kearns Goodwin, *No Ordinary Time* (New York: Simon & Schuster, 1994), p. 162.

59 "only insofar": Lash, p. 532.

59 "intrusive and impulsive": Ibid.

59 In June 1941: Interview with James Farmer and James Farmer, *Lay Bare the Heart* (New York: Arbor House, 1985), pp. 68–70.

61 Tuskegee, Alabama: Goodwin, p. 423.

61 At moments: Lash, pp. 522–23.

62 A warm woman: Ibid., p. 523.

62 "How can anyone": Patricia Sullivan, *Days of Hope: Race and Democracy in the New Deal Era* (Chapel Hill: University of North Carolina Press, 1996), pp. 160–61.

62 She was everything: Quoted in ibid., p. 159.

62 "Eleanor Clubs": Goodwin, pp. 371–72.

63 "[Y]our letter": Murray, *Song*, p. 190.

63 "a central figure": Ibid., p. xii.

63 "a painful meeting": Pauli Murray interview, OH/FDRL.

64 "We used to say": Ibid.

64 At the 1944 commencement: Murray, *Song*, p. 244.

65 "lost in a maze": Lillian Smith, *Killers of the Dream* (New York: Norton, 1961), p. 61.

65 In 1942: Anne C. Loveland, *Lillian Smith: A Southerner Confronting the South* (Baton Rouge: Louisiana State University Press, 1986), p. 35.

65 "It was one thing": Richard King, *A Southern Renaissance: The Cultural Awakening of the American South* (New York: Oxford University Press, 1980), p. 176.

65 "You should know": Pauli Murray to Lillian Smith, 7/13/56, PM.

65 "If anyone": Quoted in Loveland, p. 268.

66 "We hope": Lillian Smith to Pauli Murray, 9/8/43, PM.

66 "We are primarily": Margaret Rose Gladney, ed., *How Am I to Be Heard?: Letters of Lillian Smith* (Chapel Hill: University of North Carolina Press, 1993), p. 50.

66 "we talked our heads": Loveland, p. 43.

67 "There'd always be": Lillian Smith, *Strange Fruit* (New York: Reynal & Hitchcock, 1944), pp. 125–26.

67 "People were rarely": Loveland, p. 74.

67 "Real history": Gladney, p. 127.

67 "The mother": Smith, *Killers*, p. 27.

68 "When we": Ibid., p. 84.

68 "[S]ome, if their": Ibid., p. 96.

68 "You are": Jo Ann Robinson, "Lillian Smith: Reflections on Race and Sex," *Southern Exposure*, 4, (1977): 46.

69 Indeed, as historian: Quoted in John Dittmer, *Local People: The Struggle for Civil Rights in Mississippi* (Urbana: University of Illinois Press, 1994), p. 67.

69 "As a Southern woman": Gladney, pp. 119–20.

69 "cannot bear not": Richard King, p. 180.

69 "conflict is inherently": William H. Chafe, *Civilities and Civil Rights: Greensboro, North Carolina, and the Black Struggle for Freedom* (New York: Oxford University Press, 1980), p. 7.

69 "Ralph has a great": Gladney, p. 64.

70 "sex-obsessed": Ibid., p. 191.

70 In his column: Loveland, p. 104.

70 "We know the situation": Ibid., p. 128.

71 "The end": Carolyn Wedin, *Inheritors of the Spirit: Mary White Ovington and the Founding of the NAACP* (New York: Wiley, 1998), p. 290.

71 "austerely beautiful": David Levering Lewis, *W. E. B. Du Bois: Biography of a Race* (New York: Henry Holt, 1993), p. 348.

71 "the high priestess": Wedin, p. 98.

72 "would come about": Lewis, *W. E. B. Du Bois*, p. 349.

72 "He does do": Ibid., p. 483.

73 "Don't blame people": Wedin, p. 266.

73 "place the N.A.A.C.P.": Joanne Grant, *Ella Baker: Freedom Bound* (New York: Wiley, 1998), p. 54.

74 "in the long run": Lerner, p. 347.

74 "getting them comfortable": Interview with Lawrence Guyot.

Chapter 4

76 "As a colored": Mary Church Terrell, *A Colored Woman in a White World* (New York: G. K. Hall, 1996), p. 384.

77 "extremely difficult": Ibid., p. 22.

77 "I am persuaded": Ibid., p. 94.

78 "When my feet": Sterling, *Black Foremothers*, p. 155.

78 "When I was a youngster": Interview with Eleanor Holmes Norton.

79 "While I am grateful": Terrell, p. 427.

80 "He was beyond": Richard Kluger, *Simple Justice: The History of Brown v. Board of Education and Black America's Struggle for Equality* (New York: Knopf, 1976), p. 454.

80 "Then," recalled: Bob Smith, *They Closed Their Schools* (Chapel Hill: University of North Carolina Press, 1965), p. 34.

81 "We hate to impose": Kluger, p. 470.

81 "no less promising": Ibid., p. 471.

82 "Don't let": Ibid., p. 478.

82 "I would speak out": Smith, p. 54 and p. 60.

82 "This schools thing": Adam Fairclough, *To Redeem the Soul of America: The Southern Christian Leadership Conference and Martin Luther King, Jr.* (Athens: University of Georgia Press, 1987), p. 21.

83 In his book: Quoted in Lord, p. 62.

84 "After commenting": Florence Mars, *Witness in Philadelphia* (Baton Rouge: Louisiana State University Press, 1977), pp. 52–53.

84 "In this atmosphere": Quoted in William H. Chafe, "The Civil Rights Revolution, 1945–1960: The Gods Bring Threads to Webs Begun," in Robert H. Bremner and Gary W. Reichard, eds., *Reshaping America: Society and Institutions, 1945–1960* (Columbus: Ohio State University Press, 1982), p. 86.

84 "Apparently a 'moderate'": Carl Rowan, *Go South to Sorrow* (New York: Random House, 1957), p. 206.

84 "There is an increasing": Loveland, p. 80.

85 In January 1955: Ann Waldron, *Hodding Carter: The Reconstruction of a Racist* (Chapel Hill: Algonquin, 1993), p. 241.

85 "a Magna Carta": Lillian Smith to Pauli Murray, 5/27/54, PM.

85 "everything on my writing": Lillian Smith to Pauli Murray, 2/17/56, PM.

86 "the most influential": Mars, p. 71.

86 "Southern people": Robert Sherrill, *Gothic Politics in the Deep South* (New York: Grossman, 1968), p. 211.

Chapter 5

88 "Buses weren't": Richard Willing, "Fame Eluded 2 Women Arrested Before Parks," *The Detroit News*, Dec. 3, 1995.

88 Drivers heaped: Jo Ann Robinson, *The Montgomery Bus Boycott and the Women Who Started It* (Knoxville: University of Tennessee Press, 1987), p. 36.

88 Less than a week: Stewart Burns, ed., *Daybreak of Freedom: The Montgomery Bus Boycott* (Chapel Hill: University of North Carolina Press, 1997), p. 57.

89 "one of the most": Interview with Joe Azbell, PV.

89 "as happy": Robinson, p. 15.

90 "I felt": Ibid., p. xiii.

90 "In all these": Ibid., p. 16.

90 "private guerrilla": Mary Fair Burks, "Trailblazers: Women in the Montgomery Bus Boycott," in Vicki L. Crawford et al., *Women in the Civil Rights Movement:Trailblazers and Torchbearers, 1941–1965* (Brooklyn: Carlson, 1990), p. 76.

91 "said they would": Interview with Tacky Gayle, PV.

92 "the Negroes": Virginia Durr to Clark Foreman et al., 2/24/56, VD.

92 "really hurt": Rosa Parks, *Rosa Parks: My Story* (New York: Dial, 1992), p. 111.

92 "Everyone would": David J. Garrow, *Bearing the Cross: Martin Luther King, Jr., and the Southern Christian Leadership Conference* (New York: Morrow, 1986), p. 14.

92 "outtalk": Ellen Levine, *Freedom's Children* (New York: Putnam, 1993), p. 27.

92 "That's as much": Ibid., p. 22.

93 "No," she said: Burns, p. 6.

93 "Bless her heart": Interview with Irene West, PV.

93 "created tremendous": Quoted in John A. Salmond, *The Conscience of a Lawyer: Clifford J. Durr and American Civil Liberties, 1899–1975* (Tuscaloosa: University of Alabama Press, 1990), p. 174.

94 "I am not": Burns, p. 6.

95 "We weren't": *The Detroit News*, Dec. 3, 1995.

95 "I never cut": Cynthia Stokes Brown, ed., *Ready from Within: Septima Clark and the Civil Rights Movement* (Navarro, Calif.: Wild Trees Press, 1986), p. 16.

95 "I don't know": Parks, p. 30.

96 "What I learned": Ibid., p. 49.

96 "Rosa's schoolmates": Burks, p. 71.

96 "I had an aversion": Parks, p. 55.

97 "Every time": Ibid., p. 69.

98 "Everything possible": Cynthia Stokes Brown, "Close Bonds: The Strength of Three Women," 3, VD.

98 "granddaddy": Johnnie Carr interview by Steven Millner, in David J. Garrow, ed., *The Walking City: The Montgomery Bus Boycott, 1955–56* (Brooklyn: Carlson, 1989), p. 527.

98 "overwhelmed": Parks, p. 94.

98 "I know one thing": Ibid., p. 79.

98 "I had decided": Ibid., p. 112.

99 "I felt": Brown, "Close Bonds," 4, VD.

99 "The woman": Virginia Durr, *Outside the Magic Circle: The Autobiography of Virginia Foster Durr* (Tuscaloosa: University of Alabama Press, 1985), p. xii.

99 "something noble": Ibid., p. 44.

100 "I am not so Freudian": Virginia Durr to Clark Foreman, 11/5/56, VD.

100 "I'm not going to eat": Durr, p. 17.

100 "If you have": Virginia Durr interview, CRDP.

101 "That's why": Quoted in Henry Hampton and Steve Fayer, eds., *Voices of Freedom: An Oral History of the Civil Rights Movement from the 1950s Through the 1980s* (New York: Bantam, 1990), p. 28.

101 "beauty": Eliza Heard (Virginia Durr pseudonym), "The Emancipation of Pure, White, Southern Womanhood," *New South*, winter 1971, p. 51.

101 "so I was rather": Ibid.

101 "be a belle": Virginia Durr interview, SOHP.

101 "He did everything": Durr, p. 47.

102 "[T]he only time": Durr interview, CRDP.

102 "You sweet": Undated newspaper clipping, VD.

102 "[T]hese were ladies'": Durr interview, CRDP.

103 "her insatiable": Jessica Mitford, *Daughters and Rebels* (Boston: Houghton Mifflin, 1960), p. 257.

104 "We could hardly": Virginia Durr to Clark Foreman, 2/15/54, VD.

104 "A vicious": Virginia Durr interview, OHP/LBJ.

104 "I know": Durr, p. 172.

104 "nigger girl": Virginia Durr interview, OHP/LBJ.

105 "This hearing": Virginia Durr statement, VD.

105 "You goddamn": Durr, p. 263.

106 "Why was it you": Virginia Durr interview, CRDP.

106 "I didn't get over": Ibid.

106 "tense, nervous": Brown, *Ready from Within*, p. 17.

106 "We forgot": Parks, pp. 105–6.

107 "A healing presence": Josephine Carson, *Silent Voices: The Southern Negro Woman Today* (New York: Delacorte, 1969), p. 70.

107 "was afraid": Aldon D. Morris, *The Origins of the Civil Rights Movement: Black Communities Organizing for Change* (New York: Free Press, 1984), p. 149.

107 "nothing would": Brown, *Ready from Within*, p. 33.

107 "you had to be": Parks, p. 107.

108 "Let me have": Ibid., p. 115.

108 "People always say": Ibid., p. 116.

108 "I had decided": Radio interview with Sidney Rogers, Pacifica Radio, April 1956, in Burns, p. 84.

108 "Here was an individual": Pauli Murray speech, Nov. 7, 1965, in PM.

109 They hugged: Parks, p. 123.

Chapter 6

110 "Oh, Rosa": Quoted in Giddings, p. 265.

111 "Mrs. Carr": Interview with Johnnie Carr.

111 "I had no": Parks, p. 125.

111 After they talked: Robinson, p. 45.

113 What was going on: Jo Ann Robinson interview by Steven Millner, in Garrow, *The Walking City*, p. 570.

113 When Rosa Parks awoke: Lanker, p. 16.

113 "You mean": Coretta Scott King, *My Life with Martin Luther King, Jr.* (New York: Holt, Rinehart & Winston, 1969), pp. 94–95.

114 "At least": Ralph David Abernathy, *And the Walls Came Tumbling Down* (New York: Harper-Perennial, 1990) p. 126.

114 "were planning": Robinson, p. 53.

114 "didn't pick": Interview with Johnnie Carr.

114 "The maids": Quoted in Hampton, p. 29.

115 "I could feel": Lanker, p. 16.

115 "They've messed": Parks, p. 133.

115 "What the hell": Quoted in Howell Raines, *My Soul Is Rested: The Story of the Civil Rights Movement in the Deep South* (New York: Putnam, 1977), p. 49.

115 "We've worn": Taylor Branch, *Parting the Waters: America in the King Years, 1954–1963* (New York: Simon & Schuster, 1988), p. 136.

116 "out of a sense": Abernathy, p. 150.

116 Rosa Parks: Parks interview by Steven Millner, *The Walking City*, p. 563.

117 Women like Irene West: Josephine Carson, p. 85.

117 When that downpour: Carr interview by Steven Millner, *The Walking City*, 529.

117 "the soldiers": Quoted in Burns, p. 16.

118 "Everybody would": Robinson interview by Steven Millner, *The Walking City*, p. 572.

118 "You're the biggest": Durr, p. 283.

118 Dealy Cooksey: Dealy Cooksey interview, PV.

119 In one of the letters: Robinson, p. 102.

119 "the big buck nigger": Clara Rutledge interview, PV.

120 "are fighting": Ralph Abernathy, "The Natural History of a Social Movement," in *The Walking City*, p. 121.

120 "[T]he white women": Juan Williams, *Eyes on the Prize: America's Civil Rights Years, 1954–1965* (New York: Viking, 1987), p. 85.

120 "Dear Friend": Parks, p. 146.

121 "Sometimes, I'd": E. D. Nixon interview, CRDP.

121 "One feels": Letters to the editor, *The Montgomery Advertiser*, December 12, 1955.

121 From the day: Virginia Durr to Anne Braden, 4/20/59, BP.

122 "You're the cause": Parks, p. 147.

122 One night: Robinson, p. 139.

122 "[I]f we went": MIA executive committee minutes, 1/30/56, PV.

123 "Certainly [King]": Robinson, p. 78.

123 "he's too much": MIA minutes, PV.

124 "I'll tell you": Bus driver interview, PV.

124 "More than any other": Quoted in Burns, p. 15.
124 "Well, really": Irene West interview, PV.
125 "I sense": Donald Ferron to Preston Valien, PV.
125 "Women listened": Erna Dungee Allen interview by Steven Millner, *The Walking City*, p. 522.
125 "[S]omehow": Belinda Robnett, *How Long? How Long?: African-American Women in the Struggle for Civil Rights* (New York: Oxford University Press, 1997), p. 59.
125 "made a great show": Parks, p. 157.
126 "He didn't want": Ibid., p. 158.
126 "if the man": Irene West interview, Oral History Collection, Martin Luther King, Jr., Library.
126 "What could they": Joe Azbell interview, PV.
126 "I'll never forget": Fred Powledge, *Free at Last? The Civil Rights Movement and the People Who Made It* (Boston: Little, Brown, 1991), pp. 90–91.
127 "If anybody": Fairclough, p. 26.
127 "King has": Virginia Durr to Clark Foreman, 2/15/57, VD.
127 "Our leaders": Burns, p. 5.
127 "You help": Letters to editor, Tuscaloosa *News*, 1/14/57.
128 "really made them": Virginia Durr to Clark Foreman, 7/22/57, VD.
128 A week later: Virginia Durr to Anne Braden, 4/20/59, BP.
128 "Mrs. Durr": Durr, p. 270.
128 "I am not a lonely": Virginia Durr to Clark Foreman, undated, VD.
129 "To be a heroine": Virginia Durr to Clark Foreman, undated, VD.
129 "blazing row": Virginia Durr to Clark Foreman, 2/15/57, VD.
129 "to take me apart": Parks, p. 153.
130 "in the shuffle": Chester Higgins column, Pittsburgh *Courier*, August 31, 1957.
130 "tracked down": Martin Luther King, Jr., *Stride Toward Freedom: The Montgomery Story* (New York: Harper, 1958), p. 29.
130 "We talked": Quoted in Grace Jordan McFadden, "Septima P. Clark and the Struggle for Human Rights," in Crawford, p. 93.
130 "If Mrs. Parks": Raines, p. 51.
131 "Everybody": Robinson interview with Stephen Millner, *The Walking City*, p. 573.
131 "The black women": Robinson, p. xv.
131 "[A] trailblazer": Burks, in Crawford, p. 71.

Chapter 7

133 "a complete": Ella Baker interview, CRDP.
133 "These were women": Grant, p. 108.
133 "[H]is rationale": Baker interview, CRDP.
134 "There was some talk": Daisy Bates, *The Long Shadow of Little Rock* (New York: David McKay, 1962), p. 15.
134 "Stop staring": Ibid., p. 17.
135 "Don't hate": Ibid., p. 29.
136 "There were times": Harry Ashmore, *Hearts and Minds: A Personal Chronicle of Race in America* (Cabin John, Md.: Seven Locks Press, 1988), p. 275.
137 "you'll be destroyed": Bates, p. 170.
137 "[J]ust as a": Pauli Murray to Spingarn Award committee, 5/30/58, PM.
138 "During these hectic": Daisy Bates to Pauli Murray, 11/21/62, PM.
138 "superstars": Jervis Anderson, *Bayard Rustin: Troubles I've Seen* (New York: HarperCollins, 1997), p. 198.
138 Greatly disturbed: Branch, *Parting the Waters*, p. 232.
139 Rustin and Levison: Baker interview, CRDP.
139 "Grandma had": Ella Baker interview in *Fundi: The Story of Ella Baker*, television documentary produced by Joanne Grant, 1981.
139 "Where we lived": Ellen Cantarow, *Moving the Mountain: Women Working for Social Change* (Old Westbury, N.Y.: Feminist Press, 1980), p. 60.
140 "[W]herever there": Ibid., p. 64.
141 "You are overstepping": Grant, p. 65.
141 "I never considered": Ibid., p. 40.
141 "I have always": Mary King, *Freedom Song: A Personal History of the 1960s Civil Rights Movement* (New York: Morrow, 1987), p. 455.

141 "shared much": James H. Cone, *Martin and Malcolm and America* (Maryknoll, N.Y.: Orbis, 1991), p. 274.
141 "Equality of women": Interview with Lawrence Guyot.
141 "Men stood": Darlene Clark Hine and Kathleen Thompson, *A Shining Thread of Hope: History of Black Women in America* (New York: Broadway, 1998), p. 185.
142 "If Baptist": Interview with Lawrence Guyot.
142 "[T]he telling": Jacquelyn Grant, "Black Women and the Church," in Gloria T. Hull et al., eds., *All the Women Are White, All the Blacks Are Men, But Some of Us Are Brave* (Old Westbury, N.Y.: Feminist Press, 1982), p. 141.
142 "The dominant": Cone, p. 276.
142 "The Negro man": Quoted in ibid., p. 277.
142 "had a hard time": Quoted in Giddings, p. 313.
142 "My father": Andrew Young, *An Easy Burden: The Civil Rights Movement and the Transformation of America* (New York: HarperCollins, 1996), p. 16.
143 "[T]hey all set": Mary King, p. 11.
143 "I want my wife": Coretta Scott King, p. 88.
143 "Martin . . . was": Garrow, *Bearing the Cross*, pp. 375–76.
143 "All of the churches": Quoted in Charles M. Payne, *I've Got the Light of Freedom: The Organizing Tradition and the Mississippi Freedom Struggle* (Berkeley: University of California Press, 1995), p. 92.
144 "we are losing": Quoted in Garrow, *Bearing the Cross*, p. 107.
144 "because a person is called": Lerner, p. 351.
145 "everything depended": Fairclough, p. 50.
145 "when the flowery": Quoted in Garrow, *Bearing the Cross*, p. 116.
145 "I wasn't an easy pushover": Ella Baker interview in *Fundi*.
145 "Ella Baker": Quoted in Anderson, p. 200.
145 "She always felt": Coretta Scott King, p. 142.
146 "This is the creative": Garrow, *Bearing the Cross*, p. 124.
147 Among them were whites: Chafe, *Civilities*, p. 118.
147 By contrast: Ibid., p. 111.
149 "As you began": Hampton, p. 65.
149 "They were most confident": Cantarow, p. 160.
149 "She didn't say": Hampton, p. 63.
149 "[S]he was concerned": Septima Clark interview, SOHP.
150 "kept daring us": Milton Viorst, *Fire in the Streets: America in the 1960s* (New York: Simon & Schuster, 1979), p. 120.
150 "our personal Gandhi": John Lewis interview, CRDP.
150 "there would be no story": James Forman, *The Making of Black Revolutionaries* (Seattle: University of Washington Press, 1997), p. 215.
150 Interview with Kwame Ture (Stokely Carmichael).

Chapter 8
151 "the humble role": Quoted in Giddings, p. 243.
152 "[O]ver and above": Cynthia Griggs Fleming, *Soon We Will Not Cry: The Liberation of Ruby Doris Smith Robinson* (Lanham, Md.: Rowman & Littlefield, 1998), p. 51.
152 "The first thing": John Lewis, *Walking with the Wind: A Memoir of the Movement* (Simon & Schuster, 1998), p. 91.
153 "Ah, Diane": Interview with Kwame Ture (Stokely Carmichael).
153 In the pageant's: David Halberstam, *The Children* (New York: Random House, 1998), p. 145.
153 "a woman": Chafe, *Women*, p. 15.
154 In a 1960 article: Lerone Bennett, "The Negro Woman," *Ebony*, August 1960, p. 40.
154 "stifled and boxed in": Mathew H. Ahmann, ed., *The New Negro* (Notre Dame: Fides, 1961), p. 45.
154 "the children": Guy and Candie Carawan, *Sing for Freedom: The Story of the Civil Rights Movement Through Its Songs* (Bethlehem, Pa.: Sing Out Corp., 1990), p. 18.
155 "this stuff": Powledge, p. 208.
155 "suddenly proud": Ahmann, p. 49.
155 "Plenty of fellows": John Lewis, p. 92.
155 "came to be seen": Ibid.

156 "some dreadful monster": Ahmann, p. 47.
156 "Because she was": Halberstam, p. 143.
156 "This is Tennessee": Powledge, pp. 208–9.
158 "We feel": John Lewis, p. 110.
159 "He was making": Powledge, p. 209.
159 "They asked me": Williams, p. 139.
160 "That's Diane Nash": Powledge, p. 209.
160 "The Chaucer classes": Ibid., p. 262.
160 "I'll be doing": "Diane Nash a Cog in Freedom Ride Move," *Jet*, June 29, 1961, p. 49.
160 "Diane was a devoted": Harry S. Jaffee and Tom Sherwood, *Dream City: Race, Power and the Decline of Washington, D.C.* (New York: Simon & Schuster, 1994), p. 38.
161 "Before the women's movement": Robnett, p. 101.
161 "important to our community": Ibid., p. 43.
161 "very nurturing": Cheryl Lynn Greenberg, ed., *A Circle of Trust: Remembering SNCC* (New Brunswick: Rutgers University Press, 1998), p. 134.
162 "There was a time": Remarks by Casey Hayden, Southern Historical Association, Atlanta, 11/8/97.

Chapter 9
163 "The truth is": Lee Graham, "Who's in Charge Here? Not Women!" *The New York Times Magazine*, September 2, 1962, p. 8.
164 "the country's most hated": "In the Same Boat," *Ebony*, October 1962, p. 72.
164 "American politics": Wini Breines, *Young, White, and Miserable: Growing Up Female in the Fifties* (Boston: Beacon Press, 1992), p. 10.
164 "There has been a tendency": *The New York Times Magazine*, September 2, 1962, p. 8.
165 "The parameters": Breines, p. 166.
165 "the southern lady": Quoted in Wolfe, p. 83.
165 "What's wrong": Hodding Carter, "Yes, Tennessee, There Are Southern Belles," *The New York Times Magazine*, October 7, 1962, p. 33 and p. 93.
166 "race traitors": Remarks by Barbara Ransby, Southern Historical Association, 11/8/97.
166 "I came here": Jane Stembridge to David Forbes, 8/14/60, SNCC.
167 "I fit exactly": Stembridge, "Some Notes on Education," undated, SNCC.
167 "We were a finishing": Interview with Connie Curry.
168 "Connie was": Constance Curry, "Wild Geese to the Past," in Constance Curry et al., *Deep in Our Hearts: Nine White Women in the Freedom Movement* (Athens: University of Georgia Press, 2000), p. 25.
168 "outrageously racy": Mary King, p. 62.
169 "a lay seminary": Interview with Casey Hayden.
170 "introduced to": Ibid.
171 "I idolized her": Tom Hayden, *Reunion: A Memoir* (New York: Random House, 1988), p. 42.
171 "on a fuller level": Ibid., pp. 39–40.
171 "We need a fresh": Gladney, pp. 209–10.
172 "what I mostly did": Interview with Jane Stembridge.
172 "yearning": Remarks by Connie Curry, Southern Historical Association, 11/8/97.
172 "We of the older": Loveland, p. 214.
173 "corpse": Anne Braden, *The Wall Between* (New York: Monthly Review Press, 1958), p. 229.
173 "You never call": Ibid., p. 21.
173 "I was so": Anne Braden to Greta (no last name), 6/2/63, BP.
173 "[t]he whole idea": Anne Braden interview, CRDP.
174 "my parents": Interview with Anne Braden.
174 "Come on": Braden, p. 29.
175 "was off somewhere": Anne Braden to Greta, 6/2/63, BP.
175 "[W]e never": "Church Leader in Kentucky Indicted for Sedition," *The Witness*, February 17, 1955.
177 "What had": Braden, 219–20.
179 "*Any* white": Anne Braden to CORE officials, 5/12/60, BP.
179 "Like the scream": Black, p. 119.
179 "means defending": Anne Braden to Ella Baker, 7/1/62, BP.
180 "[I]f it had not been": Morris, p. 171.
180 "We did that": Interview with Anne Braden.

180 "There are no adjectives": Interview with Jane Stembridge.
180 "I always considered": Sara Evans, *Personal Politics: The Roots of Women's Liberation in the Civil Rights Movement and the New Left* (New York: Knopf, 1979), p. 50.
181 "I squeeze": Ibid., p. 49.
181 "[c]onflicts": Anne Braden to Ella Baker, 7/1/62, BP.
181 "She would take": Interview with Jane Stembridge.

Chapter 10

183 On May 4: Branch, p. 413.
183 "They . . . just": Stanley Cloud and Lynne Olson, *The Murrow Boys* (Boston: Houghton Mifflin, 1996), p. 345.
184 "She's going to keep": Branch, p. 424.
184 "Well, we realize": Interview with James Farmer.
185 "You know Diane Nash": John Seigenthaler interview, CRDP.
185 "We'll be back": Halberstam, p. 295.
186 "I don't think": Harris Wofford, *Of Kennedys and Kings: Making Sense of the Sixties* (New York: Farrar, Straus & Giroux, 1980), p. 153.
187 At that moment: John Seigenthaler interview, CRDP.
187 "absolute, stark": Virginia Durr interview, SOHP.
188 Instead, she thought: Halberstam, pp. 328–29.
188 "Don't you think": Farmer, p. 205.
189 "Do not tell me": Halberstam, p. 273.
189 "I was scared": Interview with James Farmer.
189 "unbelievably horrible": John Lewis, p. 169.
189 "But, Jim": Interview with James Farmer.
190 "I guess": Ibid.
190 At first: Halberstam, p. 341.
191 In the beginning: Fleming, p. 86.
191 "The jailhouse": Farmer, p. 10.
192 "where they just": David M. Oshinsky, *"Worse Than Slavery": Parchman Farm and the Ordeal of Jim Crow Justice* (New York: Free Press, 1996), p. 229.
192 Once, as Elizabeth: Howard Zinn, *SNCC: The New Abolitionists* (Boston: Beacon Press, 1965), p. 55.
192 "instant converts": Joan Trumpauer Mulholland remarks, Tougaloo College civil rights symposium, undated.
193 Riders like Judy Frieze: Seth Cagin and Philip Dray, *We Are Not Afraid* (New York: Macmillan, 1988), p. 127.
193 "Before I left": Carawan, p. 55.
193 "Jails were not": Interview with James Farmer.
194 "the most wonderful": Black, p. 127.
194 "There were a lot": Pete Seeger and Bob Reiser, *Everybody Says Freedom* (New York: Norton, 1989), p. 65.
195 "are challenging": Branch, p. 478.
195 "I'm interested": Ahmann, p. 57.
195 "Here are people": Ibid., p. 56.
196 "I became terrified": Diane Nash remarks, Mississippi Community Foundation History Workshop, McComb, Mississippi, 1991.
196 "really scared me": Nash remarks, MCF History Workshop.
197 "I was taken seriously": Robnett, p. 102.
197 "I was the only female": Nash remarks, MCF History Workshop.
198 "went into": Cantarow, p. 87.
198 "Diane and the rest": Interview with Anne Braden.
198 "Ella reached out": Charles Jones remarks, MCF History Workshop.
198 "young people": Cagin, p. 306.
199 "morally difficult": Powledge, p. 370.

Chapter 11

202 "[T]he brunt": Hampton, p. 132.
202 "is not only prevented": Quoted in Payne, p. 269.
202 "My mom": Interview with Jacqueline Byrd Martin.

202 "We felt": Jacqueline Byrd Martin remarks, MCF History Workshop.
203 "Well, you can": Brenda Travis interview with Phil Alden Robinson.
203 Ruby Divens: Remarks by Ruby Divens, MCF History Workshop.
203 "I always knew": Interview with Jessie Divens.
203 "We would have followed": Interview with Jacqueline Byrd Martin.
203 "I'm Jessie": Interview with Jessie Divens.
203 "I just": Ruby Divens remarks, MCF History Workshop.
204 "Those women": Interview with Jacqueline Byrd Martin.
204 "Violence is a fearful": Seeger, p. 87.
204 "I think the women": Interview with Ivanhoe Donaldson.
204 "You could see": Interview with Fred Powledge.
205 "I seen": Remarks by Aylene Quinn, MCF History Workshop.
206 "To be honest": Remarks by Brenda Travis, MCF History Workshop.
207 "The teachers said": Remarks by Annie Pickett Harris, MCF History Workshop.
207 "something totally unknown": Interview with Jacqueline Byrd Martin.
208 "We have to direct": Remarks by Chuck McDew, MCF History Workshop.
208 "Grace, we": Remarks by Annie Pickett Harris, MCF History Workshop.
209 "a big star": Remarks by Caroline Quinn, MCF History Workshop.
209 "I was terrified": Interview with Willie Martin McClintock.
209 "I paid my money": Interview with Jessie Divens.
209 The defiance: SNCC report on Divens arrest, undated, SNCC.
210 "They kept asking": Interview with Jessie Divens.
210 "children reared": Ibid.
211 "Diane and *Bevel*": Halberstam, p. 399.
211 "Bevel's a genius": Interview with Ivanhoe Donaldson.
212 "As I think": Anne Braden to James Bevel, 5/10/63, BP.
212 "Judge Moore": Taylor Branch, *Pillar of Fire: America in the King Years, 1963–1965* (New York: Simon & Schuster, 1998), p. 56.

Chapter 12
214 "the government": Morris, p. 238.
214 "people would speak": Seeger, p. 120.
214 "two or three": Powledge, p. 473.
215 "freed those people": Interview with Victoria Gray Adams.
215 "[S]he wanted you": Brown, *Ready from Within*, p. 96.
215 "Being in a white": Josephine Carson, p. 17.
217 "I'd put the books": Tinsley E. Yarbrough, *A Passion for Justice: J. Waties Waring and Civil Rights* (New York: Oxford University Press, 1987), p. 53.
219 "She said she didn't": Brown, *Ready from Within*, p. 29.
220 "They asked": Ibid., p. 60.
221 "I'm really": "Cynthia Stokes Brown, 'Close Bonds,'" 17, VD.
222 "Here you are": Septima Clark interview, SOHP.
222 "develop leaders": Brown, *Ready from Within*, p. 78.
222 "Those men": Ibid., p. 77.
222 "He was not aware": Young, p. 139.
222 In a letter: Robnett, p. 95.
223 "[W]hen he gets": Josephine Carson, p. 94.
223 "the work is": Septima Clark to Martin Luther King, Jr., undated, SCLC.
223 "I believe": Anne Braden to Septima Clark, 6/15/61, BP.
224 "From one end": Brown, *Ready from Within*, p. 70.

Chapter 13
225 "[W]e would say": Williams, p. 164.
225 "perhaps the richest": W. E. B. Du Bois, *The Souls of Black Folk* (New York: Library of America, 1980), p. 76.
226 Men raced: Dick Cluster, ed., *They Should Have Served That Cup of Coffee* (Boston: South End Press, 1979), p. 12.
227 "It was like": Ibid., p. 17.
227 "Get out": Bernice Johnson Reagon, "My Black Mothers and Sisters or on Beginning a Cultural Autobiography," *Feminist Studies*, spring 1982, p. 91.

227 "Nothing like": Cluster, p. 17.
228 "I could walk": Interview with Joan Browning.
229 "I went to a black": Ibid.
229 Walking out: Branch, *Parting the Waters*, p. 534.
230 "Being alone": Interview with Joan Browning.
230 "It was just like": Ibid.
231 "Instead of people": Ibid.
231 "I do feel": Bernice Johnson statement, undated, SNCC.
231 "the police officer": Brenda Boone statement, undated, SNCC.
231 "That is just": Annie Sue Herrin statement, undated, SNCC.
232 "I have never been": Vincent Harding, "Community as a Liberating Theme in Civil Rights History," in *New Directions in Civil Rights Studies*, Armstead L. Robinson and Patricia Sullivan, eds. (Charlottesville: University Press of Virginia, 1991), p. 22.
232 "Such music": Pat Watters, *Down to Now: Reflections on the Southern Civil Rights Movement* (Athens: University of Georgia Press, 1993), p. 180.
233 "Ordinarily": Cluster, p. 19.
233 "They were saying": Alexis DeVeaux, "Bernice Reagon," *Essence*, June 1980, p. 142.
233 "I was given": Greenberg, p. 115.
233 "I had never": Williams, p. 177.
233 Bertha Gober: Carawan, p. 64.
234 "With a song": Hampton, p. 108.
235 "The civil rights revolt": Pauli Murray, "The Negro Woman in the Quest for Equality," PM.
235 "mov[ing] silently": Howard Zinn, *The Southern Mystique* (New York: Knopf, 1964), p. 162.
236 "There are three": Interview with Karl Fleming.
236 "the way crossing guards": Abernathy, p. 226.
236 "A devastating loss": Branch, *Parting the Waters*, p. 557.
237 "resisted the movement": Watters, p. 146.
237 When I read": Cluster, p. 22.
237 Johnson's passion: "Bernice Reagon," *Essence*, June 1980, p. 93.

Chapter 14

240 "We want": "Students Challenge Rural Georgia," *The Southern Patriot*, December 1962, p. 1.
240 "white people": Powledge, p. 347.
240 "How could": Penny Patch, "Sweet Tea at Shoney's," in Curry et al., *Deep in Our Hearts*, p. 137.
241 "I was not": Interview with Penny Patch.
241 "Here was evil": Ibid.
241 "All my life": Interview with Peggy Dammond Day, CRDP.
241 "felt a sense": Ibid.
242 "I would see": Patch, in Curry et al., *Deep in Our Hearts*, p. 143.
242 "What are you": "White Girl in a Mire of Hate," *New York World-Telegram*, August 4, 1962, p. 1.
243 "a gray-haired old lady": Quoted in Giddings, p. 284.
243 "I learned a lot": Patch, in Curry et al., *Deep in Our Hearts*, p. 152
243 "I was never": Ibid.
243 "I think they always": Interview with Penny Patch.
244 "[W]henever we were": Interview with Peggy Dammond Day, CRDP.
244 "I referred": Zinn, *SNCC*, pp. 137–38.
244 "We are confronting": Patch, in Curry et al., *Deep in Our Hearts*, p. 148.
245 "did not unnerve": Greenberg, p. 60.
245 When Faith: 1963 SNCC press release, SNCC.
245 "They were a wonderful": Interview with Penny Patch.
245 "I almost feel": SNCC field report, 3/9/63, p. 3, SNCC.
246 "found one": SNCC field report, 2/19/63, SNCC.
246 "Sing, Dear": SNCC field report, 5/13–26/63, SNCC.
246 "Every member": Patch, in Curry et al., *Deep in Our Hearts*, p. 149.
246 "I could not": Warren Fortson comments, "Americus Movement" symposium, Albany State College, Albany, Ga.
247 "beautiful teenage girls": Danny Lyon, *Memories of the Southern Civil Rights Movement* (Chapel Hill: University of North Carolina Press, 1992), p. 80.

Chapter 15

249 "We gonna": Cagin, p. 183.

249 "I sat there": Tracy Sugarman, *Stranger at the Gates: A Summer in Mississippi* (New York: Hill & Wang, 1967), p. 212.

250 In Ruleville: James Bevel field report to SCLC, Jan.–Feb. 1963, SCLC.

250 "All my life": Victoria Gray Adams interview, *Freedom on My Mind*, documentary.

250 "The Hattiesburg movement": Interview with Victoria Gray Adams.

251 "Who's the people": Kay Mills, *This Little Light of Mine: The Life of Fannie Lou Hamer* (New York: Dutton, 1993), p. 48.

251 "I sure do hope": Unita Blackwell interview, CRDP.

251 "Hey, if she took": Interview with Ivanhoe Donaldson.

251 "You'd come": Interview with Kwame Ture (Stokely Carmichael).

251 "I'm reminded": Cluster, p. 31.

252 "trying to bust": Matt Suarez interview, CRDP.

252 "There wouldn't": Tom Dent, "Annie Devine Remembers," *Freedomways*, 1982, p. 82.

252 "[I]f you're going": John Lewis, p. 238.

253 "worse than hard": Phyl Garland, "Builders of a New South," *Ebony*, August 1966, p. 28.

253 "He didn't have": Mills, p. 22.

254 "Just listenin' at 'em": Raines, p. 249.

254 "facto laws": Mills, p. 37.

255 "If SNCC hadn't of come": Fannie Lou Hamer interview with Anne and Howard Romaine, RP.

255 "If I get to heaven": Zinn, *SNCC*, p. 196.

255 "Fannie Lou": Mills, p. 300.

255 "She was an unbelievably": Interview with Eleanor Holmes Norton.

255 "[Y]ou've never": Mills, p. 85.

255 "I'm right pleased": Sugarman, p. 120.

256 "She is the type": Payne, p. 215.

256 In the 1950s: Ibid.

257 "But that's": Interview with Bob Zellner.

258 "For the first time": Endesha Ida Mae Holland interview, *Freedom on My Mind*.

258 "take us": Endesha Ida Mae Holland, *From the Mississippi Delta* (New York: Simon & Schuster, 1997), p. 90.

259 "like a gentleman": Ibid., p. 208.

259 "My fun": June Johnson interview by Phil Alden Robinson.

261 "I been hearing": Dittmer, pp. 170–71.

261 "I didn't have": Harvard Sitkoff, *Struggle for Black Equality, 1954–1980* (New York: Hill & Wang, 1981), p. 112.

261 "Can't you say": Fannie Lou Hamer interview, CRDP.

261 "[B]efore they stopped": Raines, p. 253.

262 "there would be": Interview with Eleanor Holmes Norton.

262 "Those are women": Young, p. 254.

263 "We wondered": Quoted in Mills, p. 70.

Chapter 16

265 "SNCC was truly": Interview with Lawrence Guyot.

265 "People had titles": Greenberg, p. 137.

265 "We came": Ibid., p. 140.

266 "ignorant whites": Joyce Ladner, "Return to the Source," *Essence*, June 1977, p. 127.

266 "When we got": Greenberg, p. 143.

266 "All these folks": Interview with Fred Powledge.

266 "If you wanted": Robnett, pp. 39–40.

267 "That was the red": Interview with Chuck McDew.

267 "That is what": Interview with Karl Fleming.

267 "I was a white woman": Robnett, p. 124.

268 "particularly rambling": Tom Hayden, p. 107.

268 "a chauvinist's paradise": Ibid.

268 "Everybody always talked": Dorothy Miller interview, CRDP.

269 "a powerful and traumatic": Mary King, p. 251.

269 "We were on [blacks'] turf": Interview with Casey Hayden.

269 "gave me a sense": Mary King, p. 229.

270 "enormously supportive book": Interview with Casey Hayden.
270 "How can you not": Ibid.
270 "wasn't something": Interview with Ivanhoe Donaldson.
270 "I didn't want": Greenberg, p. 145.
271 "created a lot of stress": Interview with Ivanhoe Donaldson.
271 "quite patriarchal": Interview with Penny Patch.
271 "Where are you": Martha Prescod interview, OH/CU.
271 "wanted to keep us": Greenberg, p. 138.
271 "Women, like Negroes": Anne Braden to unknown, 2/6/62, BP.
272 "My feminist blood": Anne Braden to Joan Browning, 3/13/63, BP.
272 "I don't think": Interview with Chuck McDew.
272 "What sustained us": Mary King, p. 74.
272 "[the movement] was everything": Ibid., p. 8.
272 "a lot of loving": Interview with Bob Zellner.
272 "We were twenty": Greenberg, p. 137.
273 "We were young": Patch, in Curry et al., *Deep in Our Hearts*, p. 155.
273 "totally entranced": Interview with Penny Patch.
273 "Twentieth-century cowboys": Staughton Lynd speech, "Feminism for Men," Youngstown State University, 3/20/98.
273 "We were": Seeger, p. 88.
273 "instant access": Fleming, pp. 135–36.
273 "[I]n a town": Raines, p. 240.
274 "We prided ourselves": Interview with Casey Hayden.
274 "without ever knowing": Roger Wilkins, *A Man's Life: An Autobiography* (New York: Simon & Schuster, 1982), pp. 57–58.
274 "We used to talk": Interview with Chuck McDew.
274 "I hear from numerous": Virginia Durr to Clark Foreman, 8/5/63, VD.
275 "Sex, enjoying": Fleming, p. 102.
275 "If you were lucky": Mary King, p. 406.
275 "sexual power games": Fleming, p. 97.
275 "get in bed": Interview with white SNCC activist.
275 "Anybody that comes": Fleming, p. 134.
275 "some antagonism": Dorothy Miller interview, CRDP.
276 "The SNCC guys": Interview with Casey Hayden.

Chapter 17

279 Richardson came: Annette K. Brock, "Gloria Richardson and the Cambridge Movement," in Crawford, *Women in the Civil Rights Movement*, p. 122.
279 The forty-year-old: Robnett, p. 112.
281 "She is a stranger": Murray Kempton, "Gloria, Gloria," *The New Republic*, November 16, 1963, p. 16.
282 "wanted things": Gloria Richardson interview, CRDP.
283 In the two weeks: Branch, *Pillar of Fire*, p. 87.
283 "The March": Thomas Gentile, *March on Washington: August 28, 1963* (Washington: New Day, 1983), p. 42.
284 She was outraged: Anna Arnold Hedgeman, *The Trumpet Sounds* (New York: Holt, Rinehart & Winston, 1964), p. 178.
285 "In light of": Ibid., p. 179.
285 "No one can": Ibid., p. 180.
285 "without causing": Gentile, p. 140.
286 "What does it profit": Pauli Murray, "Chuck, Aunt Thomasina and the Negro Revolution," 7/30/63, PM.
286 "objects of ridicule": Murray, *Song*, p. 183.
286 "Therefore": Michele Burgen, "Rev. Dr. Pauli Murray," *Ebony*, September 1979, p. 108.
286 "The fact that": Murray, *Song*, 240.
286 "In the process": Pauli Murray interview, SOHP.
287 "I could not evade": Casey Miller and Kate Swift, "Pauli Murray," *Ms.*, March 1980, p. 64.
287 "Negro women": Pauli Murray, "Negro Woman in the Quest for Equality," PM.
287 "It was one": Nan Robertson, *The Girls in the Balcony: Men, Women and the New York Times* (New York: Random House, 1992), p. 99.

287 Susanna McBee: Kay Mills, *A Place in the News: From the Women's Pages to the Front Page* (New York: Dodd, Mead, 1988), p. 95.
288 "It is ludicrous": "Newswomen Hit Press Club 'Bias,'" *The Washington Post*, Aug. 22, 1963.
288 "can only be": Pauli Murray to A. Philip Randolph, 8/21/63, PM.
288 "Those of us": Parks, p. 166.
289 "It was the nearest": Murray, *Song*, pp. 353–54.
289 "The general feeling": Gentile, p. 76.
289 "part picnic": Editorial, *The Washington Post*, August 29, 1963.
289 "Those red hills": Alice Walker, "Choosing to Stay at Home," in *In Search of Our Mothers' Gardens* (San Diego: Harcourt Brace Jovanovich, 1983), p. 160.
290 "made the black revolt": Quoted in Gentile, p. 250.
290 "A thing of beauty": Cleveland Sellers, *The River of No Return: Autobiography of a Black Militant and the Life and Death of SNCC* (New York: Morrow, 1973), p. 66.
290 "Certainly": "Marcher from Alabama," *The New York Times*, August 29, 1963, p. 17.

Chapter 18
292 "[I]t is not possible": Dittmer, p. 199.
292 "enduring a Valley Forge": Nicholas von Hoffman, *Mississippi Notebook* (New York: D. White, 1964), p. 14.
292 At first, Moses: Interview with Jane Stembridge.
292 "severe, albeit": Jane Stembridge to Anne Braden, 11/12/63, BP.
292 "With all the forces": Jane Stembridge to Mary King, 11/20/63, SNCC.
293 "We decided": Interview with Ed King.
293 "We wanted": Hampton, p. 192.
293 But according to Ed King: Interview with Ed King.
294 "happening because": Patch, in Curry et al., *Deep in Our Hearts*, p. 147.
294 "to get out": Bob Moses interview by Anne Romaine, RP.
294 "We were always": Interview with Kwame Ture (Stokely Carmichael).
294 "We don't want": Willie Peacock field report, 1/15/64, SNCC.
294 "very pragmatic": Quoted in Dittmer, p. 219.
294 "You can't tell": Ibid., p. 209.
295 "I was not part": Interview with Victoria Gray Adams.
295 "serious anti-white sentiment": Patch, in Curry et al., *Deep in Our Hearts*, p. 154
295 "centuries of degradation": Ibid., p. 155.
296 "She swept us up": Interview with Heather Tobis Booth.
296 "[T]hey all wanted": Hampton, pp. 185–86.
296 "It seemed back then": Mary Aickin Rothschild, "White Women Volunteers in the Freedom Summers: Their Life and Work in a Movement for Social Change," *Feminist Studies*, fall 1979, p. 477.
296 "In general": SNCC memo, 5/22/64, SNCC.
297 Then a strong, deep: Sally Belfrage, *Freedom Summer* (New York: Viking, 1965), p. 3.
297 "The white man": Ibid., p. 7.
298 "took great pleasure": Lewis, p. 250.
298 "was their life sentence": Belfrage, p. 80.
298 "And this raised": Ibid.
298 "They're only alike": Sugarman, p. 18.
299 "I would have": Chude Pamela Allen interview, *Freedom on My Mind*.
299 "the stark terror": Raines, p. 258.
300 "Don't you know": Interview with Heather Tobis Booth.
301 "[I]t was several": Jan Handke interview, OH/USM.
301 "I was frightened": Interview with Heather Tobis Booth.
301 "My house": Raines, pp. 279–80.
301 "was that she": Linda Seese, to "Dear Friends," 11/18/65, SHSW.
301 "thought I had": Annie Mae King interview, CRDP.
302 "We had been warned": Elizabeth Sutherland, *Letters from Mississippi* (New York: McGraw-Hill, 1965), pp. 42–43.
302 "This is Nancy": Ibid., p. 48.
302 "dusty, hot": Irene Paull essay, SNCC.
302 "like she was": Endesha Ida Mae Holland interview, *Freedom on My Mind*.
303 "I remember cooking": Hampton, p. 193.

303   "almost knock-down": Fleming, p. 171.

303   "We've been getting": Alvin F. Poussaint, M.D., "The Stresses of the White Female Worker in the Civil Rights Movement in the South," *American Journal of Psychiatry*, October 1966, p. 403.

304   "I always felt": Curtis Hayes interview, *Freedom on My Mind*.

304   "completely unorganized": Sutherland, p. 202.

304   "There was very much": Doug McAdam, *Freedom Summer* (New York: Oxford University Press, 1988), p. 110.

305   "feminist consciousness": Interview with Casey Hayden.

305   "we were the": McAdam, p. 111.

305   One male volunteer: Sutherland, p. 163.

305   "the vilest type": Poussaint, p. 401.

305   "They act": Sugarman, p. 113.

306   "The white girls": Poussaint, p. 403.

306   "To this day": Interview with Penny Patch.

306   "widespread phenomenon": Evans, pp. 79–80.

307   "I can't even": Quoted in Dittmer, p. 263.

307   "kind of [a] manic": McAdam, p. 94.

307   "The theme of sexual": Ibid., p. 93.

307   "[S]leeping with black men": Rothschild, p. 481.

308   "white women sitting": Curtis Hayes interview, *Freedom on My Mind*.

308   "Whenever I'm around": Poussaint, p. 403.

308   "black males were feeling": Interview with Casey Hayden.

308   "If you didn't [have sex]": McAdam, p. 105.

308   "There've been things": Susie Erenrich, ed., *Freedom Is a Constant Struggle: An Anthology of the Mississippi Civil Rights Movement* (Montgomery: Black Belt Press, 1999), p. 502.

309   "Sex is one thing": Paul Jacobs and Saul Landau, *The New Radicals* (New York: Vintage, 1966), p. 145.

309   "We were all there": Martha Prescod Norman, "Shining in the Dark: Black Women and the Struggle for the Vote, 1955–1965," in Gordon, p. 187.

310   "one of the roughest": Interview with Kwame Ture (Stokely Carmichael).

310   "wasn't much fun": Quoted in Evans, p. 238.

310   "out in the streets": Ibid., p. 81.

311   "For sisters": Quoted in Midge Wilson and Kathy Russell, *Divided Sisters: Bridging the Gap Between Black Women and White Women* (New York: Anchor, 1996), p. 129.

311   "Many white women": Ibid., p. 79.

311   "know that they are devalued": Gloria Wade-Gayles, *No Crystal Stair: Visions of Race and Sex in Black Women's Fiction* (New York: Pilgrim, 1984), p. 232.

311   "I spent three years": Josephine Carson, pp. 254–55.

312   "Black women have": Toni Morrison, "What the Black Woman Thinks About Women's Lib," *The New York Times Magazine*, August 22, 1971, p. 64.

312   "they'd probably be": Quoted in Evans, p. 238.

312   "just didn't get it": Interview with Casey Hayden.

312   "Times had changed": Patch, in Curry et al., *Deep in Our Hearts*, p. 160.

Chapter 19

314   "why it was": Liz Fusco, "Deeper than Politics," *Liberation*, November 1964, p. 18.

315   "I came to the movement": Interview with Lawrence Guyot.

315   "Sometimes it seems": Mills, p. 91.

317   "spirit, consciousness": Robert Moses et al., "The Algebra Project: Organizing in the Spirit of Ella," *Harvard Educational Review*, November 1989, p. 424.

317   "It is important": Grant, p. 164.

317   "We . . . were flung": Belfrage, p. 237.

318   "If we mess": Branch, *Pillar of Fire*, p. 448.

319   "All of this": Mills, pp. 120–21.

319   "saw her": Charles Marsh, *God's Long Summer: Stories of Faith and Civil Rights* (Princeton: Princeton University Press, 1997), p. 38.

319   "Mrs. Hamer had": Unita Blackwell interview, OH/USM.

320   "Senator Humphrey": Ed King interview by Anne Romaine, RP.

320   "that illiterate woman": Ibid.

320 "I'm not going": Fannie Lou Hamer interview by Anne and Howard Romaine, RP.

320 "white man": "Life in Mississippi," *Freedomways*, second quarter, 1965, p. 235.

320 "If we are free": Hamer interview by Anne and Howard Romaine, RP.

320 "said to us": Hampton, p. 203.

321 "The heat was on": Fairclough, p. 202.

321 "disappeared in the space": Julian Bond interview, CRDP.

322 "You people": Hamer interview by Anne and Howard Romaine, RP.

322 "Ignorant?": Unita Blackwell interview, OH/USM.

322 "secure in their movement": Gordon, p. 181.

322 "The big niggers": Unita Blackwell interview, CRDP.

322 "it was like": Interview with Victoria Gray Adams.

322 "I said": Fannie Lou Hamer interview with Anne Romaine, RP.

323 "When they got through": Henry Sias interview, CRDP.

323 Anthony Lewis: Quoted in Cagin, p. 421.

323 "was far better": Rowland Evans and Robert Novak column, Sept. 3, 1964.

323 "You could watch": Carl Braden interview, CRDP.

324 "the coming of political age": Marsh, p. 44.

324 "meant something": Sutherland, p. 222.

324 "The fact": Interview with Lawrence Guyot.

324 "For many": Dittmer, p. 302.

325 "The kids": Ella Baker interview, CRDP.

325 "After Atlantic City": Sellers, p. 11.

325 "[F]or three months": Seeger, p. 173.

325 "I guess the thing": Sutherland, p. 226.

326 "Mama Quin[*sic*]": SNCC field report, 9/20/64, SNCC.

326 "When in Rome": SNCC press release, 9/28/64, SNCC.

326 "They weren't": SNCC field report, 9/20/64, SNCC.

327 "Do you think": Dittmer, p. 308.

327 "I would advise them": Drew Pearson column, September 30, 1964.

327 "stooge and private gestapo": Hazel Brannon Smith, "Through Hazel Eyes," *North Side Reporter*, April 27, 1961.

328 "Mississippi today": Quoted in Cagin, p. 174.

328 "I long to see": "Holmes Negroes Chip In for Prizewinning Editor," Lexington *Advertiser*, November 23, 1965.

328 "It was not": Mars, p. xv.

329 "Well, certainly": Ibid., p. 98.

329 "We intend": Ibid., p. 138.

329 "A longtime family": Ibid., p. 192.

330 "Freedom Summer": Hampton, p. 193.

Chapter 20

331 "She looked": Patch, in Curry et al., *Deep in Our Hearts*, p. 159.

332 "tremendously painful": Interview with Penny Patch.

332 "A massive": Mary King interview, SOHP.

333 "very first feminist": Interview with Penny Patch.

333 "ahead of her time": Mary King, p. 463.

333 "vision of the leadership": Ibid., p. 472.

333 "Even though": Fay Bellamy interview, OH/CU.

333 "both within and without": Clayborne Carson, *In Struggle: SNCC and the Black Awakening of the 1960s* (Cambridge: Harvard University Press, 1981), p. 148.

334 "I proposed": Forman, p. xviii.

334 "Perhaps what": Mary King, p. 453.

334 "The women were looking": Interview with Mary King.

334 "the assumption": Quoted in Evans, p. 234.

335 "within the framework": Mary King, p. 443.

335 "I was really": Greenberg, p. 135.

335 "reached a new low": Forman, p. 436.

335 "started from": Quoted in Evans, p. 238.

336 "certain things": Fay Bellamy interview, OH/CU.

336 One evening: Mary King, p. 451.

336 "It was very": Casey Hayden remarks, Southern Historical Association, Nov. 8, 1997.

337 "The *only*": Robin Morgan, ed., *Sisterhood Is Powerful* (New York: Random House, 1970), p. 35.

337 "Of course": Interview with Kwame Ture (Stokely Carmichael).

337 "a terrible disservice": Interview with Mary King.

337 "Well, let's do": Greenberg, p. 148.

338 "we really didn't": Interview with Casey Hayden.

338 "gone underground": Interview with anonymous SNCC activist.

338 "lonely almost immediately": McAdam, p. 124.

338 "not so incipient": Interview with Penny Patch.

338 "I stood in the hallway": Patch, in Curry et al., *Deep in Our Hearts*, p. 159.

339 "That was a crucial": Quoted in Dittmer, p. 324.

339 "had as substantial": David Garrow, "Commentary," in Charles W. Eagles, ed., *The Civil Rights Movement in America* (Jackson: University of Mississippi Press, 1986), p. 58.

339 Boynton inherited: Hampton, p. 210.

340 "it was Mrs. Amelia": Carawan, p. 246.

341 "determined and persistent": Young, p. 338.

341 "I was stunned": Seeger, p. 187.

341 "He had gone": Abernathy, p. 316.

341 "[N]o small measure": Young, p. 342.

342 "The horses": Williams, p. 260.

342 "was greater": Lewis, p. 335.

343 "I got put": Parks, p. 170.

344 "very conflicted": Mary Stanton, *From Selma to Sorrow: The Life and Death of Viola Liuzzo* (Athens: University of Georgia Press, 1998), p. 92.

343 "You boys": Ibid., p. 49.

345 "The lady just": Ibid., p. 51.

345 "Evidently aware": Quoted in Stanton, p. 55.

346 "The reaction": Ibid., p. 101.

346 "accused the poor": Eliza Heard (pseudonym Virgina Durr), "Economics and a Murder Trial," *New South*, October 1965, p. 5.

346 "the most controversial": Stanton, p. 6.

346 "The road": Lewis, p. 347.

347 "not amenable": C. Vann Woodward, "What Happened to the Civil Rights Movement?" *Harper's*, January 1967, p. 34.

347 "I didn't want": John Lewis interview, CRDP.

348 "We were starting": Interview with anonymous SNCC activist.

348 "I look around": Mary King, p. 496.

348 "For a long time": Ibid., p. 558.

348 "it was no longer": Patch, in Curry et al., *Deep in Our Hearts*, p. 163.

349 "I was desolate": Ibid., p. 164.

349 "no longer relevant": Forman, p. 476.

349 "This was the worst": Powledge, p. 636.

349 "You old lady": Durr, pp. 328–29.

349 "I want so much": Virginia Durr to Helen and Corliss Lamont, 6/23/68, VD.

Chapter 21

350 very lonely: Greenberg, p. 136.

351 "That inability": Quoted in Evans, p. 236.

352 "you didn't have": Interview with Heather Tobis Booth.

353 "[T]he new left": Doug Rossinow, *The Politics of Authenticity: Liberalism, Christianity, and the New Left in America* (New York: Columbia University Press, 1998), p. 17.

353 "arrogance, elitism": Quoted in Evans, p. 154.

354 "The men were telling": Interview with Heather Tobis Booth.

354 "The civil rights movement": McAdam, p. 184.

354 "What I remember": Ibid.

355 "We went through": Interview with Bob Zellner.

356 "lived on the edge": Murray, *Song*, p. xi.

356 "I will resist:": "Pauli Murray," *Ms.*, March 1980, p. 60.

357 "This chick": Pauli Murray, "Jane Crow," 8/26/68, PM.

357 "Pauli resonated": Interview with Eleanor Holmes Norton.
357 "must prepare": Pauli Murray, "The Negro Woman in the Quest for Equality," PM.
357 "I say": Pauli Murray interview, CRDP.
357 "You and I": "Pauli Murray," *Ms.*, March 1980, p. 64.
357 "The person": Ibid.
358 "we could never": Pauli Murray interview, OH/FDRL.
358 "a rock": Virginia Durr interview, SOHP.
359 "Thank God": Carl M. Brauer, "Women Activists, Southern Conservatives, and the Prohibition of Sex Discrimination in Title VII of the 1964 Civil Rights Act," *Journal of Southern History*, February 1983, p. 43.
359 "as full of booby traps": Charles Whalen, *The Longest Debate: A Legislative History of the 1964 Civil Rights Act* (Cabin John, Md.: Seven Locks Press, 1985), p. 120.
360 "I presume": Brauer, p. 49.
360 "[I]f you do not add": "Black Women and the Constitution," *Harvard Civil Rights–Civil Liberties Law Review*, 1989, p. 11.
360 "It is incredible": Brauer, p. 50.
361 "[A]s a Negro woman": Murray, *Song*, p. 356.
361 In a letter: Ibid., p. 358.
362 "would be much": Quoted in Cynthia Harrison, *On Account of Sex: The Politics of Women's Issues, 1945–1968* (Berkeley: University of California Press, 1988), p. 188.
362 "a shapeless, knobby-kneed": Ibid., p. 189.
362 "the women's groups": Ibid.
362 "Do you suppose": Pauli Murray to Marguerite Rawalt, 7/21/65, PM.
363 "a network": Murray, *Song*, p. 366.
363 "had happened": Ibid., p. 368.
363 "Discrimination against": Marcia Cohen, *The Sisterhood: The True Story of the Women Who Changed the World* (New York: Simon & Schuster, 1988), p. 138.
364 She appointed: "An Eager New Team Tackles Job Discrimination," *BusinessWeek*, July 25, 1977, p. 116.
366 When Betty: Giddings, p. 309.
367 When the CBS: Mae C. King, "Politics of Sexual Stereotypes," *The Black Scholar*, March–April 1973, p. 20.
367 "white women": bell hooks, "Black Women: Shaping Feminist Theory," in Beverly Guy-Sheftall, ed., *Words of Fire: An Anthology of African-American Feminist Thought* (New York: New Press, 1995), p. 278.
367 "I never knew": Quoted in Giddings, p. 299.
368 "It is difficult": Quoted in Pauli Murray, "Black Theology and Feminist Theology: A Comparative Study," 5/19/76, PM.
368 "I am all for": Brown, *Ready from Within*, p. 82.
368 "Fannie told them": Mills, p. 277.

Chapter 22
369 "In the past": Phyl Garland, "Builders of a New South," *Ebony*, August 1966, p. 36.
370 "Forman was sort": Interview with Ivanhoe Donaldson.
370 "Inside SNCC": Fleming, p. 101.
371 "As Ruby Doris": Ibid., p. 158.
371 "Ruby was always": Interview with Ivanhoe Donaldson.
371 "bristl[ing] with antagonism": Mary King, p. 454.
371 "I realized": Josephine Carson, p. 255.
372 "Ruby called": Fleming, p. 178.
372 "You knew": Interview with Ivanhoe Donaldson.
372 "who is stronger": Josephine Carson, p. 254.
372 "He's getting more": Ibid., p. 253.
373 "vicious attacks": Forman, p. 480.
373 "I have a feeling": Josephine Carson, p. 255.
373 "With her life": Robnett, p. 182.
373 "What killed": "Black Scholar Interviews Kathleen Cleaver," *The Black Scholar*, December 1971, p. 55.
373 "backlash of a new male": Pauli Murray, "The Negro Woman in the Quest for Equality," PM.

374 One morning: Lee Rainwater and William L. Yancey, *The Moynihan Report and the Politics of Controversy* (Cambridge: MIT Press, 1967), p. 25.
374 "to explain to the fellows": Ibid.
374 "[H]ere is where": Ibid., p. 5.
375 Because the "matriarchal structure": Ibid., p. 75.
375 "segregation, and the submissiveness": Ibid., p. 62.
376 "Although [the report]": Giddings, p. 329.
376 "brainshattering explosion": Michele Wallace, *Black Macho and the Myth of the Superwoman* (New York: Dial, 1979), p. 12.
376 "Men may be cruelly": Frances Beale, "Double Jeopardy: To Be Black and Female," in Guy-Sheftall, p. 149.
376 "the immediate goal": Quoted in Pauli Murray, "The Liberation of Black Women," in Jean E. Friedman and William G. Shade, eds., *Our American Sisters: Women in American Life and Thought* (Lexington, Mass.: D. C. Heath, 1982), p. 582.
377 "The truth is": C. Eric Lincoln, "A Look Beyond the 'Matriarchy,'" *Ebony*, August 1966, p. 112.
377 "Now that it is": Bonnie Allen, "Essence and Other Thoughts," *Essence*, May 1980, p. 95.
377 "The black woman": Toni Cade, *The Black Woman: An Anthology* (New York: New American Library, 1970), p. 103.
378 "What is clear": Joyce Ladner, *Tomorrow's Tomorrow: The Black Woman* (New York: Doubleday, 1971), p. 285.
378 "I want to step": Calvin Tomkins, "A Sense of Urgency," *The New Yorker*, March 27, 1989, p. 50.
378 "Some of the brothers": Quoted in Giddings, p. 316.
378 "castrator": Ibid., p. 317.
379 "I realize now": Sellers, p. 182.
379 "did not see 'womanhood'": hooks, *Ain't I a Woman?* p. 1.
379 "suppress their aggression": Alvin Poussaint, "White Manipulation and Black Aggression," *The Black Scholar*, May–June 1979, p. 53.
379 "The tendency": Hine and Thompson, p. 302.
380 "Write nothing": Alice Walker, "Advancing Luna—and Ida B. Wells," in *You Can't Keep a Good Woman Down* (New York: Harcourt Brace Jovanovich), p. 94.
381 On November 17: Paula Giddings, "The Last Taboo," in *Race-ing Justice, En-gendering Power*, Toni Morrison, ed. (New York: Pantheon, 1992), pp. 457–58.

Chapter 23

383 The following month: Arthur Kinoy, *Rights on Trial: The Odyssey of a People's Lawyer* (Cambridge: Harvard University Press, 1983), p. 269.
383 Shortly before noon: Ibid., p. 272.
384 "Finally, I had": Anne Braden, "The Challenge Has Just Begun," *Southern Patriot*, February 1965.
384 "I object": Kinoy, p. 274.
384 "We did it": Ibid.
385 "with the meaning": Interview with Victoria Gray Adams.
386 "We showed them": Mills, p. 171.
386 "Plain, decent": Watters, p. 335.
387 In the spring of 1965: Mills, p. 173.
388 Sarah Johnson: Sarah Johnson interview, OH/USM.
389 On the day: Interview with Johnnie Carr.
389 A few days: Constance Curry, *Silver Rights* (Chapel Hill: Algonquin, 1995), p. 23.
390 "That could not": Ibid., p. xii.
391 "was one": *The New Yorker*, March 27, 1989, p. 63.
391 "We wanted": Annie Mae King interview, CRDP.
391 "More than any other": *The New Yorker*, March 27, 1989, p. 63.
391 "black folks": Yvonne Smith, "Marian Wright Edelman: Children's Crusader," *Essence*, September 1980, p. 101.
392 "lost the truth": Mills, pp. 229–30.
394 "She literally": Mary King, pp. 469–70.
394 ". . . [S]he loved": Unita Blackwell interview, OH/USM.
394 "SNCC told me": Crawford, p. 22.

395 "People such as": *Essence*, September 1980, p. 101.

395 "what is this": Unita Blackwell interview, CRDP.

396 "She'd been working": Unita Blackwell remarks, Tougaloo College symposium, November 9, 1978.

Epilogue

397 "protest and opposition": Greenberg, p. 217.

397 "how things were": Bernice Reagon remarks, opening of Mt. Zion Civil Rights Museum in Albany, November 16, 1998.

397 "the vast accomplishments": Grace Elizabeth Hale, *Making Whiteness: The Culture of Segregation in the South, 1890–1940* (Pantheon, 1998), p. 294.

398 "he would not": Mills, p. 312.

398 "If you had": Ibid., p. 5.

398 "the starting point": Rachel Blau DuPlessis and Ann Snitow, eds., *The Feminist Memoir Project: Voices from Women's Liberation* (New York: Three Rivers Press, 1998), p. 4.

399 "laid a groundwork": Ibid., p. 66.

399 One of them: Interview with Jacqueline Byrd Martin.

399 "I'm *Dr.* Endesha": Endesha Ida Mae Holland interview, *Freedom on My Mind.*

400 "I still think": Interview with Eleanor Holmes Norton.

401 "Mrs. Devine": Alexis Jetter, "Mississippi Learning," *The New York Times Magazine*, February 21, 1993, p. 50.

401 "I've missed her": Interview with Johnnie Carr.

401 "I am happy": Parks, p. 181.

402 "I still call it": Interview with Anne Braden.

402 "sort of a legendary": Julian Bond interview, CRDP.

402 "The major pressures": Cantarow, p. 92.

403 "I'm still an activist": Cluster, p. 29.

403 After their divorce: Halberstam, p. 533 and p. 682.

404 "I [am] very": Powledge, p. 646.

405 "Of course": Interview with Joan Browning.

405 "feel grounded": Interview with Casey Hayden.

405 "[T]here was hardly": Interview with Penny Patch.

406 "Had black-white": Patch, in Curry et al., *Deep in Our Hearts*, p. 167.

406 "accounts unsettled": Greenberg, p. ix.

406 At the Trinity: Greenberg, pp. 147–49.

407 "certain romanticization": Ibid., p. 13.

407 "The intersection": Interview with anonymous SNCC activist.

407 "After the initial": Patch, in Curry et al., *Deep in Our Hearts*, p.169.

407 "ideology as alien": Murray, *Song*, p. 392.

408 "My feeling": Pauli Murray interview, SOHP.

408 "happy chaos": Marjorie Hyer, "Episcopal Priests Ordained," *The Washington Post*, January 9, 1977, p. A3.

409 "Black, white, and red": Charles Kuralt, *On the Road With Charles Kuralt* (New York: Putnam, 1985), p. 31.

409 "There is no black Christ": Sherry Shanklin, "Old Friends Turn Out to Hear Her Sermon," Durham (N.C.) *Morning Herald*, February 14, 1977, p. 1.

409 As she spoke: Kuralt, p. 30.

bibliography

Abernathy, Ralph David. *And the Walls Came Tumbling Down*. HarperPerennial, 1990.

Ahmann, Mathew H., ed. *The New Negro*. Fides, 1961.

Anderson, Jervis. *Bayard Rustin: Troubles I've Seen*. HarperCollins, 1997.

Ashmore, Harry. *Hearts and Minds: A Personal Chronicle of Race in America*. Seven Locks Press, 1988.

Barry, John M. *Rising Tide: The Great Mississippi Flood of 1927 and How It Changed America*. Simon & Schuster, 1997.

Bates, Daisy. *The Long Shadow of Little Rock*. David McKay, 1962.

Beals, Melba Pattillo. *Warriors Don't Cry*. Pocket Books, 1994.

Belfrage, Sally. *Freedom Summer*. Viking, 1965.

Bernhard, Virginia, Betty Brandon, Elizabeth Fox-Genovese, and Theda Perdue, eds. *Southern Women: Histories and Identities*. University of Missouri Press, 1992.

Black, Allida M. *Casting Her Own Shadow: Eleanor Roosevelt and the Shaping of Postwar Liberalism*. Columbia University Press, 1996.

Blee, Kathleen M. *Women of the Klan: Racism and Gender in the 1920s*. University of California Press, 1991.

Braden, Anne. *The Wall Between*. Monthly Review Press, 1958.

Branch, Taylor. *Parting the Waters: America in the King Years, 1954–1963*. Simon & Schuster, 1988.

———. *Pillar of Fire: America in the King Years, 1963–65*. Simon & Schuster, 1998.

Breines, Wini. *Young, White, and Miserable: Growing Up Female in the Fifties*. Beacon Press, 1992.

Bremner, Robert H., and Gary W. Reichard, eds. *Reshaping America: Society and Institutions, 1945–1960*. Ohio State University Press, 1982.

Brown, Cynthia Stokes, ed. *Ready from Within: Septima Clark and the Civil Rights Movement*. Wild Trees Press, 1986.

Brundage, W. Fitzhugh, ed. *Under Sentence of Death: Lynching in the South*. University of North Carolina Press, 1997.

Burns, Stewart, ed. *Daybreak of Freedom: The Montgomery Bus Boycott*. University of North Carolina Press, 1997.

Cade, Toni. *The Black Woman: An Anthology*. New American Library, 1970.

Cagin, Seth, and Philip Dray. *We Are Not Afraid*. Macmillan, 1988.

Cantarow, Ellen. *Moving the Mountain: Women Working for Social Change*. Feminist Press, 1980.

Carawan, Guy and Candie. *Sing for Freedom: The Story of the Civil Rights Movement Through Its Songs*. Sing Out Corp., 1990.

Carson, Clayborne. *In Struggle: SNCC and the Black Awakening of the 1960s*. Harvard University Press, 1981.

Carson, Josephine. *Silent Voices: The Southern Negro Woman Today*. Delacorte, 1969.

Cash, W. J. *The Mind of the South*. Knopf, 1941.

Chafe, William H. *Civilities and Civil Rights: Greensboro, North Carolina, and the Black Struggle for Freedom*. Oxford University Press, 1980.

———. *Women and Equality: Changing Patterns in American Culture*. Oxford University Press, 1978.

Cloud, Stanley, and Lynne Olson. *The Murrow Boys: Pioneers on the Front Lines of Broadcast Journalism*. Houghton Mifflin, 1996.

Cluster, Dick, ed. *They Should Have Served That Cup of Coffee*. South End Press, 1979.

Cohen, Marcia. *The Sisterhood: The True Story of the Women Who Changed the World*. Simon & Schuster, 1988.

Collins, Patricia Hill. *Black Feminist Thought: Knowledge, Consciousness, and the Politics of Empowerment*. Routledge, 1991.

Cone, James H. *Martin and Malcolm and America: A Dream or a Nightmare?* Orbis, 1991.

Cook, Blanche Wiesen. *Eleanor Roosevelt: Volume One, 1884–1933.* Viking, 1992.

Crawford, Vicki L., Jacqueline Anne Rouse, and Barbara Woods, eds. *Women in the Civil Rights Movement: Trailblazers and Torchbearers, 1941–1965.* Carlson, 1990.

Curry, Constance, Joan C. Browning et al. *Deep in Our Hearts: Nine White Women in the Freedom Movement.* University of Georgia Press, 2000.

———. *Silver Rights.* Algonquin, 1995.

DeCosta-Willis, Miriam, ed. *The Memphis Diary of Ida B. Wells.* Beacon Press, 1995.

Dittmer, John. *Local People: The Struggle for Civil Rights in Mississippi.* University of Illinois Press, 1994.

Du Bois, W. E. B. *The Souls of Black Folk.* Library of America, 1980.

DuPlessis, Rachel Blau, and Ann Snitow, eds. *The Feminist Memoir Project: Voices from Women's Liberation.* Three Rivers Press, 1998.

Durr, Virginia. *Outside the Magic Circle: The Autobiography of Virginia Foster Durr.* University of Alabama Press, 1985.

Eagles, Charles W., ed. *The Civil Rights Movement in America.* University of Mississippi Press, 1986.

Egerton, John. *Speak Now Against the Day: The Generation Before the Civil Rights Movement in the South.* University of North Carolina Press, 1995.

Erenrich, Susie, ed. *Freedom Is a Constant Struggle: An Anthology of the Mississippi Civil Rights Movement.* Black Belt Press, 1999.

Evans, Sara. *Personal Politics: The Roots of Women's Liberation in the Civil Rights Movement and the New Left.* Knopf, 1979.

Fairclough, Adam. *To Redeem the Soul of America: The Southern Christian Leadership Conference and Martin Luther King Jr.* University of Georgia Press, 1987.

Farmer, James. *Lay Bare the Heart: An Autobiography of the Civil Rights Movement.* Arbor House, 1985.

Fleming, Cynthia Griggs. *Soon We Will Not Cry: The Liberation of Ruby Doris Smith Robinson.* Rowman & Littlefield, 1998.

Forman, James. *The Making of Black Revolutionaries.* University of Washington Press, 1997.

Fout, John C., and Maura Shaw Tantillo, eds. *American Sexual Politics: Sex, Gender, and Race Since the Civil War.* University of Chicago Press, 1993.

Friedman, Jean E., and William G. Shade, eds. *Our American Sisters: Women in American Life and Thought.* D. C. Heath, 1982.

Garrow, David. *Bearing the Cross: Martin Luther King, Jr., and the Southern Christian Leadership Conference.* Morrow, 1986.

———, ed. *The Walking City: The Montgomery Bus Boycott, 1955–56.* Carlson, 1989.

Gentile, Thomas. *March on Washington: August 28, 1963.* New Day, 1983.

Giddings, Paula. *When and Where I Enter: The Impact of Black Women on Race and Sex in America.* Morrow, 1984.

Gladney, Margaret Rose, ed. *How Am I to Be Heard?: Letters of Lillian Smith.* University of North Carolina Press, 1993.

Golden, Marita, and Susan Richards Shreve, eds. *Skin Deep: Black Women and White Women Write About Race.* Nan A. Talese, 1995.

Good, Paul. *The Trouble I've Seen.* Howard University Press, 1975.

Goodwin, Doris Kearns. *No Ordinary Time.* Simon & Schuster, 1994.

Gordon, Ann D., ed. *African American Women and the Vote, 1837–1965.* University of Massachusetts Press, 1997.

Grant, Joanne. *Ella Baker: Freedom Bound.* John Wiley & Sons, 1998.

Gray, Fred D. *Bus Ride to Justice.* Black Belt Press, 1995.

Greenberg, Cheryl Lynn, ed. *A Circle of Trust: Remembering SNCC.* Rutgers University Press, 1998.

Griffith, Elisabeth. *In Her Own Right: The Life of Elizabeth Cady Stanton.* Oxford University Press, 1984.

Guy-Sheftall, Beverly. *Daughters of Sorrow: Attitudes Toward Black Women, 1880–1920.* Carlson, 1990.

———, ed. *Words of Fire: An Anthology of African-American Feminist Thought.* New Press, 1995.

Gwin, Minrose C. *Black and White Women of the Old South: The Peculiar Sisterhood in American Literature.* University of Tennessee Press, 1985.

Halberstam, David. *The Children.* Random House, 1998.

Hale, Grace Elizabeth. *Making Whiteness: The Culture of Segregation in the South, 1890–1940.* Pantheon, 1998.

Hall, Jacquelyn Dowd. *Revolt Against Chivalry: Jessie Daniel Ames and the Women's Campaign Against Lynching.* Columbia University Press, 1979.

Hampton, Henry, and Steve Fayer, eds. *Voices of Freedom: An Oral History of the Civil Rights Movement from the 1950s through the 1980s.* Bantam Books, 1990.

Harrison, Cynthia. *On Account of Sex: The Politics of Women's Issues, 1945–1968.* University of California Press, 1988.

Hayden, Tom. *Reunion: A Memoir.* Random House, 1988.

Hedgeman, Anna Arnold. *The Trumpet Sounds.* Holt, Rinehart & Winston, 1964.

Hernton, Calvin C. *Sex and Racism in America.* Grove Press, 1965.

Hine, Darlene Clark, ed. *Black Women in American History: The Twentieth Century.* Carlson, 1990.

———, ed. *Black Women's History: Theory and Practice.* Vols. 1–2. Carlson, 1990.

———, Wilma King, and Linda Reed, eds. *"We Specialize in the Wholly Impossible": A Reader in Black Women's History.* Carlson, 1995.

———, and Kathleen Thompson. *A Shining Thread of Hope: History of Black Women in America.* Broadway Books, 1998.

Hodes, Martha. *White Women, Black Men: Illicit Sex in the 19th-Century South.* Yale University Press, 1997.

Holland, Endesha Ida Mae. *From the Mississippi Delta: A Memoir.* Simon & Schuster, 1997.

hooks, bell. *Ain't I a Woman?: Black Women and Feminism.* South End Press, 1981.

Hull, Gloria T., Patricia Bell Scott, and Barbara Smith, eds. *All the Women Are White, All the Blacks Are Men, But Some of Us Are Brave.* Feminist Press, 1982.

Jacobs, Paul, and Saul Landau. *The New Radicals.* Vintage, 1966.

Jaffe, Harry S., and Tom Sherwood. *Dream City: Race, Power and the Decline of Washington, D.C.* Simon & Schuster, 1994.

Jones, Anne Goodwyn. *Tomorrow Is Another Day: The Woman Writer in the South, 1859–1936.* Louisiana State University Press, 1981.

Jones, Jacqueline. *Labor of Love, Labor of Sorrow: Black Women, Work and the Family, from Slavery to the Present.* Basic Books, 1985.

Kemble, Fanny. *Journal of a Residence on a Georgia Plantation in 1838–1839.* Harper & Brothers, 1863.

King, Coretta Scott. *My Life with Martin Luther King, Jr.* Holt, Rinehart & Winston, 1969.

King, Martin Luther, Jr. *Stride Toward Freedom: The Montgomery Story.* Harper, 1958.

King, Mary. *Freedom Song: A Personal History of the 1960s Civil Rights Movement.* Morrow, 1987.

King, Richard. *A Southern Renaissance: The Cultural Awakening of the American South.* Oxford University Press, 1980.

Kinoy, Arthur. *Rights on Trial: The Odyssey of a People's Lawyer.* Harvard University Press, 1983.

Kluger, Richard. *Simple Justice: The History of Brown v. Board of Education and Black America's Struggle for Equality.* Knopf, 1976.

Kuralt, Charles. *On the Road with Charles Kuralt.* Putnam's, 1985.

Ladner, Joyce A. *The Ties That Bind: Timeless Values for African-American Families.* John Wiley & Sons, 1998.

———. *Tomorrow's Tomorrow: The Black Woman.* Doubleday, 1991.

Lanker, Brian. *I Dream a World: Portraits of Black Women Who Changed America.* Stewart, Tabori & Chang, 1989.

Lash, Joseph. *Eleanor and Franklin.* Norton, 1971.

Lerner, Gerda. *Black Women in White America.* Vintage, 1972.

Levine, Ellen. *Freedom's Children: Young Civil Rights Activists Tell Their Own Stories.* Putnam's, 1993.

Lewis, David Levering. *W. E. B. Du Bois: Biography of a Race.* Henry Holt, 1993.

Lewis, John. *Walking with the Wind: A Memoir of the Movement.* Simon & Schuster, 1998.

Litwack, Leon F. *Trouble in Mind: Black Southerners in the Age of Jim Crow.* Knopf, 1998.

Lord, Walter. *The Past That Would Not Die.* Harper & Row, 1965.

Loveland, Anne C. *Lillian Smith: A Southerner Confronting the South.* Louisiana State University Press, 1986.

Lutz, Alma. *Crusade for Freedom: Women of the Antislavery Movement.* Beacon Press, 1968.

Lynn, Susan. *Progressive Women in Conservative Times: Racial Justice, Peace, and Feminism, 1945 to the 1960s.* Rutgers University Press, 1992.

Lyon, Danny. *Memories of the Southern Civil Rights Movement.* University of North Carolina Press, 1992.

McAdam, Doug. *Freedom Summer.* Oxford University Press, 1988.

McMurry, Linda O. *To Keep the Waters Troubled: The Life of Ida B. Wells.* Oxford University Press, 1998.

Mars, Florence. *Witness in Philadelphia.* Louisiana State University Press, 1977.

Marsh, Charles. *God's Long Summer: Stories of Faith and Civil Rights.* Princeton University Press, 1997.

Mayer, Henry. *All on Fire: William Lloyd Garrison and the Abolition of Slavery.* St. Martin's Press, 1998.

Mills, Kay. *A Place in the News: From the Women's Pages to the Front Page.* Dodd, Mead, 1988.

———. *Something Better for My Children: The History and People of Head Start.* Dutton, 1998.

———. *This Little Light of Mine: The Life of Fannie Lou Hamer.* Dutton, 1993.

Mitford, Jessica. *Daughters and Rebels.* Houghton Mifflin, 1960.

Moody, Anne. *Coming of Age in Mississippi.* Dial, 1968.

Morgan, Robin, ed. *Sisterhood Is Powerful.* Random House, 1970.

Morris, Aldon D. *The Origins of the Civil Rights Movement: Black Communities Organizing for Change.* Free Press, 1984.

Morris, Willie. *North Toward Home.* Houghton Mifflin, 1967.

Morrison, Toni, ed. *Race-ing Justice, En-gendering Power: Essays on Anita Hill, Clarence Thomas, and the Construction of Social Reality.* Pantheon, 1992.

Murray, Pauli. *Proud Shoes: The Story of an American Family.* Harper & Row, 1978.

———. *Song in a Weary Throat: An American Pilgrimage.* Harper & Row, 1987.

Myrdal, Gunnar. *An American Dilemma: The Negro Problem and Modern Democracy.* Harper, 1941.

Oshinsky, David M. *"Worse Than Slavery": Parchman Farm and the Ordeal of Jim Crow Justice.* Free Press, 1996.

Painter, Nell Irvin. *Sojourner Truth: A Life, a Symbol.* Norton, 1996.

Parks, Rosa. *Rosa Parks: My Story.* Dial, 1992.

Payne, Charles M. *I've Got the Light of Freedom: The Organizing Tradition and the Mississippi Freedom Struggle.* University of California Press, 1995.

Powledge, Fred. *Free at Last? The Civil Rights Movement and the People Who Made It.* Little, Brown, 1991.

Raines, Howell. *My Soul Is Rested: The Story of the Civil Rights Movement in the Deep South.* Putnam's, 1977.

Rainwater, Lee, and William L. Yancey. *The Moynihan Report and the Politics of Controversy.* M.I.T. Press, 1967.

Rich, Adrienne. *On Lies, Secrets and Silence.* Norton, 1979.

Robertson, Nan. *The Girls in the Balcony: Men, Women and The New York Times.* Random House, 1992.

Robinson, Armstead L., and Patricia Sullivan, eds. *New Directions in Civil Rights Studies.* University Press of Virginia, 1991.

Robinson, Jo Ann. *The Montgomery Bus Boycott and the Women Who Started It.* University of Tennessee Press, 1987.

Robnett, Belinda. *How Long? How Long?: African-American Women in the Struggle for Civil Rights.* Oxford University Press, 1997.

Rossinow, Doug. *The Politics of Authenticity: Liberalism, Christianity, and the New Left in America.* Columbia University Press, 1998.

Rowan, Carl. *Go South to Sorrow.* Random House, 1957.

Salmond, John A. *The Conscience of a Lawyer: Clifford J. Durr and American Civil Liberties, 1899–1975.* University of Alabama Press, 1990.

Salter, John R., Jr. *Jackson, Mississippi: An American Chronicle of Struggle and Schism.* Exposition Press, 1979.

Scott, Anne Firor. *The Southern Lady: From Pedestal to Politics, 1830–1930.* University of California Press, 1970.

Seeger, Pete, and Bob Reiser. *Everybody Says Freedom.* Norton, 1989.

Sellers, Cleveland. *The River of No Return: Autobiography of a Black Militant and the Life and Death of SNCC.* Morrow, 1973.

Sherrill, Robert. *Gothic Politics in the Deep South.* Grossman, 1968.

Silver, James W. *Mississippi: The Closed Society.* Harcourt, Brace and World, 1966.

Sitkoff, Harvard. *The Struggle for Black Equality, 1954–1980.* Hill & Wang, 1981.

Smith, Bob. *They Closed Their Schools.* University of North Carolina Press, 1965.

Smith, Lillian. *Killers of the Dream*. Norton, 1961.

———. *Strange Fruit*. Reynal & Hitchcock, 1944.

Snitow, Ann, Christine Stansell, and Sharon Thompson, eds. *Powers of Desire: The Politics of Sexuality*. Monthly Review Press, 1983.

Stanton, Mary. *From Selma to Sorrow: The Life and Death of Viola Liuzzo*. University of Georgia Press, 1998.

Sterling, Dorothy. *Black Foremothers: Three Lives*. Feminist Press, 1988.

———, ed. *We Are Your Sisters: Black Women in the Nineteenth Century*. Norton, 1984.

Stoper, Emily. *The Student Nonviolent Coordinating Committee: The Growth of Radicalism in a Civil Rights Organization*. Carlson, 1989.

Sugarman, Tracy. *Stranger at the Gates: A Summer in Mississippi*. Hill & Wang, 1967.

Sullivan, Patricia. *Days of Hope: Race and Democracy in the New Deal Era*. University of North Carolina Press, 1996.

Sutherland, Elizabeth. *Letters from Mississippi*. McGraw-Hill, 1965.

Terrell, Mary Church. *A Colored Woman in a White World*. G. K. Hall, 1996.

Thompson, Mildred I. *Ida B. Wells-Barnett: An Exploratory Study of an American Black Woman, 1893–1930*. Carlson, 1970.

Viorst, Milton. *Fire in the Streets: America in the 1960s*. Simon & Schuster, 1979.

Von Hoffman, Nicholas. *Mississippi Notebook*. D. White, 1964.

Wade-Gayles, Gloria. *No Crystal Stair: Visions of Race and Sex in Black Women's Fiction*. Pilgrim, 1984.

Waldron, Ann. *Hodding Carter: The Reconstruction of a Racist*. Algonquin, 1993.

Walker, Alice. *In Search of Our Mothers' Gardens*. Harcourt Brace Jovanovich, 1983.

———. *You Can't Keep a Good Woman Down*. Harcourt Brace Jovanovich, 1981.

Wallace, Michele. *Black Macho and the Myth of the Superwoman*. Dial, 1979.

Ward, Brian, and Tony Badger, eds. *The Making of Martin Luther King and the Civil Rights Movement*. New York University Press, 1996.

Watters, Pat. *Down to Now: Reflections on the Southern Civil Rights Movement*. University of Georgia Press, 1993.

Wedin, Carolyn. *Inheritors of the Spirit: Mary White Ovington and the Founding of the NAACP.* John Wiley & Sons, 1998.

Whalen, Charles. *The Longest Debate: A Legislative History of the 1964 Civil Rights Act*. Seven Locks Press, 1985.

White, Deborah Gray. *Too Heavy a Load: Black Women in Defense of Themselves, 1894–1994*. Norton, 1999.

Wilkins, Roger. *A Man's Life: An Autobiography*. Simon & Schuster, 1982.

Williams, Juan. *Eyes on the Prize: America's Civil Rights Years, 1954–1965*. Viking, 1987.

Wilson, Midge, and Kathy Russell. *Divided Sisters: Bridging the Gap Between Black Women and White Women*. Anchor, 1996.

Wofford, Harris. *Of Kennedys and Kings: Making Sense of the Sixties*. Farrar, Straus & Giroux, 1980.

Wolfe, Margaret Ripley. *Daughters of Canaan: A Saga of Southern Women*. University Press of Kentucky, 1995.

Yarbrough, Tinsley E. *A Passion for Justice: J. Waties Waring and Civil Rights*. Oxford University Press, 1987.

Young, Andrew. *An Easy Burden: The Civil Rights Movement and the Transformation of America*. HarperCollins, 1996.

Zinn, Howard. *The Southern Mystique*. Knopf, 1964.

———. *SNCC: The New Abolitionists*. Beacon Press, 1965.

acknowledgments

This book would not have been possible without the help of many people, notably those women who gave freely of their time to discuss their experiences in the civil rights movement. I'd especially like to thank Anne Braden, Joan Browning, Connie Curry, Johnnie Carr, and Jacqueline Byrd Martin for their assistance, given in so many different ways. I also want to thank Ivanhoe Donaldson, Lawrence Guyot, Chuck McDew, and the other male activists whom I interviewed for their insights into the movement, as well as for their perceptive recollections of the women with whom they worked.

I owe special thanks to Phil Alden Robinson for his generosity in sharing with me his remarkable cache of sources and research gathered over years of working on *Freedom Song*, his fine film on the movement in Mississippi.

My appreciation, also, to Angela Whitmal, curator of the Mount Zion Albany Civil Rights Movement Museum in Albany, Georgia, and to the librarians and archivists at the following institutions: the manuscript division of the Library of Congress; the Schlesinger Library at Radcliffe College; the Moorland-Spingarn Research Center at Howard University; the State Historical Society of Wisconsin in Madison; University of Southern Mississippi; Amistad Research Center at Tulane University; Tougaloo College in Jackson, Mississippi; University of North Carolina at Chapel Hill; Columbia University; and the Southern Regional Council in Atlanta.

A word of thanks to the writers and scholars whose groundbreaking work assisted me immeasurably in writing this book. I'd like to single out Darlene Clark Hine, Taylor Branch, Charles Payne, Vicki Crawford, John Egerton, Paula Giddings, Jacqueline Dowd Hall, Anne Firor Scott, William H. Chafe, Fred Powledge, and Belinda Robnett. I am particularly grateful to David Garrow, Kay Mills, John Dittmer, and Lee Formwalt for their guidance as well as for their own brilliant scholarship.

Thanks, too, to my agent, Gail Ross, and her associate, Howard Yoon, for their support and their invaluable advice. And to Nan Graham and Sarah McGrath, my editors at Scribner, for their help in shaping and focusing this book.

My deep appreciation to a circle of wonderful friends, some who housed me on research trips, others who read part or all of the manuscript and gave me much-appreciated suggestions and encouragement. They include Karen Gilmour, Mary Barcella, Kathleen Currie, Margaret Ershler, Dorothy Dixon, Mary Goodstein, Mary Wilson, Curtis Wilkie, and Walter and Judy Olson.

Thanks to Carly Cloud for her computer wizardry, her patience and sense of humor in putting up with yet another seemingly endless book-writing adventure— and for being an all-round terrific daughter. Finally, my most profound debt of gratitude goes to my husband, Stan Cloud, who also happens to be the best editor and writer I know. He took considerable time away from his own writing to help me make this a better book, and provided unstinting counsel and support when I was going through some difficult times in the course of researching and writing *Freedom's Daughters*. I owe him more than I can say.

index

Note: Page references to illustrations are in *italics*.

Abernathy, Ralph, 250, 341
  in Albany confrontation, 236
  Freedom Riders and, 188
  Montgomery bus boycott and, 113–16,
    125–26
Abernathy, Thomas, 384
Abolitionism
  segregation of sexes in, 30
  women's rights and, 30–32, 353
  women's role in, 27–32
Abortion counseling services, 355
Abortions, first-trimester, 365
ACLU (American Civil Liberties Union),
    404
ACTION, 400
Adams, John, 31
"Advancing Luna and Ida B. Wells" (short
    story), 380
Afric-American Female Intelligence Society,
    27
Agee, James, 171
Agnes Scott College, 167
Alabama
  black voter registration in, 339–41, 386
  See also Birmingham; Montgomery;
    Selma
Alabama, University of, 48, 120
Alabama National Guard, 188
Alabama State College, 89–92, 96, 112–13
  state investigation of, 124, 131
Albany (Georgia)
  Freedom Singers in, 232–34
  harassment of women in, 245–46
  King arrested in, 234, 236
  Patch in, 243
  SNCC in
    Freedom Ride arrests, 227, 229–32
    King's involvement opposed, 234–35
    1963 organizing, 264
Albany State College (Georgia), 225–27,
    230
  expulsion of students from, 238
Albert, Carl, 384–85
Alexander, Will, 46, 48
Alexandria (Virginia), 103
Algebra Project, 401
Allen, Chude Pamela. *See* Parker, Pam

Allen, Ralph, 244
Amatniek, Kathy. *See* Sarachild, Kathie
AME (African Methodist Episcopal)
    Church, 229, 250
American Antislavery Society, 30
American Baptist College, 155, 156
American Dilemma, An (book), 217
American Field Service, 401
American Friends Service Committee, 390
Americans for Democratic Action, 315
Americus (Georgia), 246–47
Ames, Jessie Daniel, 47–50
Amite County (Mississippi), 205–6, 210
Anderson, Jack, 345
Anderson, Marian, 59, 288
Anderson, Norma, 232
Angelou, Maya, 22
Ann Arbor (Michigan), 90, 268
Anniston (Alabama), 173, 183–85
Anthony, Susan B., 30–32, 359, 360
Antislavery Convention of American
    Women, 28–29
Arkansas Gazette, 136–37
Arkansas National Guard, 135, 136
Ashmore, Harry, 136–37
Associated Press, 180
Association of Southern Women for the
    Prevention of Lynching (ASWPL),
    49–51
ASWPL. *See* Association of Southern
    Women for the Prevention of
    Lynching
AT&T, 365
Atkinson, Maxine, 165
Atlanta (Georgia)
  Ebenezer Baptist Church, 138, 142, 144,
    222
  HUAC hearings in, 178–79
  SCLC headquarters in, 221
  sit-ins in, 149
  SNCC headquarters in, 160, 171–73, 229,
    239, 268–69, 275
  women's sit-in, 333–34, 371
Atlanta Baptist College, 43, 376
Atlanta Constitution, The, 68, 70
Atlanta Journal, The, 232, 237
Atlanta University, 72

Atlantic City (New Jersey). *See* Democratic National Convention (1964)
Aurthur, Elinor Tideman, 305
Austen, Jane, 103
Austin (Texas), 168–70
Avery, Annie Pearl, 275
Azbell, Joe, 89, 126

Baker, Ella, 14, 15, 132–50, *132*, 181, 222, 394
    Albany campaign and, 234, 235
    background of, 139–40
    death of, 402
    King challenged by, 133, 215
    MFDP and, 315, 317, 325
    Moses influenced by, 203
    as NAACP Southern field secretary, 73–74, 140–41, 146
    SCEF and, 179
    SCLC's founding and, 138, 139
    as SCLC staff member, 139, 143–50, 161
    sit-ins and, 148–50
    SNCC and, 161–62, 166, 168, 208, 333, 339
        her disappointment, 347
        Highlander Folk School meeting, 197–98
    in YWCA race relations project, 169, 269
Baker County (Georgia), 231
Baldwin, James, 290
Bambara, Toni Cade, 377
Baptist Church, 46, 141–42
Baraka, Amiri, 378
Barnett, Ferdinand, 44
Barnett, Ross, 192, 328
Barrett, Joyce, 245
Barry, Marion, Jr., 159, 160, 196, 197, 206, 339, 400
Bates, Daisy, 13, 134, 288
    Little Rock crisis and, 135–38, 284
Bates, L. C., 135, 137, 284
Batesville (Mississippi), 338–39
Beauvoir, Simone de, 269
Belfrage, Sally, 298, 306–7, 317
Bell, Emma, 259, 265, 295
Bellamy, Fay, 333, 336
Bennett, Lerone, 154
Bennett College, 147
Bennettsville (South Carolina), 400
Bernstein, Carl, 78
Bethune, Mary McLeod, 52, 57–58, 62, 102, 103
Bevel, Diane Nash. *See* Nash, Diane
Bevel, James, 159, 184, 190, 197, 202, 207, 210–12, 232, 253–54, 262, 403
    Selma demonstrations and, 339, 341
Biloxi (Mississippi), 329
Bingham, Barry, 56

Birmingham (Alabama), 174, 180, 232
    church bombing in, 293
    Freedom Rides in, 183–84, 185, 194
    1963 marches in, 278, 283, 290
Birmingham Junior League, 103
Black, Hugo, 99, 101, 103, 104
Black, Josephine Foster, 99, 101
"Black and white together," 240, 294, 308, 407
Black elite, 218–19
Black family, Moynihan on, 374–76
Black men
    black women's support of, 270, 366, 369–70, 377–78
    economic competition of white men and, 36, 38
    essential movement work done by, 17
    fears of sex between white women and, 37, 104
    lack of justice for, 174
    lynching as punishment for liaisons of white women and, 39–40
    male chauvinism of, 378–81
    in March on Washington, 13, 288
    ministry as one dignified calling for, 142
    mothers' domination of, 142–43, 376
    Moynihan's report on, 375–76
    Nixon on cowardice of, 115–16
    post-Civil War tension between black women and, 43–44
    protectiveness of women by, 270–71
    rapist image of, created after Civil War, 37–39
    as robbed of manhood, 142, 202, 375
    voting rights first granted to, 31–32
    white women as "supreme tabooed object" for, 308
    See also Lynching
Black migration to the North, 35
Black Monday (book), 83–84
Black nationalism, 228, 347–48
Black power, 347, *369*, 372, 373, 382
    Moynihan theory and, 377
Blackwell, Randolph, 74
Blackwell, Unita, 250–51, 302–3, 316, 319, 322, 330, 382, 383, 392, 394–96
Black women
    in abolitionist movement, 21–22, 27–32
    Ebony's issue on, 369
    education of, after Civil War, 41–42
    feminism and, 357, 366–68
    free, 27
    as glue of the community, 251–52
    hair of, 311
    as household heads, 374–75
    in late 19th-century South, 41–43
    as leaders in civil rights movement, 13–16, 43, 124–25, 202, 204, 237, 248–51, 394

lighter skin sought by, 311
lynching of, 39
in March on Washington, 13–14, 284–85, 288
as matriarchs, 375–77
Moynihan's report on, 374–76
as nurses of white children, 100–1
persecuted by white men, 226
politicians' fear of voting by, 46
seen as sexual wantons, 25–26, 35, 381
sexual exploitation of, 22–26, 35, 46
shortage of black men for, 310–11
in slavery. *See* Slavery
today's job opportunities for, 365
traditional terms for, 173
voluntary organizations of, 27, 42
voting rights of, 31–32, 359, 382
working together with white women, 16, 26, 29, 47, 66, 106, 162, 295
    Freedom Summer, 309–12, 331–32
    after World War II, 153–54
Blake, James, 108–9, 126
Bleaching creams, 311
Boles, Jacqueline, 165
Bolivar County (Mississippi), 310, 312
Bond, Julian, 148–49, 168, 211, 268, 321, 394, 402
Boone, Brenda, 231
Boston (Massachusetts), 27–29, 67
    women's liberation movement in, 354
Boston Women's Health Care Collective, 355
Boycotts
    of Nashville stores, 158
    See also Montgomery (Alabama)
Boynton, Amelia, 339–42
Boynton, Bruce, 340
Boynton, Sam, 340–41
Boynton v. Virginia, 183, 227, 340
Braden, Anne, 173–81, 191, 198, 212, 223, 271–72, 292–93, 384, 402
    sedition charge against, 177–78
    The Wall Between, 179
Braden, Carl, 175–78, 323, 402
    jailed for contempt of Congress, 179
    sedition charge against, 177–78
Braden, Jimmie, 176
Brady, Tom, 83–84
Brandeis University, 407–8
Branton, Wiley, 244
Bread and Roses, 354, 355
Breines, Wini, 164, 165
Breckinridge, Caroline Quinn, 209, 326–27
Browder, Aurelia, 123
Browder v. Gayle, 123
Brown, Ed, 398
Brown, H. Rap, 379
Browning, Joan, 228–31, 272, 404–5
Brown University, 280

Brown v. Board of Education (1954), 75, 82–86, 88, 99, 104, 123, 138, 176, 177, 328
    implementation of, 388–90
    Southern defiance of, 134
    Waring's influence on, 217
Burke, Katherine, 185
Burks, Mary Fair, 90, 93, 95, 96, 111, 125, 131
    comment on King by, 113
Bus seats
    Clark's refusal to yield, 220–21
    Divens refusal to yield, 209–10
    integrated in Louisville, 174–75

    Murray's refusal to yield, 64
    Parks' refusal to yield. *See* Montgomery (Alabama)
Bus stations
    Albany officials agree to desegregate, 236
    segregation outlawed in, 103, 227, 260–61, 340
Butler, Pierce, 24
Byrd, Jacqueline. *See* Martin, Jacqueline Byrd

California, University of, at Berkeley, 286
    Free Speech movement at, 325–26
Cambridge (Maryland), 278–82, 378
Cambridge Nonviolent Action Committee, 280
Camilla (Georgia), 231
Campbell, Bebe Moore, 311
Campbell College, 209
Camus, Albert, 169
Canton (Mississippi), 252, 302, 401
Carmichael, Stokely. *See* Ture, Kwame
Carolina Israelite (publication), 65
Carper, Elsie, 288
Carr, Arlam, 389
Carr, Arlam, Jr., 389
Carr, Johnnie, 97, 98, 111, 114, 117, 382, 389, 401
Carson, Josephine, 222–23, 371, 372
Carter, Beverly, 390
Carter, Hodding, 45, 65, 84–85, 165–66
    Smith's feud with, 68–70
Carter, Hodding, III, 394
Carter, Jimmy, 246, 289, 364
Carter, Mae Bertha, 389–90
Cash, W. J., *The Mind of the South*, 37, 38, 217
Cason, Sandra. *See* Hayden, Sandra
Castle, Doris, 189
CBS (Columbia Broadcasting System), 142, 183, 367
CDGM. *See* Child Development Group of Mississippi
Celler, Emmanuel, 359–60
Chafe, William, 69
Chaney, James, 299–301, 396

Chapel Hill (North Carolina), 408–9
Charleston (South Carolina), 26, 215, 216, 401
    black elite of, 218–19
    citizenship teacher training in, 260
Chatfield, Jack, 245, 246, 406
Chesapeake & Ohio Railroad, 35
Chicago (Illinois), women's liberation movement in, 354
Chicago, University of, 296, 333, 352, 354
Child, Lydia Maria, 28
Child Development Group of Mississippi (CDGM), 391–92, 395
Children, neighborhood raising of, 42
Children's Defense Fund, 378, 400
Chisholm, Shirley, 368
Christian, Joanne, 245–46
Christian, LaVette (Dear), 245, 246
Christian Faith and Life Community, 168–69
CIC. See Commission on Interracial Cooperation
CIO (Congress of Industrial Organizations), 102, 175
Citizenship schools, 213–15, 219–24, 245, 256, 259, 260, 304, 305, 313–14, 326, 339
Civil Rights Act (1875), 34
Civil Rights Act (1964), 318, 328, 346–47, 374
    enforcement of, 361–65
    school desegregation and, 388–90
    "sex" amendment to, 360
Civil Rights Act (1991), 400
Civil rights movement
    "black and white together" in, 240, 294, 308, 407
    black women as leaders in, 13–16, 43, 124–25, 202, 204, 237, 248–51, 394
    as "borning struggle," 397
    as chic in the mid-1960s, 273
    Communism and, 323
    dissertation on music of, 403
    general estimate of, 397–98
    journalists' reporting of, 237
    men's competitiveness in, 235
    men's work essential to, 17
    NACW and, 43
    1944 anticipation of, 19–21
    sexism in, 13–14, 287–88, 332–38, 353–54, 406–7
        men's and women's roles, 44, 125, 161
    singing in, 232–34
    violence against black women in, 204–5
    See also Freedom Riders; specific groups
Civil War, 107
    effect of defeat of South in, 37, 45
    as Lost Cause, 45, 83
    as War Between the States, 57
Clark, Jim, 340–42
Clark, Nerie, 216

Clark, Septima, 14, 15, 107, 130, 149, 213, 403
    background of, 215–19
    on black mothers and their sons, 376
    citizenship schools of, 213–15, 219–24, 260
    Echo in My Soul, 222
    at Highlander Folk School, 219–20
    last years of, 401
    NOW joined by, 368
    threats to life of, 221
Class-action discrimination lawsuits, 364–65
Clayton (Georgia), 66
Cleaver, Eldridge, 378–79
Cleaver, Kathleen, 373
Cleveland (Mississippi), 310
Cobb, Charles, 251, 294
Coca-Cola, 226
Colleges and universities
    first to admit blacks, 77
    sexism at, 286
    women admitted to, 365
    See also specific colleges and universities
Collegiate Council of the United Nations, 168
Collins, Lucretia, 190
Color Purple, The (book), 380
Columbia (South Carolina), 216
Columbus (Mississippi), 260
Colvin, Claudette, 92–94, 98–99, 106, 109, 111, 113
    in federal desegregation suit, 123, 127
Commission on Interracial Cooperation, (CIC), 46–48
Communism
    alleged in civil rights movement, 323
    witch-hunt against, 103–6, 177
Concubinage of slave women, 22
Cone, James, 141, 142
Congregationalist Church, 152
Congress of Racial Equality (CORE), 60, 172, 179, 183, 184, 189, 357, 378
    Eleanor Roosevelt and Freedom Riders of, 194
    Mississippi work of, 252
Connor, Bull, 180, 183, 185, 236, 283, 340
Consciousness-raising, 354–55
Conwell, Kathleen, 243
Conyers, John, Jr., 130, 401
Cooksey, Dealey, 118
CORE. See Congress of Racial Equality
Cotton, Dorothy, 214, 220, 222, 262
Cotton, MacArthur, 406
Council on Human Relations (Montgomery), 106
Credit cards, 365
Crisis (magazine), 71
Cronor, Mary, 82
Crouch, Paul, 105
Crusade for Citizenship, 138–39, 143–46

Culbreth, Janie, 233
Curry, Connie, 161–62, 166, 167–68,
    170–72, 390, 400, 405
Curry, Eileen, 167
Curry, Hazel, 167

Dabney, Virginius, 68
Dachau concentration camp, 240
Dallas County (Alabama), 340
Dammond, Peggy, 240–44
Daniels, Carolyn, 244–45
"Dark Testament" (poem), 65
Daughters of the American Revolution, 59
Davis, Angela, 378
Davis, Linda, 304
Dawson, Dorothy, 169–70
Day-care centers, 355, 365
Dayton (Ohio), 216
Daytona Beach (Florida), 58
Defense industry in World War II, 61
De Lott, Elaine, 333, 334
del Pozzo, Theresa, 397
Delta Democrat-Times, 68
Democratic National Committee, poll tax
    and, 102
Democratic National Convention (1964),
    MFDP at, 312, *313*, 314–25, 339,
    383, 391–93
Democratic National Convention (1968),
    interracial Mississippi delegation at,
    324, 392
Democratic National Convention (1972),
    minorities in all delegations at, 324
Democratic National Convention (1984), 396
Dennis, David, 401
Desegregation. *See* Segregation
Detroit (Michigan), 401
    race riots in, 63
Devine, Annie, 252, 322–23, 383–85, 390,
    394, 400–1
Diamond, Dion, 273
Dirksen, Everett, 361
Divens, Jessie, *200*, 203, 208–10
Divens, Ruby, 203, 208–9
Doar, John, 198
Donaldson, Ivanhoe, 204, 211, 251, 270–71,
    299, 371, 372
Dorchester (Georgia), 213–14, 220, 221
Douglass, Frederick, 21–22, 31, 41
Draft, resistance to, 348, 372
Drew (Mississippi), 390
Du Bois, W. E. B., 71, 72, 152, 225
DuPlessis, Rachel Blau, 398
Durham (North Carolina), 53, 147
Durr, Clifford, 101, 103, 105, 109, 110, 128
    federal desegregation suit urged by, 123
Durr, Virginia Foster, 38, 64, 78, 82, 92–94,
    99–106, 166, 178, 187, 221, 274,
    346, 358, 401
    black students' racism against, 349

bus boycott and, 109, 110, 118, 120, 127
called before Eastland subcommittee,
    104–6
NOW joined by, 368
persecution of, 128

Eastland, James O., 85–86, 104–6, 120,
    177–79, 191, 198, 220, 249, 358,
    386, 388, 391, 392, 398
Ebony (magazine), 154, 164, 369–70
    black matriarchy editorial by, 376–77
Eckford, Elizabeth, 136
Edelman, Marian Wright, 378, 390, 391,
    395, 400
Edmund Pettis Bridge (Alabama), 342–44
Education
    in antebellum South, 41
    of blacks after Civil War, 41–42
    Title IX and sex discrimination in, 365
    See also Colleges and universities; School
        desegregation
Edwards, Sylvester, 95, 96
Egerton, John, 55
Egypt, bondage of Israelites in, 255–56
Eisenberg, Marilyn, 193
Eisenhower, Dwight D., in Little Rock crisis,
    136
"Eleanor Clubs," 62–63
Elections
    contested in Washington by MFDP,
        383–86
    mock, in Mississippi Freedom Vote
        (1963), 291–93, 314
    1964, 383
    See also Voting
Emancipation Proclamation, 76
Emerson, Barbara Williams, 398–99
Emerson, Ralph Waldo, 170
Emory University, 167, 229
Episcopal Church, Murray in, 408–9
Equal Employment Opportunity
    Commission (EEOC)
    enforcement of Title VII by, 362–63
    Hill and Thomas at, 380–81
    Norton as chair of, 21, *350*, 364–65
    as NOW's main target, 363–64
    telephone company lawsuits of, 365
Equal Rights Amendment, 360
Essence (magazine), 377
Evans, Rowland, 323
Evans, Sarah, 306
Evans, Walker, 171
Evers, Medgar, 190

Face the Nation (CBS program), 142
Fair Employment Practices Commission, 61
Farmer, James, 60, 183, 184, 188–91, 193,
    357
Farmville (Virginia), 79–82
Farrakhan, Louis, 403

Faubus, Orval, 135–36
Faulkner, William, 191, 191
FBI (Federal Bureau of Investigation), 63,
    255, 294
    in Goodman, Schwerner, Chaney murder
        case, 300, 328–29
    Liuzzo murder and, 345
    MFDP and, 321
Featherstone, Ralph, 309
Federal Bureau of Investigation. *See* FBI
Federal Communications Commission, 103
Feminine Mystique, The (book), 363, 367
Feminism
    black women and, 357, 366–68
    Hayden's and King's paper on, 350–53
    Murray on, 408
    1960s rise of, 354–56
    See also Women's liberation movement
Field Foundation, 168
Fifteenth Amendment, 31–32, 359, 360
First Amendment, 179
Fisk University, 125, 148, 151–55, 160
Fitzgerald, Cornelia Smith, 23, 53, 409
Fitzgerald, F. Scott, 101
Fitzgerald, Thomas, 53–54
Fitzhugh, George, 23–24
Fleming, Cynthia Griggs, 371
Fleming, Karl, 15, 37, 236, 267
*For Colored Girls Who Have Considered
    Suicide/When the Rainbow Is Enuf*
    (play), 380
Forman, James, 150, 209, 228, 229, 253–54,
    265, 275, 332, 370, 373, 403
    replaced as executive secretary of SNCC,
        369
    on Waveland retreat, 335
    women's sit-in in office of, 333–34, 371
Forrest, Nathan Bedford, 340
Fortson, Warren, 246–47
Foster, Virginia. *See* Durr, Virginia Foster
Fourteenth Amendment, 30–31, 360
Frazier, E. Franklin, 202
Free blacks, 27, 44
Freedman's Bureau, 41, 44
Freedom House (Jackson), 333, 334, 337
Freedom Riders, 14, 182–99, 340
    from Atlanta to Albany (Georgia),
        228–30
    in Birmingham, 183–84, 185, 194
    in Jackson, 189–91
    as name for all civil rights workers, 199
    Nash and, 184–85, 187–90, 194–99, 282
    national attitudes toward, 195
    non-Southerners brought in by, 194
Freedom Schools, 297. *See also* Citizenship
    schools
Freedom Singers, 225, 232–34, 238
Freedom Summer (1964), 240, 255, 291,
    293–312, 325, 328, 330, 332, 339,
    354, 406

Freedom Vote (1963) in Mississippi, 291–93,
    314
Freeman, Robertina, 246
Free Speech movement, 325–26
Friedan, Betty, 366
    The Feminine Mystique, 363, 367
    in founding of NOW, 363
Frieze, Judy, 193
From the Mississippi Delta (book), 400
Fry, Pat, 346
Fugitive Slave Act (1850), 29
Fusco, Liz, 314

Gaines, Marion, 246
Gaines, Pat, 246
Gaines, Peaches, 246
Gallup Poll, 195
Gandhi, Mohandas K. (Mahatma), 21, 121,
    155, 158
Garfield, James, 76
Garrow, David, 90, 131, 339
Gayle, Tacky, 88–89, 91, 116, 119–21, 123,
    131
Geneva (New York), 32
Georgia, 50, 66, 69
    "plantation mentality" in, 225–26
    voter registration in, 226–27, 235,
        239–40, 242–47
    See also Atlanta (Georgia)
Georgia State College for Women, 228,
    404
Georgia State University, 229
Georgia Tech, 167
Ghana, University of, 287
Giddings, Paula, 43, 376
Gilmore, Georgia, 115
Gitlin, Todd, 353
Gober, Bertha, 225, 227, 229, 230, 232, 233,
    238, 402
Golden, Harry, 65
Golden, Marita, 16
Golden Notebook, The (book), 269–70
Goldwater, Barry, 315
Goodman, Andrew, 299–301, 304, 396
Goodwin, Doris Kearns, 58
Government office, appointment of women
    to, 368
Graetz, Robert, 117
Graham, Frank Porter, 55, 56
Grambling College, 131
Grant, Jacquelyn, 142
Grant, Ulysses S., 79
Gray, Fred, 88, 93–94
    federal desegregation suit of, 122–23
    as Parks' lawyer, 111, 115, 123, 124
Gray, Victoria, 214–15, 250, 295, 315,
    320–22, 383–85, 394
Great Britain, 1840 abolitionist gathering
    in, 30
Greenburg, Cheryl Lynn, 407

Greensboro (North Carolina), 74, 146–47, 167, 168
Greenville (Mississippi), 68, 388
Greenwood (Mississippi), 14, 249, 250, 256–63, 271, 273, 292, 307, 399
Greer, Montie B., 50
Grenada (Mississippi), 221
Greyhound buses, 64, 158, 182, 186, 206
Griffiths, Martha, 360
Grimké, Angelina, 26–28, 409
Grimké, Sarah, 26–28, 409
Gurr, Lulah, 128
Guyot, Lawrence, 141, 261–62, 265, 273, 315, 324, 339

Hale, Grace Elizabeth, 397
Hall, Blanton, 227
Hall, Prathia, 161, 245
Hamer, Fannie Lou, 15, *214*, 253–56, 265, *291*, 390, 396
   Freedom Summer and, 294–95, 297–98, 305–6
   last years of, 392–93
   MFDP and, *313*, 314–16, 318–23, 382–87, 392
   on middle-class Negroes, 392
   NOW joined by, 368
   opposes expulsion of whites from SNCC, 349
   Winona beating of, 260–62, 318, 398
Hamer, Perry (Pap), 253, 254, 393
Hamer v. Campbell, 387
Hamilton, Scott, 177–78
Hampton Institute, 130
Hancock, John, 31
Handke, Jan, 301
Harlem Brotherhood Group, 241
Harlem Renaissance, 140
Harper, Frances, 32, 41, 44
Harper's Weekly, 38
Harris, David, 348
Harris, Patricia Roberta, 289
Harvard Law School, women denied admittance to, 286
Harvard University, 396
Hattiesburg (Mississippi), 214–15, 250, 266, 302, 385
Hayden, Sandra (Casey; Sandra Cason), 161, *163*, 166, 168–71, 229, 267–70, 274, 275, 400, 405
   in Atlanta apartment incident, 276–77
   feminist papers of, 333–38, 350–52
   Freedom Summer volunteers sought by, 295–96
   after leaving SNCC, 348
   marriage of, 228, 268, 270, 405
   in Mississippi, 291, 292, 305, 307–9, 312
   MFDP and, 316, 318
Hayden, Tom, 171, 228, 270
   in SDS, 267–68, 353

Hayes, Curtis, 206, 250, 304
Head Start, 390–93, 395, 401
Hebrew rabbi at Parchman penitentiary, 192
Hedgeman, Anna Arnold, 169, 284, 368
Height, Dorothy, 42, 169
Heirich, Max, 326
Help-wanted ads, sex segregation in, 365
Hennings, Sally, 25
Henry, Aaron, 320, 322
Hermann, Susan, 186
Hernandez, Aileen, 362, 363, 368
Herrin, Annie Sue, 231
Higgins, Chester, 130
Highlander Folk School (Tennessee), 99, 106–7, 108, 129
   citizenship school at, 215, 219–20
   1961 SNCC meeting at, 197–98
   police raid on, 220
Hill, Anita, 380–81
Hine, Darlene Clark, 35, 141, 379
Hitler, Adolf, 53
Holland, Ain't Baby, 258, 259, 399
Holland, Ida Mae "Cat," 14, 258–60, 302, 399–400
   From the Mississippi Delta, 400
Holmes, Eleanor. *See* Norton, Eleanor Holmes
Holmes County (Mississippi), 327–28
Holocaust, the, 240
Holsaert, Faith, 245, 246
hooks, bell, 367, 379
Hoover, Herbert, 356
Hoover, J. Edgar, 345
Hope, John, 43, 376
Horton, Myles, 215, 219–20
House of Representatives, MFDP contests 1964
   elections to, 383–86
House Rules Committee, 358, 359
House Un-American Activities Committee (HUAC), 178–79
Howard University, 19–21, 59, 64, 68, 147, 152, 153, 196, 265, 279, 289, 340, 400
   sexism at, 286
HUAC. *See* House Un-American Activities Committee
Humphrey, Hubert, 315, 318–21
Hunter College, 54
Hunton, Addie, 73
Hurley, Ruby, 235

Illinois, University of, at Champaign-Urbana, 353–54
Indianola (Mississippi), 39, 85, 249, 254, 256, 301
In Friendship (group), 133
Internal Revenue Service, harassment by, 373
Interstate Commerce Commission, 227

Issaquena County (Mississippi), 395
Itta Bena (Mississippi), 211, 263

Jackson, Jesse, 396
Jackson, Mahalia, 288
Jackson, Maynard, 400
Jackson (Mississippi)
  black psychiatrist in, 303
  civil rights protest in, 248
  Freedom Riders in, 189–91
  MFDP convention in, 316–17
  1994 SNCC reunion in, 406
  preparations for Freedom Summer in,
    299
  SNCC demonstrations in, 210–11
  SNCC office in, 300, 312
  striking McComb students in, 209–10
Jackson State University, 254, 266
Jacobs, Harriet, 22
"Jail, no bail" policy, 158, 160, 212, 236–37
Jane Crow, 286
Jasper (Florida), 67
Jefferson, Thomas, 25, 31
Jenkins, Tim, 196, 197
Jenkins, Walter, 321
Jet (magazine), 160
Jim Crow laws, 34, 39, 59, 65, 68, 69, 76, 84,
    87, 103, 116
  and Jane Crow, 286
  See also Segregation
Job discrimination in World War II, 61
Johns, Barbara, 79–82
Johns, Vernon, 80, 82
Johns Island (South Carolina), 216
Johnson, Belle, 14, 260, 263, 265, 316
Johnson, Bernice. See Reagon, Bernice
    Johnson
Johnson, Carrie Parks, 47
Johnson, Frank, 343, 389
Johnson, James Weldon, 26, 152
Johnson, June, 259–63, 318
Johnson, Lady Bird, 395
Johnson, Lyndon B., 103, 347, 390
  Civil Rights Act and, 358, 361
  MFDP and, 316–23
  Quinn's meeting over bombing with, 327
  Selma and, 343, 345
  Voting Rights Act and, 343, 387
Johnson, Sarah, 388
Jones, Boyd, 81
Jones, Charles, 126, 196–98, 275
Jones, LeRoi (Amiri Baraka), 378
Jones, Mary Dora, 301
Jones, Phoebe, 203, 204
Jubilee Singers, 152
Juries, women on, 365
Justice Department, U.S., 269, 300, 327, 340,
    386
  Sunflower County lawsuit of, 387–88
  Winona beating and, 262–63

Kelley, Asa, 233
Kemble, Fanny, 24–25
Kempton, Murray, 281
Kennedy, John F., 13, 184–86, 194–99, 318
  on Birmingham violence, 283
  civil rights bill of, 281, 283, 284, 358
  Eleanor Roosevelt and, 356
Kennedy, Robert, 318, 321
  in Cambridge (Maryland) conflict, 278,
    280, 281
  Freedom Rides and, 186, 188, 194–99
Kentucky Alliance Against Racial and Social
    Oppression, 402
Khrushchev, Nikita, 186
Killers of the Dream (book), 67–70
King, Annie Mae, 301–2, 391
King, Coretta Scott, 113, 143–45, 180
King, Ed, 292, 293, 320
King, Martin Luther, Sr., 142
King, Martin Luther, Jr., 15, 80, 147, 197,
    250, 282, 328, 370
  in Albany campaign, 212, 234, 236–37
  authoritarian manner of, 144–45, 215
  Baker's challenge of, 133, 215
  in Birmingham 1963 marches, 278, 283
  citizenship program supported by, 215
  Clark and, 222–23
  Freedom Riders and, 188, 189
  full-scale civil disobedience sought by,
    146
  Hamer compared to, 255
  Hoover's hostility to, 345
  in March on Washington, 13–14, 283,
    284
  "I Have a Dream" speech, 289–90
  MFDP and, 318, 321, 322
  Montgomery bus boycott and, 113,
    115–18, 122–27, 129, 131
  in SCLC, 138–39, 144–50
  Selma confrontations and, 339, 341–44
  sit-ins and, 148–50, 159
  Stride for Freedom memoir of, 144, 145
  and Winona assaults, 262
  women and, 142–43
King, Mary, 141, 168, 169, 268–69,
    276–77, 292, 332, 335–37, 348,
    371, 400
  "Sex and Caste," 350–53
  and sit-in in Forman's office, 333–34
King, Richard, 65
Kinoy, Arthur, 384
Kirksey, Henry, 255
Kresge's stores, 78
Ku Klux Klan (KKK; nightriders), 39, 58,
    66, 82, 86, 95, 99, 108, 168, 183, 221,
    254, 264, 297, 310, 340
  Goodman, Schwerner, Chaney murdered
    by, 299–301, 304, 329–30
  in Liuzzo murder, 344–45
  McComb terror campaign of, 326–27

in Little Rock desegregation, 137
Montgomery 1956 demonstration by, 126

Ladner, Dorie, *264*, 265–66, 295
Ladner, Joyce, 265–66, 270, 324, 377, 400
Lafayette, Bernard, 156, 159, 190, 210, 232, 340–41, 403
Lafayette, Colia, 340–41, 403
Lampkin, Daisy, 73
LaPrad, Paul, 154
Lary, Curtis, 258, 262
Latimer, Trois, 227
Law firms, sexism in, 286
Lawson, James, 154–55, 355
Leadbelly, 191, *191*
Lee, Bernard, 143
Lee, Herbert, 210
Lee, Robert E., 79
Lee County (Georgia), 242–44, 246
Lessing, Doris, 269–70
Let Us Now Praise Famous Men (book), 171
Levison, Stanley, 133, 138, 139, 145
Lewis, Anthony, 323
Lewis, David Levering, 72
Lewis, Joe, 207
Lewis, John, 150, 152, 155, 158–60, 185, 187, 189, 190, 197, 199, 252, 281, 298
   ousted as SNCC chairman, 347
   in Selma-to-Montgomery march, 342, 346
Lewis, Rufus, 91–92, 124
Lexington *Advertiser*, 327–28
Liberals. *See* Southern liberals
Liberty (Mississippi), 206
Lincoln, Abraham, 76
Little Rock (Arkansas), Central High School crisis at, 13, 134–37, 286
Liuzzo, Viola, 344–46
London (England), 1840 abolitionist gathering in, 30
Looby, Alexander, bombing of house of, 158–59
Look (magazine), 126
Louisiana, black voter registration in, 386
Louisville (Kentucky), 173, 174–78, 402
Louisville *Courier-Journal*, 56, 175–77
Louisville *Times*, 175
Loveland, Anne, 70
Lowenstein, Allard, 293, 348
Loyal Democrats (Mississippi), 392
Lynching
   black men's fear of, 38–39, 276–77
   Methodist opposition to, 46, 48–49
   in Mississippi, 200–1
   NAACP founding and, 71–72
   nonsexual reasons for, 36, 39–40
   proposed federal law against, 56
   suggested need for, 173

Wells' investigation of, 36, 39–41, 44, 48
   white women's association against, 49–50
Lyon, Danny, 247

McAdam, Doug, 307
McBee, Susanna, 287–88
McCarthy, Joseph R., 177
McCarty, Anne Gambrell. *See* Braden, Anne
McCauley, Rosa. *See* Parks, Rosa
McComb (Mississippi), 200–10, 226, 399
   arms cache discovered in, 300–1
   Quinn's house bombed in, 326–27
   school strike in, 206–9
   sit-ins in, 206
   voter registration in, 201–5, 210
   women's suit against telephone company of, 365
McCormack, John, 384
McDew, Chuck, 196, 197, 208, 267, 271–72, 274–75
McDonald, Rebecca, 250
McGhee, Clarence, 257
McGhee, Jake, 257
McGhee, Laura, 14, 256–58, 260, 316
McGhee, Silas, 256, 257
McGill, Ralph, 65, 84
   Smith's feud with, 68–70
McKissick, Floyd, 357
McLaurin, Charles, 249–50, 306, 387
McLemore, Leslie, 324
Magnolia (Mississippi), 205, 208, 272
Magruder, Irene, 301
Male chauvinism, black, 378–81
March on Washington (1963), 13–14, 15, 283–85, 289–90
   women at, 13, 284–85, 287–88
Marks (Mississippi), 301
Marriage, interracial
   social equality as code words for, 62
   Terrell on, 77
   white fear of, 37
Mars, Florence, 84, 328–29
Marshall, Burke, 185, 195, 196, 281
Marshall, George C., 61
Marshall, Thurgood, 217
Martin, Jacqueline Byrd, 202–4, 207, 210, 365, 399
Martin, Willie, 209
Maryland, Eastern Shore of, 240, 242, 278–82
Maryland, University of, 131
Maryland National Guard, 280
Maryland State University, 280
Mayersville (Mississippi), 251, 396
Mays, Benjamin, 152
Mead, Margaret, 153
Meharry Medical College, 159
Mellon family, 226

Memphis (Tennessee), 77
  lynching in, 36
Memphis *Free Speech*, 36, 40
Methodist Church, 46, 67, 104, 228
  Commission on Interracial Cooperation,
    (CIC), 46–48
MFDP. *See* Mississippi Freedom Democratic
  Party
MIA. *See* Montgomery Improvement
  Association
Michigan, University of, 90, 268
Michigan Daily, 171
Military academies, women at, 365
Milledgeville (Georgia), 228
Miller, Dorothy, 268, 273, 275–76
Million Man march, 403
Mills, Kay, 398
Mind of the South, The (book), 37, 38, 217
Minneapolis Tribune, 84, 170
Minnesota, University of, 399
Miss America, 153
Mississippi
  blacks elected in, 255, 388
  black voter registration in, 195–99,
    201–5, 210, 239–40, 242–47,
    249–60, 291–92, 304, 309–10
    restrictions eased, 386–88
  citizenship schools (Freedom Schools) in,
    256, 259, 260, 297, 304, 309,
    313–14, 326, 339
  first jury conviction in civil rights case in,
    330
  Freedom Riders in, 189–91
  Freedom Summer (1964), 240, 255, *291*,
    293–312, 325, 328, 330, 332, 339,
    354, 406
  Head Start in, 390–93, 395
  jails and prisons of, 190–94, 197, 263
  as "land of grave and home of tree," 255
  literacy campaign for poor children in,
    400
  mock elections in
    Freedom Vote, (1963) 291–93, 314
    1964, 383
  as poorest and most racist state, 200
  voter registration laws in, 201
  white anti-supremacists in, 327–29
  White Citizens Councils founded in, 86
  white civil rights workers in, 292–312
Mississippi, University of, 390
Mississippi Freedom Democratic Party
    (MFDP), 312, *313*, 314–25, 339,
    383, 391–93
  Loyalist 1968 coalition with, 392
Mississippi Free Press, 328
Mississippi National Guard, 189
Mississippi Sovereignty Commission, 327
Mississippi Supreme Court, 83
Missouri, University of, 55
Missouri Press Association, 43

Mitchell County (Georgia), 231
Mitford, Jessica, 93, 103, 274
"Moderates," 84
Mondale, Walter, 321
"Mongrelization," 83–84
Montgomery (Alabama)
  bus boycott in, *110*, 114–27
    called for, 88–89, 92, 93, 131
    December 3 leafletting, 111–14, 124
    end of boycott, 125–26
    letdown afterward, 132–33
    violence against boycotters, 122
    white support, 117, 119–20
    women's organizing, 124–25, 131
  bus segregation in, 87–91, 93–94, 98
  Colvin's and Smith's refusal to yield bus
    seat in, 93–95
  Dexter Avenue Baptist Church, 80,
    113–14, 344
  Durrs return to, 103–4
  First Baptist Church, *110*, 113, 188
  Freedom Riders in, 186–87
  Holt Street Baptist Church, 116
  Miss White's school in, 96
  NAACP in, 91, 96–98, 129
  1960 student sit-in at capitol in, 131
  Parks' refusal to yield bus seat in, 13,
    107–8, 131
  proposed sit-ins and strikes in, 293
  school desegregation in, 389
  white women watching over courts in,
    121
  See also Selma-to-Montgomery march
Montgomery *Advertiser*, 89, 119, 121, 126,
    128
Montgomery Improvement Association
    (MIA), 115, 117, 119, 122–24, 127,
    129, 133, 138, 389, 401
Moore, Russell, 212
Morehouse College, 149, 152, 167
Morgan, Juliette, 120–21, 127–28
Morgan, Robin, 337
Morgan State University, 280
Morris, Willie, 26
Morrison, Toni, 312, 368
Moses, Bob, 201–5, 208, 210, 239, 248, 254,
    258–60, 267, 271, 273, 317, 326,
    400–1, 402
  arrested and beaten, 205–6
  Freedom Summer and, 291–94, 298, 299,
    303
  at Waveland retreat, 335
  wife of, 333, 403
Moss, Tom, 36, 40
Moton, Leroy, 344–46
Move on Mississippi, 198–99, 210
Moynihan, Daniel Patrick, report by,
    374–76
Mullino, Mary Addie, 50
Murray, Harriet, 54

Murray, Pauli, *19*, 25, 51, 59, 76, 85, 108, 137–38, 172, 235, 368
  background of, 23, *53–55*, 285–87
  on black power, 373
  at Brandeis University, 407–8
  Civil Rights Act (1964) and, 361–62
  Eleanor Roosevelt and, 56, 57, 63–64, 356, 358, 409
  as Episcopal priest, 408–9
  in founding of NOW, 363
  Franklin Roosevelt denounced by, *52–53*, *55–56*, 63
  at March on Washington, 289
  1944 sit-in by, 19–21, 76, 79, 147
  Randolph attacked for sexism by, 288
  women's rights and, 356–58
  writing and poems of, 65
Myrdal, Gunnar, *An American Dilemma*, 217

NAACP. *See* National Association for the Advancement of Colored People
NACW. *See* National Association for Colored Women
Nadinola bleaching cream, 311
Nash, Diane, 14, 148, 151–61, 172, 173, *182*, 239, 264, 284, 355
  Freedom Rides and, 184–85, 187–90, 194–99, 282
  Jackson demonstrations and, 210–11
  "jail, no bail" policy of, 158, 160, 212, 236–37
  marriage of, 211–12, 403–4
  Selma demonstrations and, 339, 341
  in sit-ins, 156–59, 226
  in SNCC and SCLC, 160, 339
Nashville (Tennessee), 147, 148, 152, 154–56, 174, 184, 186, 254
  bombing of lawyer's house in, 158–59
  boycott of stores in, 158
  sit-ins in, *151*, 156–59
  SNCC chairmanship and, 160–61
Nashville *Tennessean*, 159
Nation, The (periodical), 72
National Association for Colored Women (NACW), 43, 45, 78
National Association for the Advancement of Colored People (NAACP), 43, 56, 57, 61, 70–74, 102, 107, 161, 216, 362
  Albany campaign opposed by, 235
  in Arkansas, 134
  Baker as Southern field secretary of, 73–74, 140–41, 146
  black leadership of, 73
  in *Brown v. Board of Education*, 217
  Clark fired for membership in, 219
  founding of, 71–73
  Legal Defense and Education Fund, 390
  Little Rock students receive Spingarn Award from, 137–38
  in Louisville, 175
  in Mississippi, 190, 205, 206, *255*, 266
  in Montgomery, 91, 96–98, 115, 129
  1940s growth of, 70
  in Prince Edward County case, 81–82
  sit-ins and, 146
National Black Feminist Organization (NBFO), 380
National Committee Against the Poll Tax, 103
National Conference of Negro Women, 395
National Council of Churches, 220
National Council of Negro Women, 42, 169
National Council of the Churches of Christ, 284
National Organization for Women (NOW), 363–64
National Press Club, sexism at, 287–88
National Student Association (NSA), 167, 168, 170–71, 196, 293, 352
National Urban League, 43, 55, 56
National Women's Party (NWP), 358–59
National Women's Political Caucus, 368
National Women's Press Club, 288
National Youth Administration, 58, 103
Nazi Germany, 183
NBC (National Broadcasting Company), 148, 321
NBFO. *See* National Black Feminist Organization
"Negro Family: The Case for National Action, The" (report), 374–76
Neshoba County (Mississippi), 300, 328–30
Newberry, Anthony, 69
New England, abolitionism in, 27
New Haven (Connecticut), 357
New Orleans (Louisiana), 105–6, 185, 349, 355
New Republic, The (magazine), 62, 281, 400
Newsweek (magazine), 15, 236, 267, 346
New York, State University of, at Buffalo, 399
New York *Age*, 40
New York City, 28, 31, 54–55
  Harlem, 140, 241
  Norton as chair of Human Rights Commission in, 364
  Ovington's interracial dinner in, 71
  women's liberation movement in, 354
New Yorker, The (magazine), 391
New York *Herald Tribune*, 236, 283
New York Post, 72
New York Stock Exchange, 164
New York Times, The, 43, 52–53, 69, 127, 164, 195, 266, 269, 283, 287, 290, 323, 327, 363, 381
New York Times Magazine, The, 163–65, 300
New York World-Telegram & Sun, 294
Niebuhr, Reinhold, 169

Nightriders. *See* Ku Klux Klan

Nineteenth Amendment, 46, 358, 359

Nixon, E. D., 91–92, 94, 97, 106, 121

  bus boycott and, 109–11, 115, 124, 129, 130

Nonviolence

  CORE's adherence to, 183

  Freedom Riders and, 187, 193, 195

  in Freedom Summer, 293

  met with nonviolence, 236

  Selma as "last act" of, 346

  in sit-ins, 20–21, 156–57, 170

  training in, 260

    Lawson's, 154–55, 355

Norman, Martha Prescod, *264*, 271, 309, 322, 403

Norman, Silas, 403

North Carolina, University of, *52–53*, 55, 147, 408–9

North Carolina A&T State University, 74, 146–47

Norton, Eleanor Holmes, 42, 63, 78, 255, 262, 400

  as EEOC chair, 21, *350*, 364–65

  MFDP and, 316

  National Black Feminist Organization created by, 380

  Pauli Murray praised by, *356*, 357

Novak, Robert, 323

NOW. *See* National Organization for Women

NSA. *See* National Student Association

NWP. *See* National Women's Party

Oberlin College, 77

Odum, Howard, 53

Office of Economic Opportunity (OEO), 391–92, 395

Ohio Wesleyan University, 269

101st Airborne Division, 136

Oppenheimer, Robert, 105

Our Bodies, Ourselves (book), 355

Ovington, Mary White, 71–73

Oxford (Mississippi), 263

Oxford (Ohio), 297–300, 306

Palmer's Crossing (Mississippi), 250

Palo Alto (California), 348

Parchman penitentiary (Mississippi), 191–92, 194, 197, 263, 370

Parker, Mack Charles, 201, 287

Parker, Pam (Pam Parker Allen), 299, 308–9, 354

Parks, Raymond, 96–97, 110, 129

Parks, Rosa, 64, 74, 94, 205, *213*, 284, 288

  background of, 95–96

  bus boycott and, 87, 92, 115, 116, 122, 126, 129–30

  as Conyers' administrative assistant, 130, 401

fingerprinting of, *87*

  at Highlander Folk School, 99, 106–7, 108, 219

  moves to Detroit, 130

  refuses to get off bus, 13, 107–8, 131

  on Selma-to-Montgomery march, 343–44

  trial and appeal of, 115, 123

Partipatory democracy, 150, 335

Patch, Penny, *239*, 240–44, 267, 271, 273, 405–7

  in Mississippi, 291, 293–95, 300, 306, 307, 312, 331–33, 338–39

  resigns from SNCC, 348–49

Patton, Gwen, 310

Paul, Alice, 359

Paul, Weiss, Rifkin, Wharton & Garrison, 286–87

Paull, Irene, 302

Peace Corps, 400

Peacock, Willie, 294

Pearson, Drew, 327

Pennsylvania, 240

Pervall, J. B., 82

Petersburg (Virginia), 64

Philadelphia (Mississippi), 84, 300, 328–30

Philadelphia (Pennsylvania), 28, 29

Pickett, Annie, 207, 208, 210

Pickett, Grace, 208

Pittsburgh *Courier*, 130

Player, Willa, 147

Politics, personal behavior not separate from, 66, 351, 353

Poll tax, 64, 102–4, 201, 202, 205

  outlawing of, 386, 387

Ponder, Annell, 260–62, 318, 402–3

Popkin, Ann, 354

Poplarville (Mississippi), 201, 287

Port Huron Statement, 268

Post Office Department, *Strange Fruit* banned by, 67

Potts Camp (Mississippi), 50

Poussaint, Alvin, 303, 305, 306, 308, 379

Powell, Adam Clayton, Jr., 385

Powledge, Fred, 266, 290

Pregnant women, EEOC's protection for, 364

Presbyterian Church, 46

Prescod, Martha. *See* Norman, Martha Prescod

Price, Cecil, 328, 330

Prince Edward County (Virginia), 79–82

Pritchett, Laurie, 229–31, 233, 236, 237, 245, 246

Proud Shoes (book), 65

Pseudopodia (magazine), 65

Pulitzer Prize

  Hazel Brannon Smith's, 328

  Walker's, 380

Pullman porters' union, 59

Queens College, 268
Quinn, Aylene, 205, 206, 209, 326–27
Quinn, Caroline. *See* Breckinridge, Caroline
      Quinn

Rabinowitz, Joni, 245
Race riots, 63, 71–72
Racial equality, Smith's advocacy of, 66, 69
Racial justice, World War II call for, 65
Racism
   in abolitionist movement, 31
   in *Black Monday*, 83–84
   by blacks, 349
   fascism compared to, 61
   Killers of the Dream on, 68
   in nineteenth-century North, 28–29
   people themselves as protection against,
      74
   sex and, 26, 64, 67, 83, 100, 104, 119
   in SNCC, 338–39, 349
   in suffragist movement, 359
Railroad
   Albany officials agree to desegregate, 236
   Freedom Ride on, 228–30
   segregation on, 33–35, 141, 163
Raines, "Mama Dollie," 243, 244, 247, 265
Rainey, Lawrence, 328–30
Rainey, Thomas, 37
Raleigh (North Carolina), SNCC organizing
      conference in, 160, 162, 166, 168
Randolph, A. Philip, 13, 284, 287–88, 61, 61
Randolph-Macon College, 174
Rape
   of Bates' mother, 134–35
   of black women after Civil War, 35
   as looking in "insulting" way, 174
   lynching as supposed punishment for,
      36–37, 39, 48, 49
   in Montgomery, 98
   New York Times on, 43
   1959 Mississippi lynching for, 201
   as seldom in antebellum South, 38
   sit-in in Chicago over, 352
   of slave women, 22–23
   of white women, justified by Cleaver,
      378–79
Rape crisis networks, 355
Rauh, Joseph, 315, 319
Rawalt, Marguerite, 361–63
Reagon, Bernice Johnson, 225–27, *225*,
      231–34, 237–38, 266, 373, 397, 403
Reagon, Cordell, 226, 232, 403
Reeb, James, 343, 344
Religion
   black, 229
   segregation and, 67–68
   women's activities under, 27, 46
   women's subordination under, 141–42
   See also specific groups
Reuther, Rosemary, 368

Reuther, Walter, 321
Rich, Adrienne, 47
Richards, Dona, 333, 335, 403
Richardson, Gloria, 278–82, *278*, 284, 378
Richmond Times-Dispatch, 68
Rivers, Hazel, 290
Rivers, Mendel, 360
Robertson, Nan, 287
Robeson, Eslanda Goode, 66
Robeson, Paul, 66
Robinson, Bernice, 220
Robinson, Clifford, 372
Robinson, Gwen, 303
Robinson, Jo Ann, 14, 89–91, 93–95, 98, 106
   bus boycott and, 111–13, 118, 122–25
   later career of, 131
   on Montgomery's ministers, 114
Robinson, Reggie, 370
Robinson, Ruby Doris Smith, 15, 160, 185,
      186, 191, 311
   as SNCC executive secretary, 369–73, 377
Robinson, T. J., 141
Rockefeller, John D., 29
Rock Hill (South Carolina), 160, 212, 226,
      370, 373
Rollins, Avon, 204
Romilly, Dinky, 274–75, 403
Roosevelt, Eleanor, 20, 51, *52*, 59
   accused of espionage, 105
   and blacks in World War II, 60–62
   Bradens championed by, 179
   Freedom Riders and, 193–94
   Murray and, 56, 57, 63–64, 356, 358, 409
   racist hatred of, 61–63
   Smith and, 65, 67
   Southern connections of, 56–57
   in women's movement, 356, 358
Roosevelt, Franklin D., 52–53, 55–56, 60, 67
Roosevelt, Franklin D., Jr., 362
Rosa and Raymond Parks Institute
      (Detroit), 401
Rossinow, Doug, 353
Rothschild, Mary Aickin, 307
Rowan, Carl, 84, 86
Rowe, Gary Thomas, 345, *345n*, 346
Ruleville (Mississippi), 249, 250, 253, 255,
      273, 306, 393
Russell, Kathy, 311
Rustin, Bayard, 133, 138–39, 145, 318
Rutledge, Clara, 119, 121
Ryan, William Fitts, 383–84

St. George, Katherine, 360
Salt March (India), 121
Samstein, Mendy, 326
San Jose Mercury, 303
Sarachild, Kathie (Kathie Amatniek), 337,
      354, 406
Sarah Lawrence College, 274
Sartre, Jean-Paul, 169

Saturday Evening Post (magazine), 303
Saturday Review of Literature, 70
Savannah (Georgia), 339
Savannah *News*, 71
Savio, Mario, 325
Sayre, Zelda, 101
SCEF. *See* Southern Conference Educational Fund
Schley County (Georgia), 50
School desegregation, 75, 388–90
  "freedom of choice" plans in, 389–90
  See also: Brown v. *Board of Education;*
    Little Rock (Arkansas)
School strikes, 79–82, 207–10
Schrader, Emmie, 333, 334
Schwerner, Michael, 299–301, 304, 396
SCLC. *See* Southern Christian Leadership Conference
Scottsboro Boys, 96
SDS (Students for a Democratic Society), 267–68, 348, 352
  Champaign-Urbana conference of, 353–54
  sexism in, 353
Second Sex, The (book), 269
Sedition, Bradens charged with, 177–78
Segregation
  Brown v. *Board of Education* cases, 75, 82–86, 88, 99, 104, 123, 138, 176, 177, 328
  on buses. *See* Bus seats; Bus stations
  in Cambridge (Maryland), 279–82
  "fair play," 69
  in housing, in Louisville, 175–78
  King calls for full-scale assault on, 146
  legal end to, 346–47
  Morgan's attack on, 121
  Move on Mississippi drive against, 198–99, 210
  Nash's reaction to, 154–55
  opposition to, as "Communism," 177–78
  on railroads, 33–35, 141, 183
  Southern Patriot's fight against, 180
  Supreme Court's 1956 order against, 125–26
  Waring's rulings on, 217–18
  in Washington (D.C.), 19–21, 76, 78–79
  YWCA fight against, 169
  See also Jim Crow; Sit-ins
Seigenthaler, John, 185, 187, 273
Sellers, Cleveland, 290, 325, 379
Sellers, Clyde, 120
Selma (Alabama), *331*, 404
  Johnson's mention of, 343
  voter registration in, 339–41
  white minister killed in, 343
Selma-to-Montgomery march, 342–44
Senate Internal Security subcommittee, 104–5
Seneca Falls (New York), 30

"Separate but equal," 75, 79, 81, 104, 217
"Sex and Caste" (feminist paper), 350–53
Sexism
  alleged in SNCC, 332–38
  as Jane Crow, 286
Sexual harassment, 355, 364, 365
  alleged of Thomas by Hill, 380–81
Sexual relationships in SNCC, 272–75, 295, 305–9, 336–38
Shange, Ntozake, 380
Shaw University, 140, 148–49
Sherrod, Charles, 226, 239–40, 243, 264, 271
Shriver, Sargent, 395
Shuttlesworth, Fred, 145, 180, 184–85
Sias, Henry, 322–23
Singing
  in Albany campaign, 232–34
  at March on Washington, 288
  at Parchman penitentiary, 192, 232
Sisterhood Is Powerful (book), 337
Sit-ins, 146–49
  in Austin, 169, 170
  in Cambridge (Maryland), 280
  Greensboro, 74, 146–47, 168
  Lillian Smith's support of, 171–72
  in McComb, 206
  of MFDP at Democratic National Convention, 321–22
  Nashville, *151*, 156–59
  1944 Washington, 19–21, 76, 79, 147
  in the North, 168, 241
  Rock Hill, 160, 212, 226, 370, 373
  at University of Chicago health office, 352
  by women in Forman's office, 333–34, 371
Sitkoff, Harvard, 290
60 Minutes (TV program), 367
Slavery
  black women's harsh treatment under, 22, 25
  Grimké sisters' opposition to, 26–28
  King on black man's loss of manhood under, 142
  lynchings not a feature of, 38
  marriage of Baker's grandmother under, 139
  reading and writing of slaves forbidden under, 26, 41, 214
  sexual attitudes under, 22–26
  Underground Railroad and, 29, 32
  white women's lives under, 23–25
Smith, Frank, 23, 403
Smith, Hazel Brannon, 327–28
Smith, Howard, 358–60
Smith, Howard K., 183
Smith, Jean Wheeler, 403, 406
Smith, Lillian, 15, *52*, 64–70, 100, 166
  arson against, 85
  background of, 67–68
  biracial gatherings of, 66, 85

Brown v. *Board of Education* welcomed by, 84–85
Killers of the Dream, 67–70
Morgan's support of, 121
Now Is the Time, 85
sit-in movement supported by, 171–73
Strange Fruit, 66–67, 174
Smith, Mary Louise, 94, 107, 111
in federal desegregation suit, 123
Smith, Mary Riffin, 23
Smith, Ruby Doris. *See* Robinson, Ruby Doris Smith
Smith, Sidney, 23
Smith College, 151, 193
Smithsonian Institution, 403
SNCC. *See* Student Nonviolent Coordinating Committee
Snelling, Paula, 65
Social equality, as code words, 62, 72
South Carolina
employees of, not allowed to join civil rights organizations, 219
sit-in in, 160, 212, 226
See also Charleston
Southern California, University of, 399–400
Southern Christian Leadership Conference (SCLC), 14, 161
citizenship program of, 215, 220–24
controlled by men, 141, 221–23
Crusade for Citizenship of, 138–39, 143–46
founding of, 138–39
King's role in, 138–39, 144–50
lack of civil rights initiatives by, 234
Nash as local staff member of, 160
voter registration by, 341–42
Southern Conference Educational Fund (SCEF), 178–79, 220, 355, 402
Southern Conference for Human Welfare, 64, 102–4, 178
Southern liberals
Brown v. *Board of Education* and, 84–85
Smith's attacks on, 68–70
Southern Manifesto, 134
Southern Patriot (newspaper), 180
Southern Regional Council, 404, 405
South of the Border diner (McComb), 205, 326
South Today (magazine), 65
Spelman, Laura, 29
Spelman College, 152, 160, 167, 235, 289, 370
Spendrup, Ellen, 328, 329
Springfield (Illinois), 71
Stanford University, 293, 301, 367
Stanton, Elizabeth Cady, 30–32, 359, 360
State Press (Arkansas newspaper), 135, 137
"States' rights," 75, 83
Stembridge, Jane, 161–62, 166–67, 172, 173, 180, 181, 201, 292–93

Stennis, John, 391, 392
Stevenson, Adlai, 151
Stewart, Maria, 27
Stimson, Henry, 59, 61
Stowe, Harriet Beecher, 62
Strange Fruit (novel and play), 66–67, 174
Stratford College, 174
Stride for Freedom (King's memoir), 144, 145
Student Nonviolent Coordinating Committee (SNCC), 15, 21, 126, 150, 158
Albany campaign of. *See* Albany (Georgia)
alleged sexism in, 332–38, 406–7
"beloved community" of, 162, 272, 307, 312, 332, 338, 347, 406
black nationalism in, 347–48
Bradens and, 180
Cambridge Nonviolent Action Committee and, 280
Carmichael as chairman of, 347–48
community support in South of, 251–52
Eleanor Roosevelt's support of, 194
Freedom Rides and, 194, 196, 228–30
Freedom Singers of, 225, 232–34, 238
Freedom Summer (1964) and, 240, 255, 291, 293–312, 325, 328, 330, 332, 339, 354, 406
Highlander Folk School meeting of, 197–98
leadership of, 265–67, 270
Robinson as executive secretary, 369
See also Forman, James
McComb school strike and, 208–10
March on Washington and, 284, 290
MFDP and, 323–25
Move on Mississippi drive of, 198–99, 210
Nash as staff member of, 160
1960 conference of, 171–73
1960–1964 growth of, 332
1964 Waveland retreat of, 332, 334–38
1988 and 1994 reunions of, 406–7
NSA support of, 170–71
as nurturing and loving, 161
racism in, 338–39
SCEF and, 179
sexual relationships in, 272–75, 295, 305–9, 336–38
speakers of, 254–55
Student Voice (newspaper) of, 180
voter registration by, 195–99, 201–5, 210, 239–40, 242–47, 249–60, 291–92, 304, 309–10, 340–41
white-black community envisioned by, 162, 275–77
whites forced to leave, 348–49
white women in, 161–62, 166, 239–47, 267–71, 292, 294–305, 331–32, 335–36, 348–49, 371, 404–7

Student Nonviolent Coordinating
    Committee (SNCC) (cont.)
    estrangement from black women, 305–12,
        331–32, 335, 338, 349, 406–7
Students for a Democratic Society. See SDS
Student Voice (newspaper), 180
Suarez, Matt, 252
Suburbs, all-white, 165
Suffragists, 45–46, 77–78, 358–59
Sugarman, Tracy, 255–56
Sullivan, Joseph, 329
Sumter County (Georgia), 246
Sunflower County (Mississippi), 249, 254,
        256, 301, 386, 389–90, 393
    Justice Department lawsuit against,
        387–88
Supreme Court, U.S.
    Boynton v. Virginia, 183, 227, 340
    Brown v. Board of Education, 75, 82–86
    bus segregation ended by, 125–26
    sex discrimination rulings by, 365
    Washington segregation case of, 79
Swarthmore College, 240, 241, 273, 280
Sweeney, David, 348
Sweet Honey in the Rock, 403

"Take Back Your Mink" (song), 153
Talbert, Mary, 73
Tennessee State Fair, 154
Terkel, Studs, 99
Terrell, Mary Church ("Mollie"), 45, 66, 72,
        75–79, 75, 102, 386
Terrell, Robert, 76
Terrill County (Georgia), 242, 244–45
Texas, justifiable homicide in, 164
Texas, University of, 169, 170
Texas, University of, at El Paso, 389
Thirteenth Amendment, 30
Thomas, Clarence, 380–81
Thomas, Eliza, 246
Thompson, Kathleen, 141, 379
Thoreau, Henry David, 155, 170
Till, Emmett, 201, 269
Tilley, John, 144, 145
Tillich, Paul, 169
Tillman, Ben, 38, 46
Time (magazine), 85, 127
Title VII. See Civil Rights Act (1964)
Title IX, 365
Tobis, Heather, 291, 296, 300, 301
    as feminist, 352–54
Tougaloo College, 266, 293, 332
Trailways buses, 182, 183, 227, 383
Travis, Brenda, 202–3, 206–7, 210
Trenholm, H. Councill, 112–13
Trinity College, 406–7
Trumpauer, Joan, 192
Truth, Sojourner, 32, 35, 87, 88, 265, 386,
        409
Tubman, Harriet, 29, 32, 265, 279, 357–58

Ture, Kwame (Stokely Carmichael), 15, 150,
        152, 211, 251, 294, 310, 370, 394
    Black Power of, 347, 369
    misquoted remark by, 336–37
    Robinson and, 371–72
Tuscaloosa News, 127–28
Tuskegee Airmen, 61
Tuskegee Institute, 57, 339–40, 349
Tyler, Reverend, 256

Underground Railroad, 29, 32
Union Theological Seminary, 166
United Auto Workers (UAW), 321
United Daughters of the Confederacy, 45
United Press International, 180
United States Army, in World War II,
        60–61

Vandiver, Ernest, 228
Vardaman, J. K., 46
Victoria (Texas), 169
Villard, Oswald, 72
Virginia, black school strike in, 79–82
Vivian, C. T., 159
Voter Education Project, 244, 292, 398
Voting
    by black men in South after Civil War,
        37
    black registration for
        citizenship schools, 213–15, 219–24,
            245, 256, 259, 260, 304, 305,
            313–14, 326, 339
        eased in Mississippi, 386
        federal examiners mandated, 386–87
        in Georgia, 226–27, 235, 239–40,
            242–47
        Kennedys' support, 195–97
        in Mississippi, 249–50
        in Montgomery, 91, 98
        1920s Savannah, 339
        SCLC Crusade for Citizenship, 138–39,
            143–46
        in Selma, 340–41
        SNCC and, 195–99, 201–5, 210,
            239–40, 242–47, 249–60, 291–92,
            304, 309–10, 340–41
        Sunflower County, 393
    by blacks in primaries, 217, 314–15, 382
    denied to women after Civil War, 31–32
    by Maryland blacks, 279
    Supreme Court decisions on, 70
    women's suffrage movement and, 45–46,
        77–78
    See also Poll tax
Voting Rights Act (1965), 343, 346–47, 385,
        404
    practical effect of, 386–88

Wade, Andrew, 175–76, 178
Wade-Gayles, Gloria, 311

Walker, Alice, 289, 380
Walker, Wyatt Tee, 149, 220
Wallace, Henry, 103
Wallace, Michele, 376, 380
Wall Between, The (book), 179
Wall Street Journal, The, 362
Walthall County (Mississippi), 205
Waring, Elizabeth, 216–19
Waring, J. Waties, 216–19
War on Poverty, 390, 391
Warren, Earl, 82
Washington, Cynthia, 310, 312, 337
Washington (D.C.)
    Blackwell's lobbying trips to, 395
    integrated servicemen's club in, 62
    Randolph's 1941 call for march on, 61
    segregation in, 19–21, 76, 78–79
    suffragists in, 45, 77
    See also March on Washington
Washington County (Mississippi), 388
Washington *Daily News,* 289
Washington Post, The, 78, 287–89
Washington Star, 283–84
Washington University, 377
Watkins, Hollis, 206, 250
Watters, Pat, 232, 237, 386
Watts (Los Angeles), 347
Waveland (Mississippi), SNCC gathering at, 332, 334–38
Wayne State University, 346
Wellesley College, 99, 101
Wells, Ida B. (Ida Wells-Barnett), *33*, 64, 88, 380, 386
    lynching investigation by, 36, 39–41, 44, 48
    marriage of, 44
    in NAACP founding, 72
    newspaper attacks on, 42–43
    railroad segregation fought by, 33–36
    in women's suffrage movement, 45
Welty, Eudora, 191, *191*
West, Ben, 158, 159
West, Irene, 93, 117, 124, 126
Western College for Women. *See* Oxford (Ohio)
West Virginia State College, 404
Wheeler, Jean, 251, 265, 271
White, Walter, 57, 59, 61
White backlash, 347, 373
White Citizens Council, 264
    citizenship education opposed by, 221
    founding of, 85–86
    Lexington *Advertiser*'s denunciation of, 327–28
    loss of influence of, 330
    Montgomery bus boycott and, 120, 124
    Morgan's fate and, 127–28
    in Selma, 340, 346
White men
    assault on black women by, 22–23, 35

cowardice of, 127–28, 297
sexual fears by, 267
Southern post-Civil War changes and, 37
toasts to Southern women by, 37, 48
See also Southern liberals
Whiteness, blacks' obsession with, 54
White women
    in abolitionist movement, 26–28
    black men's pursuit of, 308, 311
    Braden's encouragement of, 180–81
    fear of rape by, 38–39
    idealization in South of, 23–24, 37, 40, 48–49, 68, 83–84, 101, 165–66, 242, 346
    Lost Cause supported in South by, 45
    lynching as punishment for liaisons of black men and, 39–40
    Nineteenth-century legal position of, 23–24, 26, 27
    Northern organizations of, 27
    poll tax on, 102
    in SDS, 268
    and sex with black men, 37, 104, 267, 274–75
    in SNCC, 161–62, 166, 239–47, 267–71, 292, 294–305, 331–32, 335–36, 348–49, 371, 404–7
        estrangement from black women, 305–12, 331–32, 335, 338, 349, 406–7
    Southern husbands' betrayal of, 23, 25
    watching over courts by, 121
    working together with black women, 16, 26, 29, 47, 66, 106, 162, 295
        Freedom Summer, 309–12, 331–32
    after World War II, 165–66, 353
Whitten, Jamie, 315
Wilbur, Susan, 186, 187, 273
Wilcher, Johnnie, 202, 207, 365, 326
Wilkins, Collie Leroy, Jr., 345, 345*n*, 346
Wilkins, Roger, 378
Wilkins, Roy, 13, 58, 71, 274, 282, 285, 318, 322
Williams, Aubrey, 103
Williams, Hosea, 342, 399
Williams, Tennessee, 165
Wilson, Midge, 311
Winona (Mississippi), police beatings at, 260–63, 318, 398
Winston-Salem (North Carolina), 147
Wirth, Louis, 22
Wise, Stanley, 371
Wofford, Harris, 186
Women
    Braden on liberation of, 271–72
    discrimination against. *See* Sexism
    EEOC and, 363–65
    essential behind-the-scenes work by, 235
    example of support network of, 223

Women (*cont.*)
  as 50 percent of all Democratic Party
    delegations, 324
  maiden name kept by, 333
  men accepted as leaders by, 125, 161
  as minority similar to blacks, 164
  1950s double bind for, 153
  ordination of, 408
  personal and political equated by, 66, 351,
    353
  presidential commission on, 356, 358,
    361
  as "second-class citizens," 163–64
  See also Black women; White women
Women's Era (newspaper), 43
Women's liberation movement
  consciousness-raising in, 354–55
  dissension within, 366–68
  Freedom Summer a "seedbed" for, 325
  general estimate of, 398–99
  impact of, 365–66
  1960s mushrooming of groups in, 354
  See also Feminism
Women's Political Council (WPC;
    Montgomery), 89–93, 106
  bus boycott and, 111–14, 123, 131
Women's rights
  abolitionism and, 30–32
  Nineteenth-century movement for, 27, 28,
    353
  SNCC and, 266–67
Women's Rights Convention (1848), 30

Women's suffrage movement, 45–46, 77–78,
    358–50
Woodruff, Robert, 226
Woodward, Bob, 78
Woodward, C. Vann, 84, 347
Woolworth's stores, 74, 146–47, 157, 206
Works Progress Administration (WPA), 55,
    58
World War II, 59, 60–64, 73
  racial justice called for during, 65
  women's wartime jobs during, 164
WPA. *See* Works Progress Administration
WPC. *See* Women's Political Council
Wright, Marian. *See* Edelman, Marian
    Wright
Wyckoff, Elisabeth, 192

Yale University, 196, 262, 285, 293, 316,
    358, 390
YMCA (Young Men's Christian
    Association), 170
Young, Andrew, 142, 220–22, 262, 282, 318,
    341, 394, 400
Youth Committee Against War, 60
YWCA (Young Women's Christian
    Association), 169–70, 218, 269

Zellner, Bob, 228, 239, 257, 268, 272–74,
    355, 403
  expelled from SNCC, 349
Zellner, Dorothy, 349, 355, 371, 403
Zinn, Howard, 235